FUNDAMENTALS OF RESEARCH ON CULTURE AND PSYCHOLOGY

This is the first book that provides detailed guidelines of how to conduct multi-disciplinary research to study people's behaviors in different cultures. Readers are encouraged to look beyond disciplinary boundaries to address issues between individuals and their socio-cultural environments so as to design the most effective studies possible. The core philosophical and theoretical assumptions that underlie the strategies, designs, and techniques used when researching cultural issues are examined. The book reviews all the steps that go into doing cultural research from formulating the research problem to selecting the most appropriate method for data analysis. Realist and interpretivist paradigms together with the theory of cultural models and quantitative, qualitative, mixed-method, and multiple-design strategies are reviewed. Case studies, ethnographies, and interviewing techniques are emphasized throughout. Chapters open with learning objectives and end with a conclusion, a glossary, questions, exercises, and recommended readings. Numerous multidisciplinary examples, tables, and figures demonstrate and synthesize the analysis of data. *Information boxes* provide historical notes and *how-to boxes* provide tips on methodological issues.

Highlights include:

- Encourages researchers to breach disciplinary boundaries to address the problems of human functioning in different cultures (Chapters 1 and 2).
- Introduces readers to the theory of cultural models that helps bridge the human mind and socio-cultural realities (Chapters 2 and 10).
- Propagates the realist and interpretivist philosophical paradigms for doing cultural studies and demonstrates how to use these approaches when studying people in different cultures (Chapters 3 and 4).
- Helps readers formulate productive research questions, articulate concepts, and understand the role theories play in cultural research (Chapters 5 and 6).
- Reviews research designs including case-based and variable-based ones, person-centered ethnography, interviewing, and quantitative studies (Chapters 7–10).
- www.routledge.com/9780415820325/ provides instructors with PowerPoints, additional references and studies, and questions for discussion and evaluation for each chapter and offers students chapter outlines and objectives, key terms and concepts with a hotlink to the definition, and suggested readings and websites.

Intended for advanced undergraduate or graduate courses that conduct cultural or cross-cultural research including cross-(cultural) psychology, culture and psychology, or research methods/design courses in psychology, anthropology, sociology, cultural studies, social work, education, geography, international relations, business, nursing, public health, and communication, the book also appeals to researchers interested in conducting cross-cultural and cultural studies. Prerequisites include introductory courses on research methods and cross-cultural/cultural psychology.

Valery Chirkov is Professor of Psychology at the University of Saskatchewan, Canada.

FUNDAMENTALS OF RESEARCH ON CULTURE AND PSYCHOLOGY

Theory and Methods

Valery Chirkov

NEW YORK AND LONDON

First published 2016
by Routledge
711 Third Avenue, New York, NY 10017

and by Routledge
2 Park Square, Milton Park, Abingdon, Oxon, OX14 4RN

Routledge is an imprint of the Taylor & Francis Group, an informa business

© 2016 Taylor & Francis

The right of Valery Chirkov to be identified as author of this work has been asserted by him in accordance with sections 77 and 78 of the Copyright, Designs and Patents Act 1988.

All rights reserved. No part of this book may be reprinted or reproduced or utilized in any form or by any electronic, mechanical, or other means, now known or hereafter invented, including photocopying and recording, or in any information storage or retrieval system, without permission in writing from the publishers.

Trademark notice: Product or corporate names may be trademarks or registered trademarks, and are used only for identification and explanation without intent to infringe.

Library of Congress Cataloging-in-Publication Data
Chirkov, Valery I. author.
  Fundamentals of research on culture and psychology : theory and methods / Valery Chirkov.
    pages cm
  Includes bibliographical references and index.
  1. Ethnopsychology—Methodology. 2. Cross-cultural studies—Methodology. I. Title.
  GN502.C45 2016
  155.8′201—dc23
  2015017177

ISBN: 978-0-415-82031-8 (hbk)
ISBN: 978-0-415-82032-5 (pbk)
ISBN: 978-1-315-76832-8 (ebk)

Typeset in ApexBembo
by Apex CoVantage, LLC

Printed and bound in the United States of America by
Edwards Brothers Malloy on sustainably sourced paper

BRIEF CONTENTS

Preface	*xiii*
Acknowledgments	*xvii*
About the Author	*xviii*

PART I
Thinking and Reflecting   **1**

1. Disciplinary Thinking: From Anthropology to Psychology   3

2. Theoretical Thinking: Four Perspectives in Studying Psychology in Sociocultural Contexts   32

3. Philosophical Thinking: Induction, Deduction, and Positivism   56

4. Philosophical Thinking: Abduction, Retroduction, Interpretivism, and Realism   78

PART II
Planning Research   **115**

5. Research Problem, Purposes, and Research Questions   117

6. Working with Concepts, Terms, and Theories   141

7. Research Strategies and Designs   170

PART III
Practical Aspects of Doing Research   **199**

8. The Types of Studies on Culture and Psychology   201

9. Quantitative Comparative Studies: Equivalence, Translation, and Measurement Invariance — 226

10. Ethnography — 257

11. Ethical Concerns — 282

Conclusion: Final Words of Encouragement — 299

Index — *301*

CONTENTS

PART I
Thinking and Reflecting   1

1 Disciplinary Thinking: From Anthropology to Psychology   3
   Introduction   3
   Cultural and Social Anthropology   4
      The Main Theories of Culture   6
   Psychological and Cognitive Anthropology   11
   Cross-Cultural Psychology   15
      Definition   15
      Understanding of Culture   16
   Cultural Psychology   19
   Indigenous Psychology   21
      Summary   24
   Conclusion   25
   Questions   25
   Glossary   25
   Recommended Reading   27
   References   27

2 Theoretical Thinking: Four Perspectives in Studying Psychology in Sociocultural Contexts   32
   Introduction   32
   Theoretical Thinking   32
   The Physical Science Perspective   33
      Understanding of Culture   34
      Understanding the Nature of Psychological Functioning   35
      Methodology and Methods of Research   36
      The Main Disciplines   37
   The Biological Science Perspective   37
   The Sociocultural Sciences Perspective   40
      Methodology and Methods   43

The Agentic-Interpretive Perspective   43
   Theory of Cultural Models   44
   The Main Forms of Doing Research   50
Conclusion   51
Questions   51
Glossary   52
Recommended Reading   52
References   53

3 Philosophical Thinking: Induction, Deduction, and Positivism   56

Introduction   56
The Ultimate Goals and Challenges of Scientific Research   57
Two Main Constituents of Philosophical Thinking About Research   58
   Induction and Deduction   59
   Radical Empiricism, Enumerative Induction, and the Deductive-Nomological
      Mode of Inference as the Basis of the Positivist Paradigm   66
Conclusion   73
Questions   73
Glossary   74
Recommended Reading   76
References   76

4 Philosophical Thinking: Abduction, Retroduction, Interpretivism, and Realism   78

Introduction   78
The Abductive and Retroductive Modes of Inference   78
   Charles Peirce and the Abductive/Retroductive Modes of Inference   79
The Abductive Mode of Inference and the Interpretivist Paradigm   82
   A Brief History of the Antipositivist Reaction   83
   Investigation of Meaning, Act of Interpretation, and the Abductive
      Mode of Inference   84
   Interpretation and Understanding   87
   Problems and Controversies with the Interpretivist Paradigm   92
   Summary of Interpretivism   94
The Retroductive Mode of Inference and the Realist Paradigm   95
   History of the Realism Paradigm   96
   The Main Features of the Retroductive Mode of Inference   99
   How Can the Results of Positivist and Interpretivist Studies be Used by
      Realist Researchers?   101
   Procedures and Techniques for Facilitating Retroductive Inferences   103
   Summary of Realism   107
   Critique of the Realist Paradigm   107
Conclusion   108
Questions   109
Glossary   109
Recommended Reading for Interpretivism   111
Recommended Reading for Realism   111
References   111

PART II
Planning Research   115

5 Research Problem, Purposes, and Research Questions   117

    Introduction: Formulating a Research Problem   117
        Importance of Problematization   117
        Theoretical and Applied Problems   119
        How to Formulate a Research Problem: The Thesis–Antithesis–Synthesis Logic   121
    Research Purposes   124
        The Descriptive Purpose   125
        The Explanatory Purpose   128
        Prediction and Explanation: Is Prediction a Legitimate Purpose of Research?   129
    Formulating Research Questions   131
        Types of Research Questions   132
        How to Generate Research Questions   132
        Research Questions and Hypotheses   135
        Relations Between Research Questions and Research Design   136
    Conclusion   137
    Questions   138
    Glossary   138
    Recommended Reading   139
    References   139

6 Working with Concepts, Terms, and Theories   141

    Introduction   141
    Concepts, Variables, and Hypothetical Constructs   142
        Why Conceptualization is Important for Scientific Research   142
        Concepts, Terms, and Variables   143
        Realism and Nominalism in Concept Development   144
        Empirical and Theoretical Concepts; Hypothetical Constructs   145
        Scientific Concepts and Everyday Language: Vagueness and Ambiguity of Our Words, Terms, and Concepts   146
        Defining the Concepts: Importance and Various Forms of Definitions   148
    What Is Theory and How is It Defined in Different Paradigms?   157
        Theories in Different Paradigms   159
    Conclusion   166
    Questions   166
    Exercises   167
    Glossary   167
    Recommended Reading   167
    References   168

7 Research Strategies and Designs   170

    Introduction: Research Strategy   170
    A Fundamental Concern about the Relations Between General and Particulars   171
        Nomothetic and Idiographic Sciences and Approaches   171

Extensive and Intensive Research Strategies 176
The Variable-Based Design 180
The Case-Based Design 183
  What is a Case in Case-Based Research? 184
  Why should the Case-Based Design, and not the Variable-Based One,
    Dominate in Research on Psychology and Culture? 185
The Problem of Sampling 186
  Why is Sampling Important? 186
  What should be Sampled in Culture and Psychology Research? 187
Conclusion 193
Questions 193
Exercise 194
Glossary 194
Recommended Reading 195
References 195

PART III
Practical Aspects of Doing Research   199

8   The Types of Studies on Culture and Psychology   201
  Introduction: Monocultural Studies 201
    Disciplinary Distinctions 201
    Positions of Researchers 202
    Methodology of Monocultural Studies 202
  Multicultural Comparative Studies in Anthropology, Cultural Psychology,
    and Cross-Cultural Psychology 207
    Advantages of the Comparative Method 208
    A Comparative Case-Based Design 208
    Comparative Anthropological and Cultural Psychological Studies:
      A Comparative Mode of Research Within the Interpretive and Realist Paradigms 211
    Comparative Cultural Psychological Studies 212
    Cross-Cultural Psychological Studies: A Comparative
      Variable-Based Approach 213
    Different Levels of Comparison: Country-Level Versus
      Individual-Level Studies 216
    The Dangers of Ecological Fallacy and the Fallacy of Composition 218
    Cross-Cultural Research and Ecological Fallacy 219
    Measures to Prevent Ecological Fallacy in Cross-Cultural
      Psychological Research 219
  Conclusion 220
  Questions 220
  Exercises 221
  Glossary 221
  Recommended Reading 222
  References 222

9 Quantitative Comparative Studies: Equivalence, Translation, and Measurement Invariance 226

   Introduction 226
   When Is the Translation of Data Generating Instruments Required? 227
      When to Adopt? 227
      Adaptation and Modification of Existing Instruments 227
      Developing a New Instrument Suitable for Source and Target Cultures 227
   The Problem of Equivalence in Cross-Cultural Research 228
   Types of Equivalence 228
      Construct Validity and Equivalence 229
      Statistical Testing of Construct Validity and Equivalence 235
      Content Validity and Equivalence 237
      Linguistic Equivalence 238
   Measurement Invariance Testing 245
      MACS Analyses 246
      Full and Partial Invariance 248
      Measures to Prevent Noninvariance 250
   Conclusion 250
   Questions 251
   Exercise 251
   Glossary 251
   Recommended Reading 252
   References 253

10 Ethnography 257

   Introduction 257
   What is Ethnography? Ethnography's Complexities and Problems, and Their Resolutions 258
      The Challenges of Ethnography and Their Resolutions 258
   Some Practical Issues of Ethnographic Fieldwork 261
      Selecting Settings and Entering the Field 261
      Generating Data in the Field 264
      Person-Centered Ethnography and Interviewing 268
      Recording Ethnographic Data 274
      Analyzing Ethnographic Data 276
   Conclusion 278
   Questions 278
   Exercise 279
   Glossary 279
   Recommended Reading 280
   References 280

11 Ethical Concerns 282

   Introduction 282
   Major Ethical Concerns 283

Informed Consent 283
Positions of Researchers: Insiders Versus Outsiders 286
Researchers' Ethnocentrism 288
Building Rapport 289
Sharing Results 291
Outlining Possible Standpoints 294
Conclusion 295
Questions 296
Glossary 296
Recommended Reading 297
References 297

Conclusion: Final Words of Encouragement   299

Index   *301*

PREFACE

More and more events, incidents, and happenings that occupy the informational space of various media are accompanied by the adjectives *cultural, cross-cultural, multicultural,* or their derivatives. These media stories are "cultural" in addressing sociocultural institutions like religion, ethnicity, nation, nationality, marriage, work, education, health, and how people interact and sometimes clash with these institutions. We hear and read about the religious radicalization of youth, the integration and acculturation of immigrants and native populations, violence against women, the changing definition of marriage, sports-driven riots, the multicultural workforce, and people of diverse ethnic, religious, sexual, and other backgrounds and orientations developing their new and mixed identities, to name only a few. In all these instances, individuals collaborate or collide with existing sociocultural realities and either change these realities or change themselves. Some results of these interaction are dangerous and harmful, both for people and for communities.

Research with the adjectives *cultural, cross-cultural, multicultural,* and similar terms are soaring around the world. Think about the multitude of international students who face not only the difficulties of learning new subjects, but also the challenges of new cultural rules, norms, and regulations that are sometimes more strenuous than the academic learning itself; or international companies that are mushrooming around the world and hiring personnel of all possible ethno-cultural and linguistic backgrounds; or immigrants who arrive in foreign countries to make their fortunes and are encountering the challenges of adaptation, acquiring new identities, and negotiating their old and new cultural baggage; or members of developing countries that have started processes of democratization, urbanization, and industrialization and face the challenges of adapting their traditional ways of living to the new demands of a developing world. And these examples can be multiplied. Recently, the term culture has moved from the traditional domains of ethno-cultural communities to areas where it was never used before, like the *culture of corruption,* the *culture of poverty,* the *culture of safety,* the *rape culture, gang cultures,* and so on. It is clear that all kinds of *cultural* research are crucial and important in the modern world. For psychologists who are doing this type of studies, the primary focus is on individuals—people who need to navigate these sometimes known and friendly, sometimes hostile and sometimes exciting sociocultural worlds that are full of opportunities of cultural learning and cultural emancipation, and who need a better understanding of what is going on with them, with their families or communities and what adjustments need to be made. Psychologists have to help them get this knowledge, help them comprehend and adjust to the changes that are occurring, and assist them in harmonizing their existence and bringing happiness and satisfaction to their lives.

In order to educate and empower these people, psychologists have to have knowledge about the nature and complexities of people's interaction with cultures. In order to have this knowledge, they have to conduct productive and insightful research. But how can they do this type of research on culture and psychology, how can they avoid wasting time and resources on unproductive and outdated methods of scientific investigation, how can they be prolific and also receive personal satisfaction through these scientific accomplishments? This book addresses these and other questions that students and young and not so young researchers on culture and psychology may have during their investigations.

I intentionally use the expression "research on culture and psychology" instead of labelling the specific disciplines. By "culture and psychology research," I am referring to all types of investigations where researchers are interested in examining people's psychological functioning in different sociocultural environments. Such examinations can be done within cultural and cross-cultural psychology, psychological, cognitive, and medical anthropology, transcultural psychiatry, cross-cultural education research, nursing or management studies, and many other disciplines. What is common to all these investigations is that the main interest of scholars is a person and his or her behaviors and experiences that are happening in a variety of sociocultural settings. The primary purpose of this book is to instruct students how to approach and study these behaviors and experiences. It mostly aims toward senior undergraduate and junior graduate students in psychological and social sciences that investigate people's behavior and experience in different cultures. It is expected that students are familiar with basics of cultural and cross-cultural psychology, cultural anthropology, research methods, elements of the philosophy of science and multivariate statistics. More experienced researchers can also find some inspirational ideas in this textbook.

Outstanding Features of This Textbook

There are several features of this textbook that make it different from other textbooks in this area. First of all, it is strongly committed to the belief that **the primary goal of science is to make discoveries**, to get to the unknown, to solve problems, and to decipher enigmas and puzzles. This textbook articulates the rules and prescriptions of how to make these discoveries. The paradigms and methodologies that do not lead to such discoveries should be either abandoned or used with restrictions.

Second, in order to be productive, to be able to advance knowledge and to make a substantial contribution to our understanding of ourselves in the modern world, **research should be problem-oriented.** This means that students and researchers should not simply be curious about their topics, but should have problem-driven curiosity. A problem is a paradox, a puzzle, or inconsistencies that exist out there in the worlds or inside our internal realm of thoughts, feelings, and experiences. If there is no problem, then nothing new, surprising or innovative can be revealed. No problem—no discovery.

Third, it strongly emphasizes that productive scientific research is a skillful use of intelligence, not of statistical programs. Any scientific research, and research on culture and psychology is no exception, is **first of all thinking**, and only then, doing. Students must think about the nature of objects of investigation, think about the theories that explain these objects, think about the ways of approaching them in an investigation. Such thinking should also be accompanied by **reflections** and reflective questions such as: Why am I studying this topic? Why am I using this particular theory? Why am I applying this specific philosophical paradigm? Disciplined thinking and reflections are at the core of scientific inquiries.

Fourth, this book propagates and is based on a **realist paradigm** of philosophical and methodological thinking which is relatively new for psychologists. This paradigm, which has been around as long as human beings have been curious, has recently become popular in the social sciences as a productive alternative to statistics-oriented positivist thinking as well as to social constructionist and some other postmodernist trends. Realist thinking is accompanied in this textbook by a deep appreciation and utilization of the **interpretivist paradigm,** with its desire to penetrate into the deep layers of cultural and personal systems of meaning.

Fifth, the **methodology** and the specific methods of research should always **follow problematization** and **thinking**. Methods are tools, and the tool any craftsperson should use depends on what he or she wants to do and what materials are available. Researchers have to identify the problem, conceptualize ideas about their investigation, hypothesize the structures and powers that function within these objects, and only then decide what instruments to use to approach these challenges in the most efficient and fruitful way. I like to think of a researcher as a detective whose goal is to solve a crime and who is ready to use all available means and methods to do this. A detective does not state that regardless of the nature of the crime he or she will use only, for example, hard-core evidence and DNA analysis, ignoring psychological profiling or eyewitness accounts because these methods are deemed either 'unscientific' or too 'soft' for a good investigation. If this is unthinkable for a criminal investigator, then why do scientific investigators sometimes do this, by favoring one method over all others independently of what they strive to research?

Sixth, this textbook invites culture and psychology researchers to **breach disciplinary boundaries** and learn about and utilize all possible knowledge available in various domains of psychology, anthropology, sociology, history, politics, and other disciplines. Going back to the researcher-as-a-detective metaphor, detectives never reject ballistic expertise or autopsy evidence because they belong to disciplinary domains far away from their specialization. They strive to use all possible information and knowledge to solve the crime, independent of their sources. So, why do psychologists sometimes deny ethnographic and anthropological knowledge when addressing the problems of human functioning in different cultures? Why do they routinely focus on a pretty narrow range of psychological theoretical accounts and often remain intentionally quite ignorant of vast domains of the historical, political, ethnographic, economic, and geographic knowledge that is related to communities of inquiry? They should do everything they can, as in the case of a good detective, to solve the puzzle. It should not matter where this information came from.

Seventh, this textbook acknowledges the importance and complexities of the **concept of culture** that are often ignored or simplified in mainstream psychological research. This book is built on the conviction that without understanding the nature of culture as a complex sociosymbolic, mental, and intersubjective phenomenon, no progress can be achieved in culture and psychology research. The theory of cultural models is suggested here as a productive option for cultural psychological studies.

Eighth, this textbook has a **critical stance** toward various theoretical, philosophical, and methodological approaches that stand in the way of productive and innovative solutions of scientific problems. Applying a mechanical metaphor of understanding how humans operate to research people's cultural functioning is not a productive tactic for modern cultural research. Using the positivist paradigm to think about scientific investigation is an outdated and unconstructive way to conduct culture and psychology studies (as well as other psychological and social-psychological studies). Ignoring the idiographic approach, case studies, and the intensive design impoverishes options and opportunities for curious and innovative researchers; embracing statistical analysis at the expense of thorough and inquisitive ethnography is an inexcusable limitation of any culture and psychology inquiry to understand the cultural world. This textbook criticizes the tendency some psychologists have toward the uncritical and unreflective applications of particular ways of thinking and doing research as the only ways that are scientific and correct. I label this tendency *research habitus*, and try to convince readers that this type of habitus kills science.

Structure of the Book

This textbook is organized in three parts and 11 chapters. Part I is about thinking and reflecting. It invites readers to execute disciplinary thinking in Chapter 1, theoretical thinking in Chapter 2, and philosophical contemplations in Chapters 3 and 4. The content of these four chapters is interrelated, and the textbook helps readers connect different disciplines, theoretical perspectives, and philosophical paradigms in a logical and congruent way. Part II is devoted to planning research where discovering and formulating a problem is of the greatest importance. Chapter 5 discusses this problematization together with the articulating the purposes of a study and asking research questions. Chapter 6 focuses the readers' attention on choosing concepts and working with the conceptual and theoretical foundations of an upcoming inquiry. And Chapter 7 targets such components of research strategies as nomothetic and idiographic approaches, variable- and case-based studies, as well as extensive and intensive designs and problems of sampling. Although the textbook may seem quite theoretical, my strong conviction is that not a single practical implementation can be done competently without seriously considering all these aspects. Part III elaborates on several practical aspects of doing research. Chapter 8 deals with mono- and comparative cultural studies both in anthropology and psychology; it discusses different levels of analysis and warns about the danger of ecological fallacy. Chapter 9 moves to some of the central topics of cross-cultural research: the equivalence of concepts, the translation of instruments, and the verification of the instruments' measurement invariance. Chapter 10 introduces ethnography, a topic that is a pretty rare guest in modern textbooks on research methods in culture and psychology. The book concludes with Chapter 11, which covers some of the most urgent and crucial aspects of conducting ethical cultural psychological research.

Pedagogical Elements

There are several features in this book to help readers learn the material. Each chapter starts with a **list of the content objectives** that will be covered in the chapter and a short **introduction**. These will inform readers what to expect in the upcoming chapter and set a stage for a more in-depth and informed reading of the material presented. Within chapters, several types of boxes are inserted: **information boxes** that complement the main text by historical notes and definitions, **boxes with examples** of studies, and **how-to boxes** that provide advice and prescriptions on methodological issues. There are also **figures and tables** that illustrate some propositions and help readers comprehend issues and themes. Each chapter ends with **questions** to help check students' understanding of the topics and to assist them and their instructors in organizing discussions. Some chapters also have **exercises** that allow students to showcase the skills learned in the chapters. There are **glossaries** of concepts and terms that were introduced in the corresponding chapters. These glossaries may serve as starting points for conceptualizing readers' own research. There are also **recommended reading** lists and **references** at the end of each chapter. French scholars used to talk about scientific research in terms of *"la cuisine scientifique,"* My goal in this textbook is to supply readers with the basic ingredients and main recipes to make any scientific 'meal' not only edible, but also tasty. Good luck with your cooking!

Website

The accompanying website (http://www.routledge.com/9780415820325/) features additional resources for instructors and students. The password protected instructor's section has PowerPoint slides for each chapter, additional references that complement the primary reading, and bonus questions that can be used for group discussions or as essay questions to evaluate students' knowledge. The students' section will have outlines of each chapter and chapter objectives together with key concepts to focus on, including a hotlink to the glossary definition.

ACKNOWLEDGMENTS

The author wants to thank Dr. Aaro Toomela and Dr. Lutz Eckensberger for their helpful comments on some of the chapters. He is also grateful to his students who read, commented on, and successfully incorporated early versions of chapters into their own research.

A very special thanks and deep appreciation go to the author's long-time friend and the language editor of this book, Joseph Naphin, whose vast knowledge of the English language, rich editorial experience, and strong dedication to this project helped to make this book happen.

I would like to thank the reviewers who provided valuable feedback: Osman Ozturgut, University of the Incarnate Word; David W. Shwalb, Southern Utah University; Elizabeth Trejos-Castillo, Texas Tech University; and two anonymous reviewers.

ABOUT THE AUTHOR

Valery Chirkov is a Professor of Psychology in the Department of Psychology at the University of Saskatchewan, in Saskatoon, Canada. He has authored and co-authored several books, book chapters, and articles on the topics of human autonomy, autonomous agency, and people's well-being in different cultures. He also conducts research and theorizing in the area of the psychology of immigration and acculturation and is interested in the philosophy and methodology of social and human sciences.

PART I
Thinking and Reflecting

One objective of this textbook is to highlight the importance of thinking about, reflecting upon, and planning research before any decision about methodology, design, and data generation technique is made. The second objective is to teach students that all studies must be problem-oriented. These two key points should drive research and determine its strategy, purpose, and methods for data collection and analysis.

Part I is devoted to three domains of thinking about research: *disciplinary*, *theoretical*, and *philosophical*. These three types of thinking guide researchers in understanding their stance within corresponding disciplines and their position in relation to content-related theories and philosophical paradigms. Each researcher has to have a clear understanding of the assumptions, underlying beliefs, and ideas that implicitly or explicitly guide his or her research activities. As we will discuss later, one of the objectives of such a strong emphasis on research-related reflections is to help readers discover and minimize *research habitus*, a taken-for-granted, habitual and unreflected set of beliefs about research (see Chapter 3). Chapter 1 will cover some areas of disciplinary thinking for research on culture and psychology, including anthropology—social, cultural, psychological, and cognitive—and psychology—cross-cultural, cultural, and indigenous. In Chapter 2, we will discuss four theoretical perspectives on understanding the psychological functioning of people in sociocultural environments. These perspectives are metaphorically labelled *Homo Mechanicus, Homo Bios, Homo Socius, and Homo Interpretans*. Chapters 3 and 4 will introduce three philosophical paradigms—positivism, interpretivism, and realism, together with related modes of inference—enumerative-inductive, deductive-nomological, abductive, and retroductive, where the last two are categorized as the ampliative-inductive and ampliative-deductive ways of inference.

1

DISCIPLINARY THINKING

From Anthropology to Psychology

This chapter will:

- Provide a brief historical account of social and cultural anthropology
- Discuss the main theories of culture
- Introduce the idea of cultural relativism and the etic and emic approaches to research on culture and psychology
- Analyze the emergence of and some contribution to psychological and cognitive anthropology
- Examine the accomplishments and weaknesses of cross-cultural psychology
- Consider cultural and indigenous psychology

Introduction

Research on culture and psychology is part of the social sciences that are concerned with investigating societies and people's functioning within these societies at different levels: individual, social, cultural, and national. These sciences encompass such disciplines as anthropology, economics, sociology, political science, and some fields of psychology. *Social* in the name of these sciences denotes the sociocultural, socioeconomic, sociopolitical and sociopsychological aspects of people's lives in the modern world. A goal of this chapter is to provide a survey of the main disciplines that aim at studying human functioning in different sociocultural contexts, mostly in various domains of anthropology and psychology. An additional purpose of this chapter is to show the interdisciplinary nature of culture and psychology research and to demonstrate that compartmentalized disciplinary thinking is unproductive for such investigations. Each of the analyzed fields of study has the potential to make important contributions to understanding people's behaviors and experiences in sociocultural environments. I also want to demonstrate that both cross-cultural and cultural psychology are members of a large family of disciplines where scientists want to understand how people, their actions, and experiences contribute to the development of their sociocultural worlds, and how these worlds shape and regulate their behaviors and lives. The third objective of this chapter is to help young researchers to position themselves disciplinarily and reflect on the connections with and insights from other disciplines. Here these reflections are called *disciplinary thinking*.

This chapter will provide a brief history and a major focus on the methodology of social and cultural anthropology as well as on psychological and cognitive anthropology and cross-cultural,

cultural, and indigenous psychologies. These disciplines will be defined and their approaches to culture and people's behavior and psychological functioning will be outlined. Finally, I will demonstrate how these disciplines may complement each other in resolving the enigma of humans' sociocultural existence.

Cultural and Social Anthropology

The term *anthropology* comes from Greek *anthrōpos*—human being and *logia*—study. This etymological definition means a study of humans or a science of human beings. But the more accepted interpretation of anthropology is a study of humankind, of human communities of different sizes and their ways of life, rituals, norms, and values. Anthropology is a social science, but it has several divisions, like physical, biological, and evolutionary anthropology, that connect it with natural sciences, biology first of all. There are also divisions, like linguistic anthropology, anthropology of art, religion, and history, that are closely connected to the humanities. The subfields of psychological and cognitive anthropology are the closest to psychology. These varieties of anthropology make it one of the richest social/human sciences, and psychologists interested in studying human functioning in different cultures will benefit by learning more about this discipline.

Anthropology has a long history driven by the interest and fascination that travelers, tradespeople, missionaries, and scholars experienced upon encountering exotic tribes, their unusual rituals and beliefs, paradoxical social arrangements, and many other peculiarities of people's social lives that seemed amusing and unexplainable at a first glance (see some of their accounts in Launay, 2010). A systematic study of these 'other' ways of life started in Continental Europe, where works by German philosophers **Immanuel Kant** (1724–1804)—his lectures *Anthropology From a Pragmatic Point of View* were published in 1798—and **Johann Gottfried von Herder** (1744–1803)—his 1784 book *Outlines of a Philosophy of the History of Man*—laid the basis of the studies of culture. It is believed that their precursors were Italian humanist **Giambattista Vico** (1668–1744) and French lawyer and philosopher **Baron de Montesquieu** (1689–1755), who each provided a new and revealing look and analysis of the development of human societies (Eriksen & Nielsen, 2001). These thinkers produced the idea of *volkergeist*, or "spirit of the people" or "spirit of nations" as a precursor to the idea of culture that is shared by people and molds their psychological existence. An important figure, especially for culture and psychology studies, was German scholar **Adolf Bastian** (1826–1905), who contributed to anthropology, psychology, and the humanities. Bastian suggested the important notion of "the psychic unity of mankind" for investigating the functioning of people in different sociocultural worlds. Under this concept, he understood a set of "elementary ideas" (*Elementargedanken*) that are universal for all people and that manifest themselves in varieties of "folk ideas" (*Volkergedanken*) that are peculiar for each sociocultural community (Koepping, 1983). It is believed that Bastian's notion of elementary ideas contributed to the structuralist hypotheses of Levi-Strauss as well to the insights of Carl Jung about the universal themes of collective unconscious. Although there are debates among anthropologists about how to interpret and apply this notion of "the psychic unity of mankind" (see Shore, 1998, for a discussion), it is considered one of the basic principles of modern anthropology and psychology, which states that "humans [are] everywhere born with roughly the same potentials, and inherited differences are negligible" (Eriksen & Nielsen, 2001, p. 17). British anthropologists of the 19th and 20th centuries **Edward Burnett Tylor** (1832–1917) and **Sir James George Frazer** (1854–1941) and French social scientists **Marcel Mauss** (1872–1950) and **Claude Levi-Strauss** (1908–2009) are considered to be the founding fathers of modern anthropology.

Nowadays the majority of the anthropologists who identify themselves with the social sciences are divided between *social* and *cultural anthropology*. *Social anthropology* is mostly associated with the

British (and partly French) tradition of studying the diversity of human societies. It treats cultures as the outcomes of the social structures and social relations that exist in these societies. According to these scholars, the social is primary while cultural and symbolic are secondary. *Cultural anthropology* is considered a mostly North American tradition where the cultural is believed to be the primary factor that determines social conditions. There is a tendency in modern anthropology to combine these two disciplines under the title of *sociocultural anthropology* (Carrier & Gewertz, 2013), similar to merging social and cultural psychology under the umbrella of *sociocultural psychology* (Valsiner & Rosa, 2007).

Social anthropology has its roots in the works of **Alfred Reginald Radcliffe-Brown** (1881–1955), **Bronislaw Malinowski** (1884–1942), **Sir Edward Evan Evans-Pritchard** (1902–1973), and some other British and Continental social scientists. Most of them were strongly influenced by Darwin's idea of evolution, which they applied to the realm of the social and cultural development of humankind and their civilizations. Following Radcliffe-Brown, many embraced *structural functionalism,* which treats societies as complex systems, like organisms, where all their components work together to support the main functions of survival of, coordination, and balance among the people within their social milieu. For psychologists, it is important to consider Malinowski's functionalist idea that cultures and societies serve as mediators and facilitators for the satisfaction of human physiological and psychological needs. It is believed that this idea laid the foundation of the culture and personality studies later in the United States (J. D. Moore, 1997).

Disciplinarily speaking, social anthropology has been much closer to sociology than to psychology, and its boundaries with sociology are pretty blurry. It had been thought that social anthropology should have been focusing more on primitive societies, whereas sociology should have been studying modern and industrialized societies. Today this division no longer exists, as social anthropologists intensively study various domains and aspects of life both of underdeveloped and of developed and highly industrialized countries (Fardon et al., 2012). It was also believed that anthropologists should have mostly employed holistic ethnographic methods of living and observing natives in their natural environments, while sociologists should have used a more analytical approach, very often quantitative, to study the organizations and functioning of human social communities and societies. This division no longer works either, as sociologists successfully employ ethnographic methods to do their work just as anthropologists do (Hammersley & Atkinson, 2007).

A strong critical analysis of British social anthropology was provided by American anthropologist George Peter Murdock (1951), which still bothers these scholars (see Fardon et al., 2012). Murdock's statements, that social anthropologists are closer to sociologists than to anthropologists if culture is considered the primary topic of anthropology and that in their theorizing they are indifferent to psychology, are important for psychologists who work with social anthropologists. Although the authors of two volumes of *The Sage Handbook of Social Anthropology* (Fardon et al., 2012) try to delineate the disciplinary and thematic boundaries of this discipline, many of the critical reflections of Murdock remain unaddressed.

Cultural anthropology was born in the United States and spread to other countries. German-trained physics student **Franz Boas** (1858–1942) became a prominent American anthropologist and the father of American anthropology. He was a student of Bastian, who moved to northwestern Canada to study how native people perceive the color of ice and seawater. This topic was driven by his interest in the psychophysics of vision. Then, he naturally moved to study the universal and relative aspects of psychological processes, and these studies provoked his thinking in relativistic terms, emphasizing that each community creates its unique cultures and social institutions that determine the distinctive configurations of the psychological processes of its members. Thus, an idea of *culture* as a powerful determinant of mental and behavioral differences emerged in anthropology and gave a whole new direction of thinking in comparison to social anthropology. By placing culture at the center of anthropological research, the problem of understanding what culture is and developing theoretical accounts of this phenomenon became important for these scholars.

This *culturalist* direction of cultural anthropology has been involved in studying the development and evolution of cultures and discovering the regularities and patterns of these developments, comparing cultural communities, and, finally, developing theories of culture. Cultural anthropologists became the leading theoreticians of culture in the social sciences for many years (Harris, 2001; Keesing, 1974, 1990; Kroeber & Kluckhohn, 1952; J. D. Moore, 1997). This strong emphasis on culture makes them believe in the primacy of culture in determining social structures and human behaviors, and thus they believe that by studying cultures they will provide answers to both the social and psychological concerns of people and their communities. This type of thinking made a crucial contribution to the development of the *Homo Socius* perspective, which is discussed in Chapter 2. In the second half of the 20th century, the notion of culture moved from anthropology to become an important notion in other social sciences, including psychology (Baldwin, Faulkner, Hecht, & Lindsley, 2005).

The Main Theories of Culture

The first and the most popular definition of culture came from Edward Tylor (1871/1958): "Culture or civilization, taken in its wide ethnographic sense, is that complex whole which includes knowledge, belief, art, orals, laws, custom, and any other capabilities and habits acquired by man as a member of society" (p. 1). This all-encompassing, descriptive, and eclectic definition of culture is still used nowadays. Another similarly descriptive and attractive definition of culture was provided by cultural anthropologist Melville Herskovits (1955): "Culture is the man-made part of the environment" (p. 305). Since the publication of Tylor's definition, anthropologists developed dozens of definitions of culture, making it very challenging for social scientists to use this concept for their research. Some kind of analysis and categorization of all these definitions of culture has become necessary. Kroeber and Kluckhonh (1952) implemented such a work by collecting 164 definitions of culture and examining them through a systematic and comparative analysis. This monumental work has maintained its importance and informative value to this day. But still, to understand culture, researchers have to rely not on its definitions, which can sometimes be short and simplistic, but they must think of theories of culture as a set of propositions that uncover the nature, structure, functions, and mechanisms of this phenomenon. That is why in the next sections I provide a brief account of these theories.

Adaptationist Theories of Culture

One group of culture theories comes from anthropologists who treat culture as an aggregation of tools, technologies, and practices through which human communities adapt to their environments and available resources (Harris, 2001; Keesing, 1974; J. D. Moore, 1997). *Cultural adaptationists* believe that human communities had (and still have) the ultimate goal of organizing their lives in the existing environments in such a way that promotes survival and reproduction. In order to do this successfully, people invent cultures and related institutions, like marriage, religion, laws, technologies, education, and many other conventions that help them to adapt. This is where the *"onion peeling" metaphor* of the relation between culture and pan-human nature in psychology came from: the idea that if researchers "peel off" the layers of sociocultural adaptations and conventions, they will discover primary human nature, including people's universal psychological makeup. This metaphor is still popular in cross-cultural psychology, and it implicitly or explicitly guides discussions of evolutionary psychologists about evolution and culture (see Dunbar & Barrett, 2007). Keesing (1974) summarized the main propositions of cultural adaptationists in the following way:

a. Cultures are systems (or socially transmitted behavior patterns) that serve to relate human communities to their ecological settings. These ways-of-life-of-communities include technologies

and modes of economic organization, settlement patterns, modes of social grouping and political organization, religious beliefs and practices, and so on.
b. Cultural change is primarily a process of adaptation and what amounts to natural selection. . . . Seen as adaptive systems, cultures change in the direction of equilibrium within ecosystems; but when balances are upset by environmental, demographic, technological, or other systemic changes, further adjustive changes ramify through the cultural system.
c. Technology, subsistence economy, and elements of social organization directly tied to production are the most adaptively central realms of culture. It is in these realms that adaptive changes usually begin and from which they usually ramify.
d. The ideational components of cultural systems [beliefs, values, mythology, systems of knowledge production, etc.] may have adaptive consequences in controlling population, contributing to subsistence, maintaining the ecosystem, etc.; and these, though often subtle, must be carefully traced out wherever they lead. (pp. 75–76)[1]

Adaptationist theories of culture are closely bound with the *Homo Bios* theoretical perspective that will be presented and discussed in the next chapter.

Cultures as Systems of Ideas or Ideational Theories of Culture

Kessing (1974) differentiated several subtypes of ideational theories of culture: *cultures as cognitive systems*, as *structural systems*, and as *symbolic systems*.

Many cultural anthropologists perceive *culture as cognitive systems:*

> A society's culture consists of whatever it is one has to know or believe in order to operate in a manner acceptable to its members. Culture is not a material phenomenon; it does not consist of things, people, behavior, or emotions. It is rather an organization of these things. It is the form of things that people have in mind, their models for perceiving, relating, and otherwise interpreting them ([Goodenough] p. 167).
>
> (Keesing, 1974, p. 77)

Close to this definition is the interpretation of culture as "a social stock of knowledge," suggested by sociologists Berger and Luckmann (1966/1989). This stock of knowledge consists of the accumulated experience and knowledge of community members "which is transmitted from generation to generation and which is available to the individual in everyday life" (p. 41). Such a stock of skills and information is made up of "recipe knowledge, that is, knowledge limited to pragmatic competence in routine performances" (p. 42), such as how to do things like cook food, parent a child, or go on a date. "The stock of knowledge further supplies me with the typificatory schemes required for the major routines of everyday life, . . . typification of all sorts of events and experiences, both social and natural" (p. 43). Finally, such stocks supply people with the 'lenses' of how to perceive and categorize events and things in the worlds. The communal stock of knowledge is an integrated whole that embraces all aspects of people's lives and provides individual members with all the necessary knowledge and decision-making rules that allow them to live coherent and meaningful lives within their communities.

The understanding of culture as a system of knowledge is different from the adaptationists' theories, where cultures are mostly represented by habitually performed activities, patterns of behavior and related institutions that connect communities to their environments. Tylor's definition above

---

1 Republished with permission of *Annual Reviews*, from Keesing, R. M. (1974). Theories of culture. *Annual Review of Anthropology, 3*, 73–97; permission conveyed through Copyright Clearance Center, Inc.

of culture comprises the elements of both the adaptationist and culture-as-knowledge approaches. Proponents of culture as a system of knowledge theories have also suggested using concepts such as 'cultural grammar,' 'semantic fields or 'zones of meaning,' 'cultural scripts,' and other ideas that use language as a metaphor for understanding and studying cultures (Keesing, 1974; Wierzbicka, 1996, 2002). Do not confuse this with *linguistic anthropology,* which studies language, speech, and communication as major institutions of culture (Salzmann, Stanlaw, & Adachi, 2014).

Talking about culture as a system of knowledge, it is relevant to acknowledge a *structuralist approach* to the nature of social that was initiated by social anthropologist Claude Lévi-Strauss (1967). This scholar was concerned not with culture per se, or with the functioning and experiencing of individual minds in societies; rather, he was concerned with the deep structures of cultures and societies that underlie their institutions, traditions, rituals, and beliefs. His emphasis was on the logic of structural connections rather than on the content of what is connected.

> Lévi-Strauss (1963:3) argues that "Social anthropology is devoted especially to the study of institutions considered as systems of representation." Lévi-Strauss uses 'representation' as did Durkheim, to refer to beliefs, sentiments, norms, values, attitudes, meanings [understood as collective and not individual phenomena]. Those institutions are cultural expressions that are usually unexamined by their users; in that narrow but fundamental sense, anthropology examines the *unconscious* foundations of social life: "anthropology draws its originality from the unconscious nature of collective phenomena" (Lévi-Strauss 1963:18). This search for the underlying structure of social life led Lévi-Strauss to explore three principal areas: systems of classification, kinship theory, and the logic of myth.
>
> (J. D. Moore, 1997, p. 219)

Lévi-Strauss's search for the deep underlying structures of the social corresponds well with the idea of deep hermeneutics and of realism in their application to sociocultural worlds (see Chapter 4).

Culture as symbolic systems is another variant of the ideational theories of cultures. **Victor Turner** (1920–1983), **David Schneider** (1918–1995), and **Clifford James Geertz** (1926–2006) are the best known representatives of this direction of thinking. For Geertz,

> The concept of culture . . . is essentially a semiotic one. Believing, with Max Weber, that man is an animal suspended in webs of significance he himself has spun, I take the culture to be those webs, and the analysis of it to be therefore not an experimental science in search of law but an interpretative one is search of meaning.
>
> (1973, p. 5)

According to this approach, cultures are understood as systems of shared symbols and meanings (Keesing, 1974, p. 79). For Geertz, cultural institutions, like a Beethoven quartet, a cock fight, or a funeral, are ideational phenomena, meaning that what is essential for them is not the physical entities per se, like the musicians as individuals, their attire, musical instruments, or their audiences, but the ideas or systems of meaning that cultural communities impose on this assemblage of physical entities. On one occasion, these systems of meaning construct out of human individuals and their actions the musicians and the musical concert; in another instance, out of another gathering of similar human individuals, they create a funeral. These codes of meaning are shared by members of communities, and the task of anthropologists is to discover them through interpretation. Thus, in this perspective, anthropology is seen as an interpretive science (see Chapter 4 on interpretivism). At the same time, Geertz denied that these meanings and ideas reside in individuals' minds, that they are intrapsychic by their nature. He believed that these meanings are public and *intersubjective*, implying that they exist in between the subjectivities of individual minds. Cultural meanings exist 'out there' in the communities, and people are born into them, learn them, and thus become socialized and enculturated individuals and full-fledged members of their cultural communities. This means that cultures are not patterns of behaviors and rituals, not collections of knowledge and decision-making prescriptions; rather, they are a network of symbols and codes of meaning through which people's behaviors and actions are regulated. As do the majority of social and cultural anthropologists, Geertz holds an antipsychologist position, meaning he does not use psychology to explain culture, but uses culture to explain psychology (see Chapter 2). Despite Geertz's antipsychologism, some of his ideas were further developed by cognitive anthropologists (D'Andrade, 1984) and are relevant for cultural psychologists.

It is important to emphasize that all these theoreticians were concerned with understanding the nature and structures of 'social' and 'cultural' as large systemic wholes, where the understanding of individual minds, culturally relative configurations of human mentalities, and the dynamics of interactions of culture with the human minds were not a priority. Although they have to be well educated about the developments of cultural theorists, researchers on culture and psychology cannot take these interpretations of cultures as directly and unequivocally applicable to cultural psychological research. An adjustment and even a reconceptualization of these theories has to be made in order to include individuals' minds into the broad picture of social and cultural realities.

Cultural Relativism

Boas's idea of culture as a powerful determinant of humans' psychological and social functioning inevitably implied a notion of *cultural relativism*: the idea that the ethno-racial, mental, and behavioral differences among communities of people are determined, not by biological, but by cultural factors. This idea was revolutionary for the colonial and ethnocentric thinking of European and North American scholars and has become a major maxim of modern anthropology. Later it was defined as a view that people's values, beliefs, and practices should be understood in terms of their own cultures and that judgments and moral evaluations of cultures cannot be done using criteria external to them.

Another idea conceptually close to cultural relativism is the distinction between the *etic* and *emic* approaches in studying cultures and people's behavior, suggested by American linguist and anthropologist Kenneth Pike (1967). He provided the following definition of these approaches: "The etic viewpoint studies behavior as from outside of a particular system, and as an essential initial approach to an alien system. The emic viewpoint results from studying behavior as from inside the system" (p. 37). This distinction between the etic or 'outsider' and emic or 'insider' positions of researchers toward their objects of investigation is an important methodological requirement for culture and psychology research and will be discussed in more detail in Chapters 7 and 11.

Methodologically, both social and cultural anthropologists emphasize the emic approach to study cultures and an 'insider' position of researchers toward the objects of their investigation. Because of this conviction, *ethnography* has been the main instrument for their investigations, including naturalistic and participant observation, interview, mapping and census taking, life history analysis, artifact analysis, and many other methods and techniques that allow researchers to get into the cultural communities of others and investigate their main characteristics 'from within.' Anthropologists strongly believe that only by living with and observing the practices of others as they unfold in their contexts will they get an opportunity to describe and understand the structures and dynamics of the social and symbolic fabric of these communities. Thus, an ethnographic fieldwork has become a stamp of anthropological research inquiries.

Why is ethnography so important for anthropologists? First, because knowledge about sociocultural communities is contextual and situated, meaning that it exists within particular communities, inhabited by particular people at particular locations and points of time. Researchers can make an account of this situatedness of knowledge by positioning themselves in the same locations and contexts. Second, because sociocultural arrangements are perceived as systems that function as wholes which cannot be reduced to their components. To grasp the systemic nature of cultures, researchers have to study them in a nonreductionist way. Third, there is a strong conviction that for valid anthropological research, it is most important to consider what people *do*, first of all, and only then to consider what they *say*. To know what people do, researchers have to be where the actions are happening. These arguments are also relevant for psychologists, who strive to understand why people do what they do in different sociocultural settings. There are numerous arguments from different streams of psychology that ethnography should be returned to sociocultural psychological research (see Fish, 2000; Jessor, Colby, & Shweder, 1996; Miller, Hengst, & Wang, 2003). Nowadays ethnography is often discussed under the rubric of qualitative research (Kopala & Suzuki, 1999; Nagata, Kohn-Wood, & Suzuki, 2012).

It is important to mention Malinowski's contribution to the methodology of ethnography. He revolutionized ethnographic fieldwork by incorporating participant observation (see Chapter 10).

> Malinowski invented intensive ethnographic fieldwork as a scientific ideal, involving prolonged residence in the field, command of the local language, "participation" in the activities and relationships of the community, and reconstructing "the native's point of view" of cultural practices through a combination of observation, verbal reports, and the accumulation of case material. The anthropologist became a simulated insider as well as a scholarly investigator, seeking to identify the local meanings of practices that would be opaque to less intensive investigation.
> (LeVine & New, 2008a, p. 14)

Right from their beginnings, both social and cultural anthropology have been considered the sciences of comparative studies of human societies and communities where the *comparative approach* has played an important role in achieving their goals (Evans-Pritchard, 1963; Hammel, 1980; Mace & Pagel, 1994; Radcliffe-Brown, 1951). (See Chapter 8 for more on the comparative method). The emergence of the comparative method and simultaneously the statistical method is traced back to Tylor's (1889) paper, where he compared 350 different societies on the institutions and customs of marriage and the dynamics of social development and demonstrated that statistical associations exist between the cultural practices and customs extracted from different societies. For example, they occur between forms of marriage and patriarchical or matriarchical arrangements of family structures. When presented with this report, Francis Galton raised the concern that many cultural practices that are spread to other regions and communities often come from the same source, and because of this, they cannot be treated as independent instances. This consideration, if it is true, substantially reduces the strength and, consequently, the importance of such correlations. This concern is known in comparative anthropology as *Galton's problem*, which is based on the proposition that "cultures are not independent but rather may share many cultural elements by virtue of common ancestry and proximity" (Mace & Pagel, 1994, p. 549). Galton's problem sets a serious challenge for all cross-cultural comparisons, and researchers should pay careful attention to controlling for cultural dependence when doing statistical comparative analysis.

Anthropologists are convinced that only through an in-depth analysis of cultural communities and following comparisons along various etic- and emic-based criteria will they be capable of contemplating about the stages and mechanisms of cultural development, of establishing causal relations among different elements of these systems as well as relations between sociocultural characteristics and the behavioral and mental attributes of the members of these communities. The comparative method also allows anthropologists to investigate the culture-specific and culture-universal aspects of sociocultural systems. One of the fundamental challenges for both anthropology and psychology has been the reconciliation of the thesis of the psychic unity of mankind, accompanied by discovering humans' psychological and behavioral universals, with the existence of culture-relative and specific components of people's mental lives. Thus, in their investigations, anthropologists have targeted both the differences and commonalities of people's cultural and mental existence. At Yale University, Murdock and his colleagues created the *Human Relations Area Files*, a database of anthropological data drawn from many cultures and societies that are arranged in a way that allows any interested researcher to use them for cross-cultural comparisons. Scholars may visit their site to gain access to this database: http://hraf.yale.edu/online-databases/ehraf-world-cultures/. Murdock is also known for publishing the *Outline of World Cultures* and the *World Ethnographic Sample*, the first cross-cultural data set consisting of 565 cultures coded for 30 variables (http://en.wikipedia.org/wiki/George_Murdock). Along this line of searching for universals, one may find the popular book of anthropologist Donald Brown, *Human Universals* (1991), useful.

Hammel (1980) identified the four major challenges that the comparative method in anthropology has to face and address:

1. The identification and classification of the cultural items to be compared.
2. The scope of the comparison in time and space or, more generally, in the degree of expected difference between the pairs of social units compared.
3. The aims of the comparison. Is the intent of the comparison the formulation of scientific "laws" of functional relationship, or is it the reconstruction of history from subsequent materials? Are the comparisons made for descriptive or analytic purposes? Is the style of argument inductive or deductive?
4. The design of the comparison. How much control can be exercised over exogenous variation? How much attention is paid to sampling and statistical reliability? (pp. 147–148)[2]

In modern anthropology, comparative studies are known as *cross-cultural research* (Ember & Ember, 2009); we will discuss some of their problems in Chapter 8.

Anthropologists have not been alien to quantitative methods like surveys, psychological tests, and questionnaires, but they treat their results with great caution. "One criticism of the cross-cultural survey method is that cultural elements abstracted from cultural contexts are not comparable (because they are not identical); another is that cultures are functionally integrated wholes that can be studied only as totalities" (Rossi & O'Higgins, 1980, p. 94).

Psychological and Cognitive Anthropology

In the 1920s–1940s, several students of Franz Boas—Ruth Benedict, Geoffrey Gorer, Adam Kardiner, Ralph Lipton, Margaret Mead, and some others—initiated a set of studies of the national character of people from different countries accompanied by theorizing about the interactions of sociocultural environments with human psyche and personality, known in anthropology as *culture and personality studies* (LeVine, 2001). This was probably the first attempt in the history of human sciences of a mutual penetration by anthropology and psychology, when such psychologists as Gardner Murphy and David McClelland used anthropological arguments and ethnographic evidence in their theorizing about personality (LeVine, 2001). Many find the roots of this movement in the works of **Sigmund Freud** (1856–1939), who extended an application of his ideas about the

---

[2] Republished with permission of Cambridge University Press from Hammel, E. A. (1980). The comparative method in anthropological perspective. *Comparative Studies in Society and History, 22*(2), 145–155.

structure and dynamics of psyche to cultures and societies. *Psychoanalytic anthropology* (Paul, 1989) has emerged as a discipline to reconcile the ideas of psychoanalysis and studies of culture.

One of the main ideas of culture and personality studies was the cultural patterning of personality that results in the development of a national character of people in every country or nation (Hsu, 1972, p. 3). Another way to say this is that in these studies, and followed from *psychological anthropology*, an individual and his or her personality and mental life has become a focus of a cultural analysis and is seen not as a hypothetic and average bearer of various cultural systems, as social and cultural anthropologists treated individuals, but as embodied human beings that act and function by interacting with their cultural milieu. Ethnographic studies of child rearing practices as the basis of adult personality structures and modes of functioning also started within this domain of research (LeVine & New, 2008b). Culture and personality studies were also driven by applied purposes because the government of the USA was interested in understanding the attitudes and predicting the behaviors of authorities and citizens of the countries with which the United States was building its relations, like Japan, which was defeated and occupied after WWII, Soviet Russia as an enemy in the unfolding Cold War, and some other nations of political interest. In other chapters, I will use the works of Benedict, and Gorer and Rickman for illustrative and analytical purposes.

What is remarkable about these studies from the methodological perspective is that researchers had limited, if any, opportunities to travel to the countries of interest to do their fieldwork. So, starting with Benedict's study of the Japanese national character, scholars utilized *anthropology at a distance*, when they used indirect evidence from various sources to describe and analyze the cultural patterns and national characters of interest. A brief survey of the content of Mead and Metraux's (1953/2000) *The Study of Culture at a Distance* gives a good impression of the methodological breadth of this area of research: "Group research; work with informants; written and oral literature; film analysis, and projective techniques" (pp. vii–ix). This volume can definitely extend the methodological expertise of culture and psychology researchers.

In 1972, American anthropologist Francis Hsu (1972) suggested to continue culture and personality studies within the new discipline of *psychological anthropology*. "Psychological anthropology is the study of the behaviors, experience and development of individuals in relation to the institutions and ideologies of their sociocultural environments, across all populations of the human species" (LeVine, 2010a). Hsu (1972) outlined the following differences of psychological anthropology from the exclusively psychological studies of individuals:

> the psychic material which psychological anthropology deals with are (a) the conscious and unconscious ideas shared by a majority of individuals in a given society as *individuals* . . . and (b) the conscious and unconscious psychic materials governing the action patterns of many individuals as a group. . . . Both of these are different from the unique psychology of the individual.
>
> (p. 10)

This quote leads us directly to the main focus of culture and psychology research as it is outlined in this book. In particular, it states that in order to fully understand why people do, think, and feel as they do in particular cultural communities (and people always act, feel, and think in particular sociocultural circumstances), it is important to, first, investigate collective intersubjective ideas of communities about various domains of people's lives (what is later called *public aspects of cultural models*), and then study the learned and internalized facets of these models (*internalized aspects of cultural models*); then, finally, examine how these aspects interact with each other and determine people's experiences and behaviors. Psychological anthropology and, closest to it, cultural psychology, are the core disciplines within which culture and psychology research is to unfold.

Psychological anthropologists study a wide variety of topics: "[They] tend to focus on psychocultural processes: e.g. human adaptation, learning and development, integration and disintegration at individual and societal levels, viewed from cultural, biological, psychological and sociological perspectives" (LeVine, 2010, p. 3). The leading topics of their interest have been the child development, emotions, motivation, and cognition of people in different sociocultural niches (for review see Bock, 1999; LeVine, 2010b; Lindholm, 2007). The studies of cognition gave rise to cognitive anthropology, which we will discuss shortly. One of the central topics of modern psychological anthropologists is the issue of *self* and *experience*. Some even consider the problem of human self and identity to be so important that they define the whole discipline of psychological anthropology around it:

> [Psychological anthropology] undertakes the cross-cultural study of the social, political, and cultural-historical constitution of the self; it also analyzes the manner in which human identity is variously disintegrated and reintegrated, conceptualized and realized, in diverse cultural and temporal settings. Because of its comparative thrust and its effort to reach universal truths while still giving credit to cultural specificities and the agency of individuals, psychological anthropology offers us materials and means to think more clearly and objectively about issues of selfhood and identity . . . The fundamental claim is that the individual exists only within a social and cultural context. Therefore, we can really know ourselves only if we know others, and we can really know others only if we know the cultures in which they (and we) exist.
>
> (Lindholm, 2007, p. 10)

But the study of a person's self and the investigation of how an individual forms oneself as a center of experience and action in different sociocultural communities, and how he or she reflects on this experience, are important questions for psychologists also. Psychologists who try to investigate the psychological functioning of people while ignoring the cultural contexts remove a fundamental factor that forms a person's self, his or her identity, experiences, and behaviors (Morris, 1991, 1994). And it is hard to disagree with Lindholm that in order to know humans' psychology we need to know their cultures. The topic of self inevitably leads scholars to the vast and challenging area of the agency of self and its autonomy and self-determination in the face of sociocultural prescriptions and constraints. (See the *Homo Interpretans* perspective in Chapter 2).

Closely related to the topic of self is the concept of *experience*, which is frequently labelled *subjectivity*. An idea of experience relates to the processes and results of people's first-hand contacts with the world, its events, other people, and themselves. These are the sensations, thoughts, and feelings that accompany everything people do: study, work, make love, joke, interact with other people, stay alone, meditate, and sleep. Experience is shaped by our sense of self and our identities, the feeling of who we are. Culture enters in this process in two ways: first, as a source of humans' experiences in the form of the cultural intentional things that are the primary objects of our experiences, and, second, by shaping the frame of reference through which we interpret these things. (See about intentional cultural things in Chapter 2). Thus, the study of cultural experience becomes the task of both anthropologists and psychologists (C. C. Moore & Mathews, 2001). Studies of experience move researchers to the domain of phenomenology and the phenomenological-interpretive research within *phenomenological anthropology* (Jackson, 1996) and the *anthropology of experience* (Turner & Bruner, 1986). These are important directions of psychological anthropological studies, but they have one caveat: by their very nature they are descriptive, and despite how well these descriptions are made, they do not move researchers to understand the sources of these experiences and their determinants and mechanisms. But some anthropologists become critical of these exclusively descriptive studies and invite researchers to look for the causal factors that work behind them. This is how cognitive/psychological anthropologist Roy D'Andrade (1999) worded this idea:

> Cultural meanings, social exigencies, cognitive capacities, emotional proclivities, etc., are not unrelated causal forces which can be studied each in isolation from the other.
>
> Cultural norms, beliefs and values, the social system, the economic system, different psychobiological processes, etc., all interact in complex ways to affect action. Rather than continuing to make interpretations forever, anthropology should turn to working on the way these causal systems interact with each other. (p. 101)

Methodologically psychological anthropologists follow the tradition of ethnographic research. An important innovation they have made is *person-centered ethnography* (Hollan, 2005; Levy & Hollan, 1998). This type of ethnography invites researchers to study cultures 'through the eyes' of their members, by analyzing their experiences of the cultural events, things, traditions, and rituals that exist in their communities.

> In contrast to standard ethnography which, according to LeVine, "produces a cultural description analogous to a map or aerial photograph of a community," person-centered ethnography "tells us what it is like to live there—what features are salient to its inhabitants" (1982: 293).
>
> (Hollan, 2001, p. 48)

Person-centered ethnography approaches members of communities both as informants, who give accounts of their culture, and as participants, who describe their own experience of living in these cultures. By creating this duality, anthropologists try to connect the 'cultural' and 'psychological' within one unit of analysis—an embodied, live, and functioning individual, a member of his or her cultural community (see Chapter 10.) Psychological anthropologists also use psychological tests, scales, and inventories, but try to avoid mechanistic and a-contextual analysis, the analysis that is very commonly used by cross-cultural psychologists.

Another domain of anthropology that is strongly related to psychology is *cognitive anthropology* (D'Andrade, 1995; Kronenfeld, Bennardo, de Munck, & Fischer, 2011; Shore, 1998).

> *Cognitive anthropology is the study of the relation between human society and human thought.* The cognitive anthropologist studies how people in social groups conceive of and think about the objects and events which make up their world—including everything from physical objects like wild plants to abstract events like social justice.
>
> (D'Andrade, 1995, p. 1)

Cognitive anthropology is seen by some of its representatives as a part of psychological anthropology and close to cognitive psychology, whereas others position it within cultural anthropology, close to linguistic anthropology. For culture and psychology researchers, the psychological trend in cognitive anthropology is the most valuable. The main idea of this trend is that human cognition is structured to a large extent by culture, by folk models and scripts that people learn and internalize in their communities. The primary agenda of cognitive anthropologists is to study this cultural content of people's mental schemas and models. They are also strongly interested in the systems of meaning, both cultural and personal, in how these systems are created, learned, and used by people in their everyday lives (D'Andrade, 1984). The most valuable contribution of cognitive anthropology to culture and psychology studies is the *theory of cultural models* that we will discuss in detail in Chapter 2 and apply to ethnographic research in Chapter 10. Theoretically speaking, the majority of psychological and cognitive anthropologists can be associated with the fourth perspective—*Homo Interpretans*—presented and discussed in the next chapter.

Summary

Anthropological studies provide a rich and diverse background for culture and psychology studies. One of their most important contributions is inventing and putting the concept of culture in the foreground of social research. Second, they have elaborated upon the ethnographic method and its numerous variations. This method should be more broadly introduced to cultural psychological studies. Comparative ethnographic investigations constitute another important contribution of anthropology to this area of research. Relations between anthropology and psychology have never been smooth and harmonious, but still, many anthropologists have high respect for psychological studies and their contribution to the broad domain of understanding people's functioning in sociocultural contexts. Theoretically, most modern anthropologists share various forms of the *Homo Socius* and *Homo Interpretans* perspectives, which shape the way they articulate their problems and work toward their resolutions. Biologically oriented anthropologists mostly work within the *Homo Bios* theoretical orientation.

In the next sections, we move to the areas of psychology that identify culture and psychology as their primary objects of study. The discussion starts with *cross-cultural psychology* and then moves to *cultural* and *indigenous psychology*.

Cross-Cultural Psychology

A new subdiscipline of psychology related to studying human behavior cross-culturally started emerging in the second half of the 20th century. First, the *Journal of Cross-Cultural Psychology* began publishing in 1970 and then the *International Association for Cross-Cultural Psychology* was formed in 1972. The practitioners of this new discipline, which they labeled *cross-cultural psychology*, have continued the traditions of mainstream psychology (mostly social psychology), but they decided to include culture and cross-cultural comparisons into their agenda. Their overarching goal has been to inquire about the psychological functioning of people in different cultures and theorize about the universal and unique aspects of human psychological makeup. Psychologists from North America and several European countries were the founders of this discipline, including (in alphabetical order) **John W. Berry** (Canada), **Pierre R. Dasen** (Switzerland), **Walter J. Lonner** (USA), **Ype H. Poortinga** (The Netherlands), **Marshall H. Segall** (USA), and **Harry C. Triandis** (USA).

Definition

The founders defined it in the following way: "Cross-cultural psychology is the study of similarities and differences in individual psychological functioning in various cultural and ethnocultural groups; of the relationships between psychological variable and socio-cultural, ecological and biological variables; and ongoing changes in these variables" (Berry, Poortinga, Segall, & Dasen, 1992, p. 3). The starting point of the psychological approach to culture and psychology was the thesis that, by using advanced scientific methodology, Western psychologists have built a body of knowledge in social, developmental, cognitive, and personality psychology that they believe reflects the universal (or near universal) laws of human psychological functioning. The knowledge that has been developed in the purity of experimental laboratories that has not been contaminated by situational and contextual factors (including cultural) is considered the core knowledge about psychological processes and states of any human being. Among them there are works on cognitive universals related to perceptions and thinking, basic emotions, obedience, causal attributions, self-concepts, invariant personality-trait structures, various theories of human development, and many others. But one question has been constantly haunting these Western psychologists: How universal are all these discoveries and regularities? Do they really reflect the laws of human nature or are they just the artifacts of being developed in a particular part of the world? This is how the founders of cross-cultural psychology worded this proposition:

> Many cross-cultural psychologists allow for similarities [universality of humans' psychological make-up] due to species-wide basic processes but consider their existence subject to empirical demonstration. This kind of universalism assumes that basic human characteristics are common to all members of the species (i.e., constituting a set of psychological givens) and that culture influences the development and display of them (i.e., culture plays different variations on these underlying themes . . .).
>
> (Segall, Lonner, & Berry, 1998, p. 1104)[3]

That is why one of the goals of cross-cultural psychology is to investigate psychological universals and variations of psychological states and processes across different cultural communities and to differentiate on an empirical basis the universal and culture-dependent components of human psychological functioning. The ultimate goal of these investigations is to "generate . . . nearly universal psychology, one that has pan-human validity" (Segall et al., 1998, p. 1102). As the history of science has demonstrated, the best way to achieve these goals is to use the comparative method, and hence, there are cross-cultural comparative studies in psychology. Modern cross-cultural psychology blends two theoretical perspectives discussed in Chapter 2, *Homo Mechanicus* and *Homo Bios*, and the philosophical paradigm of positivism (discussed in Chapter 3). These theoretical and philosophical underpinnings shape most main propositions of this discipline.

Understanding of Culture

Cross-cultural psychologists have a complex relationship with the concept of culture. On one hand, it is the central concept of this discipline and they fully appreciate its importance for psychology. On the other hand, these scholars emphasize its complexity, vagueness, and difficulty for operationalization, and, because of this, debate abandoning it altogether or replacing it with other more definite constructs and variables. Within the first trend, cross-cultural psychologists think about culture in the following way:

> To the cross-cultural psychologist, cultures are seen as products of past human behavior and as shapers of future human behavior. Thus, humans are producers of culture and, at the same time, our behavior is influenced by it. We have produced social environments and continually serve to bring about continuities and changes in lifestyles over time and uniformities and diversities in lifestyles over space. How human beings modify culture and how our cultures modify us is what cross-cultural psychology is all about.
>
> (Segall, Dasen, Berry, & Poortinga, 1999, p. 23)

This idea of the mutual co-construction of culture and human mentality is at the core of all culture and psychology research and constitutes the major postulate of this area of studies. But when it comes to empirical research, cross-cultural psychologists are determined either to abandon this idea

---

3 Reprinted with permission of American Psychological Association from Segall, M. H., Lonner, W. J., & Berry, J. W. (1998). Cross-cultural psychology as a scholarly discipline: On the flowering of culture in behavioral research. *American Psychologist, 53*(10), 1101–1110.

or to replace it with various proxies, such as countries/nations, ethnic/racial self-identifications, a set of cultural dimensions, or several eco-social variables.

> Pleas and attempts to define culture anew, however well-meaning and creative, are irrelevant to the conduct of cross-cultural research.
>
> (Segall, 1984, p. 153)

> In this comparative mode, [in cross-cultural psychological research] culture is treated as comprising a set of independent or contextual variables affecting [causality language] various aspects of individual behavior (Lonner & Adamopoulos, 1997; Segall, 1984). Cross-cultural research typically seeks evidence of such effects.
>
> (Segall et al., 1998, p. 1102)

One of the best examples of the application of such thinking is discovering and utilizing the dimensional approach to culture executed by Dutch cross-cultural organizational psychologist Geert Hofstede. He conducted factor analysis of job attitude surveys conducted by the IBM company in nearly 70 countries, and he first extracted four dimensions and later added a fifth one (Hofstede & Hofstede, 2005). It is important to mention that Hofstede used countries as the units of analysis and the extracted factors apply to countries, not people (see different levels of analysis in Chapter 8). These dimensions together with their theoretical justification constitute Hofstede's *cultural dimensions theory*. The primary dimensions are: (1) *small or large power distance*; (2) *individualism-collectivism*; (3) *masculinity* versus *femininity*; (4) *uncertainty avoidance* versus *uncertainty acceptance*. The fifth dimension was added based on studies in Asian countries (Hofstede & Bond, 1988) and was labelled (5) *short-term* versus *long-term orientation*.

Hofstede and his colleagues calculated scores on these dimensions for about 100 countries (see www.geert-hofstede.com), and these data have become popular in country-level cross-cultural studies (Minkov, 2013). According to this theory, each national culture can be represented by a five-dimension profile that opens vast opportunities to correlate these dimensions/variables with numerous political, economic, health, psychological, and other outcome variables (see review in Minkov, 2013). The cultural dimensions theory has become so popular among some social and behavioral scholars that many consider it to be one of the major contributions of cross-cultural psychology to social scientific knowledge and to theorizing about cultures. This theory provides a nearly perfect representation of the culture-as-a-combination-of-variables approach and has been embraced by many statistically minded cross-cultural psychologists.

Within the same variable-based thinking about culture, one can also find research driven by Harry Triandis's traditional classification of cultural components into individualism and collectivism, both of which may be horizontal or vertical and have tight or loose dimensions (Gelfand et al., 2011; Oyserman, Coon, & Kemmelmeier, 2002) as well as the theory of cultural values of Shalom Shwartz (2004; 2011), and a hypothesis about social axioms proposed by Kwok Leung and colleagues (2002).

Another direction of thinking about culture within this discipline is different versions of adaptationist and functionalist interpretation of culture, where culture is treated as a way of adjusting inherent human biological and psychological capacities—needs, cognitive mechanisms, personality proclivities—to natural environments and existing resources. This trend has a long history in anthropology (see above) and biology (Boyd & Richerson, 2005; Pagel, 2012), and cross-cultural and evolutionary psychologists find this thinking appealing and productive for their research.

With regard to **human psychological functioning**, cross-cultural psychologists continue the traditions of mechanistic and physicalistic thinking (see Chapter 2, the first perspective) within the positivist paradigm (see Chapter 3). Human behavior is seen as a result of causal 'pushes' from external and internal stimuli and determinants and it is believed that discovered statistical associations represent substantial and potentially causal relations among these variables. Despite the formal announcement of the mutual constitution of culture and the human psyche, no relevant mechanisms of such constitution have been hypothesized and validated within this stream of research. Humans' agency, their ability to interpret their environments, and pro-active attitudes toward their sociocultural milieu are out of scope for cross-cultural psychologists.

A different interpretation of how the human psyche works is suggested by evolutionary informed cross-cultural psychologists. They believe that people's behaviors and experiences are realizations of inherent evolutionarily constructed motivational and cognitive mechanisms that shape culture; together with the culture, they influence all psychological and behavioral manifestations. This is a more dynamic and complex representation of how mind and culture work together, where the dichotomy of nature (evolutionary-formed mental proclivities) versus nurture (culture) is at the center of debates (see the second perspective in Chapter 2).

The above considerations about psychological functioning lead directly to the main *methodological* tools that cross-cultural psychologists use: a variable-based analysis of sociocultural and psychological states and processes on the individual and country levels, a comparative approach, and the intensive utilization of a quantification and statistical analysis. The following chapters will address most of these methodological approaches and outline their benefits and disadvantages. Here I want to reiterate the words of the founders of cross-cultural psychology:

> Because cross-cultural psychology is descended from modern, scientific, general psychology, it is part of an intellectual tradition, rooted in Europe but developed mainly in America, that was a reaction to an earlier European tradition of political and social philosophy. Rejecting this as "soft," the late 19th century founders of psychology followed the Wundtian laboratory tradition and adopted the controlled experiment as the sine qua non of scientific research.
>
> (Segall, et al., 1999, p. 1106)

This methodological conviction of 'hard,' experimental, and quantitative thinking is still alive today and exists in a variety of modern designs and techniques (Matsumoto & van de Vijver, 2011). The rejection of the 'soft' (interpretivist, ethnographic, qualitative) approaches in doing research on culture and psychology also exists among these scholars.

Despite the initial enthusiasm of early cross-cultural researchers regarding their ability to operationalize and quantify culture as another independent variable, such an approach raised serious critiques both outside and within the discipline (Boesch, 1996; Chirkov, 2009; Fish, 2000; Gergen, Gulerce, Lock, & Misra, 1996; Misra & Gergen, 1993; Moghaddam & Studer, 1997; Shweder, 1991). Some of their arguments, which are often rooted in this science's theoretical orientation being based on the *Homo Mechanicus* perspective and the philosophy of positivism, can be summarized around the following points.

Cross-cultural psychology continues the tradition of the domains of social and behavioral sciences that assume that every sociocultural and psychological phenomenon can and should be studied based on the natural sciences methodology, mostly by applying experiments and various forms of measurement and quantifications. This assumption violates one of the most important rules of the philosophy of science—that the way a phenomenon is studied has to be congruent with the nature of this phenomenon. Cross-cultural psychologists should inquire into phenomena that are constituted by the intentional and intersubjective realities that are mediated by symbolic forms of communications and guided by human rationality and consciousness by using the theoretical and empirical tools that are more relevant to the phenomena that do not presuppose those attributes.

Cross-cultural psychologists implicitly or explicitly assume the universality of the psychological phenomena discovered in Western psychology and impose this understanding on the investigations of psychological processes in other cultural communities. A Western ethnocentrism is well known. The emergence of indigenous psychologies in different geographical regions is a reaction to such ethnocentrism, when local psychologists and social scientists propose to study the social and mental lives and behaviors of their compatriots based on the cultural traditions and folk psychologies of their own communities. Related to this is cross-cultural psychologists' strong conviction of the importance of establishing the equivalence of constructs and measures (see Chapter 9) and on the standardization of instruments across samples, which leads to the forceful imposition of the meanings and operationalization of various psychological processes that were developed in one set of cultural communities (primarily Western ones) on representatives of different cultural communities. As a result of this ethnocentrism, the unique interpretations of the culturally diverse forms of manifestations of the psychological phenomena under investigation can be missed.

Cross-cultural psychologists typically utilize the etic approach in their studies and examine cultural communities from an 'outsider' position, which is inevitably accompanied by some level of reification of cultures. They do not usually incorporate the emic approach and they make few attempts to understand people's experiences and behaviors from 'within' their particular culture.

Finally, if it is agreed that the ultimate goals of culture and psychology studies are to understand the psychological functioning of people in different sociocultural environments and explain the mechanisms of their mutual constitution and interdependence, then the many cross-cultural psychological studies that are conducted on the level of statistical generalizations among variables do not address these mechanisms and do not promote the understanding of such a mutual constitution. These statistical regularities provide little opportunity for theorizing about the nature of human psychological functioning, cultural reality, and their interactions. It is fair to say that cross-cultural psychology does a good job cataloging various interesting and important cross-cultural phenomena and the relations among them that can be subjected to a more thorough investigation using the emic approach and the abductive and retroductive modes of inference.

Cultural Psychology

Cultural psychology is a discipline that has been developed partly from within psychological anthropology and partly as a response to the criticism of a mainstream cross-cultural psychological research. It was initiated by the psychologists and psychological and cultural anthropologists who wanted to include culture and sociosymbolic environments as an undeniable part of any psychological research. The following scholars stand at the foundation of this new discipline that was developed in the second half of the 20th century, mostly in the USA, (in an alphabetical order): **Jerome Bruner, Michael Cole, Patricia Greenfield, Hazel Markus, Richard Nisbett, Richard Shweder, Jaan Valsiner**, and many others. Although a variety of different ways of thinking is hidden under the umbrella of this science (Kitayama & Cohen, 2007), there are main features and propositions across these differences that make this discipline unique and distinct.

In **defining** this discipline I will follow the theorizing of American cultural anthropologist/psychologist Richard Shweder (1991):

> Cultural psychology is the study of the way cultural traditions and social practices regulate, express, and transform the human psyche, resulting less in psychic unity of humankind than in ethnic divergences in mind, self, and emotion. Cultural psychology is the study of the way subject and object, self and other, psyche and culture, person and context, figure and ground, practitioner and practice, live together, require each other, and dynamically, dialectically, and jointly make each other up. (p. 73)

Following this definition, several features of cultural psychology can be outlined. First, it emphasizes a mutual constitution of human psychological functioning and sociocultural worlds and stresses that psychology and culture cannot be understood and studied separately from each other. Second, it highlights that the diversity of people's psychological makeups and behavioral manifestations is primarily a function of the cultural regulations that exist in people's cultural communities. And third, it underscores that cultures are dependent on people's psyche and behaviors to exist. People's mental and behavioral processes dynamically and dialectically participate in making these cultures up. Although these propositions are similar to what cross-cultural psychologists formally announced about their attitudes toward culture, cultural psychologists actually stay within these convictions in their theoretical and methodological aspects of research.

Understanding of culture is the first point where cultural psychologists remain faithful to the definition of their discipline and deviate from their cross-cultural colleagues. Shweder (1991) was one of the first social scientists who brought the concepts of *intentionality* (*intentional thing, intentional worlds, intentional states*) into culture and psychology research and who defined the concept of culture through this application; through this, he built a bridge between 'cultural' and 'psychological.'

> A sociocultural environment is an intentional world. It is an intentional world because its existence is real, factual, and forceful, but only so long as there exists a community of persons whose beliefs, desires, emotions, purposes, and other mental representations are directed at, and thereby influenced by, it.
>
> International worlds are human artifactual worlds, populated with products of our own design. An intentional world might contain such events as 'stealing' or 'taking communion' such processes as 'harm', or 'sin', such stations as 'in-law' or 'exorcist' such practices as 'betrothal' or 'divorce', such visible entities as 'weeds' and invisible entities as 'natural rights', and such crafted objects as a 'Jersey cow', and 'abacus', a 'confessional booth', a 'card catalogue'. An 'oversize tennis racquet', a 'psychoanalytic couch, or a 'living room'.
>
> Such intentional (made, breed, fashioned, fabricated, invented, designated, constituted) things exist only in intentional worlds. What makes their existence intentional is that such things would not exist independently of our involvements with and reactions to them; and they exercise their influence in our lives because of our conceptions of them. Intentional things are causally active, but only by virtue of our mental representations of them.
>
> Intentional things have no 'natural' reality or identity separate from human understandings and actions. Intentional worlds do not exist independently of the intentional states (beliefs, desires, emotions) directed at them and by them, by the person who live in them. (p. 75)

This idea of the intentionality of cultural worlds has been complemented by the concept of the *intersubjectivity* of cultural intentional states. This idea could be traced back to phenomenological sociologist Alfred Schutz (1954) and was advanced to cultural research by cognitive anthropologist Roy D'Andrade (1995). A mutual intersubjective understanding of the meaning of cultural intentional things works as the glue that makes cultural communities cohesive and their members' lives meaningful and comprehensible. Second, this intersubjectivity opens the cultural worlds for investigating by means of interpretation and understanding (see Chapters 4 and 10). These two concepts of intentionality and intersubjectivity make the cultural psychologists' approach to the notion of culture and its relation to human psychology more powerful and promising than the one of cross-cultural psychologists.

The cultural psychological definition of culture inevitably brings to light the complex nature of human interactions with their sociocultural worlds. On one hand, people share and execute the practices and meanings that they learn and internalize in their communities and use them to guide and regulate their lives. But on the other hand, cultures exist only because members of cultural communities intend, share, and execute those practices and meanings that are rooted in corresponding intentional states. But even more, because of the agency that people acquire in their lives, they possess the capacity to make changes to their cultural worlds and through these changes they can change themselves. Such an understanding of psychological functioning makes the cultural psychological approach more advanced than the cross-cultural psychological approach in understanding how culture and the human psyche constitute and change each other (Valsiner, 2014). In addition, it has a high humanistic potential in helping people to deal with their social and cultural problems.

Cultural psychologists do not deny the thesis about the 'psychic unity of mankind' but focus mostly on the variability of human psychology across cultures. Shweder (2000) provided a useful conceptualizations regarding this issue. He suggested differentiating the universal human 'mind' from the multiplicities of cultural 'mentalities.' The term 'mind' refers to humans' universal brain-determined and mind-related cognitive, emotional, and motivational mechanisms that constitute humans' universal biological-physiological-psychological propensities. This is the set of universal capacities that makes all human beings members of the same species *Homo sapiens*. According to Shweder, the term 'mentality' refers to the actual mental composition of people's minds in particular cultural communities. These mentalities include people's styles of thinking about and cognizing the worlds, culturally specific emotions and motivations, and culturally unique personality proclivities. Mentalities are formed by adjusting the universal mind to particular sociocultural environments. Hence, the Chinese mentality, Western mentality, Soviet mentality, and so on. Thus, "cultural psychology is the study of 'mentalities'" (Shweder, 2000, p. 211).

Theoretically, cultural psychology balances between the *Homo Socius* and *Homo Interpretans* perspectives (see Chapter 2). Philosophically, cultural psychologists are mostly interpretivists and some of them gravitate toward realist thinking. They are strong proponents of the 'emic' approach to studying cultures. Following their anthropological predecessors, they believe that the only appropriate way to study the culturally shaped mentalities of people is to look at the behaviors and experiences of people from 'within' their cultures.

This emic approach requires methodology that is different from the experimental thinking of cross-cultural psychologists, with their desire to standardize and quantify all the variables in a study. In their studies, cultural psychologists rely on ethnography, observations, and interviews followed by interpretation and understanding of the hidden parameters of cultural models and culture-shaped mentalities (see Chapters 4, 7, 8, and 10).

Cultural psychology is not free from critique, and often is the recipient of the critique that is applicable to most interpretative sciences. The critics question whether it is possible to 'read others' minds' (which means getting into the intentional worlds of cultural communities and understanding the mentalities of their people) objectively and scientifically; they are also concerned about the subjectivity of the accounts produced by cultural psychologists without hard-core evidence and criteria for establishing their truthfulness and validity. These and related points of criticism will be addressed in the Chapter 4 regarding the interpretivist paradigm.

Indigenous Psychology

Indigenous psychology may be considered a form of cultural psychology (Shweder, 2000) that invites researchers to investigate cultural communities using the concepts, categories, and cultural models of mental functioning that are developed in these communities. The indigenous psychology movement was initiated in the second half of the 20th century by a group of academics from different countries who, after receiving training in Western universities, mostly in the US, returned to their countries and became disillusioned with the applicability of the problems, ideas, theories, paradigms, and methods learned in these universities to the issues, problems, and challenges that their countries and people were experiencing. Many of them realized that they were replicating American psychology but only in the Chinese, Indian, or Latin American contexts, without actually tackling what people in these countries or regions have developed regarding their own understanding of what human psychology is. They realized that they were forced to ignore the hundreds and thousands of years of experience and knowledge about human psychology that their ancestors and compatriots had developed, and that they were imposing Western frames of thinking on realities that did not fit within them (or fit in them only partially) (Owusu-Bempah & Howitt, 2000). Taiwanese psychologist Kuo-Shu Yang (1997), one of the major proponents of Chinese indigenous psychology, described his transition from Western-based psychological thinking to an indigenous one:

> I finally found the reason why doing Westernized psychological research with Chinese subjects was no longer satisfying or rewarding to me. When an American psychologist, for example, was engaged in research, he or she could spontaneously let his or her American cultural and philosophical orientations and ways of thinking be freely and effectively reflected in choosing a research question, defining a concept, constructing a theory and designing a method. On the other hand, when a Chinese psychologist in Taiwan was conducting research, his or her strong training by overlearning the knowledge and methodology of American psychology tended to prevent his or her Chinese values, ideas, concepts and ways of thinking from being adequately reflected in the successive stages of the research process. Research of this kind resulted in an Americanized Chinese psychology without a Chinese "soul." Research findings in such an imposed, "soulless psychology" would not do much good in explaining, predicting and understanding Chinese behavior, simply because the imported Westernized concepts, theories, methods and tools habitually adopted by Chinese psychologists could not do justice to the complicated, unique aspects and patterns of Chinese people's psychological and behavioral characteristics. (p. 65)

It is natural that non-western communities have their own ideas about the human mind, consciousness, human development, cognition, emotion, self, and all other manifestations of people's psychological functioning. They have created systems of categories and propositions about the human psychological world, people's consciousness, selves, feelings, motivations, thoughts—almost everything that constitute the world of experience and behavior. Every large cultural community has its system of psychological thoughts and practices: African (Nobles, 2006), Chinese (Bond, 2010; Hwang, 2012; Kao & Sinha, 1997), Filipino (Enriquez, 1993) Indian (Kao & Sinha, 1997; Paranjpe, Ho, & Rieber, 1988; Rao, Paranjpe, & Dalal, 2008), Islamic (Haque & Mohamed, 2008; Utz, 2011), Latin American (Ardila, 1993), Japanese (Doi, 1973, 1986), and many others. So, the indigenous psychologists approach a study of the mentalities of members of their communities from within these indigenous systems of psychological knowledge. Cultural psychologists, as was mentioned above, also apply the emic—from within—position to their research, but still the majority of cultural psychologists are Westerners who faithfully try to implement the *outsider-to-insider* perspective (see Chapters 8 and 11). Indigenous psychologists, who are predominantly the nationals of the countries they investigate and members of these cultural communities, intend to occupy the pure *insider position* and look at the psychological functioning of their compatriots from within their communities' historical, philosophical, and religious heritage.

Indigenous psychology is defined "as a system of psychological thought and practices rooted in a particular cultural tradition" (Enriquez, 1990, cited in Yang, 2000, p. 245). Following Kim and Berry (1993), this definition can be extended by saying that indigenous psychology is a scientific study of the psychological functioning of people in various cultural communities by using the cultural models of mind, experience, and behavior that were developed in these particular countries or regions. It's a type of psychology that is rooted and is based on indigenous psychological knowledge. If we look at the psychology that exists in the West through these 'indigenous lenses,' it is possible to say that Western psychology is a version of indigenous psychology that has been developed based on the values and world views rooted in the Judeo-Christian European-American cultural traditions (Gergen et al., 1996). If this is true, then the psychology that we study and that has emerged from the laboratories of European and North American psychologists cannot be considered as the basis for the universal human psychology, but should be treated only as one of the many versions of culture-specific indigenous systems of psychological knowledge. Many psychologists consider that only the blind ethnocentrism of European-American psychologists could drive them to think that the way they study, conceptualize, and understand human psychology is actually how all human beings on earth think and feel about psychology (Harre, Clarke, & De Carlo, 1985).

To summarize the main propositions of indigenous psychology, I will use a modified form of its characteristics presented in Kim and Berry (1993) and Kim, Yang and Hwang (2006).

1. Indigenous psychology is the study of human experience and behavior in context: cultural, ecological, communal, familial, and others. This means that in order to understand people and their problems, researchers have to study these people exactly where they live and use the categories and concepts that these people operate with in managing their everyday lives.
2. Indigenous psychology is not a study of Third World communities and/or native people in their reserves and settlements, but an investigation of the cultural models of the human mind and behavior that have been developed in all countries, including the developed ones, and which constitute a mosaic of worldwide cultural diversity. To some extent, indigenous psychology is based on and operates using the concept of 'folk psychology,' a set of schema and models that ordinary people use to explain and predict their own and others' behaviors and mental states. Indigenous psychologists study the culturally determined aspects of folk psychology and inquire about people's problems through these people's cultural conceptualizations of the worlds.
3. Indigenous psychological studies are rooted in the philosophical and religious texts and traditions that lay the basis of communities' spiritual, intellectual, and mental lives. That is why indigenous psychological-cultural analysis should start with reading and analyzing these texts and building bridges between these broad and inclusive traditions and the psychological makeup and constitution of the people who share them. Indigenous psychologists emphasize that they are coming from the cultural science tradition (in this textbook, the interpretivist paradigm), not from the natural sciences or the positivist paradigm. Theoretically, these scholars use the *Homo Socius* and *Homo Interpretans* perspectives (see Chapter 2)
4. Indigenous psychologists raise an old argument about who—insiders or outsiders—are better to study the cultural models of cultural communities (see Chapter 11). Some scholars believe that only insiders, researchers who share the same cultural background, language, and world outlook with their informants and participants, can understand and investigate the cultural basis of their experience and psychology. The main argument here is that these researchers best know the objects of investigation as they live with this cultural knowledge and have direct access to it. Others argue that insiders take many aspects of their own culture for granted and because of this they miss many important characteristics of it. That is why outsiders, researchers

who are alien to a particular culture, can provide more critical and, thus, more exhaustive and comprehensive analyses of indigenous cultural models. As usual, the practical advice combines these two oppositions: a research team that consists of both 'insiders' and 'outsiders' is probably the best option to do any psychological research on culture.

5. An investigation of indigenous cultural models includes an examination of several facets of these models: (1) categorical and conceptual frameworks for everyday lives that people use to classify and structure the worlds around them; (2) patterns of typical and taken-for-granted behaviors and practices; (3) systems of values, norms, and moral codes that regulate these practices; (4) interpretive cognitive schemas that lay persons utilize to make sense of the worlds; and (5) sanctions that communities use to control the behavior of members. Researchers may be interested in cultural models of self, emotions and motivation, health and illness, and other aspects of indigenous psychological knowledge. Discovering these models may be especially productive for interventions in these communities.

6. Indigenous psychology utilizes multiple methodological approaches and paradigms and is not limited to the narrow set of 'scientific' methods that are so frequently propagated by Western psychologists who are infected by the positivist methodolatry (see Chapter 5). Some indigenous researchers suggest that in addition to indigenous psychological knowledge, their communities also possess unique indigenous methodologies, or exclusively indigenous ways of constructing knowledge, and, therefore, indigenous psychologists should adapt these ways of doing their research in order to completely 'indigenize' their academic inquiries (Denzin, Lincoln & Smith, 2008; Kovach, 2010; Smith, 2012) (see also Chapter 11). Such a call for a methodological indigenization is often justified by the fact that many indigenous communities have been oppressed by, mostly, white people and Western cultural traditions, and that by indigenizing the knowledge construction, indigenous scholars will help emancipate the oppressed and give them power through knowledge acquisition. These scholars fight against the ethnocentric European-American academic thinking that only Western researchers are at the center of legitimate knowledge. Although this trend toward the indigenization of knowledge and its production is a significant and important achievement of indigenous scholars, many questions remain to be answered about the coexistence and mutual cross-fertilization of the indigenous and Western academic traditions.

Indigenous psychologists continue to work on their conceptualization of culture, but as the analysis of their works indicates, they are more in line with anthropological and especially cognitive anthropological theories of culture. It is clear that indigenous psychologists are much closer in their thinking to cultural psychologists and psychological anthropologists than to cross-cultural psychologists, and their productive coexistence with the former is a route to success for this discipline.

Summary

Psychologists have diverse relationships with culture and represent a wide spectrum of approaches to culture and psychology research. Cross-cultural psychology tried to propagate the 'scientific' way of studying cultures and the human psyche, but in doing this, they lost touch with both culture and human mentality. What stands between these researchers and their objects are etically (from 'etic') derived variables with their equivalent and invariant assessments across diverse and by no means culturally equivalent and invariant samples, various statistical models based on sophisticated but formal and often meaningless covariances among these variables, sometimes poor theoretical accounts for discovered relations and, finally, impoverished philosophical and theoretical ways of thinking. Cultural and indigenous psychologists rebel against such treatment of culture and human mentalities and both constitute viable and potentially productive ways of guiding culture and psychology research.

Conclusion

The content for the disciplinary thinking that is presented in this chapter constitutes the first, out of three, aspects of a research-related form of reasoning that constitutes the intellectual foundations of inquiries on culture and psychology. Disciplinary thinking embraces several features. First, it gives knowledge about the disciplines that are relevant to this type of research and about their potential contributions to solving the research problems at hand. The idea is that when researchers face a scientific problem, all possible knowledge, theories, and methods—independent of their disciplinary origin—should be used to solve this problem. Second, disciplinary thinking helps researchers to position themselves within the social sciences and reflects on the advantages and disadvantages of these positions. Third, the disciplines covered in this chapter have connections to both the theoretical perspectives and philosophical paradigms that constitute the other two aspects of research-related thinking. That is why when researchers start thinking discipline-wise, they inevitably continue reasoning theoretically and philosophically. These connections create a dialectical circle of intellectual contemplations about the nature of the subject, methodology, and a researcher's outlook on them.

Questions

1. Differentiate between social and cultural anthropology. You may be required to do some additional reading.
2. Reflect on the main theories of culture in cultural anthropology and examine their applicability for culture and psychology research.
3. Why does ethnography constitute the main tool for anthropological studies?
4. How do you understand psychological anthropology? What is its relevance for culture and psychology studies?
5. How can research on phenomenological anthropology and the anthropology of experience complement studies on psychology and culture?
6. Define cross-cultural psychology and outline its main advantages and weaknesses.
7. What is cultural psychology? Articulate its differences from cross-cultural psychology.
8. What are the differences between the cultural anthropological understanding of culture and the cultural psychological one?
9. Is indigenous psychology closer to cultural or cross-cultural psychology? Justify your answer.
10. Why do you think a movement toward the indigenization of psychology has emerged?

Glossary

Anthropology is a study of humankind, of human communities of different sizes and their ways of life, rituals, norms, and values.

Anthropology (ethnography) at a distance is a set of methodological tools developed and implemented by scholars of culture and personality studies to investigate the national characters of citizens of countries while having a limited access to fieldwork there.

Cognitive anthropology is the study of the relation between human society and human thought. "The cognitive anthropologist studies how people in social groups conceive of and think about the objects and events which make up their world—including everything from physical objects like wild plants to abstract events like social justice" (D'Andrade, 1995, p. 1).

Cross-cultural psychology "is the study of similarities and differences in individual psychological functioning in various cultural and ethnocultural groups; of the relationships between psychological variable and socio-cultural, ecological, and biological variables; and ongoing changes in these variables" (Berry, et al., 1992, p. 3).

Cultural anthropology is considered mostly a North American tradition where culture is believed to be the primary factor that determines social conditions.

Cultural psychology is a branch of psychology that studies the interdependence of the mental and cultural components of people's psychological and behavioral functioning. It is a study of the culture-shaped mentalities of people.

Cultural relativism (1) the idea that the ethno-racial, mental, and behavioral differences among communities of people are determined not by biological, but by cultural factors; (2) a view that people's values, beliefs, and practices should be understood in terms of their own cultures and that judgments and moral evaluations of cultures cannot be done by using criteria external to those cultures.

Culture theory is a set of propositions that uncover the nature, structure, functions, and mechanisms of this phenomenon.

Etic and emic approaches to studying culture and people's behavior: "The etic viewpoint studies behavior as from outside of a particular system, and as an essential initial approach to an alien system. The emic viewpoint results from studying behavior as from inside the system" (Pike, 1967, p. 37).

Galton's problem: a proposition that "cultures are not independent but rather may share many cultural elements by virtue of common ancestry and proximity" (Mace & Pagel, 1994, p. 549).

Indigenous psychology is a scientific study of the psychological functioning of people in various cultural communities by using the cultural models of mind, experience, and behavior that were developed in these particular countries or regions. It's a type of psychology that is rooted and is based on indigenous psychological knowledge.

Intentional things, states, and worlds: a unique condition of human existence when intrinsically irrelevant mediums (colored papers, a piece of fabric on a wooden rod, or a collection of people) acquire meaning, institutionalization, and power over peoples' lives and behaviors by the virtue of these people's thoughts, beliefs, and emotions (intentional states) about these mediums as real and meaningful things: money, a national flag, or wedding. When these states are enacted through social interactions, intentional things are maintained and their power over people's actions is executed.

Intersubjectivity is a uniquely human way of sharing intentional states. Members of a cultural community mutually understand what intentional things mean and how to deal with them. An intersubjective understanding of the meaning of culturally intentional things works as the glue that makes cultural communities cohesive and their members' lives meaningful and comprehensible.

The psychic unity of mankind: a principle suggested by German social scholar Adolf Bastian. His interpretation of it corresponds to a set of "elementary ideas" (*Elementargedanken*) that are universal for all people and that manifest themselves in varieties of "folk ideas" (*Volkergedanken*) that are peculiar to each sociocultural community (Koepping, 1983). The modern interpretation of this idea states that "humans [are] everywhere born with roughly the same potentials, and inherited differences are negligible" (Eriksen & Nielson, 2001, p. 17).

Psychological anthropology: "Psychological anthropology is the study of the behaviors, experience and development of individuals in relation to the institutions and ideologies of their sociocultural environments, across all populations of the human species" (LeVine, 2010b, p. 1).

Social anthropology is mostly associated with the British (and partly French) tradition of studying the diversity of human societies. It treats cultures as outcomes of social structures and social relations that exist in these societies. According to social anthropologists, social is primary, and cultural and symbolic are secondary.

Sociocultural anthropology reflects a tendency of anthropologists to combine the social and cultural branches of the discipline.

Taken-for-granted is the nearly automatic and nonreflective way of using cultural prescriptions and cultural models after they have been internalized by members of a cultural community.

Recommended Reading

Baldwin, J. R., Faulkner, S. L., Hecht, M. L., & Lindsley, S. L. (Eds.). (2005). *Redefining culture: Perspectives across the disciplines*. Mahwah, NJ: Lawrence Erlbaum Associates.

Berry, J. W., Poortinga, Y. H., Breugelmans, S. M., Chasiotis, A., & Sam, D. L. (2011). *Cross-cultural psychology: Research and applications* (3rd ed.). Cambridge, UK: Cambridge University Press.

D'Andrade, R. G. (1995). *The development of cognitive anthropology*. Cambridge, UK: Cambridge University Press.

Fardon, R., Harris, O., Marchand, T.H.J., Nuttall, M., Shore, C., Strang, V., & Wilson, R. A. (Eds.). (2012). *The Sage handbook of social anthropology*. Los Angeles, CA: Sage.

Keesing, R. M. (1974). Theories of culture. *Annual Review of Anthropology, 3*, 73–97.

Kim, U., & Berry, J. W. (1993). *Indigenous psychologies: Experience and research in cultural context*. Newbury Park, CA: Sage.

Kitayama, S., & Cohen, D. (Eds.). (2007). *Handbook of cultural psychology*. New York, NY: Guilford Press.

LeVine, R. A. (Ed.). (2010). *Psychological anthropology: A reader on self in culture*. Malden, MA: Wiley-Blackwell.

Moore, J. D. (1997). *Visions of culture: An introduction to anthropological theories and theorists*. Walnut Creek, CA: AltaMira Press.

Peoples, J., & Bailey, G. (2014). *Humanity: An introduction to cultural anthropology* (10th ed.). Belmont, CA: Cengage Learning.

Shweder, R. A. (1991). Cultural psychology: What is it? In R. A. Shweder (Ed.), *Thinking through cultures: Expeditions in cultural psychology*. (pp. 73–11). Cambridge, MA: Harvard University Press.

References

Ardila, R. (1993). Latin American psychology and world psychology: Is integration possible? In U. Kim & J. W. Berry (Eds.), *Indigenous psychologies: Research and experience in cultural context*. (pp. 170–176). Newbury Park, CA: Sage.

Baldwin, J. R., Faulkner, S. L., Hecht, M. L., & Lindsley, S. L. (Eds.). (2005). *Redefining culture: Perspectives across the disciplines*. Mahwah, NJ: Lawrence Erlbaum.

Berger, P. L., & Luckmann, T. (1966/1989). *The social construction of reality: A treatise in the sociology of knowledge*. New York, NY: Anchor Books.

Berry, J. W., Poortinga, Y. H., Segall, M. H., & Dasen, P. R. (1992). *Cross-cultural psychology: Research and application*. Cambridge, UK: Cambridge University Press.

Bock, P. K. (1999). *Rethinking psychological anthropology: Continuity and change in the study of human action*. Prospect Heights, IL: Waveland Press.

Boesch, E. E. (1996). The seven flaws of cross-cultural psychology: The story of conversion. *Mind, Culture, and Activity, 3*(1), 2–10.

Bond, M. H. (Ed.). (2010). *The Oxford handbook of Chinese psychology*. New York, NY: Oxford University Press.

Boyd, R., & Richerson, P. J. (2005). *The origin and evolution of cultures*. New York, NY: Oxford University Press.

Brown, D. E. (1991). *Human universals*. Philadelphia, PA: Temple University Press.

Carrier, J. G., & Gewertz, D. B. (Eds.). (2013). *The handbook of sociocultural anthropology*. New York, NY: Bloomsbury Academic.

Chirkov, V. (2009). Introduction to the special issue on critical acculturation psychology. *International Journal of Intercultural Relations, 33*(2), 87–93.

D'Andrade, R. G. (1984). Cultural meaning systems. In R. A. Shweder & R. A. Levine (Eds.), *Culture theory: Essays on mind, self, and emotion* (pp. 88–119). Cambridge, UK: Cambridge University Press.

D'Andrade, R. G. (1995). *The development of cognitive anthropology*. Cambridge, UK: Cambridge University Press.

D'Andrade, R. G. (1999). Culture is not everything. In E. L. Cerroni-Long (Ed.), *Anthropological theory in North America* (pp. 85–103). Westport, CT: Bergin and Garvey.

Denzin, N. K., Lincoln, Y. S., & Smith, L. T. (Eds.). (2008). *Handbook of critical and indigenous methodologies*. Los Angeles, CA: Sage.

Doi, T. (1973). *The anatomy of dependence*. Tokyo: Kodansha International.

Doi, T. (1986). *The anatomy of self: The individual versus society*. Tokyo, Japan: Kodansha International.

Dunbar, R. I. M., & Barrett, L. (Eds.). (2007). *Oxford handbook of evolutionary psychology*. Oxford, UK: Oxford University Press.

Ember, C. R., & Ember, M. (2009). *Cross-cultural research methods*. (2nd ed.). Lanham, MD: Altamıra Press.

Enriquez, V. G. (1993). Developing a Filipino psychology. In U. Kim & J. W. Berry (Eds.), *Indigenous psychologies: Research and experience in cultural context* (pp. 152–169). Newbury Park, CA: Sage.

Eriksen, T. H., & Nielsen, F. S. (2001). *A history of anthropology*. London, UK: Pluto Press.

Evans-Pritchard, E. E. (1963). *The comparative method in social anthropology*. London, UK: Athlone Press.

Fardon, R., Harris, O., Marchand, T. H. J., Nuttall, M., Shore, C., Strang, V., & Wilson, R. A. (Eds.). (2012). *The Sage handbook of social anthropology*. Los Angeles, CA: Sage.

Fish, J. M. (2000). What anthropology can do for psychology: Facing physics envy, ethnocentrism, and a belief in "Race." *American Anthropologist, 102*(3), 552–563.

Gelfand, M. J., Raver, J. L., Nishii, L., Leslie, L. M., Lun, J., Lim, B. C., . . . Yamaguchi, S. (2011). Difference between tight and loose cultures: A 33-nation study. *Science, 332*(6033), 1100–1104.

Gergen, K. J., Gulerce, A., Lock, A., & Misra, G. (1996). Psychological science in cultural context. *American Psychologist, 51*(5), 496–503.

Hammel, E. A. (1980). The comparative method in anthropological perspective. *Comparative Studies in Society and History, 22*(2), 145–155.

Hammersley, M., & Atkinson, P. (2007). *Ethnography: Principles in practice* (3rd ed.). London, UK: Routledge.

Haque, A., & Mohamed, Y. (2008). *Psychology of personality, Islamic perspectives*. Singapore: Cengage Learning Asia.

Harre, R., Clarke, D., & De Carlo, N. (1985). *Motives and mechanisms: An introduction to the psychology of action*. London, UK: Methuen.

Harris, M. (2001). *The rise of anthropological theory: A history of theories of culture*. Walnut Creek, CA: AltaMira Press.

Herskovits, M. J. (1955). *Cultural anthropology*. New York, NY: Knopf.

Hofstede, G., & Bond, M. H. (1988). The Confucius connection: From cultural roots to economic growth. *Organizational Dyamics, 16*(4), 5–21.

Hofstede, G., & Hofstede, G. J. (2005). *Culture and organization: Software of the mind*. (2nd ed.). New York, NY: McGraw-Hill.

Hollan, D. W. (2001). Developments in person-centered ethnography. In C. C. Moore & H. F. Mathews (Eds.), *The psychology of cultural experience* (pp. 48–67). Cambridge, UK: Cambridge University Press.

Hollan, D. W. (2005). Setting a new standard: The person-centered interviewing and observation of Robert I. Levy. *Ethos, 33*(4), 459–466.

Hsu, F. L. K. (1972). Psychological anthropology in the behavioral sciences. In F. L. K. Hsu (Ed.), *Psychological anthropology* (pp. 1–19). Cambridge, MA: Schenkman Publishing.

Hwang, K.-K. (2012). *Foundations of Chinese psychology: Confucian social relations*. Dordrecht, The Netherlands: Springer.

Jackson, M. (Ed.). (1996). *Things as they are: New directions in phenomenological anthropology*. Bloomington, IN: Indiana University Press.

Jessor, R., Colby, A., & Shweder, R. A. (Eds.). (1996). *Ethnography and human development: Context and meaning in social inquiry*. Chicago, IL: University of Chicago Press.

Kao, H. S. R., & Sinha, D. (Eds.). (1997). *Asian perspectives on psychology*. New Delhi, India: Sage.

Keesing, R. M. (1974). Theories of culture. *Annual Review of Anthropology, 3*, 73–97.

Keesing, R. M. (1990). Theories of culture revisited. *Canberra Anthropology, 13*(2), 46–60.

Kim, U., & Berry, J. W. (1993). *Indigenous psychologies: Experience and research in cultural context*. Newbury Park, CA: Sage.

Kim, U., Yang, K.-S., & Hwang, K.-K. (Eds.). (2006). *Indigenous and cultural psychology: Understanding people in context*. New York, NY: Springer.

Kitayama, S., & Cohen, D. (Eds.). (2007). *Handbook of cultural psychology*. New York, NY: Guilford Press.

Koepping, K.-P. (1983). *Adolf Bastian and the psychic unity of mankind: The foundations of anthropology in nineteenth century Germany*. St. Lucia, Australia: University of Queensland Press.

Kopala, M., & Suzuki, L. A. (Eds.). (1999). *Using qualitative methods in psychology*. Thousand Oaks, CA: Sage.

Kovach, M. E. (2010). *Indigenous methodologies: Characteristics, conversations, and contexts*. Toronto, ON: University of Toronto Press.

Kroeber, A. L., & Kluckhohn, C. (1952). *Culture: A critical review of concepts and definitions* Cambridge, MA: Peabody Museum.

Kronenfeld, D. B., Bennardo, G., de Munck, V., & Fischer, M. D. (Eds.). (2011). *A companion to cognitive anthropology*. Malden, MA: Wiley-Blackwell.

Launay, R. (Ed.). (2010). *Foundations of anthropological theory: From classical antiquity to early modern Europe*. Chichester, UK; Malden, MA: Wiley-Blackwell.

Leung, K., Bond, M. H., De Carrasquel, S. R., Munoz, C., Hernandez, M., Murakami, F., . . . Singelis, T. M. (2002). Social axioms: The search for universal dimensions of general beliefs about how the world functions. *Journal of Cross-Cultural Psychology, 33*(3), 286–302.

Lévi-Strauss, C. (1967). *Structural anthropology* (C. Jacobson & B. G. Schoepf, Trans.). Garden City, NY: Doubleday.

LeVine, R. A. (2001). Culture and personality studies, 1918–1960: Myth and history. *Journal of Personality, 69*(6), 803–818.

LeVine, R. A. (2010a). Introduction. In R. A. LeVine (Ed.), *Psychological antropology: A reader on self in culture* (pp. 1–6). Malden, MA: Wiley-Blackwell.

LeVine, R. A. (Ed.). (2010b). *Psychological anthropology: A reader on self in culture*. Malden, MA: Wiley-Blackwell.

LeVine, R. A., & New, R. S. (2008a). Introduction: Discovering diversity in childhood: Early works. In R. A. LeVine & R. S. New (Eds.), *Anthropology and child development: A cross-cultural reader* (pp. 11–17). Oxford, UK: Blackwell.

LeVine, R. A., & New, R. S. (Eds.). (2008b). *Anthropology and child development: A cross-cultural reader*. Oxford, UK: Blackwell.

Levy, R. I., & Hollan, D. W. (1998). Person-centered interviewing and observation. In H. R. Bernard (Ed.), *Handbook of methods in cultural anthropology* (pp. 333–364). Walnut Creek, CA: AltaMira.

Lindholm, C. (2007). *Culture and identity: The history, theory, and practice of psychological anthropology*. Oxford, UK: Oneworld Publications.

Mace, R., & Pagel, M. (1994). The comparative method in anthropology. *Current Anthropology, 35*(5), 549–564.

Matsumoto, D., & van de Vijver, F. J. R. (Eds.). (2011). *Cross-cultural research methods in psychology*. Cambridge, UK: Cambridge University Press.

Mead, M. and R. Metraux (Eds.) (1953/2000). *The study of culture at a distance*. New York, NY: Berghahn Books.

Miller, P. J., Hengst, J. A., & Wang, S.-h. (2003). Ethnographic methods: Applications from developmental cultural psychology. In P. M. Camic, J. E. Rhodes & L. Yardley (Eds.), *Qualitative research in psychology: Expanding perspectives in methodology and design* (pp. 219–242). Washington, DC: American Psychological Association.

Minkov, M. (2013). *Cross-cultural analysis: The science and art of comparing the world's modern societies and their cultures*. Thousand Oaks, CA: Sage.

Misra, G., & Gergen, K. J. (1993). On the place of culture in psychological science. *International Journal of Psychology, 28*(2), 225–243.

Moghaddam, F. M., & Studer, C. (1997). Cross cultural psychology: The frustrated gadfly's promises, potentialities and failures. In D. Fox & I. Prilleltensky (Eds.), *Critical psychology: An introduction*. London, UK: Sage.

Moore, C. C., & Mathews, H. F. (Eds.). (2001). *The psychology of cultural experience*. Cambridge, UK: Cambridge University Press.

Moore, J. D. (1997). *Visions of culture: An introduction to anthropological theories and theorists*. Walnut Creek, CA: AltaMira Press.

Morris, B. (1991). *Western conceptions of the individual*. New York, NY: Berg.

Morris, B. (1994). *Anthropology of the self: The individual in cultural perspective*. London, UK: Pluto Press.

Murdock, G. P. (1951). British social anthropology. *American Anthropologist, 53*(4), 465–473.
Nagata, D. K., Kohn-Wood, L., & Suzuki, L. A. (Eds.). (2012). *Qualitative strategies for ethnocultural research.* Washington, DC: American Psychological Association.
Nobles, W. W. (2006). *Seeking the Sakhu: Foundational writings for an African psychology.* Chicago, IL: Third World Press.
Owusu-Bempah, K., & Howitt, D. (2000). *Psychology beyond Western perspectives.* Leicester, UK: Wiley-Blackwell.
Oyserman, D., Coon, H. M., & Kemmelmeier, M. (2002). Rethinking individualism and collectivism: Evaluation of theoretical assumptions and meta-analysis. *Psychological Bulletin, 128*(1), 3–72.
Pagel, M. (2012). *Wired for culture: Origins of human social mind.* New York, NY: Norton.
Paranjpe, A. C., Ho, D.Y.F., & Rieber, R. W. (Eds.). (1988). *Asian contributions to psychology* New York, NY: Praeger.
Paul, R. A. (1989). Psychoanalytic anthropology. *Annual Review of Anthropology, 1,* 177–202.
Pike, K. L. (1967). *Language in relation to a unified theory of the structure of human behavior.* The Hague, The Netherlands: Mouton.
Radcliffe-Brown, A. R. (1951). The comparative method in social anthropology. *The Journal of Royal Anthropological Institute of Great Britain and Ireland, 81*(1/2), 15–22.
Rao, K. R., Paranjpe, A. C., & Dalal, A. K. (Eds.). (2008). *Handbook of Indian psychology.* New Delhi, India: Cambridge University Press.
Rossi, I., & O'Higgins, E. (1980). Anthropological methods. In I. Rossi (Ed.), *People in culture: A survey of cultural anthropology* (pp. 79–102). New York, NY: Praeger.
Salzmann, Z., Stanlaw, J., & Adachi, N. (2014). *Language, culture, and society: An introduction to linguistic anthropology.* Boulder, CO: Westview Press.
Schutz, A. (1954). Concepts and theory formation in the social sciences. *The Journal of Philosophy, 51*(9), 257–273.
Schwartz, S. H. (2004). Mapping and interpreting cultural differences around the world. In H. Vinken, J. Soeters & P. Ester (Eds.), *Comparing cultures: Dimensions of culture in a comparative perspective.* (pp. 43–73). Leiden, The Netherlands: Brill.
Schwartz, S. H. (2011). Values: Cultural and individual. In F.J.R. van de Vijver, A. Chasiotis & S. M. Breugelmans (Eds.), *Fundamental questions in cross-cultural psychology* (pp. 463–493). Cambridge, MA: Cambridge University Press.
Segall, M. H. (1984). More than we need to know about culture, but are afraid not to ask. *Journal of Cross-Cultural Psychology, 15*(2), 153–162.
Segall, M. H., Dasen, P. R., Berry, J. W., & Poortinga, Y. H. (1999). *Human behavior in global perspective: An introduction to cross-cultural psychology* (2nd ed.). Boston, MA: Allyn & Bacon.
Segall, M. H., Lonner, W. J., & Berry, J. W. (1998). Cross-cultural psychology as a scholarly discipline: On the flowering of culture in behavioral research. *American Psychologist, 53*(10), 1101–1110.
Shore, B. (1998). *Culture in mind: Cognition, culture, and the problem of meaning.* New York, NY: Oxford University Press.
Shweder, R. A. (1991). Cultural psychology: What is it? In R. A. Shweder (Ed.), *Thinking through cultures: Expeditions in cultural psychology.* (pp. 73–11). Cambridge, MA: Harvard University Press.
Shweder, R. A. (2000). The psychology of practice and the practice of the three psychologies. *Asian Journal of Social Psychology, 3*(3), 207–222.
Smith, L. T. (2012). *Decolonizing methodologies: Research and indigenous peoples* (2nd ed.). London, UK: Zed Books.
Turner, V. W., & Bruner, E. M. (Eds.). (1986). *The anthropology of experience.* Urbana, IL: University of Illinous Press.
Tylor, E. B. (1871/1958). *Primitive culture.* New York, NY: Harper &Row.
Tylor, E. B. (1889). On a method of investigating the development of institutions; applied to laws of marriage and descent. *The Journal of the Anthropological Institute of Great Britain and Ireland, 18,* 245–272 (retrieved from http://rbedrosian.com/Historiog/Tylor_1889_Method.pdf).
Utz, A. (2011). *Psychology from the Islamic perspectives.* Riyadh, Saudi Arabia: International Islamic Publishing House.
Valsiner, J. (Ed.). (2014). *The Oxford handbook of culture and psychology.* Oxford, UK: Oxford University Press.
Valsiner, J., & Rosa, A. (Eds.). (2007). *The Cambridge handbook of sociocultural psychology.* Cambridge, UK: Cambridge University Press.

Wierzbicka, A. (1996). Japanese cultural scripts: Cultural psychology and "cultural grammar". *Ethos, 24*(3), 527–555.
Wierzbicka, A. (2002). Russian cultural scripts: The theory of cultural scripts and its applications. *Ethos, 30*(4), 401–432.
Yang, K.-S. (1997). Indigenizing westernized Chinese psychology. In M. H. Bond (Ed.), *Working at the interface of culture: Eighteen lives in social science.* (pp. 60–73). London, UK: Routledge.
Yang, K.-S. (2000). Monocultural and cross-cultural indigenous approaches: The royal road to the development of a balanced global psychology. *Asian Journal of Social Psychology 3*(3): 241–264.

2
THEORETICAL THINKING

Four Perspectives in Studying Psychology in Sociocultural Contexts

This chapter will:

- Introduce four theoretical perspectives:
  1 The physical science perspective or *Homo Mechanicus*
  2 The biological science perspective or *Homo Bios*
  3 The sociocultural sciences perspective or *Homo Socius*
  4 The agentic-interpretive perspective or *Homo Interpretans*
- Discuss theories of culture within each perspective
- Articulate the theory of cultural models

Introduction

One of the fundamental postulates of the philosophy of science is that the methods of research should be appropriate to the nature of the objects of a study. This means that if the objects of a study—a person, group of people, community, or culture—are interpreted as composites of relatively independent entities which mechanistically influence each other, then the research design and methods for this study should differ from a case when the same objects are treated as systems that dialectically constitute each other through mutual interdependence. Therefore, it is important for empirical researchers to reflect on the ways they think about the nature of the social, cultural, and psychological phenomena they want to investigate in order to choose an adequate methodology and methods. In order to conduct meaningful and productive research, scholars must explicitly articulate their theoretical assumptions about the objects of their investigation, hence demonstrating *theoretical thinking*. There are different theoretical accounts related to the understanding of culture, human psychological functioning, and their interactions, and the following chapter will analyze these perspectives and provide some guidelines for their utilization.

Theoretical Thinking

There are two kinds of theoretical assumptions that guide any research: one is about the nature of the phenomena to be studied—*content-related theoretical assumptions*. The second addresses suppositions about the ontology, epistemology, and methodology of research—*metatheoretical philosophical assumptions*. Both of these sets of propositions are crucially important for empirical research to be sound and productive. They provide a foundation for the conceptualization and solution of a research problem, and they guide the methodology of a study. In this chapter, we will examine the content-related theoretical perspectives while in Chapters 3 and 4 we will investigate the metatheoretical philosophical propositions.

Content-related theoretical assumptions in sociocultural sciences have often been articulated in terms of "scientific world views" (D'Andrade, 1986) or "models of studying people and society" (Van Langenhove, 1995, p. 13). Typically these models have been associated either with the major divisions of science—natural, biological, social, and human—or with different disciplines—physics, biology, semiotics, and others. Van Langenhove (1995) used two models for his analysis: "the model of the natural sciences" and "the model of hermeneutics" (p. 13). D'Andrade (1986) utilized three scientific world views: "the world view of the physical sciences," "the world of the natural sciences" (mostly biology), and "the world of the semiotic sciences" (pp. 20–22). This chapter will present a four-fold categorization of understanding the nature of human psychology, culture, and their interactions: the physical science perspective; the biological science perspective; the sociocultural science perspective, and the agentic-interpretative perspective (there is no particular disciplinary connection associated with this perspective). This classification is derived from the works of two scholars who independently suggested it: Joseph Rychlak (1993) and Lutz Eckensberger (2011). Although the classifications proposed by these scholars are compatible, I will mostly rely on the one formulated by Eckensberger because it was primarily created to address research on culture and psychology. Each perspective will be presented through the following subsections: major metaphors, interpretation of culture and sociosymbolic environments, understanding of the nature of psychological functioning, dominant methodological strategies, and the main disciplines that embrace these perspectives. The content of this chapter is connected to the discussion in the previous chapter. To create a more coherent understanding of the disciplinary-theoretical basis of research, read them together.

The Physical Science Perspective

Major metaphors for this perspective are: *Homo Mechanicus*—"humans as mechanisms" (Eckensberger, 2011, p. 412) and *"Physikos"* (Rychlak, 1993, p. 936). The first metaphor—humans as mechanisms—has a long history that can be traced back to Descartes and Hobbes and their thinking about the nature of human beings, which was inspired by the mechanistic interpretation of the universe provided by Copernicus, Galileo, and Kepler (Morris, 1991). This metaphor survived through centuries and provided the conceptual foundation for materialism, empiricism, and behaviorism in psychology. Make sure not to confuse it with the idea of searching for causal mechanisms of different phenomena that is propagated by the realist paradigm (see Chapter 4). The second metaphor—*Physikos*—highlights physics, mostly the classical mechanical version of it, as the model for scientific psychology to be built upon. It also emphasizes that humans should be treated as another instance of the natural physical world and functions under its same laws, energy harnessing, and expenditure processes.

> In psychology, when Clark Hull (1937, p. 2) argued that human behavior is merely a complication of the same factors that go to make up the actions of a raindrop, he was basing his explanation on the *Physikos*. At the most fundamental assumptive level, he recognized no difference between animate and inanimate substances in motion. (Rychlak, 1993, p. 936)

And also:

> Science can be viewed as an organized system of statements about objects and events. Just as other scientists look at and listen to slides, stars, and whooping cranes, the psychologist looks at and

listens to the behavior of organisms. As a scientist he makes statements about the events which he has observed. In this respect he does not differ from the bacteriologist, astronomer, or ornithologist. . . . In this regard the language of psychology is no different from the language of astronomy; one is largely about the behavior of organisms, the other about the behavior of stars and galaxies.

(Mandler & Kessen, 1964, p. 34)

Understanding of Culture

Culture as a complex sociosymbolic phenomenon does not exist in this perspective. It is reduced to convenient proxies (ethnicity or nationality) or to a set of variables/dimensions, like Hofstede's dimensions (see Chapter 1).

> Most cross-cultural psychologists, whose ultimate concern is with individual behavior, use the concept of culture either to identify context or to designate a set of antecedent variables.
> Typically, culture is used as a label for a group within a set of groups (e.g., groups constituting nationalities resident in different parts of the world or ethnic groups, often of varying national origins, living within a multicultural society) being compared on some behavioral dimension. As such, the term is an overarching label for a set of contextual variables (political, social, historical, ecological, etc.) that are thought by the researcher to be theoretically linked to the development and display of a particular behavior.
>
> (Segall, Lonner, & Berry, 1998, p. 1105)

Psychology historian Gustav Jahoda (2011) summarized this perspective's approach to culture in the following way: "cultures are treated as stable, bounded, relatively homogenous and ahistorical entities, more often than not equated with nations" (p. 51). Eckensberger (2011) commented on this approach to culture:

> The *cultural context* is defined by indexing cultures in terms of (in most cases, single) variables/categories like individualism/collectivism, which may be applied in single comparisons or multi-level analyses. In principle, cultural context is a part of the variance of the independent variable(s), and thus its importance/deepness is defined in terms of this variance. Hence cultural context is basically interpreted as a causal antecedent of psychological variables; it is therefore basically limited to the notion of environment/milieu.
>
> (p. 418)

Within the mechanistic perspective, culture exists relatively independent from humans, as an "omnipresent, general force" that is capable of "automatically" influencing human behavior (Breugelmans, 2011, pp. 135–136). Researchers within this perspective do not investigate the dynamics and processes of these influences, and try to avoid the concept of culture as much as possible.

A Danger of Culture Reification

Culture as a sociosymbolic reality is the product of human collective activity (We will discuss this in more detail later in this chapter). It does not exist outside communities of people and their social engagement. People are the authors and producers of their culture. And, when culture is created, it constitutes a powerful mechanism for regulating communal social life and its members' behavior. This ability of culture to manage people's actions and work as an external controlling device gives people the impression that their culture is not a human product but something that exists outside of human affairs and is even alien to them. Culture becomes perceived as an external reality, similar to a physical reality, with its own nature and powers over which people have no or limited control. This situation, when a product of human activity is perceived as an alien entity which is beyond people's control and which may function independently of their actions, is labeled *reification*. This is how phenomenological sociologists Berger and Luckmann (1966/1989) described the reification of sociocultural worlds:

> *Reification* is the apprehension of human phenomena as if they were things, that is, in non-human or possibly supra-human terms. Another way of saying this is that *reification is the apprehension of the products of human activity as if they were something else than human products*—such as facts of nature, results of cosmic laws, or manifestations of divine will. Reification implies that man is capable of forgetting his own authorship of the human world, and further, that the dialectic between man, the producer, and his products is lost to consciousness. *The reified world is, by definition, a dehumanized world* [here and above emphases in italics are added]. It is experienced by man as a strange facticity, an *opus alienum* [Lat.: alienated creation] over which he has no control rather than as the *opus proprium* [Lat.: creation that is one's own] of his own productive activity. (p. 89)

It is dangerous to reify sociocultural worlds because this reification creates the illusion that culture can be studied the same way as one studies a natural/physical entity. Researchers may feel that it can be measured, evaluated, calculated, and included into various equations and experimental designs as an independent variable. This thinking is sometimes called the *essentialization* of culture, meaning that culture is presented as a set of relatively stable and measurable dimensions that constitute its essence. When culture is reified and essentialized, the socially mediated, intentional, and intersubjective nature of it is completely lost and, ultimately, culture as a phenomenon disappears. Within the *Homo Mechanicus* perspective, reification and essentialization of culture are common phenomena and, if they are not reflected upon, these two processes constitute a serious hazard for productive research.

Understanding the Nature of Psychological Functioning

Following this mechanistic metaphor, individuals' psychological functioning is interpreted as the performance of relatively complex machines—similar to watches, telephone-telegraph relaying stations, or computers. All these machines have constituent parts that cause other parts to perform their functions. For example, springs or batteries in watches cause wheels and cogs to transform their energy into the hands' movement. Psychologists within this perspective try to find similar causes for people's behaviors, different mental states, and modes of psychological functioning. From this perspective, understanding human experience, behavior, and psychology requires reducing (i.e., *reductionism*) the objects of inquiry into their respective constitutive elements (*elementarism, atomism*) such as variables, traits, and dimensions in various forms (Eckensberger, 2011, p. 416), and then analyzing the relations, covariances, and potential causes of these variables. But the understanding of causality here is a peculiar one. It is built on a long history of replacing an examination of actual causality with an investigation of conjunctions and covariances of events, conditions, and variables. This line of thought started with Scottish empiricist philosopher **David Hume** (1711–1776), was continued by British philosopher **John Stuart Mill** (1806–1873) and, finally, asserted by British statistician **Karl Pearson** (1857–1936). According to Hume, researchers can only experience regular conjunctions of events and, based on these experiences, create ideas of relations among the mental impressions of these events and then interpret these ideas as causal relations among the events. To Hume, causality is not a matter of facts, but is an idea built by reflections about conjunctions of events. Mill extended this conception by announcing that the laws of the mind, which constitute the primary objects of psychological research, are "the uniformities of succession" that exist among mental events (Mill, 1843/1965, p. 27). Finally, Pearson (1892/1957) announced that searching for causality is an ephemeral endeavor, whereas searching for statistical covariances between alleged causes and effects is a much more productive idea. This British empiricist line of thoughts has strongly influenced thinking about research in many areas of psychology and other social sciences. This type of thinking also led to the extensive use of various statistical techniques in investigating the relations between sociocultural and psychological variables. And despite a mantra-like assertion that 'correlation does not mean causation,' researchers frequently talk the causality language—"culture influences . . . ," "social environment determines or affects behavior and mental states"—even though their research was based exclusively on covariances and statistical associations. To substantiate their causality claims, these researchers may use different forms of longitudinal design and experiments. These methodological tools may provide more convincing hypotheses about causal relations. But still, if research is guided by the positivist paradigm, an application of experiments for extracting causal relations may have limited utility (see Chapter 4). Despite utilizing various complex designs to establish causality within the *Homo Mechanicus* perspective, the nature of such relations remains the same: they reflect a conjunction, juxtaposition, or concurrence of empirically verifiable events and can be expressed by a simple formula: If A, then B (see Chapter 3).

These alleged causes can be located outside a person—e.g., in various social, economic, political, and cultural processes and conditions—or inside an individual—e.g., values, attitudes, personality traits, motives, and needs. One of the best examples of applying such a way of thinking is behaviorism, where human behavior is determined by contingencies of reinforcement and in order to control and predict behavioral acts, it is important to know and manipulate these contingencies. Another example is utilizing dimensional approaches to culture (like Hofstede's dimensions) and trait theories in personality (like the Big Five personality theory). Traits are "enduring characteristics of a person that can serve an explanatory role in accounting for the observed regularities and consistencies in behavior" (Reber & Reber, 2001, p. 758). The trait theories of personality "operate under the assumption that one's personality is a compendium of traits" (p. 525), meaning a mechanical constellation of several components. To study personality and to predict a person's behavior, researchers need to identify these traits and calculate their relationships with various behavioral manifestations and then infer causality. For instance, discovering a significant correlation between extraversion and the number of friends a person has allows trait psychologists to state that extraversion may cause a person's sociality and then make a prediction based on an individual's score on an extraversion questionnaire.

Methodology and Methods of Research

The methodology and research within this perspective were influenced by the same conviction to empiricism/positivism and the replacement of the idea of causation by investigating the statistical covariances among behavioral and mental variables. *Methodology* refers to the logic that frames a research process for answering research questions, and *methods* are conceptual and technical tools for generating and analyzing data. This theoretical perspective is often associated with the *nomothetic* methodological approach, understood as a scientific quest toward discovering the universal laws of phenomena (see Chapter 7). The main question here is: what is understood by the notion of 'scientific laws?' Because most adherents to this perspective deny the existence of unobservable entities, they follow the tradition of positivism to understand the laws of nature as a set of stable empirical regularities among various events, states, and conditions. Because of this conviction, the methodology of research within this perspective is straightforwardly predetermined:

a   The units of analysis are "variables" (a so-called "variable-based approach"; see Chapter 7). The phenomena under investigation—individuals, groups, communities, or cultures—are decomposed into a set of variables which constitutes the main focus of research. These variables are operationalized and measured through different tests, scales, questionnaires, or inventories. The psychometric quality of these measures is tested; the questionnaires and scales are applied to samples of people.

b   Associations among variables are calculated using various statistical techniques; these associations and other statistical indices (means, standard deviations, etc.) are used as the primary sources to test research hypotheses. These empirical regularities are generalized from samples to populations and conclusions about the generality, systematicity, and invariance of these relations are then asserted.

c   Experiments, longitudinal designs, and other techniques are used to verify or test for potential causal relations among the variables.

d   An etic or 'outsider' position of a researcher (see Chapters 1, 7, and 8) is another distinguishing feature used in the *Homo Mechanicus* methodological approach. Researchers typically take the position of a *detached observer*, which is considered by Blaikie (2010) to be a traditional "scientific" stance (p. 50). This means that when studying either human beings or various sociocultural entities, a researcher approaches them as if he or she is an unbiased, value-neutral, and objective observer, effectively adopting the same stance to objects of investigation that natural scientists have.

g   Philosophically speaking, this approach is based on the positivist paradigm (see Chapter 3). All the advantages and weakness of this philosophical paradigm apply to this perspective. Eckensberger (2011) succinctly summarized the major methodological highlights of the *Homo Mechanicus* perspective:

> (1) *materialism* and *elementarism*, have to be underlined (it is assumed that phenomena can be investigated by means of controlling (singular) variables, which usually also implies decontextualization), (2) *measurement* (tests, scaling) is essential . . . and (3) (usually linear) *causal explanation* and *prediction* as a hard test of causality are part of this perspective. So the language of *mathematics/statistics* enters the perspective in two respects: as data and measurement theory to define measures/variables, and as descriptive/inferential statistics to test relations between variables as similarities or differences. (pp. 417–418)

The Main Disciplines

Some areas of mainstream psychology, including the fields of social and personality studies, are still influenced by this mechanistic approach. The strong presence of this perspective in cross-cultural psychology has been constantly emphasized, but was convincingly criticized by Eckensberger (2011). He also remarked that "it is this perspective on which most textbooks on method in psychology as well as in cross-cultural psychology are based" (p. 418). This conclusion is supported by this textbook. A continuation of uncritical utilization of this paradigm in research on culture and psychology prevents any further developments and breakthrough of new knowledge in this area.

The Biological Science Perspective

The major metaphor is *"Bios"*—humans as biological organisms (Rychlak, 1996, p. 936). This metaphor means that evolution and the biological basis of human organisms are the starting points for understanding psychological functioning. Researchers within this perspective try to find the essence of being a human in people's biology and in the functioning of their bodies and brains. Biological organisms are animated functional units where such categories as life, environment, reproduction, survival, and adaptation replace the concepts of matter, physical causes, forces, and the mechanistic causality of the previous perspective. An evolutionary perspective, together with a developmental one, plays an important role in this type of thinking: most states and processes in human functioning are perceived as phylogenetic evolutionary acquisitions and as ontogenetically unfolding individual adaptations. The discipline of biology is modeled and copied within this perspective as a framework to think not only about individuals but also about societies and cultures. Eckensberger noted that "this theoretical perspective . . . is considered to represent a real paradigm shift [in comparison to the *Mechanicus* perspective] because it took a totally new look at the adaptive processes of organisms in their environment" (pp. 419–420).

Culture in this perspective is considered to be a specifically human way of adapting to environmental demands for securing the survival of human communities and their members. In Chapter 1, we discussed anthropology's adaptationist theories that treat culture as the collective way communities adapt to their environments. Some of these theories have been influenced by the *Homo Bios* theoretical perspective. Many psychologists, especially after the rise of evolutionary psychology, have acquired a strong inclination to apply the same adaptationist and evolutionary thinking to their understanding of culture and its role in psychological functioning (Barkow, Cosmides, & Tooby, 1992). Evolutionary biologists also cannot avoid the concept of culture and use their biological thinking to decipher it (Boyd & Richerson, 2005; Pagel, 2012). Despite some disciplinary distinctions, there are several common propositions of how representatives of this perspective treat culture. Most of them accept that humans possess several innate biological and psychological proclivities, like physiological and psychological needs, emotions, cognitive predispositions, and personality tendencies. An important nuance here is that many adaptationists believe that people inherit not only basic bio-physiological features but also almost all essential human psychological capacities: language, complex social cognition, memory, hypothetical reasoning, emotions, personality traits, and morality (Buss, 1995, 2001). Matsumoto and Juang (2013), for example, labelled these psychological capacities the "universal psychological toolkit" (p. 11) with which humans are endowed by evolution to assist them with gratifying their basic needs (p. 11). The concept of genes plays an important role; some biologists believe genes are responsible for both the development of the innate bio-psychological proclivities of individuals and for the emergence of culture (Pagel, 2012). When humans are positioned in a specific ecological environment and experience the demand to use existing resources for survival, they utilize their universal psychological toolkit to invent environment-specific practices and technologies to extract and utilize these resources. By using these practices, they generate and accumulate the knowledge and skills that help them deal with the demands and challenges of their settings. These sets of practices, skills, and knowledge are labelled culture. Culture then is transmitted to younger generations by imitation, teaching, and learning; it is transformed and modernized, and then transmitted again. An important distinction is that adaptationists argue that psychological capacities develop first and culture, as an instrument for adaptation, develops second. This is the point with which many disagree, insisting that culture is responsible for developing all their species-specific psychological capacities in humans. Finally, culture in this perspective is seen as an exclusively human-specific survival tool, or as Pagel (2012) called it, a "cultural survival vehicle" (p. 12). He used the analogy of a body of a living organism, which biologists named 'survival vehicles.' By this analogy,

> our species evolved to build, in the form of their societies, tribes, or cultures, a second body or vehicle to go along with the vehicle that is their physical body. Like our physical bodies, this cultural body wraps us in a protective layer, not of muscles and skins but of knowledge and technologies, . . . it gives us our language, cooperation, and a shared identity. (pp. 12–13)

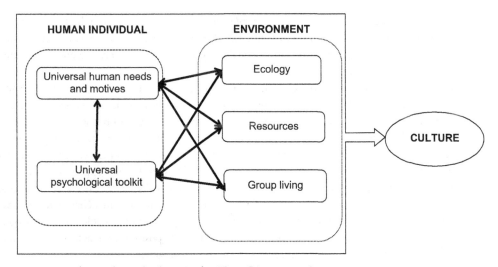

FIGURE 2.1 Understanding of culture in the *Homo Bios* perspective

Figure 2.1 depicts the understanding of culture within the *Homo Bios* perspective.

The discussion about culture brings us directly to the understanding of **psychological functioning** within the *Homo Bios* perspective. Similar to culture, mental phenomena and various forms of behavior are interpreted as sophisticated adaptations of living organisms. Such phenomena as cognition, emotion, and motivation are understood in terms of their function to efficiently guide organism-environment interaction loops by generating adaptive behavioral patterns. That is why *functionalism* is one of the main intellectual instruments for thinking about this subject matter. Every psychological process, state, or trait is interpreted here in terms of its function within an organism and/or within a system of organism-environment relations for the purpose of adaptation and survival (see also Chapter 1).

> In psychology this perspective is applied literally in the interpretation of behavior by referring to a general phylogenetic function of survival (like in attachment theory; see Bowlby, 1969) or in applying sociobiological thinking . . . [where] social behavior is understood as mainly serving the function of increasing the inclusive fitness of genes.
>
> (Eckensberger, 2011, pp. 419–420)

In addition to functionalism, the principle of *holistic organismic thinking* is another way of reasoning within the *Homo Bios* perspective. This principle means that in order to understand the purposes and functions of different physiological and psychological processes and states, an organism and the mind have to be considered not as the mechanical compositions of various components, but as organic wholes or systems where all these components are interdependent and where the phenomena of interest should be considered only within the systemic wholes where they were generated. For example, in order to understand the role and purpose of a cardiovascular subsystem, a physiologist has to look into its functions within the entire human body and understand how blood circulation contributes to the maintenance and performance of other of the body's subsystems and the organism as a whole. In addition to the ideas of evolution, adaptation, function, and organismic-systemic thinking, the concept of development is also brought into focus here. Psychological adaptations are considered in terms of their development or genesis, both phylo- and ontogenetically.

An advantage of this perspective is that *function, adaptation, system,* and *genesis,* which are interrelated, are used to answer the *why* question about the proximal and distal causes and mechanisms of psychological functioning. Some elements of realist thinking are definitely present within this paradigm's thinking (see Chapter 4).

The notion of causality is also more complex in this perspective than in the previous one. Such potential causal factors as genes, environmental pressures, adaptation tasks, universal needs, the universal psychological toolkit, and cultures all interact with each other in producing the adaptive behavior of organisms and their survival. Sociopsychological functioning of people is presented here not as a result of linear causal processes but as an outcome of the complex systemic relations among the participating determining factors in a context (Eckensberger, 2011, pp. 419–420).

The **methodology and methods** are copied from the biological sciences: population analysis; case analysis; historical and developmental studies of various biological and behavioral systems. "Measurement, particularly operationalization and statistics, play [sic] a minor role" (Eckensberger, 2011, p. 420) within this perspective. Researchers occupy the etic position of a 'detached observer' and use a mixture of nomothetic thinking, based on applying the general laws of evolution, genetics, and biology, and idiographic reasoning, where individual organisms and their development are studied as units of analysis.

The **main disciplines** are evolutionary biology, anthropology and psychology, sociobiology, and developmental and cross-cultural developmental psychology. Some ideas, especially with regard to the notion of culture, are incorporated by mainstream cross-cultural psychology.

The Sociocultural Sciences Perspective

The **major metaphors** for this perspective are *Socius,* meaning humans as social and institutionalized creatures (Rychlak, 1993, p. 936; Berger & Luckmann, 1966/1989, p. 51), and *Animal Symbolicum* (symbolizing animal) (Cassirer, 1944/1974, p. 26). The first metaphor means that in order to be *sapient,* human beings have to be social and interact with each other to produce a specifically human milieu where they become fully human. "Man's self-production is always, and of necessity, a social enterprise. Men together produce a human environment, with the totality of its socio-cultural and psychological formations" (Berger & Luckmann, 1966/1989, p. 51). The second metaphor clarifies the features around which sociality is involved. This feature is the humans' capacity to organize an environment where something always stands for something else, where things symbolize other things, events, and processes. Such a *symbolic environment* is a purely human habitat for development and functioning. Mitchell (1995) clarifies: "man, for many philosophers both ancient and modern, is the 'representational animal,' *homo symbolicum,* the creature whose distinctive character is the creation and manipulation of signs—things that 'stand for' or 'take the place of' something else" (p. 11). Regarding this metaphor, Cassirer (1944) wrote:

> No longer can man confront reality immediately; he cannot see it, as it were, face to face. Physical reality seems to recede in proportion as man's symbolic activity advances. . . . He has so enveloped himself in linguistic forms, and artistic images, in mystical symbols or religious rites that he cannot see or know anything except by the interposition of this artificial medium. . . . [S]ymbolic thought and symbolic behavior are among the most characteristic features of human life, and . . . the whole progress of human culture is based on these conditions. (pp. 25–27)

The dialectics of these metaphors are that 'social' and 'symbolic,' hence 'cultural,' are inseparable features of exclusively human environments: symbols are created, maintained, and function through social interactions, both verbal and physical, and these social interactions are directed and guided by various symbolic systems. The social and symbolic components of these exclusively human environments are mutually constitutive, therefore the terms *sociocultural worlds* and *sociocultural environments*.

Culture within this perspective is interpreted as a system of knowledge comprised of collections of recipes for acting and decision-making as well as a sociosymbolic reality that is saturated with various systems of meaning that play important roles in shaping social structures and institutions, human beings, their psychology, and behavior. In Chapter 1, we discussed three types of anthropological theories of culture. The adaptationist theories successfully survive within the biological perspective of *Homo Bios* discussed above. Within the *Homo Socius* framework, culture is conceptualized by various ideational theories. Cultures exist out there; people are born into them, and cultures regulate people's behavior by supplying them with knowledge, structures, and meanings. Within such a framework, culture is defined not only as a symbolic meaning system but as a regulative mechanism that guides human behavior and makes it meaningful, goal-oriented, and rational (read the discussion below).

A construction of institutionalized knowledge and meaning systems is the result of cultural evolution and of the uniquely situated histories of communities of people where these cultures develop. Cultural symbols and their meanings are created by communities for the coordination of members' behaviors, and they execute this function by being shared intersubjectively, "where the term 'intersubjectivity' refers to a state of affairs in which two or more people understand that they are experiencing events the same way" (D'Andrade, 1986, p. 31). When all people at a wedding interpret the unfolding of events the same way, they share the meaning of the wedding ceremony intersubjectively and therefore maintain the existence of it. Only under the condition of intersubjectivity can this event become real. Different layers of intersubjective systems of meaning and how to approach them will be discussed in Chapter 4.

Another important characteristic of cultures, understood as meaning systems, is that for people who were born into these cultures, who were enculturated and socialized within them, these cultural realities exist as natural and are therefore *taken-for-granted*. They believe that this is their 'real' and 'valid' reality, that this is how things really are. This perception becomes people's second nature, and they follow these cultural meanings, practices and prescriptions semiautomatically and without serious reflections of their nature: "This is how things are done here." This taken-for-grantedness of cultural things provides people with a sense of ontological security that is important for their optimal functioning and feeling of well-being. But the taken-for-grantedness and automaticity of the cultural representations create a serious challenge for researchers to study them and especially for using interviews and self-reflections to study culture. (We will also discuss intersubjectivity and taken-for-grantedness within the fourth perspective later in this chapter.)

With regard to people's **psychological functioning**, this perspective can be characterized by the idea of *cultural determinism*. This means, on one hand, that culture supplies all the necessary prerequisites for people to become fully functioning individuals, thus determining their mental and behavioral composition. It determines the psychological makeup and rules of psychological functioning of individuals. On the other hand, cultural determinism means that culture can be understood without any reference to the mental and behavioral functioning of members of this culture.

Anthropologists and other social scientists who endorse the first aspect of cultural determinism believe that culture is a fundamental factor that shapes people's selves, motivations, personalities, emotions and, finally, their behaviors and experiences, and that in order to understand people, scholars have to describe and analyze the cultures where people live. D'Andrade (1999) expressed this idea in the following way: "There is a notion widespread among American cultural anthropologists which holds that 'culture is everything.' According to this view, culture is the dominant *causal* force in human life" (p. 85). Without culture, human beings would remain mostly animals. "Men unmodified by the customs of particular places do not in fact exist, have never existed, and most important, could not in the very nature of the case exist" (Geertz, 1973, p. 35). To know people, you need to know their culture. This stance of cultural determinism was propagated by interpretative anthropologist Gilford Geertz (1973):

> I want to propose two ideas. The first, of these is that culture is best seen not as complexes of concrete behavior patterns—customs, usages, traditions, habit clusters—as has by and large, been the case up to now, but as a set of control mechanisms—plan, recipes, rules, instructions (what computer engineers call 'programs')—for the governing of behavior. The second idea is that man is precisely the animal most desperately dependent upon such extragenetic, outside-the-skin control mechanisms, such cultural programs, for ordering his behavior. . . .
>
> Undirected by culture patterns—organized systems of significant symbols—man's behavior would be virtually ungovernable, a mere chaos of pointless acts and exploding emotions, his experience virtually shapeless. Culture, the accumulated totality of such patterns, is not just an ornament of human existence but—the principal basis of its specificity—an essential condition for it.
>
> (pp. 44–46)

Cognitive anthropologist Brad Shore (1998) added to this position, saying that anthropologists moved culture "from the peripheries of human life into its very center as a postnatal completion of human development. The study of human nature minus culture does not produce a more basic understanding of the human but an understanding of a protohuman, a creature that is all bioessence but lacking recognizable qualities of human existence" (p. 33). Thus, any theory about being a human must include culture—the system of social institutions and meanings. Therefore, according to this perspective, an understanding of human psychology depends most of all on understanding people's sociocultural environments and institutions into which human beings are socialized and enculturated and which regulate people's behaviors and experiences.

Evolutionary psychologists Tooby and Cosmides (1992) as well as cognitive psychologist Steven Pinker (2002) called this cultural deterministic approach the *Standard Social Science Model*. According to this model, the human mind of a newborn child is metaphorically represented as a general-purpose computer that is programmed by culture through socialization and enculturation. As a result of this programming, people's minds and consequently their behaviors are perceived as more or less a mirror reflection of their society's sociocultural norms, prescriptions, and regulations.

Less important for social scientists, but crucial for psychologists, is the second aspect of cultural determinism that excludes humans' mental functioning from the process of culture production, making cultures external factors and conditions that exist independently of the involvement of people's minds. Shore (1998) articulated this last aspect the following way:

> These versions of culture [based on the *Homo Socius* metaphor] tended to give us disembodied systems, structures, or programs—knowledge without any particular knower in mind and structures of thought that lacked any flesh-and-blood thinkers. Real people were replaced by hypothetical entities—'the savage mind,' the 'typical' or 'average' members of a community. People appeared more as the passive sites of cultural programming than as purposeful agents, strategists, and meaning makers. (p. 54)

Excluding people's mental and behavioral functioning from the construction of culture is fraught with the danger of reifying culture and may lead to all the consequences that were outlined above. In addition to potential damage for the culture being researched, the reification of culture also has an important existential component relevant to people's everyday living. Berger and Luckmann (1966/1989) warned that, "The reified world is, by definition, a dehumanized world" (p. 89). If we reify the 'culture of poverty,' 'criminal culture,' the 'culture of corruption,' etc., we alienate these cultures from the people who produce and maintain them. By this, we imply that people are powerless victims of these cultures' forces over which they have no control. Thus, we remove from people their essential capability to produce, maintain and change their sociocultural environments; we dehumanize them by transforming them into the powerless pawns of alienated cultural forces.

Methodology and Methods

The researchers who endorse the *Homo Socius* perspective utilize diverse approaches and methodologies that we will be discussing throughout this book: the interpretivist paradigm (Chapter 4), the case-based approach together with the emic or 'insider' position of a researcher (Chapter 7), as well as the comparative (Chapter 8) and ethnographic methods in all their diversities (Chapters 4 and 10).

It is important to note that this perspective is so closely intertwined with social and cultural anthropology (Chapter 1) that it is logical to blend them together. That is why I suggest reading this subsection along with the previous chapter.

The main disciplines: social and cultural anthropology, sociology, some domains of psychological and cognitive anthropology.

The Agentic-Interpretive Perspective

The main metaphors are *Homo Interpretans* (Man the Interpreter) (Eckensberger, 2011, p. 424) and *Logos* (Rychlak, 1993, p. 936). These metaphors mean that human beings are perceived as mindful, reflective, rational, and interpreting agents. They are actively involved with their sociocultural worlds. Human beings are not only shaped by these worlds (as the previous perspectives suggest), but they also actively interact with their cultures and are capable of maintaining, modifying, and changing them. Another aspect of this metaphor is that humans are not only the bearers and executors of the public cultural meaning, but also the creators of their own idiosyncratic meaning about the world, other people, and themselves. Thus, they are perceived as "meaning-creating creatures" (Eckensberger, 2011, p. 424) and as the agents of their own lives. Such assumptions dramatically change how people's actions and experiences within different sociocultural environments are understood and should be studied.

Culture within this approach is the central factor for the development of consciousness and the reflective capacities of people, similar to the sociocultural perspective. But culture here is presented not as an omnipotent external determinant of human existence, but as a set of *cultural models* that are co-created by members of cultural communities and that, after being learned and internalized, regulate their behaviors (D'Andrade & Strauss, 1992; Shore, 1998). People can potentially reflect on these learned models and, because of their acquired agentic powers, evaluate their importance, relevance, and appropriateness. In this perspective, culture "does not represent an avoidable unidirectional influence, but rather a systemic framework circumscribing possible courses of action. . . . That is, the quality and extent of cultural penetration varies significantly between individuals because each individual constructs his/her 'personal culture'" (Helfrich-Holter, 2006, p. 255). Therefore, individuals are capable of having control over cultural influences.

As was mentioned above, within this perspective, a productive approach to culture is to interpret it as a system of cultural models, an idea that has been developed and successfully used by cognitive anthropologists (D'Andrade, 1995; D'Andrade & Strauss, 1992; Holland & Quinn, 1987; Shore, 1998). "A particularly powerful way of thinking about culture: as an extensive and heterogeneous collection of 'models,' models that exist both as public artifacts 'in the world' and as cognitive constructs 'in the mind of members of a community" (Shore, 1996, p. 44). An advantage of the *cultural models theory* is that, instead of categorizing the realities of human existence into three relatively independent domains—'social,' 'cultural,' and 'psychological'—it connects individuals' mental regulations with their sociocultural environments by a structured set of cultural models that are maintained and instantiated by people's actions. In the theory of cultural models, the core concepts of culture and psychology research—sociocultural institutions, the mind, behavior, experiences—are synthesized into a system where all these components are dialectically interconnected.

Theory of Cultural Models

Before presenting this theory, it is important to introduce the idea of *mental models* (Shore, 1998):

> Mental models are personal, internal representations of external reality that people use to interact with the world around them. They are constructed by individuals based on their unique life experiences, perceptions, and understandings of the world. Mental models are used to reason and make decisions and can be the basis of individual behaviors. They provide the mechanism through which new information is filtered and stored. (Jones et al., 2011, (p. 46)).

Mental models consists of various mental representations: of a prelinguistic as well as of a symbolic and linguistic nature. Prelinguistic representations of a visual, audio, kinesthetic, and tactile nature are sensed by people with no or with minimal verbal coding. A soft touch of a mother's hand is a prelinguistic component of the mental model a child develops of her mother. Linguistic mental representations are verbally coded symbolizations of various aspects of objects and their characteristics. When a child thinks about her mother as a loving and caring person, she entertains the linguistic components of the mental model of her mother. The definition above describes the *"personal mental models"* (Shore, 1996, p. 46) that are idiosyncratically developed by each person through interactions with his or her environment. Without constructing such models, humans are incapable of navigating their worlds, both natural and sociocultural. The development of idiosyncratic personal models is an essential aspect of cognitive development, as these models constitute major components of meaning-making and interpretive activities.

In addition to personal mental models, people possess mental representations of a social stock of knowledge, information, and meanings that communities develop through their history. Shore (1998) labelled these sets of representations *"conventional mental models"* (p. 47), or here, *internalized aspects of cultural models*. These models or aspects consist of concepts and categories about the worlds, decision-making rules and recipes for how to live life, how to give birth, how to love, how to eat, to sleep, to marry, to live together, and myriads of other things that people do. Individual members of a community are born into these stocks of knowledge and meanings, they learn them through the processes of socialization and enculturation, and they internalize them. This means that, in addition to the personal mental models of her mother, a child possesses the representations that are prescribed by the social conventions of the child's cultural community of how to be a good and loving daughter and how a good daughter should treat her mother. This child internalizes some of these prescriptions and uses them to guide her relationship with the mother in a way that is congruent with the conventions of her cultural community. By guiding this relationship according to those cultural conventions, the child not only creates congruence of her behavior with the behavior of other people around her, but she also maintains and reinforces these conventions by intending and enacting them. These stocks of information and meanings together with their mental representations are labeled *cultural models* by cognitive anthropologists. Based on this description, cultural models are composed of *external/public* and *internal/mental* aspects. They are external, such as wedding, banking, university education, workplace, health care, or any other social institutions are, because these institutions are public conventions that exist 'out there' in cultural communities. But cultural models are also internal to the members of these communities (conventional mental models), who use them, together with their personal mental models, to guide and regulate their behavior. The external and internal aspects are interconnected through social interactions (see Fig. 2.2.).

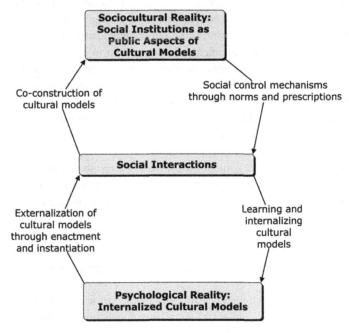

FIGURE 2.2 Theory of cultural models. This concept map was made with IHMC Cmap Tools

Theorists define cultural models in the following ways:

> Cultural models are presupposed, taken-for-granted models of the world that are widely shared (although not necessarily to the exclusion of other, alternative models) by the members of a society and that play enormous role in their understanding of that world and their behavior in it.
> (Quinn & Holland, 1987, p. 4)

> "Cultural models," [are] the presupposed, taken-for-granted, commonsensical, and widely shared assumptions which a groups of people hold about the world and its objects.
> (Hollan, 1992, p. 285)

> Cultural anthropologists assume that cultural models are intersubjective representations, constructed by individuals in relation to social environment.
> (Shore, 1998, p. 49)

Cultural models can be characterized by the following features:

1. *Cultural models are intentional, agreed-upon conventions that have real power for regulating behavior.* The intriguing paradox of these models is that they consist of things that, on one hand, are collective public institutions existing outside of individuals and influencing their behaviors, and, on the other hand, they are all products of humans' cooperation and co-construction that cannot

exist without human mental and physical involvement with them. Consider the collective institution of money and everything that is related to it—earning, saving, and spending. Any bill is a piece of paper that has no value in itself. Its value comes from a collective agreement among people, supported by governmental institutions, that some specific paper with printed symbols should be treated as "money" and should be used for all forms of economic transactions. Money is a negotiated social convention; yet it is tangibly real. You cannot avoid using it in a store or in other business institution. This characteristic of sociocultural conventions, to exist as real entities because people think about them in a certain way and behave based on this thinking, is called *intentionality*, and their corresponding things and entities are labeled "intentional things" (Shweder, 1991, p. 75) or "culturally created entities" (D'Andrade, 1984, p. 91). Therefore, "money," "marriage," "theft," "education at a university," and myriads of other acts, things, and events that are created by cultural communities are intentional things (see Chapter 1). As Shweder (1991) writes:

> What makes their existence intentional is that such things would not exist independently of our involvements with and reactions to them; and they exercise their influence in our lives because of our conceptions of them. Intentional things are causally active, but only by virtue of our mental representations of them.
>
> Intentional things have no "natural" reality or identity separate from human understandings and actions. Intentional worlds do not exist independently of the intentional states (beliefs, desires, emotions) directed at them and by them, by the person who live in them. (p. 75)

Cultural models consist of such intentional things by the virtue of their conceptions in people's minds. Shweder labeled mental representations of intentional things "intentional states," like the belief that money is very important, which leads to the intention to earn more money or the feeling of despair when an account runs low. The inseparable existence of intentional things and their corresponding intentional states eliminates the dichotomy between "sociocultural" as external and "mental" as internal factors that regulate human behavior. The elimination of this dichotomy is one of the major advantages of the theory of cultural models.

2. *Cultural models are intersubjectively shared among members of cultural communities.* Members of a community mutually understand that others have the same representations of intentional things and that all others comprehend and use these things in the same way. Each individual member also knows that other people know that each member understands intentional things the same way: "I know that you know that I know what this intentional thing means." It is this mutual co-understanding of conventional intentional things that makes it possible for people to "read others' minds" and coordinate social interactions. If this sharing did not exist, we would not be able to manage our social lives, and they would become extremely chaotic. Thus *intentionality* and *intersubjectivity* are the two main attributes of public conventional cultural models.

3. *Cultural models are learned and internalized by individuals.* In order for a cultural model to become a regulator of behavior, it has to be learned and internalized by members of cultural communities. Internalization means that some externally existing regulatory systems are taken inside a person's intrapsychic regulation and incorporated into his or her governing mechanisms. Clinical psychologists, starting with Freud, developmental psychologists, starting with Vygotskii, and social psychologists, starting with Berger and Luckmann, all talk about internalization as the primary mechanism for creating an intrapsychic regulatory system (see Schafer, 1968; Wallis & Poulton, 2001). When a father teaches his son to wash his hands and explains how and why he has to do this, the son learns the cultural model of hand-washing as a form of the

conventional institution of hygiene and health care; and later on, when the boy simply cannot exit a bathroom without washing his hands, this model becomes co-opted into his regulatory mental mechanisms; hence, it is internalized. These two processes of learning and internalizing cultural models constitute the essence of making collective cultural models available to individuals as the regulators of their behaviors. These two processes constitute the essence of the socialization and enculturation of a child in any cultural community. As Shore (1998) commented, the internalized cultural models lose their nuances and factual richness by becoming a conventional mental schema for interpreting a situation and acting within it. The schematic form of the conventional mental models makes their use economical and efficient. Bourdieu (1977) called these internalized mental schema the *habitus* that guide people's preferences, decision-making, and actions (see Chapter 6).

4. *When internalized, cultural models acquire the motivational power to initiate and regulate people's actions.* The internalization of many cultural models occurs through several stages (D'Andrade, 1995; Spiro, 1987). As an example, think about the indoctrination of a person into a religious faith. First, that person learns the basics about a particular faith from a social stock of knowledge without full acceptance and understanding of its meaning. Second, he or she learns the meaning and significance of this public model and accepts it as true, right, and correct. But this acceptance is more normative than an understanding that provides real guidance for life. Spiro called such partly internalized models "clichés" (p. 164) that are not supported by motivational or emotional involvement. "Spiro uses the example of people who say they believe Jesus died for their sins, but who have no sense of sin" (D'Andrade, 1995, p. 228). At the next level, the internalized models are not only accepted as true and right, but they also structure and guide a person's actions and feelings. "When the proposition that Jesus died for man's sin is acquired at this level, the individual feels a sense of sin and is concerned to perform the actions necessary to achieve redemption" (p. 228). The internalized cultural model at the fourth level not only guides a person's actions, but it actually instigates them, and these culturally instigated actions are motivationally and emotionally loaded. "Believing that Jesus died for man's sin, the believer is filled with anxiety about his own sins, and driven to try to atone for these sins in prayer and deeds, and filled with relief and joy at evidence to be saved" (p. 228). Only the third and fourth levels correspond to a full internalization of the cultural model. At these levels the models become strong motivational forces in determining people's behaviors and experiences (D'Andrade, 1992).

5. *People are not directly aware of the internalized cultural models, which are experienced as taken-for-granted.* The internalized cultural models become an easy-to-use and taken-for-granted way of perceiving, classifying, and evaluating realities and acting upon them (see the *Homo Socius* metaphor). For people, they become natural, valid, and the only correct ways of dealing with the worlds. The internalization of cultural models means that they function on a prereflective level, and people do not spend their time contemplating their content and appropriateness: "This is how things are, and this is how they should be done here." For them, they represent a "real reality" that is valid and true. Such acceptance of these models creates a feeling of ontological security that is crucial for people's unimpeded everyday functioning.

6. *Cultural models are designed for separate domains of everyday life.* Lives of cultural communities happen within different domains: familial—marriage, parenting, education; work-related—professional training, employment, career development; health care—healthy lifestyle, illness, medical treatment, and myriads of other domains. Each domain is regulated by a set of corresponding cultural models. Members of communities internalize all these models and hold complex constellations of their mental representations. Extracting and understanding these constellations is one of the main goals of cultural psychological research.

7. *Cultural models are distributed through a population, and they have a structure.* Although cultural models serve the important function of coordinating and regulating people's behaviors, this does not mean that all members share exactly the same models and use them in exactly the same way. Externalized cultural models are always richer and broader than any of their internalized versions. From their parents and their environments, children may learn different aspects of the same cultural model of being a good son or daughter. Also, people who share cultural models in one domain may not share cultural models in other domains. Plus, the level of models' learning and internalization may strongly differ from person to person within the same community. All these factors tell us that cultural models are distributed among populations in complex patterns and each member has an idiosyncratic constellation of them.

    It is inevitable that in order to ease the use of cultural models, they have to be structured and hierarchized. Shore (1998) suggests the following structure of cultural models:

    > At the greatest level of particularity are (1) *specific cases*, concrete experiences which provide the most direct basis for general reasoning. More abstract and institutionalized are (2) *instituted models*, which are the behavioral equivalent of conventional "categories" for experience. Instituted models are usually labeled or otherwise explicitly coded by members of community, so that they are easily recognized forms of institutionalized experience. Most abstract are (3) *foundational schemas*. Foundational schemas are very general models which work across empirically heterogeneous domains of experience and underlie a community's worldview. Foundational schemas are usually only tacitly known and explicitly cognized by members of a community. Few people are able spontaneously to describe their operative foundational schemas. (p. 366)

    This multilayered structure of cultural models means that a person has to simultaneously handle several systems of meaning and synthesize them in such a way that makes sense for him or her in a particular situation. Shore (1998) labelled this process by which a person manages these dynamics "meaning construction" (p. 7).

    > I discovered that meaning is not given to us ready-made, simply immanent either in cultural forms or in mind. Meaning could be understood only as an ongoing process, and active construction by people, with the help of cultural resources. (p. 7)

    If this idea of actively constructing meaning out of available cultural forms is correct, then it is necessary to accept the active and agentic nature of each and every member of a cultural community. This acceptance moves the application of the theory of cultural models to the level of human agency and autonomy within the existing set of cultural models.

8. *When cultural models are expressed, they become externalized and instantiated.* Internalized cultural models in the form of conventional mental models may or may not get expressed. When they are expressed, scientists talk about their *externalization*, which means that something that had been internal becomes visible, touchable, recognizable, and externally verifiable. The externalization of cultural models is responsible for the existence of these models as components of sociocultural worlds in the forms of social institutions and conventions (see Fig. 2.2.). The externalization of mental models in the form of particular actions and behaviors of people is labelled *instantiation*. When a person is accepted into a university, he or she learns the cultural model of university education. When he or she starts choosing courses, attending lectures, and doing homework, he or she instantiates this cultural model through these actions. The instantiation is always different

from both the public and internalized cultural models. For instance the cultural model of a university education, as a generic schema, requires students to do their homework and be prepared for tests. And they accept this. But it does not say where, when, with whom and for how long they have to do this. They have to decide these aspects for themselves, depending on specific conditions and situations.

9. *Cultural models cannot exist and function without social interactions among the members of a cultural community.* As a system of intersubjectively shared intentional things, cultural models acquire their power only if they are intended and enacted by people through interactions with their fellow community members who have the same models in their minds. Thus, social interactions, both behavioral and verbal, become vehicles of cultural models in their move from externalized to internalized forms and back. The role of these interactions and the overall representation of the theory of cultural models is depicted in Fig 2.2.

10. By socializing into the cultural models of their communities, people also develop a specifically human capacity of perceiving themselves as the center of their experiences and actions, or a *sense of self*. With this sense of self comes the ability of every human being to reflect on these models, to interpret and reinterpret them, to use them creatively in different situations, to either accept or reject them, and, finally, either to maintain or transform them. The human ability not to be pawns of the cultural models but to be the master and able to transform these models constitutes the essence of human autonomy, agency, and self-determination (Chirkov, 2010, 2014) and constitutes the strong humanistic appeal of the theory of cultural models (Shore, 1998). Psychological autonomy and agency mean that in lieu of their socialization and enculturation, people may develop their own values, principles, and goals that may be different from the ones prescribed by their cultural models and then actively use these values to guide their lives. The dynamic of interactions between autonomous agentic individuals and their cultural contexts constitutes one of the most intriguing and challenging aspects of culture and psychology research.

The **understanding of psychological functioning** within the *Human Interpretans* metaphor logically follows the ideas of the person–culture interactions described above. People are seen as products of cultures, as co-creators of culture, and as active agents that may reflect upon and change the dynamic of person-culture interactions to their advantage. The primary proposition here is that people are agents of their own lives: they are capable of being psychologically autonomous and self-determined despite the fact that they are products of their culture. The nature of these capabilities lies in human consciousness, language, and rationality. Starting with the ancient thinkers in Greece, China, and other civilizations, the ability of humans to be reflective and reasonable and, as a result, to be capable of guiding their lives according to their own values and goals based on rational and moral decisions has been highlighted as one of the fundamental features of human nature (see Fromm & Xirau, 1979). Despite being socialized in and enculturated by their cultures, people are not slaves of their cultural models. People are capable of reflecting on them, and they may stay attached to or rebel and act against these prescriptions; they can even modify and change them and thus transform their cultural milieu. Accepting all these human capabilities makes understanding people's actions, motivations, and experiences a very challenging enterprise. A direct mechanistic, biological, or cultural determinism does not work here. There is a complex dialectic between conscious and reflective individuals and their sociosymbolic environments that they themselves have created and maintained. The unidirectional causality of the previous perspectives is replaced here by a systemic, reciprocal and dialectical cocreation and codetermination of human agents and their cultural systems. Within this perspective, human acts are not driven by causes but are based on reasons that are interconnected with the meaning that people have assigned to the worlds, to other people, and to themselves.

There are several distinctive directions of psychological research that have been executed within this perspective:

a. The sociocultural-historical approach of **Lev Vygotsky** (1896–1934), and based on it the activity/agency theories of human actions and sociocultural psychology. The main contributors: Michael Cole, James Wertsch, Jaan Valsiner, and their numerous followers (see Valsiner, 2014; Valsiner & Rosa, 2007; Yasnitsky, Van der Veer, & Ferrari, 2014). According to this approach, human cognitive and personal development happens through social interactions with their symbolic environment mediated by other people. People learn and internalize external regulatory structures which become their intrasubjective systems for managing their experiences and behaviors.
b. Research in social and cultural developmental sciences, including the topics of cognitive (Piaget, 1947/2001; Tomasello, 1999, 2014), moral (Kohlberg, 1984), and self-development (Brandtstädter & Lerner, 1999). This is a diverse range of developmental studies that are very close in many aspects to the sociohistorical approach, and that emphasize the proactive nature of an individual and the complex dynamics of his or her interactions with the sociocultural worlds.
c. Humanistic and existential-phenomenological psychology represented by Rollo May, Abraham Maslow, Carl Rogers and other psychologists (Severin, 1965); phenomenological psychology (Sokolowski, 2000; Spinelli, 1989) including phenomenological cognitive psychology (Gallagher & Zahavi, 2008) and phenomenological neuroscience (Thompson, 2007; Varela, Thompson, & Rosch, 1991). These varied approaches focus on how and by what mechanisms an individual interprets and understands his or her life and existence. A person's sense of self and the "first person perspective" are among the main concepts of this domain. Researchers also address the interaction between humans' experiences in different symbolic environments and the functioning of their brains.
d. Studies on the psychology of human agency, self-determination, and autonomy (Chirkov, Ryan, & Sheldon, 2010; Martin, Sugarman, & Hickinbottom, 2009; Martin, Sugerman, & Thompson, 2003; Ryan & Deci, 2004; Rychlak, 2003). These personality and motivation approaches emphasize the agentic and proactive nature of human functioning and fight against mechanistic and reductionist thinking about human psychological functioning.
e. Modern German research on culture, psychology, and action. The main representatives are Ernst Boesch (1991), Lutz Eckensberger (1995), and the Saabaden school (Straub, Weidemann, Kolbl, & Zielke, 2006).

Eckensberger (2011) summarized this approach by saying: "It is particularly productive for psychology to keep and even cultivate this perspective" (p. 425).

The Main Forms of Doing Research

Within the *Homo Interpretans* perspective, researchers utilize both the interpretive and realist philosophical paradigms with a rich arsenal of methods and techniques: naturalistic and participant observation, interviews, various forms of ethnography (see Chapter 10), case analysis, and comparative analysis (see Chapters 7 and 8); phenomenological analysis and interpretive phenomenology, psychological tests and questionnaires, and experiments. The specific design and the set of methods used in each research project depend on the problem to be solved and the theoretical orientations of researchers.

The main disciplines: cognitive and psychological anthropology, some forms of cultural and indigenous psychology; some domains of personality, social, and developmental psychology; humanistic cultural psychology.

Conclusion

Fig 2.3 depicts a graphic representation of the four perspectives.

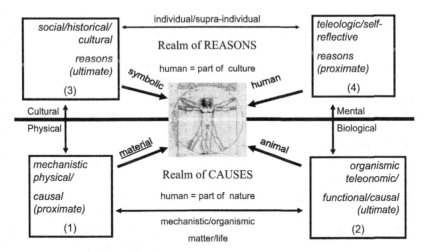

FIGURE 2.3 The four perspectives in studying culture and psychology. Adapted from Eckensberger, 2011; used with permission of the author and Cambridge University Press

Questions

To better comprehend the material and answer the questions fully, readers may wish to review the content of both Chapter 1 and Chapter 2.

1. Identify the main attributes of the *Homo Mechanicus* perspective in cross-cultural psychological research. Do you have concerns with the application of this perspective in culture and psychology research? Outline main features of this application and justify your answer.
2. Discuss the *Homo Bios* perspective: What are the advantages and disadvantages of using it in culture and psychology studies? In addressing what culture and psychology research problems would you use this perspective?
3. Compare the *Bios* perspective with the adaptationist theories of culture in anthropology. Outline the similarities and differences between these two approaches.
4. Combine the *Homo Socius* perspective with the examination of cultural anthropology in Chapter 1. How do they complement each other and what role is assigned to individuals' minds in these thoughts/ideas?
5. Explain the *Homo Interpretans* perspective. What are the advantages of such an approach to culture and psychology? Why do you think Eckensberger said that "It is particularly productive for psychology to keep and even cultivate this perspective?" Do you agree with his assessment? Justify your answer.
6. How do you understand the theory of cultural models? What advantages does it bring compared to other conceptualizations of culture?
7. If you were to adapt the *Homo Interpretans* perspective for your research, in what terms would you think about it and how would you do your study?
8. Describe how each of the four perspectives defines the causality of human actions. Reflect on how these different definitions may influence the methodology of investigations within each of the perspectives.

Glossary (some terms are cross-listed in the Glossary for Chapter 1)

Cultural determinism means that on one hand, culture supplies all the necessary prerequisites for people to become fully functioning individuals, thus determining their mental and behavioral composition. It determines the psychological makeup and rules of psychological functioning of individuals. On the other hand, cultural determinism means that culture can be understood without any reference to the mental and behavioral functioning of members of this culture.

Cultural models are regulatory mechanisms that mediate interactions of people within their cultural communities. They have the public aspects that are instantiated in different social institutions and the internalized aspects that resides in people's minds. Cultural models reflect the knowledge and prescriptions that these communities possess and are intersubjectively shared by members of communities.

Functionalism is an approach to interpreting various processes and states in terms of their functions within larger systems or organisms.

Holistic organismic thinking means that in order to understand the purposes and functions of different physiological and psychological processes and states, an organism and the mind have to be considered not as the mechanical compositions of various components, but as organic wholes or systems where all these components are interdependent and where the phenomena of interest should be considered only within the systemic wholes where they were generated.

Internalization is a process by which some externally existing regulatory systems are taken inside a person's intrapsychic regulation and incorporated into his or her governing mechanisms.

Reification of culture: Because culture is able to manage people's actions and to work as an external controlling device, some people feel that their culture is not a human product but something that exists outside of human affairs and that it is even alien to them. Such a belief is called reification of culture.

Standard Social Science Model: According to this model, the human mind is metaphorically represented as a general-purpose computer that is programmed by culture through socialization and enculturation. As a result of this programming, people's minds and consequently their behaviors are perceived to more or less mirror their society's sociocultural norms, prescriptions, and regulations.

Recommended Reading

Bennardo, G., & de Munck, V. (2013). *Cultural models: Genesis, methods, and experiences.* Oxford, UK: Oxford University Press.

D'Andrade, R. G. (1986). Three scientific world views and the covering law model. In D. W. Fiske & R. A. Shweder (Eds.), *Metatheory in social science: Pluralisms and subjectivities.* (pp. 19–41). Chicago, IL: University of Chicago Press.

Eckensberger, L. H. (2011). Cross-cultural differences as meaning systems. In F. J. R. Van de Vijver, A. Chasiotis & S. M. Breugelmans (Eds.), *Fundamental questions in cross-cultural psychology* (pp. 407–441). Cambridge, MA: Cambridge University Press.

Geertz, C. (1973). *The interpretation of cultures.* New York, NY: Basic Books.

Holland, D., & Quinn, N. (Eds.). (1987). *Cultural models in language and thought.* Cambridge, UK: Cambridge University Press.

Segall, M. H., Lonner, W. J., & Berry, J. W. (1998). Cross-cultural psychology as a scholarly discipline: On the flowering of culture in behavioral research. *American Psychologist, 53*(10), 1101–1110.

Shore, B. (1998). *Culture in mind: Cognition, culture, and the problem of meaning.* New York, NY: Oxford University Press.

Tooby, J., & Cosmides, L. (1992). The psychological foundations of culture. In J. H. Barkow, L. Cosmides & J. Tooby (Eds.), *The adapted mind: Evolutionary psychology and the generation of culture* (pp. 19–136.). New York, NY: Oxford University Press.

References

Barkow, J. H., Cosmides, L., & Tooby., J. (Eds.). (1992). *The adapted mind: Evolutionary psychology and the generation of culture*. Oxford, UK: Oxford University Press.
Berger, P. L., & Luckmann, T. (1966/1989). *The social construction of reality: A treatise in the sociology of knowledge*. New York, NY: Anchor Books.
Blaikie, N. (2010). *Designing social research: The logic of anticipation*. (2nd ed.). Cambridge, UK: Polity.
Boesch, E. E. (1991). *Symbolic action theory and cultural psychology*. Berlin, Germany: Springer.
Bourdieu, P. (1977). *Outline of a theory of practice* (R. Nice, Trans.). Cambridge, UK: Cambridge University Press.
Boyd, R., & Richerson, P. J. (2005). *The origin and evolution of cultures*. New York, NY: Oxford University Press,.
Brandtstädter, J., & Lerner, R. M. (Eds.). (1999). *Action and self-development: Theory and research through the life span*. Thousand Oaks, CA: Sage.
Breugelmans, S. M. (2011). The relationships between individual and culture. In F. J. R. van de Vijver, A. Chasiotis & S. M. Breugelmans (Eds.), *Fundamental questions in cross-cultural psychology* (pp. 135–162). Cambridge, UK: Cambridge University Press.
Buss, D. M. (1995). Evolutionary psychology: A new paradigm for psychological science. *Psychological Inquiry*, 6(1), 1–30.
Buss, D. M. (2001). Human nature and culture: An evolutionary psychological perspective. *Journal of Personality*, 69(6), 955–978.
Cassirer, E. (1944/1974). *An essay on man: An introduction to a philosophy of human culture*. New Haven, CT: Yale University Press.
Chirkov, V. (2010). Dialectical relationships among human autonomy, the brain, and culture. In V. I. Chirkov, R. M. Ryan & K. M. Sheldon (Eds.), *Human autonomy in cross-cultural contexts: Perspectives on the psychology of agency, freedom, and well-being* (pp. 65–92). Dordrecht, The Netherlands: Springer.
Chirkov, V. (2014). The universality of psychological autonomy across cultures: Arguments from developmental and social psychology. In N. Weinstein (Ed.), *Human motivation and interpersonal relationships: Theory, research, and applications*. (pp. 27–52). Dordrecht, The Netherlands: Springer.
Chirkov, V., Ryan, R. M., & Sheldon, K. M. (Eds.). (2010). *Human autonomy in cross-cultural contexts: Perspectives on the psychology of agency, freedom, and well-being*. Dordrecht, The Netherlands: Springer.
D'Andrade, R. G. (1984). Cultural meaning systems. In R. A. Shweder & R. A. Levine (Eds.), *Culture theory: Essays on mind, self, and emotion*. (pp. 88–119). Cambridge, UK: Cambridge University Press.
D'Andrade, R. G. (1986). Three scientific world views and the covering law model. In D. W. Fiske & R. A. Shweder (Eds.), *Metatheory in social science: Pluralisms and subjectivities*. (pp. 19–41). Chicago, IL: University of Chicago Press.
D'Andrade, R. G. (1992). Schemas and motivation. In R. G. D'Andrade & C. Strauss (Eds.), *Human motives and cultural models*. (pp. 23–44). Cambridge, UK: Cambridge University Press.
D'Andrade, R. G. (1995). *The development of cognitive anthropology*. Cambridge, UK: Cambridge University Press.
D'Andrade, R. G. (1999). Culture is not everything. In E. L. Cerroni-Long (Ed.), *Anthropological theory in North America* (pp. 85–103). Westport, CT: Bergin and Garvey.
D'Andrade, R. G., & Strauss, C. (Eds.). (1992). *Human motives and cultural models*. Cambridge, UK: Cambridge University Press.
Eckensberger, L. H. (1995). Activity or action: Two different roads towards an integration of culture into psychology? *Culture and Psychology*, 1(1), 67–80.
Eckensberger, L. H. (2011). Cross-cultural differences as meaning systems. In F. J. R. Van de Vijver, A. Chasiotis & S. M. Breugelmans (Eds.), *Fundamental questions in cross-cultural psychology* (pp. 407–441). Cambridge, MA: Cambridge University Press.
Fromm, E., & Xirau, R. (Eds.). (1979). *The nature of man*. New York, NY: Macmillan.
Gallagher, S., & Zahavi, D. (2008). *The phenomenological mind: An introduction to philosophy of mind and cognitive science*. London, UK: Routledge.
Geertz, C. (1973). *The interpretation of cultures*. New York, NY: Basic Books.
Helfrich-Holter, H. (2006). Beyond the dilemma of cultural and cross-cultural psychology: Resolving the tension between monothetic and idiographic approaches. In J. Straub, D. Weidemann, C. Kolbl & B. Zielke (Eds.), *Pursuit of meaning: Advances in cultural and cross-cultural psychology* (pp. 253–268). Bielefeld, Germany: Transcript-Verlag.

Hollan, D. W. (1992). Cross-cultural differences in the self. *Journal of Anthropological Research, 48*(4), 283–300.

Holland, D., & Quinn, N. (Eds.). (1987). *Cultural models in language and thought*. Cambridge, UK: Cambridge University Press.

Jahoda, G. (2011). Past and present of cross-cultural psychology. In F. J. R. van de Vijver, A. Chasiotis & S. M. Breugelmans (Eds.), *Fundamental questions in cross-cultural psychology* (pp. 37–63). Cambridge, UK: Cambridge University Press.

Jones, N. A., Ross, H., Lynam, T., Perez, P., & Leitch, A. (2011). Mental models: An interdisciplinary synthesis of theory and methods. *Ecology and Society, 16*(1), 46. Retrieved from http://www.ecologyandsociety.org/vol16/iss41/art46

Kohlberg, L. (1984). *The psychology of moral development: The nature and validity of moral stages*. San Francisco, CA: Harper & Row.

Mandler, G., & Kessen, W. (1964). *The language of psychology*. New York, NY: Wiley.

Martin, J., Sugarman, J., & Hickinbottom, S. (2009). *Persons: Understanding psychological selfhood and agency*. New York, NY: Springer.

Martin, J., Sugerman, J., & Thompson, J. (2003). *Psychology and the question of agency*. Albany, NY: State University of New York Press.

Matsumoto, D., & Juang, L. (2013). *Culture and psychology* (5th ed.). Belmont, CA: Wadsworth.

Mill, J. S. (1843/1965). *On the logic of moral sciences*. Indianapolis, IN: Bobbs-Merrill.

Mitchell, W. J. T. (1995). Representation. In T. McLaughlin & F. Lentricchia (Eds.), *Critical terms for literary study*. (pp. 11–22). Chicago, IL: University of Chicago Press.

Morris, B. (1991). *Western conceptions of the individual* New York, NY: Berg.

Pagel, M. (2012). *Wired for culture: Origins of human social mind*. New York, NY: Norton.

Pearson, K. (1892/1957). *The grammar of science*. New York, NY: Meridian Books.

Piaget, J. (1947/2001). *The psychology of intelligence*. London, UK: Routledge.

Pinker, S. (2002). *The blank slate: The modern denial of human nature*. New York, NY: Viking.

Quinn, N., & Holland, D. (1987). Culture and cognition. In D. Holland & N. Quinn (Eds.), *Cultural models in language and thought* (pp. 3–42). Cambridge, UK: Cambridge University Press.

Reber, A. S., & Reber, E. (2001). *The Penguin dictionary of psychology*. New York, NY: Penguin.

Ryan, R. M., & Deci, E. L. (2004). Autonomy is no illusion: Self-determination theory and the empirical study of authenticity, awareness, and will. In J. Greenberg, S. L. Koole & T. Pyszczynski (Eds.), *Handbook of experimental existential psychology*. New York, NY: Guilford Press.

Rychlak, J. F. (1993). A suggested principle of complementarity for psychology: In theory, not method. *American Psychologist, 48*(9), 933–942.

Rychlak, J. F. (2003). *The human image in postmodern America*. Washington, DC: American Psychological Association.

Schafer, R. (1968). *Aspects of internalization*. New York, NY: International Universities Press.

Segall, M. H., Lonner, W. J., & Berry, J. W. (1998). Cross-cultural psychology as a scholarly discipline: On the flowering of culture in behavioral research. *American Psychologist, 53*(10), 1101–1110.

Severin, F. T. (Ed.). (1965). *Humanistic viewpoints in psychology: A book of readings*. New York, NY: McGraw-Hill.

Shore, B. (1998). *Culture in mind: Cognition, culture, and the problem of meaning*. New York, NY: Oxford University Press.

Shweder, R. A. (1991). Cultural psychology: What is it? In R. A. Shweder (Ed.), *Thinking through cultures: Expeditions in cultural psychology*. (pp. 76–112). Cambridge, MA: Harvard University Press.

Sokolowski, R. (2000). *Introduction to phenomenology*. Cambridge, UK: Cambridge University Press.

Spinelli, E. (1989). *The interpreted world: An introduction to phenomenological psychology*. London, UK: Sage.

Spiro, M. E. (1987). Collective representations and mental representations in religious symbol systems. In B. Kilborne & L. L. Langness (Eds.), *Culture and human nature. Theoretical papers of Melford E. Spiro*. (pp. 161–186). Chicago, IL: University of Chicago Press.

Straub, J., Weidemann, D., Kolbl, C., & Zielke, B. (Eds.). (2006). *Pursuit of meaning: Advances in cultural and cross-cultural psychology*. Bielefeld, Germany: Transcript-Verlag.

Thompson, E. (2007). *Mind in life: Biology, phenomenology, and the science of mind*. Cambridge, MA: Belknap Press.

Tomasello, M. (1999). *The cultural origins of human cognition*. Cambridge, MA: Harvard University Press.

Tomasello, M. (2014). *A natural history of human thinking*. Cambridge, MA: Harvard University Press.

Tooby, J., & Cosmides, L. (1992). The psychological foundations of culture. In J. H. Barkow, L. Cosmides & J. Tooby (Eds.), *The adapted mind: Evolutionary psychology and the generation of culture* (pp. 19–136.). New York, NY: Oxford University Press.

Valsiner, J. (Ed.). (2014). *The Oxford handbook of culture and psychology*. Oxford, UK: Oxford University Press.

Valsiner, J., & Rosa, A. (Eds.). (2007). *The Cambridge handbook of sociocultural psychology*. Cambridge, UK: Cambridge University Press.

Van Langenhove, L. (1995). The theoretical foundations of experimental psycohology. In J. A. Smith, R. Harre & L. Van Langenhove (Eds.), *Rethinking psychology* (pp. 10–23). London, UK: Sage.

Varela, F. J., Thompson, E. T., & Rosch, E. (1991). *The embodied mind: Cognitive science and human experience*. Cambridge, MA: MIT Press.

Wallis, K. C., & Poulton, J. L. (2001). *Internalization: The origin and construction of internal reality*. Buckingham, UK: Open University Press.

Yasnitsky, A., Van der Veer, R., & Ferrari, M. (Eds.). (2014). *The Cambridge handbook of cultural historical psychology*. Cambridge, UK: Cambridge University Press.

3

PHILOSOPHICAL THINKING

Induction, Deduction, and Positivism

This chapter will:

- Articulate the fundamental problem of scientific research
- Highlight the importance of philosophical thinking in addressing this problem
- Outline two constituents of the philosophical foundations of research: *modes of inference* and *philosophical paradigms*
- Introduce and discuss two modes of inference: *inductive*, which is split into *enumerative* and *ampliative forms*, and *deductive*, which is divided into *deductive-nomological,* and *ampliative-deductive* forms
- Introduce the concepts *contexts of discovery, context of justification, empiricism,* and *rationalism*
- Discuss and criticize the philosophical paradigm of *positivism*.

Introduction

Chapters 1 and 2 introduced the basis for disciplinary and theoretical thinking while doing research on culture and psychology. But these are only a part of researchers' intellectual deliberations. Another part is reasoning related to the philosophy of science, which means a theorizing about the *ontology, epistemology,* and *methodology* of a research and its objects. It is called philosophical or metatheoretical thinking.[1] Let me remind readers that *ontology* addresses the questions about the nature and structure of the realities under investigation; *epistemology* provides assumptions about the nature and sources of knowledge that a scholar is planning to discover; and *methodology* answers the questions about the main ways of obtaining knowledge about these realities. To address these philosophical aspects, each researcher implicitly or explicitly uses particular assumptions, modes of thinking, and systems of conjoined philosophical principles. These assumptions, modes, and principles require knowledge from the philosophy of science and the skills of using this knowledge advantageously to do sound research. French scholars call this

---

1 The term 'theoretical' is used in this book in relation to theories of the phenomena that researchers investigate—content theories; conversely, the terms "metatheoretical" or "philosophical" are reserved for theorizing about theories, for reflecting upon the philosophical basis of content theories and the processes of their construction.

intellectual equipment *"la cuisine scientifique"* (Znaniecki, 1934, p. 216). This chapter will supply readers with the basic ingredients and main recipes to make any scientific "meal" not only edible, but also tasty.

The Ultimate Goals and Challenges of Scientific Research

All researchers face questions about the ultimate goal of their scientific endeavor: What is the final objective of my research? What do I want to discover? What kind of knowledge do I want to convey to people? Different scholars give different answers. I support the ones who say that they strive to understand the nature of things, to uncover the laws and causal mechanisms that drive nature, societies, cultures, human organisms, and their minds in order to understand and explain the various events, things, practices, and problems that people encounter in their lives. To say it succinctly, they try to discover the *essence* of things and to find out how things work. In the case of culture and psychology research, the ultimate goal is to understand how societies and cultures work and to explain how they interact with humans' minds and behaviors.

But how do we get to the essence of things and the corresponding laws and causal mechanisms that are hidden and not directly given to people? Researchers only have direct contact with what they can experience, see, hear or touch. They only have access to a limited number of instances of things and events, and they have serious cognitive limits regarding detecting unobservable essences and causal mechanisms. They also conduct their research at particular places and at particular times and have pre-existing biases, cultural presuppositions, values, practices, and many other very human attributes that may stand in the way of an unbiased investigation of the world. Taking all these factors into account, one could even make a pessimistic conclusion that objective scientific investigation is impossible.

Since ancient times, scholars and philosophers have delved into the possibilities of the human mind to discover the truth about the worlds. They have come up with several major presuppositions, which are true of any research: First, the worlds—natural, psychological, and sociocultural[2]—exist "out there" independently of people's thoughts and theories about them; these worlds are governed by laws and causal mechanisms which determine events and their patterns of regularities. Second, scholars have no direct access to the essence of these worlds and the things that constitute them. Scientists do not know from the first glance how things really are. They deal only with the appearances of things, with manifestations of their essences, with their *phenomena*. If they could get to the nature of things by simply looking at objects, if the essence of things were available directly to their senses, the sciences would not be necessary. Third, researchers always investigate particulars—concrete and specific events, things or people, their groups, certain communities, or countries. All these particulars exist at a certain time and in a particular place. From these particulars researchers have to generalize to universal axioms, laws, or mechanisms that explain all the particulars of a certain kind. This means that, for example, social scientists observe the actions and experiences of particular people and the activities of particular

---

2 The idea of the three worlds that researchers deal with—the natural or physical, the psychological, and the sociocultural—is taken from the works of Austrian-British philosopher of science **Karl Popper** (1902–1994) (Popper & Eccles, 1977). He labelled the natural world—"World 1," the psychological one—"World 2," and the sociocultural one—"World 3.". These worlds should be addressed as three forms of the reality that scientists are investigating. That is why I will use the plural—*worlds*—meaning these three.

institutions within particular cultures and communities, but strive to understand the driving forces, structures, and powers that explain the actions of people and activities of institutions far beyond the observed instances. These three postulates lay the basis of the fundamental problem of any scientific research that can be formulated as follows:

> **The problem of any scientific research is how to get from appearances to the essence and from particulars to the general**

It is impossible to address this problem without articulated metatheoretical thinking based on knowledge of the philosophy of science, so I turn to some of its basics.

Two Main Constituents of Philosophical Thinking About Research

It is useful to identify two constituents of the philosophical thinking important for research: *modes of inference* and *philosophical paradigms*. The *modes of inference* prescribe how to reason about the main steps and final goals of a scientific inquiry. The *paradigms* embrace particular modes of inference and provide the basis for resolving the above problem of scientific research by answering ontological, epistemological, and methodological questions about an inquiry. We begin with two main modes of inference: *inductive* and *deductive*. Then we will divide induction into *enumerative* and *ampliative modes*, and deduction into *deductive-nomological* and *ampliative-deductive modes*. By combining enumerative induction and deductive-nomological inference, the *positivist paradigm* will be introduced. A combination of other forms of induction and deduction will be discussed in the next chapter.

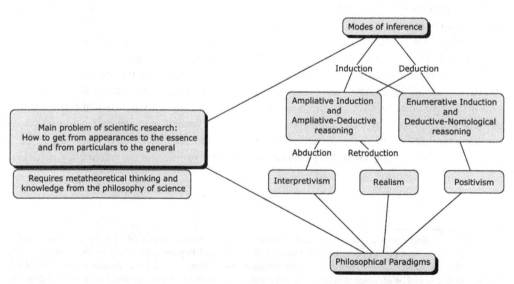

FIGURE 3.1 Main components of philosophical thinking about research. This concept map was made with IHMC Cmap Tools

INFORMATION BOX 3.1. WHY PHILOSOPHICAL THINKING IS IMPORTANT FOR EMPIRICAL RESEARCHERS

Social scientific research is a tremendously challenging and complex enterprise. Social and human sciences researchers try to get to the essence of the social and cultural worlds and the forces that drive people's behavior and shape their lives in these worlds by means of their reason, knowledge, disciplined imagination, and intuition assisted by various methods and techniques. This is in no way a simpler endeavor than striving to investigate the structure of the universe, the nature of matter, the genetic composition of living organisms, or the functioning of neurons in the brain. The intellectual tools social researchers use to decipher the codes of human behavior in different social and cultural contexts should be adequate to meet the complexity of the objects of their investigation. Simplification of research thinking—the reduction of the methodology of these studies to a limited number of approaches and techniques—does not benefit the goal of uncovering the mysteries of human societies, cultures, and people's social existence. It is impossible to sufficiently address the complexity of the sociocultural and psychological worlds without deliberating about the nature of sociocultural realities, accompanied by a deep understanding of the nature of scientific inquiries and different ways of scientific reasoning, and without serious reflections on one's own positions on these matters.

The primary proposition of this book is that any scientific inquiry is first thinking, then doing. By thinking, I mean reasoning on the level of the metatheoretical paradigms as well as on the level of content-based theories and concrete disciplines

Another reason for the emphasis on metatheoretical and theoretical thinking is that in scientific research (as in any other domain of people's functioning in sociocultural worlds) many aspects of this social activity become habitual and taken for granted. This means that researchers accept some paradigms about how the worlds operate and how they should be studied as unquestionable truth without critical analysis and reflection. Following Bourdieu, this taken-for-granted aspect of scientific activity may be labelled *research habitus*, when researchers accept one or several philosophical paradigms under an implicit assumption that these paradigms are correct and, as a result, uncritically follow their prescriptions of how to think about a study, what methods to use, and how to collect and analyze data. This blind following of research habitus, which often goes from supervisors to their students, eradicates the very essence of any scientific inquiry: to be problem-orientated, to be accompanied by reflective and critical thinking and to generate creative and innovative solutions—all the components that make science such an attractive and thrilling enterprise. Research habitus goes hand-in-hand with *methodolatry*, which is discussed in Chapter 5. In this case researchers are less concerned with a problem and a creative way to solve it, and more focused on the proper execution of the algorithm that they believe constitutes the 'correct scientific approach'.

Induction and Deduction

Induction and Its Forms

The most ancient and fundamental way of thinking from particulars to the general is *induction*, otherwise known as *inductive inference* or *inductive reasoning*. As a mode of inference, induction encompasses 'bottom-up' thinking from particulars to generals and can be traced back to ancient Greek philosophers like skeptic **Sextus Empiricus** (c. 160–210 AD), then through medieval scientists like **Roger Bacon** (1220–1292), English inductivists like

Francis Bacon (1561–1626), empiricists like **David Hume** (1772–1772) and **John Stuart Mill** (1806–1873), and finally to modern scientific thinking.

Induction is a form of reasoning comprised of inferences from a limited number of observed or experienced instances to general propositions. Induction is one of the forms of rational thinking that secures a successful way of people's functioning in pluralistic worlds. Our mind is predisposed to "jump" from particular instances to general conclusions. We use inductive reasoning in our everyday lives very frequently. Imagine a situation when you meet several representatives of a particular ethno-cultural group and all of them are sociable and friendly with you. You quickly conclude that all people from this group are sociable and friendly. Based on this generalization, you build your relations with all other members of this group accordingly and meet everyone with open arms and a broad smile. Or, in another example, a couple of your friends have cars of a particular model. They cannot stop dragging them into a repair shop. If you were in the market to purchase a car, you likely would not consider buying a car of that makeup. This inductive generalization helps you make a decision in buying a new car. The inductive inference is fundamental for scientific reasoning because scientists always have access to a limited number of cases, instances, and particulars, but want to make inferences and conclusions far beyond these observations. The main questions regarding scientific induction are: What are these generalizations about? How broadly can scientists generalize from these instances? And how reliable are these inductive generalizations?

To address these questions it is useful to differentiate two forms of inductions. The first, since the time of Bacon, has unanimously been called *enumerative* or *naïve induction* (Bacon, 1620/2000; Snyder, 2006; Znaniecki, 1934) and the other one has been labeled *substantive* (Snyder, 2006), *analytic* (Znaniecki, 1934) or *explanatory induction* (Rozeboom, 1997). My preferred term is *ampliative induction* (Douven, 2011; Skyrm, 1999).

INFORMATION BOX 3.2. BACON ON TWO FORMS OF DISCOVERING SCIENTIFIC TRUTH

Francis Bacon was the first to differentiate two forms of inductive inference in his book *Novum Organum* or *The New Organon* (1620/2000).[3] The translation of the title of his book as "The New Instrument for Rational Thinking" (see footnote 3) means that the "old" instrument for rational thinking has already been in place and the author is suggesting the new one. Below are his statements about these two instruments:

XIX

There are, and can be, only two ways to investigate and discover truth. The one leaps from sense and particulars to the most general axioms, and these principles and their settled truth determine and discover intermediate axioms; this is the current way. The other elicits axioms from sense and particulars, rising in a gradual and unbroken ascent to arrive at last at the most general axioms; this is the true way, but it has not been tried. (p. 36)

---

3 Bacon took the concept of "Organon," which means "instrument for rational thinking" (Introduction to Bacon (1620/2000), p. xii) from Aristotle's works on logic. Thus, his title should be interpreted as "The New Instrument for Rational Thinking" (Urbach, 1987) or "A True Guide to Interpretation of Nature."

XXII

Both ways start from senses and particulars, and come to rest in the most general; but they are vastly different. For one merely brushes experience and particulars in passing, the other deals fully and properly with them; one forms certain abstract and useless generalities from the beginning; the other rises step by step to what is truly better known by nature. (p. 37)

XXVI

For the purposes of teaching, we have chosen to call the reasoning which men usually apply to nature *anticipation of nature* (because it is a risky, hasty business), and to call the reasoning which is elicited from things in proper ways *interpretation of nature*. (p. 38)

XXVIII

In fact *anticipations* are much more powerful in winning assent than *interpretations*; they are gathered from just a few instances, especially those which are common and familiar, which merely brush past the intellect and fill the imagination. *Interpretations*, by contrast, are gathered piece by piece from things that are quite various and widely scattered, and cannot suddenly strike the intellect. So that, in common opinion, they cannot help seeming hard and incongruous, almost like mysteries of faith. (p. 38)

Following this logic of Bacon, we may equate the *anticipation of nature* with the *enumerative* form of *induction*, and the *interpretation of nature* with the *ampliative* one. Going back to the example of friendly strangers, anticipation of nature happens when we quickly form a very broad generalization that all members of this community are friendly and treat every new encounter through this generalization until we meet a mean person. When our unjustified overgeneralization fails, we start our quest for understanding the national character of the members of this community all over again.

In the case of interpretation of nature, the questions to be asked after the first friendly encounters should be: Who are these people really? Are they all so friendly or is this their hospitality ritual? Do they have aggressive and violent urges? Can they be mean to other people? After asking these and similar questions, you should, according to Bacon, start gathering information "piece by piece from things which are quite various and widely scattered, and cannot suddenly strike the intellect." Because of these factors, interpretations—in our language ampliative inductions—". . . to common opinion, . . . cannot help seeming hard and incongruous, almost like mysteries of faith" (p. 38).

The essence of the enumerative induction is that researchers observe a limited number of instances and then induce and generalize the discovered regularities to a larger number of similar instances that have not been observed. The results of the enumerative induction are conditional statements like: "If A, then B;" or "If people are from the ethnic community A, then they are all friendly;" or "If a car is of that particular make, then it is of low quality." Some researchers consider discovering these *empirical generalizations* to be the goal of scientific research, as it allows them to explain and predict events and also to generate hypotheses to discover new regularities. Such an assumption constitutes one of the pillars of positivism, which will be discussed later in this chapter.

There are two main features of enumerative induction. One is that researchers inductively generalize from the observed to nonobserved instances, thus increasing the number of cases to which the discovered regularity is applied, hence, "enumerative." Second, these inductive generalizations possess nothing new over and above what was observed in the initial sample. Follow these examples: Premise 1: *I have met three individuals from a particular ethno-cultural group;* or *researchers studied the self-construals of students from Asia in Western universities.* Premise 2: *All three of them have been extremely friendly*; or *researchers discovered that these participants possess interdependent self-construals.* Enumerative inductive inference/generalization: *All members of this group are friendly; all Asian people have interdependent self-construals.* Researchers started with a sample of people and then generalized to a larger population, and these generalizations have exactly the same information about friendliness or possession of a particular self-construal that the premises have. Enumerative inference does not generate new knowledge over and above what has already been empirically discovered. This form of induction has limited usefulness for scientific research because it does not allow researchers to make a breakthrough toward the essence of things beyond the empirical regularities established in a sample. This characteristic of the enumerative induction was acknowledged as early as the 17th century by Bacon, who condemned this way of conducting research as inefficient and, finally, useless: "For the induction which proceeds by simple enumeration is a childish thing, its conclusions are precarious, and it is exposed to the danger of the contrary instance; it normally bases its judgment on fewer instances than is appropriate, and merely on available instances" (Bacon 1620/2000, p. 83). It is fair to say that in some studies, like marketing research and election or opinion polling surveys, researchers may be explicitly interested in enumerating their findings to larger populations, and these are the legitimate ways of using this mode of inference.

Ampliative induction, as the term implies, allows researchers to generate new knowledge that is not given in the premises. Let's return to the example of low quality cars. If a buyer of a new car decides to follow an ampliative mode of induction, he or she should ask questions like: Are these cars really so bad? What do other owners say about their quality? How have my friends taken care of their cars? Do my friends have good driving skills? In this case you cannot use enumerative induction but have to do a more thorough investigation of the quality of these cars and strive to make a conclusion that goes beyond your first impression. You should strive to amplify your knowledge about the real quality of these cars. Consider another example: people all over the world have observed that a child becomes an intelligent and social person only after systematic interactions with adults around him or her. These are empirical observations of particular instances. Developmental researchers, starting with **Lev Vygotskii** (1896–1934), have proposed that during these interactions children internalize external symbolic regulatory systems that are held by adults and make these systems their own mental regulatory structures, thus becoming reasonable, self-conscious, and socialized individuals. The proposed explanation goes beyond the observed facts and their regularities and constitutes the amplification of knowledge toward the mechanisms of human socialization.

Many philosophers and researchers, again starting with Bacon, believe that only ampliative induction has value for scientific research because, unlike enumerative induction, it increases our knowledge about the worlds (McMullin, 1992; Peirce, 1960; Skyrm, 1999; Urbach, 1987). "But the induction which will be useful for the discovery and proof of sciences and arts should separate out a nature, by appropriate rejections and exclusions; and then, after as many negatives as are required, conclude on the affirmatives" (Bacon, 1620/2000, pp. 83–84). In executing the ampliative inductive inference, there is always a gap between the information presented in the premises and information stated in the conclusion, and the question is: How do researchers bridge this "gap" and "jump" from their premises to viable conclusions? I will provide answers to this question in the next chapter on *abductive* and *retroductive modes of inference*.

A serious problem accompanies both forms of induction. Their conclusions are always inconclusive and falsifiable. As soon as you find a mean person in the friendly community, your inference that *all* members of that community are friendly is falsified and becomes useless. In a similar way, the mechanism of internalization that explains the socialization of children will be rejected as soon as a new mechanism is proposed and empirically verified. This weakness of induction has been called the *problem of induction*; philosophers of science of different epochs, like Sextus Empiricus, Hume, and Popper, have tried to resolve it.

Before moving to the deductive modes of inference, I will introduce several new concepts from the philosophy of science: the *contexts of discovery* and *justification* and *empiricism* and *rationalism*.

Empiricism and Rationalism Within the Contexts of Discovery and Justification as the Foundations for Generating Scientific Knowledge

Context of Discovery and Context of Justification

As I have already been mentioned, the scientific inquiry consists of two interrelated parts: discovering new knowledge and then verifying its validity. Philosophers of science recognized this division long ago and correspondingly identified two contexts that they focus their attention on: the *context of discovery* and *context of justification* (Reichenbach, 1958; Schickore & Steinle, 2006). Their emphasis within the context of discovery has been directed toward the logical, psychological, social, and historical factors that lead to finding new knowledge about how the worlds operate and about the structures and mechanisms that explain empirical events and their regularities. It is the context within which new insights, ideas, intellectual breakthroughs, and productive hypotheses emerge. Discovery is the essence and the center of any scientific inquiry. Researchers' focus within the context of justification is an assessment of the validity and truthfulness of discovered theoretical statements.

Historically, the mainstream philosophy of science has considered the context of discovery to be a domain of psychological insight and intuition that cannot be subjected to the rules of normative logic, and, because of this, should be abandoned as a matter of logical and philosophical investigations (Mandler & Kessen, 1964). The discovery of new knowledge and formulating a corresponding theory is "the creative function of a genius" as Reichenbach (1958, p. 231) worded it.

Typically, philosophers of science have been concerned with the justification of already discovered knowledge. In the context of justification,

> the focus is on normative criteria for holding a theory true, or acceptable, or justified. Philosophers of science try to develop general methodological requirements for a scientific theory, for example, the degree to which the conclusions are empirically or logically supported . . . In the traditional view, philosophy of science is only about justification, not about the social or psychological circumstances of the problem-solving situation. (Bem & de Jong, 2006, p. 16)

To make any scientific investigation productive, researchers have to know how to make a discovery, because until this discovery is made, there is nothing to justify. Therefore to decipher the logic of discovery is crucial for new knowledge production, and this logic will be addressed through the abductive and retroductive modes of inference.

Empiricism and Rationalism

Any scientific inquiry has two sources of information to discover the truth: (1) *empirical*—observed facts that are perceived through the senses and experienced by researchers as representations of phenomena in the worlds, and (2) *rational*—knowledge, logical inferences, conjectures, insights, and interpretations that bind these empirical impressions into coherent wholes and allow researchers to make inferences about the essences and causes of things and events. Thus, empirical and rational components are always intertwined in any scientific investigation. They are inseparable, and it is impossible to imagine an inquiry without either of these constituents. That is why the division of arguments between empiricists and rationalists, although useful for analytical philosophical reasons, is misleading and confusing for empirical researchers who think philosophically about their investigations.

The main arguments between empiricists and rationalists have been regarding the *context of discovery,* or about how researchers come up with new knowledge. Philosophers have emphasized these two components differently at different times in history. The precursor of modern natural and human scientists were ancient natural philosophers who aimed toward the rational understanding of nature, humans, and their communities (Grant, 2007). Ancient Greek philosophers are the best representatives of this way of studying the world. The natural philosophical thinking was based mostly on intellectual speculations about the objects of inquiry supported by nonsystematic observations and experiences. Thus, the empirical component was weak and unsystematic, whereas the rational component predominated.

Then came the Middle Ages, when scholars emphasized neither of these components but focused on the interpretations of old texts. Every time medieval scholars wanted to discover the truth about the physical or social worlds, they consulted authorities or ancient texts and conducted their inquiries by interpreting Plato, Aristotle, and/or the writings of the founding fathers of the Catholic Church. This was the search for knowledge by referring to authorities. It is fair to say that the rudiments of modern science emerged at that time in the works of the medieval scholars from Europe and Asia (Grant, 1996; Hannam, 2011).

Most believe that the breakthrough to modern scientific thinking happened in Britain by introducing and emphasizing the empirical component of scientific inquiries. Thus, *empiricism* as a paradigm emerged in the philosophy of science. The British empiricists, such as **John Locke** (1632–1704), **George Berkley** (1685–1753), and **David Hume** (1711–1776), were followed by the 19th century philosophers, where the most prominent was **John Stuart Mill** (1806–1873).

Empiricism is a philosophical doctrine that states that scientific knowledge should be based solely on empirical, or sense, data and the generalizations that are rooted in these data. When confirmed, empirical generalizations acquire the status of scientific laws and, from these laws, by using the deductive mode of inference, scientists justify this knowledge by providing explanations and predictions of events and by generating new hypotheses. Although the rational aspect in the form of the deductive mode of inference is present in empiricist thinking, it plays a secondary role; it is used to justify the acquired knowledge and not to discover new knowledge. According to radical empiricists, references to unobservable entities should be abandoned as nonscientific metaphysical speculations. Taken to its extreme, this doctrine lies at the foundation of *logical positivism* or *logical empiricism,* one of the most influential metatheoretical paradigms in the philosophy of science in the 20th century (Carnap, 1966/1995).

Since the very beginning of empiricist thinking, it was contrasted with *rationalism* as a different way of discovering new knowledge. The rationalist doctrine was generated and used by several Continental philosophers including **René Descartes** (1596–1650), **Baruch Spinoza** (1632–1677), and **Gottfried Wilhelm von Leibnitz** (1646–1716). The main idea of rationalism is that to discover truth, it is not enough to simply consider empirical facts and sense data. Rationalists emphasize a nonempirical rational way for acquiring new knowledge. Their fundamental principle has been that in order to get to the essence of things, scholars have to use rational insights and get to the truth by the power of their reason. A modern interpretation of rationalism (Markie, 2008) highlights that there is a possibility to obtain knowledge that could not have been gained through sense experiences. This knowledge is obtained by intuition (intuited knowledge), rational insight, and hypothesizing about what is not directly given or observed. Based on these intuited hypotheses, rationalists deduct probable empirically observable instances which may provide either verification or falsification of these hypotheses.

> Intuition is a form of rational insight. Intellectually grasping a proposition, we just "see" it to be true in such a way as to form a true, warranted belief in it. Deduction is a process in which we derive conclusions from intuited premises through valid arguments, ones in which the conclusion must be true if the premises are true. (Markie, 2008, para. 8)

Rationalists also state that the knowledge obtained through rational insights is superior to any knowledge based on empirical sense data, which is always superficial and does not reflect the essence of things (Markie, 2008, para. 9).

Now let's turn to the deductive mode of inference.

A Definition of Deduction and Two Forms of Deductive Inferences

Induction as a "bottom-up" logic of inference has always been complemented by the logic of deduction or the "top-down" form of inquiry. In a general form, deductive reasoning moves from a general statement considered universally true to a conclusion about the present or future states of particular cases. As with the inductive mode of inference, the deductive one is deeply rooted in our everyday thinking. For example: Premise 1 – empirical generalization or near-universal scientific law states: *Every morning the sun rises in the East*. Premise 2 – a particular event is presented: *It is morning*. Conclusion—a deductive predictive inference: *The sun will rise in the East*. Because an ideal deductive inference is built on valid and true premises, it always leads to a valid conclusion. And this certainty of deductive conclusions has acquired high respect among philosophers of science and made them the main mode of reasoning for justifying existing knowledge.

In the previous section, induction was differentiated into two forms—enumerative and ampliative, and it is logical to suggest that deduction may also be represented in two forms: one that follows the enumerative generalizations and the other related to an ampliative generation of new knowledge. In both forms, the deductive reasoning goes from general to particular, but the contents of the "general" and "particular" in these two forms are different. Deduction from the empirical generalizations, which logical positivists consider to be scientific laws (or *nomos*), was labeled a *deductive-nomological mode of inference* (Hempel & Oppenheim, 1948). Philosophers also called such a combination of enumerative induction with a deductive–nomological mode of inference a *covering laws model of science*, a term that also was coined by Hempel (1965; Kim, 1999). The covering law model of science has been used by positivists as their main model of science (Polkinghorne, 1983). Following the above example, a deductive-nomological inference will sound like this: Premise 1. Empirical generalization (law): *All Asian people possess an interdependent self-construal*. Premise 2. A particular case is present: *Lee is from China*. Premise 3. Deductive conclusion: *Lee possesses an interdependent self-construal*.

The second form of deduction that follows the ampliative inductive inferences did not acquire a specific term. Markie (2008) talked, for example, about intuition-deduction (para. 5). It is logical to label it the *ampliative-deductive mode of inference,* which means a deductive inference from the rational insights produced by the ampliative inductive inferences. The structure of logic of this form of inference is very similar to the deductive-nomological one, but the content is different: a researcher proposes a conjecture/hypothesis about a possible causal mechanism of a phenomenon and then hypothesizes that, if this conjecture is correct, particular empirical evidence could be observed. For example, based on systematic observations of children's socialization a researcher proposes a hypothesis: Premise 1. Ampliative inductive inference: *Children become conscious and rational individuals through the internalization of the social mechanisms of behavior regulation that exist in the sociocultural community.* Premise 2. Deduction from the above hypothesis: *If this hypothesis is correct, then a child who was not socialized in human society will not become a conscious and rational individual.* 3. Empirical verification of the hypothesis: *A researcher tests this hypothesis by finding children who were either not raised by humans or had serious problems of socialization. If he or she finds such cases and discovers that the cognitive development of these children is seriously thwarted, then he or she may say that the hypothesis about the internalization mechanisms of human mental development has been supported.* In the case of the ampliative deduction, the conjecture/hypothesis provides access to potentially new knowledge about unobservable entities and powers (in the above example, the mechanism of cognitive development through internalization); a verification of the formulated hypothesis provides evidence that hypothesized entities and mechanisms do have the chance to exist. As a result of such verification, a new theory can be developed and new knowledge achieved. In the case of the classical deductive-nomological mode, researchers usually deduce from the existing empirical generalization to new, previously unstudied instances of the phenomenon and extend, not knowledge, but the number of instances to which the same empirical regularities are applied. Thus, it is possible to say that the enumerative inductive and deductive-nomological modes of inference produce little advancement of knowledge; conversely, the ampliative induction and ampliative-deductive modes of reasoning provide the basis for substantial advancement of knowledge and should serve as the foundation for any scientific research.

Radical Empiricism, Enumerative Induction, and the Deductive-Nomological Mode of Inference as the Basis of the Positivist Paradigm

Now we have all the components to formulate the *positivist paradigm*. This paradigm is a doctrine in the philosophy of science that can be characterized by the following features. Ontologically, it follows shallow or naïve realism, meaning that the reality for positivists is represented only by the sense data that correspond to the appearances or surface layers of the realities. Positivists deny the existence of unobservables, or, as they label them, metaphysical entities with causal powers that constitute deeper layers of reality. Epistemologically, positivists rely on radical empiricism, believing that scientific knowledge is comprised of statements about empirical regularities among and generalizations about particular instances. They rely on enumerative induction and the deductive-nomological mode of inference for explaining the phenomena, predicting new ones, and extending this knowledge to unstudied events and things (see Fig. 3.2.). The positivist paradigm is based on the covering law model of science. Methodologically, modern positivist researchers usually use variable-based approaches accompanied by various sampling procedures (see Chapter 7). The positivist paradigm is also notoriously known for its reliance on using statistical methods for trying to come to scientific conclusions.

To better comprehend this paradigm, I will analyze the main steps of a prototypical positivist logic of research. It starts with empirical observations of the phenomenon of interest. Then, researchers develop corresponding empirical concepts and define them. They transform these concepts into variables through operational definitions (see Chapter 5). Then they measure these variables in a sample of participants and analyze them and their relationships through statistical methods. Thus, researchers establish empirical regularities among the measured variables on

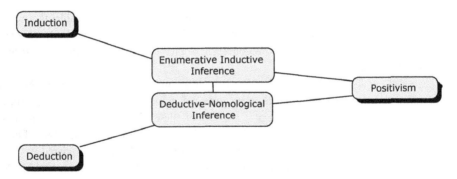

FIGURE 3.2 Structure of positivist thinking. This concept map was made with IHMC Cmap Tools

particular samples of participants. Investigators assume that these regularities reflect necessary relations among variables and, in order to gain the status of nearly-universal laws, should be confirmed on larger samples. This assumption is the basis of enumerative inductive reasoning and constitutes the essence of positivist thinking. As was mentioned above, these generalizations are composed of statements about relations among variables that are extended from observed instances to nonobserved ones. By repeated confirmations of these generalizations on different samples, they acquire the status of near-universal empirical laws, and until they are falsified by new data, they are used as the basis for deductive-nomological inferences, predictions, and explanations. This sequence of steps is applicable to any social or behavioral research that is driven by the positivist paradigm. Triandis (1993), one of the founders of cross-cultural psychology, articulated his understanding of scientific cross-cultural research in the following manner (this is his discussion with the proponents of the interpretivism approach to study culture and psychology):

> The authors [interpretivists] tell us that: "That search for stable patterns and long range predictions in human psychological phenomenon would probably not be the proper goal for the science." Just because their methodology cannot make such predictions it does not mean that they should not be made. Such predictions are exactly what science is all about. What they advocate is the prescientific step of thick descriptions, which is a fine step but not enough.
>
> *The glory of science is generalization* [emphasis added]. It is showing that the laws that account for the falling apples and the movement of planets are the same (. . .). *Predictions about how experimental subjects, randomly assigned to conditions, will behave on diverse continents have been made and supported. It is towards that kind of generalization that science should aim* [emphasis added]. (p. 250)[4]

Empirical generalizations may be used by positivists to explain newly observed events, to predict the state of nonobserved cases, or to hypothesize new associations and regularities. If all these stages are successfully implemented, then, according to this paradigm, the research cycle is completed, and scientific progress is secured. Positivist researchers believe (see Mandler & Kessen, 1964) that

---

[4] Republished with permission of John Wiley and Sons from Triandis, H. C. (1993). Comment on Misra and Gergen's: Place of culture in psychological science. *International Journal of Psychology, 28*(2), 249–250.

through a patient and systematic collection of empirical regularities among variables that represent events, things, and their attributes, they will come up with a nearly complete body of scientific knowledge. According to this paradigm, this collection of facts and their associations constitute the ultimate goal of any scientific inquiry.

Let's have a closer look at how this is done in culture and psychology research. Acculturation researchers discovered that, when they use particular questionnaires to assess immigrants' attitudes toward their acculturation, specific clusters of these attitudes emerge. These clusters were labelled: integration, assimilation, marginalization, and separation (Berry, 1997). They also discovered that one of these clusters—"integration"—has frequently been associated with scores of immigrants' well-being, levels of stress, and adaptation (Berry, Phinney, Sam, & Vedder, 2006). Based on these associations, these researchers came up with the following empirical generalization: 'If immigrants endorse integrationist acculturation attitudes, then their adaptation will be successful.' Many followers of this conclusion uncritically treat this generalization as a nearly universal 'law of acculturation,' which allows researchers and practitioners to explain and predict the dynamics of adaptation of any group of immigrants. Consider immigrants who are unsuccessful in their acculturation. Acculturation researchers may explain this condition by saying that these immigrants are poorly adjusted because they do not adopt integration attitudes toward their acculturation. The same "law of acculturation" may be used to predict the states of new cases and to expand the boundaries of scientific knowledge. When a new group of immigrants arrives in a country and their attitudes toward acculturation are measured, these scholars may predict that if these immigrants are "integrationists," then they will adapt successfully to a new society. It is important to note that in this prediction, acculturation psychologists generate new knowledge about the future success of immigrants based not on sense data, but on deductive logic. When empiricism, which states that knowledge should be based only on sense data, is complemented by knowledge generated through a deductive logic, it transforms into *logical positivism/empiricism*. According to logical positivists, the above statements, both explanatory and predictive, are scientific conclusions that are based on solid empirical evidence and a strong logical foundation.

The same logic of prediction can be used to generate new research. Instead of the above prediction, researchers may use the "law of acculturation" as a hypothesis for their study. They may test actual attitudes of newly arrived immigrants and then follow their adaptation and acculturation. If their hypothesis is confirmed, then the universal law of acculturation is verified and is extended to a new group of immigrants. These researchers implemented the *hypothetico-deductive* way of expanding scientific knowledge. This logic of explaining, predicting, and expanding knowledge creates an impression that positivism is a solid and unshakable foundation of science. Unfortunately, it is not. Next I will provide a critical analysis of this paradigm and its extensive use of statistics to discover new knowledge about the worlds.

Possible Applications of the Positivist Paradigm

1. By observing the worlds and analyzing people's experiences, positivists come up with a set of concepts and conceptual frameworks that may be insightful and interesting and may be extended to and successfully used within the interpretivist and realist paradigms (with some modifications).
2. By establishing associations among variables, researchers learn empirically about regularities that exist in the sociocultural and psychological worlds; in many cases, these regularities may be helpful for predicting some events and keeping track of the factors that may facilitate or hinder phenomena of interest. *Necessary* regularities, in contrast to *accidental* ones, are the most obvious

indications that some systematic forces are working in producing them, and such assumptions may lead researchers to productive conjectures and hypotheses about the causal mechanisms of the events; therefore, discovered empirical regularities may be good starting points for abductive or retroductive research.
3. For some types of social research, like voters polling, census, and marketing research, enumerative induction may be useful to move from a small number of surveyed instances in probability samples to larger populations.
4. In some applied psychological studies, like predicting the academic success of students based on their entrance exam scores, the positivist paradigm may serve as useful background.

A Critique of Positivism

There are more disadvantages than advantages to using the positivist paradigm. In this section I compile the points of its critique provided by philosophers and social researchers (Bhaskar, 1975/2008; Collier, 1994; Polkinghorne, 1983; Sayer, 1992).

1. Positivist research is not capable of generating new knowledge over and above empirical patterns in the forms of statistical associations, frequencies, and regularities discovered on samples of people. Enumerative induction and deductive-nomological inferences are circular and tautological and because of this they are scientifically unproductive.
2. Many positivists accept the radical empiricist approach that rejects the existence of unobservable generative powers and causal mechanisms. This denial prevents any possibility of an intellectual insight into the essences of things. Positivists consider new discoveries to be blessings; they believe that the ability to come up with creative insights cannot be taught and constitutes an area of the psychology of creativity and not part of the training of researchers.
3. For positivists (see Mandler & Kessen, 1964) the goal of science is an accumulation of statements about the patterns and regularities among variables; scientists are perceived as "research workers" (p. 150) whose job is making science by patiently and systematically generating and collecting empirical regularities (see more in Chapter 7).
4. Theoretical analysis is considered to be too metaphysical, the unnecessary luxury of exceptional scholars and a waste of time for regular research workers (see also Chapter 5 on theories in positivism). The poverty of theoretical accounting and ultimately the inability to get into the nature of things and understand and explain the world are hallmarks of positivism.
5. The education of students within this paradigm is based on teaching the philosophy of positivism, the rules for operationalizing and measuring variables, and the statistical analysis of these data. *Methodolatry* is common within this paradigm (see Chapter 5).
6. In the domain of society and culture, this type of research does not address the intentional and intersubjective nature of these realities (see Chapter 2) or the roles cultural meanings play in people's lives and behaviors. Positivist social researchers instead transform these realities into sets of variables (for example, individualism and collectivism) and make them measurable in a standard way across samples from different cultural settings. They do not consider each cultural community as a unique sociosymbolic system that should be explored and analyzed from the "inside."

The Use of Statistics Within Positivist Research and Its Critique

Because positivist researchers are primarily concerned with discovering patterns of associations and regularities among variables, measurements and an application of statistics constitute the dominant methodology of modern positivist research. This issue of the dominance of quantification and statistics in conducting social and psychological research has been the main focus of critique of the positivist paradigm since the 19th century. Below is a summary of the main arguments.

1. The fundamental questions for any form of quantification and application of statistics are: "What must objects be like for it to be possible to quantify them?" and "What must real objects and processes be like for mathematical representations of them to be practically adequate?" (Sayer, 1992, p. 176). It is possible to quantify and measure only one-dimensional and qualitatively homogeneous and invariant substances. Such substances have to stay the same regardless of the place and time they are measured. Social, cultural, and psychological phenomena are complex, multidimensional, and qualitatively heterogeneous. They change across time and space and depend on the contexts where they happen and the histories of their bearers. By their very nature, such phenomena cannot be reduced to one number that represents all their complexity, and thus, they are unsuitable for quantification and statistical analysis. Hammersley (2012) worded this critique in the following way:

> A central problem in social science measurement, long recognized, is that there is often a gap between the meaning of concepts as these function within theories or explanations, and the meaning that is implied by the procedures used to measure objects in terms of relevant variables. (p. 33)

Think about quantifying culture in a set of numbers on Hofstede's dimensions: individualism-collectivism, power distance, and masculinity-femininity scales, or presenting the acculturation of immigrants by four numbers that reflect four acculturation strategies. Do these numbers reflect all the richness and complexities of the phenomenon of national cultures or a deeply intimate phenomenon of acculturation? Probably only to a little extent. Numbers reduce the phenomenon to a mere point on a measurement scale. Do you think Aristotle could ever have imagined that the highly complex concept of eudaimonia (a feeling of happiness that accompanies a process of self-realization) would be represented in the 21st century by a number, or that researchers would be desperately trying to find the averages of eudaimonic happiness across different communities? Or that they would be measuring such immeasurable phenomena as the meaning of life, love, aggression, gratefulness, kindness, loneliness, prejudice, alienation, grief—anything you can imagine!—and doing complex statistical manipulations with them to try to understand their nature? All units of analysis within statistical positivism are designated as variables, which are indifferent to the qualitative substance of the phenomena that they represent (see Chapter 7 on a variable-based design).

The quantification of sociocultural and psychological phenomena creates an impression of dealing with "objective," "hard-core" data that can be analyzed and understood in an objective and straightforward manner and that allows researchers to minimize or eradicate the role of judgment (Hammersley, 2012, p. 33). This argument attracts many new students to the social and psychological sciences who are interested in research careers and who strive to discover "objective" truths about the sociocultural and psychological worlds. This is an illusion from several points. It is impossible to eradicate all judgments from any scientific inquiry. The numbers that are assigned to phenomena are not arbitrary but based on some theoretical considerations and put forward through specific procedures of concepts operationalization and, thus, cannot be treated as objective, bias- and value-free facts. These "facts" have to be interpreted within a particular theory and have to account for any limitations due to their operationalization and analytical procedures and, thus, will inevitably be biased and subjective. Even when a researcher applies various statistical procedures to the numbers, these analyses require interpretations; think about the challenges of interpreting the results of factor analysis or structural equation modeling. Studies based on the positivist paradigm provide no more "objectivity" than studies based on other paradigms.

2. If we accept that the final goal of any scientific explanation is understanding the causes of events or phenomena, or at least identifying the type of relationships (accidental, necessary, causal,

functional, contingent, reciprocal, etc.) that exist among these events and their components, statistical analysis provides little or no information about what types of relationships researchers are dealing with. Statistical models cannot represent causal relations because they are based on and account for a-causal quantitative variations among variables. "Unfortunately the belief that finding a way of calculating something is necessarily the same as giving a causal explanation of what produce it is endemic" (Sayer, 1992, p. 178). Statistical associations may reflect any relationship that exists among variables or be purely accidental. Without using rational reasoning based on existing theories, it is impossible to categorize and differentiate these relationships. Statistical models, most of which are based on general linear modeling, establish mathematical relations between y and x. They do not reflect the nature of y and x and represent only "that quantitative variation in y is formally (not substantially) related in some way to quantitative variation in x" (p. 179), and as a result of this, "when quantified, relations which are in fact substantial (i.e., involving material connections between objects), internal and/or causal become indistinguishable from purely formal and contingent relations" (p. 180).

3. It is a common sense understanding that the unit of analysis for psychological and sociocultural sciences should be individuals or communities of people functioning in different sociocultural contexts. This means that the focus should be on intra(within)-individual and intra- societal and cultural processes. Modern positivist research deals with inter(between)-individual covariances among variables that may not correspond to the intra-individual regularities. In many positivist studies, researchers are trying to use the between-participants variations of variables to represent the within-case dynamics of psychological and sociocultural processes, thus committing *ecological fallacy* (see Chapter 8).

4. Sociocultural and psychological phenomena are complex systems that are open to change and operate within particular contexts and conditions. Relationships and processes that operate within these systems are not linear and not one-directional; they are reciprocal and interdependent. These systems also acquire *emergent properties* that do not exist outside them. There are causal mechanisms and generative powers that produce the events and changes in such systems. The sociocultural and psychological events and processes are interdependent and mutually constitutive. The goal of science is to describe and account for these complexities and their relationships. Positivists are incapable of addressing the systemic nature of sociocultural and psychological phenomena. They reduce these systems into sets of variables and, through statistical relations among them, try to understand how these systems work:

> Knowledge of the system, object or process does not mean knowledge of each of the characters separately, but of all of them together as interdependent. Any progress in knowledge involves not only the discovery of new characters, but also a different and better understanding of the way all the characters, new and old, are combined in the given system. (Znaniecki, 1934, p. 231)

Statistical methods, with their ability to discover only linear relations among a limited number of variables, are unable "to represent internal relations and hence structures [and systems]" (Sayer, 1992, p. 180). And also,

> a fundamental limitation in the statistical method which can never be overcome: it is the practical impossibility of taking into account combinations of more than a few characters—combinations of four characters are already very difficult to handle statistically. This limitation prohibits absolutely any progress in the intensive study of facts. (Znaniecki, 1934, pp. 230–231)

5. Statistical modeling creates its own language and a "reality" of the constructed symbolic representations that exists separately and relatively independently from the reality where the phenomena under investigation exist and function. Thus, the reality of sociocultural and psychological phenomena is substituted by formal statistical models that consist of a set of variables connected by formal statistical relations based on between-subject variations. Unfortunately, the producers and users of this information pretend that these statistical models are nearly perfect representations of what is going on inside individuals or between them and their sociocultural environments and, therefore, they believe that these models can be used as valid scientific knowledge about the realities.

> By making the study of facts subservient in advance to its final purpose of a mathematical play with symbols, not only does it fail to stimulate progress in the analysis of these facts, but actually obstructs it. Thus, the worst mistake of mediaeval scholasticism is here repeated: juggling with concepts instead of investigating reality has to be again accepted as the essence of science. (Znaniecky, 1934, p. 231)

Modern social researchers echo this claim:

> Mishler (1986), who, when speaking about a survey research, notes that when "summary scores [are] aggregated across separate . . . [cases] each response is a fragment removed from the social and psychological context. . . . When these responses are assembled . . . the results are artificial aggregates that have no direct representation in the real world of communities, social institutions, families, or persons (p. 26). (Miles & Huberman, 1994, p. 208)

6. Statistically-oriented researchers cannot handle exceptions and outliers that do not fit their models. They try to exclude them or somehow account for their presence statistically. Thus, reality that does not fit statistical models is simply cut off and ignored. How reality appears does not matter as long as the statistical manipulations can be performed unobstructively. But exceptions, outliers, and contradictory cases often constitute an "essential instrument of scientific progress" (Znaniecki, 1934, p. 232) and avoiding or eliminating them prevents this progress from happening.

> Science is reason challenging experience and forcing it into a rational order. An exception is a revolt of experience [of reality] against reason. Statistical science, faced with such revolt, passively relinquishes its claims and withdraws from the struggle into the realm of pure mathematical concepts. (p. 233)

7. Znaniecki (1934) also boldly stressed that the obsession with statistics in the social sciences, where "Statistical Methods of Data Analysis" is a main course in almost all graduate programs in psychology, sociology, and related social science disciplines, which has a detrimental effect on the quality of future generations of researchers. First, such an obsession abolishes teaching graduate students the skills of creative and imaginative thinking and deliberation and "consists of substituting tabulating technique for intellectual methods, and thus eliminating theoretic thinking from the process of scientific research" (p. 235). Second, the graduate education of the research process is reduced to the skills of mere data collection and of algorithmic statistical analyses. Scientific progress, which should be based on an innovative, divergent and open-minded approach, is instead reduced to statistical data manipulations that can be learned and performed by individuals with

mediocre abilities and with no capacities for imagination and innovation (p. 235). To say it succinctly, in statistics-driven research, human intellect falls into background, and a statistical program leads to "scientific discovery."

Some more technical limitations of statistical methods have been outlined by Hammersley (2012).

8. To make valid enumerative inferences from a sample to a population, this sample has to be probability-based and representative. Social scientists in the domain of culture and psychology—mostly cross-cultural psychologists—rarely use probability sampling; as a result the enumerative generalizations that they try to make are unjustified (see more on sampling in Chapter 7).

9. In the positivist paradigm, important decisions about discovered relationships and their patterns are based on *significance testing*, an arbitrarily established criterion for rejecting the null hypothesis that differences are due to chance. Using the formal criterion of $p < .05$, which was suggested by British statistician Ronald Fisher simply out of convenience, statistical positivists make decisions about the importance and meaningfulness of relations among things and events (Cohen, 1994). Consider the fact that, when a sample is large enough, even small and practically irrelevant relations become statistically significant and should be formally considered by researchers; this is the problem of the effect size. If gender differences in a particular variable are not significant, men and women in the sample are treated as creatures without gender. The majority of editors of mainstream psychological journals will not accept a manuscript if a reported statistical model does not fit the data. Thus, formal statistical criteria decide if there is or is not a scientific discovery. (I refer interested readers to the books on how statistical considerations create obscured pictures of the world (Kline, 2004; Thompson, 2004; Ziliak & McCloskey, 2008).

Conclusion

There are different ways of addressing the fundamental problem of scientific studies, namely the problem of getting from the surface to the essence of things and from particulars to the general. These ways are outlined by philosophical paradigms and different modes of inference that researchers accept for their studies. To be aware of these paradigms and successfully use different modes of reasoning requires researchers to have knowledge and skills of metatheoretical thinking within the philosophy of science. The main mode of inference for all empirical researchers is induction, which is not a unified process but covers at least two different forms: enumerative and ampliative. For many years, enumerative induction was considered to be the only form of induction and when combined with the deductive-nomological way of reasoning it forms the basis of positivism. The positivist paradigm mostly works within the context of justification of existing knowledge and is nearly useless for making new discoveries. Only the ampliative form of induction leads to advancement of knowledge. To be that productive, this form of reasoning has to be complemented by the ampliative-deductive form of inference; these two processes constitute the essence of retroduction and abduction. The disadvantages and weaknesses of the positivist paradigm make its usefulness for social scientific investigations very questionable.

Questions

1. Explain in your own words how you understand the fundamental problem of research. Why is it a *problem* and why is it the *fundamental* one?
2. There is a long history of abandoning philosophical thinking in the teaching of research methods and design. Starting with the arguments in the textbook, add your own thoughts and arguments why philosophical thinking is important for empirical researchers.

74 Thinking and Reflecting

3. Both "enumerative" and "ampliative" forms of induction go from the particular to the general. What are the differences between the two forms of induction?
4. What is the difference between the *deductive-nomological* and *ampliative-deductive* modes of inference? Both go from general to particular, so why are the two forms suggested?
5. What are the main differences between *empiricists* and *rationalists* with regard to conducting research?
6. In your own words, articulate the main premises of the *positivist paradigm*. How do you understand and apply its ontological, epistemological, and methodological propositions? What is "empirical" and what is "logical" in logical empiricism/positivism?
7. Why do some scholars argue that positivism does not generate new knowledge? What are their arguments?
8. Why do some scholars think that the quantification of sociocultural and psychological phenomena is not a productive idea? Use arguments from the textbook and try to add your own considerations.
9. How do you understand the proposition that "Positivists are incapable of addressing the systemic nature of sociocultural and psychological phenomena"?
10. Are there any points of the positivism critique that you do not agree with? Why? Justify your position. What arguments can you post in defense of positivism? Justify them and discuss in class.

Glossary

Context of discovery and context of justification: The focus of attention of researchers within the context of discovery is directed toward the logical, psychological, social, and historical factors of discovering new knowledge about how the worlds operate. The subject of thoughts within the context of justification is an assessment of the validity and truthfulness of discovered theoretical statements.

Deduction: Deductive reasoning moves from a general statement considered universally true to a conclusion about the present or future states of particular cases.

> **Ampliative-deductive mode of inference**—a deductive inference from the rational insights or hypotheses about generating powers and mechanisms produced by the ampliative induction to the empirical evidence that can justify such insights.
>
> **Deductive-nomological mode of inference**—a deductive reasoning that is based on the enumerative generalization, as a general statement, as it is applied to particular cases. **Nomological**—"relating to or denoting natural laws . . . from Greek *nomos* 'law'" + medieval Latin *logia (-logy or—ology)* "subject of study" (Soanes & Stevenson, 2008).
>
> **Hypothetico-deductive**—the hypothetico-deductive way of expanding scientific knowledge uses deductive-nomological reasoning by proposing hypotheses about nonobserved cases based on empirical generalizations.

Emergent properties are properties of systems that emerge based on the relations among the system's components and are not reducible to properties of the separate components. Life, consciousness, social causation, human autonomy, and agency are some examples of emergent properties.

Empirical: Any research that is based on collecting evidence from observations and direct experiences. This evidence may be presented in words or numbers and may be analyzed either by qualitative or quantitative techniques.

Empiricism is a philosophical epistemological doctrine that states that scientific knowledge should be based solely on empirical, or sense, data and the generalizations that are rooted in these data.

Empiricism constitutes the core of the positivist paradigm. It also denies the existence of unobservable entities that may stand behind the empirical facts and regularities.

Essence: "the intrinsic nature or indispensable quality of something, which determines its character . . . Philosophy: a property or group of properties of something without which it would not exist or be what it is. . . . ORIGIN Middle English: via Old French from Latin *essentia*, from *esse* 'be'" (Soanes & Stevenson, 2008).

Induction: Inductive reasoning moves from a limited number of observed or experienced instances to a conclusion about general propositions.

> **Ampliative induction: Ampliative** (from Latin *ampliare*, "to enlarge"), a term used mainly in logic, meaning "extending" or "adding to that which is already known" (http://en.wikipedia.org/wiki/Ampliative). **Ampliative induction** is an intellectual operation by which a researcher makes hypotheses about unobservable generating powers and mechanisms that are not explicitly given in the empirical evidence. Also: analytic or substantive, or explanatory induction, and theoretical generalization.
>
> **Enumerative induction** is an intellectual procedure by which researchers induce/generalize empirical regularities discovered on a limited numbers of cases to more cases, or enumerate the regularities to a larger number of instances. Also, enumerative generalization.

Phenomenon (plural phenomena): "from Greek *phainomenon*, 'things appearing to view'" (Soanes & Stevenson, 2008). This concept refers to appearances of objects or events as well as the experiences that a human being has about these objects and events. "In philosophy this concept means any object, fact, or occurrence perceived or observed. In general, phenomena are the objects of the senses as contrasted with what is apprehended by intellect" (*Encyclopedia Britannica*: http://www.britannica. com/EBchecked/topic/455614/phenomenon). A phenomenon requires explanation by discovering its causes.

Positivism is a broad and complex philosophical paradigm, which is typically divided into classical positivism, logical positivism/empiricism, and postpositivism. Regardless of these variations, there is a set of core ideas that unites all these subforms into one metatheoretical doctrine: shallow realism, empiricism, and the enumerative inductive and deductive-nomological modes of inference. In modern days, positivism is associated with a variable-based approach accompanied by a statistical analysis.

Rational: Conclusions based on knowledge, logical inferences, conjectures, insights, and interpretations that bind empirical evidence into theoretically coherent wholes and allow researchers to make inferences about the essences and causes of things and events.

Rationalism is a philosophical epistemological doctrine that states that scientific knowledge should be based exclusively on reason and rational thinking. It is contrasted with empiricism. Rationalists believe that rational knowledge takes priority over empirical knowledge. In scientific research, collecting empirical evidence and rationally thinking about it are two sides of the process of scientific discovery and justification.

Research habitus (plural) is a concept based on Bourdieu's notion of habitus in its application to research activity. Research habitus are taken-for-granted unreflected-upon attitudes that one or several philosophical paradigms are correct and scientific, followed by uncritical realizations of these paradigms' prescriptions of how to think about a study, what methods to use, and how to collect and analyze data. It is an implicit way of perceiving and interpreting the research activities of oneself and other scholars. Existing research habitus are results of the internalization of mainstream university teaching, editorial and funding policies, and general public discourse of what science is about. Unreflected habitus kill scientific discoveries.

Recommended Reading

Bem, S., & de Jong, H. L. (2006). *Theoretical issues in psychology: An introduction.* (2nd ed.). London, UK: Sage.
Carnap, R. (1966/1995). *An introduction to the philosophy of science.* New York, NY: Dover.
Hammersley, M. (2012). What's wrong with quantitative research? In B. Cooper, J. Glaesser, R. Gomm & M. Hammersley (Eds.), *Challenging the qualitative-quantitative divide: Explorations in case-focused causal analysis* (pp. 27–56). London, UK: Continuum.
Hempel, C. G. (1965). *Aspects of scientific explanation.* New York, NY: Free Press.
Markie, P. (2008). Rationalism-Empiricism. In E. N. Zalta (Ed.). *The Stanford Encyclopedia of Philosophy.* Retrieved from http://plato.stanford.edu/entries/rationalism-empiricism/
Polkinghorne, D. (1983). *Methodology for the human sciences: Systems of inquiry.* Albany, NY: State University of New York Press.

References

Bacon, F. (1620/2000). *The new organon.* Cambridge, UK: Cambridge University Press.
Bem, S., & de Jong, H. L. (2006). *Theoretical issues in psychology: An introduction.* (2nd ed.). London, UK: Sage.
Berry, J. W. (1997). Immigration, acculturation, and adaptation. *Applied Psychology: An International Review, 46*(1), 5–68.
Berry, J. W., Phinney, J. S., Sam, D. L., & Vedder, P. (Eds.). (2006). *Immigration youth in cultural transition: Acculturation, identity, and adaptation across national contexts.* Mahwah, NJ: Lawrence Erlbaum.
Bhaskar, R. (1975/2008). *A realist theory of science.* London, UK: Verso.
Carnap, R. (1966/1995). *An introduction to the philosophy of science.* New York, NY: Dover.
Cohen, J. (1994). Earth is round (p < .05). *American Psychologist, 49*(12), 997–1003.
Collier, A. (1994). *Critical realism: An introduction to Roy Bhaskar's philosophy.* London, UK: Verso.
Douven, I. (2011). Abduction. In E. N. Zalta (Ed.), *The Stanford Encyclopedia of Philosophy.* Retrieved from http://plato.stanford.edu/entries/abduction/
Grant, E. A. (1996). *The foundations of modern science in the Middle Ages: Their religious, institutional, and intellectual contexts.* Cambridge, UK: Cambridge University Press.
Grant, E. A. (2007). *History of natural philosophy: From the ancient world to the nineteenth century.* Cambridge, UK: Cambridge University Press.
Hammersley, M. (2012). What's wrong with quantitative research? In B. Cooper, J. Glaesser, R. Gomm & M. Hammersley (Eds.), *Challenging the qualitative-quantitative divide: Explorations in case-focused causal analysis* (pp. 27–56). London, UK: Continuum.
Hannam, J. (2011). *The genesis of science: How the Christian Middle Ages launched the scientific revolution.* Washington, DC: Regnery.
Hempel, C. G. (1965). *Aspects of scientific explanation.* New York, NY: Free Press.
Hempel, C. G., & Oppenheim, P. (1948). Studies in the logic of explanation. *Philosophy of Science, 15*(2), 135–175.
Kim, J. (1999). Explanation. In R. Audi (Ed.), *The Cambridge dictionary of philosophy* (pp. 298–299). Cambridge, UK: Cambridge University Press.
Kline, R. (2004). *Beyond significance testing: Reforming data analysis methods in behavioral research.* Washington, DC: American Psychological Association.
Mandler, G., & Kessen, W. (1964). *The language of psychology.* New York, NY: Wiley.
Markie, P. (2008). Rationalism-empiricism. In E. N. Zalta (Ed.), *The Stanford Encyclopedia of Philosophy.* Retrieved fromhttp://plato.stanford.edu/entries/rationalism-empiricism/McMullin, E. (1992). *The inference that makes science.* Milwaukee, WI: Marquette University Press.
Miles, M. B., & Huberman, A. M. (1994). *Qualitative data analysis: An expanded sourcebook.* (2nd ed.). Thousand Oaks, CA: Sage.
Peirce, C. S. (1960). *Collected papers of Charles Peirce* (Vol. V-VI). Cambridge, MA: Belknap Press.
Polkinghorne, D. (1983). *Methodology for the human sciences: Systems of inquiry.* Albany, NY: State University of New York Press.
Popper, K. R., & Eccles, J. C. (1977). *The self and its brain.* New York, NY: Springer.
Reichenbach, H. (1958). *The rise of scientific philosophy.* Berkeley, CA: University of California Press.

Rozeboom, W. W. (1997). Good science is abductive, not hypothetico-deductive. In L. L. Harlow, S. A. Mulaik & J. H. Steiger (Eds.), *What is there were no significance tests?* (pp. 335–391). Mahwah, NJ: Lawrence Erlbaum.

Sayer, A. (1992). *Methods in social science: A realist approach.* (2nd ed.). London, UK: Routledge.

Schickore, J., & Steinle, F. (Eds.). (2006). *Revisiting discovery and justification: Historical and philosophical perspectives on the context distinction.* Dordrecht, The Netherlands: Springer.

Skyrm, B. (1999). Induction. In R. Audi (Ed.), *The Cambridge dictionary of philosophy* (pp. 425–426). Cambridge, UK: Cambridge University Press.

Snyder, L. J. (2006). *Reforming philosophy: A Victorian debate on science and society.* Chicago, IL: University of Chicago Press.

Soanes, C., & Stevenson, A. (Eds.). (2008). *Concise Oxford English dictionary* (11th ed.). Oxford, UK: Oxford University Press.

Thompson, B. (2004). The "significance" crisis in psychology and education. *Journal of Socio-Economics, 33*(5), 607–613.

Triandis, H. C. (1993). Comment on Misra and Gergen's: Place of culture in psychological science. *International Journal of Psychology, 28*(2), 249–250.

Urbach, P. (1987). *Francis Bacon's philosophy of science: An account and a reappraisal.* La Salle, IL: Open Court.

Ziliak, S., & McCloskey, D. (2008). *The cult of statistical significance: How the standard error costs us jobs, justice, and lives.* Ann Arbor, MI: University of Michigan Press.

Znaniecki, F. (1934). *The method of sociology.* New York, NY: Rinehart.

4

PHILOSOPHICAL THINKING

Abduction, Retroduction, Interpretivism, and Realism

This chapter will:

- Introduce *abduction* and *retroduction* as modes of inference for the context of discovery
- Connect abduction with the *interpretivist paradigm*
- Discuss the interpretivist paradigm that aims at *interpreting* and *understanding* different *systems of meaning*
- Link retroduction to the *realist paradigm*
- Discuss the realist paradigm that targets generating powers and causal mechanisms of things, events, and actions.

Introduction

The previous chapter introduced the four modes of research inference: enumerative and ampliative modes of induction and deductive-nomological and ampliative-deductive modes of deduction. In this chapter, I will present the other two modes of reasoning: abductive and retroductive. Both of these modes are rooted in the ampliative form of induction and deduction. Then I will introduce the paradigm of interpretivism, which is based on abduction and is applied to different systems of meaning, and the paradigm of realism, which embraces the retroductive mode of reasoning for discovering generating powers and causal mechanisms of phenomena.

The Abductive and Retroductive Modes of Inference

Let's return to the example from Chapter 3 about acculturation research within the positivist paradigm. Imagine that a researcher who is trying to think outside of the box of positivism wants to study the acculturation of immigrants beyond simple correlations of acculturation strategies with immigrants' well-being. He or she may come up with the following questions: What is actually going on with immigrants when they settle in a new country? Is it possible to talk about the psycho-sociocultural mechanisms of acculturation that regulate the behaviors and experiences of immigrants? If so, what are their constituents and how do these components work? What are the differences among the four acculturation strategies with regard to the constituents, powers, and dynamics of these mechanisms? Do these mechanisms allow researchers to explain why different strategies have different relations to immigrants' well-being?

These questions are nearly impossible to answer within the positivist paradigm because, first, they refer to unobservable structures and processes. Second, these questions ask about causal relations that cannot be discovered through statistical methods. And third, positivist research prefers to represent individuals and cultures through a set of variables and their covariances, instead of studying them as open systems embedded into particular contexts. Therefore, to answer these questions, a researcher has to look for other philosophical paradigms and has to learn different modes of reasoning. I will now address how to answer these questions by applying the *abductive* and *retroductive* modes of inference within the *interpretivist* and *realist paradigms*.

Charles Peirce and the Abductive/Retroductive Modes of Inference

Readers should remember the denial of philosophers of science to unlock the mysteries within the context of discovery while focusing their efforts on the context of justification, a trend that was especially strong within the positivist paradigm. The previous chapter showed that this paradigm and the enumerative induction and the deductive-nomological mode of inference related to positivism do not lead to scientific discoveries and do not generate new knowledge. Then what do modes of inference do? The answer is that the ampliative induction and related to it the ampliative-deductive mode of inference are the gateways to genuinely new scientific knowledge through the context of discovery.

American philosopher **Charles Peirce** (1839–1914) is one of the first modern philosophers of science who focused his attention on the context of discovery and made attempts to articulate a specific mode of inference and logical conditions for scientific breakthroughs (Peirce, 1960). This is how Polkinghorne (1983) presents Peirce's line of thoughts about a scientific discovery:

> The process of discovery begins with a shock of an experience which does not fit into one's system of thought and sets off doubt. A problem arises when the uniformity of nature which one thinks one has understood is disrupted by an experience that causes one to question and change previous understanding. One then begins a scientific inquiry with a conjecture (a hypothesis) which attempts to explain the disrupting phenomenon. (p. 121)

Peirce used the term abduction for the method of developing such a conjecture and then using it to guide research to explain the formulated problems. "Abduction consists in studying facts and devising a theory to explain them. Its only justification is that if we are ever to understand things at all, it must be in that way" (Peirce, 1960, vol. 5, p. 90). As he said, "[a]bduction is the process of forming an explanatory hypothesis. It is the only logical operation which introduces any new idea" (p. 106); elsewhere he said that "A man must be downright crazy to deny that science has made many new discoveries. But every single item of scientific theory which stands established today has been due to Abduction" (p. 106). Peirce's message is clear: if a researcher aims toward a new discovery, he or she has to use the abductive mode of inference. This is how he formalized the logic of that inference:

> The surprising fact, C, is observed
> But if A were true, C would be a matter of course
> Hence, there is reason to suspect that A is true. (p. 117)

As with induction and deduction, abduction is a part of our everyday thinking. Imagine that you notice a dark wet stain under your car. Immediately a set of questions and hypotheses start rushing through your head: Is oil leaking? Is the air conditioning cooling fluid seeping? Is there a leak in the radiator? This abductive way of thinking is offering you the best possible explanations of the problem. Recalling that the day was hot and that you drove with the AC running, and that you recently changed the oil and flushed the radiator, the explanation of the stain as a result of condensed water from the AC seems the most probable. To test this explanation, you take a sample of the liquid and realize that it is water. Your explanation was correct. Modern philosophers of science also call abduction "inference to the best explanation" (Lipton, 2004). Abduction lies at the core of scientific discoveries, medical and psychological diagnoses, and is used almost everywhere where scientists have to explain a set of problematic empirical evidence (Douven, 2011; Hanson, 1958; Rozeboom, 1997). It is considered so important for scientific discoveries that McMullin (1992) defined it as "The inference that makes science".

In this interpretation, abduction and ampliative induction actually become the same process of "jumping" from the patterns of empirical facts to conjectures and hypotheses about the causes that determine and explain them. This is how Peirce articulated the idea that abduction is actually an ampliative induction:

> The great difference between induction [enumerative induction] and hypothesis [abduction in Peirce's terms] is, that the former infers the existence of phenomena, such as we have observed in cases which are similar, while hypothesis supposes something of a different kind from which we have directly observed, and frequently something which it would be impossible for us to observe directly (1857; Vol. 2, p. 388). (Cited in Rozeboom, 1997, p. 367)

Although Peirce suggested abduction to be another mode of inference that complements induction and deduction, it is logical to equate abduction with ampliative induction and the ampliative-deductive mode of inference, while binding the enumerative induction with the deductive-nomological mode of inferences.

Abduction starts with the empirical evidence that represents a problem, unresolved issue, or with contradictions between what is known and what exists. Think about the diversity of species of animals and their fascinating ability to adapt to life in the air, in the water, on the ground or beneath the ground. One may ask: How could these diversities and adaptations have happened? Observing these and many other empirical facts about biological species, a researcher may come up with conjectures about what may be behind this diversity and its perfect adaptations. Based on these conjectures, a researcher deduces hypotheses about how these unobservable structures and powers may work, and he or she tests them with the consequent empirical studies. This is a process of ampliative-deductive inference discussed in Chapter 3. And, finally, if scientists' hypotheses are verified, they develop theories about the mechanisms of the phenomena they investigate.

One researcher who was especially fascinated with this empirical evidence was **Charles Darwin** (1809–1882), who came up with the hypothesis that the processes of natural selection may lie behind the evolution, development, and diversification of all species on earth, including humans. This was his brilliant abductive or ampliative-inductive penetration into the realm of unobservables—the real and powerful sources of species evolution. This hypothesis was a product of deep knowledge of the phenomena under scrutiny, intuition, disciplined imagination, and rational thinking. Darwin developed his ideas based on the existing systematizations of the biological forms, on the evolutionary ideas of British geologist **Charles Lyell** (1797–1875), which were complemented by his own systematic observations. Darwin developed the theory of evolution by natural selection, which allowed biologists to generate hypotheses about the functioning and manifestations of the mechanisms of natural selection in different domains. For example, biologists may hypothesize that if the theory of evolution is correct, then there should be genetic similarities between related species, such as humans and big apes. And in fact there is almost 98.5% of commonality of their genetic makeup (http://humanorigins.si.edu/evidence/ genetics). The whole new science of evolutionary biology has been developed to do the job of generating and testing hypotheses about the mechanisms and outcomes of natural and sexual selection. Hence, we have the theory of evolution with solid theoretical and empirical backgrounds.

INFORMATION BOX 4.1. TWO IMPORTANT POINTS ABOUT ABDUCTION

1. Empirical evidence provides only a starting point for developing testable hypotheses and then a theory. Theory here is not a set of statements about empirical regularities and generalizations, but a set of statements about unobservable generating powers and causal mechanisms. These hypotheses are rational, meaning they come from the mind and not directly from sense data (hence, this is the rationalist approach) and are based on knowledge, imagination, insight, and reasoning, and not exclusively on empirical facts and regularities. Thus, we have the amplification of knowledge based on rational thinking. If positivism is rooted in radical empiricism as the basis of scientific knowledge, abduction mostly relies on empirical facts and rational forms of reasoning about the essence of these facts.
2. Second, going back to the example of Darwin's theory of evolution, it is important to highlight that the processes of natural selection, which everybody now accepts as the real and powerful force behind the functioning of the biological world, are unobservable, hidden, and never given directly to scientists. Biologists do not operationalize natural selection and do not directly measure it; they infer the ideas of these processes and use these ideas to generate hypotheses that can be either verified or falsified by empirical evidence. The hidden causal mechanisms are not the objects of empirical operationalization, but only of rational abduction.

The theory of evolution is not the only example of an application of the abductive mode of inference. In psychology, think about Freud's theory of unconsciousness and mechanisms of defenses, Piaget's theory of cognitive development and the mechanisms of accommodation and assimilation that drive it; or Vygotskii's idea of internalization as a mechanism of human socialization. These theories were developed by great minds who stepped beyond direct empirical evidence and used the abductive inference to generate ideas that form the most influential theories in psychology. Learning the right way of reasoning can help each and every reader of this textbook make similar breakthroughs in their inquiries.

Another term that Peirce used synonymously with abduction is *retroduction* (but he preferred the former one); he applied both of them to the natural sciences. In modern thinking (Bhaskar, 1979/2015; Blaikie, 2007, 2010; Danemark, Ekstrom, Jakobsen, & Karlsson, 2002; Shank, 1998) these two terms are differentiated in the following way. The term abduction has been assigned to the process of uncovering the meaning of different events, practices, and experiences that people live through in their sociocultural worlds (Blaikie, 2010; Danemark, et al., 2002, Shank, 1998). According to this understanding abduction belongs to the interpretivist paradigm, which addresses the realm of meanings that exist in people's intentional worlds and which are hidden and not given directly. The term retroduction has been reserved for the process of discovering causal powers, their dynamics, and related mechanisms that generate both observed empirical regularities and systems of meaning; it is the process of understanding the essence of things and how they work. Following this logic, the retroductive mode of inference belongs to the realist paradigm and could (and should) be applied in all sciences, including natural, social, and psychological (Bhaskar, 1979/2015).

The Abductive Mode of Inference and the Interpretivist Paradigm

As soon as positivists started claiming that their logic of a scientific inquiry could easily be applied to the social, historical, and human sciences, and that this paradigm should serve as the universal background for research in any domain of science, resistance emerged. Antipositivist attitudes came from the fact that people, as objects of scientific inquiry, in comparison to objects of the nonanimated natural world, are conscious, reflective, reasonable and agentic creatures who produce intentional sociocultural realities where they live and function. Human beings are capable of producing *meaning*, where something stands for something else, and they act because of this meaning. The sociocultural and psychological worlds are saturated with different systems of meanings and these meanings and their significance, and not the "objective" stimuli which are stripped of any sense for a human being, are the conditions and contexts where the actual behaviors, thoughts, and feelings of people emerge and unfold.

INFORMATION BOX 4.2. A VARIETY OF MEANINGS OF THE TERM *MEANING*

A nominal definition of "meaning" says that it is "what is meant by a word, text, concept, or action" (Soanes & Stevenson, 2008).

The *linguistic meaning* of words and sentences explains what words and utterances stand for; what things, events, attributes, qualities, etc. these linguistic constructions represent. Linguistic meaning includes the *semantic meaning* of words and the *pragmatic meaning* of the spoken language. We find semantic meaning in dictionaries. We learn semantic and pragmatic meaning when we learn and use a language.

Sociocultural meaning is a system of signification that sociocultural communities construct for their needs, when something stands for something else. For example, a piece of paper stands for money. A piece of fabric on a wooden rod stands for a banner or flag and symbolizes a nation. People learn these sociocultural systems of meaning through enculturation. For members of a particular sociocultural community, these systems of meaning are taken for granted and constitute their valid reality for functioning. Sociocultural meaning is enacted in people's everyday practices, habitual gestures, rituals, and can also be represented in various artifacts (published texts, pieces of art, etc.). These systems of meaning are not explicitly given and have to be extracted through *interpretation,* abduction, and *understanding*.

The *idiosyncratic meaning* of people's actions and lives is a system of signification that each individual creates to make sense of his or her own life and actions in particular contexts. Idiosyncratic meaning partly consists of internalized sociocultural meanings and is partly a result of people's own interpretations of their histories, situations, contexts, and actions. Every person has access to his or her idiosyncratic meaning through his or her reflective consciousness. Outsiders do not have direct access to this system unless they use special methods of extracting and interpreting the manifestations of this meaning. Again, interpretation, abduction, and understanding are the intellectual tools to study this type of meaning.

A Brief History of the Antipositivist Reaction

The history of searching for systems of scientific inquiry suitable for the social and human sciences can be traced back to the works of Italian Renaissance scholars, where humanist **Giovanni Battista Vico** (1668–1774) was one of the leading figures. The full range of the development of the philosophy and methodology of such a system in relation to psychology is attributed to **William Dilthey** (1833–1911). The works within the phenomenological, hermeneutic, and existential paradigms presented by **Edmund Husserl** (1859–1938), **Martin Heidegger** (1889–1976), **Hans-Georg Gadamer** (1900–2002), **Maurice Merleau-Ponty** (1908–1961), **Jean-Paul Sartre** (1905–1980), and many other philosophers substantially contributed to the development of social and human sciences methodology (see Polkinghorne, 1983 and Blaikie, 2007 for a review). With regard to understanding the sociocultural domain, the most prominent scholars were **Max Weber** (1864–1920), **Paul Ricœur** (1913–2005), **Karl-Otto Apel** (1922–), **Jürgen Habermas** (1929–), and **Erick Donald Hirsch** (1928–). All these thinkers were convinced that the exclusively human way of existence consists of never-ending processes of conscious and reflective interpretations of the worlds wherein people live, their historical conditions, the behavior of other people, the aspirations and practices that people are involved with, and myriads of other things and events that constitute their sociocultural environments. Humans also constantly make sense of their own actions, thoughts and feelings, thus making their own lives the objects of permanent meaning-making and interpretations. People's proclivity toward reflections, interpretations and reinterpretations make them unique objects of scientific inquiries that have no analogies in the existing natural worlds, and, thus, require different modes of thinking and inferences. Positivists are not aiming toward and are not capable of addressing these systems of human meanings and processes of interpretations. The paradigm that has emerged to study people operating within their meaningful worlds was initially labelled *hermeneutics* (see Box 4.3.) and later *interpretivism* (Polkinghorne, 1983).

Another fundamental attribute of human existence, according to the above-mentioned scholars, constitutes the human-made sociocultural worlds that people mutually create and where they actually live and act. Without these worlds, labelled as "society" and/or "culture" or "sociosymbolic worlds," humans cannot emerge and function as fully conscious and rational individuals. These specifically human contexts of living and acting exert powerful influences on people's behavior and cannot be ignored in the scientific studies of human behavior. But the artificial, intentional, and intersubjective character of these contexts requires specific intellectual and technical tools in order to investigate and explain these worlds.

It is important to note that all these scholars were addressing two interrelated but relatively separate systems of meaning (see also the Box 4.4.). One system of meaning operates within sociocultural structures, which, together with related practices, norms, and beliefs, are created by particular communities and which provide a normative context for people's lives. It has been labelled either the "social stock of knowledge" (Berger & Luckmann, 1966/1989) or "cultural models" (in their public aspects) (D'Andrade, 1995; Shore, 1998). A second system of meaning that governs people's experiences and actions is the meanings that people idiosyncratically develop and hold with regard to their personal lives and actions (Shore, 1998). There are dialectical relationships between the first, normative and external, and the second, idiosyncratic and internal, systems of meaning. The second one is possible only because people are born into the first one. But they are not the slaves of it. Because people are socialized into the normative system of meaning, they become conscious, rational, and reflective individuals and develop a capacity to contemplate the sociocultural systems of meaning. Based on these contemplations, they are able to either accept or reject them. In addition to this, by using the power of reason, people can develop unique meanings for their lives, which may be different from the normative ones, and live according to them. This means that people possess a potentiality toward psychological autonomy, agency, and self-determination in their lives (Chirkov, 2010, 2014).

Investigation of Meaning, Act of Interpretation, and the Abductive Mode of Inference

Regardless of what system of meaning researchers decide to address, there is one common denominator: the meaning is hidden; it is not explicitly given and has to be discovered. "'Meaning' is not a phenomenon that can be subjected to empirical observation" (Polkinghorne, 1983, p. 49). The systems of meaning do not exist in any materialistic or tangible forms because they are either intersubjective (exist in between members of sociocultural communities) or intrasubjective (exist inside the psyche of individuals). But nevertheless, meaning is real: real because we really think it, real because it exists independently of what the bearers of meaning – laypeople or researchers – think it to be, and real because it possesses power that can determine and change people's lives and actions. Thus, meaning can be and should be an object of scientific investigation. Because meanings are hidden behind the surface of cultural rituals, social institutions, people's actions, their conversations, thoughts, and feelings, there should be special intellectual tools to uncover them. This intellectual tool is abduction.

> When we consider the world not as a compendium of facts but as a web of meanings . . ., then we go beyond concepts like environments and settings, to concepts like the world as . . . a "lived world," where the things we observe take on significance. It is our job to read those observations in order to determine their significances. This act of reading consists of treating observations not for themselves, but as signs of other things. Since we don't know for sure what they signify, we can only guess. Therefore, if we do indeed live in a world of signs, our most basic actions consist in reading those signs. Consequently, the *process of abduction* [emphasis added] runs through our very act of living in a world that makes sense. Where that sense breaks down, our abductions need to become explicit and reflective. (Shank, 1998, p. 852)

Blaikie (2010) defines the abductive mode of inference in the following way:

> This [abductive] research strategy involves constructing theories that are derived from social actors' language, meanings and accounts in the context of everyday activities. Such research begins by describing these activities and meanings and then deriving from them categories and concepts that can form the basis of an understanding of the problem at hand.
>
> The Abductive research strategy incorporates what the Inductive [enumerative induction] and Deductive [deductive-nomological mode of inference] research strategies ignore—the *meanings* and *interpretations,* [emphasis added] the motives and intentions, that people use in their everyday lives, and which direct their behavior—and elevates them to the central place in social theory and research. (p. 89)

The act of *interpretation* is at the heart of abduction as it allows researchers to infer that something observable stands for something else that is unobservable, where these unobservables are different meanings. Interpretation can be defined as a sequence of intellectual processes of discovering systems of meaning in the sociocultural worlds as well as in the worlds of personal lives, actions, and experiences and detecting their dimensions and structures.

We are constantly involved with the process of interpreting signs, symbols, actions, utterances, gestures, and other events around us in order to comprehend their meaning. The act of interpretation is thus a fundamental part of our everyday cognitive interactions with the world. Interpretation is also a pan-scientific intellectual tool, as quantitative or qualitative research results, statistical results, ethnographic notes, structured surveys, personal diaries, and almost everything that constitutes data in scientific research can and must be interpreted. Interpretation "is the act of clarifying,

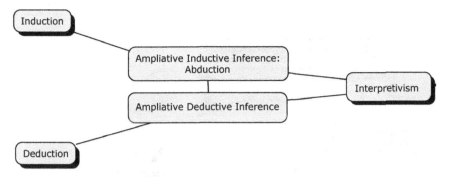

FIGURE. 4.1 Structure of interpretivist thinking. This concept map was made with IHMC Cmap Tools

explicating, or explaining the meaning of some phenomenon" (Schwandt, 2007, p. 158). The centrality of interpretation as the abductive mode of inference in the social and human sciences gave the title of the philosophical paradigm—*interpretivism* (see Fig. 4.1.). Hence, interpretive anthropology, interpretive sociology, and interpretive psychology.

INFORMATION BOX 4.3. HERMENEUTICS AS A SCIENCE OF INTERPRETATION AND THE FOUNDATION OF INTERPRETIVISM

The interpretivist paradigm is rooted in the philosophy and practices of *hermeneutics*. Hermeneutics (named after the Greek god Hermes, who served as a messenger of the gods and a mediator and interpreter between gods and people) is the systematic study of the acts of interpretation of various texts, pieces of art, legal documents, and other systems of symbolic signification. "Hermeneutics deals with clarifying the meaning of a text, and by extension the meaning of any human action, product, or expression that can be treated as a text" (Diesing, 1991, p. 105). Although it started as the science of interpreting texts, this philosophy has since been employed to study societies and cultures, human actions, conversations, and discourses.

Hermeneutics supplies and justifies the main methodological technique for interpretation: *the hermeneutic circle* (THC) (Gadamer, 1959/1988) (see Fig. 4.2.). Hermeneutics scholars believe that THC lies at the core of any interpretative act and constitutes the essence of interpretation. THC means that an interpreter of any symbolic document moves in circles from grasping the meaning of the parts, based on a pre-understanding of the whole, then using this knowledge to move back to interpreting the meaning of the whole; after grasping the meaning of the whole, the interpreter returns to (re-)interpret the parts and, when their meaning is clarified, resumes the investigation of the meaning of the whole. This circle ends when a satisfactory level of understanding is attained, but this understanding is never final and never absolutely correct. Thus, the results of interpretations are always inconclusive and falsifiable. Any interpretation, as any abductive inference, is a best guess that needs verification.

Hermeneutic scholars also provide the ontological basis of meaning by identifying its several layers, such as "surface semantics" and "depth semantics" (Ricœur, 1981, p. 217) and correspondently, "surface hermeneutics" and "depth hermeneutics" (Diesing, 1991, p. 107). Surface hermeneutics deals with the interpretation of overt messages in texts, human actions,

86 Thinking and Reflecting

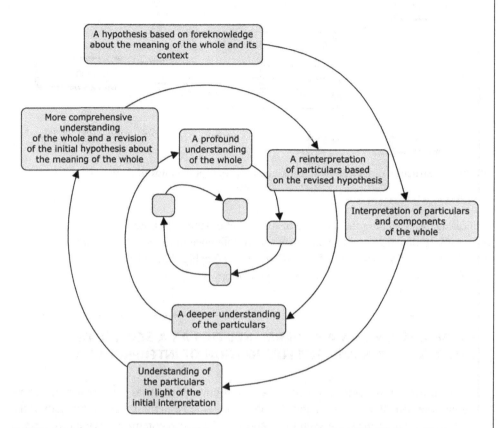

FIGURE. 4.2 The hermeneutic circle. This concept map was made with IHMC Cmap Tools

or cultural rituals. It focuses on the meaning that lies and/or is presented directly in what a researcher sees, reads, and experiences. Depth hermeneutics is concerned with concealed messages or covert meanings of texts, verbal statements, human actions, or cultural customs. Authors, actors, and agents are frequently not aware of the in-depth meanings that drive their discourses, behaviors, and actions. The acceptance of the existence of concealed or depth meanings and the importance of their discovery constitutes an ontological basis for abduction within the interpretivist paradigm: A researcher has to hypothesize about the meanings that are not given directly. Such arguments make the paradigm of interpretivism not only congruent with but also complementary to the paradigm of realism, because in-depth systems of meaning could be important components of the causal factors and powers that produce the sociocultural and psychological phenomena of interest.

The identification of surface and depth hermeneutics leads directly to a corresponding methodological dichotomy, namely between "a surface interpretation" and "a depth interpretation" (Ricœur, 1981, p. 218), also referred to as "thin" and "thick descriptions," suggested by British philosopher Gilbert Ryle (1971). The latter terms were applied by American anthropologist Clifford Geertz (1973) to anthropology and other interpretive sciences. A thin description addresses and explores the surface semantics and constitutes the surface interpretation, whereas a thick description tries to get to the complexity of depth semantics using the depth interpretation.

Interpretation and Understanding

Another concept that is closely related to the notion of interpretation is *understanding*. These two concepts came to the social sciences from the German intellectual tradition. The German word for interpretation is *auslegung* and for understanding is *verstehen* but the latter term has been used as a synonym for both concepts. For example, Weber coined the term *Verstehende Soziologie,* which was translated into English as "Interpretative Sociology" (Schwandt, 2007, p. 315). *Verstehen* was also translated as "interpretive understanding" (p. 316), or a way of elucidating and grasping the meaning of actions and sociosymbolic systems. A challenge of using the term understanding is that it "refer[s] both to the aim of human sciences as well as their method" (p. 314). As an intellectual tool, understanding is a synonym to interpretation, but as the aim of human sciences, it is either complemented or contrasted with *explanation* (see Chapter 5). Weber also talked about "'explanatory understanding,' which required grasping the motivation for human behavior by placing the action in some intelligible, inclusive context of meaning" (p. 315). In this textbook, when speaking about the process of grasping and elucidating meaning, the concept of interpretation is used. As a result of the act of interpretation, a researcher comprehends the meaning of actions and cultural traditions and attains their understanding.

"Interpretation begins with a general, vague hypothesis about the topic of the concealed message" (Diesing, 1991, p. 107). A basis for such a hypothesis is found in "foreknowledge" (p. 108), or pre-understanding, meaning that "we form an expectation about the unknown from what we 'know'" (p. 108). The idea of foreknowledge can be traced back to the works of Hans-Georg Gadamer (1998); it constitutes a crucial step for any act of elucidating meaning. The interpretive researcher's foreknowledge consists of several components.

a. General knowledge about the type of material to be interpreted—cultural rituals, a memorandum of a social institution, everyday interactions in a community, love letters, dream report, personal diary, or transcript of an interview (Diesing, 1991, p. 107).
b. Knowledge about various forms of social, psychological, behavioral, and experiential manifestations of different meanings extracted from books, previous research, and personal experiences.
c. Knowledge of the history and the context of the phenomenon to be interpreted: the history of a community of interest and its current conditions, the personal history of an individual and the context of his or her recent interactions that led to a problem being investigated (p. 107).
d. A researcher's background—researchers have their own experiences, personal worldviews, values, knowledge, intuitions, and expectations that unavoidably influence their perception, thinking, and interpretation. They have their own agenda, want to prove certain points, gain public acceptance, get published, and so forth. Interpretative researchers are embedded in their cultural traditions and work within particular historical and social contexts.

All these conditions may influence the direction in which scholars guide their attention, the events that interest them and the angle from which they look at them. Thus, data for the interpretative-abductive mode of inference are also "theory-laden."

> Our foreknowledge may be mistaken, or partial and misleading, or inapplicable to this text [or other objects of interpretation]; but in that case the interpretation will run into trouble. If our foreknowledge is weak, we may begin with two or contrary expectations and see which one works out better, or more likely will simply fail to see what is going on. (Diesing, 1991, p. 108)

As the interpretation continues, the hermeneutic circle swings with its full power.

> The initial hypothesis guides the search for and interpretation of details, which in turn revise the hypothesis, which leads to reinterpretation and further search and so on. In case of conflict, the circle tends to widen farther and farther into the context on the one side and our foreknowledge on the other side. (p. 109)

An interpretive researcher who aims toward studying cultures starts by observing and/or participating in events and practices that are complemented by the verbal accounts of the actors. It includes registering the context, the temporary sequence of actions, the patterns of interactions among involved parties and other aspects related to the phenomena under scrutiny. This part of the interpretative research is similar to the observation of events conducted in any inductive enquiry with registering instances and their regularities (see Chapter 10 on ethnography).

If an interpretative scholar works with informants, interviewees or clients/patients, then more complex processes are taking place. A researcher has to know these particular people, and they have to have an opportunity to learn about and to understand the researcher. Based on this mutual understanding, the process of "melting-together" or the "fusion of horizons," as Gadamer labeled it, is taking place (Diesing, 1991, p. 123). This means that "the two [researcher and informant] construct a common culture in place of shared tradition, and thereby learn to understand each other" (p. 123). But this "fusion of horizons" does not mean that the words of an informant disclose the hidden meaning that becomes directly available to the researcher. They do not. An interpretivist researcher has to interpret the informant's interpretations, thus performing "double hermeneutics" or the interpretation of interpretations. This means that the informant's accounts are simply another piece of evidence to work with. Diesing (1991) provided several reasons for not accepting the informant's interpretations at face value. "First, the informant is never conscious of the full meaning of a practice. Culture is largely carried on as unconscious statements and responses that maintained a shared practice" (p. 126). As mentioned in Chapter 2, meanings of cultural practices are mostly taken for granted by people, and, while interpreting the surface meanings, informants typically do not have access to the deep cultural meanings of their actions. "Second, the informants' interpretation of their own practice normally pretty it up" (p. 126), meaning that the informants will try to show themselves and their compatriots in a favorable light, depict an idealized practice, and be biased and selective in choosing examples. Sometimes they may give a researcher incomplete, abridged, or trivial accounts. It is also important to mention that a researcher may acquire different roles in the native community like "stranger or spy, novice or meddler [interfering in something that is not one's concern], contact and messenger to the outside world, and eventually friend, member, or even expert" (p. 124). Depending on what role a scholar acquires in a community, he or she may receive different accounts of the same practice.

> Expressed differently, each message, practice, or interpretation is directed to a particular ethnographer's role. If the ethnographer is seen as spy or boyfriend, he will get one message or practice. The ethnographer as novice or student will get a deeper message or practice; . . . as trusted member of the culture, a still different one; and so on. (p. 127)

The interpretation of cultural phenomena is similar to the interpretation of any "semiological system" (Ricœur, 1981, p. 219), where something stands for something else. It moves from a surface meaning to a depth meaning, and its grasping constitutes the ultimate goal and purpose of

TABLE 4.1 Four types of interpretation

	Sociocultural normative systems of meaning	*Individual systems of meaning*
Surface hermeneutics **Thin description**	1. A description and labeling of contexts, actions, and practices. *Method*: naturalistic observation.	3. A description and labeling of informant subjective experiential meanings. *Methods*: interview, observation, standardized assessment.
Depth hermeneutics **Thick description/ interpretation**	2. Interpretation of the intersubjective constitutive meanings. *Methods*: participant observation, interview, ethnography, the hermeneutic circle, abductive reasoning.	4. Interpretation of the internalized constitutive intersubjective and the personal idiosyncratic systems of meanings. *Methods*: deep interview, person-centered interview, the hermeneutic circle, abductive reasoning.

understanding. Thus, a final product of successful interpretation is the developing an understanding of systems of deep meaning in order to comprehend and/or explain events, situations, and people's actions. A systematic verbal account of such an understanding in the form of theoretical statements should be available to broader scientific and public communities and should be accepted by them. These accounts constitute the essence of the theories in the interpretivist paradigm (see Chapter 5 on theories).

A Variety of Types of Interpretation

Interpretation is a complex and challenging procedure. For educational purposes, it is helpful to systematize various forms of interpretation by using the classifications suggested in Boxes 4.2 and 4.3. As a result of the categorization of the two systems of meanings—sociocultural and individual-idiosyncratic—and the two layers of hermeneutics—surface and depth—four types of interpretations can be created (see Table 4.1.).

Let's start with the thin description of sociocultural systems of meaning: Cell 1. In doing this type of analysis, a researcher focuses on describing the main behavioral acts and practices, learning the vocabulary—words, terms, and categories—that people in a community use within a particular domain, and, finally, providing pictures of particular episodes, their contexts, and components. Researchers describe actions within particular contexts: Who or what performed them, when and under what conditions? They also collect verbal accounts that informants supply with their actions. All these descriptions are made in a researcher's own concept and worded in his or her own language. The main body of the "thin" description consists of such "observational statements" that resemble video recordings of events by providing a detailed factual representation of events. Weber (1947) called this "the direct observational understanding" (p. 94).

Cell 2 represents the "thick" description of cultural systems of meaning. Using Taylor's (1971) conceptualization, the content of the depth hermeneutics is comprised of "intersubjective constitutive meanings" (p. 27). *Constitutive* means that these meanings construct various cultural practices out of people's physical movements. For example, some cultural communities' constitutive meanings create a disciplining practice out of a parent's hand movement toward the bottom of a child. Members of a different cultural community may assign a different meaning to the same movement and construct out of it a practice of child abuse. These meanings of various social practices are *intersubjective* because members of a community not only understand the meanings of these practices themselves, but they also understand that other members understand them the same way. They also know that other members of a community know that the rest of the community treats these practices with similar respect. Intersubjectivity means that these meanings are not located exclusively in the mind of the members of a community "but are out there in the practices themselves, practices which cannot be conceived as a set of individual actions, but which are essentially modes of social relations, of mutual actions" (Taylor, 1971, p. 27). When the intersubjectivity of the practices' meaning is established, then such practices become *cultural practices* that are accepted and legitimized by the cultural community. For example, spanking a child becomes accepted as an appropriate disciplining practice. In another community, spanking becomes child abuse because people there have a different intersubjective constitutive meaning behind the same physical movements. A goal of a "thick" description is to make these systems of meanings explicit, to identify and describe them and to articulate the ways they guide and control people's actions. This is how Geertz (1973) explained the difference between thin and thick descriptions:

> But the point is that between what Ryle calls the "thin description" of what the rehearser (parodist, winker, twitcher . . .) is doing ("rapidly contracting his right eyelids") and the "thick description" of what he is doing ("practicing a burlesque of a friend taking a wink to deceive an innocent into thinking a conspiracy is in motion") lies *the object of ethnography: a stratified hierarchy of meaningful structures in terms of which twitches, winks, fake-winks, parodies, rehearsals of parodies are produced, perceived, and interpreted, and without which they would not . . . in fact exist, no matter what anyone did or didn't do with his eyelids* [emphasis added]. (p. 7)

It is important to mention that these constitutive meanings are systems that do not exist in isolation, but are organized into coherent structures:

> Things only have meaning in the field, that is in relation to the meanings of other things. This mean that there is no such thing as a single unrelated meaningful element; and it means that changes in the other meanings in the field can involve changes in the given element. Meanings cannot be identified except in relation to others. (Taylor, 1971, p. 11; used with permission of *The Review of Metaphysics*)

Different domains of communal life have corresponding systems of meaning that regulate the activities of the people within them. Take, for example, parenting. Spanking as a disciplining practice is related to the meaning of a child as an individual who cannot regulate his or her actions, who does not differentiate right from wrong and, thus, requires parental guidance. Conversely, interpreting spanking as a form of child abuse is associated with regarding a child as a human being that should be treated with respect and dignity. Therefore, in interpreting the meanings of the disciplining practices it is nearly impossible to avoid tackling the broader meanings that are assigned to a child as a human being. Cultural psychologists should focus on these normative systems of meanings as they constitute a starting point for the internalized individual systems of meanings that guide the behavior of individuals.

Let's have a look at Ruth Benedict's (1946/1974) reflections on how she conducted her ethnography at a distance in order to uncover the codes of the Japanese culture (more on this research is in Chapter 5). Her final goals were to "try to understand Japanese habits of thought and emotion and the patterns into which these habits fell. We had to know the sanctions behind these actions and opinions" (p. 4). "The goal of such study as this is to describe deeply entrenched attitudes of thought and behavior. . . . This book . . . is about habits that are expected and taken for granted in Japan" (p. 16). Benedict stressed that her job as an anthropologist is different from simply accumulating the knowledge of her informants and the writers who provided various accounts of the

Japanese life. She saw her goal as uncovering the hidden meanings, rules, and norms that structure and guide the lives of people in another nation:

> The student who is trying to uncover the assumptions upon which Japan builds its way of life has a far harder task than statistical validation. The great demand upon him is to report how these accepted practices and judgments become the lenses through which the Japanese see existence. He has to state the way in which their assumptions affect the focus and perspective in which they view life. He has to try to make this intelligible to Americans who see existence in very different focus. (p. 17)

The only way Benedict could penetrate the unknown culture in such depth was to use abductive thinking. In her attempt to get behind the observable empirical facts, the researcher's abductive inferences were similar to the thinking of natural scientists. Here is Benedict's account of this abductive process:

> I read this [Japanese] literature as Darwin says he read when he was working out his theories [sic] on the origin of species, noting that I had not the means to understand. What would I need to know to understand the juxtaposition of ideas in a speech in the Diet? What could lie back of their violent condemnation of some act that seemed venial and their easy acceptance of one that seemed outrageous? I read, asking the ever-present question: What is "wrong with this picture?" What would I need to know to understand it? (p. 7)

If a study stays only within the analysis of the normative intersubjective constitutive systems of meaning, the researcher remains an anthropologist. In order to act as a cultural psychologist, he or she has to turn his or her attention to the individual members of a cultural community, addressing the question of what drives their actions in a particular context and what is the structure of their experiences of sociocultural systems of meaning? To what extent are they driven either by the internalized cultural models/constitutive systems of meanings, by the idiosyncratic systems of personal meanings, or by a combination of both? These and related questions could be answered within cells 3 and 4. The meanings that a researcher strives to investigate in these cases were labeled by Taylor as the "experiential meaning" (p. 12) that an agent has about a situation in a particular context. There are two subsystems of meanings that a person holds about his or her actions, and a situation where these actions occur. The first one is comprised of representations of the intersubjective constitutive systems of meaning that members of the community internalized during their enculturation and socialization. Without such a system, individual members would not be capable of culturally competent interactions with other members and would be unable to efficiently navigate in their sociocultural community. The second subsystem is made up of the personal idiosyncratic structures of meanings that each member of a community develops based on his or her unique life history and personal experiences. Without that system, a person would not be an agentic individual but a puppet of sociocultural forces. To interpret and understand people's actions in a cultural context is to uncover the unique blend of these two subsystems of meanings and to make them explicit for individual agents and for the community.

For cell 3—a thin description of the idiosyncratic systems of meanings—a researcher investigates a person's behavior and his or her verbal accounts of his or her actions, interactions with other people, expressed motives and feelings, thoughts, and reflections. All these manifestations should be registered by a psychologist in order to build a basis for a subsequent thick description/interpretation. A person's self-observations, reflections, and interpretations, although very informative and crucial for further investigation, cannot be the ultimate source of information for understanding this person's actions. "According to Kant, introspection could only give knowledge of appearances, while the real world remains hidden: "I know myself by inner experience only as I *appear* to myself (1974:22)" (Langenhove, 1995, p. 14). That is why special acts of interpretation are required to get beneath the surface interpretations of an individual.

A transition to the thick description/interpretation of the idiosyncratic systems of meanings (cell 4) is probably one of the most challenging and most complex tasks that human scientists can undertake. At this phase, the goal of a researcher is to interpret the meaning of a person's actions and the meaning of a situation for an actor, and by establishing coherence between these two systems of meaning he or she can understand and explain the action. The main challenge here is that people are typically unaware of the deep meanings and driving forces behind their actions and behaviors. These forces are based on taken-for-granted internalized cultural meanings and un/subconscious urges, meanings, and connotations and are not directly available for reflection and understanding by an individual consciousness. Only an interpretive scientist has the skills and knowledge to delve into their depth. Weber (1947) referred to this act as "explanatory understanding" (p. 95). Here the hermeneutic circle becomes an indispensable intellectual tool. But to apprehend the meaning of actions within a particular situation is nearly impossible without considering the bigger whole within which this action is taking place: the constitutive systems of meaning that structure this and other situations, an actor's personality, his or her social positioning, the history of this actor's previous actions, other actors in this situation, and many other aspects. Particular actions can be correctly interpreted only when considering this larger context. But individual actions are never a replica of the larger whole; they always have their unique and idiosyncratic particulars. Thus making sense of these particulars always enriches and expands a researcher's reading and understanding of the whole. Such circular interpretations and understandings continue until a researcher reaches a satisfactory comprehension of the actions. One of the methods of extracting the learned and internalized cultural systems of meanings, or cultural models, is person-centered ethnography, which will be discussed in Chapter 10. Abductive reasoning and other techniques (some of which we will discuss in the next section about the retroductive inference) should also be creatively used during this process.

Problems and Controversies with the Interpretivist Paradigm

The interpretive sciences are not free from problems and critiques, which is most frequently directed at them from positivists.

a. Critics question whether it is possible to "read others' minds," which means getting into the intentional worlds of cultural communities and understanding the mentalities of their people objectively and scientifically. This is one of the fundamental concerns of anti-interpretivists. To address this concern it is helpful to bring back the idea of the intersubjective nature of sociocultural meaningful realities. Researchers can reliably read the minds of others because of the intersubjective nature of the fabric of cultural meaning systems. When a researcher starts living in a community and participating in its cultural practices, he or she inevitably gains access to the intersubjectively shared ideational components of its culture and builds his or her own mental representations of them. If a researcher is successful in utilizing these cultural practices and is accepted by the members of a community through performing them accurately, then he or she starts sharing the cultural model of that community, and, thus, can read the minds of other members of the community by reflecting and interpreting his or her own mental representations of their cultural model. The interpretive researcher is able to read the intersubjectively shared part of others' minds but has much more difficulty getting to their idiosyncratic components (See also Chapter 10 on ethnography).
b. Positivists are also concerned with the validity of interpretations: Aren't the products of the interpretive sciences too subjective, with no hard evidence that can be evaluated against the

standards of truthfulness and validity? This concern is often accompanied by the allegations that interpretivism is not a science but more an art. To address it, it is necessary to remind readers about the nature and challenges of any abductive/retroductive inferences. Abduction is an educated and knowledgeable guess, and as with any guessing, it is subjective and fallible. A patient goes to one doctor and gets a diagnosis, and if he or she goes to another doctor, he or she may get a different one. There is no 100% certainty in any medical diagnosis because of the abductive nature of making them. The same holds true with any interpretations. They are guesses of the best explanation that is never considered certain or absolutely true and requires further verification and validation. We will talk more about the validity of retroductive inference in the next section on realism, which also applies to the validity of interpretations. Hirsch (1967) stated that there are no rules to make good guesses, but there are methods for validating guesses and he provides an elaborate account of the validation of "an interpretive hypothesis" (p. 183). Diesing (1991) recommended including a cross-case verification of the presence of the same facts/instances/events within similar contexts to see if the interpreted meaning holds across them; he also suggested reflecting on the foreknowledge that may lead to extracting meanings that are not coherent within themselves and across cases (p. 101). Blaikie (2010) also provided an important criterion for validating interpretive accounts of cultural meanings: the social actors and members of the studied cultural communities have to recognize themselves in the ethnographer's description.

> [I]f social actors cannot recognize themselves and their colleagues in the social scientist's accounts, then the latter must have produced a distortion of the social actor's world. This process of checking social scientific accounts with the social actors' accounts is sometimes referred to as "member validation" or "member check" and is a major form of validity checking in qualitative research. However, this process is not without its difficulties. (p. 51)

c. There is an assertion that for interpretivists "everything goes" and every interpretation is acceptable if it fits the text or the practice. This assertion means that there is no ultimate truth in interpretations. Polkinghorne (1983) presented this critique in the following way:

> The positivists were opposed to the use of the *verstehen* mode on the ground that different interpreters could come to different understandings of the same phenomena. Understanding was said by positivists to be merely speculative and therefore open to challenge; they attacked it for lacking certainty and refused to include it in science (*epistēme*). (p. 22)

The question about the truth behind any scientific statement is one of the most challenging concerns for all paradigms. If we accept that there are deep layers of meaning that need to be understood, then the truth is hidden and there is no direct access to it. Meaning is arranged in systems with different constituents and complex relations. These systems can be approached from different perspectives and different angles: "The hermeneutic philosopher has a conception of multiple complementary truths about a complex practice or text" (Diesing, 1991, p. 142). Thus, to elucidate the truthfulness of interpretation, a researcher has to test and retest his or her interpretations and understandings. "The validity of interpretation can be increased (1) through the many checks occurring in the hermeneutic circle, and (2) through the correction of perspectives during the development of a tradition; but we never arrive at the one absolute truth" (p. 142).

d. Positivists blame the interpretive sciences for their inability to establish causal relations between cultural and psychological variables, arguing that they do not operate in the scientific mode of empirical sciences and that ultimately they are not scientific enough. The question of establishing causality is a universal concern for all scientists. We have already mentioned that positivists do not establish causality as they deal only with the conjunctions of events and the correlations among them. But some interpretivists talk about and infer causality. Ricœur (1981) equated causality with discovering a deep meaning that has explanatory power for the practices under investigation.

> The kind of explanation which is implied by the structural model [the models that imply a hidden structure of meaning] appears to be quite different from the classical causal model, especially if causation is interpreted in Humean terms as a regular sequence of antecedents and consequents with no logical connections between them. Structural systems imply relations of a quite different kind, correlative [systemic and interdependent] rather than sequential or consecutive. (p. 219)

Taylor (1971) also talked about causally explaining actions by accounting for their underlying meanings. We will talk about inferring causality based on case methods in Chapter 7.

e. Positivistically oriented psychologists often consider interpretation as a preliminary method of describing sociocultural contexts and people's behavior before applying more rigorous and precise measurements and experiments. It is not considered a full-fledged scientific method. This critique can be sorted out if we go back to the distinction between the two metatheoretical paradigms: positivism and interpretivism. As was highlighted above: Positivists apply enumerative methodology to psychological and sociosymbolic phenomena, while interpretivists search for an understanding of a co-construction of sociocultural environments and human mentalities along with the meanings that accompany these processes (the amplification of knowledge). In the interpretivists' view, this goal makes social and human sciences different from the enumerative sciences in principle and thus it is difficult to combine and compare them.

Summary of Interpretivism

The interpretivist paradigm is a full-fledged scientific paradigm directed toward investigating and understanding human-made meaningful realities using scientific thinking and systemic methods and techniques. Ontologically, it deals with the realities of the different systems of meanings—either sociocultural intersubjective or individual idiosyncratic, or both. These systems have surface and deep layers of signification. Such a multi-layered reality requires systematic and scientific investigation to interpret, understand, and explain it. Although these systems of meaning are socially constructed, they are real and have inherent structures and generating powers that should be scientifically investigated. Epistemologically, interpretivists agree that knowledge about meaning requires both empirical and rational components, and that access to the hidden layers of deep meaning is available only through the rational act of abduction performed through interpretation and understanding. They also endorse the idea of a relativity of scientific knowledge, meaning that all scientific hypotheses and theories are fallible—hence, they are *fallibilists* accepting the uncertainty and imperfection of human knowledge. Methodologically, interpretivists work with cases as units of their observation and analysis. They deny a variable-based approach. They implement normative and person-centered ethnography as their main instrument, accompanied by naturalistic and participant observation, interviews, document and archive analyses for thin descriptions, and the hermeneutic circle and abductive reasoning for the thick interpretation.

The Retroductive Mode of Inference and the Realist Paradigm

At the beginning of the previous chapter, I mentioned that the ultimate goal of scientific research is discovering the essence of things—getting to the bottom of the causes and powers that determine events, actions, and various phenomena. In culture and psychology research, this goal could be translated into uncovering the generative powers of the sociocultural worlds, the mechanisms of their influence on people's development, their behaviors and problems. This goal should also be expanded to explaining why people in different communities do what they do, think what they think, and feel what they feel. Does searching for empirical regularities, like in positivism, or abducting different systems of meaning, like in interpretivism, achieve this goal? Many researchers say "Yes" to this question and continue working within these two paradigms.

But the most curious and determined investigators may still feel unsatisfied. They may wonder: What actually stands behind the patterns and regularities of empirical facts? What factors determine different systems of meaning—including social intersubjective and mental intrasubjective? Are there ultimate causal structures and powers, like the law of gravity or the mechanisms of natural selection that underlie a wide diversity of phenomena in the sociocultural and psychological worlds? There are a growing number of social and human scientists who answer the above questions positively. They say that, although positivism and interpretivism constitute valuable options for resolving particular problems, neither of their objectives can be treated as the ultimate goals of scientific inquiry in the social and human sciences. These scholars argue that both empirical regularities and systems of meaning are produced by some hidden structures and powers that together with their regulatory propensities constitute *the mechanisms of the sociocultural and psychological worlds.* Scientists who share this view have been called *realists* and their metatheoretical position has been labeled the *realist paradigm* (Bhaskar, 1975/2008, 1979/2015; Chakravartty, 2010; Leplin, 1984; Niiniluoto, 1999).

INFORMATION BOX 4.4. DIFFERENT FORMS OF REALISM

Real—from late Latin *realis*, from Latin *res* "thing;" actually existing or occurring in fact; not imagined or supposed (Soanes & Stevenson, 2008). **Reality**—the state of things as they actually exist, as opposed to an idealistic or notional idea of them; the state or quality of having existence or substance; philosophy—existence that is absolute or objective and not subject to human decisions or conventions (Soanes & Stevenson, 2008).

Philosophical (ontological) realism is a doctrine that the world exists independently of our conceptions of and knowledge about it. Philosophical realism applies equally to the physical, social, and psychological worlds (see Popper's three worlds in Chapter 3) (Bhaskar, 1975/2008, 1979/2015; Manicas, 2006; Manicas & Secord, 1983).

Naive (direct, shallow, or empirical) realism accepts that what we perceive represents how the world really is; the real world is the world that appears to us (Blaikie, 2007).

Depth realism insists that beneath the surface of empirical events functions a layer of processes and mechanisms that produce these events. "The aim of science based on this ontology is to explain observable phenomena with reference to underlying structures and mechanisms" (Blaikie, 2007, p. 16).

Meaning realism is a belief that the meanings that people assign to things and events in the worlds exist independently of what people, including researchers, know or think about them; meaning is subjective, but real. (See the section on interpretivism above and the discussion in Schwandt, 2007.)

> *Scientific realism* is a combination of philosophical and depth realism in relation to research activities. The world is not only independent of our knowledge, but it also possesses unobservable internal structures and generating powers that constitute the subject matter of scientific theories. Uncovering these powers and the dynamics of their functioning constitutes the goal of all sciences, including the social and human ones. Scientific knowledge in the form of theories is the best explanation of a phenomenon available at a particular time. This knowledge is fallible and can be proved to be wrong; thus, scientific theories are only an approximation of truth (Boyd, 2002; Leplin, 1984).
>
> *Critical realism* is the form of scientific realism mostly associated with the works of Roy Bhaskar (1975/2008, 1979/2015) (who called it *transcendental realism*). There is also a reference to *critical scientific realism* (Niiniluoto, 1999). The adjective "critical" emphasizes an analysis of the advantages and faults of other philosophical paradigms, as well as the emancipatory nature of the knowledge about how the world really works.
>
> The power of realism is that by postulating the deep unobservable but real structures and generative mechanisms that determine things, events, their regularities, and systems of meaning, it invites scholars to discover these entities and, by theorizing about them, develop explanations of events and, thus, generate new knowledge about the worlds.

History of the Realism Paradigm

In Box 3.2., I introduced two modes of inference proposed by Bacon: the anticipation and interpretation of nature, and I commented that while the anticipation of nature can be equated with the conventional enumerative form of induction, the interpretation of nature represents the ampliative form of induction. Applying the interpretation of nature toward unobservable causal structures and mechanisms constituted the essence of retroduction, thus Bacon could be designated as one the first realists proposing retroduction as the primary method of scientific inference (McMullin, 1992; Urbach, 1987).

> Bacon's antipathy to simple enumeration as the universal method of science derived, first of all from his preference for theories that deal with interior physical causes, which are not immediately observable. Simple enumeration cannot do this, for it generalises only upon what is 'known and ordinary.' (Urbach, 1987, p. 30)

Urbach summarized Bacon's view on scientific theories in the following way:

> These theories should preferably concern the underlying physical, causal mechanisms and ought, in any case, to go beyond the data which generated them. They are then tested by drawing out new predictions, which, if verified in experience, may confirm the theory and may eventually render it certain, at least in the sense that it very difficult to deny. (p. 49)

William Whewell (1794–1866), an English philosopher of science and natural scientist, was a follower of Bacon and one of the inductivists who further developed the realist paradigm in the natural sciences (Snyder, 2000, 2006). Whewell believed in ampliative inductive reasoning (he called it "discoverers induction" (Snyder, 1997)) and developed the realist paradigm to its next level. He differentiated "natural kind" phenomena—real things with their generative mechanisms—and "event kind" phenomena—observable manifestations of the functioning of the natural kinds. He provided one of the first definitions of the concept of a *mechanism* that constitutes the central notion of modern realism (Bechtel, 2008; Bhaskar, 1975/2008; Hedstrom, 2005; Sayer, 1992). Whewell also formulated the criteria for evaluating the validity of the hypotheses about unobservable mechanisms, which are: *prediction, consilience,* and *coherence.* (See more about these criteria in Chapter 6).

In the social sciences, one of the strongest defenders of realism was Polish-American sociologist **Florian Znaniecki** (1882–1958). He coined the term *analytic induction* (Znaniecki, 1934), which has gained acceptance in modern sociology (Hammersley, 2012; Robinson, 1951) and psychology (Smith, Harre, & Langenhove, 1995). This form of induction represents the breakthrough of a researcher's thinking from observable events to the unobservable mechanisms of social, cultural, and psychological events. Another sociologist, **Herbert Blumer** (1900–1987), strongly supported the realist interpretation of social phenomena (Blumer, 1969/1986). The realist position has been assigned to the works of French sociologist and anthropologist **Pierre Bourdieu** (1930–2002) and British social philosopher **Anthony Giddens** (1938–) (Danemark et al., 2002).

Some anthropologists are also gravitating toward this paradigm. For example, when describing the intentional nature of sociocultural reality, Shweder (1991) said:

> A sociocultural environment is an intentional world. It is an intentional world because its existence is *real, factual,* and *forceful* [emphasis added] but only so long as there exists a community of persons whose beliefs, desires, emotions, purposes, and other mental representations are directed at, and thereby influenced by, it. (p. 74)

He talked about intentional sociocultural worlds as real and forceful and stated that they are endowed with causal powers that may influence the lives of people and communities. These forceful powers originate in the intriguing networks of intentional and intersubjective relations among members of cultural communities. D'Andrade (1999) also argued about the causal powers of intentional things and advocated for turning from a pure interpretivist approach in anthropology to, what we call, the realism paradigm:

> Cultural norms, beliefs and values, the social system, the economic system, different psychobiological processes, etc., all interact in complex ways to affect action. Rather than continuing to make interpretations forever, anthropology should turn to *working on the way these causal systems interact with each other* [emphasis added]. (p. 14)

The way Benedict thought about and conducted her study of Japanese culture can also lead to it being classified as a realist research.

In psychology the realist paradigm is much less popular than in the other social disciplines (see invitation of psychologist to this philosophy in Manicas & Secord, 1983). One may conclude that the implicit realist intentions are pretty strong among psychology researchers, as they are constantly striving to get to the causal structures of human behavior and experience; but, because of the limits of the positivist paradigm within which most of them work and especially because of the correlational nature of discovered relations, they cannot get to these structures in principle. Cognitive psychologists work most closely to or directly within the realist paradigm and they contemplate the mental mechanisms of human cognition (Bechtel, 2008; Bechtel & Richardson, 2010).

EXAMPLE BOX 4.5. EXAMPLES OF REALIST STUDIES IN THE SOCIOCULTURAL AND PSYCHOLOGICAL SCIENCES

The study by British cultural anthropologist Kate Fox (2004) *Watching the English: The hidden rules of English behavior* is an example of a realist study in anthropology. In this project the researcher aimed "to discover the hidden, unspoken rules of English behavior, and what these rules tell us about our national identity. The object was to identify the commonalities in rules governing English behavior— the unofficial codes of conduct that cut across class, ages, sex, region, sub-culture and other social boundaries" (p. 2). It is fair to notice, that although this research can be considered realist, the search for the patterns and regularities of typical English behavior was also one of the objectives of this project. The author operated broadly by the notion of the meanings of different things for English people as well. This means that elements of both the positivist and interpretivist paradigms were present there. I categorize this study as a realist one because the researcher's ultimate goal was to go beyond both the behavioral regularities and meanings into the unobservable determining powers of culturally driven behavior: its hidden rules.

The second realist feature of this research is its methodology, the way the researcher thought about and conducted her study. It started with naturalistic and participant observations to discover stable patterns and regularities in the behavior of the people in England. These observations were accompanied by interviews with relatives, friends, and strangers about these patterns. Then hypotheses were developed about the nature of the hidden rules of these behaviors. After that, various field experiments and manipulations were implemented to test the validity of these hypotheses.

> Having observed some regularity or pattern in native behavior, and tentatively identified the unspoken rule involved, an ethnographer can apply various "tests" to confirm the existence of such rule. You can tell a representative selection of natives about your observations of their behavior patterns, and ask them if you correctly identified the rule, convention or principle behind this pattern. You can break (hypothetical) rule, and look for signs of disapproval, or indeed active "sanctions." In some cases . . . you can "test" the rule by obeying it, and note whether you are 'rewarded' for doing so. (pp. 8–9)

Following this methodology, Fox entered all possible domains of life of English people: home, driving, work, play, dressing, food, sex, and various rites of passage. In addition to behavioral rules, she uncovered hidden rules of conversations about weather, humor, grooming-talk, pub-talk, and linguistic class codes. Finally, the underlying structure of Englishness was proposed (p. 401).

Another example is a realist research program on understanding the cultural basis of human cognition and communication that was undertaken by an American psychologist Michael Tomasello (1999, 2014). (This research program will also be discussed in Chapter 5). The goal of one of his projects was to investigate the cultural origin of human cognition. First, Tomasello formulated the problem for his research that, within the time frame of the six million years that it took humans to become Homo sapiens equipped with human-specific cognitive skills and symbolic communication, it is nearly impossible to explain these acquisitions by the biological mechanisms of evolution. If not biological evolution, then what mechanisms were responsible for the emergence of human consciousness and cognition? His solution was to hypothesize that this mechanism is a species-specific mode of cultural transmission which leads to "cumulative cultural evolution" and which is responsible "for many of human beings' most impressive cognitive achievements" (p. 7). At the core of human cognition, Tomasello sees our unique capacity for understanding conspecifics as intentional and mental beings like themselves (p. 10). Thus, the objectives of his empirical research were to demonstrate how this capacity evolves in children ontogenetically within their sociosymbolic environments, and how it lays the basis for the higher forms of human cognition and communication. That is, the project was about the hidden mechanisms of the symbolic representations of other intentional beings and the development of a child's own intentionality through meaningful social interactions with adults. As you may imagine, these mechanisms, which, following Vygotskii, could be labelled the mechanisms of the internalization of sociocultural regulations, are unobservable and can never be made visible. Tomasello formulated a set of hypotheses about how these mechanisms may work and tested them through a series of experiments, including comparative studies with chimpanzees.

The Main Features of the Retroductive Mode of Inference

As was mentioned, Peirce used the terms abduction and retroduction interchangeably to name the process of hypothesizing a potential causal explanation of surprising facts. Both of these modes of inference represent the ampliative form of induction. Following the suggestions of some scholars (see above), abduction has been assigned to the interpretivist paradigm, and retroduction has been reserved for the realist paradigm (see Fig. 4.3.).

This is how Sayer (1992) defined retroduction:

> Merely knowing that "C" has generally been followed by "E" is not enough: we want to understand the continuous process by which "C" produces "E," if it did. This mode of inference in which events are explained by postulating (and identifying) mechanisms which are capable of producing them is called *"retroduction."* (p. 107)

Retroductive thinking leads directly to the causal explanation that primarily answers the question: "What processes have to take place in order for the evidence of interest to be observed?" This question invites scholars to think back from the observed events to their causes, thus, *retro-* + in*duction* (McMullin, 1992).

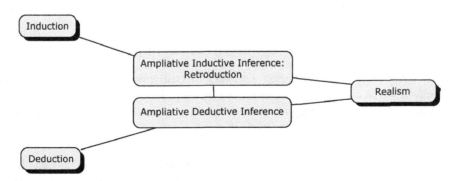

FIGURE. 4.3 Structure of realist thinking. This concept map was made with IHMC Cmap Tools

As a mode of inference, retroduction starts with a conceptualization, meaning that the components of the proposed causal mechanisms have to be identified, labelled, and defined. "*Conceptual abstraction* by means of structural analysis is the core function of social science conceptualization, and from this follows *realist causal analysis*" (Danemark et al., 2002, p. 41). When researchers use concepts to frame a theory of the discovered mechanisms, conceptualization is both the starting point of a realist inquiry and its final product.

The concept of *mechanism* is pivotal for the realist paradigm. Each and every phenomenon that exists in the world is produced by particular mechanisms. There are chemical, evolutionary, cellular, neural, cognitive, sociocultural, psycho-social, political, and economic mechanisms, among others. To explain a phenomenon is to hypothesize about its mechanisms. This concept has recently become popular in the social (Bunge, 1997; Hedstrom, 2005), biological (Craver & Darden, 2013), and psychological sciences (Bechtel & Richardson, 2010; Hogan & Bolhuis, 1994; Wright & Bechtel, 2007).

Bechtel and Wright (2009), philosophers of the mind, provided the following definition of a mechanism:

> A mechanism is simply a composite system organized in such a way that the coordinated operations of the component parts constitute the mechanistic activity identified with the explanandum [what needs to be explained]. Hence, a central feature of mechanisms is that they are mereological: the mechanism as a whole is comprised of component parts, the orchestrated operation of which constitute its function(s). Not infrequently, the parts of a mechanism, are themselves mechanisms consisting of component parts at lower levels, which implies that mechanisms are intrinsically hierarchical. (p. 119)

Sociologists define social mechanisms as:

> a constellation of entities and activities that are linked to one another in such a way that they regularly bring about a particular type of outcome. We explain an observed phenomenon by referring to the social mechanism by which such a phenomenon is regularly brought about. (Hedstrom, 2005, p. 11)

Social and psychological sciences, similar to the natural ones, should strive to discover these mechanisms:

> The task of sociology, according to Pierre Bourdieu (1989a:7), is "to uncover the most profoundly buried structures of the various social worlds which constitute the social universe, as well as the 'mechanisms' which tend to ensure their reproduction or their transformation." (Bourdieu & Wacquant, 1992, p. 7)

Medical anthropologist Arthur Kleinman (1977) directed researchers to study "the complex mechanisms by which culture affects emotions and psychopathology" (p. 5).

A unique example of the explanation through mechanisms in the sociocultural domain is provided by Bourdieu (1984):

> Because it can only account for practices by bringing to light successively the series of effects which underlie them, analysis initially conceals the structure of the life-style characteristic of an agent or class of agents, that is, the unity hidden under the diversity and multiplicity of

the set of practices performed in fields governed by different logics and therefore inducing different forms of realization, in accordance with the formula: [(habitus)(capital)] × field = practice. (p. 101)

This quote can be interpreted in the following way. The ultimate goal of social research is to explain why people execute various social practices in their environments. Bourdieu suggested four main concepts as the components of the explanatory mechanism of such practices: "practice," "habitus," "capital," and "field." In the above quote, he directly spoke of discovering the mechanism that generates these practices ("account for practices by bringing to light successively the series of effects which underlie them"). A researcher investigates the diversity of the practices that people perform in a particular domain and then retroducts the unifying mechanism behind them (discovers "the structure of the life-style characteristics of an agent or class of agents, that is, the unity hidden under the diversity"). The hypothesized mechanism consists of "habitus"—"necessity internalized and converted into a disposition that generates meaningful practices and meaning-giving perceptions" (p. 170)—which interact with "economic," "cultural," and "social capital" "as the set of actually usable resources and powers" (p. 114). This mechanism functions in "fields" of forces that "induc[e] different forms of realization" (p. 114) of it. Bourdieu used this theoretical explanation of social actions to analyze particular practices and specific domains; for example, the choices of arts, recreational, and exercise activities of people belonging to different classes. (See more in Chapter 6).

Explaining a phenomenon by referring to its mechanism was labelled by Bunge (1997) *mechanismic explanation* (p. 411), and Bechtel and Richardson (2010) called it "mechanistic explanation" (p. 17). Mechanisms are real structures and powers of the worlds, and knowledge about them is reflected in incomplete and fallible scientific theories: "mechanisms are not pieces of reasoning, but pieces of the furniture of the real world" (Bunge, 1997, p. 414).

The concept of mechanism is inseparable from the notion of *system* (see Bechtel and Wright's definition above). Systems—political, sociocultural, psychological, etc.—have structures comprised of different components; these components interact with each other and produce the processes that generate the phenomenon of interest. Thus, the mechanismic explanation consists of two parts: a *componential analysis* of the structure of the hypothesized mechanisms and a *processual analysis* of how these components work together. Mechanisms are not induced from empirical data; they have to be retroducted based on these data. Thus, retroduction can be referred to as the process of hypothesizing or conjecturing the explanatory mechanisms of a phenomena. After the explanatory mechanisms are conceptualized and theorized, a researcher has to provide evidence that these mechanisms actually exist and function.

Knowledge of the mechanisms is necessary not only for explaining the phenomenon, but also for efficiently intervening with the goals of eliciting, changing, or preventing that phenomenon. Successful interventions cannot be based on the positivists' regularities like "If A, then B," because interconnections between As and Bs in each particular case vary tremendously from the statistical regularity established by researchers. Only knowledge about the mechanisms—"how it really works"—and about the contextual factors and conditions that influence these mechanisms can provide the basis for a successful intervention.

How Can the Results of Positivist and Interpretivist Studies be Used by Realist Researchers?

Realist researchers do not reject the data obtained by positivists and interpretivists, rather they use them as important sources of information that can help generate and verify their hypotheses. A realist researcher can be compared with a criminal investigator who has to solve a murder case where the victim is dead and the perpetrator is on the run. The opportunity of directly observing the behavior of the perpetrator against the victim is lost forever. The investigator is left with possible evidence: forensic, ballistic, witnesses' accounts, psychological profiling, recognizable patterns of executing the crime, etc. Based on carefully collected pieces of evidence, he or she has to come up with one or two plausible hypotheses about the murder and then work to verify or falsify them by utilizing all possible methods and evidence available. Similar to a criminal investigator, a realist researcher who is investigating the hidden mechanisms of events and behaviors should use all possible evidence to come up with hypotheses and then work to test them. Recall the advice of Bacon (1620/2000) for those who are doing interpretations of nature:

> *Interpretations* by contrast are gathered piece by piece from things which are quite various and widely scattered, and cannot suddenly strike the intellect. So that, to common opinion, they cannot help seeming hard and incongruous, almost like mysteries of faith. (p. 38)

That is why almost everything that pertains to a researcher's case—statistical frequencies and regularities, records of naturalistic and participant observations, interview transcripts, diaries, letters, pictures and other visualizations, various layers of meanings—should be used to solve a research problem.

There are two main forms of empirical regularities, *necessary* and *accidental*. *Necessary empirical regularities* are manifestations of the causal mechanisms that produce them. Therefore, discovering them is an important step in starting a realist investigation. *Accidental regularities* do not reflect a manifestation of the mechanisms and should be ignored. Statistical associations do not differentiate between these two, and the goal of realist researchers who decide to use empirical regularities discovered by positivists is to separate accidental regularities from the necessary ones and focus on the analysis of the latter.

Even more important for realist researchers are data obtained by interpretivists through interpretation and abduction. Realists accept that the meanings (especially the in-depth taken-for-granted ones) that people use to guide and direct their actions, thoughts, and feelings may constitute important components of the causal mechanisms and, thus, are crucial to explaining people's behavior.

> Social worlds are inherently meaningful. It is necessary to understand the meaning people assign to their actions in order to understand the actions. The actions in their turn mediate everyday social phenomena as well as deeper underlying structural relations, which are constitutive of the society under study. (Danemark, et al., 2002, p. 36)

But in contrast to interpretivists, who believe that providing interpretations of lives, actions, and meanings constitutes the ultimate goal of sociocultural sciences, realists encourage researchers to look behind these meanings and search for the explanatory mechanisms behind them.

> In opposition to some interpretative social science approaches, we [realists] claim that an interpretation of the "second order" [the same as double hermeneutics] does not constitute a social scientific explanation either. It is not enough just to build on various social agents' own descriptions and understandings of themselves and of existence. As we have already pointed out, social phenomena have material dimension, and it is essential to explore how people's notions and concepts are related to social practices of various kinds. (p. 37)

By acting in a particular way and being driven by the meanings of a situation and one's own actions, an actor remains unaware of the structures and forces that created the situation and required him or her to deal with it. The agent is also unaware that by acting he or she reproduces the very forces that stand behind the whole situation. "People can be coerced into consenting to arrangements by forces that they do not understand, and in doing so, they can produce and reproduce social structures of whose existence they may be entirely unaware" (Shapiro, 2005, p. 32). To uncover these forces and structures is the precise goal of a realist social or human scientist. To do this efficiently, realist researchers should generate and use both 'quantitative' and 'qualitative' data. Realists labelled this multidata multimethod approach "critical methodological pluralism" (Danemark et al., 2002, p. 152). This means that for realists, all empirical evidence is relevant once these data address the problem to be resolved. Other terms that realists use to describe their methodological approach to research are the contrasting terms *extensive* and *intensive designs* (Danemark et al., 2002; Sayer, 1992). I will discuss these two forms of design in Chapter 7.

Procedures and Techniques for Facilitating Retroductive Inferences

As we discussed above, the retroductive inference constitutes the logical basis of the context of discovery. Within this context, a researcher has to make a breakthrough from the evidence to a hypothesis about the hidden, unobservable structures and generative powers that produce this evidence. But how can this breakthrough be made? In the section on interpretivism, we discussed the technique of the hermeneutic circle that is used to extract deep layers of meanings. Below we present other techniques that are suggested for conducting retroductive inferences.

Shank and Cunningham (1996) recommend that researchers treat empirical evidence: numbers, regularities, actions, artifacts, recorded thoughts, emotions, interpreted meanings, etc., as *clues directing toward* or *signs of hidden mechanisms*. Once these clues and signs become plentiful and reliable, it is more likely that these causal mechanisms will be discovered. By using the evidence as symptoms, a researcher resembles a physician who is trying to diagnose a disease in a patient based on test results and a patient's own verbal accounts. The same authors cite *argument by analogy* and *metaphorical thinking* as other methods that can be used to move from empirical premises to ampliative inductive conclusions. Abbott (2004) believes that making an analogy is "in many ways most important of the general heuristics" (p. 114), where general heuristics "are tested ways of broadening what you are doing, ways to come up with new ideas, new methods, or new data, ways to get unstuck for coming up with new ideas" (p. 112). A researcher uses a metaphor or an analogy with existing processes, phenomena, or mechanisms from other disciplines or domains of life to shed light on his or her particular case and to help compile collected evidence into a coherent hypothesis about the hidden mechanisms. For example, in his attempt to understand and explain people's social behavior, social psychologist Ervin Goffman (1959) used the analogy of a theatrical performance: meaning that he saw people's behavior on a social scene to be analogous to actors' performance in a theater, where actors manipulate people's perception and judgment about them by using various methods and techniques. This analogy helped Goffman to provide one of the most influential accounts of the hidden mechanisms of social behavior. Danemark et al. (2002) complemented these techniques with: *counterfactual thinking*, *social experiments and thought experiments*, *studying pathological and extreme cases*, and *comparative case studies* (pp. 100–106).

INFORMATION BOX 4.6. INSIGHT AND INTUITION IN RETRODUCTION

Insight and intuition are two processes that are frequently mentioned with regard to retroduction. Insight is "the capacity to gain an accurate and deep understanding of something" (Soanes & Stevenson, 2008), whereas intuition is "the ability to understand something immediately, without the need for conscious reasoning" (Soanes & Stevenson, 2008). Waller (1934) put insight at the center of any scientific inquiry. He based his logic of insightful scientific inquiry on the ideas of the Gestalt psychologists who stated "that mental events do not occur as separate and discrete sensations, but in organized wholes" (p. 285). Their major experiments were conducted on human perception and indicated that whatever configurations of dots, shades, or other elements are presented to participants, they see and infer particular patterns (gestalts) that make these configurations more or less meaningful to them. If we move to the domain of scientific inquiries, the search for and discovering of gestalts among evidence, thoughts, arguments, and hypotheses constitute the essence of intellectual insight, or "Eureka!" Think about the insights regarding the periodic table of chemical elements by Mendeleev: "It is sometimes said that he played 'chemical solitaire' on long train journeys using cards with various facts of known elements" (from http://en.wikipedia.org/wiki/History_of_the_periodic_table). Kekulé's benzene formula reflects this process as well:

> He said that he had discovered the ring shape of the benzene molecule after having a reverie or daydream of a snake seizing its own tail. This vision, he said, came to him after years of studying the nature of carbon-carbon bonds.... He told yet another anecdote in 1890, of a vision of dancing atoms and molecules that led to his theory of structure. This happened, he claimed, while he was riding on the upper deck of a horse-drawn omnibus in London. (from http://en.wikipedia.org/wiki/Friedrich_August_Kekulé_von_Stradonitz).

Modern philosophers move to defend insight as a legitimate component of clinical scientific reasoning (Braude, 2012).

Counterfactual thinking is based on a disciplined imagination of the possible presence or absence of conditions that produce or change the phenomena under scrutiny. This type of thinking is accompanied by abstraction and reasoning based on existing knowledge about the object of a study by asking counterfactual questions like, What if . . .? Or What would happen if . . .? (Abbott, 2004, pp. 158–161).

> Counterfactual thinking is fundamental for all retroduction. We ask questions like: How would this be if not . . . ? Could one imagine X without . . . ? Could one imagine X including this, without X then becoming something different? In counterfactual thinking we use our stored experience and knowledge of social reality, as well as our ability to abstract and to think about what is not, but what might be. (Danemark, et al., 2002, p. 101)

Counterfactual thinking is based on deliberating "contrary to the facts," meaning imagining what a phenomenon under study may look like if it possessed or did not possess particular qualities and characteristics. What if money disappeared? What if all the oil on the earth disappeared?

> If we consider presence and absence, the necessary and contingent, the constitutive and the non-constitutive as opposites, we can say that counterfactual thinking is at the same time dialectics, since in this reasoning we examine something in relations to its opposite (p. 101)

Counterfactual thinking also allows researchers to understand more deeply what they discover and to create better arguments by posing their cases against the counterfactuals. In studying sexuality a researcher may ask: What if people's sexual lives unfolded without restrictions from their community and society? Answering this and similar questions may provide a researcher with the opportunity to better understand the nature and purpose of social rituals, taboos, restrictions, and sanctions regarding sexuality.

Experiments in Retroductive Realist Research

Since its emergence at the dawn of scientific empirical thinking during the Middle Ages, an *experiment*—a purposeful manipulation of environmental conditions in order to control for changes in the object of a study—has been considered the primary technique to discover scientific laws and to establish causal relations between variables. Experiments are used both within the positivist and realist paradigms, but they have different logic and different implications.

In the positivist paradigm, an experiment is no more than a well-refined establishment of an empirical regularity among events or among the conditions and events, like "If A, then B." In a precise and controlled way, it sets up a situation when, if condition or event A is present, then event B happens. Based on the requirements of randomness of participants' assignments to the conditions and on a tight control for confounding conditions, experimentalists make an inference about the causal relations between A and B: If the hypothesized relation between A and B is experimentally verified, then it is possible to say that A causes B. This is an old and mainly rejected interpretation of causality that is based on Hume's idea that "causal relations are regular contingent relations between events" (Manicas & Secord, 1983, p. 400). The benefits of experiment here are that in comparison to other methods, like observation, interview, or survey, experiment provides a more refined articulation of necessary conditions for the dependent variable to emerge or change, thus providing strong evidence of potential causal relations. But in reality, this form of experiment does not go above and beyond covariances between events/conditions/variables, similar to what well-developed surveys do. And because covariances do not necessarily mean causality, this type of experiment does not generate knowledge about the unobservable causal mechanisms of events, although it can be useful in leading researchers in this direction.

The realist paradigm provides a different rationale for experiments. Realist experiments are not about establishing necessary connections among events, "but are about the causal properties of structures that exist and operate in the world. This difference is crucial" (p. 402). Based on the hypothesis/theory that a causal mechanism produces a phenomenon, an experimenter specifies the conditions under which this mechanism will produce the phenomenon and under which it will not. The realist researcher manipulates these conditions within an experiment while keeping irrelevant contextual factors under tight control. Realists would say that an experiment allows them to test their hypotheses under the condition of *closed systems*, meaning systems that are artificially protected from the influence of factors that operate in the real world of *open systems*. Under these *conditions of closure* (Bhaskar, 1975/2008), realists isolate the causal mechanisms and verify the lawful way they operate. A successful experiment verifies a hypothesis about the causal properties of the mechanism and allows the researcher to propose an explanatory theory about the phenomenon under scrutiny. Real world open systems function not only under the influence of the discovered causal mechanism but also under the influence of other mechanisms and numerous external and internal conditions that moderate and mediate these mechanisms' work. Following this predicament, applied researchers may test what conditions facilitate and what conditions hinder the function of these mechanisms in the real world, and they may study the ways different causal mechanisms interact with each other. The fact that under some conditions these mechanisms do not necessarily produce predicted events does not mean that the theory is not valid, rather that a researcher needs to discover the conditions under which the mechanisms operate.

EXAMPLE BOX 4.7. AN EXAMPLE OF REALIST EXPERIMENTATION IN SOCIAL RESEARCH

Consider an example from the Englishness project of Fox (2004), which I used as an illustration of a realist study in Box 4.5:

> I am sitting in pub near Paddington station, clutching a small brandy. It's only about half past eleven in the morning—a bit early for drinking, but the alcohol is part reward, part Dutch courage. Reward because I have just spent an exhausting morning accidentally-on-purpose bumping into people and counting the number who said 'Sorry;" Dutch courage because I am now about to return to the train station and spend a few hours committing a deadly sin: queue jumping.
>
> I really, really do not want to do this. I want to adopt my usual method of getting an unsuspected research assistant *to break sacred social rules* while I watch the result from a safe distance. But this time, I have bravely decided that I must be my own guinea pig. I don't feel brave. I feel scared. My arms are all bruised from the *bumping experiments* [emphasis added]. I want to abandon the whole stupid Englishness project here and now, go home, have a cup of tea and lead a normal life. (p. 1)

This anthropologist is conducting the social experiment of breaking sociocultural norms and rules and observing people's reactions. The experimenter did the "bumping experiment" to test the hypothesis about the rules of English polite behavior in that only English people will apologize for the inconveniences created by others. Now the researcher is preparing to do another experiment: queue jumping. The first experiment is not directed toward establishing the regularity "If I bump into an English person, he or she will be the first to apologize," but to test the hypothesis that overpoliteness is one of the rules of English behavior. (The researcher could complement her experiment in London with the same experiment in, for example, Moscow, and observe how frequently or infrequently Russians are overpolite). In the second experiment, her goal is not to discover the regularity that "If I jump a queue, people will be angry with me," but to test a hypothesis related to the problem of typical English behavior and the English identity that "fair play" is at the essence of the English character.

It is important to mention that realist research is primarily case-based and not variable-based, as the majority of positivist studies are. The differences between these two forms of study designs as well as the differences and commonalities between nomothetic and ideographic studies will be discussed in Chapter 7. Here I only mention the application of *pathological circumstances* and *extreme cases* as the means to promote retroductive thinking (Danemark et al., 2002).

> To get an answer to the question 'How is X possible?' we can study various cases where the preconditions for X appear much more clearly than in others. There are at least two types of cases where social conditions and mechanisms are very obvious: first, those where the conditions are challenged and the mechanisms are disturbed; and second, extreme cases where mechanisms appear in an almost pure form. (p. 104)

Bhaskar (1979/2015) also mentioned that generative structures may be more available for understanding and researching in periods of transition and crisis. Such pathological and extreme cases as well as conditions of crisis make the causal mechanisms more obvious, facilitating the retroductive thinking about their properties. Take, for example, the process of acculturation of immigrants. Moving to another country, facing a new language, new traditions, and norms is definitely a stressful period for immigrants and their families. This is a time when their home culture based sociocultural norms of behavior regulation are not in power any more while the new ones are not yet learned. Consider such pathological cases when male immigrants have killed their wives or daughters only because these women did not comply with the rules and regulations that existed in their home sociocultural communities and instead started embracing the rules and norms of their new social lives. In these cases the mechanisms of acculturation went wrong, leading to horrible results. Studying such extreme cases is a productive way for realist researchers to delve into these mechanisms. Thinking further, one may see immigration as a period of transition where the sociocultural and agentic forces of people's social behaviors interact in the most obvious ways. Thus, immigration may be the ideal case to investigate the mechanisms of the functioning of sociocultural structures and human agency, which is one of the fundamental problems of modern social theories. Studying this period of transition will be especially fruitful if a researcher has a theory of the mechanisms of human agency which can be tested under the different socio-cultural conditions that immigrants go through.

Summary of Realism

Ontologically, as is clear from the name of the paradigm, its representatives are deep realists. First, they believe that the worlds exist "out there" independently of our thoughts and conceptions about them. Second, these real worlds are comprised of unobservable structures and generative powers that determine and guide events, people's systems of meaning and their actions. These unobservable mechanisms are not directly accessible, but they are knowable; and discovering them constitutes the ultimate target of any scientific research. Epistemologically, realists believe that knowledge about unobservables is fallible (hence, they are *fallibilists*) and is a social, cultural, and historical product (hence, they are *epistemological social constructionists*). Regardless of these limitations, realists believe that scientific theories reflect and represent the deep layers of reality—however incomplete or falsifiable these theories may be. Methodologically, realists conduct problem-oriented research and endorse all possible methods pertaining to the resolution of these problems (critical methodological pluralism). The main intellectual tool of realist thinking is retroduction, which represents the ampliative forms of induction and deduction. Realists almost completely deny the variable-based approach but endorse case-based analysis in its numerous variations accompanied by a multiplicity of techniques and procedures (see *intensive* versus *extensive research design in* Chapter 7).

Critique of the Realist Paradigm

Despite its fundamental importance for scientific research, realism is not widely accepted in many social and behavioral sciences, including cultural psychology. In addition, there are intensive philosophical debates between realists and antirealists of various strains, which I can only briefly mention here.

The antirealist paradigms are represented by strong versions of social constructionism, pragmatism, conventionalism, and some other idealist and postmodernist philosophical doctrines. Antirealists argue, first of all, that we do not know if reality exists out there and, even if it exists, they believe that we can never get to know it. Antirealists claim that "the world is just what we take it to be according to our current interpretative practices" (Schwandt, 2007, p. 258). They believe that the validity of scientific propositions and theories is not in their reflection of the real mechanisms of phenomena; rather, it is a matter of conceptual frameworks and linguistic constructions—"a particular habit of construing evidence according to some logic of inquiry that we have adopted that answers to our own ideas of what is good in the way of belief" (p. 258). These are some of the criticisms of the realist position that are continuously debated in the philosophy of science (See, Chakravartty, 2013; Leplin, 1984).

Moving to research methodology, I will address two concerns raised by Alvesson & Skölberg (2009). These authors argued that the realists' claim that methods of research should be congruent with the nature of the object of a study (a claim that is strongly endorsed and propagated in this textbook), or, worded differently, that the object of the study should direct the methodology of its investigation, is a "naïve conception" (p. 45). In their opinion, what constitutes the object of a study and its necessary constituent properties depends on the views and perspectives of the researchers. This means that reality is defined and constructed by researchers and does not exist independently of them: "uses of different perspectives would probably lead to different properties and different produced objects" (p. 45). Such an argument is a classic example of the *epistemological fallacy* that realists try to avoid (Bhaskar, 1975/2008, p. 36). The epistemic fallacy consists of reducing ontological questions to epistemological ones (Collier, 1994, p.9). This means that instead of inquiring about the nature of reality (an ontological question), scholars argue about the social construction of the theoretical accounts of this reality (an epistemological question). The consequences of the epistemic fallacy is that the researchers who are prone to it do not study the reality, rather they study their own verbal projections of it, and they are primarily concerned with the terms, definitions, and other semantic constructions that are involved in formulating the researchers' statements. Such concerns create an illusion of scientific activity, while in fact the scholars are actually playing endless and ultimately useless "language games" instead of addressing the realities around them. As a result, real psycho-social problems such as the honor killings of immigrant women, bullying, hate crimes, and many other social pathologies remain unexplained, while researchers compete with each other over the fanciness of their epistemological perspectives on these events. The sad part is, as they argue about the relativity of what "honor killings" may stand for, these killings continue.

Alvesson & Skölberg's other complaint is about "the unproductive concepts of structure and mechanism" (p. 46) which, in their opinion, are vague and, finally, fruitless. Let's take, for example, their interpretation of the concept of mechanism. They deny that the idea of mechanism can be applied to social phenomena: "Described in these terms [in terms of mechanisms], social phenomena come across as mechanical and often they run the risk of being overtly simplified" (p. 48). They continue: "it is not always clear what mechanisms are, for instance as distinguished from underlying patterns (the latter are said to be revealed by abduction, the former via 'retroduction,' and it is rather unclear what the difference really is)" (p. 48). In our opinion this is another example of critiquing a theoretical position without demonstrating its deep and comprehensive understanding or having an *a priori* biased attitude that the authors want to promulgate. As was mentioned above, the concept of mechanism is a complex one, requiring deep theoretical and empirical investigation. For some students, it may seem like a mechanical, rigid, inflexible, one-way, and deterministic way of viewing a phenomenon that may stand in contrast with the demand for an approach that reflects a modern, flexible, multi-perspectival approach to sociocultural and sociopsychological phenomena. This is an erroneous understanding of this very powerful idea, and its complexity is not the basis for its critique and denial.

Conclusion

The ampliative ways of research thinking are the most mysterious and inexplicable forms of rational reasoning. To account for them, philosophers of science introduced two concepts: abduction and retroduction, which both allow researchers to hypothesize about unobservable meanings, mechanisms, and generating powers. Researchers should use abduction in relation to extracting different systems of meaning within the interpretivist paradigm. Interpretation and understanding are the core processes of such abductive inferences. The hermeneutical circle, which is based on dialectical circling between the whole and the particulars, is proposed as the main technique for interpretation. It is also suggested to differentiate the thin form of description from the thick version of interpretation that can be applied to sociocultural and idiosyncratic systems of meaning. Retroduction is associated with the realist paradigm and aims toward discovering unobserved causal mechanisms by going back from empirical facts to the causes that produce them. Retroductive inferences can be facilitated by using various techniques and methods for breaking through empirical facts to unobservables.

Questions

1. Provide examples from your everyday life when you have used abductive/retroductive thinking. Analyze the structure of this thinking and identify its main components and dynamics.
2. Why are both abduction and retroduction considered to be ampliative forms of induction and deduction? Justify your answer.
3. Why did McMullin call abduction/retroduction "the inference that makes science?"
4. Following the example of Darwin, provide your own reflections on the abductive/retroductive nature of the development of some of the well-known theories by Freud, Piaget, Vygotskii, or others.
5. What is *meaning* with regard to human behavior and experience? What two systems of meaning are discussed in the chapter?
6. What is *hermeneutics* and how do you understand *the hermeneutic circle* (THC)? Take an instance of behavior or conversation with your colleague(s) and apply THC to extract the meanings of these actions or utterances. Reflect on the dynamics of your thinking.
7. The chapter labelled *interpretation* as a form of abduction. Justify this claim.
8. Discuss in class the four types of interpretation and provide examples of each.
9. Use the interpretation of your colleague's behavior from question 6 and apply to it all the points of critique outlined in the chapter. Support and justify that interpretation is a valid scientific way of thinking.
10. Is human mental life *real*? Justify your answer.
11. Provide examples of realist retroductive thinking in psychology.
12. What is *mechanism* with regard to people's functioning in different cultures? How do you understand the *mechanismic explanation*?
13. Compare positivist, interpretivist and realist thinking about the same phenomenon (for example: the acculturation of immigrants, bullying, family violence, people's happiness).
14. How can realists use the results of positivist and interpretivist studies?
15. Discuss the main techniques for retroductive thinking.
16. Provide critical reflections on the realist paradigm.

Glossary

Abduction (the **abductive mode of inference**) is a way of thinking that occurs when a researcher starts with a problem and empirical evidence regarding it and then suggests a hypothesis of why this problem exists and how the empirical evidence can be explained. This mode of inference is also called *inference to the best explanation*. In the original version, Peirce used this term as a synonym of retroduction. Later scholars suggested using the term abduction to describe the process of interpretation and extracting different forms of meaning.

Hermeneutic circle, the: a rational process of apprehending particulars based on their relations to the whole and then enriching the whole by the new knowledge of particulars. The hermeneutic circle lies at the core of most forms of interpretation.

Interpretation is a sequence of intellectual processes to discover systems of meaning and their dimensions and structures, both in the sociocultural worlds and in the worlds of personal lives, actions, and experiences. It is considered to be the core element of abduction in its use in the interpretivist paradigm. After grasping these meanings, researchers provide logical and linguistic arrangements of the explicated ideas by connecting them to available evidence, previous research, and other interpretations. Based on these acts of interpretation, researchers reach an understanding of sociocultural and mental-experiential phenomena. Interpretation and interpretative understanding are the main analytical tools that make interpretative human and social sciences different from the natural ones.

Interpretivism: a philosophical paradigm rooted in the hermeneutic tradition that is based on the assumption that in order to understand peoples' lives in their sociocultural contexts, it is important to interpret the symbolic systems that exist in these contexts as well as in people's idiosyncratic systems of meaning.

Meaning (also, **systems of meaning**): a signification of something by something else. A piece of paper is called money and has trade value in societies. There are linguistic, sociocultural, and idiosyncratic forms of meaning. All forms of meaning are arranged in systems, where meanings of events, things, and actions are built into a coherent but flexible structure that works as a context for and as a determinant of human actions and experiences. *Sociocultural systems of meaning*—intersubjective collective significations of the world, other people and individual selves. *Idiosyncratic systems of meaning*—intrasubjective significations that are unique for each person.

Realism (also, *scientific* and *critical realism*) is a philosophical paradigm that ontologically differentiates empirical—sensed and measurable—from real—unobservable and causally powerful—levels of any reality. The goal of science is to retroduct the unobservable mechanisms at the level of the real in order to explain the empirical facts and evidence. Retroducted hypotheses are the products of the social activity of scientists (socially constructed) and are falsifiable. The hypotheses that continue receiving empirical support become theories that serve as the basis for interventions.

Reality: this term represents how things and events really are rather than as they appear to be or are experienced by us. Reality exists independently of our knowledge about it. Our knowledge about it can be true, partially true, or false, but never absolute and complete. Reality possesses generative powers and causal mechanisms that determine constellations and regularities of empirical events. Our experience of these events does not give us direct access to the mechanisms of reality. This term is applied to nature (natural or physical reality), human mental life (psychological or mental reality) and sociocultural worlds (sociocultural reality). Any paradigm that denies the existence of reality cannot serve as a basis for scientific inquiries.

Retroduction: (*retro- induction*—thinking back from empirical evidence to their causes); (**the retroductive mode of inference**) was initially used as a synonym for abduction, but later became associated with hypothesizing about causal mechanisms and generative powers of different things, events, and processes. Many philosophers of science associate it with the realist paradigm.

Thin and thick descriptions (also *surface hermeneutics/interpretation* and *depth hermeneutics/interpretation*): two types of description/interpretation that are used by interpretivists. Thin description is an account of actions, events, and practices by usually naming them and providing their descriptive report. Thick description/interpretation is a process of abducting deeper layers of "intersubjective constitutive meanings" (Taylor, 1971, p. 24) that stand behind the observed actions and practices and provide their explanation. Thick description may also be applied to individuals' intrasubjective constitutive systems of meanings.

Understanding (*Verstehen*, German) is a term for the process and result of comprehension of the meaning of intentional realities as well as the sense that individual agents assign to the actions of others as well as their own behaviors. It is a pan-human universal phenomenon that applies both to people's everyday comprehensions as well as to human and social scholars' grasping of different systems of meaning during their studies. Understanding that is based on the interpretation of different systems of meaning was labelled *interpretive understanding*.

Recommended Reading for Interpretivism

Blaikie, N. (2007). *Approaches to social enquiry: Advancing knowledge*. Cambridge, UK: Polity.

Diesing, P. (1991). *How does social science work? Reflections on practice*. Pittsburgh, PA: University of Pittsburgh Press.

Polkinghorne, D. (1983). *Methodology for the human sciences: Systems of inquiry*. Albany, NY: State University of New York Press.

Ricœur, P. (1981). *Hermeneutics and the human sciences: Essays on language, action and interpretation*. Cambridge, UK: Cambridge University Press

Taylor, C. (1971). Interpretation and the science of man. *The Review of Metaphysics, 25*(1), 3–51.

Recommended Reading for Realism

Bhaskar, R. (1975/2008). *A realist theory of science*. London, UK: Verso.

Bhaskar, R. (1979/2015). *The possibility of naturalism: A philosophical critique of the contemporary human sciences* (4th ed.). Oxon, UK: Routledge.

Blaikie, N. (2010). *Designing social research: The logic of anticipation*. (2nd ed.). Cambridge, UK: Polity.

Danemark, B., Ekstrom, M., Jakobsen, L., & Karlsson, J. C. (2002). *Explaining society: Critical realism in the social sciences*. London, UK: Routledge

Manicas, P. T., & Secord, P. F. (1983). Implications for psychology of the new philosophy of science. *American Psychologist, 38*(4), 399–413.

Rozeboom, W. W. (1997). Good science is abductive, not hypothetico-deductive. In L. L. Harlow, S. A. Mulaik & J. H. Steiger (Eds.), *What if there were no significance tests?* (pp. 335–391). Mahwah, NJ: Lawrence Erlbaum

Sayer, A. (1992). *Methods in social science: A realist approach*. (2nd ed.). London: Routledge.

References

Abbott, A. (2004). *Methods of discovery: Heuristics for the social sciences*. New York, NY: Norton.

Alvesson, M., & Sköldberg, K. (2009). *Reflexive methodology: New vistas for qualitative research* (2nd ed.). Los Angeles, CA: Sage.

Bacon, F. (1620/2000). *The new organon*. Cambridge, UK: Cambridge University Press.

Bechtel, W. (2008). *Mental mechanisms: Philosophical perspectives on cognitive neuroscience*. New York, NY: Routledge.

Bechtel, W., & Richardson, R. C. (2010). *Discovering complexity: Decomposition and localization as strategies in scientific research* (2nd ed.). Cambridge, MA: MIT Press.

Bechtel, W., & Wright, C. D. (2009). What is psychological explanation? In J. Symons & P. Calvo (Eds.), *The Routledge companion to philosophy of psychology* (pp. 113–130). London, UK: Routledge.

Benedict, R. (1946/1974). *The chrysanthemum and the sword: Patterns of Japanese culture*. Boston, MA: Houghton Mifflin.

Berger, P. L., & Luckmann, T. (1966/1989). *The social construction of reality: A treatise in the sociology of knowledge*. New York, NY: Anchor Books.

Bhaskar, R. (1975/2008). *A realist theory of science*. London, UK: Verso.

Bhaskar, R. (1979/2015). *The possibility of naturalism: A philosophical critique of the contemporary human sciences* (4th ed.). Oxon, UK: Routledge.

Blaikie, N. (2007). *Approaches to social enquiry: Advancing knowledge.* Cambridge, UK: Polity.

Blaikie, N. (2010). *Designing social research: The logic of anticipation.* (2nd ed.). Cambridge, UK: Polity.

Blumer, H. (1969/1986). *Symbolic interactionism: Perspective and method.* Berkeley, CA: University of California Press.

Bourdieu, P. (1984). *Distinction: A social critique of the judgement of taste* (R. Nice, Trans.). Cambridge, MA: Harvard University Press.

Bourdieu, P., & Wacquant, L. J. D. (1992). *An invitation to reflexive sociology.* Chicago, IL: University of Chicago Press.

Boyd, R. (2002). Scientific realism. In E. N. Zalta (Ed.), *The Stanford encyclopedia of philosophy.* Retrieved from http://plato.stanford.edu/archives/sum2010/entries/scientific-realism/ (Summer 2010 ed.).

Braude, H. D. (2012). *Intuition in medicine: A philosophical defense of clinical reasoning.* Chicago, IL: University of Chicago Press.

Bunge, M. (1997). Mechanism and explanation. *Philosophy of Social Science, 27*(4), 410–465.

Chakravartty, A. (2010). *A metaphysics for scientific realism: Knowing the unobservable.* Cambridge, UK: Cambridge University Press.

Chakravartty, A. (2013). Scientific realism. In E. N. Zalta (Ed.), *The Stanford Encyclopedia of Philosophy.* Retrieved from http://plato.stanford.edu/entries/scientific-realism/ (Summer 2013 ed.).

Chirkov, V. (2010). Dialectical relationships among human autonomy, the brain, and culture. In V. I. Chirkov, R. M. Ryan & K. M. Sheldon (Eds.), *Human autonomy in cross-cultural contexts: Perspectives on the psychology of agency, freedom, and well-being* (pp. 65–92). Dordrecht, The Netherlands: Springer.

Chirkov, V. (2014). The universality of psychological autonomy across cultures: Arguments from developmental and social psychology. In N. Weinstein (Ed.), *Human motivation and interpersonal relationships: Theory, research, and applications.* (pp. 27–52). Dordrecht, The Netherlands: Springer.

Collier, A. (1994). *Critical realism: An introduction to Roy Bhaskar's philosophy.* London, UK: Verso.

Craver, C. F., & Darden, L. (2013). *In search of mechanisms: Discoveries across the life sciences.* Chicago, IL: University of Chicago Press.

D'Andrade, R. G. (1995). *The development of cognitive anthropology.* Cambridge, UK: Cambridge University Press.

D'Andrade, R. G. (1999). Culture is not everything. In E. L. Cerroni-Long (Ed.). *Anthropological theory in North America* (pp. 85-103). Westport, CT: Bergin and Garvey.

Danemark, B., Ekstrom, M., Jakobsen, L., & Karlsson, J. C. (2002). *Explaining society: Critical realism in the social sciences.* London, UK: Routledge.

Diesing, P. (1991). *How does social science work? Reflections on practice.* Pittsburgh, PA: University of Pittsburgh Press.

Douven, I. (2011). Abduction. In E. N. Zalta (Ed.), *The Stanford Encyclopedia of Philosophy.* Retrieved from http://plato.stanford.edu/entries/abduction/

Fox, K. (2004). *Watching the English: The hidden rules of English behavior.* London, UK: Hodder & Stoughton.

Gadamer, H.-G. (1959/1988). On the circle of understanding. *Hermeneutics versus science?* In J. M. Connelly & T. Keutner (Eds.). *Three German views.* (pp. 68–78). Notre Dame, IN: University of Notre Dame Press.

Gadamer, H.-G. (1998). *Truth and method* (2nd rev. ed.). New York, NY: Continuum.

Geertz, C. (1973). *The interpretation of cultures.* New York, NY: Basic Books.

Goffman, E. (1959). *Presentation of self in everyday life.* Garden City, NY: Doubleday.

Hammersley, M. (2012). Qualitative causal analysis: Grounded theorizing and the qualitative survey. In B. Cooper, J. Glaesser, R. Gomm & M. Hammersley (Eds.), *Challenging the qualitative-quantitative divide: Explorations in case-focused causal analysis* (pp. 72–95). London, UK: Continuum.

Hanson, N. R. (1958). *Patterns of discovery: An inquiry into the conceptual foundations of science.* Cambridge, UK: Cambridge University Press.

Hedstrom, P. (2005). *Dissecting the social: On the principles of analytical sociology.* Cambridge, UK: Cambridge University Press.

Hirsch, E. D. (1967). *Validity in interpretation.* New Haven, CT: Yale University Press.

Hogan, J. A., & Bolhuis, J. J. (Eds.). (1994). *Causal mechanisms of behavioural development* Cambridge, UK: Cambridge University Press.

Kleinman, A. M. (1977). Depression, somatization and the "new cross-cultural psychiatry". *Social Science & Medicine, 11*(1), 3–10.

Langenhove, L. V. (1995). The theoretical foundations of experimental psychology and its alternatives. In J. A. Smith, R. Harre & L. V. Langenhove (Eds.), *Rethinking psychology* (pp. 10–23). London, UK: Sage.

Leplin, J. (Ed.). (1984). *Scientific realism*. Berkeley, CA: University of California Press.

Lipton, P. (2004). *Inference to the best explanation*. London, UK: Routledge.

Manicas, P. T. (2006). *A realist philosophy of social science: Explanation and understanding*. Cambridge, UK: Cambridge University Press.

Manicas, P. T., & Secord, P. F. (1983). Implications for psychology of the new philosophy of science. *American Psychologist, 38*(4), 399–413.

McMullin, E. (1992). *The inference that makes science*. Milwaukee, WI: Marquette University Press.

Niiniluoto, I. (1999). *Critical scientific realism*. Oxford, UK: Oxford University Press.

Peirce, C. S. (1960). *Collected papers of Charles Peirce* (Vol. 5–6). Cambridge, MA: Belknap Press.

Polkinghorne, D. (1983). *Methodology for the human sciences: Systems of inquiry*. Albany, NY: State University of New York Press.

Ricœur, P. (1981). *Hermeneutics and the human sciences: Essays on language, action and interpretation*. Cambridge, UK: Cambridge University Press.

Robinson, W. S. (1951). The logical structure of analytic induction. *American Sociological Review, 16*(6), 812–818.

Rozeboom, W. W. (1997). Good science is abductive, not hypothetico-deductive. In L. L. Harlow, S. A. Mulaik & J. H. Steiger (Eds.), *What if there were no significance tests?* (pp. 335–391). Mahwah, NJ: Lawrence Erlbaum.

Ryle, G. (1971). *Collected papers. Volume II: Collected essays, 1929–1968*. New York, NY: Barnes & Noble.

Sayer, A. (1992). *Methods in social science: A realist approach*. (2nd ed.). London, UK: Routledge.

Schwandt, T. A. (2007). *The SAGE dictionary of qualitative inquiry*. (3rd ed.). Thousand Oaks, CA: Sage.

Shank, G. (1998). The extraordinary ordinary powers of abductive reasoning. *Theory & Psychology, 8*(6), 841–860.

Shank, G., & Cunningham, D. J. (1996). *Modeling the six modes of Peircean abduction for educational purposes*. Paper presented at the Annual Meeting of the Midwest AI and Cognitive Science Conference, Bloomington, IN. Retrieved from http://www.cs.indiana.edu/event/maics96/Proceedings/shank.html

Shapiro, I. (2005). *The flight from the reality in the human sciences*. Princeton, NJ: Princeton University Press.

Shore, B. (1998). *Culture in mind: Cognition, culture, and the problem of meaning*. New York, NY: Oxford University Press.

Shweder, R. A. (1991). Cultural psychology: What is it? In R. A. Shweder (Ed.), *Thinking through cultures: Expeditions in cultural psychology*. (pp. 73–112). Cambridge, MA: Harvard University Press.

Smith, J. A., Harre, R., & Langenhove, L. V. (1995). Idiography and the case-study. In J. A. Smith, R. Harre & L. V. Langenhove (Eds.), *Rethinking psychology* (pp. 59–69). London, UK: Sage.

Snyder, L. J. (1997). Discoverers' induction. *Philosophy of Science, 64*(4), 580–604.

Snyder, L. J. (2000). William Whewell. In E. N. Zalta (Ed.), *The Stanford Encyclopedia of Philosophy*. Retrieved from http://plato.stanford.edu/entries/whewell/

Snyder, L. J. (2006). *Reforming philosophy: A Victorian debate on science and society*. Chicago, IL: University of Chicago Press.

Soanes, C., & Stevenson, A. (Eds.). (2008). *Concise Oxford English dictionary* (11th ed.). Oxford, UK: Oxford University Press.

Taylor, C. (1971). Interpretation and the science of man. *The Review of Metaphysics, 25*(1), 3–51.

Tomasello, M. (1999). *The cultural origins of human cognition*. Cambridge, MA.: Harvard University Press.

Tomasello, M. (2014). *A natural history of human thinking*. Cambridge, MA: Harvard University Press.

Urbach, P. (1987). *Francis Bacon's philosophy of science: An account and a reappraisal*. La Salle, IL: Open Court.

Waller, W. (1934). Insight and scientific method. *American Journal of Sociology, 40*(3), 285–297.

Weber, M. (1947). *The theory of social and economic organization*. New York, NY: Oxford University Press.

Wright, C. D., & Bechtel, W. (2007). Mechanisms and psychological explanation. In P. Thagard (Ed.), *Philosophy of psychology and cognitive science* (pp. 31–80). Amsterdam, The Netherlands: North-Holland.

Znaniecki, F. (1934). *The method of sociology*. New York, NY: Rinehart.

PART II
Planning Research

Having a clear disciplinary (or interdisciplinary) position and a strong knowledge of theories and philosophical paradigms does not guarantee the advancement of scientific knowledge. To make such advancement, all this baggage has to be applied to solve a problem that is vital to science and/or to the communities and people who live there. That is why every research project has to have a problematization phase, the phase when the problem, purpose, and research questions for the project are formulated. Through this stage the disciplinary, theoretical, and philosophical knowledge are transformed into tools for a solution to the problem, and thus they become a powerful force of science advancement. This section will introduce ideas that are important for the *problem formulation* and *conceptual framing* of a research. In Chapter 5 we will discuss how this formulation can be done and how it is related to stating the project *purpose* and constructing *research questions*. Chapter 6 will deal with the conceptual issues of an emerging project. It will discuss the nature of *concepts* and *terms*, their definitions and the challenges of proper use. Special attention will be paid to the nature and role *theories* play in research. Chapter 7 starts with the concept of *research strategies*—ways of approaching research problems within available resources. Then it will discuss *nomothetic* and *idiographic approaches* to an investigation and corresponding *variable-based* and *case-based* designs. This chapter will be concluded by discussing different aspects of sampling in cultural research.

5
RESEARCH PROBLEM, PURPOSES, AND RESEARCH QUESTIONS

This chapter will:

- Highlight the importance of problem-oriented research
- Identify a way to formulate a research problem
- Present and discuss several research purposes
- Stress the significance of good research questions
- Warn against methodolatry.

Introduction: Formulating a Research Problem

Importance of Problematization

In the previous chapter we discussed the proposition that without making discoveries, there is no progress in science. In this chapter, readers will learn that a scientific discovery can be made only within a problem-oriented research—research that tackles a challenge driven by unknown and unexplained causes, factors, and conditions. The ultimate goal of science is to surprise us; it should tell us something we did not already know (Bhaskar, 1979/2015, p. 10). It also has to explain or to clarify something that we did not understand or were confused about. In order to get this surprise effect and/or to clarify something, every research project has to address a *scientific/research problem* (or a set of problems): a puzzle or enigma that exists in the worlds and in our understanding of them. Many philosophers of science (Kuhn, 1962/1996; Peirce, 1957; Popper, 1965) have highlighted the importance of articulating a scientific problem for a research in order to be able to advance knowledge, to make science efficient and useful. In the previous chapter, we discussed that any intellectual breakthrough to the unknown through abduction or retroduction is only possible when this unknown is formulated as a research problem. When the unknown is not explicitly stated, there is nothing to discover. A flow chart of research problematization is depicted on Fig. 5.1.

Formulating a research problem serves several important functions within a project: (1) The problem directs a researcher's thinking and as a result predetermines the purposes of a study and its research question; (2) together with understanding the nature of the phenomena under investigation, it dictates the methodology and design of the research; and (3) when the study is finished and the problem is addressed, nobody will ask the questions "So what?" or "What was the point of the

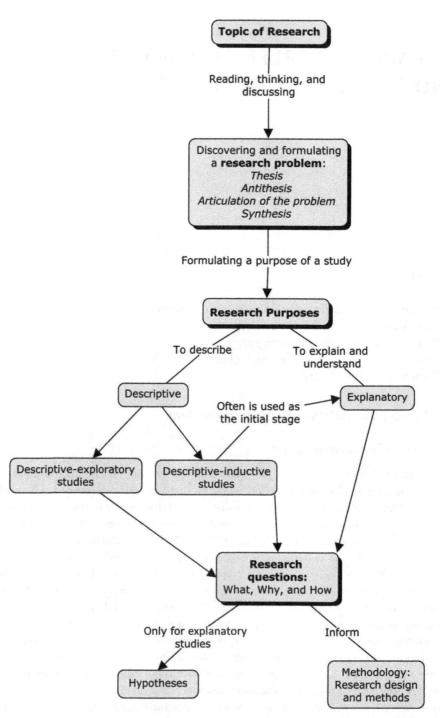

FIGURE 5.1 Research problem, purposes, and research questions. This concept map was made with IHMC Cmap Tools

study?" because the importance of the problem and the suggested solution of it should be obvious to even the most oblivious critics. A valid solution of a well-justified and well-articulated problem always contains new pertinent knowledge, so the "So what?" question is naturally dropped.

Another important function of a well-formulated research problem is (4) its capacity to motivate and provide meaning for a researcher's current project and even to his or her further research career. A researcher has to believe in the significance of finding a solution to the problem he or she is trying to solve and have deep faith that this solution is vital for scientific communities and societies at large. It is desirable that a researcher becomes invested with his or her problem and even starts seeing it as his or her personal problem that craves a resolution. The research has to become meaningful in a broad societal context as well as in the researcher's individual life; the meaningfulness of a solution to the problem should generate an enjoyable, intrinsically motivated, and, finally, successful research project. Question yourself about why are you involved in this enterprise and in studying this particular topic and problem: "Why did I choose this topic and this problem? Do I really want to study it? What is behind my interest in this topic? What are my motivation, interests, and values in pursuing this topic?" Continue these reflections throughout your research and your professional career. To be a reflective scholar is one of the most important qualities that a researcher needs to cultivate in order to be successful.

Theoretical and Applied Problems

There are two types of research problems: *theoretical* and *applied*. These are accordingly dealt with either by *basic* or *applied research*. *Basic research* focuses on discovering the mechanisms of the phenomena under investigation and formulating theories that describe these mechanisms and explain the phenomenon. If new and puzzling facts are discovered that cannot be explained by the existing theories, then a theoretical problem emerges and basic science researchers have to address it. Theoretical problems in culture and psychology research are contradictions, tensions, and omissions that exist in a researcher's explanation of the states and processes that unfold when people function in different cultural contexts; these problems are gaps in the understanding of the mechanisms that account for these states and processes. Solutions of theoretical problems are addressed both theoretically and empirically. Theoretical solution means that researchers reconsider existing concepts and theoretical propositions about the causal mechanisms and either reformulate them or generate new ones that better explain the phenomenon of interest. To verify these new hypothetical mechanisms, a researcher has to generate new evidence that support them; thus, new data collection and new experiments are conducted. A researcher uses new evidence, logic, and existing knowledge to modify the theory.

EXAMPLE BOX 5.1. AN EXAMPLE OF A THEORETICAL RESEARCH PROBLEM

As an example of a theoretical problem in culture and psychology research, I will take the work of Michael Tomasello, an American developmental psychologist and the codirector of the Max Planck Institute of Evolutionary Anthropology. In his book *The Cultural Origins of Human Cognition* (1999), he formulated what he called "the basic puzzle" (p. 2) that he wanted to address in his project. The puzzle is that the two million years that it took for the representatives of the species "Homo" to become "Homo sapiens" are not enough to explain the emergence of humans' species-specific cognitive abilities by the mechanisms of biological evolution. There should be another explanation of this unique emergence. Tomasello's proposed solution of this puzzle is the mechanism of "social or cultural transmission, which works on time scales many orders of magnitude faster than those of organic evolution" (p. 4). Cultural transmission of the knowledge and skills through generations together with the cultural learning of these skills by human individuals lead to "cultural cumulative evolution [which] is thus the explanation for many of human beings' most impressive cognitive achievements" (p. 7). Cultural cumulative evolution has happened through inventing linguistic symbols, developing symbolic mental representations, and the emergence of new species-specific human cognitive capabilities. Thus, the purpose of Tomasello's project was to demonstrate through what sociocultural and psychological processes human beings acquired their cognitive abilities and how the symbolically mediated social interactions within cultural environments emerge and function as primary mediums for human socialization. The researcher also wanted to show that neither existing biological adaptations can explain human cognition without taking into account the historical and ontogenetic process of cultural transmission and cultural learning. This clear articulation of the scientific problem led this scholar to develop straightforward objectives for his project as well as to create hypotheses about how and through what specific mechanisms social symbolic environment leads to the emergence of unique human cognitive capacities. All these attributes of Tomasello's project on cognitive development made this research one of the most distinguished achievements of modern cultural and developmental psychology.

Applied research problems stem from practical issues related to people's functioning in societies, with regulating their behaviors in different sociocultural environments, and with challenges related to people's undesirable behaviors, thoughts, and emotions. Applied problems emerge when people's conduct and actions become problematic for their own well-being, the well-being of communities, and of society at large. People's clashes with existing or new cultural realities, conflicts with existing social norms, and confusions with their own urges and desires are some of the sources of applied/practical problems for cultural psychologists. Successful applied researchers use the knowledge of the mechanisms of various behaviors that were articulated in the basic research and then study the conditions under which these mechanisms either work or do not work in a particular sociocultural context.

EXAMPLE BOX 5.2. AN EXAMPLE OF AN APPLIED PROBLEM

For this example let us examine the study by Ruth Benedict (1946/1974) to uncover the national character of Japanese people: *The chrysanthemum and the sword: Patterns of Japanese culture*. In 1944, Ruth Benedict, one of the best known American cultural anthropologists, was approached by the American government's Department of Information with a request to study the Japanese national culture and the national character of Japanese people in order to anticipate and predict how the Japanese would react to their defeat and the potential occupation of Japan by US troops. This information was vital for planning final military operations and following diplomatic steps and programs. These are the questions that Benedict was asked to address: "What would the Japanese do? Was capitulation possible without invasion? Should we bomb the Emperor's palace? What could we expect of Japanese prisoners of war? What should we say in our propaganda to Japanese troops and to the Japanese homeland that could save the lives of Americans and lessen Japanese determination to fight to the last man? (. . .) When peace came, were the Japanese a people who would require perpetual martial law to keep them in order? Would our army have to prepare to fight desperate bitter-enders in every mountain fastness of Japan? Would there have to be a revolution in Japan after the order of the French Revolution or the Russian Revolution before international peace was possible? Who would lead it? Was the alternative the eradication of the Japanese?" (p. 3).

In order to answer these and related practical questions, the anthropologist studied Japanese culture, which she articulated as the "design for living" (p. 12); "deeply entrenched attitudes of thought and behavior" (p. 16), "the assumptions upon which Japan builds its way of life" (p. 17), "the lenses through which the Japanese see existence" (p. 17), "the basic assumptions which any nation makes about living" (p. 19). Culture, according to Benedict, regulates people's behaviors by providing "common rationale and some common motivations" (p. 12) and, because of this commonality, makes their lives meaningful, ordered, and cohesive.

Since the US was at war with Japan, Benedict could not travel there to implement an anthropologists' main methodological tool: ethnographic fieldwork. Thus, she was forced to perform "anthropology at a distance" by using other sources of information, such as interviews with Japanese-Americans who were reared in Japan and books about Japan written by Japanese citizens, Western travelers, researchers, and writers. She also watched movies produced in Japan and discussed them with the Japanese people and conducted a thorough analysis of the Japanese culture and compared it to similar and distant cultural systems. However, this collection of information would be useless for the objectives of the project if the author failed to get inside the hidden assumption of the Japanese way of life by using her knowledge, experience, imagination, and logic. This insight made by a talented mind, and not simply an accumulation of ethnographic facts, made this project a classic in anthropology and cultural psychology.

Time is the best judge of the success of a scientific enterprise. The most recent edition of the book was published in 2013 and was described in glowing terms: "essential reading for anyone interested in Japanese culture, this unsurpassed masterwork opens an intriguing window on Japan" (www.amazon.com). Even more, this book was translated into the Japanese language and was published in Japan in 1948, and it helped the Japanese to reflect on their own postwar cultural identity and new position in the world. It was also translated into Chinese and was used by the Chinese government as a source of information about Japan when tensions between the two countries rose.

How to Formulate a Research Problem: The Thesis-Antithesis-Synthesis *Logic*

Problems are not given; they need to be discovered and formulated, and they need to be accepted by other members of scientific and/or civil communities as a problem. Scientific problems have to be formulated in such a way that will allow researchers to address them at the existing level of knowledge. Therefore, finding and formulating the problem for one's research should be an important but challenging intellectual exercise. Several authors (Abbott, 2004; Blaikie, 2010; Kumar, 2005; Maxwell, 2005; Punch, 2013; White, 2009) have suggested strategies and practical techniques (heuristics) for formulating a problem. Combining these suggestions with my own pedagogical experience, the following framework can be offered. Follow the flow chart on Fig. 5.1.

1. *Choose the topic for your future research program.* Select a matter that concerns you, that highly interests you, a matter that you believe is of high importance and significance to people's lives, communities' wellness, and societies' development. It is important to choose a topic that will support your long-lasting interest and intrinsic motivation. This topic may be a part of your own experience, or it may correspond to your deeply accepted values and life philosophy. Keep in mind that sound research programs should extend in time and should be relatively resistant to fluctuations in popular public and media interests. The topic is not a

problem; it is an area of your personal and scientific interests and concerns. The topic is the most general foundation for your research. Be precise and definite with the terms and concepts that you use to articulate your topic.

2. ***Start working on collecting information to formulate the problem for your particular research project.*** Should you start formulating the problem before or after reading the literature on the topic? The answer to this question depends on your familiarity with the topic, your own experience, and the amount of information available to you (White, 2009). Conventional wisdom is to start with the literature, using the concepts from your topic as the search words, while being open to discussions in the media, public presentations, and general discourses in the scientific community. Consult with experienced colleagues working within the same area and addressing the same or similar topics. Examine literature references provided in special journals or publications like *Annual Reviews in Psychology*,[1] *Genetic, Social, and General Psychology Monographs, Review of General Psychology, Psychological Review,* and *Psychological Inquiry*. It is important to be sensitive to the nature of the phenomena that you choose for your topic; you may decide to spend some time on thinking and defining what exactly constitutes your topic. Be aware that despite using the same terms, understandings of the phenomena under investigation may vary substantially among researchers; every time you read a source, look for definitions of the main concepts.

HOW-TO BOX 5.3. A WORD OF WARNING: *DO NOT OVERREAD!*

If you are a novice researcher, you may be overpowered by the authority of published authors, and this may kill your own interest, innovativeness and creativity with regard to the topic. Common conclusions and thoughts may be: "Everything has been done and I have nothing to contribute;" or "Researchers that are smarter than I am are struggling with this topic/problem, so what can I do in this area? I cannot contribute anything new" or "There is no point of doing research in this area because it has been so intensively researched already." These and similar demotivating and discouraging thoughts are inevitable at this stage of problem formulation, and you need to teach yourself how to deal with them.

First, do not overread: do not allow the information from the published sources to kill your own ideas or deemphasise them; try to stay sensitive to your own thoughts, be proud of them and cherish them. Do not lose sight of what is important and interesting *to you*. Make your reading and thinking in iterative circles. Start by generating general ideas about the topic and the aspects of interest within it; then do some reading. Return to thinking about the relevance of this information to your ideas; refine your topic and your understanding of it. Then do a more refined reading, clarify the terms and concepts, and follow this with a more precise formulation of the topic; discuss your ideas with experienced colleagues; do more reading and so forth. . . . An important outcome of this cycle is the creation of a *conceptual framework*, a network of the main concepts that will frame your future project that builds your vocabulary of how to think and talk about your topic and problem. You will continue building and refining this framework along the way (see Chapter 6 on concepts).

---

[1] There are similar *Annual Reviews* publications in almost all social science disciplines. In addition, all social sciences have special journals focused on providing reviews in their disciplines, and readers should consult with their libraries to find the review publications that can be useful for them.

At some point you need to disengage with the literature, stop reading, and start to independently interpret the received information and find the problematic points within it. "Disengaging with the literature can cause a great deal of anxiety as it represents moving from the comfortable world of the ideas of others into the uncertain world of your own research" (White, 2009, p. 16). You may find that the literature has limited information about your topic, so you may decide to conduct an exploratory study to collect more information in order to formulate a problem that could be a constructive and important option.

3. *Apply the "thesis-antithesis-synthesis" strategy to formulate the problem.* If we look carefully at the way scholars formulate problems for their research, we may discover a long-standing and efficient pattern of logical thinking and reasoning to problematize this process. This pattern is the time-tested paradigm of dialectical thinking: *thesis-antithesis-synthesis*. First, state your *thesis*: formulate well established facts, taken-for-granted opinions or propositions, existing and accepted theoretical accounts for the states of modern day affairs or findings from existing research with regard to the phenomenon of interest. These facts, findings, and accounts should exist independently of your opinion about them; they should be justified by previous research and supported by empirical evidence. In Tomasello's (1999) work, the reconstructed thesis could be formulated as *human beings possess unique cognitive abilities mediated by language that cannot be found in any other species.*

Then, formulate an *antithesis*: a statement that the facts, findings, and accounts explicated in the thesis either contradict each other or contradict some broader presumptions, existing theories, accepted expectations, or even common sense. Try to justify your *thesis* and *antithesis* with literature, empirical data, and logic. Be very precise with the terms and concepts that you use to word your problem. The antithesis in Tomasello's research could be stated as *human beings' unique cognitive abilities could not have been developed within the two million year timeframe through only the mechanisms of the biological evolution.* The main point of formulating a problem is to discover and state a contradiction between the thesis and antithesis, to articulate a dialectical tension between them. (This is dialectical because there is no right or wrong position here, and because thesis and antithesis are never fixed and permanent). In our examples, the problem is the tension between the fact that humans have unique cognitive capabilities, but their emergence within the two million year timeframe cannot be explained through biological evolution. How then could they have emerged?

A scientific research project is the resolution of this tension. A solution to the problem, or a *synthesis,* is the formulation of hypotheses and propositions that reconcile the thesis and antithesis in a logical and empirically verifiable way. Such synthesis is usually arranged as a scientific theory if the proposed hypotheses have been verified. The logic of science development will inevitably lead to formulating a new thesis which will be followed by another antithesis and a new tension between them. Thus, the circle of scientific progress will move forward, determining the advancement of scientific knowledge.

This classical *thesis-antithesis-synthesis* strategy to formulate a problem may be considered the most general and ideal way of problematizing any scientific research. The real practices of many scientists demonstrate that research may vary with regard to how it is problematized. It may be driven by pure curiosity, by the desire to collect and accumulate facts that may emerge in puzzling patterns, or by the desire to further develop existing constructs and concepts by collecting or getting access to various databases. But regardless of these pathways, all research must have implicit problems deep at the core, and making these problems explicit is an important task of any researcher.

> **HOW-TO BOX 5.4. GUIDELINES FOR USING THE *THESIS-ANTITHESIS-SYNTHESIS* STRATEGY EFFICIENTLY**
>
> Ask yourself the following questions:
>
> 1. What should the **thesis** in your formulation of the research problem be? Formulate a statement (or statements) of a relatively obvious, well-accepted state of affairs within the area of your research interest; for example: *a. Children are naturally cooperative, helpful, and supportive. b. People have a universal capacity for self-determination and autonomous agency. c. Men are predisposed to actions and agency, whereas women are hardwired into relations and nurturing.*
> 2. Now formulate your **antithesis**. Consider what facts, theories, or propositions demonstrate the limitations of your thesis, its inadequacies and/or insufficiencies. Formulate this contradiction as clearly as possible. Use existing data, social statistics, previous research, logic—everything possible to formulate the antithesis and its contradistinction to the thesis. *a. Children easily become involved in aggressive and cruel acts such as different forms of bullying, which may injure or even kill other kids. b. In many societies and under specific conditions, people deny their capacity toward self-determination and autonomy and try to obediently follow norms and practices that may be harmful to them and their communities in the long run. c. There are many examples of women being agentic, taking actions into their own hands, and even subordinating men.*
> 3. Formulate *what actually constitutes the problem* within the discovered contradistinction. Different scholars may formulate different problems out of the same thesis and antithesis. The problem should be framed and articulated. The formulation of a problem is a distinct and challenging part of any research project, so take your time to come up with the proper problem, as this will benefit your research in the long run. *a. If children are helpful and considerate by nature, then why and under what conditions do they become nasty and cruel bullies? What kills their kindness? b. How can the inherent human tendency toward autonomy and self-determination be destroyed by sociocultural norms, prescriptions and practices? What are these norms and practices and how do they work? c. What is the balance between agency and relatedness in human beings, especially in males and females, and how do they emerge and interact with various sociocultural environments?*
>
> Some heuristics that may facilitate the problematization stage of research can be found in Abbott (2004).

Research Purposes

With the formulation of the problem, the problematizing phase of research planning is only starting. Depending on the state of the problem and the readiness of a researcher to address it, the upcoming study may have different purposes. Conventionally, textbooks distinguish two main purposes of research: *descriptive* and *explanatory*. These two purposes seem straightforward at first glance. Both of them are comprised of a complex network of ideas and related research strategies and practices.

The purpose *of describing* typically includes a depiction of the phenomenon in its various aspects: behavioral, phenomenological, narrative, statistical, demographic, historical, socioeconomic, and political. This purpose may include pure exploratory objectives (descriptive-exploratory studies), when almost nothing or very little is known about the phenomenon, problem, or population of interest, or this purpose may be situated within an inductive research strategy (descriptive-inductive studies). Descriptive studies rarely constitute the ultimate goals of a project; instead they usually serve as the initial phase of an explanatory investigation. The purpose *of explaining* typically pertains to providing answers to the following questions: Why does the phenomenon of interest take place? What factors cause it to occur? What are the mechanisms that make it happen? How would understanding these mechanisms help to solve the problem? Almost all these questions are concerned with making the phenomenon intelligible and understandable. An explanation, and related to it an understanding, may be approached through either of the discussed philosophical paradigms, but the nature of explanation in each case will be different.

The Descriptive Purpose

It is possible to differentiate *descriptive-exploratory* and *descriptive-inductive* studies by the level of structure of their conceptualization, data generation, and analysis.

Descriptive-exploratory studies are often used as a step in formulating the research problem, while they may also be the starting stage of an explanatory research project (Stebbins, 2001). To *explore* usually means to develop an initial rough description of a phenomenon, to survey the contexts and conditions of its existence; as a part of the formulation of a problem, the phenomenon in question is examined in its wholeness and totality.

> Exploratory research is necessary when very little is known about the topic being investigated, or about the context in which the research is to be conducted. . . . Essentially, exploratory research is used to get better idea of what is going on and how it might be researched. (Blaikie, 2010, p. 70)

Blaikie also highlighted the fact that Herbert Blumer—a well-known sociologist—was a strong defender of exploratory studies in the social sciences. According to him, researchers have to gain an adequate understanding of the segments of the sociocultural realities that they want to investigate before moving on to actual research.

> The purpose of exploratory investigation is to move towards a clearer understanding of how one's problem is to be posed, to learn what are the appropriate data, to develop ideas of what are significant lines of relation, and to evolve one's conceptual tools in the light of what one is learning about the area of life. (Blumer, 1969/1986, p. 40)

Descriptive-exploratory studies are usually relatively open-ended and loosely structured, both conceptually and method-wise. An example of such a study would occur when a cultural psychologist, anthropologist, or sociologist is entering a field with only vague ideas of the specific directions of his or her research. *Exploratory studies* are directed toward generating more information; in contrast, *confirmatory studies* test and verify a priori developed hypotheses and propositions.

EXAMPLE BOX 5.5. EXAMPLES OF DESCRIPTIVE-EXPLORATORY STUDIES (JUST ABSTRACTS)

Deborah L. D., & Wilsnack, S. C. (1979). Alcohol abuse among lesbians: A descriptive study. *Journal of Homosexuality, 4*(2), 123–142. (Abstract is republished with permission of Taylor and Francis. Get the full article at http://www.tandfonline.com/doi/pdf/10.1300/J082v04n02_01#.VRhzLuEmz7A)

> Intensive interviews with 10 lesbian alcohol abusers revealed strong dependency needs, low self-esteem, and a high incidence of depression. Drinking increased power-related behaviors, enhanced self-esteem, and, for many subjects, increased feelings of depression. The findings suggest that lesbians with alcohol problems need (a) therapists who will accept their sexual orientation and (b) treatment that will help them increase their sense of power and self-esteem without alcohol.
>
> Braun, Kathryn L., & Nichols, Rhea. (1997). Death and dying in four Asian American cultures: A descriptive study. *Death Studies, 21*(4), 327–359. (Abstract is republished with permission of Francis and Taylor. Get the full article at http://www.tandfonline.com/doi/pdf/10.1080/074811897201877#.VTfcnpMmz7A)
>
> Among ethnic minorities, the Asian and Pacific Islander (API) American group is the fastest growing, and, as a whole, is quite longevous. Although there is significant literature on the history and religious traditions of API cultures, little has been published on death rituals and beliefs of the American descendants of these groups. The purpose of this study was to begin to explore cultural variations in response to the process of dying and grieving among four Asian American populations—Chinese, Japanese, Vietnamese, and Filipino. To this end, key informants and focus group interviews were conducted with members of these ethnic groups, and significant differences among, and within, groups were found. The small size and Hawaiian base of the sample preclude generalization of findings to the United States as a whole. However, this study provides health care workers with information that can increase their awareness of and sensitivity to Asian American approaches to death and dying.
>
> These are typical modern descriptive studies conducted with qualitative methodology. The samples are purposeful or convenient; there are no well-defined conceptual frameworks to guide the studies, but these frameworks may be articulated after the research. The methods are usually open-ended interviews structured around describing and analyzing the experiences of participants within particular issues. Typically, such studies do not explain the phenomenon and do not provide solutions to the problems, but as a beginning step they can be very useful.

Descriptive-inductive studies are another form of descriptive studies which are more structured, tightly conceptually interwoven and focused more on answering specific research questions rather than pure exploratory ones. Blaikie (2010) defined this type of descriptive studies in the following way: "To *describe* is to provide a detailed account, or the precise measurement and reporting, of the characteristics of some population, group or phenomenon, including establishing regularities" (p. 69). There are several differences between this type of descriptive studies and the exploratory ones described above. Descriptive-inductive studies are guided by specific research questions and have a priori developed conceptual frameworks and operationalizations of these concepts; they include various forms of assessing and/or measuring the phenomenon under scrutiny and different forms of analyzing the obtained data: tabulation, descriptive statistics, correlations, and some others. But these studies, in comparison to explanatory and confirmatory ones, are not assenting. They do not have hypotheses about the mechanisms of the phenomena and are not guided by the desire to confirm some ideas or propositions, as they are still open-ended. They look at what is going on, but are doing this in a more structured and refined manner than pure exploratory studies. There are usually several goals of such studies: (1) to provide descriptions of a particular phenomenon in precise and statistics-available forms; (2) to look for the patterns in presentations of the variables or for regularities of relationships among the variables. An example of an inductive-exploratory study is a census survey regarding the demographic, socioeconomic, and psychological characteristics of minority groups in a multicultural society. Another example is a clinician who is administering a battery of tests and questionnaires to patients to build their psychological profiles in order to identify patterns; this in turn may lead to a successful diagnosis.

EXAMPLE BOX 5.6. EXAMPLES OF DESCRIPTIVE-INDUCTIVE STUDIES (JUST ABSTRACTS)

Caron, J., & Liu, A., 2010. A descriptive study of the prevalence of psychological distress and mental disorders in the Canadian population: Comparison between low-income and non-low-income populations. *Chronic Diseases in Canada, 30*(3), 84–94. (© All rights reserved. Reproduced with permission from the Minister of Health, 2015).

Objective: This descriptive study compares the rates of high psychological distress and mental disorders between low-income and non-low-income populations in Canada.

Methods: Data were collected through the Canadian Community Health Survey—Mental Health and Well-being (CCHS 1.2), which surveyed 36,984 Canadians aged 15 or over; 17.9% (n = 6620) were classified within the low-income population using the Low Income Measure. The K-10 was used to measure psychological distress and the CIDI for assessing mental disorders.

Results: One out of 5 Canadians reported high psychological distress, and 1 out of 10 reported either substance abuse or at least one of the five mental disorders surveyed. Women, single, separated or divorced respondents, non-immigrants and Aboriginal Canadians were more likely to report suffering from psychological distress or from mental disorders and substance abuse. Rates of reported psychological distress and of mental disorders and substance abuse were much higher in low-income populations, and these differences were statistically consistent in most of the sociodemographic strata.

Conclusion: This study helped determine the vulnerable groups in mental health for which prevention and promotion programs could be designed.

Tsai, J. L. Ying, Y-W, & Lee, P. A. 2000. The meaning of "being Chinese" and "being American": Variation among Chinese American Young Adults. *Journal of Cross-Cultural Psychology, 31*(3), 302–332. (Republished with permission of Sage Publications, Inc.; permission conveyed through Copyright Clearance Center, Inc.).

Few studies have investigated how the meanings attached to being of a particular culture vary within cultural groups. The meanings of "being Chinese" and "being American" were compared among three Chinese American groups: 122 American-born Chinese (ABC), 119 immigrant Chinese who arrived in the United States before or at age 12, and 112 immigrant Chinese who arrived in the United States after age 12. Participants completed the General Ethnicity Questionnaire (abridged version). For each group, the relationship between "being Chinese" and "being American" and the specific cultural domains (e.g., engagement in American activities, Chinese language proficiency) on which they were based were assessed. Results suggest that "being Chinese" and "being American" were unrelated for ABC, but were negatively related for immigrant Chinese. Results also suggest that for immigrants, the domains on which "being Chinese" and "being American" are based change with increased time living in the United States.

These two studies, although entirely descriptive, try to come up with generalizations in order to identify problems or vulnerable groups to study further. Both studies are conceptually articulated and have well-defined variables and their assessment. They use various forms of analysis to come to their generalizations. That is why they are descriptive and inductive at the same time.

The Explanatory Purpose

Explanation as a purpose and goal of a study is even more complex and multifaceted than description. The concept of explanation, together with the concept of understanding, has several meanings and denotes different things, depending on the philosophical paradigms of researchers (Mahajan, 1998; von Wright, 1971). In addition, the verb *to explain* is used in our everyday language, which also adds to the multiplicity of its meanings. Blaikie (2010) provided the following definition of explanation:

> Explanation is making intelligible the events or regularities that have been observed and which cannot be accounted for by existing theories. Explanations eliminate puzzles and provide intellectual satisfaction. To explain some phenomenon is to give an account of why it behaves in a particular way or why particular regularities occur. (p. 71)

The way this intelligibility is achieved depends on a researcher's philosophical paradigms: positivism, interpretivism, or realism. Positivists use the deductive-nomological mode of explanation by subsuming a specific case to a general empirical regularity or law (see Chapter 3). "The observations we make in everyday life as well as the more systematic observations of science reveal certain repetitions or regularities in the world. . . . The laws of science are nothing more than statements expressing these regularities as precisely as possible" (Carnap, 1966/1995, p. 3). Here an explanation comes from applying an a priori established regularity to particular cases and instances and concluding that these cases are parts of this regularity and, thus, are explained by it. "No explanation—that is, nothing that deserves the honorific title of 'explanation'—can be given without referring to at least one law" (p. 6). Carnap used the following example: Jimmy hit Tommy in the nose. Why is little Tommy crying? The events, facts, or states that require explanation are called *explanandum*. There is a law to be used for this explanation: if somebody hits another person in the nose, it will be painful and the person will cry. This empirical generalization is called *explanans* or something that explains. We explained why Tommy is crying by referring to the empirical psychological law (p. 7). Here is an example of this type of explanation within cross-cultural psychological research: Matsumoto and Fletcher (1996) discovered that individualism as a cultural dimension is positively associated with a prevalence of cardiovascular diseases across several countries. This is an empirical generalization established through the descriptive-inductive study of the associations of Hofstede's cultural dimensions with the spread of various illnesses in different countries. This is the *explanans*. Now imagine that we have a community of people who on average have high blood pressure, and we want to explain the occurrence of this disease. This is our *explanandum*. In the positivist's mode of explanation, the *explanandum* should be deduced from the *explanans*: the average high blood pressure in a community can be explained by the fact that this community endorses an individualistic culture. Thus, if people in a community have a high prevalence of cardiovascular disease, it is probably because they live in an individualistic culture.

Within the realist paradigm (see Chapter 4), to explain means "to establish elements, factors or mechanisms that are responsible for producing the state of or regularities in a social phenomenon" (Blaikie, 2010, p. 69), or to propose generating powers and causal mechanisms that determine the phenomenon of interest. Realists do not consider subsuming to an empirical regularity a legitimate explanation because such a subsumption does not reveal the mechanisms of the regularity. Also, they scoff at this subsumption because the very regularity—for example, that the individualistic dimension is associated with the prevalence of cardiovascular disease—by itself requires explanation. Going back to our example above, critical realists may ask: why and through what processes may the endorsement of individualistic values on a society level determine the high blood pressure in its members? Such elements of individualism as a fast pace of life, competitiveness, strong goal orientation, and some others should be carefully studied and their influence on the increase of blood pressure should be determined. Explanation within the interpretivist paradigm is discussed in Chapter 6, p. 158–159.

Prediction and Explanation: Is Prediction a Legitimate Purpose of Research?

Another potential but controversial purpose and objective of research is *to predict* behavior or the outcomes of events. Many psychology textbooks and manuals for research design announce prediction to be one of the goals of scientific psychological research. This is the correct fact that certain areas of psychology are built around psychological predictions: educational testing—predicting the educational performance of students; personnel selection—prediction of job candidates' future performance; marketing and advertisement psychology—predicting consumers' behavior; criminal psychology—predicting inmates' behavior after incarceration and assessing their probability to reoffend; and counselling and clinical psychology—predicting the outcomes of treatment. Any scientific prediction should be based on both empirically and theoretically solid backgrounds. But the meaning of what is entailed by "solid background," "empirical data," and "theoretical basis" depends on the philosophical position of a researcher.

The most evident possibility for prediction comes within the positivist paradigm. It is based on the same logic as explanation but works in the opposite direction. Within positivism, the basis for both explanation and prediction is the lawful empirical regularity established during the inductive (enumerative) stage of the study. Let's follow Carnap's example provided above. The *explanans* is *'If somebody hits another person in the nose, it will be painful and the person will cry'*. What will happen if Jimmy hits Tommy in the nose? Based on the provided law, we may predict that Tommy will cry. In the example of associations between the cultural dimensions and frequencies of various diseases, the regularity established by these researchers allows them to state that people from communities with individualism will have a higher probability of cardiovascular diseases. They predicted the unknown occurrences of diseases by deducing them from the existing lawful regularity. The logic here is the same as in the case of explanation: people have cardiovascular disease because they belong to individualistic cultures. In the deductive thinking within the positivist paradigm, such logical congruency of explanation and prediction is called the *symmetry of prediction and explanation* (Bhaskar, 1975/2008), where explanation goes back from the *explanans* and prediction goes forward from it. Keep in mind that this positivist version of prediction is not the prediction of a future state of affairs. It is a so-called *categorical prediction*—a prediction of people being placed into a particular category based on previously established cross-sectional statistical analysis. If a community is positioned into the category of "individualistic cultures," then it acquires an attribute of being prone to high rates of cardiovascular diseases. To provide predictions for the future, researchers have to establish an empirical regularity based on a longitudinal design or, as personnel test developers say, establish a predictive validity of a test/*explanans*.

More careful analysis of these forms of explanation and prediction within positivism raises questions about the applicability and finally, the usefulness of these modes of inference. As an astute reader may notice, these manipulations of *explanans* and *explanandum* generate nothing new about their relations, as researchers are working around the same regularities but applying them within explanatory or predictive objectives. This way of thinking is redundant and cyclical (Polkinghorne, 1983). Although it may be practically useful in some applied areas, philosophers of science abandoned this logic for scientific explanation a long time ago.

Proponents of realism do not support the idea of prediction in the social sciences (Bhaskar, 1979/2015). One of the reasons for this is that prediction is only possible in closed systems that are somehow isolated from external and uncontrollable influences. Sociocultural worlds and people's functioning within them are open systems, systems that are subjected to the influences of numerous contextual and conditional factors that are practically impossible to control. That is why even if researchers know the causal mechanisms that produce events, they cannot predict these events because the conditions that moderate these mechanisms are either unknown or uncontrollable. According to realists, it is possible to explain events based on discovering the causal mechanism, but not possible to predict them; thus, the symmetry between explanation and prediction does not hold for them.

The purpose "to understand" is closely related to explanation and some of its details were discussed in the previous chapter about the interpretivist paradigm. In the philosophy of science, explanation is conventionally associated with the positivist paradigm and understanding or *verstehen* with the interpretivist one (Mahajan, 1998; von Wright, 1971).

> The difference between them is a matter of *how intelligibility* [of the phenomenon] *is achieved*; by *causal explanation* or by *reason explanation*. Explanations identify causes of events or regularities, the factors or mechanisms that produce them, whereas understanding is provided by reasons or accounts social actors give to their actions. The latter is also associated with the *meaning of an event or activity* in a particular social context, either that given by social actors or meaning that researchers derive from social actors' accounts. *Explanations are produced* by researchers who look at a phenomenon *from the "outside,"* whereas *understanding is based on an "inside" view* in which researchers grasp the subjective consciousness, the interpretations, of social actors involved in the conduct [emphases added]. (Blaikie, 2010, p. 72)

> To *understand* is to establish reasons for particular social action, the occurrence of an event or the course of a social episode, these reasons being derived from the ones given by social actors. (p. 69)

Weber (1947) tried to reconcile these two purposes by introducing two forms of understanding, *direct observational understanding* and *explanatory understanding*, in relation to studying social actions. In observational understanding, a researcher tries to grasp "the subjective meaning of a given act as such, including verbal utterances" (p. 94). When we see and hear particular facial and verbal expressions, we can immediately understand if a person is happy, angry, sad, etc. Upon observing students in a library, we may immediately deduce that they are reading books and writing papers. This type of understanding refers to the surface hermeneutics and thin descriptions that were discussed in the previous chapter. In the process of explanatory understanding,

> we understand in terms of *motive* the meaning an actor attaches to the proposition twice two equals four, when he states it or writes it down, in that we understand what makes him do this at precisely this moment and in these circumstances. (p. 95)

When we encounter an angry person, we try to comprehend why he or she is angry; when we see students reading books, we wonder whether they are preparing for exams, writing their theses, or reading just for pleasure. These explanatory understandings correspond to the depth hermeneutics and thick description/interpretation discussed in the previous chapter.

With the variety of meanings of the purposes of description, explanation, and understanding, it is clear that serious theoretical work is required by a researcher to formulate his or her philosophical position, to understand the ontology of the phenomenon that he or she wants to study, and to choose an appropriate purpose of research providing a complete account of what he or she understands under these purposes. The provided account also indicates that any research is a cyclical process where theoretical assumptions, research problems, formulated purposes, and methodology are constantly interacting with each other, creating a chain of interdependent steps and processes.

Formulating Research Questions

Sometimes experienced researchers may skip an explicit formulation and justification of the purposes of their studies, but they typically cannot avoid the formulation of *research questions* (RQs). A statement of RQs logically follows the formulation of a research problem and the purposes of the studies. Many research design textbooks highlight the importance of RQs for the successful implementation of research studies (Blaikie, 2010; Flick, 2011; Green, 2008; Leong, Schmitt, & Lyons, 2012; Punch, 2013; White, 2009).

Why are research questions important? Because they are the foundation of good research. RQs translate the research problem and purpose of a study into more precise and practical guidelines of what to study and how to conduct these studies. They determine the design and methods used, structure data generation and analysis, and provide logic for data interpretation and discussion. Thoroughly answered RQs provide solid grounds to address the research problem and obtain new knowledge. Without well-articulated and justified questions, all these stages of research may fall apart and a study may become a collection of purely technical manipulations of different methods that may result in a potentially useless conglomerate of data.

EXAMPLE BOX 5.7. EXAMPLES OF RESEARCH QUESTIONS

Let's consider the study of Whiting and Whiting (1975) about cultural influences on child development. The authors started their book with RQs and the model for research, and only later in the text introduced the problem they wanted to address. It can be reconstructed in the following way: Up until recently, the majority of child development studies have been monocultural. Several studies have shown some "differences between social classes or between ethnic groups. . . . Culture as a variable has been used implicitly rather than explicitly" (p. 2). This means that culture as one of the influential factors of child development has not been explicitly stated, operationalized, and studied. They continue: "the meaning of the differences [between classes and ethnic groups] in terms of cultural values was rarely explored systematically" (p. 2). The authors also mentioned that "when culture has been taken as a variable to be studied, the beliefs, values, and techniques of the whole society . . . have been given unitary values as though everyone in the group accepts them. Variations of individuals within the society have been wiped out on the assumption that custom compels consensus" (p. 2). The research problem for this study was based on a gap in knowledge of what culture is and the role it plays in child development. This gap was addressed by the following research questions:

> Are children brought up in societies with different customs, beliefs, and values radically different from each other? Do differences attributable to sex, age, and birth order override these cultural differences? Does the situation and setting influence a child's behavior or are his actions similar across environments? Or, to ask these questions in a summary form, if you want to predict the behavior of a preadolescent child, which would it be most important to know: his or her sex, age, birth order, the culture into which he was born, or the situation he was in at the moment you made your prediction. (p. 1)

> With regard to its purpose, this study has descriptive elements, as many relations among the concepts were unknown, but at the same time the authors set a goal of explanation, as they strove to uncover the causal mechanisms of cultural influences on human development. They pronounced several hypotheses and strived to establish "the direction of causation in social change" (p. 3). The research questions were complemented by the researchers' theoretical assumptions about the study and its methodology. They used a variety of anthropological and psychological theories that were prevalent at the time. The study is located within the domain of comparative ethnography with sets of intra- and intercultural comparisons. The research problem, purposes, and research questions were located within a theoretical model for psycho-cultural research, which outlined the researchers' main components of potential causal mechanisms: environment, history, maintenance systems, child-rearing environment, learned and innate capacities of children, and projective expressive systems. Each domain was characterized by a set of concepts, forming the conceptual framework of the study. The domains in this model are connected by arrows, which indicate the researchers' understanding of their relationships and influences. This study has all the components we discussed above and is a good example of a cultural developmental investigation.

As the pedagogical practices show, the formulation of RQs is one of the most challenging parts of the research planning process for students. Without focusing on this process and applying some techniques and skills, the formulation of RQs may easily be overlooked and simplified. This would greatly diminish the quality of the research.

Types of Research Questions

The type of RQs to be asked follows the purpose of a specific study: descriptive or explanatory; exploratory or confirmatory. Typical RQs suggested by textbooks are questions that start with "What," "Why," or "How." Blaikie (2010) related them to the three main purposes of research that he outlined: description, explanation/understanding, and change. Other authors extend this list by including: "Who," "Where," "How many," and "How much" (Yin, 2003). White (2009) argues that some of these questions are redundant or ambiguous. For example, he stated that "Why" questions may mean causes, motives, reasons, processes, purposes, and justifications. He suggested avoiding them by replacing with more clearly specified formulations: "What reason?" "What purpose?" or "Through what process?" Some authors (Hamblin, 1967) raised similar concerns regarding the ambiguity of the word "How," which may mean "How does a phenomenon come into being?" (genesis), or "How does a phenomenon unfold?" (process and duration). Hamblin suggested formulating all the "W" questions through "What" questions: "When"—at what time; "where"—at what place, "who"—what type of people; "why"—because of what reasons/causes; and "how"—through what mechanisms.

How to Generate Research Questions

Most of the textbooks mentioned above suggested strategies and steps for developing RQs. Their summary is presented below.

For the first step, *brainstorm as many questions as possible*: descriptive, exploratory, explanatory—all possible types. Blaikie (2010) commented: "The purpose is to try to expose all the ideas that you have on the research problem, particularly those that may be taken for granted and which later you wish you have been fully aware of at the design stage. No questions should be censored, even if it may seem to be marginal, outrageous or impractical" (p. 63).

At the next step, *review, select, and structure* the generated RQs. This stage includes finding overlapping and redundant questions, identifying marginal, impractical, and unsuitable ones, categorizing them with regard to the purposes of your studies and, finally, structuring them as *main* and *subsidiary questions*. Blaikie defined *main questions* as the ones that "will form the core of the research project, the key questions that are to be answered." (p. 64). The "subsidiary questions will include those that deal with background information or issues, that are supposed by one or more major questions that, while being necessary, are not absolutely central to the project" (p. 64). He provided the following example:

Main research question

- To what extent is environmentally responsible behavior practiced?

Subsidiary research question:

- To what extent are household waste products recycled?
- To what extent is buying environmentally damaging products avoided?
- To what extent is public transport and cycling used in preference to private motor vehicles? (p. 65)

In the next step, work on *wording* your RQs. Let's consider the problem of explaining immigrants' acculturation. The main question can be formulated like this: "Why do immigrants stay strongly connected to their home country norms and traditions even at the expense of their smooth adaptation to a host country?" Let's analyze the wording of this question more thoroughly. *Why* implies a search for an explanation. Following the above suggestion, *why* can be replaced by more direct indication of what a researcher is looking for: "Because of what determining factors and through what processes does the phenomenon in question happen?" *Immigrants*: who enters into this category? Refugees, voluntary migrants, business immigrants, family reunion immigrants? Other categories? What about other characteristics such as age, gender, socioeconomic status, and some other basic demographic variables? These variables can be clarified in the subsidiary questions. *Strongly*—this is a very ambiguous word: what does *strongly* mean in this context? How will the researcher measure this strength? *Connected*: what is the nature of this connection? Is it typified by things like thinking about their homes, eating only home-country food, and similar behaviors? Anything else? *Home country norms and traditions*: there are assuredly hundreds of different norms and traditions that can be found in any country. Which in particular are of interest to the researcher? *Even at the expense of . . .* this is again a colloquial expression that is difficult to address in research. Do the immigrants take all the money they earn in a host country and send it back home, forcing them to live in squalor in their adopted home? Do immigrants refuse to follow the rules of a host country and do everything according to their home country prescriptions? *Smooth adaptation* is another nice sounding but ambiguous expression: what is *adaptation*? Following the everyday rules, participating in municipal elections, contributing to charities? What is the nature of immigrant adaptation, and what are its indicators? *Smooth*: What does this mean? No problems with the law? Having a job? A high salary? Marrying a local woman or man? *Host country*: the host country may be big, having different regions with different climates, physical and sociocultural differences; do researchers mean the specific place where the research will be conducted? Will they be able to make generalizations from this place to the whole country?

It is clear that the original question is too vague and requires either refinement or to be complemented by subsidiary research questions. A potential refinement could be the following: *What cultural, social, and psychological processes explain why young male refugee immigrants from South American countries continue to exercise the culture of machismo, even when this tradition stands in their way of education and employment in the Toronto region of Canada?* The subsidiary research questions could be worded to make the main question clearer: What are the gender and age differences among immigrants with regard to their adherence to home culture norms and traditions? To what domains of their home culture's norms and traditions are immigrants of different genders and ages mostly dedicated? (Consider family relations, parenting, education, work relations, health maintenance). In what areas and domains of life do immigrants of different ages and genders experience the most serious problems while adapting to their host country? These and many potential subsidiary questions clarify the groups of immigrants to be investigated, articulate the domains of the home and host cultures to be studied, and clarify the final point of the inquiry.

As in the above example, a researcher has to pay serious attention to the wording of RQs and to the usage of terms and concepts. We have already discussed the ambiguity of "How" and "Why" questions. Textbooks warn about the ambiguity of almost every word we use in our discourses, especially evaluative terms such as "successful," "effective," "satisfactory," "frequent," "rare," and "detrimental." Such a concern may be raised with regard to the very first question in the Whiting & Whiting study: "Are children brought up in societies with different customs, beliefs, and values radically different from each other?" The expression "radically different" is evaluative and vague. What does "radically" mean? How radical is radical? "Different"—with regard to what characteristics? The way to correct this ambiguity is either to reword the question with more precise terms or to treat this question as the main one and complement it with a set of subsidiary questions that clarify the terms and intentions of the main question. Whiting and Whiting did the latter: they suggested further questions about gender, age, and birth order differences in the social behavior of children, and clarified cultural "radical differences" as the differences that override any gender, age, or birth order's intracultural variability. My advice is that every concept and term used for wording the questions should be carefully selected, justified, and defined. And remember, a researcher must also keep in mind the relations between the RQs and the purposes and problem of the project.

Do not confuse the research questions with the data generating questions. Researchers must be careful not to confuse the RQs with the questions they intend to ask their participants in surveys or interviews. Sometimes inexperienced researchers want their participants to answer research RQs directly; they want their participants to do their job for them by providing the answers to their RQs right away. The main difference between these two types of questions is that research questions are about the essence of things, about the laws of nature and unobservable mechanisms and powers; conversely, the interview and survey questions are about the experiences of people, their opinions, thoughts, and beliefs, or the processes that constitute the phenomena that require explanation. A researcher should collect all possible evidence about the phenomena of interest, including individuals' personal accounts of their behaviors and experiences, and then make inferences about the hidden and unobservable powers that produced those phenomena. Only a scientist is positioned to make such inferences, whereas his or her participants cannot. One may argue that for people, as conscious and motivated agents, their own motives, goals and intentions are the driving forces of their actions, so why is a researcher unable to ask them about their motivation? In fact a researcher can ask participants such questions, but should not treat their answers as valid reflection of actual forces that drive people's behavior. Keep in mind that people's behavior is strongly driven by "taken-for-granted" aspects of culture, which often occur automatically with minimal conscious reflection. People also have subconscious motivation that is not reflected in their conscious accounts. When formulating the answers to interview questions, there are invisible forces of social desirability, striving to be a "good participant," making efforts to gain the respect of the researcher and many other motivations contributing to the shaping of final answers. A researcher has to treat these data (survey and interview answers) the same way as a criminal investigator treats eyewitness accounts: as evidence which should be intelligently combined with other evidence (forensics, ballistic expertise, DNA analysis and many others) to develop justified hypotheses about the causes and dynamics of a crime. Researchers should ask every participant-immigrant, for example, for their account of why they behave and act the way they do in a new country, but they should not treat these answers as a valid representation of the unobservable mechanisms of acculturation. Researchers must do naturalistic observations and collect information from teachers, employers, and other members of immigrants' acculturative situations. They have to compare their responses with well-adapted and with ill-adapted compatriots, and compare them with immigrants from different cultural and ethnic communities. Only after gathering all this information can researchers start generating hypotheses about the mechanisms of acculturation.

The next step is a *critical reflection on each question*, similar to what was suggested with the formulation of a problem. A researcher is advised to ask him or herself: Why am I asking this question? How is it related to the research problem and what purpose does it serve? Why do I want to know the answer to it? When I answer this question, will I be able to address my research problem? How does it relate to my other questions? Is its researchable? What methods should I use to answer these questions? Can I manage all these questions? Blaikie (2010) recommended that:

> This process [of critical reflection on RQs] needs to be taken very seriously and not glossed over quickly. It is very easy to include questions because "that would be interesting to explore," or "I would really like to know about that." This critical examination needs to be ruthless. (p. 65)

Kumar (2005) provided the following example of a student reflecting and rewording her RQ for a qualitative study. Her initial question was: What does it mean to live with an autistic child? The immediate response she received from her supervisor and some mothers of such children was: "What do you mean by" what does it mean' to live with an autistic child?" Then she started working on rewording this question. This work included looking into the literature, reading accounts of the parents of autistic children and of autistic adults themselves, which ended up with a reformulation of her research question.

At their starting point, many ethnographic and qualitative studies are exploratory in their nature, and RQs may be generated after the project has commenced and may undergo a pretty lengthy process of formulation and reformulation. The same may be true for more traditional empirical studies: RQs are never carved in stone and should be reflected upon and corrected if needed as the research project unfolds.

Research Questions and Hypotheses

The methodologists discuss the relations between RQs and research hypotheses as well as the role these hypotheses play in research (Blaikie, 2010; Green, 2008). From the positivist point of view, "An **hypothesis** is a conjecture about relationship between relevant variables, cast as a statement that is testable. It provides a clear (if tentative) proposition of what might be the case, that is then subjected to verification via empirical investigation" (Green, 2008, p. 56). Researchers deduct hypotheses from *explanans* or empirical laws and apply these hypotheses to particular cases. From the realist perspective, hypotheses are conjectures about the causal mechanisms that should explain the phenomenon. They are retroducted by a researcher and provide tentative answers to "Why" (because of what causes and/or reasons) and "How" (through what processes) the phenomenon happens. In both cases hypotheses follow the formulation of RQs and do not substitute for them. In a more specific sense, hypotheses present tentative answers to the RQs. Not all research requires hypotheses: descriptive and exploratory studies that strive to answer "What" questions do not need them. But for explanatory studies, hypotheses are crucial as they provide tentative ideas about what may be the causes of a problem. That is why RQs should play a primary role in guiding research and hypotheses should complement them. Blaikie (2010) also warned about not confusing theoretical and statistical hypotheses. Theoretical hypotheses are substantive explanatory conjectures, whereas statistical hypotheses are used to establish whether the observed statistical relations occurred by chance or whether the regularities found in a sample could be expected in the population (p. 147). Statistical testing is only one of the ways to provide evidence to verify a theoretical hypothesis. "Decisions about whether data confirm or refute a theoretical hypothesis cannot be settled by the use of tests of statistical significance" (p. 147).

Relations Between Research Questions and Research Design

One of the most important functions of RQs is to determine the research design and specific method to be used in the empirical investigation. Let's consider, for example, the first question of the Whiting and Whiting study (1975): "Are children brought up in societies with different customs, beliefs, and values radically different from each other?" (p. 1). This question implies that the future design should be comparative in nature, addressing patterns of children's behaviors across different sociocultural environments. This comparison, as the authors further discussed, could be done either by conducting observations in natural settings or by doing experimental studies under more rigorously controlled conditions. The authors decided that for their project, naturalistic observation was the best fit to answer their research questions. This decision was made because of the strong exploratory component in their question and because of the desire to include a wide range of actual environmental factors related to children's socialization.

Consider Tomasello's (1999) study about the influence culture has on human cognitive development. His question seems similar to the RQ in Whiting and Whiting's study. But in Tomasello's study, culture is considered less as a particular natural sociocultural environment, and more abstractly as "the species-typical and species unique 'ontogenetic niche' for human development" (p. 79). (In these two studies, the concept of "culture" is defined quite differently. Consider how these differences shape the designs of each study). Because Tomasello was not interested in a particular culture, but in culture as a context of meaningful interactions with adults by means of symbolic forms, he decided to use a comparative experimental design for his studies. He compared the behavior of apes (mostly chimpanzees) and children in different experimental situations. The same results could not have been achieved through naturalistic observations. His design allowed Tomasello to answer his explanatory question more directly: "Through what process and mechanisms does culture participate in the cognitive and linguistic development of humans?"

Green (2008) suggested that researchers ask the following question in order to ensure consistency between RQs and the methodology of a research project:

- What methodological strategies are implied by the purposes and objectives of your research question?
- What methods of data collection are most consistent with the objectives of the research, as they are embedded in the question?
- Does your question need adjusting in light of your proposed research design, or could you rework your research design on the basis of your reconsidered question? (p. 58–59)

The most important message for readers to understand is that research inquiries should be driven by a research problem and research questions; methods should be secondary and determined by them. Scientific research should be problem-driven and not method-driven, because unlike a skillful application of data-generating and analytical techniques, the problem solution guarantees new discoveries and knowledge generation. The prevalence of methods over the essence of a scientific inquiry is labelled *methodolatry* (see Box 5.8. below), and should be strongly avoided.

INFORMATION BOX 5.8. DANGER OF METHODOLATRY

Collins Dictionary defines *methodolatry* as the "worship of a method that employs it uncritically regardless of ever-changing particulars and steadfastly ignoring past negative results." (http://www.collinsdictionary.com/submission/3666/methodolatry). Denzin and Lincoln (2003) defined methodolatry as "a preoccupation with selecting and defending methods to the exclusion of the actual substance of the story being told" (p. 48). Methodolatry is "method-oriented" thinking in research, and it is a serious concern for psychologists (Chamberlain, 2000; Reicher, 2000), sociologists (Emke, 1996), qualitative (Denzin and Lincoln, 2003), educational (Martin & Sugarman, 1993), and market researchers (Stokes & Bergin, 2006). In actual empirical research, methodolatry means that researchers know what method they intend to use before they problematize and plan their research. They know that they will choose experiment, or survey, or discourse analysis, or ethnography—independently of the nature of the problem to be solved. They were taught these methods, know how to conduct them and how to analyze the data, and feel confident about using them. They are specialists in methods, not in problem solving. The question of fit between their research questions and methodology is secondary in such cases because, regardless of what the problem or RQs are, researchers will use the same set of tools every time.

In one of my research methods classes, students compare observation, interview, and survey methods for doing social psychological research. One day, I brought three devices to keep loose sheets of paper together: a small paper clip, a large spring-based bundle clip, and a paper folder with a hole puncher. I then asked the students which of these devices is the best for keeping the sheets together. The answer was unanimous: "It depends." It depends on the number of sheets we have and for what purpose we want to bundle them together. After that I immediately asked them which one of the studied methods is the best. Before this demonstration, when answering the same question, some of the students preferred interview together with observation, some survey. Now, they were all impelled to say: "It depends." Research methods are the tools that a researcher should use depending on the nature of the problem and the type of questions he or she is trying to answer. The choice of methods should be contingent upon the objectives of the study, and not vice versa. Methodolatry jeopardizes the quality of research, provides much less if any useful knowledge about a phenomenon, kills the creativity of a researcher (Emke, 1996) and, finally, undermines the reputation of science because of the method-driven studies' limited capability to solve problems that communities and societies are facing. The best remedy against it is informing researchers about the hazard of methodolatry, proliferating "problem-oriented" thinking in research communities, and teaching students a wide variety of techniques and methods of data collection and analysis so they are capable of applying them to fit the problem at hand.

Conclusion

Every study starts with discovering and formulating a research problem. A research problem is a central and fundamental factor, or a pivotal axis, around which the project should be organized. Problems can be theoretical or applied. Finding and formulating a problem is a challenging intellectual exercise. It starts with a general topic which interests a researcher. The topic should also be relevant and important to scientific and sociocultural communities. The schema Thesis-Antithesis-Synthesis can be used as a guideline for formulating a problem. There are two main purposes of any research: to describe and to explain. These purposes should be coordinated with the research problem that researchers aim to address. Descriptive-exploratory and descriptive-inductive studies differ with regard to their conceptual frameworks, the degree of the structure provided, and differences in theoretical backgrounds. Explanation, as a purpose of a study, is the ultimate goal of any research. What it means to explain depends on the philosophical paradigm that a researcher endorses. Understanding, as a purpose of a study, has different meanings in research on culture and psychology. It is usually associated with the interpretivist paradigm. Some researchers use the research purposes of explanation and understanding as synonyms. Research purposes are carried through research questions. There are several types of research questions, which correspond to different purposes of studies. Different strategies can be used to facilitate a formulation of these questions. Research questions link the research problem and research purposes with the research design, and they structure the ways of finding a solution of the research problem. In order to be successful, any research project should be problem-oriented and, through the research questions, its design and methods have to be determined. Method-oriented studies should be avoided as they may lead to methodolatry, which is detrimental to the success of any research.

Questions

1. Why does this textbook strongly emphasize the advantages of problem-oriented research? What advantages does a well-articulated problem bring to research?
2. Consider the research project that you are involved with and try to formulate the problem that this project strives to address.
3. After formulating this problem, go through the four functions of the problem and try to apply them to the problem at hand.
4. Read a set of articles related to the topic of your interest. Try to identify the way the authors formulated the problem for their studies. Look for the T-A-S logic in them. Are there any other strategies that the authors used for their problematizations?
5. Compare articles with a relatively good formulation of problems to articles with a relatively unclear and vague formulation of problems. Follow how the good formulation structured the whole study. Look for disadvantages caused by a weak formulation of a problem.
6. Identify the purposes of the studies that you are analyzing. How are these purposes related to the problem and research questions? If there is no articulation of the purposes, try to reconstruct them.
7. Examine a few explanatory studies. Are their explanations really explanatory? Within what paradigm are they operating?
8. Identify research questions either in your own research or in the articles that you are analyzing. How are these research questions logically connected with the problem and purpose of the studies? How well are they worded? Watch for the links between research questions and the studies' designs and methodology. If you are working with your own project, play with different formulations of the research questions.
9. Discuss the issue of methodolatry in class. Provide examples. Compare "problem-oriented" studies with "method-oriented" ones. Contemplate the advantages and disadvantages of this approach.

Glossary

Descriptive purpose (to describe) is to provide a broad account of the phenomenon of interest, its context, regularities, and manifestations. A descriptive purpose usually precedes explanatory research.

Explanatory purpose (to explain): making something clear and intelligent; to uncover the causes, powers, and mechanisms that make a phenomenon happen.

Exploratory versus **confirmatory** studies: The **exploratory purpose** is close to the descriptive one and aims at investigating a phenomenon in its complexity of manifestations, conditions, and contexts of its occurrences. **Confirmatory studies** have an a priori idea, hypothesis, or conjecture that researchers aim to confirm or falsify. Exploratory ones do not have such ideas and serve as the basis for the formulation ideas for confirmatory studies.

Methodolatry is a tendency of researchers to plan their studies based on the methods that they will use, regardless of the problem they are trying to solve. Methodolatry is considered a serious offense in all disciplines and should be avoided. Robust scientific research should be problem-oriented and the methodology a researcher selects should be contingent on the nature of the problem and the paradigm of the researcher.

Research problem is rooted in the tension between existing knowledge and new evidence, facts and phenomena that need explanation. **Theoretical problems** are determined by the inability of existing theories to explain new facts, regularities and generalizations; **applied problems** reflect the tensions, conflicts, and challenges that people experience in their communities.

Research questions are building blocks of any empirical research project. They identify what aspects of the problem will be addressed and specify conditions and factors that will be involved in the research. Conventional research questions are: "What" (exploratory and descriptive), "Why" (explanatory: because of what causes and reasons), and "How" (explanatory: through what mechanisms).

Thesis-Antithesis-Synthesis strategy for problem formulation: a set of logical steps to identify a current state of affairs in the area of interest (thesis), followed by the discovery of omissions that exist in the thesis with regard to the complexities of the phenomenon under investigation (antithesis); a researcher then formulates a tension between thesis and antithesis (statement of a problem), and designs a study to reduce these tensions and resolve the problem (synthesis).

Recommended Reading

Abbott, A. (2004). *Methods of discovery: Heuristics for the social sciences*. New York, NY: Norton.

Bechtel, W., & Wright, C. D. (2009). What is psychological explanation? In J. Symons & P. Calvo (Eds.), *The Routledge companion to philosophy of psychology* (pp. 113–130). London, UK: Routledge.

Blaikie, N. (2010). *Designing social research: The logic of anticipation*. (2nd ed.). Cambridge, UK: Polity.

Green, N. (2008). Formulating and refining a research question. In G. N. Gilbert (Ed.), *Researching social life* (3rd ed., pp. 43–62). Los Angeles, CA: Sage.

Kumar, R. (2005). *Research methodology: A step-by-step guide for beginners* (2nd ed.). London, UK: Sage

Leong, F.T.L., Schmitt, N., & Lyons, B. J. (2012). Developing testable and important research questions. In H. Cooper (Ed.), *APA handbook of research methods in psychology* (Vol. 1. Foundations, planning, measures, and psychometrics., pp. 119–132). Washington, DC: American Psychological Association.

Punch, K. F. (2013). *Introduction to social research: Quantitative and qualitative approaches* (3rd ed.). Thousand Oaks, CA: Sage.

White, P. (2009). *Developing research questions: A guide for social scientists*. New York, NY: Palgrave Macmillan.

References

Abbott, A. (2004). *Methods of discovery: Heuristics for the social sciences*. New York, NY: Norton.

Benedict, R. (1946/1974). *The chrysanthemum and the sword: Patterns of Japanese culture*. Boston, MA: Houghton Mifflin.

Bhaskar, R. (1975/2008). *A realist theory of science*. London, UK: Verso.

Bhaskar, R. (1979/2015). *The possibility of naturalism: A philosophical critique of the contemporary human sciences* (4th ed.). Oxon, UK: Routledge.

Blaikie, N. (2010). *Designing social research: The logic of anticipation.* (2nd ed.). Cambridge, UK: Polity.

Blumer, H. (1969/1986). *Symbolic interactionism: Perspective and method.* Berkeley, CA: University of California Press.

Carnap, R. (1966/1995). *An introduction to the philosophy of science.* New York, NY: Dover.

Chamberlain, K. (2000). Methodolatry and qualitative health research. *Journal of Health Psychology,* 5(2), 285–296.

Denzin, N. K., & Lincoln, Y. S. (2003). *Strategies of qualitative inquiry.* 2nd ed. Thousand Oaks, CA: Sage.

Emke, I. (1996). Methodology and methodolatry: Creativity and the impoverishment of the imagination in sociology. *The Canadian Journal of Sociology, 21*(1), 77–90.

Flick, U. (2011). *Introducing research methodology: A beginner's guide to doing a research project.* Thousand Oaks, CA: Sage.

Green, N. (2008). Formulating and refining a research question. In G. N. Gilbert (Ed.), *Researching social life* (3rd ed., pp. 43–62). Los Angeles, CA: Sage.

Hamblin, C. (1967). Questions. In P. Edwards (Ed.), *The encyclopedia of philosophy.* (pp. 49–53). New York, NY: Macmillan.

Kuhn, T. S. (1962/1996). *The structure of scientific revolutions.* (3rd ed.). Chicago, IL: University of Chicago Press.

Kumar, R. (2005). *Research methodology: A step-by-step guide for beginners* (2nd ed.). London, UK: Sage.

Leong, F.T.L., Schmitt, N., & Lyons, B. J. (2012). Developing testable and important research questions. In H. Cooper (Ed.), *APA handbook of research methods in psychology* (Vol. 1. Foundations, planning, measures, and psychometrics., pp. 119–132). Washington, DC: American Psychological Association.

Mahajan, G. (1998). *Explanation and understanding in the human sciences* (2nd ed.). Oxford, UK: Oxford University Press.

Martin, J., & Sugarman, J. (1993). Beyond methodolatry: Two conceptions of relations between theory and research in research on teaching. *Educational Researcher, 22*(8), 17–24.

Matsumoto, D., & Fletcher, D. (1996). Cross-national differences in disease rates as accounted for by meaningful psychological dimensions of cultural variability. *Journal of Gender, Culture, and Health, 1*(1), 71–82.

Maxwell, J. A. (2005). *Qualitative research design: An interactive approach.* (2nd ed., Vol. 41). Thousand Oaks, CA: Sage.

Peirce, C. S. (1957). *Essays in the philosophy of science.* Indianapolis, IN: Bobbs-Merrill.

Polkinghorne, D. (1983). *Methodology for the human sciences: Systems of inquiry.* Albany, NY: State University of New York Press.

Popper, K. (1965). *Conjectures and refutations: The growth of scientific knowledge.* New York, NY: Basic Books.

Punch, K. F. (2013). *Introduction to social research: Quantitative and qualitative approaches* (3rd ed.). Thousand Oaks, CA: Sage.

Reicher, S. (2000). Against methodolatry. *British Journal of Clinical Psychology, 39*(March), 1–6.

Stebbins, R. A. (2001). *Exploratory research in the social sciences.* Thousand Oaks, CA: Sage.

Stokes, D., & Bergin, R. (2006). Methodology or "methodolatry?" An evaluation of focus groups and depth interviews. *Qualitative Market Research: An International Journal, 9*(1), 26–37.

Tomasello, M. (1999). *The cultural origins of human cognition.* Cambridge, MA: Harvard University Press.

von Wright, G. H. (1971). *Explanation and understanding.* Ithaca, NY: Cornell University Press.

Weber, M. (1947). *The theory of social and economic organization.* New York, NY: Oxford University Press.

White, P. (2009). *Developing research questions: A guide for social scientists.* New York, NY: Palgrave Macmillan.

Whiting, B. B., & Whiting, J.W.M. (1975). *Children of six cultures: A psycho-cultural analysis.* Cambridge, MA: Harvard University Press.

Yin, R. K. (2003). *Application of case study research* (2nd ed.). Thousand Oaks, CA Sage.

6
WORKING WITH CONCEPTS, TERMS, AND THEORIES

This chapter will:

- Highlight the crucial importance of well-defined *concepts*
- Discuss that concepts are ideas wrapped in the "shell" of *terms;* if they are measured and vary across entities of interest, they become *variables*
- Clarify that variables are manifestations of concepts through *operational definitions*
- Differentiate *empirical* and *theoretical concepts,* or *hypothetical constructs*
- Discuss arguments between *realists* and *nominalists* regarding the nature of concepts
- Introduce the *vagueness* and *ambiguity* of scientific terms and concepts and stress the importance of their *definitions*
- Examine the concept of *scientific theory* and analyze it within the three paradigms.

Introduction

In order for researchers to identify the phenomena they want to study, to formulate problems regarding these phenomena, and to answer research questions, they have to have special intellectual devices or tools to identify different components of the socio-cultural and psychological worlds and operate them within the logic and structure of a scientific investigation. Scientists cannot approach their subjects with empty hands, the naked eye, and the mindset of naïve laypersons. The intellectual tools that make any scientific research possible are concepts, conceptual framework, and theories.

> Throughout the act of scientific inquiry concepts play a central role. They are significant elements of the prior scheme that the scholar has of the empirical world; they are likely to be the terms in which his problem is cast; they are usually the categories for which data are sought and in which the data are grouped; they usually become the chief means for establishing relations between data; and they are usually the anchor points in interpretation of the finding. Because of such a decisive role in scientific inquiry, concepts need especially to be subject to methodological scrutiny. (Blumer, 1969/1986, p. 26)

As sociologist Herbert Blumer stated above, concepts are the pivotal component of any scientific inquiry, and they deserve researchers' special attention and scrutiny. Generating and using concepts constitutes complex dialectics in a research process, as scientific concepts and theories are both *instruments for* and *products of* scientific inquiries. Scholars use concepts to dissect realities and to analyze the facts, events, and experiences that they study. Theories tie concepts together into conceptual frameworks and explain the phenomena that researchers investigate. Establishing theories with well-validated explanatory power is considered to be the ultimate objective of scientific inquiries. In addition to the explanatory function, scientific theories are used to guide other cycles of research to get a deeper and better understanding of the ways the worlds work.

When a young scholar joins researchers of culture and psychology, he or she encounters a specific vocabulary about "culture(s)," "cultural models," "society," "social communities," "internalization," "personality," "human agency," "engagement," "experience," "attitudes," "social control," "self," "self-regulation," "extraversion," "methodology," "research design," "philosophical paradigms," and thousands of other ideas pertaining to this type of research. These concepts have been created to describe and explain things, events, actions, and their mechanisms, as well as different aspects of the research processes in the sciences of mind and culture. What are scientific concepts? What is their nature and how do they differ from our everyday words? What is their structure? How are these concepts created and how are they related to and used during a research process? Why is it important to seriously consider concepts and to pay close attention to their use? These and related questions are the focus of this chapter. We will cover the roles that concepts and theories play in shaping social research in general and in studies on culture and psychology specifically, and discuss such categories as: *concepts, terms, variables, empirical and theoretical concepts, hypothetical constructs, hypotheses, empirical and theoretical laws, and theories.*

Concepts, Variables, and Hypothetical Constructs

Why Conceptualization is Important for Scientific Research

To deal efficiently with the worlds, humans have to partition them into categories, into manageable units so the human mind can handle the diversity and multiplicity of these worlds. The cognitive process of categorization is a fundamental feature of human interactions with the worlds, other people, and oneself. Typically, these categorizations are arranged in a variety of patterns of symbolic mental representations such as the classifications of plants and animals, the systematizations of kinship, the categorizations of people based on race and ethnicity, the classification of mental processes and myriads of other classificatory systems that guide people's experience of and actions in the worlds. Scientific concepts are special forms of the symbolic mental representations developed by scientists for the purpose of research. These concepts are the building blocks of scientific knowledge. As fragile blocks will contribute to erecting a weak building, vague and poorly defined concepts will make the building of scientific knowledge porous, shaky, and, finally, unusable. Following Blumer, we may say that, if the concepts about the worlds are clear, well-defined, and well-articulated, then connections between researchers' thinking and these worlds will be well-established and have a solid foundation.

People use words to describe their daily lives. Similarly, researchers use concepts and terms to describe the phenomena of their interest and the process of doing their research. No scientific and research deliberations can happen without concepts. The process of developing concepts is called *conceptualization,* which is a pivotal and universally important aspect of any scientific inquiry, independent of the philosophical paradigm of a researcher or the objects of his or her inquiry. Blaikie (2010) uses the term "the language of *conceptualization*" to identify

> the language that social scientists use to communicate their theoretical ideas and research findings to each other; it is the language of both abstract theoretical notions and means of identifying observable phenomena. In the context of a research project, this language is used

to identify key concepts and to state relationships between these concepts, to state research questions and hypotheses. (p. 116)

Consider, for example, the research program of Tomasello about the cultural origin of human cognition (1999, 2014). To tackle this topic, which includes investigating the interactions between the sociocultural and psychological worlds of a developing child, the researcher created a system of ideas about the aspects of "culture" he included in the investigation, about the components of "origin" or "development" he wanted to consider, and regarding the constituents of "human cognition." This system of ideas became the conceptual framework of his investigation. Thus, before, during, and after his research project, Tomasello generated several concepts pertaining to this topic and expressed them in one or several words, such as: "the species-typical 'ontogenetic niche' for human development," "cognitive habitus," "cognitive ontogeny," "joint attention," "understanding of others as intentional beings like the self" and many others, which, finally, constituted the structure of his theory. As a surgeon uses a scalpel to perform an operation, this researcher used concepts to dissect the interactions between sociocultural environments and growing human individuals in order to address the enigma of human cognitive development.

Concepts, Terms, and Variables

The central notion for this chapter is the notion of *concept*. "A concept is an idea that is expressed in words" (Blaikie, 2010, p. 111). Concepts are "'*mental representations*', often called *ideas*, serving their classificatory function presumably by resembling the entities to be classified" (Yagisawa, 1999, p. 170). "Concepts . . . are the units of meaning and hence the building blocks of rational discourse. We use concepts to form propositions" (Bunge, 1996, p. 49).

The linguistic labels that are used to express conceptual ideas are called *terms*. When they are applied to scientific concepts, they constitute *scientific terms*. We may think about any concept as a nut that has an idea at the core, and the term(s) which express this idea as the shell. For the sake of simplicity, in this section we will use concepts that are expressed in one term: such as "culture," "personality," "community," "agency" etc., although, as I showed above, many concepts can be represented by several terms. Sometimes *concept* and *term* are used as synonyms: an "observational concept" = an "observational term" or a "theoretical concept" = a "theoretical term" (Kaplan, 1964). For the sake of clarity it is better to keep these two notions separate because, as I will show later, the same ideas (concepts) may be expressed by different terms and the same terms may be used to express different ideas.

Kaplan (1964) differentiates *substantive* and *notational* terms. (In this case, the author uses "term" and "concept" as synonyms.) "Substantive terms cannot be eliminated without loss of conceptual content, but notational terms are fundamentally abbreviations, and could be replaced" (p. 49). For example, the concept/term "symbol" is substantive. It represents the idea that something stands for (symbolizes) something else, and this concept cannot be removed from scientific discourse without losing the idea of symbolization. On the other hand, some terms like "MMPI" (the Minnesota Multiphasic Personality Inventory) are useful notations. This differentiation is important to keep in mind because some researchers have a tendency to use sophisticated notations to cover rudimentary ideas, and it is important not to confuse a bright shell for an impoverished conceptual content. Often psychologists use various mathematical abbreviations and symbols to cover a lack of substantial ideas beneath these notations. Such terms do not progress science.

> Nothing is easier than to say "Let $y = f(x)$", but nothing is gained if we do not have the faintest idea of how to solve the equation, or even how to characterize the function sufficiently so as to allow for the further use of the notation in taking derivatives or whatever. Substantive terms remain fundamental. (Kaplan, 1964, p. 50)

Realism and Nominalism in Concept Development

Scientific concepts have two sides: With one side they represent the worlds' events, things, and processes, and with the other they reflect the researchers' ideas about these events and things and constitute the content of the scientists' reasoning about the objects of their inquiries. For example, on the one hand, Tomasello's concept "the species-specific 'ontogenetic niche' for human development" represents the sociosymbolic environments into which any child is born. On the other hand, this concept represents his idea that a human child can only evolve as a fully functioning human being in such an environment; that the sociosymbolic context is a necessary condition specific for human development. Thus, this concept connects the researcher's idea about children's development with particular aspects of the necessary conditions for such development.

Understanding concepts as representations of different aspects of realities typically corresponds to the *ontological tradition* of conceptualization. "The ontological tradition is concerned with establishing a set of concepts that identifies the basic features of the social world, and that are essential for understanding societies, major social institutions or, perhaps, small-scale social situations" (Blaikie, 2010, p. 113). Think of such concepts as "society," "community," "a niche for development," "social institutions," "power," "human agency," "cultural systems," and many more that were developed to address various aspects of the sociosymbolic and psychological worlds of people. Without such concepts, these worlds would have been perceived as undifferentiated conglomerates of human collectivities, as unstructured arrangements of unreflected interactions of people within social groups, accompanied by the mysterious emergence of different consequences and effects that people cannot understand and foresee. The emphasis on the second aspect of concepts, that they reflect scientists' thinking about the worlds, can be traced back to Kant, who emphasized that people impose on the world their understandings of it, and through the concepts they structure the world for its better understanding. This position is labeled here the *epistemological tradition* of conceptualization.

This introduction of the two traditions of conceptualization brings to our attention the centuries-old argument between *realists* and *nominalists* about the nature of concepts/terms and theories. *Realists* believe that scientific concepts reflect properties of the real worlds and that the objects of a conceptualization have real existence independently of their naming. Thus, according to realists, society, as "the aggregate of people living together in a more or less ordered community" (Soanes & Stevenson, 2008), has real existence independently of how laypersons or social researchers think about and conceptualize it. Realists mostly work within the ontological tradition. *Nominalists* believe that concepts are convenient labels, notifications, or names that logically and conveniently arrange humans' perceptions and experiences. According to nominalists, concepts have no correspondence with reality, which is unavailable for people to know (see, for example, Nunnally & Bernstein (1978) on constructs). Nominalists strongly emphasize the epistemological aspect of conceptualization. For example, in psychology there have been long-standing debates about whether personality traits, which have been discovered through a statistical analysis of adjectives that describe a human personality, are simply convenient linguistic labels or if they reflect the real properties of a person that exists independently of psychologists' factor analytic techniques and corresponding theorizing (Allport, 1927; D'Andrade, 1965). D'Andrade (1965) analyzed the logic of trait psychology and demonstrated that many traits are pure verbal constructions (nominalism) while others represent psychological reality (realism). Many psychologists believe that the Big Five personality traits are real and universal across cultures, have an evolutionary basis, and exert a real determining force on human behavior (Matsumoto & Juang, 2013). Similar discussions and arguments have unfolded around the concept of "causation." Realists believe that there are actual powers and determining forces that cause human actions and experiences, and that the goal of science is to discover these powers by proposing and testing theories about their existence. David Hume's notorious interpretation of causality states that people can only perceive the conjunctions of events and, based on these perceived conjunctions, they form an idea of causality that has nothing to do with representing the real forces that make such conjunctions happen. Thus, Hume treated the idea of causality as a nominalist. Modern scientists who try to talk about the causes of human actions based only on the statistical analysis of covariances between variables follow the same nominalist tradition but in a more sophisticated and disguised form.

Empirical and Theoretical Concepts; Hypothetical Constructs

Concepts are the main instruments for describing and explaining phenomena under scrutiny. Therefore, there are *descriptive* or *empirical concepts* and *explanatory* or *theoretical concepts*.

Descriptive Concepts and Variables

Descriptive concepts are ideas that are based on categorizing and identifying the pieces of physical, sociosymbolic, and psychological realities. These concepts represent the way researchers "perceive" these realities. If a behaviorist talks about "stimuli," this is how he or she perceives and describes the factors that influence individuals' behavior. When anthropologists talk about a "kinship hierarchy," they describe structures of extended families and then use these descriptions for further analysis. What is conceptualized through empirical concepts becomes intellectually visible and comes into existence for researchers, and what is not conceptualized remains invisible and nonexistent for the scientists' intellectual gaze. A conceptualization often means bringing phenomena or their aspects to life and making them the focus of researchers' attention. Therefore, the richer the descriptive conceptualization of the objects of inquiry, the more the objects' nuances, aspects, and particulars will become the points of researchers' attention.

An important type of scientific idea widely used in empirical research is the concept of *variable*. Researchers apply this concept to those phenomena or their parts that vary. Variables may acquire several values to which numbers can be attached. When measured by a personality questionnaire, a personality trait that demonstrates variability among individuals becomes a *personality variable*. This variable is expressed by numbers to which various statistical procedures can be applied. Hofstede's cultural dimensions (Hofstede & Hofstede, 2005) are represented by numbers that vary across different nations and, thus, become *cultural variables*. Variables are usually created through *operational definitions* of the corresponding concepts. (We will talk about operational definitions later in this chapter). Modern empiricists believe that establishing statistical regularities among psychological, social, and cultural variables constitutes the main task of psychological and sociocultural sciences. Because of this, in some branches of social sciences that endorse the empiricist paradigm, like cross-cultural psychology, macrosociology, mainstream social psychology, and some areas of personality research, variables are the main intellectual and methodological devices to think about and to conduct their investigations. This approach is frequently called the *variable-based* design, which is contrasted with the *case-based* design (see Chapter 7).

Explanatory Concepts

Concepts are the main devices for penetrating the surface of empirical events and getting to the meanings and mechanisms that produce and connect these events. In this function of representing the in-depth reality of the worlds, concepts constitute core elements of scientific theories and are labelled *explanatory* or *theoretical concepts* or *hypothetical constructs*. Theoretical concepts are the ideas that make reference to unobservable factors, their structures, and powers in the social and/or psychological functioning of people in different communities. These concepts are expressed by *theoretical terms*.

Another notion that psychologists usually like to use to express their explanatory ideas is *hypothetical construct*. MacCorquodale & Meehl (1948) proposed that "the term 'hypothetical construct' be used to designate theoretical concepts which . . . refer to processes or entities that are not directly observed (although they need not be in principle unobservable)" (p. 104). According to them, such a term presupposes "the existence of nonobserved entities or the occurrence of unobserved processes" (p. 103). Hypothetical constructs are used when scientists hypothesize the existence of nonobserved or unobservable processes such as "internalization," "accommodation and assimilation," "an understanding of others as intentional beings like the self," "enculturation," "acculturation," and many other phenomena that may or may not be directly observed and recorded, such as "personality," "self," "self-concept," "personality traits," "culture," "society" "social norms," and many others.

The fundamental question about the nature of hypothetical constructs, as in the case of concepts in general, is: are these constructs simply convenient linguistic notations used by researchers to structure their knowledge of social interactions, people's behavior, and communities functioning, or do they refer to real psychological and sociocultural processes? Again this is the argument between nominalists and realists, but in this case it is in regard to theoretical ideas and notations and the existence of unobservable entities. In modern philosophical discussions, nominalism is often represented in the form of a *strong version of social constructionism* (Burr, 2003; Gergen, 2009; Lock & Strong, 2010; Schwandt, 2000). This philosophical doctrine

> appear[s] to deny any **ontology** of the real whatsoever. Gergen, for example, argues that "one must be suspicious of all attempts to establish *fundamental* ontologies—incorrigible inventories of *the real*" . . . Taken literally, that may well mean that everything in the world and about the world is nothing but sociolinguistic product of historically situated interactions, a kind of linguistic or semiotic **idealism**. (Schwandt, 2007, p. 40)

According to social constructionists, social scientists place importance not on if there is real reality behind these historically situated interactions, rather on what type of linguistic reality people create through them. These scholars believe that these linguistic realities are important because individuals live and act in constructed linguistic worlds, not in the unknowable "real" worlds. Therefore, various linguistic forms, terms, wordings, narratives, discourses, and "voices" become the objects of social constructionist inquiries, leaving social and psychological realities abandoned and unexplored.

Realists, on the other hand, focus their inquiries on uncovering the mechanisms and causal powers of the social-cultural and psychological worlds. They treat verbal constructions: concepts, hypothetical constructs, and theories, as fallible representations of these realities. These verbal representations may happen to be false, and thus can be abandoned; but some of them may correspond to what is really happening "out there" and form a basis of scientific knowledge about the worlds. Yes, scientific theories are socially constructed, because they are developed through social communication and linguistic exchanges among researchers in scientific communities that function in particular places and in particular times. But such theories are worthless if they are not about the reality they are intended to explain. The socially constructed component of scientific theories within a realist doctrine is a good example of a *weak form of social constructionism* (Schwandt, 2000), which is explicitly or implicitly embraced by most scientists.

Scientific Concepts and Everyday Language: Vagueness and Ambiguity of Our Words, Terms, and Concepts

Many concepts used in the social and human sciences are rooted in everyday language, which is their birthplace and the main source of problems.

The common language is not only a prerequisite for science, but in effect the very basis on which scientific language is built. This is the case not only for the development of a more appropriate vocabulary and grammar, but also for the initial categories and generalizations from which the scientist proceeds. (Mandler & Kessen, 1964, p. 18)

Our natural language names things, events, and conditions in the worlds and it is expected that an *equivalence function* (Mandler & Kessen, 1964, p. 12) exists between the words and the objects of their representation. Language does not work if the word "child" is not equivalent to an actual young human being. In the same way, scientific concepts should always functionally correspond to events, things, their properties and relations in the real worlds. (Refer to the ontological tradition of conceptualization and the realist position described above). But this equivalence of words in representing the worlds does not always hold true, and this creates problems of *vagueness* and *ambiguity*. These issues are the main problems of using concepts in the social and human sciences (Mandler & Kessen, 1964; Blumer, 1969/1986; Sennet, 2011).

Vagueness of scientific terminology means that terms/concepts are uncertain with regard to their signification, uncertain about what they actually represent (Sennet, 2011). This may happen when concepts are not well defined and terms are confusing. Despite the existence of numerous professional dictionaries and encyclopedias, many scientific concepts and terms in the social sciences are vague, especially when they are used in empirical research. *Ambiguity* is another serious problem of scientific concepts. It means that a term or an utterance has several meanings which depend on the context of their usage, on the persons who use them, or on the recipients of this information. "Ambiguity refers to the case in which the same sentence, unchanged in its linguistic structure, depends for its truth or falsity on the circumstances under which it is used" (Mandler & Kessen, 1964, p. 17). Let's take, for example, the term "intentionality," which we used to define the nature of sociocultural realities and cultural models (see Chapter 2). This term's ambiguity creates difficulty in using and understanding it in different texts. "Intentional" means "done on purpose and deliberately" (Soanes & Stevenson, 2008); it also means "aboutness" of human consciousness; the fact that humans' perceptions, ideas, thoughts, emotions are always about something. Intentionality is "the distinguishing property of mental states or psychological phenomena, implying that they have content, are directed at, about, or involved with objects, whereas physical things lack this property" (Bem & de Jong, 2006, p. 276). Shweder (1991) extended this understanding of intentionality to the realm of culture, calling such cultural artifacts as "money," "law," "divorce," "ideology," "government" and millions of other phenomena artificially created by human communities "intentional things," meaning things that exist only because people think about them and act toward them in a particular way (see pp. 75–76). Now consider a sentence from a textbook on cross-cultural psychology: "Three important features of cultural approaches include intentionality (or purposeful action), historicity of behavior and developmental change" (Berry, Poortinga, Segall, & Dasen, 2002, p. 328). In this sentence the authors speak about intentionality in Shweder's terms, but are defining this concept as a "purposeful action," creating ambiguity in their statement.

The vagueness and ambiguity of our natural language create misunderstandings in our everyday lives. Poets and fiction writers may use these properties of the language for their purposes to create rich and vivid descriptions of experiences that give their readers space for imagination and associations. But for scientific research, these pitfalls of natural language are disastrous and should be avoided at all costs. Doing good research starts with clarifying and defining your scientific language, its terms, and its concepts.

In addition to semantic (different meanings of terms) and pragmatic (different meanings that depends on speech acts and contexts) ambiguity, there is another form of a conceptual ambiguity as important and potentially harmful for a productive conceptualization and research. Kaplan (1964) called it *"functional ambiguity"* (p. 47). This idea is based on the notion that scientific concepts serve different purposes within a research activity, and if these functions are confused, then functional ambiguity takes place. Above I introduced "descriptive" or "observational" and "explanatory" or "theoretical" concepts. These concepts serve different functions in research: the former describe the phenomena and how people experience them, and the latter provide explanations of these phenomena. Functional ambiguity happens when descriptive concepts are used to explain a phenomenon. For example, personality traits like neuroticism, extraversion, openness, agreeableness, and conscientiousness are descriptive concepts. They are nothing more than the labels or notations that are attached to statistically derived groupings of the adjectives that are used in the English language to describe human personality. (This is the nominalist interpretation of the nature of personality traits). The function of these labels is to represent different groups of adjectives that were discovered through factor analytic techniques. That is why it is a mistake to use them as explanatory ones, like in the statement: "A child is happy because she is an extravert," or "This person has a problem with his mood regulation because he is a neurotic" (achieved high scores on the neuroticism scale). Categorizing a child as an extravert is to locate and describe her among the descriptive dimensions of personality. It is similar to categorizing a cat as a carnivorous mammal. It is a conceptually and logically confusing to use these categorizations to explain the characteristics of a child's emotions or a cat's behavior. To explain a child's happiness, a researcher needs explanatory concepts that refer either to the meanings of events in a child's life or to the causal factors that influence a child's mood, like "a child is happy because she feels loved."

Defining the Concepts: Importance and Various Forms of Definitions

Nominal and Theoretical Definitions

The only way to avoid having vague and ambiguous terms and concepts is to define them as clearly as possible. A definition is a "specification of the meaning or, alternatively, conceptual content, of an expression" [or a concept] (Yagisawa, 1999, p. 213). There are three types of definitions: *nominal, theoretical,* and *operational.* Let's start with the nominal and theoretical ones. As I said above, each concept consists of two aspects: an idea that a researcher wants to convey and the verbal "shell" that expresses this idea, also known as the term. The word "intentional" is a term, and this term conveys two ideas of either "doing something on purpose" or the "aboutness of mental states." A *nominal definition* is the etymological definition of a term. A *theoretical definition* is an articulation of the idea that is conveyed by the term. A simple rule of thumb to differentiate these definitions is that we look for nominal definitions in language dictionaries, and for real definitions we go to encyclopedias and specialized professional dictionaries. Nominal definitions are usually accompanied by presenting the etymological origins of the term in Greek, Latin or other languages. Let's return to the concept of "intentionality." This is how Schwandt (2007) provided the etymologically based nominal definition of the term "intentional." "Its meaning derives from the Latin root *intendo* (to aim at or to extend toward)" (p. 156). For the theoretical definition, he stated: "Intentionality signifies a state of engagement with the world; our consciousness or mental states are always 'about' something" (p. 156). It conveys the idea of "aboutness" of mental states.

The inability to differentiate between these two forms of a conceptual definition creates several problems for researchers' theoretical thinking. One case of such a problem is presented above, when two different ideas—"doing something on purpose" and the "aboutness of mental states" are represented by one term—"intentionality." The term "intentionality" has two meanings and without articulating them, this term becomes ambiguous. That is why students and even experienced researchers may sometimes argue about terms instead of looking for the theoretical articulation of the ideas behind them. One solution of such ambiguity is to introduce separate terms for each idea; for example, to use the terms "intentionality" and "aboutness." Let's take as another example the concept of "culture." The term "culture" originated either from French *culture* or directly from Latin *cultura,* which means "growing, cultivation" (Soanes & Stevenson, 2008). This term denotes "a cultivated piece of land." This is its nominal definition. Behind the same term we find several different ideas: "1 the arts and other manifestations of human intellectual achievement regarded collectively; 2 the customs, ideas, and social behaviour of a particular people or group; 3 biology; the cultivation of bacteria, tissue cells, etc. in an artificial medium containing nutrients." (Soanes & Stevenson, 2008). Because of the multiplicity of definitions of the concept *culture*, the statement: "I study culture" is ambiguous. Does this mean the person is studying arts or investigating the customs, ideas, and social behaviors of people, or exploring a culture of carcinogenic cells? Because of this ambiguity, the term culture does not meet the precision requirement for a scientific concepts definition. Another instance of semantic ambiguity happens when the same or similar ideas are conveyed by different terms. Consider the terms "instinct," "drive," and "need." All three convey a relatively similar idea of the inborn motivational predispositions of living organisms. If this similarity is not clearly articulated, academics may spend hours discussing the differences among the terms without substantially penetrating into the motivational forces of humans and animals.

One solution for this type of ambiguity is unifying the terminology to avoid a multiplicity of terms for overlapping ideas. However, the main route of fighting the vagueness and ambiguity of scientific terms/concepts is to provide their thorough and elaborated *theoretical* or, frequently called, *conceptual* or *real* definitions. As I said above, this definition is an elaborate and coherent expression of an idea of the concept. "A 'real [theoretical] definition', according to traditional logic, is not a stipulation determining the meaning of some expression but a statement of the 'essential nature' or the 'essential attributes' of some entity" (Hempel, 1952, p. 6). Such a definition is an expression of a researcher's thoughts about the nature of a phenomenon; these thoughts are expressed with the help of other concepts, both empirical and theoretical.

Operational Definition

Almost all social scientists agree that theoretical definitions are essential for concepts to become powerful intellectual tools for investigating surrounding realities. Much more controversy exists surrounding another type of scientific definitions, namely about the *operational definitions* of concepts. To define a concept operationally means to represent it through procedures (or operations) by which the concept becomes manifested and measurable. The founder of the idea of operationalization, a physicist and Nobel laureate **Percy William Bridgman** (1882–1961), declared that "we mean by any concept nothing more than a set of operations; the concept is synonymous with the corresponding set of operations" (Bridgman, 1927, p. 5). The operational definition of hypothetical constructs in psychology is a set of statements about what questions (in an interview), items (in a questionnaire), and segments of behavior (in an observation) a researcher will use to make his or her conceptual ideas empirically verifiable. Let's take for example the concept of "extraversion." "Extraversion" is theoretically defined in many trait theories as a person's sociality, as an orientation toward and preference of social interaction and communication. An operational definition of it may sound like this: extraversion is a personal predisposition that manifests itself through a number of social contacts established by an individual, by positive feelings that accompany social activities, and by a belief in the importance of social interactions for a person's well-being. Based on this operationalization, the following items were developed to assess people's extraversion: "Would you be very unhappy if you were prevented from making numerous social contacts?" "Do you usually take the initiative in making friends?" "Would you rate yourself as a lively individual?" (Eysenk,

1958, p. 15). But the operationalization of concepts is much more than developing items for corresponding questionnaires. For example, "aggressiveness" can be operationalized for naturalistic observation as the number of instances a child hits other children within 30 minutes of spontaneous playtime; "culture" can be operationalized through a set of scores on Hofstede's cultural dimensions; a person's socioeconomic status is usually operationalized by measuring his or her education, type of job, and income.

To make the application of concepts productive and efficient there should be logical relations between the theoretical and operational definitions of them. Concepts' operationalizations should represent the researchers' ideas about the nature of these concepts. Research becomes unconvincing if the theoretical definitions of concepts are not reflected in or connected with their operationalizations. Such disconnection indicates that the idea that a researcher has about a phenomenon does not guide the empirical part of his or her research. Quite often a researcher formally provides a theoretical definition of a construct but then uses scales of convenience that have little or no logical connection with the underlying idea of the concept. Let's take as an example the concept of "acculturation." The most frequently used theoretical definition of this concept by acculturation psychologists is the following: "Acculturation comprehends those phenomena which result when groups of individuals having different cultures come into continuous first-hand contact, with subsequent changes in the original culture patterns of either or both groups" (Redfield, Linton, & Herskovits, 1936, p. 149). It was developed by anthropologists who were concerned with the problems in interactions between Europeans descendants and aboriginal people in North America. It addresses the phenomenon of acculturation at a group level but poorly suits psychological studies of acculturation on an individual level (see a discussion on the definitions of acculturation in (Chirkov, 2009) and other articles in this issue of the journal). It does not provide any idea about what social and psychological processes comprise the mechanisms of acculturation. This definition is so general and vague that any operationalization can fit within it. Thus, after providing this definition, acculturation researchers very often move to operationalizations of acculturation that have nothing to do with this definition. There are now dozens of different acculturation scales with very few—if any—substantial theoretical social-psychological definitions of the concept of acculturation. The result of this is that there is an abundance of empirical articles on immigrants' adjustment and not a single theory of acculturation. As a positive example of a logical connection between the theoretical and operational definitions, we use the concept of drive. Drive is typically understood as "an innate, biologically determined urge" (Soanes & Stevenson, 2008). If drive is a biologically propelled motivational force, then, to elicit this force, an organism has to deny access to the corresponding biological substance. Thus, behaviorists successfully used the length of food deprivation as the operationalization and measure of a hunger drive.

Limitations of Operationalization

The majority of psychologists and many other social scientists have embraced the idea of operationalization wholeheartedly because it allows them to make their hypothetical constructions, such as "intelligence," "extraversion," "happiness," and thousands of others, empirically verifiable, and enables them to test these ideas through a quantification and statistical analysis (see (Langfeld, 1945) for a historical review). The reason for this popularity is rooted in the empiricist nature of many psychological and sociological studies and related theories. Due to operationalization, any empirical or theoretical concept becomes an observable and measurable variable. And, as readers remember, this is exactly the idea of empiricism: to deal only with observables and to establish relationships and regularities among them. Thus, by operationalizing all the concepts and establishing statistical regularities among them, social scientists are following the canons of the empiricist/positivist paradigm, that only the empirical and observable reality should be the source of scientific knowledge. That is why the concept *operationalism* has emerged in the philosophy of science as an alternative way to identify this paradigm, thus making the tendency toward the operationalization of all concepts its other defining characteristic (Chang, 2009).

Many scholars have criticized the excessive operationalizing of concepts in the social sciences. A first point of this critique is that an operational definition provides an overtly restrictive form of a concept (Chang, 2009). In the same vein, Blumer (1969/1986) argued that any operationalization is a limited and circumscribed representation of the idea of a concept. He used as an example the concept of "intelligence." By its theoretical idea, intelligence is a broad and multifaceted psychological phenomenon that has different manifestations in different domains of human activity, like scientific research, engineering, military operations, investment planning, hunting, lecturing, playing football, and teaching children. These activities require rational thinking and acting, but in each case the intelligence required has a different nature, structure, and manifestations. Psychologists have been inclined to reduce all this diversity to the scores on intelligence tests developed for a pedagogical purpose. "It should be immediately clear how ridiculous and unwarranted it is to believe that the operationalizing of intelligence through a given intelligence test yields a satisfactory picture of intelligence" (p. 31). Blumer further suggested studying intelligence as it unfolds in people's everyday activities: "to catch and study intelligence as it is in play in actual empirical life instead of relying on a specialized and usually arbitrary selection of one area of its presumed manifestation" (p. 31).

Second, to use the operationalizations to identify the meaning of concepts is a dangerous idea, because then these operationalizations start running the show, instead of the opposite, when the ideas and theories determine how to identify and study different manifestations of the concepts. Related to this is a concern expressed by Hempel (1966) that operationalizations of concepts may change as the theories within which these concepts are used change (p. 95), which means that operationalizations should always be secondary to theoretical ideas, never the opposite way.

Another point of critique of operationalism is that not all concepts can be or should be operationalized. For example, the theoretical concept of "evolution" has never been operationalized, but nevertheless, it has played a fundamental role in changing our understanding about how life and living organisms emerged. This is where the operationalist/empiricist/positivist position comes into a fundamental conflict with the realist paradigm. (See the discussion below).

Concepts and Philosophical Paradigms

In this section I will summarize the use of concepts and the process of conceptualization within each philosophical paradigm. The use of concepts within each paradigm is strongly determined by its main postulates and constitutes an important aspect of how these paradigms actually work within research. It is possible to say that the paradigms manifest themselves in the processes of development and the use of the concepts.

Concepts Within the Positivist Paradigm

There are three aspects of how positivists treat concepts: (a) theoretical concepts are nominal; (2) all concepts have to be operationalized and transformed into variables; (3) the concepts are developed by researchers and imposed on the objects of investigation. All three of these aspects are closely and intimately related to the main propositions of this paradigm.

Because of the strict empiricist foundation of their epistemological position, positivists do not accept the existence of unobservables and, because of this, their theoretical concepts have exclusively nominal functions—hence, the nominalist position regarding theoretical concepts. What they have labeled "theoretical terms" are so-called "auxiliary" or "nominal" terms that connect empirically verifiable concepts into a coherent conceptual framework (Hollis, 2002). They are used as "fillers" among empirical concepts to "glue" them together. This proposition determines the second conceptual rule of positivism: all concepts that are used in research have to be operationalized. This again is a direct consequence of the postulate of empiricism: scientific knowledge has to be empirically based, because only empirical and directly observable data can give researchers a solid basis for their theories. Theories here are statements about near-universal regularities among empirically given events, things, and processes. The third aspect of the positivist's conceptualization reflects the concepts' origins. In positivist research, concepts are generated by researchers based on their understanding of the phenomena, and their operationalizations are imposed on the objects of a study. Researchers' theories and operationalizations also determine the uses and interpretations of their data. Participants in such research are passive generators of answers to the imposed instruments, with no space to say anything about their own understanding of the phenomena and their meaning.

> The *operational* tradition works "top down" in the sense that it imposes a researcher's concepts on everyday life, the assumption being that the researchers is in a position to judge what concepts will be relevant because of the theoretical model or perspective that has been adopted. (Blaikie, 2010, p. 120)

Although extreme positivism and empiricism are abandoned as research paradigms in most domains of social and human sciences, their presence in the researchers' thinking may be traced by the way they use concepts in their research.

Concepts in the Interpretivist Paradigm

Researchers who work on interpreting different levels of meanings are more diverse and cautious with using their concepts. An important idea that accounts for a complex way of using concepts in interpretivist research is the idea of *double hermeneutics* of social inquiries. Positivist researchers deal with a "single hermeneutic" (Danemark, Ekstrom, Jakobsen, & Karlsson, 2002, p. 36) because they have to interpret only the data that they themselves generated. As was mentioned in Chapter 4, participants' and informants' interpretations and understandings of events that they participate in are off the radar of positivists. Double hermeneutic means that interpretivist researchers have to interpret the interpretations which their informants have already developed with regard to things, events, and actions within their sociocultural worlds. The source of this doubleness is the existence of two conceptual systems in interpretivist research: the researchers' own systems of knowledge, ideas, and meanings with which they approach the intentional worlds of others, and the system of ideas and meanings that is used by their informants, the lay members of a cultural community. To skillfully structure and efficiently use these conceptual systems during the process of double interpretation constitutes one of the main challenges of the interpretivist paradigm.

One of the most important distinctions of interpretivist and positivist conceptualizations is the sources of their concept. While positivists impose their concepts, ideas, and meanings on participants, interpretivists set their own conceptual frameworks based on ideas extracted from the everyday language and practices of their informants.

The main purpose of interpretivist research is to gain an understanding of cultural and personal meanings and the ways they are generated and utilized by members of cultural communities. Thus, the researchers have to learn about the worlds where their informants live and the meanings that they create about them. Interpretivist scholars try to look at the worlds through the eyes of their informants and to comprehend them by using their language. Geertz (2000) labelled this perspective "from the native point of view." This is how Blaikie (2010) articulated this approach:

> In the hermeneutic tradition, researchers work "bottom up" by adopting the position of learner rather than expert. Social actors have to teach the researchers how they understand their world, i.e. what everyday concepts and interpretations (lay theories) they use to make sense of it. By a complex process, researchers can use these lay concepts and methods of understanding as the ingredients for their accounts. (p. 120)

Discovering these laypersons' conceptualizations is only the initial step of developing the researchers' own concepts as tools for further investigation. Blaikie highlighted the following sequence of steps: lay concepts—> technical concepts—> more abstract and elaborated scientific concepts of a researcher (p. 120). Geertz (2000) used "experience-near" and "experience-distant" (p. 57) concepts in ethnographic inquiry, which correspond to the above continuum: folk concepts are experience near, like "fear," whereas scientific abstract concepts are experience-distant, as, for example, "phobia." These abstract concepts are used to formulate theories about people's actions and practices. Geertz highlighted the fundamental challenge of interpretive work in the following way:

> To grasp concepts which, for another people, are experience-near, and to do so well enough to place them in illuminating connection with those experience-distant concepts that theorists have fashioned to capture the general features of social life is clearly a task at least as delicate, if a bit less magical, as putting oneself into someone else's skin. (p. 58)

To illustrate this work, Geertz described his inquiry into the world of a small Javanese village to understand these villagers' interpretations of what a person is. He identified two native concepts that are used by locals with regard to personhood: *batin* and *lair*, or "inside" and "outside" words (p. 60).

> *Batin*, the "inside" word, does not refer to a separate seat of encapsulated spirituality detached or detachable from the body, or indeed to a bounded unit at all, but to the emotional life of human beings taken generally. It consists of the fuzzy, shifting flow of subjective feeling perceived directly in all its phenomenological immediacy but considered to be, at its roots at least, identical across all individuals, whose individuality it thus effaces . . .
>
> And, similarly, *lair*, the "outside" word, has nothing to do with the body as an object, even an experienced object. Rather, it refers to that part of human life which, in our culture, strict behaviorists limit themselves to studying—external actions, movements, postures, speech—again conceived as in its essence invariant from one individual to the next. Therefore, these two sets of phenomena—inward feelings and outward actions—are regarded not as functions of one another but as independent realms of being to be put in proper order independently. (pp. 60–61)

Based on the analysis of these and some other experience-near concepts (such as *alus*—"pure" or "refined" and *kasar*—"impolite" or "rough") related to the Javanese notion of personhood and people's psychological functioning, he came to the conclusion that the Javanese ideal of personal functioning consists of controlling the inner psychological world through meditation and religious discipline and controlling outward actions through etiquette, thus making a civilized human being emotionally stable with his behavior being "predictable, undisturbing, [and] elegant" (p. 61). Then Geertz proceeded to do a similar analysis of the Balinese and Moroccan cultural models of personhood and self and articulated their uniqueness and differences from the Western model.

Another difference of the interpretivists' use of concept is that their concepts, although theoretically defined, are flexible as they are involved in the hermeneutic circles of interpretations and reinterpretations. Concepts evolve as researchers discover new layers of meanings and new nuances of their applications in different domains of life. That is why strict operationalization is in sharp opposition to the main postulates of this paradigm. Blaikie (2010) accounted for this aspect in the following way:

> To use concepts as advocated by this [interpretivist] tradition is to be reflexive: to allow concepts to evolve through a process of re-examination and reflection. The meaning of a concept does not remain static; it changes as the concept evolves from the data and is applied to them. Whether concepts developed in this way can be applied in other contexts is a matter for investigation. . . . The aim of all this is to generate concepts that fit the problem at hand and work to provide useful description and understanding. (p. 120)

Geertz (2000) described this circle of constant moves from general to specific and back in the following way:

> In answering this question, it is necessary I think first to notice the characteristic intellectual movement, the inward conceptual rhythm, in each of these analyses, . . . namely, a continuous dialectical tacking between the most local of local detail and the most global of global structure in such a way as to bring both into view simultaneously. In seeking to uncover the Javanese, Balinese, or Moroccan sense of self, one oscillates restlessly between the sort of exotic minutiae (lexical antitheses, categorical schemes, morphophonemic transformations) that make even the best ethnographies a trial to read and the sort of sweeping characterizations ("quietism," "dramatism," "contextualism") that makes all but the most pedestrian of them somewhat implausible. Hopping back and forth between the whole conceived through the parts which actualize it and the parts conceived through the whole which motivates them, we seek to turn them, by a sort of intellectual perpetual motion, into explications of one another. (p. 70)

As an attentive reader may notice, this is a well-articulated description of the hermeneutic circle that was presented in Chapter 4.

Concepts in the Realist Paradigm

Representatives of the realist paradigm have both similarities and differences with positivists and interpretivists regarding the use of concepts. Realists accept the necessity and importance of the empirical concepts—concepts that describe, classify, and categorize empirical reality—and the possibility of their operationalization. But, as readers remember, according to realism, theoretical concepts and many hypothetical constructs do not require operationalization because they represent the realm of unobservables: powers, structures, and mechanisms, which by their very nature are unavailable for direct empirical verification. Think about the concept of "natural selection," which reflects a set of unobservable processes that act on biological populations over a very long period of time. No one can observe and manipulate it. That is why it is impossible and unnecessary to operationalize it. Researchers may theorize what processes constitute natural and sexual selections, and how they work and then test their hypotheses about these processes through a variety of methods. Operationalization in this case is not required and cannot be done. Think about such concepts as "unconscious," "ego," "internalization," "accommodation," and many others that are used by researchers as useful explanatory tools, but which are not available for operationalizations. Realists believe that their theoretical concepts are not simply the nominal language constructions that are created to connect empirical facts and label their associations, but that they reflect real entities (until they are falsified), their properties, and the powers that drive them. For realists, theoretical concepts are intellectual devices to help infer hypotheses that could be tested empirically. The descriptive and empirical concepts should be operationalized and used to verify the proposed hypotheses.

Realists mostly use concepts that are generated by researchers but they do not deny the possibility of using concepts extracted from the agents' own experience and interpretations. Realist-interpretivist research that aims at discovering deep layers of meaning may start with the experience-near concepts and then move to more experience-distant ones, establishing a fruitful conceptual framework using the bottom-up strategy of conceptualization.

Differences Between Realists and Interpretivists

Realism invites sociocultural researchers to go beyond the first order interpretations of everyday life provided by informants and also surpass the second order interpretations provided by researchers. For realists, descriptive concepts, the ones that are applied to the meanings of things as well as to structures of experiences of members of communities, are not as important as theoretical concepts, which should "go beyond more superficial and accidental circumstances, including ideologically conditioned understandings of various kinds" and should "speak of the mechanisms that produce courses of events" (Danemark et al., 2002, p. 37), people's actions, thoughts, and meanings. The development of these theoretical concepts constitutes one of the most important objectives of a social realist research. Realists

> claim that an interpretation of the "second order" does not constitute a social scientific explanation either. It is not enough just to build on various social agents' own descriptions and understanding of themselves and of existence, . . . social phenomena have a material dimension, and it is essential to explore how people's notions and concepts are related to social practices of various kinds. (p. 37)

When we deal with theoretical concepts in the realist paradigm, it is practically impossible to give them a concise definition. Usually they require an elaborated description and explanation in order to help other scholars grasp their meaning and to understand the role they play in explaining the phenomena under research. An encyclopedia article or even a book may be necessary to explain them thoroughly. In Box 6.1 I discuss the concept of habitus—one of the most deep and complex theoretical concepts in sociocultural realist sciences.

EXAMPLE BOX 6.1. THE CONCEPT OF HABITUS AS AN EXAMPLE OF A THEORETICAL CONCEPT IN REALIST SOCIAL RESEARCH

As an example of a theoretical concept within the realist paradigm, let's examine Pierre Bourdieu's idea of *habitus*. **Pierre Bourdieu** (1930–2002), a French anthropologist, sociologist, and philosopher, is known for his ethnographic and sociological research conducted inside and outside of France. Many scholars consider Bourdieu to be realist in his theorizing and research. Combined with the concepts of "capital" (economic, social, and cultural), "field," and "practice," Bourdieu's concept of *habitus* comprises the conceptual framework for his theory of regulating human actions by sociocultural structures. He is known for introducing a theoretical law of human social actions, or *practice*: "[(habitus)(capital)] x field = practice." (Bourdieu, 1984, p. 101). But let's go back to the concept of *habitus*.

Every sociocultural community develops particular ways of dealing with everyday situations, events, and circumstances: how to make love, how to marry, how to give birth, how to bring up a child, how to eat, how to sleep, how to perceive the world, how to classify it, and the myriads of ways of interpreting and understanding what counts in their world as beautiful, ugly, just, wrong, inappropriate, and thousands of other aspects of communal living. As cultural communities evolve, these ways of dealing with events are refined, polished and, finally, inscribed into the social fabric of a community as the proper ways of perceiving, categorizing, interpreting, and doing things. They become habitual, taken-for-granted manners of acting within, reacting to and interacting with the sociocultural world. This is a social constituent of what Bourdieu designates as "habitus." Any new member of a community has to internalize these habitual and customary behaviors and accept them as valid and trustworthy methods for organizing all aspects of his or her life without reflection or hesitation. As a result of this internalization, the everyday world opens to people as "a commonsense world endowed with the *objectivity* secured by consensus of the meaning (*sens*) of practices" (1977, p. 80). This is an intrasubjective component of *habitus*. This means that people with internalized *habitus* perceive their social worlds as "immediately intelligible and foreseeable, and hence taken for granted" (p. 80). This taken-for-grantedness is very important for people's feeling of security and predictability of the world where they live. *Habitus* allow members of a community to understand each other and coordinate their actions based on this mutual understanding in a way that provides the smooth and harmonious coordination of social actions (unfortunately it is not always that smooth). According to Bourdieu, social life is possible because of *habitus*.

Bourdieu assigned several functions in regulating human practices to the internalized *habitus*. "The habitus is necessity internalized and converted into a disposition that generates meaningful practices and meaning-giving perceptions; . . . habitus [are]—systems of generative schemes" (1984, p. 170). For Bourdieu, *habitus* are systems of dispositions, reproductive programs, and principles that participate both in the perception and interpretation of information from the social worlds and in initiation and regulation of people's actions. *Habitus* is "an acquired system of preferences, of principles of vision and division (what is usually called *taste*), and also a system of durable cognitive structures (which are essentially the product of the internalization of objective structures) and of schemes of actions which orient the perception of the situation and the appropriate response" (1994, p. 25). "Habitus are generative principles of distinct and distinctive practices—what the worker eats, and especially the way they eats it, the sport he practices and the way he practices it, his political opinions and the way he expresses them are systematically different from the industrial owner's corresponding activities" (1994, p. 8). He also called them the "generative principle of regulated improvisations" (1977, p. 78), meaning that habitus not only generate practices, but they also set a range within which a person may improvise with these practices by exercising his or her agency.

Another important attribute of habitus as internalized disposition is that they act automatically with or without minimal conscious control. When asked about these habitual practices, a person may answer that this is how these practices are done here. "The habitus is the universalizing mediation which causes an individual agent's practices, without either explicit reason or signifying intent, to be none the less 'sensible' and reasonable'" (1977, p. 79). He compared the experience of habitus with "what is called in sport a 'feel' for the game, that is, the art of *anticipating* the future of the game, which is inscribed in the present state of play"

(1994, p. 25). On a final note, it is important to say that habitus is not directly and obviously given to either an actor or a researcher; researchers cannot discover habitus by interviewing members of a community about them or conducting surveys on them. Habitus can only be inferred (we may say, retroducted) by a researcher based on a set of empirical evidence comprised of observations, ethnography, interviews, and surveys that are glued together by the knowledge, reason, imagination, and intuition of a researcher. The nonobservable nature of habitus and its unavailability to direct empirical methods through operationalizations make this concept a realist theoretical construct in its purest form.

What is Theory and How is It Defined in Different Paradigms?

"A theory-driven empirical study" is a conventional statement about, and an important requirement for, good research. At meetings of graduate students' advisory committees, it is common to hear: "What theory did you use for your study?" Or, "Your project cannot be a-theoretical." But what is *theory* in research on psychology and culture? How can we define these theories, what are their functions in empirical studies, and how can they be used efficiently? These are the questions for the rest of this chapter.

We have just talked about various aspects of dealing with scientific concepts and here we may start applying these aspects to the concept of *theory*. Let's start with the nominal definition: The term "theory" came into life "via late Latin from Greek *theōria*—contemplation, speculation" (Soanes & Stevenson, 2008). Here are several theoretical definitions of this concept.

> Theory [is] a supposition or a system of ideas intended to explain something, especially one based on general principles independent of the thing to be explained. (Soanes & Stevenson, 2008)

> *Social theories are explanations of recurrent patterns or regularities in social life.* They are answers to questions or puzzles about why people behave in the way they do in particular social context, and why social life is organized in the way it is. In the context of research design, *a theory is an answer to a "why" question*; it is an explanation of a pattern or regularity that has been observed, the cause or reason for which needs to be understood. (Blaikie, 2010, pp. 124–125)

> A theory is more than a synopsis of the moves that have been played in the game of nature; it also sets forth some idea of the rules of the game, by which the moves become intelligible. (Kaplan, 1964, p. 302)

Theories are rational and logical verbal constructions that consist of theoretical concepts and propositional statements that connect these concepts. Theories are created to explain phenomena, events, and things upon which researchers focus in their investigations. A common denominator of the above definitions is that in their statements, theories go beyond observable events and their regularities; they explain them both. They explain them by providing the general principle, the theoretical laws of why and how these events and their patterns have occurred.

It is not a coincidence that we discuss the meaning of the concept *theory* in the same chapter where we examine scientific concepts. Concepts for a theory are as firewood for a campfire. As Kaplan (1964) explains, "it follows that concept formation and theory formation in science go hand in hand—another great insight owed to Kant" (p. 52). Kaplan also warned researchers about the complex dialectics between concepts and theories, or about *"the paradox of conceptualization."* This paradox means that "the proper concepts are needed to formulate a good theory, but we need a good theory to arrive at the proper concepts" (p. 53). Another side of this paradox is the fact that the growth of scientific knowledge is accompanied by more refined and well-articulated conceptualizations—not heavily reliant on the descriptive, but mostly theoretical.

The major constituents of a theory are *theoretical concepts* and *theoretical laws* (Kaplan, 1964, p. 297). As we discussed in the previous sections, theoretical concepts are the ideas that make reference to unobservable factors, their structures, and powers in the social and/or psychological functioning of people in different communities. What are *theoretical laws*? It is perhaps easiest to explain them by comparing them to *empirical laws* or *empirical regularities*. The statement "the sun rises every morning in the east" is an example of an empirical regularity, which acquires the status of an empirical law because it works universally. Thorndike's law of effect, that behavior that is reinforced has a high probability to be repeated, is a behaviorist empirical law. All generalized statements based on statistical regularities are other instances of empirical laws. Empirical laws, thus, are statements of invariant regularities among events, things, behavioral acts and other empirically observable instances. Very often we can see these regularities (as in the case of the rising sun) and confirm their validity by simply witnessing them.

Theoretical laws, on the other hand, are statements of systematic relations among unobservable entities. These entities are identified by theoretical concepts. Let's look again at Tomasello's (1999) theory of the cultural origin of human cognition. One of the pivotal statements that he put forward to explain the emergence of human cognition was "the ability of individual organisms to understand con-specifics as beings *like themselves* who have intentional and mental lives like their own" (p. 5). This is a statement about the dynamics among several unobservable entities through the processes of intersubjective sharing of similar mental representations. "The ability . . . to understand . . ." "to understand con-specifics as beings like themselves," "intentional and mental lives" are theoretical concepts, created by the researcher to describe unobservable components of the process of human sociocultural bases of cognitive development. None of these theoretical entities are empirically verifiable, but were inferred through retroduction by the scientist based on his studies and are rooted in knowledge about the human socialization and enculturation. The above statement about the relationships among these concepts may be called a theoretical mechanism or law of the culturally acquired basis of social cognition. To word this law differently: in their socio-symbolic environments, all human beings acquire an ability to understand other people as beings like themselves, having their own mental worlds and psychological lives.

There are several distinguishing features of theoretical laws. (1) They do not generalize empirical regularities from samples to populations (*enumerative generalization;* see Chapter 3), rather they generalize the unobservable entities and their relations that are abstracted from particular empirical instances to other instances—*theoretical generalization*. (2) They aim at explaining not only why the theoretical entities are interconnected but also what the rules, principles, and nature of this interconnectedness are (see Kaplan's definition of a theory above). Tomasello's theoretical law not only states the inherent sociality of humans' mental development, but it also clarifies the nature of this sociality, specifically that it is based on the shared intersubjectivity of human individuals and their ability to understand others though this intersubjectivity. Hence, this law reveals not simply that people have to be socially connected in order to become human beings, but that the essence of this sociality lies in their shared intersubjectivity: "I know that you think and feel like me, and I also know that you know that I know this, and we together have the same understanding of the world." This intersubjectivity is the basis of culture and of exclusively human forms of social cognition. (3) Theoretical laws cannot be observed directly; they are inferred. A researcher's rational thinking and creative imagination are crucial for this inference. "[A]rriving at workable theories calls for the exercise of creative imagination, as has been emphasized by countless working scientists, from Einstein on down" (Kaplan, 1964, p. 308).

(4) Another fundamental component to construct a theory is having deep knowledge about the phenomenon under investigation, about other theories, their empirical evidence, and their critiques. Researchers must have all available facts about the phenomenon. Knowledge from any adjacent disciplines is also important. (5) Theories are a set of theoretical laws that explain the phenomenon of interest and address the problem that has driven the research. Explanation is a major function of a theory and, hence, of theoretical concepts and theoretical laws.

In culture and psychology studies, the notion of explanation is a controversial one, as many scholars, especially interpretivists, question the possibility of explaining human actions, suggesting instead an interpretative understanding of them. Is it possible to explain human action in various sociocultural contexts? What kind of statements should account for the explanations in these cases? Consider an immigrant father originally from Afghanistan who killed his daughters because they became too strongly acculturated into Canadian teenage culture and thus brought "dishonor" to him and his family (see the Shafia family murders at http://en.wikipedia.org/wiki/Shafia_family_murders). One form of explanation is to refer to this father's thoughts, feeling, beliefs, and reasoning that he provided to justify his action. This is an explanation through understanding a person's meanings, reasons, and intentions. Interpretivists often subscribe to this type of interpretative explanation. Realist researchers may want to explain why these meanings, reasons, and motives emerged—what were the ultimate causes not only of these particular actions, but of the motives, reasons, and interpretations behind them? And this is where a theory is crucial. Although "honour killings" frequently happen in the native country of the people involved, in our case it is definitely related to the problem of the acculturation of the father and his daughters to the Canadian way of life. Thus, a theory of acculturation is needed here. Because there is no such a theory, I will use Bourdieu's theory of practice and his concept of habitus to explain this murder. It is possible to state that the father brought with him from Afghanistan deeply internalized cultural habitus about family honor, the role women play in maintaining this honor, and the sanctions that can be implemented to restore this honor when it is stained. These habitus were engraved in his mind as the only valid way to perceive, interpret, and deal with the world. After immigrating to Canada, the same habitus continued guiding his perception and actions. But in this Western country, his old habitus became useless and led him to the catastrophic actions. This man did not reflect on his new surroundings, did not take the time to learn the new habitus relevant to the culture of Canada and, finally, failed in his Canadian life. In this theorizing, we find the ultimate cause of this person's behavior, feelings, and motivation is relying upon the unreflected old habitus, which became a causal explanation of this murder. If we accept this theoretical explanation, then the following questions can be asked: why do other immigrants from the same country not kill their daughters? Why did the Shafia father fail to acculturate to Canada while other fathers succeeded in acculturating? What are the mechanisms of acculturation and why did they go wrong in the Shafia case?

Thus, we may state that explanation through understanding, as a first level explanation, and explanation through causal powers, as a deeper level of explanation, may work together, but for analytical purposes, they have to be kept separate (Shapiro, 2005).

Theories in Different Paradigms

The interpretation of the concept of theory and everything related to it in the above section associates to the realist paradigm, with some aspects pertaining to interpretivism. In this section I will elaborate more on understanding theories in positivism and interpretivism. It is good to start with the following quotation:

> Bacon himself characterizes the scientist as neither wholly speculative and like a spider spinning his web from his own substance, nor wholly empirical and like an ant collecting data

into a heap, but like the bee feeding on the nectar it gathers, digesting it, and so transmuting it into the purest honey. (Kaplan, 1964, p. 308)

This quote identifies three ways of doing science. The spider spins the web of meanings by imposing the subjectivities of researchers' thinking on the realities under investigation. The ant collects empirical facts and regularities to compile them into a usable heap. Lastly, the bee collects nectar to produce honey, as a scientist collects empirical data in all their forms to produce a well-researched theory. Hence, three metatheoretical paradigms are presented here: interpretivism (in one of its forms), positivism, and realism.

Theories in Positivism

For positivists, theories are descriptive by their nature. Recall that because the positivism paradigm is rooted in extreme empiricism, its followers deny the existence of nonobservable entities and, therefore, all scientific elaborations, both descriptive and explanatory, should be contained within the empirical realm. To positivists the main languages are the language of observable empirical events and the language of operationalization (Blaikie, 2007). All scientific concepts should be reducible to this empirical and observational languages. This is how the positivist psychologists articulate their view of scientific theory:

> Our preliminary outline of the use of the notion of theory has brought us this far: A theory, through a set of definitions or rules for interpretation, must be about something (it has empirical reference); a theory is a more-or-less complex anticipation system (it permits prediction); a theory must be stated in a way that is communicable (it is public). (p. 139) . . . Theories are sets of statement, understandable to others, which make predictions about empirical events. (Mandler & Kessen, 1964, p. 142)

Bem and de Jong (2006) provided a similar definition: "a theory is a set of statements that organizes, predicts and explains observations; it tells you how phenomena relate to each other, and what you can expect under still unknown conditions" (p. 18). As demonstrated in Chapter 3, for positivists predictions can be done through the deductive-nomological mode of inference by using established empirical regularities as near-universal laws.

> [T]he original idea (with the logical positivist) was that theories have a formal structure, like abstract calculus, and deriving predictions [and explanations] is considered an exercise in formal logic. . . . In the history of psychology, however, Hull's attempt to build a formal deductive system for the prediction of behavior was a failure. (p. 18)

Positivists also separate empirical and theoretical aspects of research making them relatively independent forms of research activity. This is how Mandler and Kessen (1964) articulate this separation:

> Throughout the history of modern science there has been a running debate between two groups of researchers on the issue of the utility of theories. On one side have appeared the defenders of *abstraction and speculation*, the people who, like James (1892) calling for a "Lavoisier or Galileo of psychology," see theory as an essential step in the scientific process. *For them, the mere recitation of accumulated 'facts' would never constitute a system of knowledge, but rather they seek the greater theoretical insight that will reveal the secrets of nature.* Counter to this devotion to generalized statement is the attitude of the *research workers* who are usually

called *'pure empiricists.'* From Newton's (1713) celebrated but probably misunderstood *'Hypotheses non fingo"* to Skinner's (1950) "Are learning theories necessary?" there has been a steady line of defense drawn for the position that *what matters in science is the patient collection of data*, to which end worrying about *heady abstractions will be more of a diversion* and *waste of time than a help to prediction and control* [emphases added]. (p. 149–150)

The positivist position is clear here: they are "research workers" who are "pure empiricists" and they are patiently collecting data for the purpose of "prediction and control." It is presumed that the data out there are objective, independent of research workers' conceptions of them, and are waiting to be picked up. The fellows from another stream of thinking are trying to "reveal the secrets of nature" with regard to people's functioning; they invite psychologists to theorize based on "accumulated facts." The research workers reject this invitation to be involved with "heady abstractions," because such involvement is "a diversion and waste of time" and distracts research workers from doing the science of prediction and control. Thus "pure empiricists" naïvely believe that they can successfully run their experiments without any concern about the theories behind them, and call this enterprise true scientific research. When too many psychologists and social scientists endorse such thinking, the result for the science and its effectiveness could be disastrous: science transforms itself into a library of empirical facts and regularities, and knowledge does not progress.

Another side of the same type of thinking is the possible existence of a "theoretical psychology" relatively independent of empirical research. This happens when scholars believe that theorizing can be separated from empirical investigations and may constitute a separate and relatively independent form of research activity. In some instances, theoretical psychologists work with empirical data that have been collected by other researchers and that are waiting to be theoretically systematized. But the fact here is that in cases of such "pure" theorizing, the unity of the empirical and theoretical sides of a problem-oriented research is broken and assigned to different people, and such division of labor can be problematic. This unity is restored under the realist paradigm.

Let us first summarize the main features of a theory in the positivists' understanding. (1) A theory has to consist only of empirically measurable and verifiable concepts/variables; no non-observable theoretical entities are allowed. In some instances, positivists may strive to go beyond pure descriptions of events and their regularities, and may introduce " *'auxiliary'* theoretical terms" (Niiniluoto, 1999, p. 111). These auxiliary terms are semantic constructions that allow researchers to connect observational concepts and statements into a coherent logical system (pp. 109–113). But nothing is implied to exist behind these terms; they are simply verbal notifications. (2) A positivist theory is a set of statements that describe relations among empirical variables and clarify the conditions under which these relations are the strongest. (3) The main purpose of these theories is to predict outcomes, usually different forms of human behavior, and not their causal explanations. (4) All manipulations with the variables and tests of their predictive powers have to be done by statistical analysis. (5) These theories are usually relatively flexible, allowing for the inclusion or exclusion of some of the variables; such theories have no potentiality for an in-depth understanding of the nature of behavior, but may be utilitarian for the practical prediction of different instances of human actions, including actions related to health, work, or education.

Theories in Interpretivism

Does interpretivism require theories? Does an interpretivist research aim at developing a theory? Is a theory actually a relevant concept for this type of research? These are the questions that researchers who identify themselves with this paradigm ask themselves. If interpretivism is about interpretation and understanding cultural and personal meanings, what should theories in this paradigm be about?

We may identify two forms of interpretivism: in one, a researcher, as the spider in the above quotation, creates meaning out of linguistic and conversational interactions with texts or persons; in the other, a researcher, as the bee mentioned above, uses interpreted meanings to understand them and develop some theoretical accounts for these meanings and their developments. The first form of interpretivism is similar to a strong version of social constructionism, whereas the second one is considered to be a part of the realist paradigm. I have a strong conviction that the denial of reality in any of its forms cannot coexist with science and scientific research, so, I set aside the discussion of the first version of interpretivism and send interested readers to authoritative sources (see above).

I have already presented some of the theoretical ideas of Pierre Bourdieu within the realist paradigm, and now, as an example of productive theoretical work in the domain of interpretivism, I will use the works of another French anthropologist and sociologist, **Marcel Mauss** (1872–1950). Mauss published several books that refer to their theoretical content even in the titles: *The gift: Forms and functions of exchange in archaic societies* (1925/1967), *A general theory of magic* (1950/1990), and *Sacrifice: Its nature and function* (together with Henri Hubert, 1964, later this was translated as *Understanding religious sacrifice*, Routledge, 2001). His most renowned text is considered to be *The gift*, where he made an attempt to understand the functions and purposes of exchanging gifts. The research question that drove his inquiry was: "What power resides in the object given that causes its recipient to pay it back?" (1922/1990, p. 33). It immediately becomes clear from this question that the author wants to go beyond the ritual of gift exchange and wants to understand the power that drives this ritual and especially the act of reciprocation. This question indicates that Mauss had strong realist inclinations to get into the causal driving forces of the phenomenon he interpreted and tried to explain.

In constructing his theory Mauss, first, provided an analytic description of different rituals of gift exchange in Polynesia, Melanesia, among American Northwest Indians, and in some other regions. He started with using descriptive concepts extracted from the studied communities like, "potlach," "tongo," "kula," and many others. These are the experience-near concepts that label various gift exchange rituals and their aspects in the language of native people. Based on these descriptions, the scholar introduced theoretical experience-distant concepts, which became the building blocks of his theory of gift exchange: "the notion of honour," "social statuses," "the obligation to give," "the obligation to receive," and "the obligation to reciprocate." The more encompassing concept "the institution of 'total service'" combines these three obligations into a theory of gift exchange. Next, Mauss introduced ideas of the forces and powers that accompany the ritual of gift exchange. His theoretical conclusion is that gift exchange is a powerful ritual that is driven by the notions of honor, prestige, wealth demonstration, status maintenance, and social bonds establishment. It is powerful because a tremendous part of the social fabric of the analyzed societies resides in this ritual. As the consilience criteria (see below), Mauss traced the signs of this ritual in modern morality, laws, and economic activities and demonstrated the continuity of many of its aspect into modern times.

We may conclude that interpretivist research may have a theoretical focus over and above the descriptive goals of ethnography and the interpretive objectives of understanding meanings of observed practices and rituals. In this case, theorizing is directed toward locating the phenomenon under investigation within the field of forces of a particular collectivity and demonstrating what forces are at work and how they generate and regulate the phenomenon of interest. In this case, theories are sets of statements about the mechanisms that function behind the scene of observable events and actions and their meanings. The abductive and retroductive modes of inference are the primary ways of reasoning here. Interpretivist theoreticians do not develop hypotheses about the mechanisms and do not usually put them to the test through experiments. But it is fair to say that these theories can be falsified by discovering societies or cultural communities where the rituals work under different laws. Therefore, interpretivist theories, just as any other scientific theories, can be falsified. For example, Testart (1998) and Laidlaw (2000) criticized Mauss's theory of gift exchange by describing practices of "free" gifts, those forms of gift exchange that Mauss proclaimed do not exist.

Theories in the Realist Paradigm

Realists start their theoretical work by studying patterns of events that are observed and established through different methods and that constitute a problem or puzzle for scientists.

> The ultimate objects of scientific understanding are . . . the things that produce and the mechanisms that generate the flux of the phenomena of the world. Scientists attempt to discover the way things act, a knowledge typically expressed in laws; and what things are, a knowledge . . . typically expressed in real definitions. (Bhaskar, 1975/2008, p. 66)

To move from the empirical to the real realm, realists use retroduction to infer the unobservable mechanisms of events and their patterns. Theoretical concepts are used to express ideas about the unobservable components of these mechanisms. These concepts are articulated through theoretical (or real) definitions. Relations among theoretical concepts are expressed in the form of theoretical laws. These laws are used to identify the dynamic aspects of the interactions of the structural components and the causal generative powers that produce the configurations of events. Realist theories are sets of statements about components and powers that make the causal mechanisms work in producing the phenomena of interest. Bourdieu's realist position in studying society and people's action in it is presented like this:

> The task of sociology, according to Pierre Bourdieu (1989a:7), is "to uncover the most profoundly buried structures of the various social worlds which constitute the social universe, as well as the 'mechanisms' which tend to ensure their reproduction or their transformation." (Bourdieu & Wacquant, 1992, p. 7)

One of the fundamental features of using the realist approach on a theoretical activity is that it is not separated from the empirical work of data generation, collection, and systematization. Realists start their research by identifying a scientific problem and creating conjectures to explain it. These conjectures are hypotheses, foreknowledge or nascent theories that are used to generate data for testing them. In the social and psychological sciences there are no pure objective facts; these facts depend on researchers' conceptualizations of the corresponding realities and their events. Scientific concepts create social facts. But concepts are constituents of theories; thus, facts based on observations, surveys or experiments are always theory-laden. Facts do not "speak for themselves;" they need to be generated and interpreted. Conjectures, hypotheses, and theories also set the framework for this interpretation. If the data support the conjectures and hypotheses that were proposed upfront, these hypotheses can be worded as theories that need further theoretical elaboration and empirical verification in order to become a valid explanation of the problem. If the mechanisms hypothesized by the theory exist and are real driving forces of a particular behavior or social event, then researchers may expect that particular events in particular conditions should take place. Researchers either create artificial conditions to make these events happen (realist experiments) or search for naturally occurring events and explore the conditions that make them come about (realist case-based research). Thus, every step of realist research blends theoretical thinking with empirical testing, making these two aspects of a research activity inseparable. Once again, the research approach of Bourdieu provides a good example of such unity:

> Bourdieu maintains that every act of research is simultaneous empirical (it confronts the world of observable phenomena) and theoretical (it necessary engages hypotheses about the underlying structure of relations that observations are designed to capture). Even the most minute empirical operation—the choice of a scale or measurement, a coding decision, the construction of an indicator, or inclusion of an item in a questionnaire—involves theoretical choices, conscious or unconscious, while the most abstract conceptual puzzle cannot be fully clarified without systemic engagement with empirical reality. (Bourdieu & Wacquant, 1992, p. 35)

Criteria of Validity for Realist Theories

An important question about realist theories is: what are the criteria for testing their validity? As readers will remember, the theories that are created by the abductive and retroductive modes of inference are based on the disciplined imagination, intuition, and reasoning of researchers. Are there limits to their imagination? Can their fly-off creativity be systematically evaluated? The answer is "Yes," and the scholar who has most contributed to the development of these criteria is **William Whewell**, an English philosopher, researcher, and scholar of encyclopedic erudition and knowledge. He may be named as one of the fathers of the realist approach in modern sciences (Snyder, 2006). Whewell proposed three criteria for the verification of the validity of a theory: *prediction*, *consilience*, and *coherence* (Snyder, 2000, 2005).

Prediction. The criterion of prediction is pretty straightforward: if the theorized mechanism exists, then, when the conditions are right, a researcher can expect a particular phenomenon to happen. Ability to foretell the events is, in his opinion, a strong indicator of the validity of a theory.

> He [Whewell] believed that "to predict unknown facts found afterwards to be true is . . . a confirmation of a theory which in impressiveness and value goes beyond any explanation of known facts" (1857/1873, II, 557). Whewell claimed that the agreement of the prediction with what occurs (i.e., the fact that the prediction turns out to be correct), is "nothing strange, if the theory be true, but quite unaccountable, if it be not (1860a, 273–4). (Snyder, 2000, para. 16)

As an example of this criterion, we will again use Tomasello's research. This researcher proposed that cooperation—and not competition—constitutes the basis of human sociality and the development of social cognitions. This hypothesis may be labelled as the theory of the cooperative basis of human development. If this theory is true, then the tendency for cooperation must have intrinsic properties: people, especially children, have to have a natural tendency to cooperate, to help, and to sacrifice without any extrinsic rewards. But, if parents or teachers use external rewards for cooperation and helping activities, then this intrinsic inclination could be undermined. To test this prediction, Warneken and Tomasello (2008) conducted an experiment where 20-month-old children were given material rewards for helping adults and, as a result of this manipulation, their desire to help diminished. This experiment confirmed that a tendency toward cooperation is not a learned but an inherent proclivity of humans, and it probably lies at the foundation of our sociality.

Readers may ask, if prediction is also a criterion for the positivist theories, then what is the difference between using it as a validation criterion in positivism and realism? The difference is tremendous. Let's take as an example the prediction of sea tides. Since ancient times, people in coastal areas have developed very accurate tables for predicting tides depending on place, time of year, and time of day. These predictions are based on the universal regularity with which tides occur. For a pure practical purpose, such predictions are very useful and applicable. But this is not a science, because such tables do not provide an explanation of why tides occur and what their mechanisms are. It is known now that they are "caused by the combined effects of the gravitational forces exerted by the Moon and the Sun and the rotation of the Earth" (http://en.wikipedia.org/wiki/Tide). The science of tides and theories of tides are about the forces that bring tides to life. Predictions of tides based on these theories serve the purpose of validating the theory but are not a utilitarian one. Thus we may say that predictions in positivist theories serve utilitarian purposes, while predictions within the realist paradigm serve the purpose of validating a theory about the mechanism of a phenomenon.

Consilience. The second criterion of the validity of a realist theory, according to Whewell, is *consilience*. His classic example is the consilience of Newton's law/theory of gravity.

> What Newton found was that these different kinds of phenomena—including circumjovial orbits, planetary orbits, as well as falling bodies—share an essential property, namely the same cause. What Newton did, in effect, was to subsume these individual "event kinds" into a more general natural kind comprised of sub-kinds sharing a kind essence, namely being caused by an inverse-square attractive force. Consilience of event kinds therefore results in causal unification. (Snyder, 2000, para. 19)

The consilience criterion means that if a proposed theory about the mechanism of a phenomenon is correct, then it is highly probable that the same mechanism works for events and phenomena that are different from those that were used to generate the theory. Whewell defined it in the following way: "The Consilience of Inductions takes place when an Induction, obtained from one class of facts, coincides with an Induction, obtained from another different class. This Consilience is a test of the truth of the Theory in which it occurs" (cited in Wilson (1999, pp 8–9). Darwin used the consilience criterion to defend his theory against numerous critiques.[1] Snyder (2006) provided the following accounts of his use of consilience: 1. "Darwin's theory explains not just many facts, but many *kinds* of facts" (p. 192). This means that the theory of evolution not only explains the adaptedness of organisms, but "the theory provides an explanation for facts in the realm of classification, geography, paleontology, embryology, comparative anatomy, and geology" (p. 192). 2. In his theory, Darwin used laws discovered in other disciplines and tried to causally unify these laws. "Thus Darwin stressed that his theory explained phenomenal laws such as the law of embryonic resemblance" (pp. 192–193). 3. Finally, Darwin stressed that his theory provides causal explanations that none of the other theories can. For example, only his theory explains the homological structures of different organisms. The common ancestor and the process of gradually branching off of different species are causally responsible for the existence of these structures (p. 193). The same criteria of validity can be applied to some theories of interpretivists. Recall that Mauss applied his theory of gift exchange to modern economics, law, and morality and some other spheres of people's lives that are far away from the ethnographic setting where this theory was developed.

---

1 It is interesting to note that one of the most disturbing points of early critiques against Darwin was that his theory was not sufficiently "inductive" and that he "departed from the true inductive track" (Snyder, 2006, p. 190). "Hostile reviewers were demanding 'direct proof'—by which they seemed to mean something like the blind collection of facts and simple inductive generalization of the 'naive inductive' method" (p. 190). Darwin commented to a sympathetic reviewer that "until your review appeared I began to think that perhaps I did not understand at all how to reason scientifically" (p. 190). Darwin replied to one these "inductivists," that "on his standards of proof, *natural* science would never progress" (p. 190). The problem for Darwin was the clash between the enumerative and ampliative forms of inductions; in his thinking the latter he utilized, while his critical reviewers were preoccupied with the former.

Coherence. The third criterion for validating theories—*coherence*—is closely related to the second one. For this criterion, "Whewell claimed, 'the system [theory] becomes more coherent as it is further extended. The elements which we require for explaining a new class of facts are already contained in our system. . . . In false theories, the contrary is the case' (1858b, 91)" (Snyder, 2000, para. 20). Because a theory continually develops and progresses, with time it will require less and less reconceptualization in order to accommodate and explain new facts or new types of phenomena.

Because the realist paradigm is not well articulated in culture and psychology research, more elaboration and thinking is required to make such theories an effective tool for investigations.

Conclusion

Concepts or ideas are building blocks of any research inquiry. They identify the aspects of realities to be investigated and determine what will be considered as "facts" in an inquiry. Concepts are arranged in the form of terms, or linguistic representations of the ideas. Nominalists believe that concepts are names or constructions that conveniently arrange humans' perceptions and experiences. Realists suppose that concepts reflect entities that have real existence. Empirical or descriptive concepts represent various categorizations of realities, whereas explanatory concepts are used to explain phenomena of interest. To avoid vagueness and ambiguity of terms and concepts, they have to have nominal and theoretical definitions. When concepts are operationalized using operational definitions, they are transformed into variables. Theoretical concepts connected by theoretical propositions constitute the essence of scientific theories. Theories address theoretical laws that explain the phenomena of concern. Theories are instruments for and products of scientific research. Conceptualizations and theories' constructions unfold differently in different philosophical paradigms.

Questions

1. Why are concepts and the process of conceptualization considered to be the pivotal aspects of research?
2. Reflect on ontological and epistemological traditions in conceptualization: Is there tension between them? If yes, what is the nature of this tension? In your thinking and discussion, use the arguments between realists and nominalists.
3. Try to understand the strong and weak versions of social constructionism in relation to concept generation and in relation to linguistic and sociocultural realities. This is a challenging question that may require more research.
4. Provide examples of the vagueness and ambiguity of scientific terms in your area of research. Reflect on the consequences of these pitfalls in conceptualization.
5. How do you understand the "functional ambiguity" of concepts? Provide examples of it.
6. Provide several examples of theoretical and operational definitions of the concepts you deal with. Reflect on their differences. Watch for the correspondence between the theoretical and operational definitions of the same concepts.
7. Discuss the limitations of operational definitions. Why do many researchers object to the intensive operationalization of social and psychological concepts?
8. Discuss the application of concepts in three philosophical paradigms. Try to identify the researchers' philosophical thinking by the way they use concepts in their research.
9. Think about theories in your area of research. What theoretical concepts do they use and what theoretical laws do they articulate? Try to differentiate theories within the three paradigms. Reflect on their differences.

Exercises

1. Select concepts that you use in your project; differentiate between empirical and theoretical concepts. What characteristics led you to differentiate them in these categories? Think about the roles that these concepts play in your research and how you use them.
2. Define these concepts; differentiate three forms of definitions; compare them.
3. Connect all the concepts in a meaningful way, creating a conceptual map of your project.

Glossary

Concepts are ideas wrapped in layers of linguistic terms.

> **Empirical concepts** describe the phenomena under investigation.
> **Experience-near** and **experience-distant concepts** (in interpretivism): experience-near concepts are ideas used by people in communities to categorize their worlds; experience-distant are concepts that are used by researchers to comprehend the experience-near categorizations.
> **Substantive and notational concepts/terms**: without substantive concepts, one cannot fully understand a problem or phenomenon; notational concepts simply identify some aspects of the phenomenon of interest.
> **Theoretical concepts** or **hypothetical constructs** represent unobservable structures and powers and explain the phenomenon.

Definition: *nominal*—articulates the etymological origins of a term; *theoretical*—expresses the idea of a concept and addresses the essence of some entity; *operational*—represents a concept through procedures (or operations) by which it becomes manifested and measurable.

Epistemological tradition in conceptualization: highlights the uniqueness of researchers' thinking about the worlds and positions his or her ideas on the phenomenon of interest. Corresponds to the nominalist system of thinking about concepts.

Ontological tradition in conceptualization: emphasizes concepts as representations of some aspects of realities that are the focus of inquiries. Corresponds to the realist approach to scientific concepts.

"The paradox of conceptualization" (by Kaplan, 1964): This paradox means that "the proper concepts are needed to formulate a good theory, but we need a good theory to arrive at the proper concepts" (p. 53). Another side of this paradox is the fact that the growth of scientific knowledge is accompanied by more refined and well-articulated conceptualizations—not heavily reliant on the descriptive, but mostly theoretical.

Theoretical laws are statements about regularities and mechanisms that explain a phenomenon.

Theories are rational verbal constructions that consist of theoretical concepts and propositional statements that connect these concepts and articulate theoretical laws. Theories are created to explain phenomena, events, and things.

Variables are aspects and parameters of phenomena that vary. Usually they are concepts that are made empirically verifiable through operationalizations.

Recommended Reading

Bem, S., & de Jong, H. L. (2006). *Theoretical issues in psychology: An introduction.* (2nd ed.). London, UK: Sage.
Blaikie, N. (2010). *Designing social research: The logic of anticipation.* (2nd ed.). Cambridge, UK: Polity.
Chang, H. (2009). Operationalism. In E. N. Zalta (Ed.), *The Stanford encyclopedia of philosophy* (Fall 2009 ed.). Retrieved from http://plato.stanford.edu/archives/fall2009/entries/operationalism/
Danemark, B., Ekstrom, M., Jakobsen, L., & Karlsson, J. C. (2002). *Explaining society: Critical realism in the social sciences.* London, UK: Routledge.

Kaplan, A. (1964). *The conduct of inquiry: Methodology for behavioral science*. San Francisco, CA: Chandler.
Schwandt, T. A. (2000). Three epistemological stances for qualitative inquiry: Interpretavism, hermeneutics, and social constructionism. In N. K. Denzin & Y. S. Lincoln (Eds.), *Handbook of qualitative research*. (2nd ed., pp. 189–213). Thousand Oaks, CA: Sage
Schwandt, T. A. (2007). *The SAGE dictionary of qualitative inquiry*. (3rd ed.). Thousand Oaks, CA: Sage.

References

Allport, G. W. (1927). Concepts of trait and personality. *Psychological Bulletin, 24*(5), 284–293.
Bem, S., & de Jong, H. L. (2006). *Theoretical issues in psychology: An introduction*. (2nd ed.). London, UK: Sage.
Berry, J. W., Poortinga, Y. H., Segall, M. H., & Dasen, P. R. (2002). *Cross-cultural psychology: Research and applications*. Cambridge, UK: Cambridge University Press.
Bhaskar, R. (1975/2008). *A realist theory of science*. London, UK: Verso.
Blaikie, N. (2007). *Approaches to social enquiry: Advancing knowledge*. Cambridge, UK: Polity.
Blaikie, N. (2010). *Designing social research: The logic of anticipation*. (2nd ed.). Cambridge, UK: Polity.
Blumer, H. (1969/1986). *Symbolic interactionism: Perspective and method*. Berkeley, CA: University of California Press.
Bourdieu, P. (1984). *Distinction: A social critique of the judgement of taste* (R. Nice, Trans.). Cambridge, MA: Harvard University Press.
Bourdieu, P., & Wacquant, L. J. D. (1992). *An invitation to reflexive sociology*. Chicago, IL: University of Chicago Press.
Bridgman, P. (1927). *The logic of modern physics*. New York, NY: Macmillan.
Bunge, M. (1996). *Finding philosophy in social science*. New Haven, CT: Yale University Press.
Burr, V. (2003). *Social constructionism* (2nd ed.). London, UK: Routledge.
Chang, H. (2009). Operationalism. In E. N. Zalta (Ed.), *The Stanford Encyclopedia of Philosophy* (Fall 2009 ed.). Retrieved from http://plato.stanford.edu/archives/fall2009/entries/operationalism/
Chirkov, V. (2009). Critical psychology of acculturation: What do we study and how do we study it, when we investigate acculturation? *International Journal of Intercultural Relations, 33*(2), 94–105.
D'Andrade, R. G. (1965). Trait psychology and componential analysis. *American Anthropologist, 67*(5), 215–228.
Danemark, B., Ekstrom, M., Jakobsen, L., & Karlsson, J. C. (2002). *Explaining society: Critical realism in the social sciences*. London, UK: Routledge.
Eysenk, H. J. (1958). A short questionnaire for the measurement of two dimensions of personality. *Journal of Applied Psychology, 42*(1), 14–17.
Geertz, C. (2000). "From the native's point of view": On the nature of anthropological understanding. In C. Geertz (Ed.), *Local knowledge: Further essays in interpretive anthropology* (pp. 55–72). New York, NY: Basic Books.
Gergen, K. J. (2009). *An invitation to social constructionism* (2nd ed.). London, UK: Sage.
Hempel, C. G. (1952). *Fundamentals of concept formation in empirical science*. (Vol. 2). Chicago IL: University of Chicago Press.
Hempel, C. G. (1966). *Philosophy of natural science*. Englewood Cliffs, NJ: Prentice-Hall.
Hofstede, G., & Hofstede, G. J. (2005). *Culture and organization: Software of the mind*. (2nd ed.). New York, NY: McGraw-Hill.
Hollis, M. (2002). *The philosophy of social science: An introduction*. Cambridge, UK: Cambridge University Press.
Kaplan, A. (1964). *The conduct of inquiry: Methodology for behavioral science*. San Francisco, CA: Chandler.
Laidlaw, J. (2000). A free gift makes no friends. *Journal of the Royal Anthropological Institute, 6*(4), 617–634.
Langfeld, H. S. (1945). Symposium on operationism. *The Psychological Review, 52*(5), 241–294.
Lock, A., & Strong, T. (2010). *Social constructionism: Sources and stirrings in theory and practice*. Cambridge, UK: Cambrodge University Press.
MacCorquodale, K., & Meehl, P. E. (1948). On a distinction between hypothetical constructs and intervening variables. *Psychological Review, 55*(2), 95–107.
Mandler, G., & Kessen, W. (1964). *The language of psychology*. New York, NY: Wiley.
Matsumoto, D., & Juang, L. (2013). *Culture and psychology* (5th ed.). Belmont, CA: Wadsworth.
Niiniluoto, I. (1999). *Critical scientific realism*. Oxford: Oxford University Press.

Nunnally, J. C., & Bernstein, I. H. (1978). *Psychometric theory* (3rd ed.). Boston, MA: McGraw-Hill College.

Redfield, R., Linton, R., & Herskovits, M. (1936). Memorandum on the study of acculturation. *American Anthropologist, 38*(1), 149–152.

Schwandt, T. A. (2000). Three epistemological stances for qualitative inquiry: Interpretavism, hermeneutics, and social constructionism. In N. K. Denzin & Y. S. Lincoln (Eds.), *Handbook of qualitative research*. (2nd ed., pp. 189–213). Thousand Oaks, CA: Sage.

Schwandt, T. A. (2007). *The SAGE dictionary of qualitative inquiry.* (3rd ed.). Thousand Oaks, CA: Sage.

Sennet, A. (2011). Ambiguity. In E. N. Zalta (Ed.), *The Stanford Encyclopedia of Philosophy*. Retrieved from http://plato.stanford.edu/archives/sum2011/entries/ambiguity/

Shapiro, I. (2005). *The flight from the reality in the human sciences.* Princeton, NJ: Princeton University Press.

Shweder, R. A. (1991). Cultural psychology: What is it? In R. A. Shweder (Ed.), *Thinking through cultures: Expeditions in cultural psychology.* (pp. 73–11). Cambridge, MA: Harvard University Press.

Snyder, L. J. (2000). William Whewell. In E. N. Zalta (Ed.), *The Stanford Encyclopedia of Philosophy*. Retrieved from http://plato.stanford.edu/entries/whewell/

Snyder, L. J. (2005). Confirmation for a modest realism. *Philosophy of Science, 72*(5), 839–849. doi: 10.1086/508113

Snyder, L. J. (2006). *Reforming philosophy: A Victorian debate on science and society.* Chicago, IL: University of Chicago Press.

Soanes, C., & Stevenson, A. (Eds.). (2008). *Concise Oxford English dictionary* (11th ed.). Oxford, UK: Oxford University Press.

Testart, A. (1998). Uncertainties of the "obligation to reciprocate:" A critique of Mauss. In M. Mauss, N. J. Allen & W. James (Eds.), *Marcel Mauss: A centenary tribute* (pp. 97–110). New York, NY: Berghahn Books.

Tomasello, M. (1999). *The cultural origins of human cognition.* Cambridge, MA: Harvard University Press.

Tomasello, M. (2014). *A natural history of human thinking.* Cambridge, MA: Harvard University Press.

Warneken, F., & Tomasello, M. (2008). Extrinsic rewards undermine altruistic tendencies in 20-month-olds. *Developmental Psychology, 44*(6), 1785–1788.

Wilson, E. O. (1999). *Consilience: The unity of knowledge.* New York, NY: Vintage Books.

Yagisawa, T. (1999). Definition. In R. Audi (Ed.), *The Cambridge disctionary of philosophy* (2nd ed., pp. 213–215). Cambridge, UK: Cambridge University Press.

7
RESEARCH STRATEGIES AND DESIGNS

This chapter will:

- Introduce the idea of *research strategies*
- Discuss differences between *nomothetic* and *idiographic* approaches to scientific inquiry
- Present *extensive* and *intensive* research strategies rooted in the realist paradigm
- Continue discussing the *etic* and *emic* positions of social researchers
- Contrast *variable-based* and *case-based designs*
- Outline the challenges and controversies of *sampling* in culture and psychology research.

Introduction: Research Strategy

A research strategy (RS) is a high level plan for answering research questions and solving research problems. Strategies are, first of all, driven by the problem, purposes, and questions of a research project. They also take into account available resources, the conditions of a study, and its time frame. A RS is a script of how to achieve the goals of research in particular conditions with the available resources and within a required time frame. Some research textbooks identify induction, deduction, retroduction and abduction (or sometimes only induction and deduction) as RSs. I called these intellectual processes *modes of inference* because they are usually not the strategic plans for a particular study, but the patterns of judgments which, together with the metatheoretical paradigms, shape how a researcher should think about generating empirical evidence and then move from this evidence to theoretical conclusions and a solution to the problem.

RSs are frequently compared with military or business strategies, which are interpreted as an attempt to get to "desirable ends with available means" (Mckeown, 2012) or "a pattern in a stream of decision making" (Mintzberg, 2011). This interpretation of RS as a justified sequence of decisions made about the most important aspects of a study is well applicable to the logic of the scientific research presented in this book. Recall that we have already identified several decisive points in conducting research. The starting point is formulating the problem and stating the study's research purpose and research questions. The next decision is about the content-related theoretical perspective and the ontological basis of the phenomenon of interest. Then there are reflections on the metatheoretical paradigms and the related modes of inference, which should be congruent with the nature of the problem and the theoretical approach. All these decisions have to be made both consequently and iteratively in order to set a clear plan for achieving the goals of a study. If these strategic decisions have not been made or have been made poorly, a proposed study may suffer from various logical and theoretical inconsistencies. Decisions also have to be made about the resources, time, and the specific conditions of the project. After these primary decisions, researchers move to decisions about the methodology of a study: What research design should be used—in what way should data generation, collection, and analysis be arranged? And the last step in the strategic planning is about selecting specific methods or techniques for implementing the research design. RSs are not given; they should be developed, tailored to a particular research problem, addressed in a particular place with a specific research team. Articulating RS is an important step in any scientific research and should be mindfully addressed. This textbook provides basic ingredients for research strategy development, but it is up to the creativity and thoughtfulness of the research team to mix them properly in order to reach the desired outcomes. Below I will present several important considerations that are directly related to strategic decision-making: *nomothetic* versus *idiographic* approaches and related to them *variable-based* and *case-based* designs.

A Fundamental Concern about the Relations Between General and Particulars

Recall from Chapter 3 that one of the aspects of the fundamental problem of any scientific research is: "How can researchers get from particulars to the general?" The struggle to answer this question goes back to the dawn of modern science when scholars were arguing about the primary axioms, first principles, or universal laws that are responsible for the essence of things and that determine their manifestations. These scholars were well aware that these primary universals are unobservable and manifest themselves in particulars: observable events, things, and conditions. This led these scholars to asking questions of how the general and particulars coexist and how to get from particulars to the general. Researchers of culture and psychology cannot avoid answering these questions either. One question that these scientists have to address is how to approach cultural communities and the psychological functioning of their members: either to take each community one at a time and to study them deeply to understand their cultural models and the psychological makeup of their people, or to approach several communities and apply to all of them the same variables and establish regularities and patterns among these variables and generalize these regularities to other communities. As the practices of empirical studies demonstrate, anthropologists and cultural psychologists are more inclined to use the former approach, which has been known as *idiographic* and/or case-based, whereas many sociologists, political scientists, and mainstream cross-cultural psychologists prefer the latter one, which has been labeled *nomothetic* and/or variable-based methodology. A struggle between these two lines of research has lasted for many decades and, finally, led to a complete divorce between the anthropological and psychological disciplines that study cultures. But without answering the above question, it is difficult for students of culture and psychology to build their research strategy competently and in line with the problem they are trying to address. The main arguments here are: What approach is truly scientific? Does studying particulars give access to general and universal knowledge? And are the general regularities applicable to and do they explain each and every particular? To address these arguments we need to start with the notions of *nomothetic vs. idiographic sciences,* then talk about corresponding approaches and finally address the differences between variable-based versus case-based designs.

Nomothetic and Idiographic Sciences and Approaches

The *nomothetic* versus *idiographic* distinction with regard to scientific inquiries was first articulated by German philosopher **Wilhelm Windelband** (1848–1915) to address two different ways of obtaining scientific knowledge (1894/1980). In 1937, personality psychologist **Gordon Allport**

(1897–1967) (1937/1963) introduced these two approaches to psychology, and, since that time, the nomothetic versus idiographic ways of thinking about doing research in social and behavioral sciences have been intensively discussed in method textbooks (Davis, 2003), in personality psychology (Lamiell, 1998), and in cultural and cross-cultural psychology (Helfrich-Holter, 2006). Initially this distinction was intended to differentiate the natural (nomothetic) sciences from the cultural (idiographic) sciences, but later it became associated with different approaches to the generation of knowledge within these sciences (Malcolm, 2004).

The *nomothetic approach*, as the term implies, is directed toward discovering the laws of the natural world, society, human mind, and behavior in order to use them to understand how these entities work, to explain them, and to make interventions possible. Windelband (1894/1980) assigned the emergence of nomothetic thinking to the natural sciences, including psychology:

> Although the phenomenon in question may be a motion of bodies, a transformation of matter, a development of organic life, or a process of imagination, emotion, and volition, the purpose of these disciplines is invariably the discovery of laws of phenomena. (p. 174)

Windelband associated the emergence of the *idiographic approach* with what he called the "sciences of the mind" (p. 173), which include history, anthropology, sociology, and some domains of psychology. These sciences "are concerned with a single event or a coherent sequence of acts or occurrences; the nature and life of an individual person or an entire nation" (p. 174). In this focus on particular cases, the sciences of the mind "provide a complete and exhaustive description of a single, more or less extensive process that is located within a unique, temporally defined domain of reality" (p. 174). In contrast to the nomothetic sciences, the object of idiographic investigation is "to reproduce and understand in its full facticity an artifact of human life to which a unique ontological status is ascribed" (p. 175).

The idiographic approach aims at describing and analyzing a single case or a set of interrelated cases in depth and to inquire about their structural patterns, and patterns of regularity of their functioning in various contextual conditions. Anthropological ethnographic studies of isolated communities are an example of such idiographic inquiry (see more in Chapters 8 and 10). Think also about clinical or counseling psychologists who work with single patients to resolve their particular problems by finding a characteristic pattern of the patients' personality and conditions of their lives in a particular family and community within a particular period of their lives; or political scientists or sociologists who study nations, provinces, cities, and neighborhoods in their entirety. They all are implementing the idiographic way of inquiring (see Ragin & Becker, 1992).

According to Windelband (1894/1980), both approaches have a right to exist and both provide valuable ways of generating knowledge in empirical sciences.[1] These two approaches reflect a complex dialectic that exists between "the relationship of the general to the particular"—the dialectic that has been considered "as the fundamental nexus of all scientific thought" (p. 175).

As history has demonstrated, both approaches may be applied to social and psychological sciences: any sociocultural or mental event can be viewed as an instance of a general regularity and

---

1 Windelband (1894/1980) classified all sciences into either "rational sciences" such as philosophy and mathematics or "empirical sciences," which require for their research a set of theoretical propositions and "the verification of facts on the basis of observation" (p. 173). The empirical sciences he differentiated into "natural sciences" (physics, biology, geology, physiology, some domains of psychology) and "sciences of the mind" (anthropology, sociology, political science, and other domains of psychology).

thus be explained through nomothetic thinking. But the same sociocultural or psychological phenomena can also be investigated in their uniqueness and distinctiveness within particular historical and contextual conditions. Unfortunately, these two approaches have been presented in these sciences as opposing and incompatible methodologies of inquiry with a preference for the nomothetic one: "Traditional nomothetic methods have dominated psychological research over the decades, centuries, and now, millennia" (Harris, 2003, p. 42). The idiographic approach has even been considered as "a non- or anti-scientific point of view" (Lamiell, 1998, p. 26). One of the main reasons for such an attitude is the widespread conviction that idiographic research does not allow for the generalizations that have been considered the most important objective of scientific inquiries (see discussions in (Gomm, Hammersley, & Foster, 2000). In addition to such polarization, the nomothetic approach has become strongly associated with the positivist paradigm and the idiographic one—with the interpretivist philosophical stance adding more to the separation of these approaches and related disciplines. It is important to say that the term "nomothetic" has become a synonym to such adjectives as "quantitative," "variable-based," "statistics-oriented," and "oriented toward discovering causality;" conversely, "idiographic" has become synonymous with "qualitative," "clinical" "ethnographic," and "holistic," and "oriented toward understanding." Such differentiation and the following division of social sciences on this methodological basis does not allow for cross-fertilization among the disciplines and does not contribute to the progression of knowledge about societies, cultures, and individuals. I am proposing a different point of view, where this sharp dichotomization of these two strategies is downplayed and these strategies are dialectically synthesized.

Empirical Generalizations and Theoretical Laws

The issue of coordinating the general and particulars that separates these two approaches actually boils down to the following questions: What constitutes the general and what are the particulars? Are they really so different that they require different and incompatible paradigms and methodologies? Can they be reconciled conceptually and methodologically? To answer these questions we need to introduce the concepts of law, different forms of generalization, cases, and variables.

Let's start with the concept of a law in the natural and social sciences. In Chapter 6, we discussed the concept of theoretical laws and highlighted two different interpretations of this concept—one belonging to the positivist paradigm and the other to the realist one. According to the conventional positivist interpretation, laws of nature are understood as reliable empirical (often statistical) associations/regularities established among variables on large samples of instances. They usually address relatively stable conjunctions of events that can be described by the formula: "If A, then B". In Chapter 3, I labeled such regularities empirical generalizations and indicated that they are discovered through enumerative induction.

> According to this [positivist] point of view, roughly speaking, laws enunciate the regular or uniform concomitance (correlation) of phenomena, i.e. features appearing in objects, states which obtain, or events which happen. The prototype instance of a law is either a universal ("all A are B") or a probabilistic correlation. (von Wright, 1971, p. 18)

Examples of such laws can be found in the book *Human behavior: An inventory of scientific findings* by Berelson & Steiner (1964):

> C29 The less use of physical punishment in childhood and the more use of reasoning, the less likely child or adolescent to engage in delinquent behavior (p. 82); B1 There is a tendency in most human societies for people to prefer their own kind and to stereotype ethnic outgroups,

especially lower status one, in a negative fashion (p. 500); B2 People prejudiced against one ethnic group tend to be prejudiced against others. (p. 502)

If one decided to evaluate these laws critically, it would become clear to any inquisitive scholar that they are not really laws of nature, which can be used to explain different phenomena, but regular conjunctions of events, or empirical regularities. These regularities cannot be treated as real laws of human behavior and cannot be the ultimate goals of scientific inquiry because of two reasons. One is articulated by Cummins (2000): the empirically established statistical conjunctions of events are *psychological effects* that themselves require explanations. These effects are useful starting points for discovering deeper layers of structures and powers that make these regularities happen. The second reason is mentioned by Bhaskar (1979/2015), when he discussed the confusion of empirical regularity with a law:

> here again failure to make an ontological distinction between causal laws and patterns of events results in absurdity. For if causal laws are constant conjunction of events then one must ask: what governs phenomena in systems where such conjunctions do not obtain. (p. 12)

When realists define the concept of law, they talk about the mechanisms of various natural, biological, sociocultural or psychological phenomena (Bhaskar, 1975/2008; Collier, 1994; Sayer, 1992) (see also Chapters 4 and 6). Causal mechanisms are unobservable structures and powers that generate, determine, and regulate phenomena and events in the worlds. These mechanisms are real and exist independently of people's knowledge and their theories about them. These mechanisms are governed by the causal laws of nature, and, when discovered, they explain the worlds. According to realists, such laws should be the primary focus of any scientific endeavor. Windelband (1894/1980) expressed this realist interpretation of the concept of law when he said:

> They [nomothetic sciences] strive to acquire knowledge of the nomological necessities whose timeless immutability governs all events. From the colorful world of the senses, the natural sciences construct a system of abstract [theoretical] concepts. The purpose of such a conceptual scheme is to comprehend the true nature of things that lies behind the phenomena: a silent and colorless world of atoms in which the earthy aura of perceptual qualities has disappeared completely: the triumph of thought over perception. (p. 178)[2]

When Windelband mentions "the nomological necessities whose timeless immutability governs all the events" and of a task "to comprehend the true nature of things that lies behind the phenomena" he talks the realist language, and Windelband's "laws of nature" become exactly these nonobservable mechanisms that realists invite scientists to discover.

German philosopher **Edmund Husserl** (1859–1938) also made a contribution to the classification of sciences and corresponding methodologies. In (1900/1970) he provided a similar interpretation of nomological sciences in terms of their goals of discovering a hidden "unifying principle . . . law" (p. 230). These nomological (or theoretical sciences, as Husserl labeled them)

---

[2] Republished with permission of *History and Theory* from Windelband, W. (1894/1980). Rectorial Address, Strasbourg, 1894. *History and Theory, 19*(2), 169–185; permission conveyed through Copyright Clearance Center, Inc.

are the ones "whose field is determined by the stand point of theory, of unity of principle, which embrace in ideal closure all possible facts and general items whose principle of explanations have a single legal base" (p. 230). Husserl contrasted theoretical sciences with practical or normative sciences that deal with specific objects of inquiry in an attempt to explain them for the purpose of practical manipulations and pragmatic utilization, like geography, history, astronomy, anatomy, etc. Practical (now known as applied) researchers build their studies on general laws and causal mechanisms discovered by theoretical scientists, and apply these laws to understand the functioning of a particular phenomenon. "It is at any rate clear that the abstract or nomological sciences are the genuine, basic sciences, from whose theoretical stock the concrete sciences must derive all the theoretical element by which they are made sciences" (pp. 230–231). It is important to stress that for Husserl practical sciences study particular objects and particular cases, or "what is individual" (p. 231), hence emphasizing the idiographic approach. For Husserl this approach means connecting "all the truths whose content related *to one and the same individual object, or to one and the same empirical genus*" (p. 230). He also outlined the connections between studying individual objects and building a theory: researchers who are interested in constructing a theory have to move from these individual cases toward theoretical generalizations by hypothesizing the underlying laws, thus providing a logical connection from idiographic to nomothetic thinking:

> practical interests can attach to what is individual, and impart the highest value to its detailed description and explanation. When, however, our purely theoretical interest sets the tone, the single individual and the empirical connection do not count intrinsically, or they count only as a methodological point of passage in the construction of a general theory. (p. 231)

Thus Husserl's conclusion supports the conviction that scientists who focus on developing a theory should extract important information by studying individual cases. Thus, the nomothetic and idiographic approaches should not be contrasted. They complement each other because hypotheses about hidden mechanisms (scientific theorizing) can be generated by studying particular instances within the competencies of idiographic or practical sciences. By working with particular cases, social researchers generalize from these instances to the underlying structures and generating powers and move from the domain of concrete idiographic sciences to the domain of theoretical ones (Ragin & Becker, 1992; Smith, Harre, & Langenhove, 1995; Valsiner, 2007). Therefore, the idiographic approach leads to theoretical (nomological) generalizations, and these two approaches become connected through their dialectical complementarity: "The particular eternally underlies the general, the general eternally has to comply with the particular" (Goethe, cited in Hermans (1988, p. 785),

In addition, the idiographic approach does not stand in contradistinction to causal analysis. Causal mechanisms work within entities where the effects happen: within individuals who experience happiness, in communities where crime rates are rising, in societies that modernize themselves, cultures that promote corruption, and nations that intimidate other nations. These units of analysis are systems that have components that through their complex interactions produce the phenomena of interest. These units are embedded into particular ecological, social, cultural, economic, and political contexts that facilitate or hinder the functioning of these mechanisms. If a researcher wants to theorize about causal mechanisms, he or she has to study these individual units and retroduct hypotheses about these mechanisms. Realists emphasize that an investigation of various mechanisms and the conditions of their work can be done through the idiographic system of inquiry and an *intensive design* (Easton, 2010). (See later in this chapter).

Nomothetic and Idiographic Approaches in Interpretive Sciences

How does this distinction work within the interpretive sciences, which conventionally have been considered the idiographic sciences? The idiographic inquiry within the interpretivist paradigm is aimed at describing the phenomena of interest and interpreting the meanings that operate within the units of analysis. Denzin (2001) described ideographic interpretivism the following way:

> Ideographic research assumes that each individual case is unique. This means that every interactional text [i.e. everything that is created through the interactional activities of people including actual texts, rituals, sequence of actions, pieces of art, and cultures] is unique and shaped by the individuals who create it. This requires that the voices and actions of individuals must be heard and seen in the texts that are reported. Emic studies are also ideographic. They seek to study experience from within, through the use of thick description or accounts which attempt to capture the meanings and experiences of interacting individuals in problematic situations. They seek to uncover the conceptual categories persons use when they interact with one another and create meaningful experience. Emic investigations are particularizing. Etic research is generalizing. (pp. 20–21)

The question may be asked, "Are nomothetic generalizations (generalizations of the laws of a phenomenon) possible within this paradigm?" And the answer is: "Yes, it is possible." According to Denzin (2001), several symbolic interactionists, such as Goffman and Garfinkel, who were in the interpretivist camp of social scholars, conducted research that produced nomothetic results. Goffman, for example, sought for "general patterns" (p. 20) of everyday interactions (Goffman, 1967) and patterns of self-presentation during these interactions (Goffman, 1959, 1966). In these studies, "specific configurations of meaning that operate within a single case, or culture, are set aside in favor of cross-case universals" (Denzin, 2001, p. 20). According to Denzin, this means that Goffman generalized across cases in order to come up with universal laws of everyday interactions or self-presentations. These nomothetically oriented interpretivists who were looking for underlying rules and patterns of human behavior and/or experiences can be identified as social realists looking for the underlying mechanisms of social behavior. Thus, even within the interpretivist paradigm, it is possible to identify both the *interpretive idiographic* and *interpretive nomothetic* approaches. The dialectic here is that a researcher comes to nomothetic conclusions only through studying individual cases.

An idiographic inquiry typically starts with an application of different ethnographic and conventional qualitative methods (see (Denzin & Lincoln, 2012)). One may stay within such descriptions or may move toward a thick description of different systems of meaning that stand behind the discovered patterns of interactions (see Chapter 4). By conducting abductive inference within the hermeneutic circle of interpretations, researchers may reach the deep layers of hidden meanings and ultimately the driving forces behind them. Within the interpretive nomothetic and realist paradigms, case studies may be complemented by analytical procedures such as analytic induction (Hammersley & Cooper, 2012; Smith et al., 1995; Znaniecki, 1934), causal networking (Miles, Huberman, & Saldana, 2014), grounded theorizing (Glaser & Strauss, 1967; Hammersley, 2012), and qualitative comparative analysis (Ragin, 1998; Ragin & Amoroso, 2011).

Extensive and Intensive Research Strategies

Instead of using the terms nomothetic and idiographic approaches, realist scholars use the concepts of *extensive* and *intensive* designs or strategies to characterize different research strategies related to the general and particulars (Danemark, Ekstrom, Jakobsen, & Karlsson, 2002; Sayer, 1992). According to realists, the entities in the sociocultural and psychological worlds—individuals, neighborhoods, cultural communities, and nations—are complex, *heterogeneous* (diverse in character or content (Soanes & Stevenson, 2008)) and *polyvalent* (having many different functions, forms, or facets (Soanes & Stevenson, 2008)) systems that have numerous properties (Sayer, 1992, p. 241). The dilemma for researchers is whether to study a large number of entities identified by a small number of common properties or a small number of entities characterized by a large number of properties, or as it frequently presented: "depth versus breadth" (Sayer, 1992, p. 242). Realists labeled the first approach *extensive* and the second *intensive* research strategies. (They actually labeled them 'designs' but according to our categorization it is better to call them strategies, because they do not represent a particular plan for doing a research; they are just broad research strategies within which different designs can be implemented. The term design is used with regard to being either variable-based or case-based, among other forms of designs: cross-sectional, longitudinal, and experimental to name a few). The summary of these two strategies is presented in Table 7.1.

TABLE 7.1 Intensive and extensive strategies

	Extensive examines a large number of entities with a small number of common properties	*Intensive* examines a small number of entities with a large number of diverse properties
Goals and purposes of research inquiry	To establish empirically verifiable patterns of associations among properties of the entities; to generalize these empirical regularities to a large number of entities; to articulate socio-cultural or psychological "effects" (Cummings, 2000), like "If A, then B."	To provide thick description and interpretation; to discover generative mechanisms and explain the phenomena; to articulate conditions that facilitate or hinder the functioning of these mechanisms; to generalize these mechanisms across entities.
Most typical RQ	What are regularities and patterns of associations among variables in the sample? How widely are these regularities and patterns distributed or represented in the population?	What did the agents actually do? What is the deep meaning of their actions? How does the process unfold? How does a hypothesized causal mechanism work in a particular case or in a limited number of cases?
Units of observation and analysis	Samples (preferably probability and representative) from populations; distributions of the variables and covariances among them.	Separate entities (cases) or groups of entities, both similar and different, in their contexts; cases may be purposefully selected based on the hypotheses about the generative mechanisms.
The nature of units of analyses and type of relations	Statistical aggregates; formal relations of similarity and/or covariance.	Open systems in contexts and with histories; substantial relations of connection and interdependence.
Typical methods	Surveys with standardized questionnaires or interviews; statistical analysis; analysis of existing national and international databases.	Ethnography, naturalistic and participant observation; semistructured interviews, artifacts analysis; structural, or causal analysis.
Type of account produced	Patterns of empirical regularities; allowing for some forms of predictions but lacking explanatory power.	Causal explanation through mechanisms of production of certain actions, things, or events; conditions that moderate these causal mechanisms.
Type of generalization	Enumerative generalization from a sample to the population.	Theoretical generalization of hypotheses/ theories about causal mechanisms to other cases of a particular kind.
Limitations	Does not allow a researcher to get to the "essence" of things; serves only descriptive and some predictive purposes.	Actual concrete patterns and contingent relations within cases are unlikely to be "representative" or "average" and thus unlikely to be enumeratively generalizable.

Adapted from Danemark et al., 2002, p. 165; republished with permission of Routledge, Taylor & Francis Group

I want to conclude this discussion by saying that nomothetic and idiographic distinctions in studying sociocultural and psychological phenomena should not separate researchers but should provide better opportunities for advancing knowledge. Following Husserl, dialectical thinking on this matter is advocated here: individual events and particulars can be studied on their own for their better understanding and for practical purposes, but they may also serve as windows into deeper layers of reality, which are accessible by applying abductive and retroductive thinking to these cases. But the nomothetic versus idiographic confrontation does not end at the philosophical level; it extends to a more practical level of research design, in particular, the choice between the *etic* and *emic* positions of a researcher and *variable-based* or *case-based* designs.

Etic Versus Emic Positions

In Chapter 1, I introduced two research positions for approaching subject matters in anthropology and psychology: the etic and emic stances, suggested by Kenneth Pike (1967). As readers remember, the etic strategy approaches cultures, communities, or individuals from outside of these systems, similar to the traditional nomothetic position of natural scientists. The emic approach requires studying behavior or cultures from within these systems, similar to what is required by idiographic scientists. Pike provided the following ten characteristics of these two researchers' stances (numbers are added).

1. The etic approach treats all cultures or languages—or a selected group of them—at one time. It might be called "comparative" in the anthropological sense. . . . The emic approach is, on the contrary, culturally specific, [and] applied to one language or culture at a time.
2. Units available in advance, versus determined during analysis: Etic units and classifications, based on prior broad sampling or surveys . . . may be available before one begins the analysis of a further particular language or culture . . . emic units of a language [culture and behavior as well] must be determined during the analysis of that language; they must be discovered, not predicted—even though the range of kinds of components of language has restrictions placed upon it by the physiology of the human organism.
3. Creation versus discovery of a system: The etic organization of a worldwide cross-cultural scheme may be created by the analyst. The emic structure of a particular system must, I hold, be discovered.
4. External versus internal view: description or analyses from the etic standpoint are "alien" in view, with criteria external to the system. Emic descriptions provide an internal view, with criteria chosen from within the system. They represent to us the view of one familiar with the system and who knows how to function within it himself.
5. External versus internal plan: An etic system may be set up by criteria of "logical" plan whose relevance is external to the system being studied. The discovery or setting up of the emic system requires the inclusion of criteria relevant to the internal functioning of the system itself. (pp. 37–38).

These five criteria describe how researchers approach objects of their study from these perspectives. Etic scholars prepare their research plan before their investigation; they treat cultures, communities, or individuals as outsiders to these systems and apply their a priori created criteria to evaluate them. Emic scholars take into consideration the nature of these systems and tackle them "from within" by understanding the logic of their organization.

6. Absolute versus relative criteria: The etic criteria may often be considered absolute, or measurable directly. Emic criteria are relative to the internal characteristics of the system, and can be usefully described or measured relative to each other.

7   Nonintegration versus integration: The etic view does not require that every unit be viewed as part of a larger setting. The emic view, however, insists that every unit be seen as somehow distributed and functioning within a larger structural unit or setting, in hierarchy of units and hierarchy of settings as units.
8   Sameness and difference as measured versus systemic: Two units are different etically when instrumental measurements can show them to be so. Units are different emically only when they elicit different responses from people acting within the system.
9   Partial versus total data: Etic data are obtainable early in analysis with partial information. In principle, on the contrary, emic criteria require a knowledge of the total system to which they are relative and from which they ultimately draw their significance.
10 Preliminary versus final presentation: Hence, etic data provide access into the system—the starting point of analysis. They give tentative results, tentative units. The final analysis or presentation, however, would be in emic units. In the total analysis, the initial etic description gradually is refined, and is ultimately—in principle, but probably never in practice—replaced by one which is totally emic (pp. 37–39).

The last five criteria reflect the nature of objects of investigation and the logic of their analysis. The emic position is systemic, where all components are considered in their interconnectedness and as parts of larger units. The etic perspective is more mechanical, where each constituent can be analyzed independently of other components. That is why etic knowledge is preliminary and partial, and emic knowledge is complete and exhaustive.

This etic versus emic distinction is important for any culture or psychology researcher to consider because it identifies the two positions that a researcher may occupy in relation to his or her object of study, and as a result, determines and shapes all the aspects of research methodology. Let's take as an example Levin's et al. (2001) cross-cultural study of helping behavior, which is etic in its approach. The researchers decided to study and compare helpfulness to strangers across 23 countries. They decided a priori what types of behavior (units of observation) they would designate as "helpful" and thus investigate, and how these behaviors would be generated and assessed. The researchers used standardized behavioral measures when trained research assistants (1) dropped a pen in front of a pedestrian going in the opposite direction; (2) while wearing a leg brace and walking with a heavy limp, they dropped a pile of magazines and struggled to pick them up; and (3) dressed as blind people, assistants stood at a street corner and intended to cross a road. The researchers quantified the reactions of people in these situations and made quantitative comparisons across countries.

The following characteristics of the etic versus emic approach are present in this study: **Characteristic 1.** Researchers simultaneously approached 23 countries with the intention to compare then on the helpfulness of their citizens. They did not study helpfulness within one cultural group or one country. **2 & 3.** They decided a priori the reactions to particular behavioral acts that they would count as helpfulness; thus the units of observation were available in advance. They did not study different reactions in each country according to its cultural understanding of helpfulness. **4 & 5.** The researchers occupied an external viewpoint to the system of ethical ideas of each culture and expected that members of all the countries would interpret and react to the assistants' difficulties in the same way. They did not state and try to answer questions like: Who are considered strangers in this cultural community? How are strangers treated in this culture? What does helpfulness to another person mean? When is it appropriate to demonstrate such helpfulness? **6.** The criteria of helpfulness were absolute and directly measurable and were brought from outside of the cultural system of the countries. They did not consider such relativity criteria, for example, as the "debt of honor," when helping a stranger may indebt this stranger to reciprocate and, because he or she is unable to do this, such helping may be viewed as "not helpful" in the long run. **7.** The researchers treated helpfulness to strangers as an isolated act and did not consider it within a broader system of ethical and moral codes that exist in each country. **8.** Helpfulness was compared and the quantitative measures directly demonstrated that, for instance, citizens of Rio de Janeiro, Brazil are the most helpful people in the world. The researchers did not compare the emotional, cognitive, and behavioral reaction of people according to each country's moral codes of helping others. **9.** This study presents only partial information about both the behaviors of people and the codes of conduct that exist in these countries. If other researchers want to investigate this phenomenon further, they have to take into account other behaviors within the system of moral values that exist in each country. And, finally, **10.** This study could be a starting point for a more inquisitive study of helpfulness within each country, but it cannot be considered a complete and final comparative investigation of human helpfulness.

The Variable-Based Design

The variable-based design lies at the basis of statistically driven quantitative studies rooted in the positivist paradigm. Studies that are organized by such a design are guided by theories (in the positivist meaning of this term) that provide conceptual frameworks and designate variables to be studied:

> The variable-oriented approach is theory-centered. It is less concerned with understanding specific outcomes or categories of outcomes and more concerned with assessing the correspondence between relationships discernible across many societies or countries, on the one hand, and broad theoretically based images of macrosocial phenomena, on the other. (Ragin, 1987, p. 53)

This definition, which was articulated by a sociologist, is well applied to cultural and psychological studies too. It is possible to say that researchers on culture and psychology apply the variable-based design when they are concerned with assessing a correspondence between their theories of how various constructs should be related within and between personality and culture domains and how these variables should be connected to each other in different sociocultural contexts. They are concerned with studying the empirically verifiable relations among these variables and how these relations correspond to their theories. Variable-based studies start by delineating basic concepts and their theory-based connections that are typically presented as a study's "theoretical model." These concepts represent the most general and common attributes of individuals or cultural communities, which are then operationalized through different scales, questionnaires, indicators, and indices. Cases for a study—participants, countries, or communities—are selected and then the corresponding variables are measured. The data set usually takes the form of a matrix where cases are arranged in rows and variables in columns (see Fig 7.1.)

For variable-based studies, such a matrix is dissected vertically by variables, which become the primary units of analysis. Researchers collapse their data across cases, aggregate the variables' scores, and subject them to various forms of statistical analyses: they calculate their means, standard deviations, distributions, and frequencies. Based on the quality of the sample, researchers may also generalize these parameters to the population from which the sample was drawn. Researchers also calculate associations among these variables based on the covariances among them by using correlation, factor, and regression analyses, as well as more advanced forms of statistical analysis. These associations are not causal and cannot be used to represent the unobservable causal mechanisms. Associations that represent the necessary relationships among variables may be used as a starting point for inferring the causal powers that make these regularities happen, but it is difficult to identify which statistical associations are accidental and which are necessary.

	Variable 1	Variable 2	Variable 3	Variable 4	Variable 5	Variable 6
Case 1						
Case 2						
Case 3						
Case 4						
Case 5						
Case 6						
Variables' scores aggregated across cases	Aggregate V1: $M_{v1}; SD_{v1}$	Aggregate V2 $M_{v2}; SD_{v2}$	Aggregate V3 $M_{v3}; SD_{v3}$	Aggregate V4 $M_{v4}; SD_{v4}$	Aggregate V5 $M_{v5}; SD_{v5}$	Aggregate V6 $M_{v6}; SD_{v6}$

FIGURE 7.1 A data matrix for a variable-based study.

Note: M stands for mean; SD for standard deviation

There are several goals in a variable-based inquiry. The first is to test the propositions of the theories by comparing the discovered statistical models with theoretical ones. The second is to establish the generalizability of the findings by extrapolating them to more cases, thus executing enumerative induction/generalization. The main assumption behind such analysis is that the statistical examination of associations across a large number of cases eliminates the particularities of individual cases and exposes near universal empirical regularities among the variables. When these regularities are generalized to larger samples and, if possible, to whole populations, they constitute the empirical laws of the phenomena under study (in the positivistic understanding of the concept of "law;" see above) and may be used to explain and predict the behavior or functioning of each entity or case. The discovery of such regularities is considered to be the goal of science and reporting them constitutes the main content of the majority of mainstream psychological articles. Associations between cultural dimensions and frequencies of different diseases (Matsumoto & Fletcher, 1996) are considered to be a substantial contribution to the body of cross-cultural psychological knowledge and worthy of publishing in journals and textbooks.

Criticism of the variable-based approach in the social sciences and psychology has lasted for decades (Allport, 1937/1963, 1962; Lamiell, 1987; Valsiner, 1986a). Recently, another wave of dissatisfaction and criticism with regard to such design and the knowledge produced by it has been raised by social and behavioral scientists (Abbott, 1992; Barlow & Nock, 2009; Byrne & Ragin, 2009; Cooper, Glaesser, Gomm, & Hammersley, 2012; Lamiell, 2013). This criticism can be summarized in the following points:

a. The actual bearers of the phenomena of interest in social and psychological sciences: people, social groups, communities, or nations, are dissected into a set of acontextual and impersonal variables, traits or dimensions, and these bearers stop to exist as independent, bounded, and structured entities. Instead they are substituted by a set of common variables, their aggregated scores, and the relationships among them. These aggregated scores do not represent any of the constituent cases and exist in an abstract statistical space. Think about the textbook example of a formal meaning of the Mean, or average score, for the income of three persons sitting on a bench in a park: a millionaire with an income of $5 million a year, a software engineer with $100,000 a year, and a homeless person with barely $20 a week (~$1000 a year). The mean for this sample is $1,700,333. This number does not represent any of the individuals in the sample and constitutes a formal aggregation of the real incomes. Mulaik (1987) labelled this *"the average man fallacy. . . .* This fallacy generalizes to all cases where a statistical (or mathematical) artifact is uncritically treated as if it were representative of a real attribute of some entity" (p. 294). Such situations exist in, for example, psychology, where embodied individuals who live in particular places and times simply stop being the focus of psychologists and are replaced by configurations of various variables. Such a situation provokes questions like, "Where is the individual subject in scientific psychology?" (Valsiner, 1986a, p. 1). Imagine a person who is interested in how watches work for the purpose of their repair. Instead of looking at one particular watch as an example of a class of particular watches, he or she collected all watches in a community, disassembled them and sorted all the extracted parts into different categories: springs, hands, cogwheels, batteries, etc. Then, by arranging them in different groups and combinations, he or she believes he or she can understand how the watches work, what their mechanisms are, and possibly repair the broken ones. It is obvious that this endeavor will fail. Psychologists who are running variable-based studies are doing exactly this by trying to study psychological or sociocultural phenomena by disassembling them into variables and by doing different arrangements of these variables. Human personality is transformed into a set of personality traits; motivation is represented by its associations among a variety of needs or motives; cultural communities are dissected into dimensions, and so forth.

b. Researchers are driven by the assumption that, because they are discovered on a large number of instances, associations among variables reflect nearly universal regularities that exist and govern each and every case in the database, and, if the sample is large and representative enough, they hold true for all the entities in the population under investigation. As early as 1903, French psychologist Alfred Binet (1903) made the following observation:

> American authors, who love to do things big, often publish experiments [des experiences] made on hundreds or even thousands of persons: they believe that the conclusive value of a study is proportional to the number of observations. That is only an illusion. (p. 300)

Researchers who use big-sample studies believe that laws of society and human behavior are expressed through between-subject variances of the variables, and that the bigger the samples, the more reliable the discovered laws. This assumption may partially work only if probability sampling is used, if the samples are representative of the population, and if researchers find criteria to differentiate accidental correlations from the necessary ones. Psychologists, in general, and cross-cultural psychologists, in particular, rarely use such sampling, and because of this, their generalizations from the convenient and nonprobability samples, often of students, do not have legitimacy for making broad enumerative generalizations. (See more on sampling later in this chapter.)

c. In continuation of the previous point, many authors mentioned that inferences from sample-based correlations to individual-level mechanisms are unwarranted because of two reasons. One is that such inferences can be made only if the cases constituting samples are qualitatively homogeneous, and, two, there is the danger of committing *ecological fallacy*. Ecological fallacy happens when statistical regularities discovered on a sample level among aggregated scores are applied to the individual level of functioning of particulars. The relationship among the same variable on the sample/aggregate and individual/case levels constitutes different levels of social or psychological realities and must not be confused in its analysis (see discussion of ecological fallacy in Chapter 8).

Participants in these samples are not qualitatively homogeneous. They are open systems that have structures and mechanisms of functioning within particular sociocultural contexts. The behavior of such systems depends on their interactions with these contexts. They may have some common attributes that researchers extract in the form of variables and correlate on a sample level. But in reality these attributes (if they even exist) work within people intraindividually in coordination with other attributes in unique ways, which are difficult, if ever possible, to express statistically.

Correlations among the variables' aggregated scores represent covariances of abstract attributes among each other and reflect formal statistical relations among data. These correlations usually have low resemblance, if any, both theoretical and applied, to the real mechanisms that work within living, historical, and cultural subjects.

d. In the variable-based design, variables become the agents and the vehicles of the phenomena of interest rather than people or other concrete entities (Valsiner, 1986b). Instead of stating that happy people acquire and possess good health, researchers note that happiness is associated with good health. Similarly individualism is associated with cardiovascular disease, rather than people living in individualistic societies suffer from this form of malaise. The reality where people live, love, suffer, or flourish is substituted by an artificial statistical simulacrum where variables, and not humans, become the agents of happiness, love, suffering, or illnesses.

e. "A fundamental rule of quantitative social science is that 'correlation is not causation.' Yet social scientists routinely make statements that one variable causes variation in another, when the evidence is based entirely on correlational patterns" (Ragin, 1992, p. 3). For example, in their chapter on sampling, which I examine later on, Boehnke, Lietz, Schreier, and Wilhelm (2011) discussed only statistical and quantitate variable-based studies yet they repeatedly used causal language to describe the intentions of cross-cultural researchers: studying factors that *influence* empathy among students in three countries (p. 113), cultural contexts *determining* adolescent xenophobia (p. 121), and the *effects* of culture on psychological phenomena (p. 124). Such confusion of statistical relations and causation can be traced back to the early days of cross-cultural psychology when its founders stated: "The second, and easily the most common, reason for doing cross-cultural *psychological* research is to examine the 'systematic co-variation (or cause) between cultural and behavioral variables' (Berry, 1980)." (Lonner & Berry, 1986, p. 89). This serious flaw of many variable-based researches indicates that, first, researchers are implicitly looking for causal relations in order to explain the phenomenon of interest. And second, they intentionally or unintentionally violate the main rule of multivariate statistics by trying to make causal inferences based on statistical covariances.

f. Finally, "certainly, nomothetic scientist approaches [in our case, variable-based studies] based on transferring the language of variables to the social world has—in brutal summary—been largely useless" (Byrne, 2009b, p. 520). Although many readers may perceive this conclusion as a bit exaggerated, it means that at the bottom line, it is often difficult or perhaps even impossible to make practical applications or interventions based on statistical associations among variables. For interventions to be successful, researchers and practitioners need to know the mechanisms of the phenomenon of concern and base their intervention on this knowledge.

Where can the variable-based approach be useful? It can be useful in epidemiological-type studies interested in distributions of and associations among various variables: frequencies of diseases and their associations with people's or communities' characteristics, like income, education, religion, political affiliation, and other factors; or frequencies of crime and their related attributes, etc. These studies have to be done on groups of people and represent general structural patterns of covariances of diseases, crimes, etc. on a sample level. They provide a relatively broad picture of different phenomena on societal or cultural levels and allow a researcher to develop hypotheses about potential causes and consequences.

The Case-Based Design

Is there an alternative to the variable–based design? The majority of social researchers find such an alternative in case-based studies and more and more social scientists are turning to them in search of a better way to understand and explain the phenomena of their inquiries (Flyvbjerg, 2006; George & Bennett, 2005; Gerring, 2007; Ragin & Becker, 1992; Thomas, 2011; Yin, 2003, 2009).

What is a Case in Case-Based Research?

The *Concise Oxford English Dictionary* (Soanes & Stevenson, 2008) defines case as "1. An instance of a particular situation; an example of something occurring . . . 2. an instance of a disease, injury, or problem." Valsiner (1986a) provided the following definition of a case (in his language "the individual subject"):

> The individual subject is a *self-contained whole, an organism in which psychological phenomena occur, and that functions as a system.* . . . [The individual subject can be not only separate individuals, but also] a social group, consisting of individual persons who are related to one another. . . . Likewise, a gang of adolescents on a city street, a group of students attending a certain grade at school, a local community, a social class (in sociological analysis), a culture (in the thinking of anthropologists), a country, and—ultimately—the whole of mankind, can be considered to be individual subjects if our interest in them emphasizes their functioning as self-contained systems. (p. 4)

Cases, which become units of observation and analysis, could be individuals (exemplary leaders, outstanding teachers, excellent and failing students, or clinical patients), communities (classes of students, work teams, gangs, cult groups, subcultures, crowds), or even whole nations; they could be particular events and incidents (industrial accidents, new implementations in organizations, processes of transition in communities or institutions) and myriads of other entities or processes, events or practices that happen to people and their communities (Yin, 2009). As shown in Fig 7.1, the variable-based design dissects the data matrix vertically by collapsing all the attributes across cases. Case-based researchers cut this matrix horizontally and analyze and compare cases as unique combinations of the variables.

Another term that requires a definition is *case-based method* or *case-base studies*. Gerring (2007) provides the following definition of case study:

> To refer to a work as a "case study;" might mean: (a) that its method is qualitative, small-N, (b) that the research is holistic, thick (a more or less comprehensive examination of a phenomenon), (c) that it utilizes a particular type of evidence (e.g., ethnographic, clinical, nonexperimental, non-survey-based, participant-observation, process-tracing, historical, textual, or field research), (d) that its method of evidence gathering is naturalistic (a 'real-life context';), (e) that the topic is diffuse (case and context are difficult to distinguish), (f) that it employs triangulation ("multiple sources of evidence"), (g) that the research investigates the properties of a single observation, or (h) that the research investigates the properties of a single phenomenon, instance, or example. (p. 17)

A case-based method is a complex research design that may range from a simple naturalistic observation to a multiyear ethnographic expedition, from a participant observation in a particular community to experimental studies. These studies are usually multimethod, extended in time and typically do not use large samples. Benedict (1946/1974) commented on her methodology:

> In such study one quickly reaches the point where the testimony of great numbers of additional informants provides no further validation. Who bows to whom and when, for instance, needs no statistical study of all Japan; the approved and customary circumstances can be reported by almost any one and after a few confirmations it is not necessary to get the same information from a million Japanese. (pp. 16–17)

Why should the Case-Based Design, and not the Variable-Based One, Dominate in Research on Psychology and Culture?

For culture and psychology researchers, the cases for analysis are individuals embedded in their communities within broader sociocultural wholes. It is important to note that the units of analysis here are not individuals or communities per se, but the members of the communities as they live and function there—individuals within the sociocultural contexts. People embedded in their sociocultural contexts constitute complex systems of social, cultural, and psychological powers. These systems interact with each other and produce the problematic phenomena that researchers study. Japanese people within their Japanese culture were the cases for Benedict in her acclaimed study. In the Whiting and Whiting research (1975), children and their families within their eco-cultural niches were the units of observation and analysis. In each case, researchers focused on systems comprised of people within their contexts in order to grasp their interdependence and mutual constitution. As the results of these studies demonstrated, only the case-based approach, and not the variable-based one, allowed them to fulfill their missions. Going back to the critique of positivism from Chapter 3, we may say that, unlike case-based studies, the variable-based design is incapable of shedding light on the systemic relations among components, factors, and powers that make up these relations.

If we accept that a main goal of sociocultural and psychological research is to explain various sociocultural and psychological phenomena by hypothesizing and theorizing about their causal mechanisms, then researchers have a serious dilemma deciding what to use as the empirical starting point for this causal theorizing. Should researchers start with correlations among variables obtained on large samples of people or start with thorough descriptions of cases, events, and practices, whereby researchers' convictions of such mechanisms may work? Our previous discussions led to the conclusion that both options can be used. A well-executed statistical analysis of valid data on representative samples may provide scientists with important clues about hidden powers and generative mechanisms. But such analysis will never pinpoint these mechanisms, and these statistical clues should be complemented by additional information. Many social researchers search for such information in case studies: "Cases have to be selected, because they exhibit or are likely to exhibit variations in the mechanism under scrutiny—or of its context" (Ackroyd, 2009, p. 539). "Case studies [within the realist paradigm] examine the operation of causal mechanisms in individual cases in detail" (George & Bennett, 2005, p. 21). Although researchers had been looking for these mechanisms in the statistical aggregates and their associations for decades, recent methodological theorizing in social and psychological research emphasizes case analysis as the primary way to discover these causal mechanisms.

> Systematic comparison based on interpretation [and analysis] of a range of cases . . . seeks to establish distinctive characteristics of particular cases or sets (ensembles) of cases and to explore how those characteristics taken together are causal to the current condition of cases. (Byrne, 2009a, p. 5)

One of the strongest objections against the case-based design is that it does not allow for generalization, which is considered to be the quintessence of any scientific inquiry. This argument can be addressed by going back to the two types of induction introduced in Chapter 3: enumerative and ampliative. As readers may remember, by conducting enumerative induction, researchers generalize a particular regularity from an observed sample to a larger number of nonobserved instances. Ampliative induction, which is accompanied either by abduction or retroduction, allows scholars to move from the observed regularities to the unobserved mechanisms behind them. Enumerative induction lies as the basis for *enumerative* or *statistical generalization* (Yin, 2009, p. 38). "In statistical generalization, an inference is made about a population (or universe) on the basis of empirical data collected about a sample from that universe" (p. 38). In *analytic* or *theoretical generalization* (p. 38), researchers start with hypotheses about causal mechanisms, test these hypotheses on some cases and then work on generalizing their understanding of these mechanisms by testing them and comparing across diverse cases. Bechtel (2009) called such generalization, from the hypotheses to theories about mechanisms, "generalization with mechanisms:"

> [G]eneralization with mechanisms does not involve simply applying a law [an empirical generalization] to other instances of the specified natural kind, but engaging in inquiry to determine what modifications are required to characterize the similar yet somewhat different mechanism active in another person or in different circumstances in the same person. (p. 125)

In conclusion, we may say that case-based studies allow researchers to do theoretical generalization about causal mechanisms by testing and expanding hypotheses about these mechanisms from one case to another. These studies do not allow researchers to do statistical generalizations that are only possible within the variable-based design. The issue of different forms of generalization is also discussed in Chapter 10.

The Problem of Sampling

Why is Sampling Important?

A discussion of different forms of generalizations inevitably leads us to the problem of sampling. This chapter was started with the question of how to move from particulars to the general, as researchers only have access to a limited number of participants, communities, or countries but want to make conclusions about the universal characteristics of people or cultures beyond the ones that were studied. Badly selected particulars for such analysis may jeopardize the very essence of the scientific research since they are the "windows" into the unobservable domains of the realities. Thus, the issue of how to select cases in order to make generalizations possible is a serious concern of not only culture and psychology researchers, but of all social and human scientists. We may also refer to another, more prosaic motto of empirical researchers: "Garbage in, garbage out." This means that if we have badly selected cases and use clumsy methodology to generate data from them, then no matter how sophisticated the analyses, it is almost impossible to achieve valid and reliable knowledge production. Whatever paradigm or theory researchers use, the particulars are the bricks for the construction of future knowledge. Thus, sampling is crucial for good research. Sampling is important for all domains of culture and psychology research, including cultural (Bernard, 2011) and comparative anthropology (Ember & Ember, 2009), cultural psychology (Heine, 2012), and mainstream cross-cultural psychology (Lonner & Berry,1986; Boenke et al., 2011).

Sampling is crucial because researchers physically cannot survey all communities or the members of a community (called population), so in order to evaluate the psychological, social, and cultural characteristics of the population, researchers draw a sample of its representatives and use them to estimate the population parameters. This is similar to the way doctors take several drops of blood to evaluate all the blood that circulates in an organism.

In order to be effective, sampling should follow the requirements of consistency with regard to the problem, theory, and philosophical assumptions that guide a research program. In the area of cross-cultural comparative psychological research, there is serious confusion with regard to sampling and its theoretical consistency with the assumptions and purposes of research. Mainstream cross-cultural psychologists strive to discover universal human psychological characteristics by comparing various psychological phenomena across cultures and nations. They strive to generalize from their comparative studies to all of humankind, or at least to large cultural communities like East and West, Western and non-Western countries, and so forth (see Chapter 1). To achieve their goals, they mostly use the positivist paradigm and variable-based designs, which both rely on enumerative generalization. Such generalization requires probability sampling, which these researchers do not typically use (Boenke et al., 2011). This is the first contradiction. To explain this reluctance to implement probability sampling, cross-cultural methodologists are forced to theorize using realist language without accepting the realist paradigm (Boenke et al., 2011). This is the second contradiction. Recently they have started discussing qualitative research and case-based design, but equate them with the traditional idiographic approach (see above) and a purely descriptive purpose, denying these approaches any capacity to generalize to the level of generative mechanisms (Boenke et al., 2011). This is the third contradiction. Because of these contradictions, it is confusing for students of culture and psychology to understand how to conduct sampling properly for their studies. In this section we will discuss the logistics of sampling within the framework developed in this textbook.

What should be Sampled in Culture and Psychology Research?

Lonner and Berry (1986) identified four levels of sampling in cross-cultural psychology study: cultures, communities, individuals, and behaviors. Boenke et al. (2011) reduced this schema to only two levels: cultural communities/countries and individuals. Anthropologists are also concerned with selecting cultures to study and to compare (Bernard, 2011; Ember & Ember, 2009). In addition, they must select informants who make a valid account of cultures (Bernard, 2011; Johnson, 1990) and choose appropriate "settings, events, times, households, or people" (Johnson, 1998, p. 152).

Sampling Culture, Cultural Communities, Countries, or Nations

The purpose of sampling cultures differs depending on the purpose and paradigm of a research project. Mainstream cross-cultural psychologists usually treat different cultures/nations as independent variables and people's behavior and their various psychological characteristics as dependent ones. This whole approach has been identified as a quasiexperimental design, with the only difference being that the independent variables cannot be manipulated and participants cannot be randomly assigned to different conditions. The logic of such a design is the following: cultural communities or countries differ with regard to various cultural or country-level dimensions. If researchers are interested in how cultures are related to human behavior and experience, they have to choose countries that vary along one or several cultural dimensions and analyze the differences in the mean level of and/or relationships among various behavioral and psychological variables measured on members of these cultures. Favorite cultural dimensions for such comparisons are the ones suggested by Triandis and colleagues (Singelis, Triandis, Bhawuk, & Gelfand, 1995; Triandis, 1995): individualism-collectivism and vertical and horizontal dimensions, and tightness and looseness (Gelfand et al., 2011), discovered by Hofstede (2005), the cultural values determined by Schwartz (2007), or by Inglehart (2003) and their colleagues. Researchers select countries that vary along one or several of these dimensions, sample individuals from these countries, and measure participants' psychological and nonpsychological characteristics: demographics, socioeconomic status, psychological attributes, health, and many others. They identify differences between these samples and attribute them to the differences in the selected cultural dimensions—individualism-collectivism, for instance. Then researchers generalize by announcing that people in collectivistic countries may be less lonely, more empathetic, have lower self-esteem, be less happy, and so forth. Researchers may also calculate intercorrelations among the psychological variables and discover, for example, that in collectivistic cultures, self-esteem co-varies less with life satisfaction than in individualistic cultures (Diener & Diener, 1995). All these conclusions directly or indirectly try to claim a near-universal generalization of how cultural dimensions shape human psychology.

> **INFORMATION BOX 7.1. CULTURAL ATTRIBUTION FALLACY IN CROSS-CULTURAL PSYCHOLOGICAL RESEARCH**
>
> Matsumoto and Yoo (2006) identified a serious flaw of many comparative cross cultural psychological studies. They labeled it *cultural attribution fallacy*. This fallacy happens when researchers discover group differences on psychological variables across samples from different ethnic, national, or cultural communities and draw the conclusion that these differences have an ethnic, national, or cultural origin, "when in fact the mere documentation of between-group differences does not justify such interpretations" (p. 235). The problem here is that even though researchers draw their samples from different nations/cultural groups, it does not guarantee that the discovered psychological differences are explained by national or cultural factors. In order to make such an assertion, they have to justify empirically that particular cultural differences, dimensions, or factors are responsible for the discovered psychological differences.

In addition to choosing countries based on "cultural dimensions," Boenke et al. (2011) suggested that researchers consider various "cultural regions" and run comparisons across them. Several regions were identified by Inglehart and colleagues and by Schwartz. Inglehart and Welzel (2010), for instance, delineated Catholic Europe, Protestant Europe, English-speaking countries, ex-Communist countries, Latin America, Africa, South Asia, and Confucian countries. Schwartz (2007) added to this classification: Orthodox East Europe, Muslim Middle East, Southeast Asia, and sub-Saharan Africa. Although these classifications are based on different foundations—religion, language, philosophy, and geography—cross-cultural methodologists recommend using them as a sampling frame for comparative psychological research of cultures.

When the sampling of countries is based on research questions and theoretical interests in particular dimensions or cultural regions, it is called a *theoretical sampling of cultures/countries* (Boenke, et al. 2011). (Keep in mind that to be fully theoretical, researchers have to answer why this particular dimension is of theoretical interest. What is unique about this dimension that makes it worthy of study? Why do researchers expect that this dimension is informative in studying particular psychological features? Only by answering these questions can the selection of countries be called theoretical in the full meaning of this term). Theoretical sampling requires that research goals guide the sampling strategy (p. 121). Depending on the interest either in the similarities or differences of people's functioning, researchers may choose countries that are either similar or different and then contemplate the sources of the discovered psychological differences. (See Mill's methods of agreement and difference in Chapter 8). Theoretical sampling implies a *purposive sampling procedure* for selecting countries. The methodologists also recommend that researchers select more than two countries for comparative studies because two-country comparisons may lead to the overemphasis or underemphasis on differences. A third country, C, is needed to calibrate and make sense of the differences between countries A and B (p. 122). Another option for cross-cultural research is *convenience sampling*, where there is no linkage between the research questions and the countries selected and where the countries are selected based on accessibility and convenience. And, finally, some methodologists (van de Vijver & Leung, 1997) recommend a *random sampling* of cultures, although the costs and practicality of such a procedure remain an issue.

Despite recent efforts of cross-cultural psychologists to amend their flaws, the biases in selecting countries still exist. In the recent highly-discussed article by Henrich, Heine, and Norenzayan

(2010), the authors stated that the mainstream cross-cultural psychologists, who claim that their aim is to discover pan-human universal human psychology, mostly employ participants from *W*estern, *e*ducated, *i*ndustrialized, *r*ich, and *d*emocratic societies. Because of such a biased selection, their participants "are among the least representative populations one could find for generalizing about humans" (p. 61). The authors called them WEIRD subjects and seriously questioned the whole enterprise of extrapolating from the studies on such samples to the pan-human psychology.

Anthropologists are mostly concerned with selecting research sites and informants for the purpose of collecting information about cultural practices, processes, and rituals. Selecting research sites implies a selection of not only appropriate cultural communities but also particular sites in these communities: villages, towns, neighborhoods, or families that will best serve the purpose of research (Bernard, 2011). Anthropologists are also concerned with selecting good *informants*, members of a community who are able to provide researchers with valid information about their cultures (Johnson, 1990, 1998; Small, 2009). *Key informants* are the most knowledgeable members of these communities with whom researchers build long-term relationships. *Specialized informants* are informants who "have a particular competence in some cultural domain" (Bernard, 2011, p. 150): parenting, healing, or food preparation. As Bernard explains, "good key informants are people whom you can talk to you easily [sic], who understand the information you need, and who are glad to give it to you or get it for you" (p. 150).

Regardless of the fact that the theoretical justification of countries or cultures selection for comparative psychological studies sounds like an important methodological requirement, it nevertheless is rare in the practice of cross-cultural research. Boenke et al. (2011) reported that after analyzing all articles published in the *Journal of Cross-Cultural Psychology* from 1996 to 2005, they discovered that only 21% of articles used theoretical sampling, and 67% of selected articles sampled countries purposefully but not theoretically. This means that the whole point of using cultures as factors that may help understand variations of human functioning is ignored in the majority of cross-cultural research, making such research nearly useless and theoretically impotent. Finally, the authors made another discouraging revelation:

> Experiential knowledge suggests that in many more than 6% of all cases, cultures were originally selected conveniently (by knowing a colleague in a country other than one's own), and the purposefulness of the selection procedure was only developed ex post facto. (p. 118)

It is up to individual researchers to decide whether they should theorize before selecting countries for comparison and let their theories lead the research, or whether they should select whatever countries are available and then trim their justification for such selection in a way that makes the publication of such a study possible.

Sampling Participants

In order to generalize from a sample to the population, this sample has to be representative of the population and drawn by a procedure that ensures that all individuals in the populations have an equal chance to be selected. Such a procedure is called *probability sampling*. Probability sampling is the only procedure that allows researchers to generalize from samples to populations.

The main advantage of probability sampling is that it facilitates statistical analysis (Boenke et al., 2011, p. 106). Because participants are selected into the sample randomly, there is high probability that, if another sample is selected, then its characteristics will not deviate too far from the first one. "This replicability of sampling that is crucial for accuracy and precision in studying any sample" (p. 106). Why? Because any estimate based on a sample has an error, and the more accurate the repeatability of the samples, the closer researchers get to obtaining the "true" population characteristics from a sample, which is exactly what every investigator strives for. Probability sampling eases the selection of participants. "The beauty of probability sampling is that the preferences of the researchers do not play a role in correctly designed and implemented probability samples because the case selection mechanism is governing solely by chance" (p. 103). In conducting a simple probability sampling, researchers

> define a population of individuals they want to study and then draw up a sampling frame, which is basically a listing of all individuals within the population. From the sampling frame, individuals are then randomly selected in a manner that ensures every member of the population has an equal chance of entering the sample. (p. 103)

This selection by chance is also expected to take care of the *representativeness* of a sample, meaning that it should reflect the composition of the population. But a simple probability sampling has a problem with securing this representativeness because populations are usually heterogeneous, consisting of people of different genders, ages, education, income, ethnic background, and myriads of other characteristics. To take care of this heterogeneity of populations and make the samples more homogeneous, using *stratified* and/or *cluster sampling* is recommended (Bernard, 2011; Boenke et al., 2011). *Stratified sampling* is based on the identification of key variables that group a population into strata established, for example, on education, religious affiliation, having or not having children, etc. Researchers split the population into subpopulations (strata), and then they select people randomly from each stratum. The number of people per stratum can be either proportionate or disproportionate in relation to the percentage of individuals from the population in each stratum (Boenke et al., 2011, p. 105). Bernard (2011) advised that "if differences on a dependent variable are large across strata like age, sex, ethnic group, and so on, then stratifying a sample is a great idea. [But] if differences are small, then stratifying just adds unnecessary work" (p. 119). If researchers are not sure what independent variable has the strongest covariance with the dependent variable, he also suggests not to stratify. *Cluster sampling* has a similar idea, but in this case population is partitioned in order to move from a large heterogeneous population to smaller, more homogeneous and more manageable clusters of respondents. This partitioning can be done based on household locations, by schools, church parishes, campuses, and so forth. Other more complex forms of sampling can be found in comprehensive handbooks (Cochran, 1977; Thompson, 2012).

Here, it is important to highlight that if researchers aim toward enumerative generalizations, they must use probability sampling; otherwise their studies will lose their credibility and validity. As you can see from this description, probability sampling is a derivate of enumerative induction and generalization, which is a move from facts established on a small number of individuals to the same facts, but generalized, on a larger number of similar individuals. Researchers can of course use nonprobability and not representative samples, but then they cannot do valid enumerative generalizations.

Why do Cross-Cultural Psychologists not use Probability Sampling and Why are They Proud of This?

In their analysis of the articles from the *Journal of Cross-Cultural Psychology*, Boenke and colleagues (2011) discovered that only "7% of all studies [they analyzed] used a probability sampling approach, whereas 93% used a nonprobability sampling strategy." About 56% used a simple convenience sampling by selecting whoever was available for researchers at the time of research (p. 122). A classic complaint about a majority of psychological studies in general, and cross-cultural in particular, is that many participants are college students who do not represent the populations to which researchers want to generalize their discoveries. Despite this nonrepresentativeness, in many cross-cultural research studies conducted on college students of different ethnic backgrounds, conclusions are made about all people of a particular ethnicity, thus generalizing from a nonprobability, nonrepresentative sample of students to the population of ethnic groups or even whole nations.

Many researchers, especially those who are serious about survey studies, have noted that cross-cultural psychologists often violate basic requirements for such types of research. Visser, Krosnick, and Lavrakas stated: "Social psychological research attempting to generalize from the college student sample to a nation looks silly and damages the apparent credibility of our enterprise" (p. 237). So why do psychologists not do probability representative sampling?

One of the answers is "because it is often difficult and expensive to draw representative random samples in culture-comparative studies, nonrandom sampling procedures have frequently been used" (Lonner & Berry, 1986, p. 89). In our opinion, this is an inexcusable reason for not following the scientific requirements. Cross-cultural psychologists strive for discovering universal psychology, which they cannot achieve through nonprobability convenience sampling. Difficulty and cost should not be barriers to true science.

Recently cross-cultural methodologists started claiming that they do not need random representative samples and can easily go with convenience sampling (Boenke et al., 2011, p. 122.). To justify such a claim they state that, first, according to some statisticians "no probabilistic considerations are necessary to test the adequacy of a sample for representing a population" (p. 123). If this were true, then the training of sociologists and cross-cultural psychologists should include such considerations; the authors would have to include them into their manuscripts, and the editors would have to consider them within their publication policy. Until this happens, such claims are irresponsible and sound like a poor excuse for choosing the easy way to do research. Cross-cultural methodologists also provide a second more theoretical argument for not using probability sampling:

> Psychologists using quantitative research methods typically do not want to generalize to the collective from which their sample was drawn but to other bearers of the psychological attribute under scrutiny in their research. . . . No random probability sampling is needed as long as the aim of the study is not to describe a collective—the population—but to enhance knowledge about the relationship of psychological phenomena in a given set of individuals. (p. 123)

Readers who have closely followed the discussion about philosophical paradigms may notice that these scholars have started talking the semirealist language, meaning that some quantitative psychologists strive not to do enumerative generalizations from samples to populations, but want to generalize about the relationship of psychological phenomena from one set of individuals to another. This argument is no less confusing than the previous one. To investigate the psychological mechanisms of human functioning requires the full-fledged realist paradigm with all of its attributes. This means accepting the reality of unobservable structures and powers that determine the phenomena of interest, aiming toward discovering causality, and not shying away from using the interpretivist paradigm to discover deep layers of meanings of events and practices. They must accept the superiority of case-based analysis and implement ampliative induction and retroductive thinking to move from empirical evidence to the hypotheses of causal mechanisms. Without such acceptance, claiming that the quantitative psychologists, who implicitly or explicitly use the positivist paradigm, try to find statistical associations among various psychological variables and treat them as proxy for causal relations, confuses the very essence of different metatheoretical paradigms and does not serve any good in training future generations of researchers in culture and psychology. If a researcher uses the positivist paradigm, he or she should be aware of this and apply the methodology that is adequate to that paradigm. If he or she wants to avoid such methodology, then he or she has to change the paradigm and not just the verbal furnishing of the same old empiricist thinking. It is obvious that there are serious problems with how quantitative positivist cross-cultural psychologists do their research, especially with regard to sampling. Instead of denying the necessity of following the scientific requirements streaming form their paradigm, they must change the paradigm. Realist and interpretivist research require different methodology overall and a different sampling approach in particular.

The umbrella term for sampling within the realist and interpretivist paradigms is *purposive sampling*. It is a set of procedures that requires that researchers select their cases—informants, participants, cultures, events, practices, settings, or processes—*on purpose*, depending on the problem and questions of their research and the theory that guide their study. Their primary purpose should be a theoretical one, meaning that the cases that can help shed light on a hypothesized theory about the causal mechanisms of a phenomenon should be selected. This is challenging, as it is not always clear what these mechanisms are and, correspondently, what cases will be the best to represent them. That is why methodologists suggest a different version of purposive sampling to help researchers articulate their theories, problems, and overall goals of research more clearly (Bernard, 2011, pp. 147–154; Boehnke et al., 2011, p. 105; Miles et al., 2014, pp. 30–37). In *by type of case sampling*, scientists select cases that represent the phenomenon of interest, like AIDS patients, victims of bulling, voluntarily childless families, etc. *Typical case sampling* should be considered when researchers are interested in typical representatives of a population, phenomenon, or process, like typical black suburban households, typical East Asian immigrants, or typical fans of a particular team. What defines "typical" constitutes a separate question. Usually researchers use cases with the most frequent attributes in a particular subpopulation. If census data indicates that a typical suburban family is comprised of, for example, white, 28–45 years old parents who both work and have two kids and one dog, then a typical household will possess the majority of these characteristics. Typical cases are contrasted with *deviant cases*, which are atypical and unusual for the phenomenon of interest at a particular place and time. Sometimes typical cases may also be called *critical cases*, meaning the cases that are the most important for providing evidence that supports a theory, cases that have inspired particular productive hypotheses. The retroduction of a theory may be facilitated by including *extreme case sampling* into the program of research, meaning sampling that is focused on the cases that demonstrate either a very high or a very low degree of the phenomenon of interest or its very atypical forms (this is also called *deviant cases* and *maximum variation sampling*). Extreme cases of successful and unsuccessful acculturation include: immigrants with atypically high levels of education and/or high political or business achievements versus immigrant families who demonstrate a low level of cultural adjustment, such as those where honor killings of female relatives have taken place. It is important to note that, for case-based studies, researchers often use the comparative design because only thorough these comparisons can the productive hypotheses about mechanisms of events and practices be retroducted. We will talk more about the comparative design of cultural studies in psychology in the next chapter.

What Should the Sizes of Various Purposive Samples be?

Bernard (2011) provides the following recipe:

> There is growing evidence that 10–20 knowledgeable people are enough to uncover and understand the core categories in any well-defined cultural domain or study of lived experience. Morse (1994) recommended a minimum of six interviews for phenomenological studies and 30–50 interviews for ethnographic studies and grounded theory studies. (p. 154)

One of the fundamental characteristics of the purposeful sampling procedure is its evolving nature (Miles, Huberman, & Saldana, 2014), meaning that it is processual and iterative in selecting, analyzing, and reanalyzing cases and then selecting new ones based on the previous steps. Such a procedure is a much better starting point for a retroductive scientific process than deciding upon a sample for survey and blindly following the dictate of the probability theory. This procession from one type of case to another may follow the development of a theory that gets more and more details and nuances by including new and more diverse instances of the phenomenon or process. Closely related to the above considerations is the *criterion of saturation* for selecting cases. When adding more cases no longer provides new information about the processes and mechanisms of interest, then sampling should be terminated, or should be changed to another strategy.

Sampling should be logically connected with all other components of the research project: problem, theory, and the philosophical paradigm. Violations of this rule as well as violations of the prescribed norms of a particular paradigm lead to invalid and unproductive studies. Researchers should follow their paradigm and be consistent with its demands.

Conclusion

This chapter started with identifying research strategies as a high level plan of solving a research problem with existing resources, conditions, and in a set time frame. To make this planning successful we discussed one of the most challenging issues of social research: relations between particulars—cases, sites, communities, or individuals, and the general—encompassing laws and regularities that determine and influence the functioning of all the particulars. Traditionally this problem has been addressed by differentiating nomothetic and idiographic sciences and the corresponding approaches for obtaining knowledge. Researchers should not polarize these approaches but should strive to discover the general through investigating the particulars and retroducting hypotheses about the underlying laws and mechanisms that will be followed by theoretical generalization and consequent empirical verifications. Extensive and intensive research strategies rooted in the realist paradigm are suggested as an alternative to the nomothetic versus idiographic division. An important distinction between the etic and emic stances of a social researcher is presented and discussed. A detailed discussion of the variable-based versus case-based design highlights numerous disadvantages of the former and invites researchers to focus on the latter design. Sampling for culture and psychology research is a challenging issue that should be predetermined by a research problem and the theoretical and philosophical assumptions of an investigator.

Questions

1. What is the logic behind the traditional differentiation between nomothetic and idiographic science? Do you agree with this classification? If not, why not?
2. Articulate two understandings of laws: from the positivist and from the realist points of view. Discuss the differences. Which understanding looks more logical? Justify your answer.
3. How does this chapter connect idiographic and nomothetic approaches? Present it in your own words. Do you agree or disagree with it? Justify your answer.
4. Do you agree that the nomothetic versus idiographic distinction may apply to interpretive sciences? Provide some examples that support your point of view.
5. Thoroughly examine Table 7.1. and discuss the differences between extensive and intensive strategies. Compare these classifications with nomothetic versus idiographic as well as the quantitative versus qualitative taxonomy of different strategies. Discuss their similarities and differences.
6. Why is the variable based design criticized in this chapter? Do you agree with this critique? What advantages do you think this design provides for culture and psychology studies? Discuss this in class and apply this critique to known studies.

7. Does the case-based design constitute a viable alternative to the variable-based one? Summarize your arguments for and against this statement. Provide examples that support your position.
8. Reflect on your own and your colleagues' practices of sampling. Do they follow all the requirements for this procedure? Do they violate some of them? Why? How are these violations justified? How is sampling related to the philosophical paradigm? Articulate your understanding of these links.

Exercise

Select studies that were conducted either from the etic or emic positions. Articulate the main distinctive features of these positions in the selected studies. Look back at your own research: do you have an etic or emic stance? Justify your answer.

Glossary

Case-based design approaches entities of investigation as units within their contextual and temporal positioning. It handles these entities as systems and tries to grasp the multiplicity of their manifestations and expressions. The emic positioning of researchers provides them with an opportunity to use the intensive strategy and inquire into deep layers of meaning and the causal mechanisms behind these manifestations.

Etic and emic positions of researchers, introduced by Pike (1967), apply to the stance of a social scholar toward his or her object of investigation. Etic is an "outside" stance, where a researcher imposes on an object of study his or her concepts, criteria of evaluation, a priori designated units of observation and some equivalent measures. Emic is an "inside" stance, where a researcher looks at an object of inquiry from "within this object." All the tools for a study—concepts, criteria, units of observations, and measurements—are selected based on the nature and qualities of these systems. These positions resemble the nomothetic and idiographic differentiation of sciences.

Extensive research strategy: realist scholars suggest this strategy to study a large number of entities with a small number of common properties. It strives to establish empirical regularities across these entities and generalize to the similar kinds. The extensive research strategy frequently uses statistics and often employs the etic position of researchers; it may be associated with the positivist/quantitative paradigm and variable-based design.

Idiographic: to describe a unique or distinct object, case, event; from *idios* (Greek) own, distinct and *graphikos* (Greek) writing; to write (from Soanes & Stevenson, 2008, and http://www.thefreedictionary.com/). In the philosophy of science, this idea reflects the investigation of a single event, entity, or individual by the extensive examination of their modes of being, history of emergence, and contextual and temporal conditions of functioning. It is often considered to be a purely descriptive enterprise.

Intensive research strategy examines a small number of entities with a large number of diverse properties. It strives to get in depth into studies to deep layers of meaning or generative mechanisms. This strategy requires investigators to take the emic stance and is often used within the interpretivist or realist paradigm and uses the case-based design.

Nomothetic: relating to laws (scientific, legislative, etc.); from *nomos* (Greek) law and *thetic* (Greek) presented dogmatically; arbitrarily prescribed (from http://www.thefreedictionary.com/). See also nomological (Chapter 3). In the philosophy of science, this concept identifies a search for the laws that govern the natural world, societies, the human's mind and behavior in order to use these laws to understand how these entities work, to explain them, and make interventions possible. Many consider discovering these laws to be the ultimate goal of science because they give humans power over these realities.

Sampling is a procedure of selecting units of observation for a study. In cultural and psychology research, investigators sample cultures, communities, sites, activities, informants, and participants. All these forms of sampling should be driven by research problems and be congruent with the theoretical and philosophical assumptions of a researcher. Violations of this congruency make social research weak and even useless. Different forms of sampling, like *probability*, *stratified*, *purposeful*, and their different variations should be thoroughly considered during the strategic planning of a project.

Strategy: "(from Greek *stratēgia* 'generalship') **1** a plan designed to achieve a particular long-term aim. **2** the art of planning and directing military activity in a war or battle" (Soanes & Stevenson, 2008). A research strategy is a script of how to achieve the goals of research in particular conditions with the available resources and within a required time frame.

Variable-based design requires splitting the entities of an investigation into measureable components: dimensions, traits, construals, etc., operationalizing them into variables and measuring them, and then subjecting them to statistical analysis. The main purpose is to discover empirical regularities among the variables, to confirm the theories and provide the basis for positivism-based explanations and predictions. It is typically conducted within the extensive strategy and requires the etic position of a researcher.

Recommended Reading

Byrne, D., & Ragin, C. C. (Eds.). (2009). *The SAGE handbook of case-based methods*. Los Angeles, CA: Sage.

Cummins, R. A. (2000). "How does it work?" versus "What are the laws?": Two conceptions of psychological explanation. In F. C. Keil & R. A. Wilson (Eds.), *Explanation and cognition*. Cambridge, MA: MIT Press.

Easton, G. (2010). Critical realism in case study research. *Industrial Marketing Management, 39*(1), 118–128.

Gomm, R., Hammersley, M., & Foster, P. (Eds.). (2000). *Case study method: Key issues, key texts*. London, UK: Sage

Johnson, J. C. (1998). Research design and research strategies. In H. R. Bernard (Ed.), *Handbook of methods in cultural anthropology* (pp. 131–171). Walnut Creek, CA: AltaMira.

Lamiell, J. T. (1998). "Nomothetic" and "idiographic:" Contrasting Windelband's understanding with contemporary usage. *Theory Psychology, 8*(1), 23–38.

Lamiell, J. T. (2013). Statisticism in personality psychologists' use of trait constructs: What is it? How was it contracted? Is there a cure? *New Ideas in Psychology, 31*(1), 65–71.

Miles, M. B., Huberman, A. M., & Saldana, J. (Eds.). (2014). *Qualitative data analysis: A methods sourcebook* (3rd ed.). Thousand Oaks, CA: Sage.

Thomas, G. (2011). *How to do your case study: A guide for students and researchers*. Los Angeles, CA: Sage.

Yin, R. K. (2009). *Case study research: Design and methods* (4th ed.). Los Angeles, CA: Sage

References

Abbott, A. (1992). What do cases do? Some notes on activity in sociological analysis. In C. C. Ragin & H. S. Becker (Eds.), *What is a case? Exploring the foundations of social inquiry* (pp. 53–82). New York, NY: Cambridge University Press.

Ackroyd, S. (2009). Research design for realist research. In D. A. Buchanan & A. Bryman (Eds.), *The SAGE handbook of organizational research methods* (pp. 532–548). London, UK: Sage.

Allport, G. W. (1937/1963). *Patterns and growth in personality*. New York, NY: Holt, Rinehart and Winston.

Allport, G. W. (1962). The general and the unique in psychological science. *Journal of Personality, 30*(3), 405–422.

Barlow, D. H., & Nock, M. K. (2009). Why can't we be more idiographic in our research? *Perspectives on Psychological Science, 4*(1), 19–21.

Bechtel, W., & Wright, C. D. (2009). What is psychological explanation? In J. Symons & P. Calvo (Eds.), *The Routledge companion to philosophy of psychology* (pp. 113–130). London, UK: Routledge.
Benedict, R. (1946/1974). *The chrysanthemum and the sword: Patterns of Japanese culture*. Boston, MA: Houghton Mifflin.
Berelson, B., & Steiner, G. A. (1964). *Human behavior: An inventory of scientific findings*. New York, NY: Harcourt, Brace & World.
Bernard, H. R. (2011). *Research methods in anthropology: Qualitative and quantitative approaches*. Lanham, MD: AltaMira.
Bhaskar, R. (1975/2008). *A realist theory of science*. London, UK: Verso.
Bhaskar, R. (1979/2015). *The possibility of naturalism: A philosophical critique of the contemporary human sciences* (4th ed.). Oxon, UK: Routledge.
Binet, A. (1903). *L'étude expérimentale de l'intelligence*. Paris, France: Scheicher.
Boehnke, K., Lietz, P., Schreier, M., & Wilhelm, A. (2011). Sampling: The selection of cases for culturally comparative psychological research. In D. Matsumoto & F. J. R. van de Vijver (Eds.), *Cross-cultural research methods in psychology* (pp. 101–129). Cambridge, UK: Cambridge University Press.
Byrne, D. (2009a). Case-based methods: Why we need them; what they are; how to do them. In D. Byrne & C. C. Ragin (Eds.), *The SAGE handbook of case-based methods* (pp. 1–10). Los Angeles, CA: Sage.
Byrne, D. (2009b). Causality and interpretation in qualitative policy-related research. In D. Byrne & C. C. Ragin (Eds.), *The SAGE handbook of case-based methods* (pp. 511–521). Los Angeles, CA: Sage.
Byrne, D., & Ragin, C. C. (Eds.). (2009). *The SAGE handbook of case-based methods*. Los Angeles, CA: Sage.
Cochran, W. G. (1977). *Sampling techniques* (3rd ed.). New York, NY: John Wiley.
Collier, A. (1994). *Critical realism: An introduction to Roy Bhaskar's philosophy*. London, UK: Verso.
Cooper, B., Glaesser, J., Gomm, R., & Hammersley, M. (2012). *Challenging the qualitative-quantitative divide: Explorations in case-focused causal analysis*. London, UK: Continuum.
Cummins, R. A. (2000). "How does it work?" versus "What are the laws?": Two conceptions of psychological explanation. In F. C. Keil & R. A. Wilson (Eds.), *Explanation and cognition*. Cambridge, MA: MIT Press.
Danemark, B., Ekstrom, M., Jakobsen, L., & Karlsson, J. C. (2002). *Explaining society: Critical realism in the social sciences*. London, UK: Routledge.
Davis, S. F. (Ed.). (2003). *Handbook of research methods in experimental psychology*. Malden, MA: Blackwell.
Denzin, N. K. (2001). *Interpretive interactionism*. Thousand Oaks, CA: Sage.
Denzin, N. K., & Lincoln, Y. S. (2012). *Strategies of qualitative inquiry*. Thousand Oaks, CA: Sage.
Diener, E., & Diener, M. (1995). Cross-cultural correlates of life satisfaction and self-esteem. *Journal of Personality and Social Psychology, 68*(4), 653–663.
Easton, G. (2010). Critical realism in case study research. *Industrial Marketing Management, 39*(1), 118–128.
Ember, C. R., & Ember, M. (2009). *Cross-cultural research methods*. (2nd ed.). Lanham, MD: AltaMira Press.
Flyvbjerg, B. (2006). Five misunderstandings about case-study research. *Qualitative Inquiry, 12*(2), 219–245.
Gelfand, M. J., Raver, J. L., Nishii, L., Leslie, L. M., Lun, J., Lim, B. C., . . . Yamaguchi, S. (2011). Difference between tight and loose cultures: A 33-nation study. *Science, 332*(6033), 1100–1104.
George, A. L., & Bennett, A. (2005). *Case studies and theory development in the social sciences*. Cambridge, MA: MIT Press.
Gerring, J. (2007). *Case study research: Principles and practices*. Cambridge, UK: Cambridge University Press.
Glaser, B. G., & Strauss, A. L. (1967). *The discovery of grounded theory: Strategies for qualitative research*. Chicago, IL: Aldine.
Goffman, E. (1959). *Presentation of self in everyday life*. Garden City, NY: Doubleday.
Goffman, E. (1966). *Behavior in public places: Notes on the social organization of gatherings*. New York, NY: Free Press of Glencoe.
Goffman, E. (1967). *Interaction ritual: Essays on face-to-face behavior*. Garden City, NY: Anchor Books.
Gomm, R., Hammersley, M., & Foster, P. (Eds.). (2000). *Case study method: Key issues, key texts*. London, UK: Sage.
Hammersley, M. (2012). Qualitative causal analysis: Grounded theorizing and the qualitative survey. In B. Cooper, J. Glaesser, R. Gomm & M. Hammersley (Eds.), *Challenging the qualitative-quantitative divide: Explorations in case-focused causal analysis* (pp. 72–95). London, UK: Continuum.
Hammersley, M., & Cooper, B. (2012). Analytic induction versus qualitative comparative analysis. In B. Cooper, J. Glaesser, R. Gomm & M. Hammersley (Eds.), *Challenging the qualitative-quantitative divide: Explorations in case-focused causal analysis* (pp. 129–169). London, UK: Continuum.

Harris, R. J. (2003). Traditional nomothetic approaches. In S. F. Davis (Ed.), *Handbook of research methods in experimental psychology* (pp. 41–64). Malden, MA: Blackwell.

Heine, S. J. (2012). *Cultural psychology* (2nd ed.). New York, NY: Norton.

Helfrich-Holter, H. (2006). Beyond the dilemma of cultural and cross-cultural psychology: Resolving the tension between nomothetic and idiographic approaches. In J. Straub, D. Weidemann, C. Kolbl & B. Zielke (Eds.), *Pursuit of meaning: Advances in cultural and cross-cultural psychology* (pp. 253–268). Bielefeld, Germany: Transcript-Verlag.

Henrich, J., Heine, S. J., & Norenzayan, A. (2010). The weirdest people in the world? *Behavioral and Brain Sciences, 33*(2–3), 61–135.

Hermans, H. J. M. (1988). On the integration of nomothetic and idiographic research methods in the study of personal meaning. *Journal of Personality, 56*(4), 785–812.

Hofstede, G., & Hofstede, G. J. (2005). *Culture and organization: Software of the mind.* (2nd ed.). New York, NY: McGraw-Hill.

Husserl, E. (1900/1970). *Logical investigations* (J. N. Findlay, Trans. Vol. 1). New York, NY: Humanities Press.

Inglehart, R. (Ed.). (2003). *Human values and social change: Findings from the values survey.* Leiden, The Netherlands: Brill.

Inglehart, R., & Welzel, C. (2010). Changing mass priorities: The link between modernization and democracy. *Perspectives on Politics, 8*(2), 551–567.

Johnson, J. C. (1990). *Selecting ethnographic informants.* Los Angeles, CA: Sage.

Johnson, J. C. (1998). Research design and research strategies. In H. R. Bernard (Ed.), *Handbook of methods in cultural anthropology* (pp. 131–171). Walnut Creek, CA: AltaMira.

Lamiell, J. T. (1987). *The psychology of personality: An epistemological inquiry.* New York, NY: Columbia University Press.

Lamiell, J. T. (1998). "Nomothetic" and "idiographic:" Contrasting Windelband's understanding with contemporary usage. *Theory Psychology, 8*(1), 23–38.

Lamiell, J. T. (2013). Statisticism in personality psychologists' use of trait constructs: What is it? How was it contracted? Is there a cure? *New Ideas in Psychology, 31*(1), 65–71.

Levine, R. V., Norenzayan, A., & Philbrick, K. (2001). Cross-cultural differences in helping strangers. *Journal of Cross-Cultural Psychology, 32*(5), 543–560.

Lonner, W. J., & Berry, J. W. (1986). Sampling and surveying. In W. J. Lonner & J. W. Berry (Eds.), *Field methods in cross-cultural research* (pp. 85–110). Beverly Hills, CA: Sage.

Malcolm, W. (2004). Nomothetic/ideograpthic. In M. S. Lewis-Beck, A. Bryman & T. F. Liao (Eds.), *The SAGE encyclopedia of social science research methods.* Thousand Oaks, CA: Sage.

Matsumoto, D., & Fletcher, D. (1996). Cross-national differences in disease rates as accounted for by meaningful psychological dimensions of cultural variability. *Journal of Gender, Culture, and Health, 1*(1), 71–82.

Matsumoto, D., & Yoo, S. H. (2006). Toward a new generation of cross-cultural research. *Perspectives on Psychological Science, 1*(3), 234–250.

Mckeown, M. (2012). *The strategy book: How to think and act strategically to deliver outstanding results.* Harlow, UK: Pearson Education.

Miles, M. B., Huberman, A. M., & Saldana, J. (2014). *Qualitative data analysis: A methods sourcebook* (3rd ed.). Thousand Oaks, CA: Sage.

Mintzberg, H. (2011). *Managing.* San Francisco, CA: Berrett-Koehler.

Mulaik, S. A. (1987). A brief history of the philosophical foundations of exploratory factor analysis. *Multivariate Behavioral Research, 22*(3), 267–305.

Pike, K. L. (1967). *Language in relation to a unified theory of the structure of human behavior.* The Hague, The Netherlands: Mouton.

Ragin, C. C. (1987). *The comparative method: Moving beyond qualitative and quantitative strategies.* Berkeley, CA: University of California Press.

Ragin, C. C. (1992). Introduction: Cases of "What is a case?". In C. C. Ragin & H. S. Becker (Eds.), *What is a case? Exploring the foundations of social inquiry* (pp. 1–17). New York, NY: Cambridge University Press.

Ragin, C. C. (1998). The logic of qualitative comparative analysis [Supplement]. *International Review of Social History, 43*, 105–124.

Ragin, C. C., & Amoroso, L. M. (2011). *Constructing social research* (2nd ed.). Los Angeles, CA: Sage.

Ragin, C. C., & Becker, H. S. (Eds.). (1992). *What is a case? Exploring the foundations of social inquiry.* New York, NY: Cambridge University Press.

Sayer, A. (1992). *Methods in social science: A realist approach.* (2nd ed.). London, UK: Routledge.

Schwartz, S. H. (2007). A theory of cultural value orientation: Explication and applications. In Y. Esmer & T. Pettersson (Eds.), *Measuring and mapping cultures: 25 years of comparative value surveys* (pp. 33–78). Leiden, The Netherlands: Brill.

Singelis, T. M., Triandis, H. C., Bhawuk, D. P. S., & Gelfand, M. J. (1995). Horizontal and vertical dimensions of individualism and collectivism: A theoretical and measurement refinement. *Cross-Cultural Research, 29*(3), 240–275.

Small, M. L. (2009). "How many cases do I need?:" On science and the logic of case selection in field-based research. *Ethnography, 10*(1), 5–38.

Smith, J. A., Harre, R., & Langenhove, L. V. (1995). Idiography and the case-study. In J. A. Smith, R. Harre & L. V. Langenhove (Eds.), *Rethinking psychology* (pp. 59–69). London, UK: Sage.

Soanes, C., & Stevenson, A. (Eds.). (2008). *Concise Oxford English dictionary* (11th ed.). Oxford, UK: Oxford University Press.

Thomas, G. (2011). *How to do your case study: A guide for students and researchers.* Los Angeles, CA: Sage.

Thompson, S. K. (2012). *Sampling* (3rd ed.). New York, NY: John Wiley.

Triandis, H. C. (1995). *Individualism and collectivism.* Boulder, CO: Westview Press.

Valsiner, J. (1986a). Where is the individual subject in scientific psychology? In J. Valsiner (Ed.), *The individual subject and scientific psychology* (pp. 1–14). New York, NY: Plenum Press.

Valsiner, J. (Ed.). (1986b). *The individual subject and scientific psychology.* New York, NY: Plenum Press.

Valsiner, J. (2007). *Culture in minds and societies: Foundations of cultural psychology.* Los Angeles, CA: Sage.

van de Vijver, F. R., & Leung, K. (1997). *Methods and data analysis for cross-cultural research.* Thousands Oaks, CA: Sage.

Visser, P. S., Krosnick, J. A., & Lavrakas, J. (2000). Survey research. In H. T. Reis & C. M. Judd (Eds.), *Handbook of research methods in social and personality psychology* (pp. 223–252). Cambridge, UK: Cambridge University Press.

von Wright, G. H. (1971). *Explanation and understanding.* Ithaca, NY: Cornell University Press.

Whiting, B. B., & Whiting, J. W. M. (1975). *Children of six cultures: A psycho-cultural analysis.* Cambridge, MA: Harvard University Press.

Windelband, W. (1894/1980). Rectorial Address, Strasbourg, 1894. *History and Theory, 19*(2), 169–185.

Yin, R. K. (2003). *Application of case study research* (2nd ed.). Thousand Oaks, CA Sage.

Yin, R. K. (2009). *Case study research: Design and methods* (4th ed.). Los Angeles, CA: Sage.

Znaniecki, F. (1934). *The method of sociology.* New York, NY: Rinehart.

PART III

Practical Aspects of Doing Research

In Part III, we will focus on the methodical and technical aspects of research on culture and psychology. Chapter 8 presents and describes the main types of studies on culture and psychology: *monocultural* and *multicultural comparative*. We will examine different *units* and *levels of analysis*, such as ecological or country level versus the individual. This examination will lead to the challenges of *ecological fallacy*, an error that may happen if researchers confuse their levels and units of analysis. Chapter 9 is devoted to one of the most complex topics of comparative research on culture, the notion of *construct comparability*. We will also examine its diagnostics and the related issues of *instrument translations* and the *statistical verification* of invariance of assessment tools. Chapter 10 will introduce *ethnography* as a major method of anthropological and cultural psychological studies. And, finally, Chapter 11 will address some major ethical aspects of cultural and psychology research.

8

THE TYPES OF STUDIES ON CULTURE AND PSYCHOLOGY

This chapter will:

- Introduce two types of studies on culture and psychology: monocultural and multicultural comparative
- Discuss the advantages of comparative case-based method
- Contrast this method with comparative variable-based studies in cross-cultural psychology
- Introduce country-level and individual-level research
- Warn against ecological and individual fallacies.

Introduction: Monocultural Studies

Monocultural studies are focused on one or several culturally similar communities, countries, or geographical regions grouped by ethnicity, race, religion, or language. These studies may strive to provide a description of these communities by presenting their ecology, economy, and history as a background for understanding their cultural models and the psychological functioning of their members. They may also attempt to understand and explain behaviors, cognitions, and other experiences of people in these communities in order to interact and do business with them, to educate their members, to implement health interventions, to help with cultural changes and transitions, and many other applied goals. A wide range of research purposes from descriptive and exploratory to interpretative and explanatory may be implemented within this type of studies.

Disciplinary Distinctions

Monocultural studies typically have two goals: one is to uncover cultural models for the domains that are at the focus of a research: parenting, marriage, health, education, illnesses, work, etc. The second one is to explore how, after being internalized, these models are experienced by people and regulate their behaviors. Some monocultural studies may focus mostly on understanding the cultural models; these are usually conducted by anthropologists with more focus on culture than on people's actions and experiences. Other studies may focus on the experiences of people in these communities, how they behave, think, and feel in their environment because of the cultural models they have internalized. Such studies are conducted by psychological/cognitive anthropologists and cultural psychologists. Indigenous psychologists conduct most of their research as monocultural and also belong to this family. A collaboration of cultural/indigenous psychologists and cultural anthropologists could be productive for such studies. Anthropologists excel at analyzing the cultural context of people's lives, whereas psychologists delve into the usages and experiences of these cultures by their members.

Positions of Researchers

In Chapter 7 etic and emic positions of researchers were discussed. Here I provide an elaboration of these positions in relation to monocultural studies. The majority of monocultural studies are conducted by researchers from Western countries who explore the sociocultural realities of non-Western communities. These researchers are coming from "outside" of these communities but strive to accommodate "a native point of view" and to see the world through the "lenses" of that particular community. We may call this an *outsider-to-insider position*. Some monocultural studies are conducted by scholars who are members of the cultural communities they want to investigate. These are monocultural *indigenous studies* (Yang, 2000).

The term "indigenous" usually refers to the research of non-Western scholars of their own communities and countries. Interestingly, when Western researchers perform this type of studies on their own communities the term "indigenous" is rarely used. Indigenous monocultural studies are conducted from what may be called an *insider position*. In addition to the traditional research purposes—description, understanding, and explanation—such studies may be conducted toward self-reflective and identification objectives, when researchers strive to better understand their own cultural communities in order to help their members to appreciate their own cultural heritage more deeply or to solve the problems that these communities may experience.

Methodology of Monocultural Studies

These studies usually start by presenting a history of the community of interest, its geography and ecology, together with its economic and demographic aspects. This is understandable, as the cultural and psychological characteristics of people emerge and unfold in a particular environmental context, have a history of their development, and are interrelated with socioeconomic parameters of their communities. As a rule, researchers travel to these communities and live there for some time. The main methodology for such studies is ethnography, with its deep involvement with and participation in the everyday lives of the communities of interest. Within ethnographic fieldwork, researchers may utilize surveys, psychological tests and questionnaires; they may incorporate experiments, both laboratory and field ones; they may use interviews and analyze life histories, artifacts, and archives. This triangulation of different methods secures efficient answers to the research questions. Monocultural studies are case-based by their design, as researchers strive to comprehend the patterns of meanings and practices of particular cultural communities and attempt to uncover the causes that determine people's functioning in these communities. Unless researchers set a specific goal of discovering the mechanisms of the sociocultural regulation of people's behavior, monocultural studies rarely aim toward generalizations, either enumerative or theoretical. They usually explore communities just for the sake of describing and understanding them. In conducting these studies, researchers may follow the interpretive or realist paradigms: either working on the systems of meanings within which members of the communities operate, or aiming toward discovering the psycho-sociocultural mechanisms of people's functioning there. The fundamental dialectic here is that the interpretative and realist positions are interrelated as these mechanisms are human-made and are saturated with meaning. Therefore abductive and retroductive thinking go hand-in-hand in this type of research. The best way to illustrate the application of all these designs and methods is to look at different monocultural studies and their methodology.

Examples of Monocultural Studies

a. Studies of national character. The seminal study of Benedict (1946/1974) on Japanese national character, which we have intensively discussed, is a classic example of a monocultural study. Among other studies conducted within the culture and personality tradition (see (Mead & Metraux, 1953/2000), is Gorer and Rickman's (1949/1962) "The people of Great Russia: A psychological study" and Mead's (Mead, 1966) study of the modal personality of Soviet people and their attitudes toward authorities. These studies were also strongly driven by the practical concerns of the American government after WWII to know more about their new enemy in the Cold War. Gorer and Rickman's book was first published in 1949, survived several editions and was concerned "with a single aspect of that very complex subject, their [the Great Russians] psychology, the shared motives and views of the worlds" (p. xxiv). John Rickman, an English physician, worked in Russian peasant communities at the beginning of the 20th century and presented his experiences in a set of ethnopsychological essays that constitute the first part of the book. In the second half, Gorer elaborated on the main characterological features of Russians and the sources of their psychological attributes. He worked within the frame of "social anthropology and whole-person psychology (including depth psychology and the developing data of ethology)" (p. xxxix-xl), interpreted several hundred interviews with refugees, immigrants, and visitors to the USA conducted by other researchers, and analyzed Russian political history and literature. Based on this evidence, Gorer identified Russians as

> oppressed by diffuse feelings of guilt and hostility, but show[s] very little anxiety. . . . They also tend to oscillate between unconscious fears of isolation and loneliness, and an absence of feelings of individuality so that the self is . . . merged with its peers in a "soul-collective." (p. 189)

The authors found the root of these feelings in the practice of swaddling toddlers, a practice that strongly restricts physical activity, later resulting in adults' emotions of rage, hostility, unfocused guilt, feelings of separateness and loneliness. These scholars not only interpreted their empirical data in terms of psychodynamic psychology, but also reotroduced a hypothesis about the causal mechanism of the Russian national character. As with any hypothesis, and especially in such a challenging issue as the national character of the people of such a large and diverse country, the swaddling hypothesis as a causal factor of Russians' psychology attracted a lot of debates, and finally was rejected (Chisholm, 2008; Mead, 1954). But some of the related hypotheses, like the idea of "the slave soul of Russia" and Russians' "moral masochism" were perpetuated by several more current studies (Rancour-Laferriere, 1995, 1999).

Another monocultural study related to a particular geographical region, or "cultural area," is Gary Gregg's (2005) study on Middle Eastern and North African (MENA) Muslim societies: *The Middle East: A cultural psychology*. Gregg is a American personality psychologist who works "in the 'study of lives' tradition pioneered by Henry Murray, Robert White, and Erik Erikson, which entails investigating single lives in depth" (from Gregg's website http://people.kzoo.edu/ggregg/). His study of MENA people is mostly descriptive in its purpose, as it strives to summarize various resources on the "psychological dimensions of traditional ways of life in Middle Eastern and North African societies, and of the impact of 'modernization' and 'underdevelopment'" (p. 3). The author's goal was to address Westerners' deep misunderstanding of the cultures and psyches of the people of the MENA countries. This study did not aim at one particular "culture" but targeted a "cultural area" (or "ethno-geographic area"), a term that was coined within culture and personality studies. This term describes a geographical area with several contiguous countries, nations, or communities that share some sociocultural and psychological characteristics. Other examples of such areas include North American Plains Indians, ex-Communist countries, and Orthodox Christian nations. Such a conceptualization gives researchers flexibility from the rigidity of the mainstream social sciences' usage of the notion of "culture" as a bounded and homogeneous set of traditions and practices within a particular nation that shape distinctive national personalities.

Gregg started his book with a list of misconceptions and stereotypes that Westerners hold about inhabitants of this region. Then he provided the social context ("social ecology") of human development of this area and the basic values that guide this ecology. The rest of the book may be characterized as an analytic ethnography of the six periods of human development: infancy, early childhood, late childhood, adolescence, early adulthood, and mature adulthood, and shows how each stage is dealt with by people in the MENA area. Methodologically the author relied on the existing literature of this cultural area, much of which was conducted by indigenous Arab psychologists and social scientists. These reviews were complemented by the author's own interviews and observations. Gregg held a typical "outsider-to-insider position" and carefully combined Western (outsider) and indigenous (insider) visions and approaches.

b. Studies of a geographical area united by the same cultural model of interest. Richard Nisbett and Dov Cohen's (1996) multimethod Western indigenous study of the culture of honor showcases several aspects of a good monocultural research: It has a clear articulated problem, a proposed hypothesis about the causes of the problem, and a set of a multimethod studies that test this hypothesis.

The problem that the researchers addressed is the higher prevalence of violence in the South of the USA in comparison to the North. "The South has long been thought to be more violent than the North, and we believe that some distinctive aspects of the South are key to this violence" (p. xv). ("The South of the USA" can be conceptualized in this research as a cultural area within a country.) They proposed that the culture of honor that was historically developed in this geographical region lies at the root of many patterns of the Southerners' tendency to violence.

I classify this study as realist research, even though the authors probably never thought about it in this way, because it nearly perfectly represents realist requirements for the intensive design: it has multimethod triangulation around a particular causal hypothesis. This is how the authors described their methodological conviction:

> In our view, the scientific study of culture in the "culture and personality" era was hampered by reliance on too narrow a range of methodologies. In addition to the methods of the ethnographer and the psychometrician, it is possible to apply the methods of the historian, the "cliometrician" (quantitative and archival studies of history and social institutions), and the survey sociologist, and the experimental psychologist. When all these methods are used to study the same set of problems and when they point toward the same conclusions, a level of inference can be achieved that is far beyond what investigators could have accomplished at an earlier time. (p. xvii)

The researchers used all the above-mentioned methods to provide a consilience of the evidence that verifies their hypothesis. This is how they describe the use of each of these methods:

> Making use of the *historical and ethnographic work of others* [all emphases are added], we have drawn a picture of traditional, herding-based cultures of honor around the world and shown their commonalities with the historical and contemporary cultures of the U.S. South. With *archival methods* using census and crime reports, we have collected evidence showing that the homicide rate of the South, especially the rural South, remains high relative to the rest of the country. Using *survey techniques*, we have collected evidence indicating that the values of southerners favor violence for purposes of protection of property, for retaliation for an insult, and for the socialization of children. Employing *experimental methods*, we have collected evidence showing that southerners respond to insults in ways that are cognitively, emotionally, physiologically, and behaviorally quite different from the pattern shown by northerners. In *field experiments*, we have shown that southern institutions are more accepting of individuals

who have committed violent crimes in defense of their honor. And with *archival methods*, we have collected evidence indicating that many of the social institutions and contemporary public policies of the South have their roots in the culture of honor—including the acceptance of violence to protect property and personal and national honor. (pp. xvii–xviii)[1]

Based on this diverse and well-justified methodological background, these scholars came to the convincing conclusion that "culture of honor" as a cultural model for the male behavior in the South does exist and, when internalized, has a strong impact on men's behavior and experience in a vast array of situations. Violence is one of the manifestations of this cultural model and can be explained by it.

c. *Studies of cultural models of family life and parenting.* The institution of the family and related to it models and practices of courtship, marriage, child-rearing, and parenting have always been a focus for psychologists and anthropologists. Therefore, it is not surprising that many researchers have targeted them in their studies (Sara Harkness & Super, 1996; R. A. LeVine & New, 2008; Rubin & Chung, 2006; Stockard, 2002).

American cognitive anthropologist Naomi Quinn (1987, 1996, 2005c) studied her country's cultural model of marriage by exploring how Americans talk and reason about the relationship between husband and wife (children excluded). (See additional details of this study in Chapter 10). The researcher targeted white, suburban, and middle-class families in the US. She asked her informants to talk about their marriages, and then conducted "the cultural analysis of discourse" (Quinn, 2005b, p. 3). By analyzing how people talk, what key words and metaphors they use, and how they reason about marriage, Quinn aimed at discovering the hidden cultural meanings about marriage that are usually not directly available for her informants' conscious reflections, but which drive their stories and actions. Because Quinn is an American researcher, this study was conducted from the insider position and may be considered as a Western indigenous investigation.

> Cultural analysis, then, refers here to the efforts to tease out, from discourse, the cultural meanings that underlie it. These cultural meanings are implicit in what people say, but rarely explicitly stated. . . . So the tacit understandings that underlie discourse must be reconstructed from the clues that this discourse provides. As I say in my volume contribution, "I came to see my analytic approach as the reconstruction, from what people said explicitly, of the implicit assumptions they must have in mind to say it (Quinn, p. 45). (Quinn, 2005b, p. 4)

The researcher developed a schedule for open-ended interviews where researchers

> ceded control of the "interviews" to the "interviewees," allowing them to decide how their interviews should be organized over all, what topics should come next and what might have been overlooked or unfinished, and when we were done. Our role was that of a good listener in a decidedly one-sided conversation. (Quinn, 2005a, p. 41)

In analyzing these interviews, Quinn searched "for a pattern across interviewees and passages, that would be evidence of shared, stable understandings" (p. 43). To do this, she focused on "the

---

[1] Copyright 1996, Nisbett, R. E., & Cohen, D. *Culture of honor: The psychology of violence in the South.* Reprinted by permission of Westview Press, a member of the Perseus Books Group.

key words and the *metaphors* in people's talk about marriage, and the *reasoning* that they did about it" (p. 44). The investigator selected these three elements of discourse because, in her opinion, they are "culturally-laden," meaning that "selection of metaphors, reasoning, and use of key words are all in different ways governed by cultural schemas, each provided and excellent window into the shared schema on which its usage was predicated" (p. 44). The results of this investigation are presented in the Table 8.1.

This table represents the eight dimensions of the cultural meaning of marriage with examples of their typical verbal indicators in the interviewees' discourses. This study is a good illustration of the abductive inference of deep layers of cultural meaning through a thick description/interpretation of people's stories and interviews. (See also Chapter 10).

Rae-Espinoza's (2010) inquiry about parenting in Ecuador is an example of a monocultural parenting study. The goal was to investigate the parenting practices and beliefs of mothers in Ecuador's largest city, Guayaquil. The researcher asked the following research questions: What is the cultural model of the long-term parenting goals of Ecuadorian mothers? What are the practices of reaching these goals? And what are the meanings of these goals and practices? Rae-Espinoza spent hours observing parent-child interactions in various households conducting ethnography—naturalistic observations accompanied by interviews of the mothers. While answering the question about the long-term parenting goals of Ecuadorian mothers, she introduced the Ecuadorian understanding of the "social" and "antisocial" person (p. 371). A *social* person is one who maintains the social order in the community, and the maintenance of this social order is considered to be the essence of the

TABLE 8.1 Characteristics of marriage commonly expressed in metaphor

1. *Sharedness*
   We are together in this.
2. *Lastingness*
   It was stuck together pretty good.
   We feel pretty confident about being able to continue that way.
3. *Mutual benefit*
   That was something we got out of marriage.
   Our marriage is a very good thing for both of us.
4. *Compatibility*
   The best thing about Bill is that he fits me so well.
   Both of our weaknesses were such that the other person could fill in.
5. *Difficulty*
   That was one of the hard barriers to get over.
   The first year we were married was really a trial.
6. *Effort*
   She works harder at our marriage than I do.
   We had to fight our way back almost to the beginning.
7. *Success or failure*
   We know that it was working.
   The marriage may be doomed.
8. *Risk*
   There are so many odds against marriage.
   The marriage was in trouble.

Eight dimensions/meanings of the cultural model of marriage for Americans. Based on the study of Quinn (1987), from D'Andrade (1995); republished with permission of Cambridge University Press cultural notion of a good person. Correspondently, an *antisocial* person refers to an individual who "actively threatens the social order and the interests of others" (p. 371). The author reported that cultivating a social personality in children is the primary goal of good parenting. The researcher then discussed different practices of reaching this goal, including discipline, control, and permission. She stated that many forms of Ecuadorian parenting practices, such as when parents fulfill almost any request from a child, could be labelled as "permissiveness" and condemned from the Western point of view. Rae-Espinoza argued against such a judgment by exploring the meaning of this permissiveness for Ecuadorian mothers. She discovered that for these mothers such "acquisitiveness" (the term that the author preferred to use) is a means to developing a social personality, whereas, according to local beliefs, rejecting a child's requests will promote antisocial characteristics. Ecuadorian mothers discipline their children by removing them from desirable social activities and interactions, thus again emphasizing the importance of positive social engagements. This study can be classified as an interpretive cultural psychological study where the researcher tried to understand the meaning of the goals of parenting practices from "within" the Ecuadorian mothers' perspectives, thus implementing an outsider-to-insider researcher's position. The author strongly argued against Western ethnocentrism regarding "proper parenting" and supported the importance of a nonjudgmental approach to the parenting practices of various cultural communities.

The above examples demonstrate that monocultural psycho-anthropological studies may embrace a wide variety of methodologies, techniques, and methods and can be conducted by anthropologists and psychologists. They provide a deep insight into the meanings, practices, and causes of people's behaviors and experiences and comprise an undeniable part of the research on culture and psychology.

I direct readers to other interesting monocultural studies, like the classical interpretation of Balinese cockfight by Geertz (1973), the analysis of the cultural scripts and cultural grammar of Japanese conducted by linguistic anthropologists Wierzbicka (1996), and the analysis of culture and personality in the drinking patterns of the Camba men in eastern Bolivia by Mandelbaum (1965). At the end of the chapter, I provide an exercise with regard to these (or similar) studies and invite readers to do it.

Multicultural Comparative Studies in Anthropology, Cultural Psychology, and Cross-Cultural Psychology

Monocultural studies are well-suited for exploratory and descriptive purposes, and sometimes they may strive for thick descriptions and causal inferences. Nevertheless, after conducting such studies, a curious researcher may be left unsatisfied, as the studies may pose more questions than provide answers. Consider the swaddling hypothesis as an explanation of the Russian national character. A researcher may ask the question: Do cultural communities other than Russia tightly swaddle toddlers? If the answer is yes, then, what are the psychological consequences for people in these communities? Are they the same as for Russians? In many Indian tribes in North and South America, mothers tightly tie their infants to a board to prevent them from harming themselves when the mother is absent. Despite this practice, the psychological characteristics of the adults in these communities have never been related to the swaddling. Chisholm (2008) provided more insight on these issues. It is a natural extension of monocultural research to want to compare sociopsychological features across cultures, thus leading to multicultural comparative studies.

The comparative approach is widely used in all social sciences: anthropology, sociology, economics, political sciences, and psychology (Bornstein, 1980; George & Bennett, 2005; Ragin, 1987). It is also notable to mention comparative linguistics, religion, art, music, and mythology. In the rest of this chapter, I will address the use of this approach by anthropologists and cultural and cross-cultural psychologists. We will discuss the utilization of a comparative design with cases and with variables, hence the two forms of comparative designs will be analyzed: *comparative case-based* and *comparative variable-based* studies (Ragin, 1987). I will also address the issue of the *levels of analysis*: *ecological* versus *individual*, and the danger of various fallacies when these levels are confused: *ecological fallacy* and *fallacy of composition*.

Advantages of the Comparative Method

A comparative mode of research is one of the most powerful ways to get to the essence of things and to theorize about their nature, functions, and causal mechanisms. Blaikie (2010) considered a comparative mode of inference to be "one of the best methods for generating theory" (p. 70). Hammersley (2012) believed that "comparative method is essential to causal analysis" (p. 39). To do this analysis, researchers have to explore similarities and differences among cases with and without the phenomenon of interest present. Factors that are present when the phenomenon exists, and absent when it does not, are the first candidates for the causes. Comparing cases with different contextual factors that interact with the causes is the best avenue to explore these hypotheses further. The comparative approach may be *historical* or *concurrent*. In the *historical comparative analysis*, researchers compare people, communities, or societies that exist at different stages of their development, or differ with regard to their history. Think about comparing humans with apes, children of different ages with adults, societies at different stages of their socioeconomic development, and so forth. Historical comparisons provide an opportunity for scientists to hypothesize about the trajectories and regularities of development and to theorize about the causal mechanisms of maturation and change. The best example of *concurrent comparisons* are comparisons of different modern societies and cultural communities as well as people from these groupings. These studies address the fundamental questions of the social sciences, including: What role do sociocultural realities play in shaping and determining people's psychological functioning? What is universal and what is culturally specific in humans' psychological makeup? Through what mechanisms should policies and interventions address societal and psychological problems? Another example of a concurrent comparison for the sake of discovering causal factors of behavior is the experimental testing when researchers compare participants from a control group to ones with an experimental condition. Or think about comparing healthy people with patients with a particular medical diagnosis for the purpose of understanding how the disease emerged and what role it plays in people's behaviors and experiences. Only through these and similar comparisons may researchers arrive to conclusions about the role culture plays in people's behaviors and experiences, the nature of human development and the causal factors of different effects, like health and illness.

A Comparative Case-Based Design

This method can be traced back to Francis Bacon's *The Novum Organon*, where he emphasized the comparison of various instances to understand their essence. John Stuart Mill (1882) was one of the first philosophers to propose particular techniques of comparison in order to arrive at causal conclusions: *method of agreement* and *method of difference* as well as *method of residue* and *method of concomitant variations*. Later Mill's approach was labeled *eliminative induction* (Hammersley, Gomm, & Foster, 2009) and contrasted with Znaniecki's *analytic induction* (Hammersley & Cooper, 2012; Robinson, 1951; Znaniecki, 1934). Social scientists continue elaborating both the case-based approach and its various comparative extensions (George & Bennett, 2005; Mills, Durepos, & Wiebe, 2009; Ragin, 1998; Yin, 2009).

Why did all these scholars emphasize cases and not variables as the units of the comparative analysis? If the goal of science is to get to the essence of things and to understand the causal mechanisms that make various events happen, then researchers have to look for these events and their mechanisms where they actually happen: within cultural communities, ethnic groups, and the individual members of these groupings. It is also important to consider the embeddedness of these cases within particular temporal and spatial dimensions. A comparative investigation starts with a single case when an individual, a community, an institution, or a nation is subjected to a detailed descriptive analysis. Miles, Huberman, and Saldana (2014) labeled it "within-case analysis," which is followed by "cross-case analysis." George and Bennett (2005) talked about "the method of process-tracing," where "researchers examine histories, archival documents, interview transcripts, and other sources to see whether the causal process a theory hypothesizes or implies in a case is in fact evident in the sequence and values of the intervening variables in that case" (p. 6). Monocultural studies may serve as examples of these within-case examinations. In a single case, a particular effect/outcome occurs because of the presence of a specific configuration of causal and contextual factors. But these factors are hidden and unknown. How do we get to them? Researchers try to discover a pattern of the factors and conditions in every case and then compare cases with different patterns of these factors, thus doing cross-case analysis. These patterns are important clues for retroducting hypotheses about the causal mechanisms, but without comparing a particular case with other cases where these patterns vary in the absence or presence of the outcomes of interest, such hypothesizing is difficult to test and confirm. Thus, comparison is crucially needed to search for generative mechanisms.

Mill identified several methods that represent the logic of comparative designs, where the majority are the *method of agreement* and the *method of difference*. The former method invites researchers, first, to identify cases that have the same phenomenon or event of interest present, such as people becoming ill from a particular disease, several individuals having exceptional longevity, immigrants becoming successful, communities having a high level of suicide, and so on. Second, among the diversity of all the features and conditions within the cases, scientists look for the factors that are common to all of these cases, like common foods eaten by all individuals older than 105 years or the health-care habits of ill people. These common factors are identified as necessary conditions for the outcome to happen and are candidates for their causes. The *method of difference* asks investigators to compare cases which have the outcome of interest (exceptional longevity) with the ones that have the opposite outcome (low life expectancy) and to infer which factors are present when the outcome takes place and which are not present when it does not. The more refined version of these two methods is *controlled comparison*: "the study of two or more instances of a well-specified phenomenon that resemble each other in every respect but one" (Georege & Bennett, 2005, p. 151). Randomized experiment is the ideal controlled comparison, but it cannot be implemented in cultural studies. Therefore, comparison among purposefully selected cases may serve as a functional equivalent for the experimental logic. And this makes a strong appeal for cultural and social comparativists. For example, researchers may decide that the nature of motivation to immigrate is one of the causes of immigrants' success. Thus, they select diverse cases of successful immigration and analyze the patterns of their motivations, trying to identify the similarities that may explain these immigrants' success (method of agreement). Then they select immigrants who are not successful and investigate whether these cases have different motivational patterns in comparison to the successful ones (method of difference). Such comparisons may support the proposed causal hypothesis. Keep in mind that to conduct a full causal analysis, it is not enough to establish that motivation is associated with the immigrants' success, but it is crucial to explore how—through what mechanisms—motivation influences their success. In addition, contextual factors that make these mechanisms work should also be the focus of such causal analysis. Thus, retroduction of the mechanisms and further process-tracing analysis of how they work are necessary.

One of the modern designs that is widely used by sociologists and political scientists is the *Qualitative Comparative Method*, proposed by sociologist Charles Ragin (1998; Ragin & Amoroso, 2011). According to Ragin, the goal of comparative analysis is to determine the configuration of the conditions that may be the determinant of a phenomenon of interest (Ragin & Amoroso, 2011, pp. 146–147). To illustrate this method Ragin and Amoroso (2011) used the hypothetical example (pp. 146–149) of 16 countries which experienced public protests in the early 80s. In half the cases, the governments violently suppressed these protest, whereas in the other half, the governments did not. The goal of the researchers is to discover what factors determined the violent repressions against the protesters. They identified four potential factors that could causally contribute to the behavior of the governments: (1) political closeness either with the Soviet Union or the West; (2) the level of industrialization; (3) the presence of a democratic government; and (4) a strong military presence in the country. To do this identification, researchers had to be familiar with the literature and have some kind of a theory of repressive governments in order to proceed with such analysis. To detect the configuration of factors that led to repressions, they arranged a table (see Table 8.2.).

The presence or absence of each factor is indicated by 1 or 0. The analysis of this table brought researchers to the conclusion that there are two combinations of factors that are associated with repressions: one is "an absence of democratic government . . . combined with strong military establishment" (p. 147), and the second is "a presence of democratic government . . . combined with an absence of significant industrialization prior to the protests" (p. 147). None of the eight countries lacking violent repressions has either the first or the second combination of factors. The researchers proposed that the identified patterns have causal explanatory power and suggested two mechanisms through which these factors might actually determine violence against protesters. In the first case,

> the military establishment has gained the upper hand in part because of the absence of checks (democratic government) on its power. The second configuration . . . suggests a situation where a breakdown of democratic rule occurred in countries that lack many of the social structures associated with industrialization (e.g., urbanization, literacy, and so on). (p. 147)

TABLE 8.2 Simple example of comparative methods.

Case	Aligned with USSR	Industrialized	Democratic Government	Strong Military	Violent Repression
1	0	0	0	1	1
2	0	1	0	1	1
3	1	0	0	1	1
4	1	1	0	1	1
5	0	0	1	0	1
6	0	0	1	1	1
7	1	0	1	0	1
8	1	0	1	1	1
9	0	0	0	0	0
10	0	1	0	0	0
11	0	1	1	0	0
12	0	1	1	1	0
13	1	0	0	0	0
14	1	1	0	0	0
15	1	1	1	0	0
16	1	1	1	1	0

Copyright, 2011; Republished with permission of Sage Publications Inc., from Ragin, C. C., & Amoroso, L. M. (2011). *Constructing social research* (2nd ed.). Los Angeles, CA: Sage; permission conveyed through Copyright Clearance Center, Inc.

The next step was to verify these hypotheses by analyzing the countries with regard to why the governmental violence happened and to confirm that the hypothesized mechanisms actually were in place at the time of the protests.

Another comparative method that also resembles some forms of quasiexperimental designs is the *before-and-after case study design* (MacDonald, 2009). As the name suggests, this method compares the state of a number of cases (people, institutions, communities, or nations) before and after a particular event, intervention, or treatment happens. The within-case analysis before an event or intervention serves as the basis for future comparisons. The events or interventions can be of a different nature: either controlled by researchers or people participating in the study, like immunization or medical treatment; or naturally occurring events, like earthquakes, flooding, or fires; or governmental policies, like a smoking ban or seat belt legislation. There are different objectives of such a design: to understand the mechanisms of the event or intervention and how and why they work or do not work; or to understand the mechanisms of people's reactions to these processes. Such studies may strongly help to plan future interventions and predict their potential outcomes.

Comparative Anthropological and Cultural Psychological Studies: A Comparative Mode of Research Within the Interpretive and Realist Paradigms

The comparative design has a long history in anthropology (Evans-Pritchard, 1963; Hammel, 1980; Radcliffe-Brown, 1951). British social anthropologist Radcliffe-Brown started his Huxley Memorial Lecture by quoting Franz Boas, who explicitly identified the role of the comparative method within the science of anthropology:

> A comparison of the social life of different peoples proves that the foundations of their cultural development are remarkably uniform. It follows from this that there are laws to which this development is subject. Their discovery is the second, perhaps the more important aim of our science. (p. 15).

Although many modern anthropologists will reject this very idea of a lawful social life and the goal of their science being to discover these laws, this question is still open for discussion (see Hammersley et al., 2009). But what is difficult to reject is Boas's idea that only through the comparative method may anthropologists discover and theorize about the uniformities and differences between people's social lives. The comparative design has been executed in anthropology through two major forms: a qualitative comparative analysis of different societies and a cross-cultural quantitative analysis across different societies and countries. In his lecture, Evan-Pritchard (1963) also explicitly talked about causal analysis and understanding the ultimate determinants of various social phenomena in different societies and communities; he saw the comparative method as perhaps the only method for establishing this causality. He was critical of the first attempts of anthropologists to look for causal factors by using the quantitative methods of survey, tabulation, and statistical analysis, which had started to emerge by that time. I want to reiterate one of his conclusions which remains true today: "The method of statistical correlation can only pose questions, it cannot give us the answers to them" (p. 14).

Comparative research in anthropology is known as *cross-cultural research* (Ember & Ember, 1998, 2009). The goal of such research is to compare various sociocultural phenomena across different cultural communities in order to "answer questions about the incidence, distribution, and causes of cultural variation.... [C]ross-cultural researchers are interested in causes and effects of cultural variation across the world or across regions of the world" (Ember & Ember, 1998, p. 648). As an example of cross-cultural anthropological research, Ember compared different cultural models for sexual intercourse for men. Some models emphasise that intercourse is debilitating; it weakens men and should be done rarely or even avoided. Other models stress the hedonistic and pleasurable aspects of sex and do not prescribe abstinence. The cross-cultural researcher asked four research questions: 1. Descriptive and statistical: "How common is the belief that sex is dangerous for one's health? What proportion of societies have it?" 2. Inquiry about the causes of such models: "Why do some societies have the belief that heterosexual sex is harmful?" Why do such variations of this cultural model happen? and What are the causes of such variations? 3. Research questions about the consequences of a particular cultural model of people's behavior and experience: What are the effects of different cultural models of sexual intercourse on men's health and behavior? (4) And relational: How do cultural models for sexual intercourse relate to the type of marriage and family organization prevalent in that cultural community and the level of fertility? (p. 650; direct quotes are in parentheses and the rest is rephrasing).

Ember and Ember (1998) also identified four dimensions along which such comparisons can be done. The first is the geography of the samples of comparison: either they are worldwide or they come only from a particular geographical area. The second is the size of the samples: "two-case comparisons, small-scale comparisons (fewer than 10 cases), and larger comparisons." Third, "whether the data used are primary (collected by the investigator in various field sites explicitly for the comparison) or secondary (collected by others and found by the investigator in ethnographies, censuses, and histories)". Fourth, "whether the data on a given case pertain to . . . just one time period (a *synchronic comparison* of cases) or two or more time periods (a *diachronic comparison*)" (p. 652). The authors concluded that "worldwide cross-cultural comparisons using secondary synchronic data . . . are the most common in anthropology" (p. 652).

Comparative Cultural Psychological Studies

In studying various social phenomena, cross-cultural anthropologists focus mostly on their cultural side, meaning that they articulate and compare the shared and public aspects of various cultural models. Conversely, cultural psychologists aim at understanding the intrasubjective or psychological side of the same models and how they relate to people's behaviors and experiences. Comparative cultural psychological studies are not frequent. I will analyze one of them as an example. Shweder and his colleagues (Shweder, Jensen, & Goldstein, 1995) compared the meaning of sleeping arrangements in India and the United States. Sleeping arrangements in different cultural communities is a classic anthropological problem, as scholars try to not only describe *how* members of different cultural communities arrange their sleeping but also answer *why* they make these particular arrangements and what moral principles underlie the configurations of arrangements. Researchers asked dozens of family members from both countries to make sleeping arrangements for seven family members: father, mother, son 15, son 11, son 8, daughter 14 and daughter 3, in various sleeping spaces: one, two, three, and up to seven rooms. Based on the analysis of these arrangements, they conjectured several moral criteria that may justify these arrangements. To test their hypotheses and also to construct the hierarchy of these principles, they asked Indian and American adults to rank a set of sleeping patterns that breach the hypothesized moral principles. Based on this ranking they ordered the sleeping arrangements from "most offensive" to "least offensive." The most informative was the request to arrange the family in only three rooms. Based on these results, the following hierarchy of moral principles was inferred. Indian principles: a. Incest avoidance: sexually mature relatives of different sexes do not sleep together; b. Care for the dependents: young children do not sleep alone; c. Female chastity anxiety: girls and young women do not sleep alone; and d. Respect for hierarchy: mature males do not sleep with other males who must defer to them because there is an implication of disrespectful familiarity. For Anglo-Americans there are three moral principles for sleeping arrangements: a. Incest avoidance; b. The sacred couple: husband and wife always sleep together; c. Respect for the privacy of an individual: individuals should sleep alone as much as conditions allow (pp. 32–33). The researchers then tested their hypotheses about these moral principles. (They did such testing only in India). They asked 160 children (ages eight to twelve) and adults to describe their family's sleeping arrangements on the previous night. Researchers wanted to see how well their principles explain the actual sleeping compositions. The results were encouraging: "In 87 percent of the Oriya household, sleeping arrangements were consistent with all four Oriya preferences. The most important principle, incest avoidance, was violated in 8 of 160 households. . . . The second most important principle, protection of the vulnerable, was never violated. The third . . . principle, female chastity anxiety, was violated in two households. The principle of respect for hierarchy was violated in twelve households" (pp. 36–37). Researchers also compared the actual Indian sleeping arrangements with the American moral principles and discovered that "the American sacred couple principle was violated in 78 percent of Oriya households" (p. 37). Only 11% of cases in India were consistent with all three American moral guidelines. I want to highlight several features of this comparative study: a. Researchers inferred their conjectures of the underlying moral principles based on how their participants made the arrangements and not on what they said about them; b. They tested their hypotheses by asking about more and less offensive sleeping compositions. This was an especially creative move, as "people are often better able to tell you what is 'out of question' than what is possible; the violations often prompt a clearer statement of principle" (Goodnow, Miller, & Kessel, 1995, p. 19); c. They tested their hypothesis against real sleeping arrangements and calculated the frequencies of how well their theory fit real life. This study may easily be qualified as an abductive interpretivist inquiry into deep layers of meaning or even as a retroductive realist investigation.

I also draw the attention of readers to an interesting comparative cultural psychological study that tested the universality and validity of Kohlberg's moral stages theory in one African cultural group (S. Harkness, Edwards, & Super, 1981), as well as a comparative psychoanalytical study of self in India and Japan (Roland, 1988).

Cross-Cultural Psychological Studies: A Comparative Variable-Based Approach

This is probably the most typical form of cross-cultural or cross-national studies known to students of psychology and other social sciences. Mainstream cross-cultural psychology has emerged as a discipline to test the psychological regularities discovered in the West cross-culturally and cross-nationally. Let's remind readers that this field of psychology is based on the assumptions that to get to the universal core of human psychology and formulate the laws of pan-human psychology, it is necessary to cross-culturally study the regularities and laws of people's psychological functioning discovered in the West. Such comparisons allow researchers to "peel off the layers of culture" (Poortinga, van de Vijver, & van de Koppel, 1987) and discover the psychological universals. The comparative mode of cross-cultural psychology is so important for this discipline that Berry (1980) suggested to search for the identity of cross-cultural psychology not in its content, but in its methodology—the comparative method. Because of such emphasis, some scholars even consider this field of studies not as a separate discipline with its specific object and paradigm of inquiry, but simply as a an extension of mainstream psychological research to a cross-national comparative mode of investigation: "Cross-cultural psychology has for a long time been treated in literature—even by its own representatives—not as a discipline of its own or an individual branch of psychology, but solely as a method or research strategy in its own right" (Simon, 2006, p. 269). Considering itself a descendant of "modern, scientific, general psychology" (Segall, Lonner, & Berry, 1998), cross-cultural psychology continues the traditions of experimental psychology as the main intellectual and methodological tool for obtaining valid and reliable data about various psychological and cultural phenomena. The idea that comparative studies follow the logic of various experimental designs, which was discussed above, is explicitly present in the works of cross-cultural psychologists (Berry, 1980; Matsumoto, 2003). In particular, Matsumoto (2003) stated that "In a strict experimental sense, these [cross-cultural comparative] studies are simply between-subject, between-group, quasi-experimental designs, in which specific cultures, typically operationalized by nationality, ethnicity, or race, serve as different levels of cultural factor" (p. 190).

What Are the Purposes of Cross-Cultural Psychological Studies?

Based on Matsumoto's (2003) classification, the following taxonomy of comparative studies may be suggested. Cross-cultural/national comparative researchers may compare psychological phenomena of interest by (a) frequencies and distributions, (b) means, and (c) associations. They may also do comparisons of experimental discoveries. These comparative studies may be conducted at individual or cultural levels.

Cross-cultural/national comparative psychological studies compare "two or more cultures on some psychological variable of interest, often with the hypothesis that one culture will have significantly higher scored on the variable than the other(s)" (Matsumoto, 2003, p. 190). Such comparative studies may address several aspects.

(a) *The comparisons of frequencies and distributions* allow researchers to discover the variability of manifestations of psychological processes across nations. In such studies, researchers identify cultural practices or variables and ask questions about their frequencies across different cultural communities or countries and the relations of these frequencies with other parameters of these communities. Let's take as an example the cross-cultural study of helping behavior conducted by Levine and his colleagues (2001). Their goal was to explore if helping strangers varies cross-culturally. The researchers asked the following research questions: a) Is helping strangers a cross-culturally meaningful characteristic of a country? b) Does helping strangers vary cross-culturally? c) What are some community characteristics that are related to helping strangers across cultures? They conducted a quasiexperimental field inquiry on convenience samples of pedestrians in large cities in 23 countries. Helping behavior was assessed by three standardized behavioral indicators: 1. Dropping a pen in front of a pedestrian going in the opposite direction. 2. While walking with a heavy limp and wearing a leg brace, the experimenter let fall a pile of magazines and struggled to reach them. 3. Dressed as a blind person, the experimenter was trying to cross the street. Experimenters calculated the percentages of the pedestrians who helped them relative to the overall number of people approached. All participating cities were ranked based on the percentage of the passers-by who offered help. These numbers were correlated with various economic and social indicators of the corresponding countries. The three most helpful cities were: Rio de Janeiro (Brazil), San Jose (Costa Rica), and Lilongwe (Malawi). The least helpful places were: Singapore (Singapore), New York (United States), and Kuala Lumpur (Malaysia). The only significant correlation discovered was between helping behavior and economic indicator: $r = -.43, p < .001$), which means that the more prosperous the country, the less helping behaviour was demonstrated.

(b) *Mean-level comparison studies* statistically compare mean scores on the same psychological variables across different countries or cultural/ethnic groups. The purpose is to establish differences in the manifestation of psychological processes, personality traits, motives, and emotions and to identify the relationships of these manifestations with cultures. Cross-cultural psychologists believe that mean-level comparative studies "have been important to the psychological literature because they have tested the limitations to knowledge generated in mainstream psychological research, and they have helped to advance our theoretical and conceptual thinking in all areas of psychology" (Matsumoto, 2003, p. 190). Let's take as an example a set of investigations of the Big Five personality model across nations (McCrae, 2001; McCrae & Allik, 2002). After establishing the universality of the five personality factors across different countries, researchers wondered if people from different nations vary with regard to these traits: are Italians more extraverted then Germans, and Russians more neurotic than British? Using the self-report NEO Personality Inventory, teams of researchers collected data from hundreds of participants in different countries, aggregated them within each country, calculated the means and standard deviations of scores on each trait, constructed personality profiles for each sample, and compared all these aggregated scores (McCrae, Terracciano, & al., 2005). There are numerous applications of such studies, such as the possibility of predicting personality disorders in different countries based on the aggregate personality scores (Terracciano & McCrae, 2006). The fundamental obstacle in conducting such mean-level comparative studies is the problem of the construct and measurement equivalence. These issues and the related problems of cross-cultural quantitative comparisons are discussed in the next chapter.

(c) *Cross-cultural structure comparison studies* evaluate associations among psychological variables and between these variables and different outcomes across countries and communities. Proponents of these studies believe that, although the means of psychological variables may be different between countries, the relations among them are important in order to understand the universality versus relativity of various psychological empirical generalizations. For example, Chirkov & Ryan (2001) investigated whether support for adolescents' autonomy associates with their well-being and academic motivation similarly in the USA and Russia. They asked the following research questions: a) Does the level of autonomy support in Russia and the US differ? and b) Does autonomy support have the same statistical relations with self-determined motivation in Russia and the US? This study combined mean-level and structural comparisons. It was expected that in the Russian sample the level of perceived autonomy support from parents and teachers would be lower than in the US because of the more controlling and authoritarian cultural models for adolescents' behavior regulation in Russia. But despite these mean differences, it was expected that the correlations between autonomy support and adolescents' well-being and autonomous academic motivation would be in the same positive direction in both samples. The results confirmed both hypotheses: the means of autonomy support were different in the predicted directions and the associations were positive across samples. These results confirmed the assumption of self-determination theory that autonomy support positively associates with students' self-determined motivation and mental health independently of the level of control/authoritarianism that exists in the countries. The same problem of construct and measurement equivalence as in the mean-level comparison studies is crucial to resolve in this type of study as well.

(d) *In experimental studies across cultures*, researchers identify a phenomenon that has been experimentally discovered in one culture and apply the same experimental procedures in other countries in order to observe the strength of the experimental effect. Researchers wonder if people from different societies behave differently under the same experimental conditions. Replications of Asch's conformity studies or Milgram's obedience studies performed in various countries are good examples (see the review in (Smith & Bond, 1999)). Let's take for example Asch's conformity experiments, where 40% of American participants could not withstand group pressure. It was natural for researchers to ask if people from other countries or cultural groups are more or less prone to the same type of conformity and why these differences take place. To answer these questions researchers replicated the same experiments across different countries. In their meta-analysis Bond and Smith (1996) analyzed 133 reports of replications of Asch's experiments in 17 countries. Although there were reports of very high effect size in some female samples and samples from India and Zimbabwe, the average effect size was relatively small—29% (range from 0% to 60%). Correlations with the cultural dimensions demonstrated that conformity was higher in collectivistic countries. Although interesting, such replications miss the main point of conducting cross-cultural replications of experiments. The experiments should be conducted to test hypotheses about possible causal mechanisms of sociocultural factors influencing psychological phenomena. A simple replication of the same experimental procedure cross-nationally without causal hypothesis brings little new knowledge over and above curious differences in the means.

These four types of comparisons describe the diversity of cross-cultural psychological research well. There is one more dimension that should addressed here: Most of these studies can be done either on the individual or country level.

Different Levels of Comparison: Country-Level Versus Individual-Level Studies

Attentive readers probably noticed that the above examples address the variables at different levels of aggregations. In Chirkov & Ryan's study, the researchers studied individuals, and although they aggregated their scores within each sample, the units of analysis were people; the counties only designated the comparison groups. In the study of helpful behavior by Lewin et al. and in the cross-cultural studies of Big Five personality traits, the researchers aggregated individual scores within each country and then used these scores for their analysis, thus making countries the units of the analysis. These differences bring to our focus the issue of *country-level* or *ecological* and *individual-level comparative* studies. Matsumoto (2003) classified country-level studies as a separate type of cross-cultural study, but this distinction can be held for each of the cross-cultural psychological studies identified above.

The main concept for this distinction is *levels of analysis* that is common and important to many social sciences. Levels of analysis "refer to sets of causal [and not only causal] processes, each representing different degrees of organizational complexity (hence the idiom of 'levels of organization' and levels of complexity')" (Jepperson & Meyer, 2011, p. 60). In addition to the terms *country-level* and *individual-level*, social researchers use such terms as micro-, meso- or institutional-, and macro- or system-levels of analysis (Pettigrew, 1996). Natural scientists also address their topics of interest at different levels of analysis: quantum-, molecular- cell-, or population-levels. These distinctions of different levels of complexities and organizations reflect a fundamental characteristic of how our natural, social, and psychological worlds are organized. Specifically, they invite scholars to see these worlds as hierarchically structured systems, where different systems are nested into larger systems and interact with each other to produce natural, social, or psychological phenomena. The organization of the sociocultural worlds starts at the level of individuals, then moves to a more complex level of institutional and organizational relations, and, finally, to the level of large entities such as nations, countries, and even the whole world. Culture and psychology researchers may address their problems either at one of these levels or they may try to approach them systemically by considering several levels simultaneously.

When researchers work at the individual level of analysis, the units of their sampling and analysis are individuals. They survey respondents and then enter their answers person-by-person into the statistical software. All the calculations are made among the individuals. This level of analysis is used when researchers investigate associations of particular psychological attributes or behaviors and strive to explore psychological mechanisms at the level of individuals. The research questions are usually: 1. What statistical regularities exist among people's psychological attributes sampled from different cultural communities? and, 2. May these regularities be used to explain the cultural differences in people's psychological makeup?

In contrast, when researchers target country-level characteristics, their units of sampling may be either individuals or countries, but the units of analysis are always countries. For such studies, scholars may survey individuals from different countries, sum up their scores, and enter these aggregates into statistical programs. These aggregated country-level scores are then used for the analysis. Researchers may also enter data that already exist only on a country-level: a country's Gross Domestic Product (GDP), mortality rate, life expectancy, human development index, etc. Later, researchers may correlate the level of GDP with, for example, a country's aggregated score on helpfulness. Country-level studies are popular among international economists, sociologists, and political scientists as they strive to understand the regularities and tendencies that exist among countries on an international level.

In recent decades, country-level studies have become popular among cross-cultural psychologists. Such popularity was promoted by the emergence of large international databases that supply social researchers with an abundance of information about countries and communities regarding a variety of political, economic, social, and psychological indicators. The purpose of such studies in psychology is not very clear. On the one hand, the reason for such interest lies in the idea that because culture is a supra-individual phenomena, it is logical to investigate it at the level where it exists: national cultures at the level of nations, communal cultures at the level of communities, and organizational cultures at the level of organizations (Smith, 2002). But when researchers strive to explain the cultural differences in human behavior (see "unpackaging studies" below) using such a design, the individuals, as units of analysis, disappear, and such a goal becomes questionable. Strong support for this direction of research came from the dimensional approach to national cultures by Geert Hofstede (2005). Studies by other researchers on values and their distribution among nations additionally fueled this type of research (see works of Shwartz (2007; 2011) and Inglehart (2003; Inglehart & Oyserman 2004) and their colleagues). A survey of cross-national psychological studies conducted within these theories at a county level was provided in Minkov (2013). On the other hand, psychologists sometimes attempt to address mean-level comparisons and relations of cultural variables with countries' economic and political indices. This is a legitimate goal for this level of analysis, but then such studies become more sociological than psychological. Researchers should justify the purposes and goals of culture-level psychological studies more vigorously. Readers who are interested in the methodology of international surveys at a country level are directed to (Davidov, Schmidt, & Billiet, 2010) and (J. A. Harkness, van de Vijver, & Mohler, 2003).

Cross-cultural researchers identified a type of studies that corresponds to country-level analysis, and labeled it "unpackaging cross-national studies" (Matsumoto, 2003; Matsumoto & van de Vijer, 2012). The schema of *unpackaging studies* is relatively straightforward. Researchers compare a set of psychological variables across two or more nations. (In this case, these nations represent loosely defined different cultures). Within each country, they identify and evaluate several specific social, economic, religious, educational, and other variables—which are called "contextual variables"— and measure the associations of these contextual variables with the psychological ones within each country. Investigators believe that by this design "they unpack the contents of the global unspecific concept of culture into specific measurable psychological [and contextual] constructs, and examine their contribution to cultural differences" (Matsumoto, 2003, pp. 190–191). Some have claimed that such studies are a step forward from direct cross-nation comparative studies because culture as an unspecified variable is replaced by more specific, measurable variables that unpack and explain cultural differences (p. 191).

An example of such a study is the project of Georgas, van de Vivjer, and Berry (2004). Its purpose was to employ the ecocultural framework (Berry, 1976) to "understand how a set of . . . contextual variables relates to a set of psychological variables" (p. 75). The researchers first selected 32 ecological and social indices from six domains: ecology, economy, education, mass media, population, and religion. Then they conducted a cluster analysis and compiled 174 nations into five "cultural areas" or clusters. Next, researchers "explore[d] relationships between country clusters . . . and psychological variables" (p. 78). What they called psychological variables were "the country-level means from studies of Hofstede (1980, 2001); Schwartz (1994); Smith Dugan, and Trompenaars (1996); Inglehart (1997) and from the studies of subjective well-being by Diener (1996)" (p. 78). The authors did not explain why they identified these cultural variables as psychological ones, but they finally correlated them with the ecocultural variables. "The most important result was the finding that differences in scores of the psychological variables showed systematic relationships with cluster membership of countries on these ecological and sociopolitical elements. Two of these elements, affluence and religion, were the most powerful constructs in this linkage"

(p. 94). Although the researchers ambitiously announced that "the present study has proposed a solution to a theoretical and methodological problem of current cross-cultural psychology, that is, the search for context variables—cultural variables—that would explain similarities and differences in psychological variables in different countries" (pp. 90–91), a critical reader may be skeptical that this type of study has any future in culture and psychology research. These are sociological-type country-level correlational studies that bring little insight into how and through what mechanisms sociocultural realities influence and regulate individual peoples' behavior and experience.

The Dangers of Ecological Fallacy and the Fallacy of Composition

The emergence of country-level cross-cultural psychological studies has raised the issue of comparing their results with the results of studies at the individual level. Is it possible to know about the behavior and psychology of individuals by studying similar factors and variables on the ecological (country, culture, or community) level? In answering this question, the problem of *ecological fallacy* has arisen. *Ecological* or *decomposition fallacy* is a fallacy of logical inference when conclusions about individual-level characteristics—probabilities or associations—are made based on ecological-level studies. A fallacious inference in the opposite direction—from an individual level to an ecological one—has been labeled the *individual fallacy* or the *fallacy of composition* (Gomm, 2012; Pettigrew, 1996). Gomm (2012) mentioned that the individual fallacy is a danger mostly for qualitative case-based researchers: "that is the unwarranted assumption . . . that the case(s) they have studied are typical of all cases, or of a major sub-division of them when this is not actually so." He also identified stereotyping as "a qualitative version of the fallacy of composition" (p. 121).

Ecological fallacy may happen in several forms. Following the example from Allport (1937/1963), if 70 out of every 100 teenagers in a community become juvenile offenders, researchers say that there is a 70% probability for teenagers' criminality. But if a researcher announces that a particular boy or girl has a 7 out of 10 chance of becoming an offender, he or she is committing an ecological fallacy. The sample-based statistical probability does not correspond to the probability of being an offender on an individual level.

Another form of ecological fallacy is an inference from correlations among aggregate variables on the ecological level (*ecological correlations* (Robinson, 1950)) to the associations of the corresponding variables on an individual level (individual correlations). A classic example of the difference between these types of correlations is provided by Robinson (1950): An ecological correlation between American state-level indicators of the foreign-born populace and the states' literacy scores is positive .63. The more immigrants in the states, the higher their literacy. On the individual level, when researchers correlated individual scores on being foreign born (Yes or No) and their literacy, the correlation became negative .11. The ecological correlation is misleading, as it actually reflects the fact that foreign-born immigrants tend to settle in states where the level of literacy is high. The individual correlation reflects reality: being foreign-born associates with being less literate.

> The ecological fallacy consists of thinking that relationships observed for groups necessarily hold for individuals: if countries with more Protestants have higher suicide rates, then Protestants must be more likely to commit suicide; if countries with more fat in the diet have higher rates of breast cancer, then women who eat fatty foods must be more likely to get breast cancer. These inferences may be correct, but are only weakly supported by the aggregate data. (Freedman, 2001, p. 4028)

The causes of differences between the levels are manyfold. One, is a systemic factor that relates to the fact that large social systems acquire *emergent properties*, properties that are not present at an individual level (Liao, 2008). Although countries' GDP reflects their wealth, this systemic indicator is not reducible to the annual income of the individuals of the countries. The correlation of GDP with life expectancy is not equivalent to the correlation of people's annual incomes and the years they lived. Other sources of differences between levels are *confounding* and *aggregation biases* (Freedman, 2001). The conclusion that "Protestants must be more likely to commit suicide" is wrong because Protestant countries may differ from nonProtestant ones in many other ways besides religion. This is an example of a *confounding bias*. An *aggregation bias* happens because aggregated data and associations based on them provide biased estimations of the data and their associations on the individual level. This term is frequently used as a synonym for ecological fallacy.

Cross-Cultural Research and Ecological Fallacy

Cross-cultural psychologists are well aware of the danger of ecological fallacy and many leading researchers warn other researchers about its danger (Hofstede, 2005; Matsumoto, 2003; Pettigrew, 1996; Smith, 2002; Smith and Bond, 1999). Despite these warnings, it still happens. For example, ecological fallacy can be found in Fischer & Boer's (2011) study aimed at investigating the country-level relationships among individualism, wealth, and a population's well-being. The sample included 63 countries, which were the units of their analysis. The ecological fallacy occurred when researchers started interpreting their results, which showed that countries with higher scores on individualism demonstrated higher scores on country-level well-being. Yet the researchers stated: "It appears that the extent to which individuals are provided with choices in their lives is a good indicator of their well-being, supporting some previous findings with positive affect indicators of well-being (e.g., Diener et al., 1995)" (p. 177) and "providing individuals with more autonomy appears to be important for reducing negative psychological symptoms, relatively independent of wealth" (p. 179). The units of analysis in this research were countries but the interpretations were made with regard to individuals. The fact that individualistic countries have higher scores of their populations' well-being does not necessarily indicate that individualistically-oriented individuals will have higher well-being.

A more common but more subtle way of committing ecological fallacy is to use the correlations among variables obtained on a sample as an approximation of the general psychological mechanisms that function within individuals. In addition to ecological fallacy based on aggregation bias, researchers who make such inferences also confuse interindividual statistical regularities with intraindividual causal mechanisms. They act on an implicit assumption that empirically verifiable sample-based regularities are reflections of necessary causal relationships that generate the behaviors and experiences of individuals.

Measures to Prevent Ecological Fallacy in Cross-Cultural Psychological Research

Schwartz suggested a way to control for ecological fallacy by laying out a clear and consistent theoretical and conceptual differentiation of culture- and individual-level variables. He repeatedly reminded his readers that he was developing two theories: the theory of basic individual values "on which individual people in all societies differ (e.g., security, achievement, hedonism, concern for others)" along with the theory of "normative value orientations on which cultures differ (e.g., hierarchy, egalitarianism, harmony)." "Basic individual values are an aspect of personality" while the normative cultural value orientations "underlie and justify the functioning of societal institutions" (Schwartz, 2011, p. 463).

Hofstede is another researcher who was vigilant with regard to ecological fallacy. He warned cross-cultural psychologists about its danger from the moment he outlined his theory of the cultural dimensions.

> Hofstede is particularly careful to emphasize that his core values apply to national cultures and not to individuals. If two nations differ on a given value dimension, it would not be logical to infer that because two cultures differ, then any two members of the cultures must necessarily also differ in the same manner. (Smith and Bond, 1999, p. 48)

To help psychologists to avoid this type of fallacy, Triandis (1995) suggested using the terms *individualism* and *collectivism* to represent these two cultural ideologies on the country level. For the corresponding orientations on the level of individuals, he suggested the terms of *idiocentric* and *allocentric* tendencies.

Many social scientists and methodologists are looking for statistical ways to address ecological fallacy, because sometimes researchers have to estimate the behavioral tendencies of individuals when only aggregate data are available. This topic is beyond the scope of this book, and I send interested readers to (Firebaugh, 2001; Grenners, 2012; Jargowsky, 2005).

Conclusion

The chapter began by presenting monocultural studies, which aim to describe particular cultural communities, countries, or cultural areas and analyze the interrelations of culture and the psychological functioning of people. Researchers may approach them from the outsider-to-insider position, when researchers from outside the community of investigation enter it and try to gain a native (insider) point of view. Or they may come from the same community and occupy the insider position. These studies are usually case-based and may be descriptive or explanatory in nature. Multicultural comparative studies analyze two or more cultural communities or countries with regard to the sociocultural attributes of these communities and their relations to the psychological makeup of their members. Such studies in anthropology and cultural psychology are based on the comparative case-based method. Comparative case-based studies can provide insights into the causal mechanisms of various phenomena, thus leading to the development of hypotheses about such mechanisms and guiding their verification. The following variations of comparative case-based designs are introduced: method of agreement, method of difference, controlled comparison, qualitative comparative method, and before-and-after case study design. The case-based method is contrasted with the comparative variable-based approach, which is frequently used in cross-cultural psychological studies. These studies compare frequencies and distributions as well as means and associations among various psychological and sociocultural variables. Such studies are conducted on levels where both countries (country-level studies) and individuals (individual-level studies) can serve as the units of analysis. Confusing these two levels of analysis may lead either to *ecological* or *individual fallacy*. Sources, examples, and countermeasures against ecological fallacy were discussed.

Questions

1. What are the purposes and goals of monocultural studies?
2. Can these studies provide an explanation of the cultural influences on human psychological function? Provide examples.
3. Where does the power of the comparative design come from? Explain why comparative studies are considered to be so important for building theories and for causal explanations.
4. Discuss and provide your own examples of the main types of the comparative approach: method of agreement, method of difference, method of controlled comparison (also known as randomized experiment), before-and-after case study design, and the qualitative comparative method.
5. Contrast the comparative case-based and variable-based designs. What are the advantages and disadvantages of each?
6. Provide your own examples of the different types of comparative variable-based studies.
7. Explain in your own words ecological and individual fallacies.

8. The textbook states that one form of ecological fallacy is using correlations among variables obtained on a sample as an approximation of the general psychological mechanisms that function within individuals. Do you agree or disagree? Justify your answer.
9. How can ecological fallacy be accounted for?

Exercises

1. Select a set of monocultural studies from the text or from your own sources. (For example, the journal *Ethos*, 2010, 38, 4 reports a set of studies on mothering in different cultural communities that can be used for this exercise).

The goal of this exercise is to analyze these studies along the main analytical lines suggested by this textbook in order to teach students to dissect the studies with regard to their major components and learn how to be analytical and critical.

Choose one study and lead students through the following questions:

   1 What problem did the researchers try to address? Were there research questions? If so, what were they?
   2 What theoretical position do the authors express? What understanding of culture, human psychological functioning and their interactions underlie these studies? Justify your answers.
   3 What philosophical paradigm guides the study? Justify your answer.
   4 What were the main methods and data gathering techniques that the researchers used?
   5 What analytical/intellectual tools did the researchers use to analyze the data?
   6 Did they answer the RQs? Have the problems been addressed?
   7 What are your comments and conclusions about the study?

2. Compare case-based and variable-based cross-cultural studies (if needed, consult Chapter 7) and evaluate which of them provides a deeper insight into the interaction of culture and psychology. Why? Justify your conclusion. Make your own conclusion about the advantages and disadvantages of different designs.

Glossary

Comparative case-based design: compares various cases (people, groups, communities, countries) as whole units with all their structural and dynamic relations kept relatively intact. Particular methods are: *method of agreement, method of difference, method of controlled comparison* (also known as *randomized experiment*), *before-and-after case study design*, and the *qualitative comparative method*.

Comparative method/design: a type of research design that compares different communities, people, or conditions in order to explore the common and unique features of these units and to infer the underlying causes of differences among them.

Comparative variable-based design groups the units of comparison into variables, quantifies them, and conducts various statistical analyses to establish regularities in these variables' associations.

Country-level ecological comparative studies use countries or communities as the units of analysis.

Ecological or decomposition fallacy: a fallacy of logical inference when conclusions about individual-level characteristics—probabilities or associations—are made based on ecological-level studies.

Individual fallacy or the fallacy of composition: a fallacy of logical inference when conclusions about ecological-level characteristics—probabilities or associations—are made based on individual-level studies.

Individual-level comparative studies use individuals as units of analysis.

Levels of analysis: "refer to sets of causal [and not only causal] processes, each representing different degrees of organizational complexity (hence the idiom of 'levels of organization' and 'levels of complexity')" (Jepperson & Meyer, 2011, p. 60).

Monocultural studies are focused on one or several culturally similar communities, countries, or geographical regions grouped by ethnicity, race, religion, or language. They provide a description of these communities in order to understand their cultural models and the psychological functioning of their members.

Multicultural comparative studies provide a comparison of the social-psychological and psychological attributes of people across different communities. These comparisons are accompanied by comparing cultural models and the sociocultural features of the corresponding cultural groups.

Recommended Reading

Blaikie, N. (2010). *Designing social research: The logic of anticipation.* (2nd ed.). Cambridge, UK: Polity.
Ember, C. R., & Ember, M. (2009). *Cross-cultural research methods.* (2nd ed.). Lanham, MD: AltaMira Press.
Harkness, J. A., van de Vijver, F. J. R., & Mohler, P. P. (Eds.). (2003). *Cross-cultural survey methods.* New York, NY: Wiley.
Mills, A. J., Durepos, G., & Wiebe, E. (Eds.). (2009). *Encyclopedia of case study research.* Los Angeles, CA: Sage.
Quinn, N. (Ed.). (2005b). *Finding culture in talk: A collection of methods.* New York, NY: Palgrave Macmillan.
Ragin, C. C., & Amoroso, L. M. (2011). *Constructing social research* (2nd ed.). Los Angeles, CA: Sage
Yin, R. K. (2009). *Case study research: Design and methods* (4th ed.). Los Angeles, CA: Sage

References

Allport, G. W. (1937/1963). *Patterns and growth in personality.* New York, NY: Holt, Rinehart and Winston.
Benedict, R. (1946/1974). *The chrysanthemum and the sword: Patterns of Japanese culture.* Boston, MA: Houghton Mifflin.
Berry, J. W. (1976). *Human ecology and cognitive style: Comparative studies in cultural and psychological adaptation.* New York, NY: Sage.
Berry, J. W. (1980). Introduction to Methodology. In H. C. Trinadis & J. W. Berry (Eds.), *Handbook of cross-cultural psychology: Methodology* (Vol. 2, pp. 1–28). Boston, MA: Allyn & Bacon.
Blaikie, N. (2010). *Designing social research: The logic of anticipation.* (2nd ed.). Cambridge, UK: Polity.
Bond, R. A., & Smith, P. B. (1996). Culture and conformity: A meta-analysis of studies using Asch's (1952b, 1956) line judgment task. *Psychological Bulletin, 119*(1), 111–137.
Bornstein, M. H. (Ed.). (1980). *Comparative methods in psychology.* Hillsdale, NJ: Lawrence Erlbaum.
Chirkov, V., & Ryan, R. M. (2001). Parent and teacher autonomy-support in Russian and U.S. adolescents: Common effects on well-being and academic motivation. *Journal of Cross-Cultural Psychology, 32*(5), 618–635.
Chisholm, J. S. (2008). Swaddling, cradleboard and the development of children. In R. A. LeVine & R. S. New (Eds.), *Anthropology and child development: A cross-cultural reader* (pp. 100–114). Oxford, UK: Blackwell.
D'Andrade, R. G. (1995). *The development of cognitive anthropology.* Cambridge, UK: Cambridge University Press.
Davidov, E., Schmidt, P., & Billiet, J. (Eds.). (2010). *Cross-cultural analysis: Methods and applications.* New York, NY: Routledge.
Ember, C. R., & Ember, M. (1998). Cross-cultural research. In H. R. Bernard (Ed.), *Handbook of methods in cultural anthropology* (pp. 647–687). Walnut Creek, CA: AltaMira Press.
Ember, C. R., & Ember, M. (2009). *Cross-cultural research methods.* (2nd ed.). Lanham, MD: AltaMira Press.

Evans-Pritchard, E. E. (1963). *The comparative method in social anthropology*. London, UK: Athlone Press.
Firebaugh, G. (2001). Ecological fallacy. In N. J. Smelser & P. B. Baltes (Eds.), *International encyclopedia of the social and behavioral sciences* (Vol. 6, pp. 4023–4026). Amsterdam, The Netherlands: Elsevier.
Fischer, R., & Boer, D. (2011). What is more important for national well-being: Money or autonomy? A meta-analysis of well-being, burnout, and anxiety across 63 societies. *Journal of Personality and Social Psychology, 101*(1), 164–184.
Freedman, D. A. (2001). Ecological inference. In N. J. Smelser & P. B. Baltes (Eds.), *International encyclopedia of the social and behavioral sciences* (Vol. 6, pp. 4027–4030). Amsterdam, The Netherlands: Elsevier.
Geertz, C. (1973). Deep play: Notes on the Balinese cockfight. In C. Geertz (Ed.), *Interpretation of cultures*. (pp. 412–453). New York, NY: Basic Books.
Georgas, J., Vijver, F. J. R. v. d., & Berry, J. W. (2004). The ecocultural framework, ecosocial indices, and psychological variables in cross-cultural research. *Journal of Cross-Cultural Psychology, 35*(1), 74–96.
George, A. L., & Bennett, A. (2005). *Case studies and theory development in the social sciences*. Cambridge, MA: MIT Press.
Gomm, R. (2012). Qualitative causal analysis and the fallacies of composition and division: The example of ethnic inequalities in educational achievement. In B. Cooper, J. Glaesser, R. Gomm & M. Hammersley (Eds.), *Challenging the qualitative-quantitative divide: Explorations in case-focused causal analysis* (pp. 96–125). London, UK: Continuum.
Goodnow, J. J., Miller, P. J., & Kessel, F. (1995). Editors' preface to "Who sleeps by whom revisited." In J. J. Goodnow, P. J. Miller & F. Kessel (Eds.), *Cultural practices as contexts for development* (Vol. 67, pp. 17–20). San Francisco, CA: Jossey-Bass.
Gorer, G., & Richman, J. (1949/1962). *The people of Great Russia: A psychological study*. New York, NY: Norton.
Gregg, G. S. (2005). *The Middle East: A cultural psychology*. New York, NY: Oxford University Press.
Grenners, T. (2012). Hofstede revisited: Is making the ecological fallacy when using Hofstede's instrument on individual behavior really unavoidable? *International Journal of Business and Management, 7*(7), 75–84.
Hammel, E. A. (1980). The comparative method in anthropological perspective. *Comparative Studies in Society and History, 22*(2), 145–155.
Hammersley, M. (2012). What's wrong with quantitative research? In B. Cooper, J. Glaesser, R. Gomm & M. Hammersley (Eds.), *Challenging the qualitative-quantitative divide: Explorations in case-focused causal analysis* (pp. 27–56). London, UK: Continuum.
Hammersley, M., & Cooper, B. (2012). Analytic induction versus qualitative comparative analysis. In B. Cooper, J. Glaesser, R. Gomm & M. Hammersley (Eds.), *Challenging the qualitative-quantitative divide: Explorations in case-focused causal analysis* (pp. 129–169). London, UK: Continuum.
Hammersley, M., Gomm, R., & Foster, P. (2009). Case study and theory. In R. Gomm, M. Hammersley & P. Foster (Eds.), *Case study method* (pp. 234–259). London, UK: Sage.
Harkness, J. A., van de Vijver, F. J. R., & Mohler, P. P. (Eds.). (2003). *Cross-cultural survey methods*. New York, NY: John Wiley & Sons.
Harkness, S., Edwards, C. P., & Super, C. M. (1981). Social roles and moral reasoning: A case study in a rural African community. *Developmental Psychology, 17*(5), 595–603.
Harkness, S., & Super, C. M. (Eds.). (1996). *Parents' cultural belief systems: Their origins, expressions, and consequences*. New York, NY: Guilford Press.
Hofstede, G., & Hofstede, G. J. (2005). *Culture and organization: Software of the mind*. (2nd ed.). New York, NY: McGraw-Hill.
Inglehart, R. (Ed.). (2003). *Human values and social change: Findings from the values survey*. Leiden, The Netherlands: Brill.
Inglehart, R., & Oyserman, D. (2004). Individualism, autonomy, self-expression: The human development syndrome. In H. Vinken, J. Soeters & P. Ester (Eds.), *Comparing cultures: Dimensions of culture in a comparative perspective*. (pp. 74–96). Leiden, The Netherlands: Brill.
Jargowsky, P. A. (2005). The ecological fallacy. In K. Kempf-Leonard (Ed.), *The encyclopedia of social measurement* (Vol. 1, pp. 715–722). San Diego, CA: Academic Press.
Jepperson, R., & Meyer, J. W. (2011). Multiple levels of analysis and the limitations of methodological individualisms. *Sociological Theory, 29*(1), 54–73.
LeVine, R. A., & New, R. S. (Eds.). (2008). *Anthropology and child development: A cross-cultural reader*. Oxford, UK: Blackwell.

Levine, R. V., Norenzayan, A., & Philbrick, K. (2001). Cross-cultural differences in helping strangers. *Journal of Cross-Cultural Psychology, 32*(5), 543–560.

Liao, T. F. (2008). Level of analysis. In P. J. Lavrakas (Ed.), *Encyclopedia of survey research methods* (Vol. 1, pp. 420–421). Los Angeles, CA: Sage.

MacDonald, V. (2009). Before-and-after case study design. In A. J. Mills, G. Durepos & E. Wiebe (Eds.), *Encyclopedia of case study research* (Vol. 2, pp. 51–54). Los Angeles, CA: Sage.

Mandelbaum, D. G. (1965). Alcohol and culture. *Current Anthropology, 6*(3), 281–288.

Matsumoto, D. (2003). Cross-cultural research. In S. F. Davis (Ed.), *Handbook of research methods in experimental psychology* (pp. 189–208). Malden, MA: Blackwell.

Matsumoto, D., & van de Vijer, F. J. R. (2012). Cross-cultural research methods. In H. Cooper (Ed.), *APA handbook of research methods in psychology* (Vol. 1, pp. 85–100). Washington, DC: American Psychological Association.

McCrae, R. R. (2001). Trait psychology and culture: Exploring intercultural comparisons. *Journal of Personality, 69*(6), 819–846.

McCrae, R. R., & Allik, J. (Eds.). (2002). *The five-factor model of personality across cultures*. New York: Kluwer Academic/Plenum Publishers.

McCrae, R. R., Terracciano, A., & et al. (2005). Personality profiles of cultures: Aggregate personality traits. *Journal of Personality and Social Psychology, 89*(3), 407–425.

Mead, M. (1954). The swaddling hypothesis: Its reception. *American Anthropologist, 56*, 395–409.

Mead, M. (1966). *Soviet attitudes toward authority: An interdisciplinary approach to problems of Soviet character*. New York: Schocken Books.

Mead, M., & Metraux, R. (Eds.). (1953/2000). *The study of culture at a distance*. New York: Berghahn Books.

Miles, M. B., Huberman, A. M., & Saldana, J. (2014). *Qualitative data analysis: A methods sourcebook* (3 ed.). Thousand Oaks, CA: Sage.

Mill, J. S. (1882). *System of logic*. New York: Harper & Brothers, Pub.

Mills, A. J., Durepos, G., & Wiebe, E. (Eds.). (2009). *Encyclopedia of case study research*. Los Angeles, CA: Sage.

Minkov, M. (2013). *Cross-cultural analysis: The science and art of comparing the world's modern societies and their cultures*. Thousand Oaks, CA: Sage.

Nisbett, R. E., & Cohen, D. (1996). *Culture of honor: The psychology of violence in the South*. Boulder, CO: Westview Press.

Pettigrew, T. F. (1996). *How to think like a social scientist*. New York: HarperCollins College Publishers.

Poortinga, Y. H., van de Vijver, F. J. R., & van de Koppel, J. M. H. (1987). Peeling the onion called culture: A synopsis. In C. Kagitcibasi (Ed.), *Growth and progress in cross-cultural psychology* (pp. 22–34). Berwyn, PA: Swets North America.

Quinn, N. (1987). Convergent evidence for a cultural model of American marriage. In D. Holland & N. Quinn (Eds.), *Cultural models in language and thought* (pp. 173–194). Cambridge, UK: Cambridge University Press.

Quinn, N. (1996). Culture and contradiction: The case of Americans reasoning about marriage. *Ethos, 24*(3), 391–425.

Quinn, N. (2005a). How to reconstruct schemas people share, from what they say. In N. Quinn (Ed.), *Finding culture in talk: A collection of methods* (pp. 35–81). New York, NY: Palgrave Macmillan.

Quinn, N. (2005b). Introduction. In N. Quinn (Ed.), *Finding culture in talk: A collection of methods* (pp. 1–34). New York, NY: Palgrave Macmillan.

Quinn, N. (Ed.). (2005c). *Finding culture in talk: A collection of methods*. New York, NY: Palgrave Macmillan.

Radcliffe-Brown, A. R. (1951). The comparative method in social anthropology. *The Journal of Royal Anthropological Institute of Great Britain and Ireland, 81*(1/2), 15–22.

Rae-Espinoza, H. (2010). Consent and discipline in Ecuador: How to avoid raising an antisocial child. *Ethos, 38*(4), 369–387.

Ragin, C. C. (1987). *The comparative method: Moving beyond qualitative and quantitative strategies*. Berkeley, CA: University of California Press.

Ragin, C. C. (1998). The logic of qualitative comparative analysis. *International Review of Social History, 43*, 105–124.

Ragin, C. C., & Amoroso, L. M. (2011). *Constructing social research* (2nd ed.). Los Angeles, CA: Sage.

Rancour-Laferriere, D. (1995). *The slave soul of Russia: Moral masochism and the cult of suffering*. New York, NY: New York University Press.

Rancour-Laferriere, D. (1999). Russians react to the idea of Russian masochism. *Journal of Psychohistory, 27*(1), 59–66.
Robinson, W. S. (1950). Ecological correlations and the behavior of individuals. *American Sociological Review, 15*(3), 351–357.
Robinson, W. S. (1951). The logical structure of analytic induction. *American Sociological Review, 16*(6), 812–818.
Roland, A. (1988). *In search of self in India and Japan: Toward a cross-cultural psychology.* Princeton, NJ: Princeton University Press.
Rubin, K. H., & Chung, O. B. (Eds.). (2006). *Parenting beliefs, behaviors, and parent-child relations: A cross-cultural perspective.* New York, NY: Psychology Press.
Schwartz, S. H. (2007). A theory of cultural value orientation: Explication and applications. In Y. Esmer & T. Pettersson (Eds.), *Measuring and mapping cultures: 25 years of comparative value surveys* (pp. 33–78). Leiden, The Netherlands: Brill.
Schwartz, S. H. (2011). Values: Cultural and individual. In F. J. R. van de Vijver, A. Chasiotis & S. M. Breugelmans (Eds.), *Fundamental questions in cross-cultural psychology* (pp. 463–493). Cambridge, MA: Cambridge University Press.
Segall, M. H., Lonner, W. J., & Berry, J. W. (1998). Cross-cultural psychology as a scholarly discipline: On the flowering of culture in behavioral research. *American Psychologist, 53*(10), 1101–1110.
Shweder, R. A., Jensen, L., & Goldstein, W. A. (1995). Who sleeps with whom revisited: A method for extracting the moral goods implicit in the practice. In J. J. Goodnow, P. J. Miller & F. Kessel (Eds.), *Cultural practices as contexts for development* (Vol. 67, pp. 21–39). San Francisco, CA: Jossey-Bass.
Simon, P. (2006). The solution of fundamental methodological problems in cross-cultural psychology by guaranteeing the equivalence of measurement. In J. Straub, D. Weidemann, C. Kolbl & B. Zielke (Eds.), *Pursuit of meaning: Advances in cultural and cross-cultural psychology* (pp. 269–292). Bielefeld, Germany: Transcript-Verlag.
Smith, P. B. (2002). Levels of analysis in cross-cultural psychology. *Online readings in psychology and culture, 2*(2). doi: http://dx.doi.org/10.9707/2307-0919.1018
Smith, P. B., & Bond, M. H. (1999). *Social psychology across cultures* (2nd ed.). Boston, MA: Allyn & Bacon.
Stockard, J. E. (2002). *Marriage in culture: Practice and meaning across diverse societies.* Belmont, CA: Wadsworth.
Terracciano, A., & McCrae, R. R. (2006). Cross-cultural studies of personality traits and their relevance to psychiatry. *Epidemiologia e Psichiatria Sociale, 15*(3), 176–184.
Triandis, H. C. (1995). *Individualism and collectivism.* Boulder, CO: Westview Press.
Wierzbicka, A. (1996). Japanese cultural scripts: Cultural psychology and "cultural grammar." *Ethos, 24*(3), 527–555.
Yang, K.-S. (2000). Monocultural and cross-cultural indigenous approaches: The royal road to the development of a balanced global psychology. *Asian Journal of Social Psychology, 3*(3), 241–264.
Yin, R. K. (2009). *Case study research: Design and methods* (4th ed.). Los Angeles, CA: Sage.
Znaniecki, F. (1934). *The method of sociology.* New York: Rinehart & Company.

9

QUANTITATIVE COMPARATIVE STUDIES

Equivalence, Translation, and Measurement Invariance

This chapter will:

- Discuss the problem of equivalence in cross-cultural research
- Examine construct validity and construct equivalence
- Investigate content validity and content equivalence
- Analyze linguistic equivalence and translation of psychometric instruments
- Review the statistical testing of instruments' measurement invariance.

Introduction

Researchers of all paradigms may face the necessity of assessing the psychological characteristics of people across different cultural communities quantitatively. Such a task may require developing and/or translating data generating instruments. There are several types of instruments that may cause concern regarding their cross-cultural use and comparability. These include ability and IQ tests (Georgas, Weiss, van de Vijver, & Saklofske, 2003; Greenfield, 1997; Malda et al., 2008), educational and performance tests (Hambleton, Merenda, & Spielberger, 2005), personality inventories (Barrett, Petrides, Eysenck, & Eysenck, 1998; McCrae & Allik, 2002; van Hemert, van de Vijver, Poortinga, & Georgas, 2002), health, psychopathology, and psychiatric assessment instruments (Butcher, Lim, & Nezami, 1998; Guillemin, Bombardier, & Beaton, 1993; Koot, Oord, Verhulst, & Boomsma, 1997), and different types of survey questionnaires developed for the practical needs of organizational psychologists, social workers, health professionals, and other specialists (Ægisdóttir, Gerstein, & Çinarbas, 2008; Beaton, Bombardier, Guillemin, & Ferraz, 2000; Cruz, Padilla, & Agustin, 2000; Riordan & Vandenberg, 1994; Schaffer & Riordan, 2003; Tran, Ngo, & Conway, 2003; Wheelan, Buzarglo, & Tsumura, 1998). These instruments differ with regard to the presence or absence of hypothetical constructs, psychometric construction, demands for their reliability, validity, and some other features. Because of these differences, the procedure for translating and adapting these instruments may vary. This chapter will cover the main steps of translating psychometric instruments and it will outline the ways of securing the equivalence of concepts, items, and tests and questionnaires. Readers who want to explore this topic in more detail are invited to consult the special publications on this topic: (Brislin, 1976; Hambleton & Zenisky, 2011; Harkness, van de Vijver, & Mohler, 2003; Tran, 2009; van de Vijver & Leung, 1997) as well as some sources referenced in the text.

When Is the Translation of Data Generating Instruments Required?

There are three options for researchers when they face the need to use cross-culturally valid assessment instruments. They may *adopt* an existing instrument; they may decide to *adapt* an existing instrument; or they may *develop* their own multilingual questionnaire or test (Harkness, van de Vijver, & Johnson, 2003; Tran, 2009). Their choice should be determined by their research goals and the availability of the required instruments.

When to Adopt?

Researchers usually adopt existing instruments because they want to compare different cultural groups on well-established constructs by using well-known and valid instruments. Think about psychological tests, such as the NEO Personality Inventory (NEO-PI), the Eysenck Personality Inventory (EPI), the Minnesota Multiphasic Personality Inventory (MMPI), the Wechsler Intelligence Scales, and many other psychological instruments that have become the staples of modern psychology. Researchers may have a research problem that requires them to conduct standardized comparisons across cultures, to replicate the existing studies in another cultural setting, or to contribute to existing databases on particular topics. In all these instances they need to use the existing instruments and translate them from an original or source version (usually in English) to the target language. Because constructs for such questionnaires have already been established and announced to be nearly universal across populations, *construct equivalence* may not be an issue here (although a thorough researcher should question this assumption of universality and check it on a target sample first). *Content equivalence* is not an issue either, as the items of the original instruments have already been selected. Researchers have to implement *centering* (Werner & Campbell, 1970), or *close translation* (Harkness, 2003), meaning translating the source language instrument to the target language as closely to the original as possible. Therefore, *linguistic* and *semantic equivalence* becomes the primary concern. After developing an adopted version of a test in another language, it should be tested psychometrically and the results should be compared with its original version. Some examples include: a set of studies on translating and psychometrically testing the NEO PI (Caprara, Barbaranelli, Bermúdez, Maslach, & Ruch, 2000; McCrae & Costa, 1997), the MMPI-2 (Butcher et al., 1998), the EPI (Barrett et al., 1998; van Hemert et al., 2002), The Child Behavior Checklist (Koot et al., 1997), and the Kaufman Assessment Battery for Children (KABC-II) (Malda et al., 2008; Malda, van de Vijver, Srinivasan, Transler, & Sukumar, 2010).

Adaptation and Modification of Existing Instruments

When an instrument in the source language was developed without cross-cultural considerations and has some elements of ethno-centeredness, researchers may choose to conduct its linguistic and cultural adaptation. This adaptation may include eliminating items that are culturally inappropriate (see some examples further in this chapter) and finding culturally and linguistically appropriate ways of addressing the same construct. *Decentering* is a procedure that is recommended (Werner & Campbell, 1970). Decentering means that researchers keep the construct intact but modify its linguistic manifestation in the target culture. Following the adaptation, a new version has to be psychometrically tested. Examples of this process include: the adaptation of the Achievement Goal Questionnaire (Sun & Hernandez, 2012), the adaptation of a measure of acculturation (Cruz et al., 2000).

Developing a New Instrument Suitable for Source and Target Cultures

There are times when there is no instrument to measure the construct or phenomenon of interest. Then researchers face the problem of developing a new test or questionnaire that will be suitable for different cultural and linguistic communities. Developing a new cross-culturally acceptable instrument may go in different ways (Harkness, van de Vijver, & Johnson, 2003). The procedure of constructing different versions of the same instrument may unfold *sequentially*, meaning that an instrument in a source language is developed first and in the target language next (similar to the adaptation procedure discussed above). "The *parallel approach* [emphasis added] incorporates cross-cultural input from all target cultures and languages while the source questionnaire is still under development" (p. 22). During *simultaneous* design, researchers "produce different language versions at the same time" (p. 22). In this case, the construct is kept intact but the items are constructed in culturally and linguistically relative forms. In the latter case, the decentering procedure is implemented. It is also recommended to include culture-universal and culture-specific items to "cover a shared set of concepts more fully" (p. 20.). Some examples of developing new cross-cultural instruments are: the Child and Youth Resilience Measure (Ungar & Liebenberg, 2011) and the Group Development Questionnaire (Wheelan et al., 1998).

The Problem of Equivalence in Cross-Cultural Research

The most fundamental problem inherently present in all aspects of adopting, adapting, or designing instruments for cross-cultural studies is the problem of *equivalence* of the original and translated versions of instruments. Do they measure the same things and with the same accuracy? Cross-cultural methodologists use two concepts in this regard: *equivalence* and *bias* (van de Vijver & Leung, 1997, 2011). "Equivalence refers to the level of comparability of measurement outcomes" (van de Vijver & Leung, 2011, p. 19). Bias is a distortion of equivalence when an instrument is applied in a different cultural setting. There are different sources of bias: construct, method and item biases, as well as ethnocentric bias, response bias, procedure bias, cognition bias, communication bias, and some others. "Bias and equivalence are two sides of the same coin. Cross-cultural equivalence requires the absence of biases, and the presence of cross-cultural bias always results in some form of inequivalence" (p. 19).

Equivalence is pivotal for comparative and cross-cultural research because these studies compare people's cognition, emotions, desires, personality characteristics, and behaviors, and it is crucial that these objects are comparable and that researchers are actually comparing apples with apples and oranges with oranges.

Types of Equivalence

There are three types of equivalence: *construct equivalence* (or *concept equivalence*), *content equivalence*, and *linguistic equivalence* (Flaherty et al., 1988). They are interrelated and should be considered as a network of interdependent ideas and practices regarding the nature and comparability of measurement instruments. If psychometric instruments are based on hypothetical constructs, then construct equivalence lies at the core of all other forms of equivalence. If there is no construct equivalence, there is no sense in testing other forms of equivalence. For many forms of surveys, researchers are interested in assessing respondents' self-reports about their behaviors, perceptions of events, opinions, and attitudes. These instruments are typically not construct-based and, therefore, can be evaluated for content and linguistic equivalence only. All three forms of equivalence should be established by a theoretical analysis of propositions behind the constructs and by cultural and linguistic analyses of the wordings of the items. When researchers are convinced by the theoretical and cultural analysis of equivalence, they may use statistical methods to verify their conclusions. This statistical verification of the comparability of measurement outcomes constitutes a *measurement equivalence/invariance*, which establishes the equivalence of measurement instruments in the quantitative forms. Measurement invariance may range from full to partial invariance and may include different forms of its analysis (see the section on the statistical analysis of measurement invariance below for more details).

Construct Validity and Equivalence

Construct equivalence is the most challenging form of equivalence, and major debates between different schools of the comparativist research unfold around it. Cultural universalists believe that there are universal behavioral forms, psychological states, and processes that can be applied to almost all people around the world and which constitute components of the pan-human psychology. They rely on the thesis of the "psychic unity of mankind" and argue that as members of the same species, people have a universal psychological makeup that could be discovered through cross-cultural comparisons. Cultural relativists do not deny the idea of the psychic unity of mankind, but emphasize that the universal features of the human mind are transformed in different cultural communities into culturally relative mentalities (see Chapter 1), and in order to understand and explain the behaviors and experiences of people from different cultural communities, researchers need to understand these mentalities. They believe that looking for the direct equivalence of various behavioral and psychological constructs across different cultural communities is a futile endeavor. They believe that the universals of human psychology should be inferred from empirical evidence based on solid theoretical considerations and not by directly measuring them by psychological tests. Because of these controversies, the process of establishing construct equivalence is a challenging task that includes theoretical, ethnographic, and psychological theorizing accompanied by a thorough statistical analysis.

What is a Hypothetical Construct?

In Chapter 6, the concept *hypothetical construct* was introduced together with the notions of *theoretical* and *empirical concepts*. The idea of hypothetical construct has become popular in psychological measurement and test design and lays the theoretical basis of modern psychometrics (Cronbach & Meehl, 1955; Nunnally & Bernstein, 1978). Let me remind readers that a hypothetical construct is an idea (hypothesis) about the unobservable features of people's personality, cognition, motivation, and other aspects of psychological functioning. Hypothetical constructs manifest themselves in specific patterns of actions, thoughts, feelings, and motives of people, and can be assessed through empirical indicators: by observing people's behavior, asking them questions, and administering standardized tests. Conventionally, psychological tests, scales, and questionnaires are based on hypothetical constructs such as "intelligence," "extraversion," "self-construal," "individualism," "locus of control," "achievement motive," and hundreds of others.

Construct Validity and Construct Equivalence

In order to understand the nature and logic of arguments around construct equivalence, it is useful to review the idea of *construct validity* (Cronbach & Meehl, 1955; Messick, 1995). If a hypothetical psychological construct is a set of ideas about psychological processes, dispositions, and states that underlie humans' actions, then the construct validity of an instrument is an indication of how well these ideas are represented in the measurement procedure, or, to say it differently, how well a test or scale reflects the main theoretical ideas about the construct that it intends to measure. It is relevant to interpret construct validity as "not a property of the test or assessment as such, but rather of the meaning of the test scores" (Messick, 1995, p. 5). This means that "what needs to be valid is the meaning or interpretation of the scores as well as any implications for actions that this meaning entails" (p. 5). And because the meaningfulness of scores is rooted in the ideas behind the hypothetical constructs, the interpretation of these scores is related to the robustness of these ideas and hypotheses. The construct validity is a set of proofs, both theoretical and empirical, that justify the construct-related meaningfulness of test scores. Investigating the meaning of these scores across samples and, based on this, their similar interpretability constitutes the essence of establishing construct equivalence. Construct equivalence means that the scores from different samples have the same theoretical and psychological meaning.

Biases That Produce the Incomparability of Test Scores

Theoretical ideas behind hypothetical constructs come from different sources. The primary sources are the psychological theories that are typically developed in Western countries. Many Western psychologists believe that these constructs are universal and applicable to all representatives of the human species. Based on this assumption, they also believe that the tests that measure these constructs are universally valid across different cultural groups. These psychologists forget that each cultural community has created its own cultural models of the human psyche and its major processes and functions—this is the main idea of all indigenous psychologies. They also forget that their theories and research operate by and within cultural models of their own cultural communities, and by conducting cross-cultural research they impose on other populations their indigenous cultural views of human psychology. Ignoring these facts makes a researcher prone to *ethnocentric bias* (Marsella, Dubanoski, Hamada, & Morse, 2000). Therefore, existing psychological constructs and the theories behind them are, in many cases, a part of indigenous world views of particular cultural communities; testing equivalence is an attempt to generate evidence that these constructs work in other cultural communities too. Thus, establishing construct equivalence is a process of finding out if a construct that is taken from one indigenous cultural model has meaning and relevance for people from other cultural communities.

Some constructs, like cognitive abilities, intelligence, personality traits, some emotions, and motives, may exist across different communities, but the meaning of them and the ideas that are assigned to these constructs may be different. In this case a *construct bias* takes place. In addition, the incomparability of scores may happen because of test items having different meanings in different cultures (*item bias*), because of different values and meanings of the testing procedures (*procedural* or *measurement bias*), because of different modes of knowing (*cognition bias*), or different conventions regarding testing as communication (*communicative bias*) (Greenfield, 1997; van de Vijver & Leung, 2011). If not taken care of, these biases can make a Western-type psychological testing in other cultures unacceptable and the obtained results nearly meaningless. Let's look at these issues in more detail. The following analysis is based on the Greenfield's (1997) work on cross-cultural ability testing analysis.

Construct bias: Constructs are understood differently across cultures. The most common source of construct inequivalence is that the construct does not exist in another community or, if it does exist, the individuals' understanding and definition of the construct may differ from the Western one. Let's look at an example. In order to assess the intelligence of Kpelle people (an African ethnic group), psychologists administered a test that required participants to classify objects into categories: instruments go with instruments, vegetables with vegetables and so on (Greenfield, 1997). Kpelle participants used a functional principle for the objects classification: a knife goes together with a potato. They argued that this was the behavior of a wise man. When asked how a fool would respond, they provided the taxonomic classification: tools are put together and vegetables together, the very principle the psychologist wanted the participants to use. The Western understanding of intelligent classification was different from the Kpelles' criterion of being wise.

> Clearly, the example raises profound questions about assuming the cross-cultural validity of IQ tests. It shows that cultural bias cannot be eliminated simply by making item content familiar. A deeper kind of cultural bias concerns what kinds of cognitive processes are more or less valued. (p. 1116)

The author continues:

> But this issue goes beyond cognitive tests: When psychologists take any instrument into another group, how do they know what that test means to the participants? The bottom line

is this: Whenever a psychological instrument and its standardized interpretation means something entirely different to participant and tester, the instrument's validity has been severely undermined for identifying cross-cultural similarities and differences in cognitive ability or for evaluating deficits in clinical assessment. (p. 1116)[1]

This quote provides a clear articulation of the problem of the construct equivalency of psychological tests across cultures. The construct bias in cognitive testing happens when "IQ tests are given to people with a radically different set of presuppositions about the nature of intelligence" (p. 1117). Ethnocentric bias—that a Western-based idea of intelligence and its testing is universally valid—is in full swing here.

Similar concerns are expressed by medical anthropologists involved with cross-cultural psychiatric studies (Kleinman, 1977; Kleinman, Eisenberg, & Good, 1978). Depression has been a focus of the analysis of the cross-cultural comparability of Western psychiatric terms and classifications for a long time. Anthropologists believe that the definition of depression as "a psychiatric syndrome characterized by specific affective, cognitive, behavioral, and somatic symptoms" (Marsella, Sartorius, Jablensky, & Fenton, 1985, p. 300), is a product of the Western cultural model of mental health. "Equivalent concepts of depression are not found among many non-European groups, including, for example, Nigerians . . . Chinese . . . Canadian Eskimo . . . Japanese . . . and Malaysians" (p. 300). Kleinman and Good (1985) continue: "'Dysphoria'—sadness, hopelessness, unhappiness, lack of pleasure with the things in the world and with social relationships—has dramatically different meaning and form of expression in different societies" (p. 3). Therefore, when Western psychiatrists use the model of depression from their own culture to study depressive-affective disorders in other cultural groups, they are committing "a *categorical fallacy*, perhaps the most basic and certainly the most crucial error one can make in cross-cultural research" (Kleinman, 1977, p. 4). This error happens when researchers "superimpose their own cultural categories on some sample of deviant behavior in other cultures, as if their own illness categories were culture-free" (p. 4). In the context of our discussion of equivalence, we may label this fallacy an *ethnocentric construct bias*, meaning that researchers assume that the constructs they study are nearly universal and their equivalence is a priori presumed without empirical evidence. As a result they are actually trying to measure a phenomenon that does not exist in another culture. Another example of construct inequivalence can be found in (Eyton & Neuwirth, 1984).

Construct bias: Bias or a cultural perspective?

An important point to highlight here is that cross-cultural psychologists act within a cultural model about human psychology and the way to study it that exists in their own cultural community. This model nearly automatically shapes their perception, categorization, and understanding of psychological processes and acceptable ways of assessment. Mainstream cross-cultural psychologists call this cultural perspective a *cultural bias* and invite researchers to eliminate it, or at least minimize it, at any cost. Greenfield (1997) finds such biases natural: "objectivity in the sense of no perspective is impossible" (p. 1118); and thus, it is nearly impossible to eliminate this form of bias. But it should be accounted for by acknowledging "(1) what perspective (or perspectives) inform a particular piece of research, (2) to what extent the researchers are aware of their perspectives, and (3) whether the perspectives illuminate or obfuscate the subject at hand [numbering is added]" (p. 1118). To answer these questions, she proposed that, in addition to ethnographic investigations of the nature of constructs under scrutiny, to include representatives of different cultures into a team for developing psychological instruments: "egalitarian, multicultural collaboration in instrument development constitutes a powerful tool to detect and prevent the cross-cultural misunderstandings that undermine validity in cross-cultural ability testing" (p. 1117).

---

[1] Reprinted with permission of the American Psychological Association from Greenfield, P. M. (1997). You can't take it with you: Why ability assessments don't cross cultures. *American Psychologist, 52*(10), 1115–1124.

Kleinman (1977) complemented this conclusion with his arguments against the essentialization of mental disorders, which leads to a preoccupation of transcultural psychiatrists "with disease as an entity, a thing to be 'discovered' in pure form under the layers of cultural camouflage" (p. 4). (Recall a cross-cultural psychologists' metaphor of looking for a 'pan-human' universal psychology by 'peeling the onion of cultural layers'). In this researcher's opinion, the *essentialist fallacy* happens because researchers forget or ignore the idea that disease

> is an explanatory model not a thing. Thus, in comparing diseases one is always comparing explanations not entities. There can be no stripping away of layers of cultural accretion in order to isolate a culture-free entity. (p. 4)

Recall our discussion above that construct validity refers to the ability of a psychologist to explain the test's scores meaningfully. A meaningful explanation is what cross-cultural researchers should be looking for by using constructs' theoretical bases. In this same way, categories of medical diseases are explanatory schemas that allow physicians to name, categorize, and explain particular configurations of symptoms. A set of symptoms including low mood, absence of pleasure from everyday activities, low motivation, fatigue, and suicidal thoughts acquire meaning by being categorized as "depression" in Western countries. Does this category provide a similarly meaningful interpretation of the same symptoms in China, for example? The answer is "No." Chinese doctors use the concept of "neurasthenia" to categorize these symptoms.

Cognition bias: A collective as an agent of cognition

Cognitive abilities are about knowing, memorizing, and thinking about the worlds. In Western psychology, the knower is always an individual who then can share this knowledge with others. "Many societies think of knowing as a group process, not an individual one. The collaborative construction of knowledge, as it often occurs in the course of conversation, is the norm" (p. 1118). Therefore, the construct of individual cognitive ability, or of a set of individual knowledge, does not exist in such cultures. Solving various cognitive tasks is a collective enterprise in these communities, as knowledge is distributed among members of the community and the generation of new knowledge occurs collectively. If we accept that there is a construct of collective cognition, then the concept of individual testing becomes nearly irrelevant in such settings and different forms of abilities testing should be used.

Cognition bias: Distinction between the process of knowing and the object of knowledge

One of the basic postulates of the Western epistemology of cognition is that there is a difference between the process of knowing and the object of knowledge. Many societies do not share this distinction because they exercise "an epistemology of mental realism." Children in such societies do not make a distinction "between their own thought or statement about something and the thing itself. Thought and the object of thought seem[ed] to be one (Greenfield & Bruner, 1969, p. 637)" (Greenfield, 1997, p. 1118). Not differentiating the theory of knowledge of local people from the knowledge or skills of a particular cognitive process may lead to a fraudulent conclusion about these people's cognitive abilities. Formal schooling is the process that brings a change to the epistemology of mental realism to cognitive relativism. which separates the object of cognition from a cognizer's own thoughts and ideas about this object. Therefore, formal schooling changes the nature of constructs to be tested and the nature of testing procedures.

The following two sources of construct inequivalence are related to interactions between researchers and participants and the very procedure of testing itself.

Procedural bias: Different functions of the test's questions

The Western cognitive testing procedure is based on the assumption that by asking a test question, a participant (usually a child) has to give a verbal answer and express his or her view. In some cultures, this may violate the local cultural model for adult-children communication, according to which, children should listen to an adult, they should not express their opinion, and on the adult's request they should respond by doing something. Therefore, it is suggested that a construct evaluation can be improved "by changing the communicative mode of the assessment from test questions to action directive" (p. 1120).

Procedural and item bias: Test's items format may not correspond to the cultural model of communication

Local cultural models of communication can assume that all given information in a conversation is relevant for a problem solution. For example, a multiple-choice format of cognitive testing contains redundant and incorrect information. This confuses participants, and because of this, the construct may not be properly evaluated. Changing the format of testing can make constructs more comparable and the testing more valid. Another obstacle for a construct evaluation is that test procedures are de-contextualized and rely on abstract and formal knowledge. Mostly unschooled and nonliterate individuals prefer to think in the context and process only situationally relevant information.

Communication bias: Impersonal communication with a stranger may not be acceptable

Several aspects of Western-based testing can go against a local model of communication with strangers. In many communities, locals do not communicate with strangers. Forcing local people to be tested without establishing at least a minimal level of personal relationship alienates the participants; a valid assessment of a construct becomes nearly impossible.

How to Deal With the Problem of Construct Inequivalence

If a cross-cultural researcher suspects or has already discovered construct inequivalence, he or she has several options to consider. The first step is to investigate if the construct of interest actually exists in another cultural group, and if it does exist, what does it mean and how does it manifest itself?

Although they accept the importance of this step, mainstream cross-cultural psychologists are unsure that it can be implemented. One of them, Ype Poortinga (1989) pessimistically stated that "the universality of high level concepts [psychological hypothetical constructs] is beyond empirical scrutiny, because it is not clear which behavioral referents form part of it and which do not" (p. 754). Using intelligence as an example, Poortinga continued: "From this perspective the question whether intelligence is a universal human characteristic, or whether there are different 'intelligences,' cannot be solved on the basis of empirical findings" (p. 754). By "empirical scrutiny" and "empirical findings", this researcher meant quantifiable results of the application of different assessment instruments. So, he suggested starting to deal with the problem of construct equivalence "from a proposition that any meaningful psychological construct by definition has to refer to a universal aspect of behavior. Any evidence of inequivalence then invariably points to measurement artifacts" (p. 753).

Cultural and indigenous psychologists as well as cultural, psychological, and medical anthropologists exercise two approaches with regard to construct comparison. More radical researchers deny the very idea that construct equivalence should be sought. They believe that each community develops its indigenous understanding of human psychology, and in order to understand the psychology of these people, they should be studied exclusively within their own framework. Imposing constructs from other indigenous systems of psychological thinking does not make sense to them, because these imposing constructs do not have roots and explanatory powers in another community.

Less radical researchers who try to do meaningful comparisons across different cultural communities suggest that any cross-cultural comparative research should start with an ethnographic study and the analysis of the cultural models that exist in cultural communities regarding cognitive abilities, personality, self, health, diseases, and many other constructs and processes as well as different ways of knowing and communicating. "The anthropological method of ethnography is an indispensable way for psychologists to enter new meaning system and to learn about culture's conventions concerning knowledge and communication" (Greenfiels, 1997, p. 1122). The same idea was expressed by Kleinman (1977), who suggested starting cross-cultural studies of mental disorder with "detailed local phenomenological descriptions." Using these descriptions, researchers would "compare indigenous and professional psychiatric explanations of these disorders along with the behavior they interpret." They also should extract and compare the "symptom terms and illness labels" between local and professional accounts. These comparisons would lay the foundation of developing models of diseases that would be used in cross-cultural comparisons (p. 4).

Thus, the ethnographic and cultural-phenomenological analysis should be the first step in discovering how members of another community understand and experience different psychological constructs. By doing naturalistic and participant observations and interviewing members of a target cultural community, cultural psychologists should extract the corresponding cultural models and try to formulate the conceptions of various psychological states and functions from the "natives' point of view." Such an ethnographic investigation ensures that the constructs of interest are protected from the ethnocentric construct bias because "a fair cross-cultural comparison can be carried out only after the investigation of each culture in its own terms" (Greenfield, 1997, p. 1123).

Greenfield's second piece of advice is that "the most valid research instruments are derived from cultural meanings in the group where the instruments are to be applied" (p. 1122). This means that "comparable abilities must be studied with different instruments in different countries" (p. 1122). But what about the comparability of these constructs and establishing the universality of psychological functions?

> Contrary to the usual assumption, culture-specific assessments are not incompatible with the demonstration of universals. In fact, they often enhance the chances for finding universals in cognitive abilities by providing culturally familiar opportunities for all participants—not merely those belonging to the culture of the test—to use and demonstrate their cognitive abilities (Greenfield, 1997). This is because universal abilities take particular forms (Greenfield, in press). (p. 1122)[2]

Greenfield's next recipe against construct bias is: "when a given instrument is used beyond the culture in which it was developed, it is necessary to research the meaning or meanings that participants in the new culture attach to the instrument and to its procedure" (p. 1123). Thus, again a thorough ethnographic study is required: now with regard to the meaning of the test and the measurement procedure that accompanies it. For more information on this topic, see (Helms, 1992; Hines, 1993)

---

[2] Reprinted with permission of the American Psychological Association from Greenfield, P.M. (1997). You can't take it with you: Why ability assessments don't cross cultures. *American Psychologist, 52*(10), 1115–1124.

Statistical Testing of Construct Validity and Equivalence

A statistical approach to construct validity testing was initiated by Cronbach and Meehl (1955). They coined not only the notion of construct validity but also the corresponding concept of *nomological network*, which has its roots in the deductive-nomological model of explanation suggested by logical positivists (see Chapter 3). This nomological network represents the theory behind the construct: "The laws in a nomological network may relate (a) observable properties or quantities to each other; or (b) theoretical constructs to observables; or (c) different theoretical constructs to one another" (p. 290). (See Fig 9.1.). According to Cronbach and Meehl, to determine the construct validity of a test is to establish relationships between the test scores and the scores of other tests that are based on theoretically relevant constructs within the nomological network. Researchers must also calculate the associations of these constructs with their observable manifestations and postulate relationships among observables as well.

To test construct validity statistically is to, first, postulate a network of constructs related to the construct of interest and, based on these assumptions, make predictions about associations among the constructs and their observable manifestations. If empirical tests confirm these predictions, then a strong justification of the test's construct validity is obtained. It is important to make these predictions BEFORE the empirical tests are undertaken, not after. Remember, we need to confirm our ideas about the constructs, not just develop this idea from the empirical data.

To test construct equivalence across different samples is to compare the nomological networks for the same construct across different cultural communities. If these networks are similar—meaning that relations of the hypothetical constructs with each other, hypothetical constructs with the observables, and the observables among themselves are all comparable—then it is possible to say that construct equivalence has been established. This way of establishing construct equivalence is known as *functional equivalence* (van de Vijver & Leung, 2011, pp. 20–21). A construct is functionally equivalent across cultures if a questionnaire that measures it has "a similar pattern of convergent and divergent validity (i.e., nonzero correlations with presumably related measures and zero correlations with presumably unrelated measures)" (p. 21).

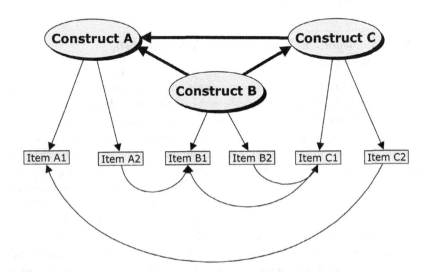

FIGURE 9.1 Nomological network with three constructs, each with two observable manifestations/items. This figure was made with IHMC Cmap Tools

Establishing *structural equivalence* of a measurement instrument across different samples is another statistical test of construct comparability (Fischer & Fontaine, 2011; van de Vijver & Leung, 2011). The notion of structural equivalence follows Cronbach & Meehl's idea of confirming construct validity by investigating the internal structure of the test's items through the analysis of their intercorrelations and factor structure. This procedure is usually applied when cross-cultural researchers are adopting an existing test, scale, or questionnaire. Factor analysis (FA) is a powerful technique to test construct validity and structural equivalence. FA aims to discover the factors that are supposed to be latent and nonobservable—hidden dimensions that 'stand behind' and account for participants' performance on the test's item (Mulaik, 1987; Pett, Lackey, & Sullivan, 2003). These factors may be identified as unobservable psychological constructs and, thus, FA can be considered a procedure that validates the existence of these constructs. If the FA procedure confirms that a test's items have the same latent factors structure across different samples, then there is strong evidence that the constructs behind this test are comparable across these samples.

Both versions of factor analysis—exploratory (EFA) and confirmatory (CFA)—are suitable for testing construct validity and comparability across samples (Brown, 2015; Thompson & Daniel, 1996). Typically, EFA is used to explore the structure of items and to identify (a) if two versions of the instrument have the same number of factors—*dimensional invariance*, (b) if the same items are associated with the same factors—*configural invariance*, and (c) if there are similar loadings of items on the corresponding factors—*metric invariance*. This exploration may provide a good approximation of the test's structural comparability and, hence, it may support construct equivalence. To obtain more precise and quantifiable indicators of the structural equivalence, the multigroup CFA is recommended (Fischer & Fontaine, 2011; van de Vijver & Leung, 1997). In conducting this analysis, researchers postulate, based on their theories, a structure of the items, and then examine if empirical data confirm this structure. They conduct this analysis simultaneously on two (or more) samples and obtain statistical indicators of how well their data fit the postulated model in all groups. Indicators of the model's fit as well as the program's suggestions for modifying the model may shed light on the sources of the structural inequivalence. This information is useful for researchers to theorize about the nature of the construct and its manifestations in each sample and make necessary adjustments either to the theory or to the instrument.

Words of Caution Regarding Relying Exclusively on Statistical Analysis for Construct Equivalence Testing

Simple logic tells us that in order to run construct validity and comparability correctly, researchers first have to test the construct theoretically and culturally, then develop items that represent it in both samples, and only after that use these items to statistically confirm the theory behind the construct. It may be tempting to develop items first, then statistically establish their structure across samples, and then based on this structure theorize about the hypothetical constructs; but this is not a procedure for the construct equivalence testing; rather it is a pragmatic way of designing a new test without theoretically justifying it. Structural equivalence should confirm the theoretical analysis of the construct. When researchers confuse these two strategies, the "inductivist fallacy" happens: "the belief that one can make inductive inferences uniquely and unambiguously from data without making prior assumptions. . . . [I]t is the fallacy behind the way many users of exploratory common factor analysis have expected the method to provide them with unambiguous results" (Mulaik, 1987, p. 298). In our case this fallacy means that EFA, when used for statistically structuring the items during test development, cannot serve as an instrument of justifying the construct validity and equivalence.

Advanced Statistical Techniques for Testing Construct Validity/Equivalence

In addition to different versions of FA, there are several other advanced statistical techniques that allow researchers to explore construct equivalence. Among them are Structural Equation Modelling (SEM) and Multidimensional Scaling (MDS). SEM allows researchers to test structural and functional equivalence simultaneously. It also provides an opportunity to do such testing in several cultural groups at the same time, providing a powerful test of the theories that underlie the constructs and their relations. SEM is well suited for testing construct equivalence as it allows investigators to simultaneously measure all components of the postulated nomological network: hypothetical constructs (latent variables in SEM's terminology) and the relations among them (functional equivalence), the relations of observables to the latent factors (structural equivalence), and the relations among the observables. This procedure also allows researchers to account for error variances and thus to achieve high precision in their assessments (Byrne, 2006; Little, 1997). Path analysis is an abbreviated version of SEM analysis, where no measurement models are tested. It can be used to test functional equivalence also (See more on SEM in cross-cultural research (Billiet, 2003; Davidov, Schmidt, & Billiet, 2010; Tran, 2009). MDS is another multivariate technique that may be used to evaluate the structure of test items and provide evidence for the comparability of constructs and their manifestations (Fischer & Fontaine, 2011; Fontaine, 2003).

Content Validity and Equivalence

Psychological hypothetical constructs may be used as theoretical concepts or as "middle level" constructs. Theoretical constructs refer to nonobservable explanatory ideas which cannot be operationally defined in any form of behavioral or experiential manifestations. Psychoanalytic constructs "libido," "ego," "id," and "superego" are of this kind. Such constructs are used exclusively for theory building. "Middle level" constructs, also known as "intervening variables" (MacCorquodale & Meehl, 1948), are ideas that can be expressed in observational, behavioral, or experiential terms through operational definitions. For this type of construct, their operational definitions are not only possible, but are sought for by researchers. Think about concepts such as "intelligence," "anxiety," "depression," "extraversion," and many others. The idea of *content validity* refers to this second type of hypothetical construct and can be briefly described as follows. The "middle level" hypothetical constructs manifest themselves in various forms. These manifestations are typically behavioral, cognitive, and affective. All these manifestations constitute a universe of possible displays related to the construct (Fitzpatrick, 1983; Flaherty et al., 1988). Because researchers cannot gain access to and evaluate all these manifestations, they sample a representative set of them, transform it into test items and then use them to assess the construct, symptom, behavioral problem or other psychological attribute. Content validity is concerned with how well the test items represent the universe of possible manifestations of the psychological attribute, covering all relevant domains. If an intelligence test contains only verbal items to assess deductive reasoning, then its content validity is low because it lacks other manifestations of intelligence, such as attention, memory, and nonverbal aspects of cognitive functioning.

Such interpretation of content validity brings us directly to the idea of *content equivalence*. If the construct of interest is comparable across samples, then researchers have to analyze whether items of the test that measure this construct represent the universes of the construct's manifestations in all the samples equally well.

> If content validity has been established in the original culture, the task is to reexamine each item's relevance in the second culture under investigation. The first question is whether the phenomenon (item) in fact occurs in and is noticeable by the members of the culture. (Flaherty et al., 1988, p. 259)

Consider the following example (Flaherty, 1988). Researchers were interested in investigating the social adaptation of Peruvian peasants who moved from Andean villages to Lima, the capital of Peru. They used a US-based set of scales for assessing social adaptation that included: "Have you had at least four traffic tickets in your life for speeding or running a light?" This item that represents an antisocial domain of the construct "social adaptation" lacks content equivalence in the Peruvian context "because none of the migrants being studied drove a car" (p. 259). Items that comprise the domain of "antisocial tendencies" represent "behavior that does not conform to the usual values of society" (p. 259). Values are different in each society; therefore behaviors that do not conform to them should also be different. A systematic infringement of traffic laws indicates the violation of the fundamental value of North American society of being a law-abiding citizen. To study antisocial tendencies in the Peruvian society, researchers have to know what laws are important there. Does law obedience constitute a fundamental value? What behaviors are considered to be a violation of this value? In another study, to ensure content equivalence, Eyton & Neuwirth (1984) suggested using open-ended interviews to explore a society's conception and explanation of illness, illness related behaviors, and modes of treatment. The interviewees should be purposefully selected and their answers subjected to a thematic analysis to extract the main dimensions of the illness, its possible manifestations, attitudes toward different treatments, and other aspects of interest. Such a procedure in its various modifications, like focus groups, can be used for both construct and content equivalence testing.

Linguistic Equivalence

By now, we have discussed the equivalence of the constructs and the comparability of the content of constructs' manifestations across cultures. Usually, these manifestations are expressed in words, and words have different meanings. Therefore, these manifestations have to have linguistically comparable connotations across samples: they have to be expressed in words and sentences that convey to participants from culturally different samples the same (or similar) meanings. It is important to note that the analysis of linguistic equivalence goes hand-in-hand with an examination of the construct and content forms of equivalence. Let's take as an example an analysis of some of the items used to assess the integration acculturation strategy (Boski, 2008). One of the items reads: "I prefer to have both Vietnamese and French friends." Boski correctly argued that the meanings of the words "friendship" and "friends" vary across different languages and/or cultural groups. For Latin Americans, a friend is "someone to spend really good times with, and to keep good memories of such moments;" in contrast, for Poles, a friend is "someone to rely upon in bad times (more than for good times), when you are in need for help and support. A friend indeed is a friend in need" (p. 144). An English definition of the word "friend" reads: "a person with whom one has a bond of mutual affection, typically one exclusive of sexual or family relations" (Soanes & Stevenson, 2008). The above item may elicit different answers not because of a difference in strength of the construct, but because of different interpretations of the word "friend."

The problem of linguistic equivalence is important for all cases of adapting, adopting, or creating new instruments. The following section will outline the basic guidelines for psychological instruments translation and the strategies for establishing this equivalence. I recommend several informative resources (Hambleton & Zenisky, 2011; Harkness, 2003; Tran, 2009) as well as publications that have stood the test of time (Brislin, 1976; Sechrest, Fay, & Zaidi, 1972; Werner & Campbell, 1970). Some practical issue of scales translation can be found in (Siaki, 2011; Sperber, Devellis, & Boehlecke, 1994; Wong & Poon, 2010)

Centered Versus Decentered Translation and Items' Linguistic Equivalence

There are two tactics to translate test items: *centered* and *decentered* translation (Werner & Campbell, 1970). In a *centered* or *asymmetrical* (also verbatim, close, or literal) translation, researchers use the language of a source instrument as the frame of reference (the center) for questionnaire development and stay loyal to it in translating it to another language. "As an undesirable example of asymmetrical translation, consider the typical practice in translating English language 'personality tests' into foreign languages. If equivalence to the original 'standardized' form is demanded, there results an awkward, exotic target-language version" (p. 399).

A *decentered* or *symmetrical* translation aims at maintaining the same construct across samples, but uses the target language's terms, colloquialisms, and expressions that are best for expressing its manifestations. Werner and Campbell (1970) provide the following example of decentered translations:

> in Navaho a coyote may be identified with witchcraft, while in European languages and cultures a black cat might perform the same function; or in translation of proverbs and poetry: English "'once in a blue moon" becomes in Spanish "every time a bishop dies." (p. 399)

In the above example of "friend," researchers have to do a semantic comparison of the key terms that constitute the test items. They may consider, for example, working with various synonyms like "pal," "buddy," "comrade" or "soul mate." These words have to be semantically compared with synonymous words in the target language. For the Peruvian example, the constructed "antisocial tendencies" must stay the same for the Peruvian peasants, but cultural values, manifestations of their violations, and wordings of these manifestations should be relevant to and understandable by the Peruvian respondents. The goal will be "to find equivalent content areas in each culture on an item-by-item basis, yielding two different instruments that are equivalent in content" (p. 259), but different in their linguistic furnishing.

Werner & Campbell advised "to regard the English [source language] version as itself continually open for revision in the process of preparing 'equivalent' tests, i.e., of decentering the translation effort" (p. 399). This means that the source language items should not be kept unchanged during the translation, but be open for syntactic and lexical paraphrasing in order to reduce ambiguities and, thus, make the process of decentering easier.

The Procedure of An Instrument Translation

The issue of translation is relevant to adopting and adapting an existing instrument. The topic of developing a new culturally relevant instrument is not considered in this section but some of its related issues will be discussed below.

Harkness (2003) suggested a five-step procedure for translating a test: *t*ranslation, *r*eview, *a*djudication, *p*retesting and *d*ocumentation (TRAPD) (p. 38). Tran (2009) recommended the following steps: translation (both forward and back), a committee appraisal of the translated items, cognitive interviews, focus groups, and pilot testing. Let's follow these steps.

A. *Translation*. Harkness offered a simple rule to guide the translation: "Ask-the-Same-Question" (p. 21), which means that whatever verbal construction is used, respondents in different cultures have to ultimately answer the same questions about the same constructs, behaviors, or attitudes. How can you follow this rule?

Researchers start with translating a test from its source language to the target one. There are different strategies suggested at this point. One is a set of *forward and back translations* (Brislin, 1976; Werner

& Campbell, 1970) and another is *a committee-based translation* procedure (Harkness, 2003, Tran, 2009). In F&BT, translator 1 makes a translation from the source language to the target one, and translator 2 does a back translation from the target to the source language. A researcher assesses the equivalence of the original and back-translated versions of the source instrument, and, based on this comparison, accepts or revises the translated version of an instrument. Brislin (1986) advised that this cycle of forward and back translations can be repeated several times with different translators. "Moving back and forth between languages in this way is the basis of decentering, since no one language is the 'center' of attention" (p. 160). This decentering ensures that the final version of a translated instrument is culturally and linguistically appropriate.

Harkness (2003) is critical about this procedure because, if a primary researcher is not bilingual, he or she is not capable of directly assessing the target language version and has to rely exclusively on the expertise of translators. She believes that researchers must have direct access to the translated version. She suggested a committee-based translation procedure. Such an adjudication committee includes the researchers who are running the project (they may or may not be bilingual), translators, specialists in questionnaire design, and experts in the source and target cultures. Translators independently translate an original instrument. Then a meeting is held where the translators and researchers "go through the entire questionnaire discussing versions and agreeing on a final review version" (p. 38). In this case, even if the researchers do not know the target language, they participate directly in the discussion of the translated version of the instrument and can develop their own opinion about its quality. Tran (2009) suggested that such a committee may work with original and translated versions as well as with back-translated versions of the instrument.

Translators should always translate into their strongest language (Harkness, 2003, p. 42), meaning, in translating a questionnaire from English to Russian, a translator should be a native Russian speaker with English as a second language. Back translation should be done by an English-speaking translator, with Russian as a second language. Bilingual researchers may serve as primary or secondary translators and participate in both processes, with an emphasis on their strongest language.

B. *Review and appraisal of the translated items.* As was mentioned above, both centered and decentered translations can be used. Experts recommend the decentered translation as the centered translation usually sounds awkward and unnatural in the target language (Tran, 2009, p. 41). Harkness (2003) mentions that "for questionnaires, close translation is a balancing act." She concluded that "translated versions that are clear and make sense to respondents may not be as close [to the original version] as researchers might like" (p. 47). It is up to researchers to finally decide how centered the translation should be. Based on Tran's recommendations, it is possible to say that well-translated items should have construct and concept relevance across samples and be culturally appropriate and linguistically clear and accessible.

Construct/concept relevance. Following these criteria, the committee members assess how well translated items represent the construct of a test or behavior, the attitudes or other psychological, social, or cultural phenomena that are to be measured. It is especially challenging to express unfamiliar or unknown concepts in the target population.

> For example, a study of Turkish peasants (Frey 1963) concluded that 'there was no nationally understood word, familiar to all peasants, for such concepts as "problem," "prestige," and "loyalty." Similarly, the Japanese concept of *giri*—having to do with duty, honor, and social obligation—has no "linguistic, operational, or conceptual corollary in Western cultures" (Sasaki 1995). (Smith, 2003, p. 71)

The primary researchers and experts in the target culture and its language should have the strongest voice in dealing with translating such concepts.

The *cultural appropriateness* of the items represents the extent to which they reflect the realities, practices, traditions, and situations of the target cultural communities; the items have to "make sense" in another culture. Asking about "dating" or "inviting a girl out" in paternalistic cultures with predominantly arranged marriages would be culturally challenging or even inappropriate. Eating preferences, sleeping arrangements, styles of communication, interactions with parents and people in authority, and myriads of other practices may drastically differ from community to community and, thus, require a thorough cultural analysis of the situations and practices included in the items. To establish the cultural relevance of the items, researchers should use ethnographic descriptions of the target cultural community, consult with specialists of this culture, conduct focus groups and interviews with members of this community to discover the most appropriate manifestations of the construct or phenomenon of interest.

Language clarity and accessibility. The use of appropriate terms and words as well as the syntax of the sentences should be evaluated by linguists, translators, and regular people from the target population. The goal is to assess how linguistically correct and how natural the items sound for the target population. Commenting on the linguistic challenge of item translations, Smith (2003), provides the following example: "for Spanish-speaking immigrants in the United States, *educación* includes social skills such as proper etiquette not included in the more academic meaning of 'education' in English (Greenfield, 1997)" (p. 71).

Smith (2003) outlines six simple rules for item wordings in cross-cultural translation.

a. "Avoid vague quantifiers (e.g., 'frequently,' 'usually,' 'regularly') since these words have highly variable understandings across both respondent and question context" (p. 88).
b. "Avoid items with ambiguous or dual meaning." Smith used an example of an item from the State-Trait Anger Expression Inventory: "I am secretly quite critical of others" (p. 88). This statement could be understood as keeping anger inside or expressing anger by criticizing people behind their backs.
c. "Ambiguity also arises from complex questions with more than one key element" (p. 88). This advice concerns long and double-barrel items that ask about several things in one statement. Rudmin and Ahmadzadeh (2001) provided an example of such a question from an acculturation questionnaire: "When I have to furnish a room, I would not buy Korean furniture because it looks so out-of-place, and also because there is so much beautiful Canadian furniture available." This is a long (28 words), double-barrel item simultaneously states rejection of Korean furniture and acceptance of Canadian furniture. Agreeing with this statement may mean only rejecting Korean furniture, only accepting Canadian furniture, or accepting both these options.
d. "Avoid hypothetical and counter-factual questions. People rarely produce coherent thoughts on most imagined situations and may not be able to even grasp the state of affairs described in the item" (p. 88).
e. Employ easy to understand terms that are widely used across different cultural communities and segments of the population. "When necessary, provide definitions to clarify the meanings of terms" (p. 89).
f. When asking about various activities, he suggested using precise time references. "For example, 'Do you fish?' might be understood to mean 'Have you ever gone fishing?' or 'Do you currently go fishing?' It would be better to phrase the question as follows: 'Have you gone fishing during the last 12 months?'" (p. 89).

242 Practical Aspects of Doing Research

HOW-TO BOX 9.1. GUIDELINES FOR ITEMS WORDING (BASED ON (BRISLIN, 1986, PP. 144–150) AND (SMITH, 2003, PP. 88–89))

1. Use short, simple sentences of fewer than 16 words. (Note: items can be of more than one sentence.)
2. Employ the active rather than the passive voice.
3. Repeat nouns instead of using pronouns.
4. Avoid metaphors and colloquialisms.
5. Avoid subjunctive verbs like "could," "would," or "should" that state a mood expressing what is imagined, wished or possible. Many languages do not have readily available words for such English subjunctives.
6. Add adjectives and even sentences to provide context to key items. Asking about a man giving up his seat on a bus to a woman should be contextualized by indicating her age. Reword key phrases to provide redundancy that may help translators grasp the main idea of the item.
7. Avoid possessive forms.
8. Use specific rather than general terms (e.g., use the specific animal such as cows, chickens, or pigs rather than the general term "livestock").
9. Avoid words indicating vagueness (e.g., probably, maybe, perhaps).
10. Use wordings familiar to translators.

In addition to the semantic clarity of items, it is important to adequately translate and evaluate the relevance of *response scales*, such as "Strongly agree," "Agree," "Disagree" and "Strongly disagree" (Harness, 2003, pp. 52–56 and Smith, 2003, pp. 73–79). People in different countries have different exposure to surveys with quantifiable answer scales and as a result they may have problems in quantifying their answers. For countries and communities with a well-established survey tradition, there will be no problem directly translating the response scales from the source language. For communities which are not familiar with the survey format, special arrangements should be made. The main issue here is that quantifiers ("Very frequently," "Rarely," "Sometimes," etc.) may mean different quantities in different languages, thus requiring special efforts to translate them correctly. If such translation becomes a problem, Smith (2003) advised using simple, usually dichotomous answers like "yes/no," "like/dislike," and "agree/disagree" (pp. 76–77). Another suggestion is to get rid of verbal labels altogether and to employ numeric, graphic, or symbolic scales. For numeric scales, numbers from 1 to 5 (or 7 or 9 or 10) are used to quantify respondents' answers. Graphic scales may use different means to represent the increase of a quantity, frequency, or agreeableness, like ladders, truncated pyramids or stepped mountains. Different symbols, like human faces, may be used to represent happiness and satisfaction or pain and suffering (ϑ—Λ). Such nonverbal scales, although not without their own problems (pp. 74–76), address the ambiguity of using linguistic quantifiers.

After the items are translated, the adjudication committee evaluates them by the above criteria. Some items may be accepted, others may be reworded and edited, and other items can simply be dropped. The evaluation of the accepted and revised items continues with cognitive interviewing and focus group procedures.

C. *Cognitive interviewing* is a procedure of investigating the process of interpreting, understanding, and answering survey items. Researchers ask respondents to describe what comes to their minds when they read the items and explain why they chose particular answers (Beatty & Willis, 2007; Nápoles-Springer, Santoyo-Olsson, O'Brien, & Stewart, 2006; Willis, 2004). Survey designers usually use two techniques: thinking-aloud and probing. During an application of the thinking-aloud method, an interviewer asks participants to verbalize as fully as possible their way of interpreting, understanding, and answering the question/item. For example, "Tell me what you were thinking about when reading this question/statement. Please tell me how you came up with your answer to it" (modified from Beatty & Willis, 2007, pp. 289–290). During this "thinking-aloud" process, an interviewer asks participants almost no questions and allows them to freely express the process of understanding and answering the items. After this, a researcher may start asking more detailed questions. He or she may ask about items' difficulty, clearness, and appropriateness. For example, "can you tell me in your own words what that question was asking?" (p. 290). The above criteria may serve as guidelines for such probing. The answers are recorded either verbatim or by using a voice recorder.

D. *Focus groups* are a popular procedure not only for planning and designing research on culture and psychology (Hughes & DuMont, 1993), but also for evaluating translated versions of surveys or questionnaires. Focus groups may be used to collect the culturally appropriate practices, situations, and experiences of people regarding the object of testing, thus providing a bank of different manifestations of the construct. Focus groups may be used to evaluate the quality of an already translated instrument (Nassar-McMillan & Borders, 2002). Participants of the cognitive interviewing should not participate in focus groups, and participants of the groups should not participate in later pilot and regular testing. The focus groups should be between 7 and 10 people and should be representative of the target population—age, gender, social status, ethnic composition, etc. It is recommended to arrange several focus groups based on the major sociodemographic, ethno-cultural or sociopsychological characteristics relevant to the developing instrument (Fuller, Edwards, Vorakitphokatorn, & Sermsri, 1993). The most typical are gender, age, socioeconomic status (level of income, level of education, main occupations, etc.), and ethno-cultural composition (membership in different ethnic groups or religious denominations). It is recommended to include people who do not know each other, as strangers are more willing to share their opinions with other strangers (Morgan, 1991). The facilitators of the focus groups should avoid illegal, immoral, or taboo topics, unless the questionnaire touches on these topics. If this is the case, the facilitators require special training and the participants should be selected carefully. The translated questionnaires are distributed prior to the group session, and participants are asked to answer them and be prepared to discuss their answers. Tran (2009) also suggested preparing a list of all the questionnaire's constructs/concepts and their indicators and discuss them too. During the interview, the same questions about how well the items represent the concepts or constructs, their linguistic clarity, and cultural appropriateness are discussed. The discussion, which may raise unforeseen but important issues about items or the testing procedure, should be video- or audio-recorded. Group facilitators, similar to cognitive interviewers, should be trained and prepared to moderate the discussions and make it interesting for participants and useful for the research team. Focus groups may last up to 1.5–2 hours, but not longer. Fuller et al. (1993) provided the following examples of the important contributions a focus group's members made to translating a questionnaire of household crowding in Bangkok:

> They [local participants of the focus group] believed that, as one example, that the phrase *too tired to do anything* would not be meaningful and that the phrase *too tired to move* would more meaningfully communicate the idea that an extreme tiredness had gripped someone. Similarly, translating the question, "During the past few weeks, how often have you felt particularly excited or interested in something?" presented difficulty because, in the Thai context,

excitement has the connotation of misfortune. Also, because Thais are supposed to remain calm and peaceful at all times, it would be socially undesirable to admit being excited.... Another item in the original scale—"feel happy all the time"—was changed to "in a good mood," because the word *happy* was deemed to be too abstract in the Thai language. A related example pertains to translation of the concept *self-respect*. The literal translation of *self-respect*... makes no sense to most Thais.... The term *dignity* could be translated in a more meaningful manner. (pp. 100–101)

Pilot testing. After collecting all this information about the instrument, an adjudication committee should evaluate the overall quality of the translation item-by-item and decide upon its proposed final version. When this version is ready, the research team should conduct *pilot testing*, which allows researchers to use psychometric indices and statistics to finalize the quality of the instrument. Pilot testing should be conducted on a representative and probability-derived (which is not often feasible) sample. The size of the sample depends on the size of the questionnaires, and it is recommended to have 5 to 10 respondents per item (Tran, 2009). The results should be compared with the psychometric parameters of the original instrument in the source language. The following are the main psychometric indices for item analysis that researchers should calculate and analyze before approaching more sophisticated forms of statistical analysis (Tran, 2009).

a. *Distribution of the scores for each item*. Each distribution of the items' scores is examined using skewness (symmetry of the distribution) and kurtosis (flatness or "peakness" of the distribution). Every statistical package has an option for such analysis. The distributions of item scores from the translated version are compared with the distributions from the original instrument. "Difference in data distribution and pattern of responses of the instrument items are early signs of differences in reliability and validity of the research instrument between the comparative groups" (p. 68). The reliability analysis that usually follows these calculations often supports the conclusion that the items with high scores on skewness and kurtosis should be reworded and reanalysed. With regard to the measurement equivalence, it is expected that these indices for each item will be similar across the compared groups. If this is not the case, then the quality of the translation should be re-examined.

b. *Distribution of responses along the answer scale*. The answer scale for the instrument may vary from dichotomous (Yes/No; Agree/Disagree), to 3-point (Agree/Uncertain/ Disagree), 5-point, 7-point or even longer. Researchers calculate how many respondents chose each response option and compare these patterns of responses across different versions of an instrument. A main clue that researchers should look for is a *response bias*, a stable tendency of respondents to answer items by using particular response options; for example, avoiding negative options or extreme points. Tran (2009) provided an example of conducting the item analysis of a depression questionnaire across four groups: white Americans, black Americans, Japanese, and Russians. It was discovered that the Japanese respondents had a stable tendency to avoid the option "Most of the time." They demonstrated a response bias of avoiding the acceptance of the depressive symptoms.

c. *Internal consistency of the items—Cronbach's alpha reliability*. The internal consistency of items belonging to the same construct is an indicator that this construct is reliably represented in the selected sample of the items and that these items are working in accord in measuring the construct they are supposed to measure. An average of the items' intercorrelations forms the basis for evaluating such consistency and is usually represented by the Cronbach's alpha coefficient of internal reliability. This coefficient is calculated for each version of the instrument and compared (for how to compare the reliability coefficients, see box 4.1. in (van de Vijver & Leung,

1997, p. 60). If they are significantly different, then a concern about the measurement invariance should be raised. To find the sources of the internal consistency differences, researchers have to look at the item score distributions (see a. above) and also calculate the item-total correlations: a correlation of each item score with a total score for the test. Low correlations, which may be related to the skewness or kurtosis of the scores distributions, may lie at the basis of low internal consistency. Such items should be reviewed and/or retranslated.

d. *Exploratory factor analysis.* The final procedure that is recommended for the item analysis is EFA. When discussing this procedure for testing construct validity/equivalence, the logic of the analysis goes from the hypothesized construct to its manifestations. In the item analysis procedure, the structure of examination goes the opposite way: from the items back to the latent factors that underlie their covariances. (For the technical aspects of the FA procedure, refer to the following sources: (Field, 2013; Pett et al., 2003; Tabachnick & Fidell, 2012). Researchers should compare factor patterns and loadings of the items on each factor across different versions of an instrument. For example, if EFA extracts the same number of factors from a translated version of the test as in its original version, then these two versions can be considered to be measurement invariant. A different factor structure is a strong indicator of construct and measurement inequality. If the equivalence of the factor pattern is established, then researchers may compare the factor loadings of each item. These loadings should be similar; strong deviations across the comparison groups indicate that the versions are not psychometrically invariant. Examples of the item analysis of translated scales with more technical details can be found in coefficients; see box 4.1. in van de Vijver & Leung, 1997 and Tran, 2009).

After the pilot testing, the adjudication committee assembles all the information about the translated version of the instrument and makes a decision about its final version. This version is then used for data collection and the results of its application are subjected to advanced statistical analysis to ensure construct and measurement comparability in the context of a particular research. It is also possible that after publishing the translated version of the instrument, other researchers may decide to use it for their studies. Although the scale or test is well translated, these researchers still have to control for its measurement invariance in their own research, while answering their research questions.

Measurement Invariance Testing

Steenkamp and Baumgartner (1998) identified three main goals for cross-cultural quantitative comparison research: "(1) exploring the basic structure of the construct cross-nationally, (2) making quantitative comparisons of means across countries, and (3) examining structural relationships with other constructs cross-nationally" [numbers are added] (p. 82). FA was introduced as a statistical method to test construct equivalence and to evaluate items' quality and comparability. With the emergence of CFA and SEM, the process of testing construct and measurement invariance (MI) has been raised to a new level. MI establishes the equivalence of the instruments in a quantitative form. The MI of an instrument means that individuals with the same amount of the construct have the same standing in either of the samples, regardless of which scale has been used: original or translated. To assess it, there is a set of strategies generally known as *multigroup mean and covariance structures analyses* (MACS analyses) (Byrne, 2006; Little, 1997; Ployhart & Oswald, 2004). This section provides the basic rationale and logic of this strategy. Readers should consult the original sources to learn more about these forms of analyses. Some examples of the application can be found in: (Chirkov, Ryan, Kim, & Kaplan, 2003; Chirkov, Ryan, & Willness, 2005; Dimitrov, 2010; Tran, 2009; Tran et al., 2003).

MACS Analyses

Little (1997) gives four reasons why these types of analyses are well suited for testing construct comparability and establishing between-group differences on measured constructs. First, they allow a researcher to simultaneously conduct a confirmatory factor analysis in two or more groups and test models with "the expected pattern of indicator-to-construct relations for both intercepts and factor loadings" (p. 54). Secondly, MACS analyses allow "tests of the cross-group equivalence of all reliable measurement parameters (i.e., again, *both intercepts and loadings*)". Thirdly, they permit a researcher to correct for measurement error and estimate the constructs' means and covariances as true and reliable values. Finally, according to Little, they give an opportunity to test "hypotheses about possible sociocultural influences on the constructs" (p. 54).

MACS analyses may help to answer research questions including: Are constructs' means similar across samples? Are associations among constructs in each group equal? Researchers want to answer these questions under the assurance that all forms of equivalence are present. For example, Chirkov and Ryan (2001) studied the level of autonomy support and its relation to academic motivation in Russia and the US. They hypothesized that Russian students would perceive their parents and teachers as being less autonomy supportive than their American counterparts will; but despite this difference, autonomy support will positively predict self-determined academic motivation in both samples. The construct, content, and linguistic equivalence of the measures had been established. They then used MACS analyses to verify their hypotheses statistically, and the results supported them. Specifically, using latent means and variances comparison, they discovered that Russian participants had a lower level of perceived autonomy support than their American counterparts. By using attenuated correlations among the latent constructs, researchers found that association between autonomy support and self-determined motivation and well-being were positive in both samples. But why were these MACS procedures necessary? Why not compare raw scores of the scales directly? And why is the calculation of latent means and the correlations among them recommended? Directly comparing the raw scores of the scales' means has some challenges. These scores represent the contributions of not only the constructs of interest, but also irrelevant constructs and various measurement errors within and between samples because of the biases (see above). Although, researchers have managed them by establishing the equivalences of the instruments at the stage of their adaptation, it is also necessary to take care of them statistically, to try to obtain an error-free estimation of the constructs and to confirm the measurements' invariance to answer research questions meaningfully. Only under this condition can any theoretically sound interpretations of cross-cultural data be drawn.

> Thus, demonstration of measurement equivalence is a logical prerequisite to the evaluation of substantive hypotheses regarding group differences, regardless of whether the comparison is as simple as a between-group mean differences test or as complex as testing whether some theoretical structural model is invariant across groups. (Vandenberg & Lance, 2000, p. 9)

MACS Procedures for Testing Measurement Invariance

A starting point of MACS analysis is presented on Fig 9.2.

Constructs A and B (latent variables) are measured in two groups by questionnaires with three items (manifest variables) each. The arrows from the constructs to the items indicate that the variations in the manifest variables are accounted for by the variations in the constructs. The measurement is imperfect, meaning that the variance of the items is also accounted for by other

Quantitative Comparative Studies **247**

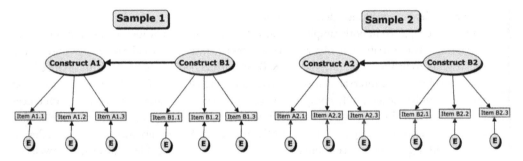

FIGURE 9.2 Comparing two constructs and their corresponding tests across two samples. This figure was made with IHMC Cmap Tools

uncontrolled latent variables and by measurement errors. That is why there are arrows from the errors of measurement (E) to the manifest variables. The higher the reliability and validity of the instruments, the lower the measurement errors. That is why reliability and validity must be evaluated and reported before such an analysis. Researchers want to compare the means of the constructs A1 and A2 and constructs B1 and B2 (mean analysis). They also want to test the equality of the relations between these constructs across groups (functional equivalence and/or equality of relations related to research questions). In order to do this correctly, they have to reassure the measurement invariance of all measures. In the following presentation, I use the reviews that summarized the measurement invariance procedures for applied researchers (Gregorich, 2006; Little, 1997; Steenkamp & Baumgartner, 1998; Vandenberg, 2002; Vandenberg & Lance, 2000).

MI analysis starts with a variance-covariance matrix with a mean vector calculated for all measured variables within each sample. The mean vector is a set of means of the variables and the variance-covariance matrix has variances of the variables on the diagonal and covariances between the variables on the rest positions. Statistical programs automatically calculate these vectors and matrices out of the raw data or transform the correlational matrices supplied with means and standard deviations for each variable into them.

a. First one should conduct "an omnibus test of the equality of covariance matrices across groups, that is, a test of the null hypothesis of invariant covariance matrices (i.e., $\Sigma g = \Sigma g'$), where g and g' indicate different groups" (Vandenberg & Lance, 2000, p. 12). It is commonly accepted that

> if covariance matrices do not differ across groups, then ME/I [measurement equivalence/invariance] is established, and further tests of the other aspects of measurement equivalence are not necessary. . . . If, however, groups' covariance matrices differ, then investigation into the specific source of the lack of equivalence is warranted. (p. 19)

b. If it is discovered that the covariance matrices differ (which is frequently the case), then *configural invariance* is tested by comparing a configuration of factor loadings of the items in each version of an instrument on the factors. The configural invariance holds when the items' loadings on nonrelevant factors are constrained to zero in both samples, and loadings on relevant factor(s) are significantly different from zero and freely estimated (no constraints imposed across samples (Steenkamp & Baumgartner, 1998; Vandenberg & Lance, 2000). Configural invariance does not require loadings of items on factors to be similar across samples; it simply indicates that a model with a specified items' configuration fits data in both samples well.

c. *Metric invariance* is established next by testing the equality of factor loadings of the same items on the same factor(s) in both samples. Because factor loadings indicate how variations in latent variables relate to variations in observed scores "metric invariance can be tested by constraining the loadings to be the same" (Steenkamp & Baumgartner, 1998, p. 80). Metric invariance indicates equality of scale intervals across countries, and when it is established "difference scores on the item can be meaningfully compared across countries, and these observed item differences are indicative of similar cross-national differences in the underlying construct" (p. 80). (See the procedures and examples in Little, 1997; Steenkamp & Baumgartner, 1998; Train, 2009). Researchers argue whether configural invariance is enough to establish construct equivalence (Steenkamp & Baumgarten, 1998) or if metric invariance must also be determined (Byrne & Campbell, 1999). But in any case, neither of these forms of invariance allows a researcher to do latent means comparisons across samples. For these comparisons scalar invariance is required.

d. *Scalar invariance* allows a researcher to make meaningful means comparisons across samples. "It addresses the question of whether there is consistency between cross-national differences in latent means and cross-national differences in observed means" (Steenkamp & Baumgartner, 1998, p. 80). This type of invariance is tested by constraining the intercepts of corresponding items' regressions on the latent variable(s) to be equal (Vandenberg and Lance, 2000, p. 12). For the technical details of how to do this, see: Steenkamp & Baumgartner (1998) and Little (1997).

Other forms of invariance testing are:

Factor covariance invariance is tested by imposing equality constraints on the covariances between/among the latent variables in all samples.

Factor variance invariance is tested by constraining the variances of the latent constructs to be the same across samples. "If both the factor variances and covariances are invariant, the correlations between the latent constructs are invariant across countries" (Steenkamp & Baumgartner, 1998, p. 80). Factor variance-covariance invariance is important for establishing the invariance of the latent constructs' associations across samples.

Error variance invariance is the final constraint that can be tested, when "the amount of measurement error is invariant across countries. . . . If items are metrically invariant, and if the error variances and factor variances are cross-nationally invariant, the items are equally reliable across countries" (p. 81). Little (1997) called this form of invariance "strict factorial invariance" (p. 55) and did not consider it suitable for meaningful cross-cultural comparisons.

Full and Partial Invariance

In testing MI for practical purposes, it is important to differentiate *full* and *partial invariance* (Byrne, Shavelson, & Muthen, 1989; Byrne & Watkins, 2003; Gregorich, 2006; Steenkamp & Baumgartner, 1998). Situations when the omnibus test of the variance-covariance matrices' equality is held are pretty rare if ever achievable. In cases when some constraints are inadmissible, researchers talk about *partial measurement invariance*. Steenkamp and Baumgartner (1998) mention that full MI is "a reasonable ideal" (p. 81), and that researchers have to expect deviations from it. But how far can such deviations go and still be considered invariant measures? To answer this question, researchers have to start with the *partial configural invariance* that takes place when different factor structures emerge in different groups because some of the items load on different factors. To conduct further analysis, there has to be a subset of factors that are configurally invariant. For a meaningful cross-cultural analysis the zero loadings and some, but not necessarily all, of the salient loadings have to be invariant (p. 81). For *partial metric invariance* researchers have to establish the equality of factor loadings across samples for the configurally invariant factors. Steenkamp and Baumgartner (1998) indicated that in order to do further cross-cultural analysis, "at least one item (other than the one fixed to unity to define the scale of each latent construct) [has to be] metrically invariant" (p. 81).

At this point, making a decision about the acceptable level of partial MI should be guided both by theoretical—"which loadings should not be constrained to be equal across countries" (p. 81)—as well as pure statistical considerations—by evaluating the magnitude of various fit indices.

> If partial metric invariance is supported, *partial scalar invariance* [emphasis added] can be tested. The intercepts of those items that are not metrically invariant across groups are left unconstrained across countries, while the intercepts of the other items are (initially) held invariant. (p. 81)

To do a meaningful cross-national comparison of latent means, "metric and scalar invariance for at least two items per construct (or per factor if the construct is multidimensional) is required" (p. 82). To improve the reliability of the means estimate, researchers may decide to work with noninvariant items psychometrically-wise in order to increase their equivalence. When making decisions based on partial metric and scalar invariances, it is important to take into account theoretical and statistical considerations.

> Partial measurement invariance can also be investigated for the factor covariances, factor variances, and error variances. In testing for the equivalence of error invariance one would logically set free the invariance constraints on error variances of those items that were found not to have cross-nationally invariant factor loadings. (p. 82)

How to Use MI in Cross-Cultural Research

As mentioned, MI testing may help with evaluating construct equivalence, with comparing a construct's means, and with investigating relationships among constructs cross-culturally. According to Steenkamp and Baumgartner (1998), for the statistical verification of construct equivalence, configural invariance has to be established, where "the same pattern of (zero and nonzero) factor loadings [has to be] found in the different countries" (p. 82). Metric invariance—the equality of factor loadings—may be searched for, but is not necessary. To verify construct equivalence statistically, it is important that items in different samples fall on the same factors, not that the magnitude of the loadings is the same cross-culturally. As was mentioned before, some scholars believe that both configural and metric invariances are needed to verify construct equivalence. To conduct latent means comparison, partial metric and scalar invariance is required (at least two items per construct should be fully invariant). "If this is not the case, comparing scores cross-nationally is meaningless since the measurement scales are fundamentally different across countries" (p. 82). If researchers strive to establish construct equivalence by relating the constructs of interest with other relevant constructs, "full or partial metric invariance has to be satisfied because the scale intervals of the latent constructs have to be comparable across countries. Scalar invariance is not required because no absolute comparisons of scale scores are conducted" (p. 82). If researchers want to compare standardized measures of associations among constructs across samples, "factor variance invariance is required in addition to metric invariance" (p. 82).

Measures to Prevent Noninvariance

In addition to considering the construct, content, and linguistic equivalence of the measures thoroughly, there are other factors that should be taken care of to avoid measurement noninvariancee of controllable sources (van de Vijver & Leung, 2011).

a. The administration procedure must be standardized. Such standardization includes but is not limited to: developing a detailed administration protocol which specifies a standard way of conducting measurement procedures, providing instructions for research assistants, prescribing how to answer participants' questions, defining the degree of details about items and constructs that may be disclosed to participants, and some others. More attention should be paid to the administration of cognitive and ability tests, where the process of interaction between the researcher and participants is more complex and diverse than in cases of paper-and-pencil surveys or personality inventories. In some cases, research assistants who will be administering such tests should receive special training.
b. Samples should have content comparable with regard to major parameters: demographics (gender, age, education, socioeconomic status), psychological, and other relevant variables. As an example, van de Vijver and Leung (2011) discussed the level of education of participants from different cultural settings: "Studies involving widely different cultural groups cannot avoid the substantial difference in the educational background of the participants, which in turn may bias the cross-cultural differences obtained." (p. 28). They suggested reducing this sampling bias by "match[ing] participants from different groups on education by stratified sampling" (p. 28). For this way of control, the representativeness of the samples should also be monitored.
c. Participants' response style may obscure measurement invariance. Some styles include: *social desirability* (answering the questions not as one feels or thinks, but as it is prescribed by or expected by social norms), *acquiescence* (the tendency of participants to agree with questions regardless of how they really think or feel) and a response pattern with a stable tendency for using either extreme or middle categories on a response scale. Researchers may control for these biases by accounting for sample content—"individuals from less affluent, more collectivistic countries show more acquiescence and social desirability" (p. 28); or researchers may make adjustments to their instruments to avoid some of these biases. For example, changing the rating scale from 5 points to 10 points removed the tendency of Hispanics toward an extreme response style (Hui & Triandis, 1989). See also (Morren, Gelissen, & Vermunt, 2012)

Conclusion

This chapter is devoted to the important and hotly debated issues of measuring and quantitatively comparing the psychological and sociocultural characteristics of people across different cultural communities. Cultural universalists, who support the idea of such measurements, and cultural relativists, who deny the opportunity to make meaningful quantitative comparisons, are at the extreme poles in such debates. Regardless of the outcomes of these theoretically relevant arguments, the practical considerations in areas of education, health, immigration, and many others require that such measurements and comparisons be done. The central issue is construct equivalence, which must be established both theoretically and culturally. The construct equivalence examination is accompanied by considering the content and linguistic forms of equivalence. These types of equivalence should be tested statistically. Special attention should be paid to establishing the metric invariance of instruments through MACS analyses. Confirmatory factor analysis and structural equation modeling should be used to establish various kinds of invariance. Both theoretical and statistical considerations should be taken into account to state the invariance of the instruments and the equivalence of their results.

Questions

1. Discuss the main points of debate between cultural universalists and relativists regarding construct equivalence. What is your personal opinion on this matter? Justify your position.
2. What are the relationships between *equivalence* and *bias* in cross-cultural testing? What types of biases exist? What are the mechanisms of these biases and how do they distort tests' equivalence?
3. Analyze the biases articulated by Greenfield and Kleinman. Provide your own examples. Think about other forms of biases pertaining to personality tests, opinion surveys, and other measurement instruments.
4. Justify the logic of *construct validity/equivalence* testing.
5. Explain in your own words what *inductivist fallacy* (by Mulaik) means when using factor analysis for construct validity testing.
6. Explain what is a test's *content validity* and *content equivalence*. How does this form of equivalence relate to *linguistic equivalence*?
7. What are the differences between *forward-and-back* and *committee-based translations* of an instrument?
8. What are the differences between *centered* and *decentered translations*? Provide your own examples.
9. What is *cognitive interviewing* and how can this procedure and *focus groups* be used to establish linguistic equivalence?
10. What is *measurement invariance*? Explain it in your own words and provide examples of invariant and noninvariant instruments.
11. Without going into many statistical details, what is the meaning of each of the following forms of invariance: *dimensional, configural, metric, scalar, factor covariance, factor variance, error variance, and full and partial invariance.*
12. What is *partial measurement invariance* and how can it be practically used in cross-cultural measurements?
13. What are the measures for preventing measurement noninvariance?

Exercise

Construct equivalence examination. Take a psychological or behavioral concept that is relevant and self-evident in your cultural community. For example, an "outgoing person," "cool person," "self-made person," "sexy person," or such notions as "friend," "boy/girlfriend" or "soul mate." Students of different specializations may wish to investigate concepts from their own disciplines; for example, medical students may choose illnesses. Explore these concepts in your own community: What do people think about them, how do they understand them, and through what manifestations do they identify the presence of these constructs or attributes? If you decide to measure these attributes, what items will you use? Imagine that you decided to measure the "coolness" of a person in another cultural community. How would you approach this task? Outline and justify your plan. If you have time, implement this plan. Try to follow and consider most of the recommendations in this chapter.

Glossary

Bias: A systematic distortion of the result of measurements due to particular factors. There are different sources of bias in cross-cultural testing: *construct, method* and *item biases,* as well as *ethnocentric bias, response bias, procedure bias, cognition bias, communication bias,* and some others.

Categorical fallacy: This error happens when researchers "superimpose their own cultural categories on some sample of deviant behavior in other cultures, as if their own illness categories were culture-free" (Kleinman, 1977, p. 4). Another term for this is *ethnocentric construct bias*, meaning that researchers assume that the constructs they study are nearly universal and their equivalence is a priori presumed without empirical evidence.

Centering (close translation) refers to a translation of the source language instrument to the target language that is as close to the original as possible.

Decentering (decentered translation) is a translation in which researchers keep the construct of instruments intact but modify its linguistic manifestation in the target (and sometimes on the source culture(s)).

Equivalence: Equivalent "from late Latin *aequivalent-, aequivalere* 'be of equal worth'. **1** equal in value, amount, function, meaning, etc. > **(equivalent to)** having the same or a similar effect as" (Soanes & Stevenson, 2008)). "Equivalence refers to the level of comparability of measurement outcomes" (van de Vijver & Leung, 2011, p. 19). Different forms of equivalence:

> **Construct (concept) equivalence** means that the test scores from different samples have the same theoretical and psychological meanings.
> **Content equivalence** is concerned with how well test items represent the universe of possible manifestations of a psychological construct, covering all relevant domains in all samples.
> **Functional equivalence:** is a form of the statistical verification of construct equivalence. A construct is functionally equivalent across cultures if a questionnaire that measures it has "a similar pattern of convergent and divergent validity (i.e., nonzero correlations with presumably related measures and zero correlations with presumably unrelated measures)" (van de Vijver & Leung, 2011, pp. 20–21).
> **Linguistic and semantic equivalence:** manifestations of a psychological construct have to have linguistically comparable connotations across samples: they have to be expressed in words and sentences that convey the same (or similar) meanings to participants from culturally different samples.
> **Structural equivalence:** one of the forms of statistical verification of construct equivalence. This form of equivalence is typically tested by applying either exploratory or confirmatory factor analysis to the items from the same instruments administered in different samples. The same number of factors and similar configurations of items across factors indicate the structural equivalence of the instrument.

Measurement invariance: establishes the equivalence of measurement instruments in the quantitative forms. Individuals with the same amount of the construct have the same standing in either of the samples, regardless of which scale has been used, original or translated. Establishing invariance allows researchers to compare the means and structural relations of the constructs error free. Forms of invariance include: *dimensional, configural, metric, scalar, factor covariance, factor variance, error variance,* and *full* and *partial invariance*.

Nomological network: represents the theory behind the construct: "The laws in a nomological network may relate (a) observable properties or quantities to each other; or (b) theoretical constructs to observables; or (c) different theoretical constructs to one another" (Cronbach & Meehl, 1955, p. 290).

Recommended Reading

Beaton, D. E., Bombardier, C., Guillemin, F., & Ferraz, M. B. (2000). Guidelines for the process of cross-cultural adaptation of self-report measures. *Spine, 25*(24), 3186–3191.

Brislin, R. W. (1986). The wording and translation of research instruments. In W. J. Lonner & J. W. Berry (Eds.), *Field methods in cross-cultural research* (pp. 137–164). Beverly Hills, CA: Sage

Flaherty, J. A., Gavira, F. M., Pathak, D., Mitchel, T., Wintrob, R., Richman, J. A., & Birz, S. (1988). Developing instruments for cross-cultural psychiatric research. *The Journal of Nervous and Mental Disease, 176*(5), 257–263.

Guillemin, F., Bombardier, C., & Beaton, D. (1993). Cross-cultural adaptation of health-related quality of life measures: Literature review and proposed guidelines. *Journal of Clinical Epidemiology, 46*(12), 1417–1432.

Hambleton, R. K., Merenda, P. F., & Spielberger, C. D. (Eds.). (2005). *Adapting educational and psychological tests for cross-cultural assessment*. Mahwah, NJ: Lawrence Erlbaum.

Harkness, J. A., van de Vijver, F.J.R., & Mohler, P. P. (Eds.). (2003). *Cross-cultural survey methods*. New York, NY: John Wiley & Sons.

Matsumoto, D., & van de Vijver, F.J.R. (Eds.). (2011). *Cross-cultural research methods in psychology*. Cambridge, UK: Cambridge University Press.

Tran, T. V. (2009). *Developing cross-cultural measurement*. Oxford, UK: Oxford University Press

References

Ægisdóttir, S., Gerstein, L. H., & Çinarbas, D. C. (2008). Methodological issues in cross-cultural counseling research: Equivalence, bias, and translations. *The Counseling Psychologist, 36*(2), 188–219.

Barrett, P. T., Petrides, K. V., Eysenck, S.B.G., & Eysenck, H. J. (1998). The Eysenck Personality Questionnaire: an examination of the factorial similarity of P, E, N, and L across 34 countries. *Personality and Individual Differences, 25*(5), 805–819.

Beaton, D. E., Bombardier, C., Guillemin, F., & Ferraz, M. B. (2000). Guidelines for the process of cross-cultural adaptation of self-report measures. *Spine, 25*(24), 3186–3191.

Beatty, P. C., & Willis, G. B. (2007). Research synthesis: The practice of cognitive interviewing. *Public Opinion Quarterly, 71*(2), 287–311.

Billiet, J. (2003). Cross-cultural equivalence with structural equation modeling. In J. A. Harkness, F.J.R. van de Vijver & P. P. Mohler (Eds.), *Cross-cultural survey methods* (pp. 247–264). New York, NY: John Wiley & Sons.

Boski, P. (2008). Five meanings of integration in acculturation research. *International Journal for Intercultural Relations, 32*(2), 142–153.

Brislin, R. W. (1976). *Translation: Applications and research*. New York, NY: Gardner Press.

Brislin, R. W. (1986). The wording and translation of research instruments. In W. J. Lonner & J. W. Berry (Eds.), *Field methods in cross-cultural research* (pp. 137–164). Beverly Hills, CA: Sage.

Brown, T. (2015). *Confirmatory factor analysis for applied research*. (2nd ed.). New York, NY: Guilford.

Butcher, J. N., Lim, J., & Nezami, E. (1998). Objective study of abnormal personality in cross-cultural settings: The Minnesota Multiphasic Personality Inventory (MMPI-2). *Journal of Cross-Cultural Psychology, 29*(1), 189–211.

Byrne, B. M. (2006). *Structural equation modeling with EQS: Basic concepts, applications, and programming*. (2nd ed.). New York, NY: Psychology Press.

Byrne, B. M., & Campbell, T. L. (1999). Cross-cultural comparisons and the presumption of equivalent measurement and theoretical structure: A look beneath the surface. *Journal of Cross-Cultural Psychology, 30*(5), 555–574.

Byrne, B. M., Shavelson, R. J., & Muthen, B. (1989). Testing for the equivalence of factor covariance and means structures: The issue of partical measurement invariance. *Psychological Bulletin, 105*(3), 456–466.

Byrne, B. M., & Watkins, D. (2003). The issue of measurement invariance revisited. *Journal of Cross-Cultural Psychology, 34*(2), 155–175.

Caprara, G. V., Barbaranelli, C., Bermúdez, J., Maslach, C., & Ruch, W. (2000). Multivariate methods for the comparison of factor structures in cross-cultural research: An illustration with the Big Five Questionnaire. *Journal of Cross-Cultural Psychology, 31*(4), 437–464.

Chirkov, V., & Ryan, R. M. (2001). Parent and teacher autonomy-support in Russian and U.S. adolescents: Common effects on well-being and academic motivation. *Journal of Cross-Cultural Psychology, 32*(5), 618–635.

Chirkov, V., Ryan, R. M., Kim, Y., & Kaplan, U. (2003). Differentiating autonomy from individualism and independence: A self-determination theory perspective on internalization of cultural orientations and well-being. *Journal of Personality and Social Psychology, 84*(1), 97–110.

Chirkov, V., Ryan, R. M., & Willness, C. (2005). Cultural context and psychological needs in Canada and Brazil: Testing a self-determination approach to internalization of cultural practices, identity and well-being. *Journal of Cross-Cultural Psychology, 36*(4), 425–443.

Cronbach, L., & Meehl, P. E. (1955). Construct validity in psychological tests. *Psychological Bulletin, 52*(4), 281–302.

Cruz, F.A.D., Padilla, G. V., & Agustin, E. O. (2000). Adapting a measure of acculturation for cross-cultural research. *Journal of Transcultural Nursing, 11*(3), 191–198.

Davidov, E., Schmidt, P., & Billiet, J. (Eds.). (2010). *Cross-cultural analysis: Methods and applications.* New York, NY: Routledge.

Dimitrov, D. M. (2010). Testing for factorial invariance in the context of construct validation. *Measurement and Evaluation in Counseling and Development, 43*(2), 121–149.

Eyton, J., & Neuwirth, G. (1984). Cross-cultural validity: Ethnocentrism in health studies with special reference to the Vietnamese. *Social Science & Medicine, 18*(5), 447–453.

Field, A. (2013). *Discovering statistics using IBM SPSS statistics* (4th ed.). London, UK: Sage.

Fischer, R., & Fontaine, J.R.J. (2011). Methods for investigating structural equivalence. In D. Matsumoto & F.J.R. van de Vijver (Eds.), *Cross-cultural research methods in psychology* (pp. 179–215). Cambridge, UK: Cambridge University Press.

Fitzpatrick, A. R. (1983). The meaning of content validity. *Applied Psychological Measurement, 7*(1), 3–13.

Flaherty, J. A., Gavira, F. M., Pathak, D., Mitchel, T., Wintrob, R., Richman, J. A., & Birz, S. (1988). Developing instruments for cross-cultural psychiatric research. *The Journal of Nervous and Mental Disease, 176*(5), 257–263.

Fontaine, J.R.J. (2003). Multidimensional scaling. In J. A. Harkness, F.J.R. van de Vijver & P. P. Mohler (Eds.), *Cross-cultural survey methods* (pp. 235–246). New York, NY: John Wiley & Sons.

Fuller, T. D., Edwards, J. N., Vorakitphokatorn, S., & Sermsri, S. (1993). Using focus groups to adapt survey instruments to new populations: Experience from a developing country. In D. L. Morgan (Ed.), *Successful focus groups: Advancing the state of the art* (pp. 89–104). Newbury Park, CA: Sage.

Georgas, J., Weiss, L. G., van de Vijver, F.J.R., & Saklofske, D. H. (Eds.). (2003). *Culture and children's intelligence: Cross-cultural analysis of the WISC-III.* San Diego, CA: Academic Press.

Greenfield, P. M. (1997). You can't take it with you: Why ability assessments don't cross cultures. *American Psychologist, 52*(10), 1115–1124.

Gregorich, S. E. (2006). Do self-report instruments allow meaningful comparisons across diverse population groups? Testing measurement invariance using the confirmatory factor analysis framework. *Medical Care, 44*(11), S78-S94. doi: 10.2307/41219508

Guillemin, F., Bombardier, C., & Beaton, D. (1993). Cross-cultural adaptation of health-related quality of life measures: Literature review and proposed guidelines. *Journal of Clinical Epidemiology, 46*(12), 1417–1432.

Hambleton, R. K., Merenda, P. F., & Spielberger, C. D. (Eds.). (2005). *Adapting educational and psychological tests for cross-cultural assessment.* Mahwah, NJ: Lawrence Erlbaum.

Hambleton, R. K., & Zenisky, A. L. (2011). Translating and adapting tests for cross-cultural assessments. In D. Matsumoto & F.J.R. van de Vijver (Eds.), *Cross-cultural research methods in psychology* (pp. 46–70). Cambridge, UK: Cambridge University Press.

Harkness, J. A. (2003). Questionnaire translation. In J. A. Harkness, F.J.R. van de Vijver & P. P. Mohler (Eds.), *Cross-cultural survey methods* (pp. 35–56). New York, NY: John Wiley & Sons.

Harkness, J. A., van de Vijver, F.J.R., & Johnson, T. P. (2003). Questionnaire design in comparative research. In J. A. Harkness, F.J.R. van de Vijver & P. P. Mohler (Eds.), *Cross-cultural survey methods* (pp. 19–34). New York, NY: John Wiley & Sons.

Harkness, J. A., van de Vijver, F.J.R., & Mohler, P. P. (Eds.). (2003). *Cross-cultural survey methods.* New York, NY: John Wiley & Sons.

Helms, J. E. (1992). Why is there no study of cultural equivalence in standardized cognitive ability testing? *American Psychologist, 47*(2), 1083–1101.

Hines, A. M. (1993). Linking qualitative and quantitative methods in cross-cultural survey research: Techniques from cognitive science. *American Journal of Community Psychology, 21*(6), 729–746.

Hughes, D., & DuMont, K. (1993). Using focus groups to facilitate culturally anchored research. *American Journal of Community Psychology, 21*(6), 775–803.

Hui, C. H., & Triandis, H. C. (1989). Effects of culture and response format on extreme response style. *Journal of Cross-Cultural Psychology, 20*,(3) 296–309.

Kleinman, A. M. (1977). Depression, somatization and the "new cross-cultural psychiatry". *Social Science & Medicine, 11*(1), 3–10.

Kleinman, A. M., Eisenberg, L., & Good, B. (1978). Culture, illness, and care: Clinical lessons from anthropological and cross-cultural research. *Annals of Internal Medicine, 88*(2), 251–258.

Kleinman, A. M., & Good, B. (1985). Introduction: Culture and depression. In A. Kleinman & B. Good (Eds.), *Culture and depression: Studies in the anthropology and cross-cultural psychiatry of affect and disorder* (pp. 1–32). Berkeley, CA: University of California Press.

Koot, H. M., Oord, G.V.D. Verhulst, P. C., & Boomsma, D. I. (1997). Behavioral and emotional problems in young preschoolers: Cross-cultural testing of the validity of the Child Behavior Checklist/2–3. *Journal of Abnormal Child Psychology, 25*(3), 183–196.

Little, T. D. (1997). Mean and covariance structures (MACS) analysis of cross-cultural data: Practical and theoretical issues. *Multivariate Behavioral Research, 32*(1), 53–76.

MacCorquodale, K., & Meehl, P. E. (1948). On a distinction between hypothetical constructs and intervening variables. *Psychological Review, 55*(2), 95–107.

Malda, M., van de Vijver, F.J.R., Srinivasan, K., Transler, C., & Sukumar, P. (2010). Traveling with cognitive tests: Testing the validity of a KABC-II adaptation in India. *Assessment, 17*(1).

Malda, M., van de Vijver, F.J.R., Spinivasan, K., Transler, C., Sukumar, P., & Rao, K. (2008). Adapting a cognitive test for a different culture: An illustration of qualitative procedures. *Psychology Science Quarterly, 50*(4), 451–468.

Marsella, A. J., Dubanoski, J., Hamada, W. C., & Morse, H. (2000). The measurement of personality across cultures: Historical, conceptual, and methodological issues and considerations. *American Behavioral Scientist, 44*(1), 41–62.

Marsella, A. J., Sartorius, N., JableBerkeley, CA: University of California Press.

McCrae, R. R., & Allik, J. (Eds.). (2002). *The five-factor model of personality across cultures*. New York, NY: Kluwer Academic/Plenum Publishers.

McCrae, R. R., & Costa, P.T. J. (1997). Personality trait structure as a human universal. *American Psychologist, 52*(5), 509–516.

Messick, S. (1995). Standards of validity and the validity of standards in performance assessment. *Educational Measurement: Issues and Practice, 14*(4), 5–8.

Morgan, D. L. (Ed.). (1991). *Successful focus groups: Advancing the state of the art*. Newbury Park, CA: Sage.

Morren, M., Gelissen, J.P.T.M., & Vermunt, J. K. (2012). Response strategies and response styles in cross-cultural surveys. *Cross-Cultural Research, 46*(3), 255–279.

Mulaik, S. A. (1987). A brief history of the philosophical foundations of exploratory factor analysis. *Multivariate Behavioral Research, 22*(3), 267–305.

Nápoles-Springer, A. M., Santoyo-Olsson, J., O'Brien, H., & Stewart, A. L. (2006). Using cognitive interviews to develop surveys in diverse populations. *Medical Care, 44*(11), S21-S30.

Nassar-McMillan, S. C., & Borders, L. D. (2002). Use of focus groups in survey item development. *The Qualitative Report, 7*(1), Retrieved from http://www.nova.edu/ssss/QR/QR2017–2011/nassar.html

Nunnally, J. C., & Bernstein, I. H. (1978). *Psychometric theory* (3rd ed.). Boston, MA: McGraw-Hill College.

Pett, M. A., Lackey, N. R., & Sullivan, J. J. (2003). *Making sense of factor analysis: The use of factor analysis for instrument development in health care research*. London, UK: Sage.

Ployhart, R. E., & Oswald, F. L. (2004). Applications of Mean and Covariance Structure Analysis: Integrating correlational and experimental approaches. *Organizational Research Methods, 7*(1), 27-65. doi: 10.1177/1094428103259554

Poortinga,Y. H. (1989). Equivalence of cross-cultural data: An overview of basic issues. *International Journal of Psychology, 24*(6), 737–756.

Riordan, C. M., & Vandenberg, R. J. (1994). A central question in cross-cultural research: Do employees of different cultures interpret work-related measures in an equivalent manner? *Journal of Management, 20*(3), 643–671.

Rudmin, F. W., & Ahmadzadeh, V. (2001). Psychometric critique of acculturation psychology: The case of Iranian migrants in Norway. *Scandinavian Journal of Psychology, 42*(1), 41–56.

Schaffer, B. S., & Riordan, C. M. (2003). A review of cross-cultural methodologies for organizational research: A best-practices approach. *Organizational Research Methods, 6*(2), 169–215.

Sechrest, L., Fay, T., & Zaidi, S. M. (1972). Problems of translation in cross-cultural research. *Journal of Cross-Cultural Psychology, 3*(1), 41–56.

Siaki, L. A. (2011). Translating questions for use with Samoan adults: Lessons learned. *Journal of Transcultural Nursing, 22*(2), 122–128.

Smith, T. W. (2003). Developing comparable questions in cross-national survey. In J. A. Harkness, F. J. R. van de Vijver & P. P. Mohler (Eds.), *Cross-cultural survey methods* (pp. 69–92). New York, NY: John Wiley & Sons.

Soanes, C., & Stevenson, A. (Eds.). (2008). *Concise Oxford English dictionary* (11th ed.). Oxford, UK: Oxford University Press.

Sperber, A. D., Devellis, R. F., & Boehlecke, B. (1994). Cross-cultural translation: Methodology and validation. *Journal of Cross-Cultural Psychology, 25*(4), 501–524.

Steenkamp, J.-B.E.M., & Baumgartner, H. (1998). Assessing measurement invariance in cross-national consumer research. *Journal of Consumer Research, 25*(1), 78–90.

Sun, H., & Hernandez, D. (2012). Testing structural invariance of the Achievement Goal Questionnaire in American, Chinese, and Dutch college students. *Measurement and Evaluation in Counseling and Development, 45*(4), 257–269.

Tabachnick, B. G., & Fidell, L. S. (2012). *Using multivariate statistics.* (6th ed.). New York, NY: Pearson.

Thompson, B., & Daniel, L. G. (1996). Factor analytic evidence for the construct validity of scores: A historical overview and some guidelines. *Educational and Psychological Measurement, 56*(2), 197–208.

Tran, T. V. (2009). *Developing cross-cultural measurement.* Oxford, UK: Oxford University Press.

Tran, T. V., Ngo, D., & Conway, K. (2003). A cross-cultural measure of depressive symptoms among Vietnamese Americans. *Social Work Research, 27*(1), 56–64.

Ungar, M., & Liebenberg, L. (2011). Assessing resilience across cultures using mixed methods: Construction of the Child and Youth Resilience Measure. *Journal of Mixed Methods Research, 5*(2), 126–149.

van de Vijver, F. J. R., & Leung, K. (1997). *Methods and data analysis for cross-cultural research.* Thousands Oaks, CA: Sage.

van de Vijver, F. J. R., & Leung, K. (2011). Equivalence and bias: A review of concepts, models, and data analytic procedures. In D. Matsumoto & F. J. R. van de Vijver (Eds.), *Cross-cultural research methods in psychology.* Cambridge, UK: Cambridge University Press.

van Hemert, D. A., van de Vijver, F. J. R., Poortinga, Y. H., & Georgas, J. (2002). Structural and functional equivalence of the Eysenck Personality Questionnaire within and between countries. *Personality and Individual Differences, 33*(6), 1229–1249.

Vandenberg, R. J. (2002). Toward a further understanding of and improvement in measurement invariance methods and procedures. *Organizational Research Methods, 5*(2), 139–158.

Vandenberg, R. J., & Lance, C. E. (2000). A review and synthesis of the measurement invariance literature: Suggestions, practices, and recommendations for organizational research. *Organizational Research Methods, 13*(1), 4–70.

Werner, O., & Campbell, D. (1970). Translating, working through interpreters, and the problem of decentering. In R. Naroll & R. Cohen (Eds.), *A handbook of method in cultural anthropology* (pp. 398–420). New York, NY: Natural History Press.

Wheelan, S. A., Buzarglo, G., & Tsumura, E. (1998). Developing assessment tools for cross-cultural group research. *Small Group Research, 29*(3), 359–370.

Willis, G. B. (2004). *Cognitive interviewing: A tool for improving questionnaire design.* Thousand Oaks, CA: Sage.

Wong, J. P.-H., & Poon, M. K.-L. (2010). Bringing translation out of the shadows: Translation as an issue of methodological significance in cross-cultural qualitative research. *Journal of Transcultural Nursing, 21*(2), 151–158.

10
ETHNOGRAPHY

This chapter will:

- Present and discuss the major objectives and challenges of using ethnography for culture and psychology research
- Connect ethnographic investigation with the theory of cultural models
- Link ethnography with the interpretivist abductive inquiry
- Examine some practical aspects of ethnography
  - Entering the field
  - Doing participant observation
  - Conducting ethnographic person-centered interviewing
  - Analyzing ethnographic data.

Introduction

The term *ethnography* comes from the Greek words *ethnos*—people, nation, tribe, and *graphia*—description, writing. It means a description of people, their ways of life, customs, and traditions. Ethnography is often discussed as *ethnographic fieldwork* or simply *fieldwork*, where "the field is the natural, nonlaboratory setting or location where the activities in which a researchers is interested take place" (Schensul, Schensul, & LeCompte, 1999, p. 70). Ethnography is a not a particular method; it is an approach that has many variations and incorporates different methods and techniques for data generation. It is also a way of thinking about sociocultural worlds and the people inhabiting them, how to research them, and how to discover new knowledge about both cultures and people.

Ethnography was initially introduced and elaborated upon by anthropologists as *the* method to study cultures and people's ways of life in these cultures. Later, it was embraced by sociologists to study different social communities from the inside, by psychologists to study people's behaviors and experiences under different conditions and in different locations, and later researchers in nursing, education, organizations, and other social institutions. Right now, ethnography is considered to be a full-fledged methodological approach by almost all social and human sciences and is treated as the most characteristic representation of a so-called "qualitative" approach to scientific research.

What is Ethnography? Ethnography's Complexities and Problems, and Their Resolutions

To define the content of ethnography for culture and psychology research, it is useful to use Richard Shweder's insights about this topic (1996, 1997). Shweder is one of the most psychologically oriented cultural anthropologists and one of the most culturally sensitive cultural psychologists, so his opinion of these two sides of the inquiry is valuable and insightful.

According to Shweder (1996), "true ethnography" (p. 15) starts with identifying "the relevant moral communities that are embedded within any complex society" (p. 34) that a researcher wants to investigate. "Moral communities" are "social collectivities" that are "'composed of individuals who are parties to sets of arrangement, conventions, and agreements,' [here he used Greenwood's definition] and they must be distinguished from mere 'aggregate groups' (for example, all Americans who happen to be Mexican decent)" (p. 34). These moral or, as they are labeled in this book, cultural communities and their members are the primary units of analysis for culture and psychology ethnographic investigations. Members of these communities have constructed "models of and for their own behavior" (p. 48). These cultural models include but are not limited to "the beliefs about person, society, and nature, as well as the worthy and unworthy motives, and desires, and goals" (p. 27), "different preferences (values, goals, tastes, desires, ideals of personal well-being)", "different constraints (information, causal beliefs, abilities, dispositions, resources, technology, systems of domination or control)" (p. 17), and different systems of meanings of events, things, activities, beliefs, and preferences. These models are used to regulate people's social interactions and practices as they unfold in their everyday lives. These models are about intentional things, like "education," "job," "dating" "marriage," "parenting," and myriads of other social institutions that are brought to life by people's intentional states: by their thoughts, expectations, feelings, and beliefs about these things (Shweder, 1991, p. 75). Cultural models are co-created by a culture's members and are intersubjectively shared by them, which makes these models an invisible but powerful causal force that drives individuals' actions and structures their experiences (see Chapter 2 on the theory of cultural models). "Members of a culture are members of a moral community who work to coconstruct a shared reality [cultural models] and who act as though they were parties to an agreement to behave rationally within the terms of the realities they share" (Shweder, 1996, p. 20). The intentional nature of cultural models that are intersubjectively shared and understood by members of cultural communities makes these models the central point of any culture and psychology research, because in such models the human psyche and social institutions become mutually constitutive parts of the co-constructed social and mental realities. Therefore, it is impossible to understand why people do what they do in different sociocultural settings without investigating the public *inter*subjective as well as the internalized and private *intra*subjective aspects of cultural models.

Thus, the objective of ethnography for culture and psychology studies is twofold: (1) to uncover the cultural models of moral/cultural communities and (2) to investigate "the structure of other minds" (p. 20). This is the central point of any culture and psychology ethnographic study: to inquire about the representative and regulative models that are collectively constructed and collectively used by members of communities, as well as the mentalities, subjectivities, and behaviors of these members as these mentalities are formed and structured by the internalized aspects of these models and people's own experiences. These two forms of ethnographic knowledge—about cultural models and about the mental representations of them in individual minds—can be used to address and further investigate the problems and issues that these communities may struggle with: unemployment, criminality, low health status, poverty, and many others.

The Challenges of Ethnography and Their Resolutions

These two facets of the ethnographic inquiry create difficulties for researchers. Let's discuss some of them.

Investigating Communal Cultural Models

The real challenge of ethnography is how to infer these models and how to get into other minds while still remaining within the frameworks of the scientific enterprise. The primary difficulty of uncovering cultural models is that they are hidden from and unobservable by both members of communities and ethnographers. They are taken for granted, which means that the members do not reflect on them and use then automatically and habitually; this makes it difficult for researchers to elicit them. With regard to reading other minds, social scholars debate if this is even possible. And if the answer is "'Yes," then they question how to do this and how valid these readings are. If the answer is "No," then the whole ethnographic enterprise as a scientific investigation is in serious jeopardy. Shweder and many other anthropologists are sure of the validity of ethnographic investigations, and their logic is the following.

Ethnography starts with investigating and describing "the sanctionable behavior (the 'normal' discourse and praxis) of members of a moral community" (p. 26). These are the ways of life of these people, their everyday practices and routines, like forms of greetings, ways of disciplining children, eating, sleeping, driving, dating, making love, their typical conversations and discourses, and many other things, events, and customs that constitute the fabric of people's social lives. In Chapter 4, listing and naming these behaviors was characterized as "thin" descriptions. These observable behaviors and verbal discourses are symptoms and manifestations of the unobservable cultural models that drive them. An ethnographer's goal is to infer these models in the form of conjectures and hypotheses, which can later be subjected to further empirical testing and verification. This is how Shweder (1996) presented this issue:

> To get things started, allow me to suggest that we think about the thing called a culture as nothing other than a plausible hypothetical model, . . . which represents the shared and relatively enduring preferences and constraints exhibited in the observable behavior of a designated network of individuals who are tied to each other as members of some self-sanctioning moral community. Accordingly, the methods of true ethnography are designed to reveal things called preferences and constraints, including those that may be taken for granted by members of a moral community, that may be implicit in their behavior, difficult for them to notice, or socially undesirable for them to articulate or disclose under even the most ideal communicative circumstances. (p. 20)

As attentive readers probably noticed, this quote nearly perfectly describes the initial stages of the process of abductive inference, which was articulated in Chapter 4 with regard to interpretivism, as it is applied to the dynamic of the ethnographic "diving" into the intentional worlds of others. Shweder agrees with this conclusion by saying that "true ethnography is an interpretive study" (p. 26).

Another concept that should be used here is a "thick" description/interpretation as it was presented in Chapter 4. A "thick" interpretation is an inference about the hidden systems of meaning, cultural models, and assumptions that guide people's everyday practices. Participant observations and interviews are the primary sources of information for these abductive inferences. Participant observation not only provides researchers with descriptive accounts of activities of interest, but it also provides an opportunity for ethnographers to learn about and internalize these models and then get access to them through personal reflections (see further in this chapter). Interviews of members of cultural communities may also provide evidence about the content and structure of cultural models, but these interviews cannot be treated as the ultimate truth about these models.

This verbal or "evaluative discourse" (p. 48), as Shweder called it, should be considered as another set of important information for abductive conjecture about the models.

> The observation of everyday evaluative discourse by members of a moral community offers the ethnographer a glimpse of the official cultural model constructed by insiders to represent to themselves and (sometimes) to others the meanings exhibited in their own behavior. (p. 48)

The art of ethnography then is to generate and collect reliable, valid, and informative observations regarding evaluative discourses, practices, and ways of life, and then skillfully infer the cultural models that may lie behind these observations. The logic of such an inquiry is in no way different from the thinking of a detective who is investigating a murder case or a physician who is working on a patient's diagnosis. An ethnographic investigation of cultural models is a legitimate scientific enterprise within the interpretivist (and in some cases realist) paradigm with the help of the abductive and retroductive modes of inference.

Getting to the Minds of Others

The challenge of getting into other minds, where researchers want to investigate what members of communities think and feel when they are guided by the cultural models in their everyday functioning, is another challenging task for an ethnographer. It is important to remind readers that this psychological aspect of ethnographic research aims toward understanding people's individual systems of meaning, which are constituted by the internalized aspects of cultural models as well as by the idiosyncratic systems representing their unique life experiences (see Chapters 2 and 4). These systems guide people's social activities and, in order to understand why people do what they do, it is important to uncover them. Is reading other minds possible? In Chapter 4 about interpretivism, the answer was "Yes, it is possible to get access to the individual systems of meanings that represent publicly shared cultural models." Ethnography is one of the best ways to do this.

> It is a central assumption of ethnography that, in order to understand what people are doing and why, one needs to understand the meanings involved: how they interpret and evaluate the situations they face, and their own identities. (Hammersley & Atkinson, 2007, p. 168)

Reading other minds is possible because of the intersubjective nature of intentional things that constitute cultural models. Intentional things exist because of the intentional states (beliefs, thoughts, feelings, and wants) members of a community have about these things. Money (an intentional thing) exists as a real enforcer and regulator of people's social actions only because people think of these pieces of paper as valuable and important commodities that they have to earn, save, spend, invest, inherit, or throw away. Money, as an intentional thing, is one of the most important components of communities' cultural models for work, entertainment, marriage, status, success, and many other things. In order for cultural models, which are based on the institution of money, to regulate people's behaviors, people have to share the intentional states that make money possible, and they need to know that others understand money the same way they do. This shared intersubjective understanding makes an investigation of other minds possible through the means of ethnography. As will be discussed further, ethnographers typically enter cultural communities to live and function there for a relatively prolonged period of time. They not only live there, but they also participate in everyday practices and customs, converse with people, listen to their stories, joke with them, and live more or less "the native way of life." This point is crucial. In order to live naturally and comfortably, an ethnographer has to learn and to some extent develop the intentional states about the intentional things that constitute natives' cultural models and ultimately their sociocultural realities. Successfully functioning in the host community means that an ethnographer has access to shared intentional states that become parts of his or her own mental representations, and it is his or her task to reflect on them, describe them, and then infer their structures, major dimensions, and modes of functioning. This is how Shweder (1997) described this aspect of ethnography:

> People have within themselves an enormous complexity of cognitive and emotional structures. Understanding others is a process by which you will find something within yourself that will be the bridge to understanding difference. It seems to me that without fieldwork it is impossible to reach that depth. (p. 162)

Thus, an ethnographer has access to other minds through entering the intentional worlds of others, through sharing with them the intersubjective mental states that are dialectically related to corresponding cultural models, and then reflecting on these models. Because these processes of entering, learning, and reflecting require time, ethnography cannot be done in a short period and requires months, if not years, of patient work to establish contact with natives, build relationships with them, and start functioning within their worlds. "True ethnography takes time. It requires some degree of rapport and a good deal of trust" (Shweder, 1996, p. 20). To infer these internalized intrasubjective components of cultural models, it requires knowledge of existing public cultural models, knowledge of the ethnographer's own cultural models that should be bracketed out at the time of an investigation, as well as a clear understanding of his or her own idiosyncratic mental representations, which should be differentiated from the learned aspects of the native cultural models. The researcher's high reflectivity, logical thinking, and insightful imagination constitute the core of the investigative process. "Ethnography is about discovery. Skillful ethnography is about making some room for the creative imagination and some disciplined intuition" (Shweder, 1997, p. 154). Although it is not that straightforward as in the case of inferring public cultural models, the process of abductive interpretation is also at the forefront here. Further on, this chapter will discuss the use of person-centered interviewing to elicit both public cultural models and individuals' internalized systems of meaning. To establish the validity of these abducted inferences, they should be empirically tested against the practices and realities of the communal life.

Some Practical Issues of Ethnographic Fieldwork

Selecting Settings and Entering the Field

Ethnography is not only about travelling abroad and investigating remote exotic communities. Ethnography can be done in your neighborhood by investigating schools, hospitals, campuses, aboriginal reserves, immigrant communities, and other local groups. In any ethnographic study, a researcher has to make several selections: to choose the settings, and within these settings to choose whom to observe and talk to, during what events and activities should these inquiries take place, and at what time and in what context this should happen. The main rule is that the research problem and research questions should be the guidelines for all these selections and considerations. But even if a problem has been clearly formulated, there is still plenty of room for choices regarding the technical aspects of research. Selecting the setting where to conduct ethnography and cases for investigation within this setting is of a primary concern to ethnographers.

Sampling the Settings

Selecting the setting or settings is the first important choice to be made. If a researcher is interested in the acculturation of immigrants, there are many communities of immigrants from different countries to choose from; if a researcher is interested in problems of aboriginal people in North America, he or she may study native people on reserves or in urban settings, may explore communities of aboriginal students on campuses, or may work in a school with a high percentage of aboriginal pupils. The choice or availability of a particular setting may correct if not change the research problem and questions. Even more, "in ethnographic research the development of research problems is rarely completed before fieldwork begins; indeed, the collection of primary data often plays a key role in that process of development" (Hammersley & Atkinson, 2007, pp. 28–29). Some research questions may not be able to be answered in a particular setting, so "the researcher is then faced with the choice of either dropping these questions from the investigation or re-starting the research in a setting where they *can* be investigated, if that is possible" (p. 29). Ultimately, the rule is that the research questions should be congruent with the settings where research will be conducted.

A typical critique about ethnography is that its results are not generalizable; specifically, it is difficult or even impossible to generalize from one or a relatively small number of settings to a larger number of similar settings. Ethnography is a typical case-based approach, and a generalization of its results is different from the empirical generalization that can be made based on the variable-based approach. Some aspects of these differences were discussed in Chapter 7. Let's repeat the basic arguments. Generalizability concerns should be addressed by, first, acknowledging that for some ethnographic studies generalization is not an issue, as researchers may be interested in investigating a particular region, settlement, or setting and discovering its cultural, social, and psychological peculiarities. Consider the monocultural studies presented in Chapter 8, where the focus was to learn about particular cultural communities and not to generalize to broader settings. If the issue of generalization emerges, then the difference between its theoretical and enumerative forms should be considered. A *theoretical* or *analytic generalization* is concerned with extending the hypothesized sociocultural and sociopsychological mechanisms of a phenomenon of interest discovered in one setting to other settings where this phenomenon takes place. Ethnography is well suited for theoretical generalizations as its rich and diverse data provide a fertile soil for the abductive and retroductive inferences that may lead to productive hypotheses. Theoretical generalization requires a theoretical sampling. Mason (2002) provides the following description of the theoretical sampling procedure:

> theoretical sampling means selecting groups or categories [or cases] to study on the basis of their relevance to your research questions, your theoretical position and analytical framework, your analytical practice, and most importantly the argument or explanation that you are developing. Theoretical sampling is concerned with constructing a sample . . . which is meaningful theoretically and empirically, because it builds in certain characteristics or criteria which help to develop and test your theory or your argument". (p. 124)

Theoretical sampling requires a purposeful selection of settings, informants, participants, their activities, and events (see Chapter 8). Thus, "strategic selection of cases can be employed in testing theoretical ideas. Here the aim is to select cases for investigation which subject theories to relatively severe test" (Hammersley & Atkinson, 2007, p. 33).

As readers may remember, the purpose of the *enumerative generalization* is to expand the regularities (usually among variables) discovered in one sample to a larger number of cases to prove the universality of these regularities. Ethnography is not well suited for this type of generalization, as it never employs probability sampling and does not operate with variables. But if the purpose of a study still requires generalizing to other settings, then Hammersley &

Atkinson (2007) and Gobo (2008) suggested using a typical setting as the starting point for such generalization:

> Where the aim is generalization to some finite set of cases, rather than the development and testing of theory, it may be possible to assess the typicality of the case or cases studied by comparing their relevant characteristics with information about the target population, if this available in official statistics or from other studies. (Hammersley & Atkinson, 2007, p. 34)

Once again, the research problem and research questions should drive these decisions.

Getting Access

The next important aspect is getting access to the selected settings. These settings may be either particular physical locations with distinct boundaries, like a village, a reserve, an organization, a school, a campus, or a hospital, or they could be a specific social group or community without visible boundaries or a particular physical location, like an immigrant community, a group of Alcoholics Anonymous, a criminal gang or a cult organization. As most ethnographic manuals (Cranq & Cool, 2007; Gobo, 2008; Hammersley & Atkinson, 2007; Liamputtong, 2008; Schensul et al., 1999), advise, there are people who control and/or provide access to the sites and who should be searched for and approached to help get access to a desired setting. These individuals are called *gatekeepers*. Gatekeepers can be official leaders, like a village chief, a chief of a band, a manager of an organization, or a principal of a school, or they can be highly respected and trusted members of a community, like elders, priests, teachers, doctors, or nurses who have worked in the community for years and have acquired a good reputation, people's confidence, and reverence. If an ethnographer wants to enter the field smoothly, where people will be eager to accept him or her, to share activities, and to talk about themselves, then finding such gatekeepers, getting to know them, and gaining their trust is crucially important. For formal organizations like schools, hospitals, or business organizations, official permission may also be needed. Several ethical, organizational, and political issues may emerge when negotiating access. How much should you tell the gatekeeper about the research? Do you even tell him or her about it at all? The issue of covert, semicovert or open research is of concern here also.

Although Hammersley & Atkinson (2007) and Gobo (2008) discussed the advantages and disadvantages of a covert ethnographic investigation, this technique is not recommended for researchers (especially young ones) for several reasons. It is immoral to deceive trusting people who may disclose intimate details without knowing how and for what purpose these revelations will be used. For this reason, it is highly improbable that an institutional review/ethics board will allow such a study. Another concern is the security of the researcher; if something happens to him or her, it will be difficult to help because of this covert identity and agenda. And, third, if the deception is discovered, then the researcher's and his or her institution's reputation will be jeopardized.

Hammersley & Atkinson (2007) argued that telling the whole truth about the study at its outset is not a wise idea. Full disclosure bounds a researcher to follow through with his or her initial promises and expectations, but new evidence or new ideas may often change the initial course of an investigation and this change may create tension with gatekeepers.

The other argument for not always providing a full account of one's purposes to gatekeepers and others at the beginning of the research is that unless one can build up a trusting relationship with them relatively rapidly, they may refuse access in a way that they would not do later on in the fieldwork (p. 57). Thus, a recommended strategy is to tell gatekeepers truthful information about the general scope and intention of the investigation at the beginning of a study and along the way; as greater trust and rapport are established, provide more details about it in order to gain access to new and more relevant informants and information. Hammersley & Atkinson (2007) also warned researchers of the downside of having a powerful and well-informed gatekeeper. As members of their communities, gatekeepers may have a vested interest in supporting researchers as well as a concern about how their communities and organizations will be portrayed (p. 51). "Gatekeepers may therefore attempt to exercise some degree of surveillance and control, either by blocking off certain lines of inquiry, or by shepherding the fieldworker in one direction or another" (p. 51). Communities may also have been frequently visited by different researchers who did not impact their lives, leading community members to decide to refrain from any further research participation. Such situations will require more efforts and strategic maneuvering to convince gatekeepers to help researchers gain access to these sites. Finally, Hammersley and Atkinson (2007) gave the following advice:

> Negotiating access is a balancing act. Gains and losses now and later, as well as ethical and strategic considerations, must be traded off against one another in whatever manner is judged to be most appropriate, given the purposes of the research and the circumstances in which it is to be carried out. Moreover, changes in judgment about what is best may need to be made as the research progresses. (p. 58)

Researchers' Identities and Roles

Another important but often hidden aspect of an access negotiation is establishing, accepting, and playing out a researcher's identity and role in the setting. As was mentioned in Chapter 4, access to information strongly depends on the identity/role members of a community assign to a researcher. Informants will eagerly convey information to a person who is considered a trusted friend or expert and will refrain from talking too much if they perceive a researcher as a spy or a meddler. In addition to these identities within the community, a researcher's professional and personal identity may also play a role. For example, depending on circumstances and settings, a researcher may decide to introduce him or herself as an anthropologist, a psychologist, a sociologist, or as an expert or a novice. Marital status, ethnic background, religious affiliation, and other aspects of his or her personal identity may be relevant to gaining access and obtaining the trust of gatekeepers and members of communities. A researcher's declared identity is only part of what his or her identity and role will finally be in the community. A researcher

> is identified with this role by the social actors, and it gives meaning to his or her presence in the community. . . . The researcher can only partially influence the role and identity attributed to him or her because the participants creatively modify the information that they receive about the researcher. (Gobo, 2008, p. 122)

By strategically managing identities and roles together with skillfully executing assigned roles, a researcher may strongly enhance the success of a study. Failure to do this may jeopardize the whole enterprise.

Generating Data in the Field

When an ethnographer is accepted in the field and is settled there, problems emerge regarding whom to observe, whom to talk to, during what events studies should take place, and at what times. One of the fundamental advantages of ethnography is that it focuses on what people do in their natural settings, first, and what they say about what they do, second. Thus, naturalistic (or direct) (Johnson & Sackett, 1998) and participant observation are the primary techniques for generating data while interview is the secondary one. In *naturalistic observation*, a researcher holds a passive position as an observer who is studying the unfolding of the everyday life of a community without participating in it. Hammersley & Atkinson (2007) used the term "the complete observer" to describe, for example, observing group interactions through a one-way mirror or watching public interactions through a window (pp. 84–85). *Participant observation*, in contrast, is studying native life by participating in its practices and rituals (Spradley, 1980). Participant observation is the key methodological tool for an ethnographer to get access to, to learn, and to internalize the cultural models of communities. Only by doing things together with members of a community and doing them right can an ethnographer gain access to the intersubjectively shared intentional world of these people. Reflections on the newly acquired intentional states that allow a researcher to be accepted by community members and successfully performing necessary activities constitute one source of information for abducting the unknown cultural models. Talking to these people and getting their accounts of what is going on, what they are doing, and why, constitutes more valuable data for making these inferences productive. Therefore, *interviewing* is another window to the unknown world of native lives.

Naturalistic observation is one of the most intriguing, challenging, and rich methods for obtaining information about contexts and events, people's behavior, emotions, and the causality of events. After introductory and exploratory scanning of the setting, a researcher may continue with more systematic observations: mapping the setting, counting, and census-taking (Schensul et al., 1999) followed by observing particular people and specific activities and events. Through *ethnographic mapping* a researcher graphically represents the setting where the study will be conducted in the form of a plan, map, or schema. Such mapping provides a space-wise representation of a community and allows a researcher to learn about it quicker and better. Mapping can be accompanied by *census-taking*, through listing "every person, household unit, or other unit (e.g., reindeer, latrines, water pumps, public telephone booths, garbage dump sites) in the research setting of interest to the researcher" (p. 103). Census-taking complements mapping in providing researchers with a broad picture of distribution of important units of analysis and their count what can be used for future sampling (p. 103). *Counting* is another useful procedure that may be done at the early stages of observation. It "refers to listing and enumerating types of people, material items, locations, or other things that are important in situating the event, location, or activity more accurately in the context of community" (p. 102). For example, people at different events are primary objects for such counting. An ethnographer should consider different numbers at an event: of what sociodemographic categories people fall into, how many people are doing different activities like talking, standing, sitting, dancing, being alone or in a group, etc. Mapping, census-taking, and counting provide a broad "bird's-eye view" perspective on the setting, people, and activities there.

Johnson and Sacket (1998) provided a detailed account of different forms of sampling in the field. People should be sampled based on the research questions, and such sampling should be complemented by categorizing them based on either "observer-identified categories" or "member-identified categories" (Hammersley & Atkinson, 2007, p. 38). This means that samples of interest are not homogeneous, but consist of different subgroups of individuals who may be categorized either by the community members themselves or by the researcher-observer. It is important to differentiate the observational units thoroughly. It is also important to do *sampling of time* (Hammersley & Atkinson, 2007) or *setting temporal boundaries* (Johnson and Sacket, 1998) to select when it is best to do observations. Researchers have to choose the right time to do a successful observation because people's activities and attitudes fluctuate over time and to "catch them" at the right moment is important for making valid hypotheses about their mechanisms. Another reason to consider the time dimension is that ethnographers cannot do their job around the clock (except perhaps in anthropological fieldwork) because of several pragmatic and practical issues: fatigue, lack of time and resources, personal schedule of researchers, etc. So they have to choose the proper time periods that are the most informative for answering the research questions.

In organizing the sampling of time, it is as important to sample the routine as it is to observe the extraordinary. The purpose of such systematic data collection procedures is to ensure as full and representative a range of coverage as possible, not just to identify and single out the superficially "interesting" events. (Hammersley & Atkinson, 2007, p. 37)

Johnson & Sacket (1998, pp. 315–322) identified several time sampling strategies for observation, like continuous monitoring, fixed-interval instantaneous sampling, random-interval instantaneous sampling, and one-zero or activity presence sampling. These advanced techniques are beyond the scope of this chapter, so interested readers should consult this source. *Sampling events* and *activities* can be closely related to time sampling. For example, in order to observe an unpredictable and quick event like a schoolyard fight, an observer has to continuously monitor pupils' behavior in the yard during breaks.

Participant Observation

DeWalt, DeWalt, & Wayland (1998) emphasized the inevitable tension between "participating" and "observing" while implementing this method. They stated that "participation implies emotional involvement; observation requires detachment" (p. 262). The art of participant observation is to balance these two extremes by avoiding "complete participation" (p. 263) or, as Hammersley and Atkinson (2007) labelled this, "going native" and establishing "overrapport" (p. 87), and being a complete observer by entirely detaching oneself from the activities of people an ethnographer wants to study. Ethnography manuals talk about a continuum of participation between these two extremes, like "'moderate participation'... when the ethnographer is present at the scene of the action but doesn't actively participate or interact, or only occasionally interacts, with people in it" and "'Active participation'... when the ethnographer actually engages in almost everything that other people are doing" (DeWalt, et al., 1998, p. 262). Observations unfold differently in these situations, and a researcher should be prepared for more challenging reflections and self-analysis in the latter case.

HOW-TO BOX 10.1. SEVEN RULES OF SUCCESSFUL PARTICIPANT OBSERVATION (FROM DEWALT ET AL., 1998, PP. 266–267)

1. "The ethnographer has to approach participating and observing any particular situation with and open mind and a nonjudgmental attitude."
2. "Almost all people love to tell their story and to share their experiences with those who take an interest in them ... if an ethnographer shows genuine interest in learning more about behaviors, thoughts, and feelings, he or she will be a welcome guest at most activities".
3. "It is normal to feel awkward and unsure when observing and participating in a new situation. The feeling of 'culture shock' (Bock 1970) when you are confronted with a wide variety of new behaviors and stimuli is something almost all ethnographers have experienced".
4. "Everyone will make mistakes, but most of these can be overcome with time and patience."
5. "It's important to be a careful observer. This is a skill that can be enhanced through practice." [Training oneself to notice small details of the surroundings, people's demeanor, conversations, nonverbal behaviors and many other nuances takes time and determination.]
6. "It's important to be a good listener.... Through language we rapidly acquire a substantial amount of information in a short time. If we listen, we will learn much more quickly."

7   "We should be open to being surprised and to learning the unexpected. This is perhaps the strength of participant observation as a method . . . participant observation puts the researcher into situations in which he or she is acquiring information in an open-ended fashion. The insights gained from this method often can and should be used later on to be verified and substantiated through more structured techniques." [Experienced ethnographers also warn about the danger of various preconceptions that a researcher brings with him or her to the field that may stand in the way of open and nonjudgmental acceptance of new and unexpected information.]

In order to participate in communal activities, an ethnographer first has to be accepted by and develop trust with the members of the community. The manuals on ethnographic fieldwork emphasize a researcher's attributes as a person and his or her style of interactions and communication as important factors in developing this trust. Regarding personal characteristics, Schensul et al. (1999) and Hammersley and Atkinson (2007) identified: gender—only men or only women can be invited to particular activities and ceremonies; race, ethnicity, and religious affiliation—sometime natives prefer to talk to people who are of a similar racial-ethnic and/or religious background; class and education background—people of a similar social origin may be considered more trustworthy and "socially close." (Some issues of the insider/outsider position of a researcher will be discussed in the next chapter). Such features as physical appearance like hair and/or eye color, body size, or other body features may play a role in building relations with locals. Other more manageable characteristics include attire and demeanor, including style of communication. Hammersley and Atkinson (2007) considered style of dressing as a form of impression management for the sake of reporting a desired identity, closeness to informants, and researcher's status. Think about what you might wear to study bikers (very often a covert ethnographic study), homeless people, students of a high status university, or nurses in a palliative care unit. Although dressing should allow blending in, it also has to convey a desired identity—an expert, a friend and collaborator, a regular person—and help a researcher in his or her impression management.

> In overt participant observation, then, where an explicit research role must be constructed, forms of dress, can "give off" the message that the ethnographer seeks to maintain the position of an acceptable marginal member, perhaps in relation to several audiences. They may declare affinity between researcher and hosts, and /or they may distance the ethnographer from constraining identities.
>
> There can be no clear prescription for dress other than to commend a high degree of awareness about self-presentation. (Hammersley and Atkinson, 2007, p. 68)

Knowledge of language and of basic rituals of greeting, of starting and maintaining conversations, of proper posture and other nonverbal behaviors should be adequate to the field settings. Working through an interpreter is another challenge that an ethnographer has to deal with if he or she does not know a local language (Bujra, 2006). Experts emphasize such ways of building trust as helping locals in their routine activities, but especially in emergencies, sharing with them some extreme or dangerous situations, and personal disclosures (see Hammersley & Atkinson, 2007, pp. 63–73 and DeWalt et al., 1998, pp. 267–270 for more on these topics).

Although participant observation may start immediately upon entering the field, it is not recommended to start looking for answers to the research questions instantly. Start slow by hanging around, observing what people are doing, talking about ordinary topics, and maintaining conventional conversations. "Especially in the early days of field negotiations it may be advantageous to find more "ordinary" topics of conversation, with a view to establishing one's identity as a "normal," "regular," "decent" person" (Hammersley & Atkinson, 2007, p. 70). An ethnographer in a new place is a stranger and novice, so his or her initial behavior should be congruent with this initial role. This role also provides a good opportunity to start asking questions, to solicit advice and to collect information that competent members of a community may take for granted. Schensul et al. (1999) informed young ethnographers about the possibility of being rejected by a community and being excluded from participating in some activities. Reasons for rejections "may include lack of trust, the community's discomfort with an outsider, community members' anticipation that a situation might be dangerous, or the community's reluctance or inability because of poverty or civil war to provide continuing support for a stranger" (p. 94). A researcher has to diagnose the signs of exclusion and rejection (sometimes there is no direct refusal, but only indirect indicators of this (see Schensul et al., 1999, p. 94) and try to identify the reasons for this and decide whether to fix the problem or to leave the field.

The procedures and techniques of participant and naturalistic observation are diverse and strongly depend on the purpose of a research project and the setting and context of the observations (Spradley, 1980). In addition to knowing the basic rules, an observer has to be creative, open-minded, and flexible in finding the best strategies of implementing observations for meeting the demands of his or her study.

Interview

If different forms of observation provide information about what is going on in the community and how a researcher sees events, interview is the only way to get the actors' account of the same events, actions, rituals, or traditions. Therefore, different forms of interviewing should complement observations. Validity concerns of such accounts exist. Critics of the interview method question whether a scientific investigation can rely on these subjective and unreliable opinions and points of view. The answer to such concerns again depends on the philosophical paradigm of a researcher. For positivists, such accounts cannot be considered scientific facts to be analyzed, because they are not quantifiable and their validity and reliability are unknown. But for interpretivists and realists, such opinions represent an important piece of evidence of how locals account for their worlds, for themselves, for their actions, and for the actions of other people; and these pieces of evidence acquire their values when they are combined with other information for abducting or retroducting hypotheses about deep layers of the meaning of systems or cultural models and their mechanisms. Therefore, validity is not in the words of the interviewees, but in the researcher's hypotheses. Again, think about a detective who uses eyewitness accounts not as facts but as another piece of evidence, which along with the analysis of the crime scene, autopsy results, and other information, can help solve the mystery of a murder. It is also important to note that the 'objects' of investigation in sociocultural research are "in fact 'subjects', in the sense that they have consciousness and agency. Moreover . . . they produce accounts of themselves and their world" (Hammersley & Atkinson, 2007, p. 97). This means that if we want to understand why people do what they do in various cultural settings, we need to listen to their accounts because they are part of the picture of causal forces that drive people's behaviors. "We can use what people say as evidence about their perspectives, and perhaps about the larger subcultures and cultures to which they belong. Knowledge of these perspectives and cultures will often form an important element of the analysis" (p. 98).

Person-Centered Ethnography and Interviewing

The last quote moves us to one form of ethnographic interviewing that has a particular value for cultural psychological research, namely *person-centered ethnography* and *interviewing* (Hollan, 2001, 2005; Levy & Hollan, 1998). As was stated at the beginning of this chapter, the main purpose of a cultural psychological ethnographic study is twofold: first, to extract and explore cultural models that function in a community and, second, to investigate how these internalized models structure the experience, motivation, and behavior of the members of a community. Person-centered interviewing is well suited for these two purposes. The creators of this type of interviewing, Levy and Hollan (1998), described it:

> There is a significant difference between asking a Tahitian interviewee something like "Please describe for me exactly how and why supercision (a penis-mutilating rite of passage) is done by Tahitians," and asking him "Can you tell me about *your* supercision?" 'What happened leading up to it?" "What happened that day?" "Did it change your life in any way?" "How?" "What did you think and feel about it then?" "What do you think and feel about it now?"
>
> The first question uses the interviewee as an informant, as an expert witness (albeit with a limited and special perspective) about some community procedure. The second set of questions treats the interviewee as a respondent, as an object of study in him- or herself; it explores what he or she [sic] makes of the procedure. The relation between the two sets of answers is directly informative (see Levy 1973:117–122) and illuminates the force of supercision on males in a way that the informant-based cultural description does not, so that the two types of description complement each other, both for social and psychological interpretations.
>
> Person-centered interviewing moves back and forth between the informant and the respondent modes. A remark of a young woman informant: "I felt very shy and embarrassed at that time" might be followed by a respondent-type probe: "Tell me more about how you felt" or by the informant-type questions: "What do girls usually feel under these circumstances?" "How do they usually act?" "If they don't feel or act like that, what do people think?" (p. 336)

The innovation here is to treat an interviewee both as an informant, who provides information about public cultural models, and as a respondent, who shares his or her experiences of being driven by these models, exposed to them, and involved in their co-construction. Its founders argue that the benefit of this type of interviewing is that mental and subjective are not separated from public and cultural, but are treated in their dialectical relations: as soon as an external public cultural model is identified, it is immediately treated as a part of the internal, subjective, and private experience of an individual who is subjected to its influence. When properly used, person-centered interviewing serves as a rich background for building theories about cultural models and the mechanisms of their functioning in people's experience and behavior. The best account of conducting this form of interviewing is provided by cognitive anthropologists Naomi Quinn, Roy D'Andrade, Claudia Strauss, and their colleagues (Quinn, 2005c)

Interviewing People as Informants

Informants are members of a community considered to be knowledgeable about particular domains of communal life and who an ethnographer decides to interview to get access to this knowledge. If the target of research is a cultural model of a particular domain, then anybody who functions in this domain is a potential informant. The task is to select informants who will provide the most exhaustive accounts of that model.

Interviews may happen spontaneously while a researcher is participating in communal activities and asks questions to clarify something, or they can be deliberately organized activities. Hammersley and Atkinson (2007) called them "unsolicited and solicited accounts" (p. 99). *Unsolicited verbal accounts* are conversations and verbal statements that a researcher heard of or participated in during observations. These are spontaneous, natural, situational, and contextual verbal accompaniments of actions and interactions. Many ethnographers highly value these accounts as they provide direct access to people's "situated vocabulary" (p. 145) which may serve as a "window" into the perception and structuring of their worlds. These accounts may be indispensable for understanding both public cultural models and their private internalized components. Some ethnographers believe that unsolicited accounts are more reliable than the solicited ones. In some cultural communities people can be suspicious of individuals who are constantly asking questions and may treat them and corresponding situations as threatening (p. 99). There is also an opinion that researchers' questions structure respondents' answers, thus eliciting reactive and to some extent artificial accounts of the topic of interviewing. Sometimes ethnographers are not capable of doing a deliberate interview and the observational results and unsolicited accounts may be the only pieces of information they have. Despite these legitimate concerns, in most cases ethnographers cannot avoid conducting a deliberate interview.

The best way to do it is to make it look like a conversation where the researcher actively and respectfully listens to an informant's accounts that are open-ended and mostly unrestricted by the interviewer. It is possible to say that informants are providing their stories or discourses about the activities, practices, categories, or events that interest a researcher who then conducts "the *cultural analysis* of [such] discourses" (Quinn, 2005b, p. 3) to uncover the underlying cultural models. The basic assumption of such cultural analysis is that cultural models are so deeply internalized by members of a community that they take them for granted as implicit but valid propositions about their lives. Because of this implicit nature, people are usually unaware of their models and have difficulty explicitly stating them when directly asked. This is how Quinn (2005a) justified this type of analysis:

> I came to see my analytic approach as the reconstruction, from what people say explicitly, of the implicit assumptions they must have had in mind to say it. My assumption is that the shared understandings I seek lie behind what people said. (p. 45)

Thus, the goal of analyzing cultural models from interviews is to reconstruct meaning, especially cultural meaning, from the clues provided by informants' discourses (Quinn, 2005b, p. 4). The ethnographer's intellectual challenges correspond well with the abductive and retroductive thinking of interpretivists or realists. The thick description/interpretation of cultural systems of meaning is also present here.

In order to conduct an interview suitable for such analysis, Quinn (2005a) suggested an open-ended unrestricted style of interviewing.

> I developed a style of interviewing in which I and my research assistants deliberately ceded control of the "interviews" to the "interviewees," allowing them to decide how their interviews should be organized over all, what topics should come next and what might have been overlooked or unfinished, and when we were done. Our role was that of a good listener in a decidedly one-sided conversation. Our only intervention was to guide speakers back to the topic when they occasionally wandered off too far. We made every effort not to interrupt. As interested listeners, however, we asked our interviewees, whenever it seemed appropriate, to expand on their points, explain what they meant, spell out the implications of examples they gave, and give examples of generalizations they made. We also made note, either mentally during the actual interview or listening to it before the next, of comments dropped, key terms or phrases used, and then, at appropriate junctures in the same or later interviews, we brought the conversation back to these topics. (p. 41)

Ethnography **271**

In this quote, Quinn has outlined most of the main features of a good open-ended unstructured interview (see also Schensul et al., 1999 and Hammersley & Atkinson, 2007). Box 10.2 below summarizes the techniques and behaviors that will help readers to conduct such interviews.

HOW-TO BOX 10.2. TIPS FOR AN OPEN-ENDED UNSTRUCTURED INTERVIEW

- Trust and rapport must be established before the interview takes place. An interviewee feels comfortable with the interviewer and is motivated to talk and to share his or her thoughts and opinions. The interviewee is aware of the general scope of research and has consented to this interview.
- Start with identifying the topic of conversation by asking a general question like: "Tell me please about how [*topic of your research*] is treated, considered, thought of, behaved toward or dealt with in your community?" Clarify the general boundaries of the domain that you want to discuss. Use the vocabulary that members of the community employ when speaking about this domain.
- Turn into a good listener with an appropriate body posture and facial expression.
- Record the interview using a high quality voice or video recorder. Video recording supplies a researcher with additional nonverbal information.
- Try not to interrupt the flow of conversation, as the sequence of themes that the interviewee brings up is important for the following analysis. Interrupt and redirect the conversation only when it veers too far off topic.
- To maintain the flow of the interview, ask probe questions to clarify unclear words, to provide definitions and explanations, to give examples, and to flesh out key ideas.
- Observe nonverbal cues for emotionally meaningful aspects of the discussion, for repeated words, abrupt changes or discontinuations of a theme, metaphors, styles of reasoning behind the statements, typical constructions of sentences, paralinguistic elements like pauses, voice inversions, speaking too loudly or too quietly, etc. You may decide to bring up these observations later on in the conversation and discuss them.

Cultural analysis of respondents' interviews. Readers may find a full account of the logic and techniques of such analysis in (Quinn, 2005a). Here are the main points. The primary analytic goal of such analysis is to find a relatively stable configuration of themes and issues that run across all the informants. A researcher should search "for patterns *across* interviewees and passages, that would be evidence of shared, stable understandings" (p. 43). The first step in this search is "grouping" by analyzing "features of discourse that did occur frequently" (pp. 43–44). In Quinn's investigation of the American cultural model of marriage, such frequent elements of discourse "turned out to be the *key words* and the *metaphors* in people's talk about marriage, and the *reasoning* that they did about it" (p. 44). There are two features that make this triad well suited for cultural analysis. First, they are "culture-laden," meaning that "selection of metaphors, reasoning, and use of key words are all in different ways governed by cultural schemes, each provided an excellent window into the shared schema on which its usage was predicated" (p. 44). Second, the use of these culture signifiers "was largely out of speakers' conscious control" (p. 44), which ensures their potential validity. Although informants intentionally choose metaphors and reasoning, they cannot choose the aspects of the cultural model that these metaphors and ways of reasoning represent. The researcher started by grouping the metaphors and discovered that "the metaphors different speakers used to talk about marriage in varied contexts fell into eight classes. These were metaphors of *lastingness, sharedness, (mutual) benefit, compatibility, difficulty, efforts, success (or failure),* and *risk*" (pp. 47–48). (See Table 8.1. in Chapter 8). This grouping of the metaphorical descriptions of marriage is like factor analysis in statistics, when a variety of scores are clumped together based on unobservable factors or hypothetical constructs that are believed to be responsible for intercorrelations among these scores. Only in the cultural analysis of marriage, it was the researcher's mind and not a statistical program that inferred the hidden factors. Quinn actually took things one step further from a simple linguistic factor analysis and created a story, or a sequential account of how eight dimensions of marriage could be threaded together in a logical sequence.

> The story behind these metaphors that I had in mind was a product of intuition I had, as an American myself, about American marriage. Roughly, I knew, people regarded their marriages as successful if they lasted. In order to last, though, a marriage had to be beneficial, and in order for it to be beneficial, its difficulties had to be overcome, requiring effort. (pp. 60–61)

This intuited inference (abduction) demonstrates that the cultural model of marriage is not a mechanical ensemble of eight dimensions, but a coherent logical system that could be used as a guide for people's motivation and behaviors in this domain. But, as was stated in Chapter 4, what is the validity of such abductions? Aren't they products of unrestricted imaginations that may lead to pure fictions and fantasies? The point here is that these inferences are hypotheses that require further exploration and verification. And this is exactly what Quinn did. She asked herself: "How could I verify this story? What kind of evidence would convince others that it existed in Americans' minds, and convince scholars like George Lakoff that it did so independently of the metaphors they used to talk about marriage?" (p. 61). And at that point of her investigation, the researcher turned to additional sources of evidence extracted from the interviews, namely, informants' reasoning.

> It occurred to me at some point to cull out and examine instances of reasoning that interviewees did about marriage, to see if this reasoning conformed to, and supported, my intuitions about what led to what in the cultural story of marriage. Lo and behold, interviewees spelled out exactly the sequence of events I had surmised, not only confirming my "story" but filling in additional pieces of it. (p. 61)

Thus, the ethnographer turned to the logic and sequence of reasoning that informants use when talking about their marriages. In addition to confirming and enriching the existing account of the cultural model of marriage, reasoning analysis allowed the scholar to make important theoretical implications. This is how she described this:

> On reflection, it is not surprising that their reasoning exposed these reasoners' cultural schema for marriage, because it is this schema that structures this reasoning. . . . I come to see that what I had been thinking of as a somewhat disembodied cultural model *of* marriage was better understood as a model *for*—a schema designed for reasoning about marriage, and that had evolved and spread just because it served this purpose well. (p. 61)

This revelation fits nicely with what Shweder said about the importance of cultural models *of* and *for* various behaviors[1] that cultural communities create to coordinate their members' experiences and actions. Quinn logically inferred that most people's reasoning about routine cognitive tasks are culturally determined, providing them with quick and economical heuristics for solving these tasks. But by using these heuristics, people also reinforce, maintain and co-construct the existing cultural models. In her opinion, metaphors and the ways of reasoning complement each other: "In the same way that metaphors are windows into shared knowledge of *cultural exemplars*, reasoning is an especially good analytic window into the *shared structure* [emphasis added] or cultural schema being used to do it" (p. 61). This important methodological conclusion can be applied to the investigation of a broad range of other cultural models. Quinn finished her cultural analysis with examining a key word that her informants frequently used while talking about their marriages: the word "love." Such an examination is rooted in the assumption that this and other key words are also culture-laden and "permit speakers [an] easy reference to the salient cultural concepts that they mark" (p. 72). Key words are arranged in a network within a cultural model of interest and should be studied in detail in order to further understand the depth and richness of the primary model.

Interviewees as Respondents

As a requirement for a successful person-centered interview, interviewees should be studied as respondents regarding their own internalized aspects of cultural models or, as Strauss (2005) worded it, about their "personal meanings of shared assumptions" (p. 208). The idea is that cultural models are public and implicit assumptions that represent parts of sociocultural reality (like marriage, being a woman, work, education, society, etc.)—or cultural models *of*. The same models also prescribe and drive people's thinking, feeling, and behaving within the corresponding domain—or cultural models *for*. Driven by these models, people interact with their worlds and gain their own experience. Along with their implicit cultural assumptions, this experience serves as "their personal interpretive framework" (p. 208) that ultimately motivates their behavior and shapes their further experiences. The goal of interviewing people as respondents is to discover their interpretive frameworks. It is important to note that Quinn conducted between-case analysis to extract the public aspects of the cultural model of marriage because this model is shared and distributed among people. When interviewing people as respondents, researchers aim at extracting the internalized aspects of cultural models that reside in their minds.

To study personal interpretive frameworks, a researcher should work within-cases and try to go deep to discover various layers of individual systems of meaning. Strauss (2005) provided a helpful account of this process. In analyzing open-ended, uninterrupted interviews about respondents' understanding of "work" in the American context, she first looked at the contiguity of the topics in the interview, meaning that if topic B follows topic A when a speaker is allowed to talk without interruption, then A and B are linked in that person's PSN [personal semantic network = personal interpretive framework]. Therefore, the first step in tracing someone's PSN is looking at what else they talk about in connection with the topic in question (p. 208).

Such an association of topics A and B indicates a semantic connection of these topics in an individual's cognitive schema. This conclusion can be supplemented by an analysis of the respondent's "voice" when talking about these topics. Strauss borrowed the concept "voice" from Mikhail Bakhtin, "who uses it to mean the characteristic verbal expression of a personality and point of view" (p. 209). Keeping the same voice indicates a strong connection between topics A and B.

---

[1] A distinction of cultural models *of* and cultural models *for* particular elements of environment and corresponding behaviors can be traced to Geertz's (1973, pp. 93–94) arguments that such a distinction is important in order for the concept of cultural models to be efficient in accounting for people's functioning.

To proceed further, Strauss collected all passages related to the primary topic of interest from the same respondent and looked at three things:

> (1) *strong versus weak associations* (strongly associated ideas are mentioned repeatedly and usually without prompting from the interviewer); (2) *self-relevant versus nonself-relevant associations* (self-relevant associations are tied to the person's self-image); and (3) *associations with emotional and motivational hot spots* (ideas connected to hot spots are expressed with strong emotions, trigger powerful memories, and are often associated with nonroutine goals speakers have pursued). (p. 209)

Then she started an analysis of individual passages by coding themes and topics, looking for their frequencies, contiguity, and associations. The result of this work was an elaborated account of how a particular individual perceives and interprets work and how work relates to his or her self-image, motivation, and other aspects of life. She concluded:

> Clearly, conducting a PSN analysis is time consuming. You may decide it is not worth the effort, given your research questions. The benefit of it, however, is an analysis that gives more insight into the cognitive and emotional meaning of keywords and concepts, evidence for patterns of subcultural variations, and understanding of how people's ideas on one subject are related to other things they say, think, and do. (p. 223)

By the end of her chapter, Strauss provided several methodological suggestions:

> For personal semantic network analysis, it is imperative to let interviewees speak as the interviewee sees fit instead of adhering to a fixed interview schedule. For interviewees to reveal their emotional hot spots, interviewers have to be nonjudgmental and friendly: A stiff, formal approach will not work. . . . The interview transcript should contain long turns by the interviewee, broken up only infrequently by the interviewer. (p. 239)

She provided some accounts of the reliability of her analysis; when Strauss's graduate student was taught semantic network analysis, she came up with the same key elements that the primary researcher discovered. But even though the reliability was not being tested, Strauss argued that providing readers with initial data and the researcher's interpretation was better than excluding such analysis or some parts of it.

Recording Ethnographic Data

The ethnographic data recording is usually called *fieldnotes*. The biggest challenge for a young ethnographer constitutes generating fieldnotes from naturalistic and participant observations. The questions are how, about what, and when should they make these notes (Hammersley & Atkinson, 2007, p. 142)? Fieldnotes may have different forms: (1) *very short unscripted memos* of occurring events taken during or immediately after an event or action. These memos serve as a memorizing tool to help a researcher recall these events at a later time. A researcher may use a small voice-recorder to unobtrusively record his or her observations (Schensul et al., 1999, p. 116). (2) *Actual fieldnotes*: a detailed description of *what* happened, to *whom*, *when*, *where* and under *what circumstances*. If these notes also contain ethnographer's personal reflections and revelations about his or her emotions, motivations, attitudes, fears, and dreams, then such notes are called an (3) *ethnographic journal*, which is a more private account of the fieldwork (Hammersley & Atkinson, 2007). Some researchers

(Schensul et al., 1999) recommend keeping the actual fieldnotes and the journal separately. Researchers' actual fieldnotes may be organized differently, but regardless of the form they must have: a full description of the setting(s) including mapping, counting, and census-taking, a detailed description of the actors, their attire, nonverbal behavior, almost everything relevant to the study; records of the conversations that accompanied the episodes, preferably in direct speech, or as close to it as possible. Keep in mind how the metaphors, logic of reasoning, and sequences of the discussed topics were important for the analyses in Quinn's and Strauss's studies. Schensul et al. (1999) use the metaphor of video recording to teach young ethnographers what to write in their fieldnotes. Instead of writing that a classroom was "bright and warm with a lot of visual stimulation," they advise ethnographers to paint a more vivid picture:

> the walls are painted in warm shades of yellow and orange. Three of the four walls have collections of between 10 and 20 photographs, posters, children's drawings, and writing samples. Some of the writing samples are on colored construction paper. Others are accompanied by colorful outlines, frames, or drawings. (p. 115)

The same rule applies when describing people's appearances and behaviors. Instead of writing that guests were elegantly dressed, an ethnographer should describe what they were wearing (p. 115). In addition, "behaviors should be defined behaviorally, rather than in terms of what they mean to the observer. . . . Researchers should describe the behavior and avoid attributing meaning to it in the fieldnotes until they discover what the behavior communicates to others in the setting" (p. 115).

Ethnographers should write fieldnotes as soon as possible after the observed actions and episodes. Hammersley and Atkinson (2007) provide the following advice:

> It is difficult to overemphasize the importance of meticulous note-taking where this is the main means of data recording. The memory should never be relied on entirely, and a good maxim is "if in doubt, write it down." Furthermore, it is absolutely essential that one keep up to date in processing notes. Without the discipline of daily writing, the observations will fade from memory, and the ethnography will all too easily become incoherent and muddled. (p. 144)

These detailed fieldnotes can be accompanied by (4) *analytic notes* and *memos* (Hammersley & Atkinson, 2007) that reflect a researcher's interpretation and understanding of the situations and events as well as hypotheses about potential meanings, powers, structures, and causal mechanisms. These analytic memos serve an important role in the transition from note taking to analysis.

> The regular production of analytic memoranda will force the ethnographer to go through such a process of explication. Ideally, every period of observation should result in processed notes and the reflexive monitoring of the research process. As the memoranda accumulate, they will constitute preliminary analyses, providing the researcher with guidance through the corpus of data. (p. 151)

This means that every observation, participation, or involvement should be reflected upon with these questions in mind: What do these data mean with regard to my study? How do these data allow me to answer my research questions? What light do they shed on resolving the research problem?

Analyzing Ethnographic Data

It is becoming an ill-defined belief and practice in many social and behavioral sciences to think about data analysis as an algorithmic, step-by-step sequence of operations that inevitably leads to particular results that constitute some kind of "discovery" that is worthy of publishing. Some feel that various uncertainties, guesses, intuitions, and other "subjective" conclusions have to be removed from such an analytic process as much as possible in order to secure an "objective" and "scientific" approach to a solution of a problem. Readers may recognize in such a conviction a consequence of the empiricist-positivist thinking, a thinking that cannot be applied to interpretivist and/or realist research. Although, securing "objective" measurements and rigorous statistical analysis provides researchers with instances of empirical and statistical regularities, these regularities nevertheless remain at the level of empirical, the level of observable manifestations. The same is true with observed actions and the recorded verbal accounts of them. These are all empirical manifestations of the unobservable forces and structures that brought them to life. In true science, researchers have to go from the surface of events to their deep meaning and generating powers. No single method, quantitative or qualitative, can do this no matter how sophisticated it is. Only the creative inquisitive mind can get to these deep meanings and powers. Therefore, the purpose of analyzing ethnographic data is to move from descriptions to meanings and mechanisms, from empirical to real, and from the surface to the essence of events, things, and actions. Not all ethnographers and social scientists will agree with this declaration, but the goal of this textbook is to emphasize exactly this point of view—the view that the analysis of ethnography is a process of abductive inference, the process of intelligent hypothesizing and imaginative penetration into the meaning of communal lives and individual actions. Summarizing the discussions on this topic in Chapter 4 and in this chapter, and using some insights from ethnography experts (Hammersley & Atkinson, 2007), the following strategy can be suggested.

Stage of Conceptualization

Clamping events, utterances, and actions into categories that may reflect underlying meanings, tendencies, powers, and ideas is a starting point of the analysis. These categories and concepts take initially unstructured data and put them into some kind of order which later can be used for a more elaborate analysis. Concepts are also elements of analytical thinking; that is why developing such elements is important for a successful analysis. Conceptual analysis starts by reflecting upon the data obtained from observations and interviews. Various systems of coding and theme identification can be useful in this reflection. Emerging concepts may be *informant-* or *observer-driven* and can be *experience-near* or *experience-distant* (see Chapter 6 for more on these concepts). Analysis of "situated vocabularies" may end up with informant-driven categories that reflect informants' interpretations of the world. When a researcher enters the field with a set of theoretical ideas of what he or she expects to find, then the concepts that organize his or her observations are observer-driven. A researcher has to maintain a balance between the observer-driven conceptual frameworks used while thinking and planning the research and the informant-driven ones by being open-minded to new data and consequently new conceptualizations that emerge during fieldwork. Emerging concepts are not isolated monads, but an integrated system that should account for the data at hand. The most productive strategy is thus reading and rereading notes and protocols followed by making a set of hermeneutic circles of inferences. A researcher starts with a purpose and goals for a project and goes to the data to understand their roles in achieving these goals. From these interpreted data, he or she goes back to the big picture of the problem that now is illuminated by the newly acquired data. A new set of data is looked at from this new perspective on the problem and these data are correspondently conceptualized and interpreted.

> [Theorizing] ought to involve an iterative process in which ideas are used to make sense of data, and data are used to change our ideas. . . . So, analysis is not just a matter of managing

and manipulating data. We must be prepared to go beyond the data to develop ideas that will illuminate them, and this will allow us to link our ideas with those of others; and we must then bring those ideas back to test their fit with further data, and so on. (Hammersley & Atkinson, 2007, p. 159)

Looking for and Discovering Patterns in Events and Actions

As readers may remember, researchers in the studies of the cultural model of marriage and in the investigation of participants' understanding of work were looking for patterns, consistent similarities in metaphors, themes, and reasoning in order to hypothesize the underlying models and systems of meaning. Finding such patterns in observations, in contextual settings, situated vocabularies and all other available empirical evidence is a productive way to move from a conceptualization of data to the hypotheses about models and systems of meaning. As Shweder advised, researchers should start by looking at the *routine* habitual activities that are already organized in patterns. These patterns make people's lives structured and provide them with a feeling of existential security. Then ask: What is behind such patterns? Why are they organized in such a way? Are there disturbances in this routine? How do people react to these disturbances?

Closely related to the analysis of habitual activities is the analysis of *rituals* (Hammersley & Atkinson, 2007, p. 169). Rituals are more symbolic than routine activities; they are set actions that have intrinsic meaning to the actors: think about religious, wedding, and military rituals. The meaning of rituals is taken for granted and often deeply internalized by the actors: "This is how things are done here." Discovering and analyzing such rituals is important to identify the collective and individual systems of meaning that drive them. There are *values* that nurture these rituals and stabilize routine. In addition, there are *rules* (p. 169), informal guidelines for behaviors in different situations. These rules not only prescribe the behaviors of community members, but they are also used for decision-making in these situations. Values, norms, and rules are the organizing principles that may stand behind routine activities and rituals and thus should be treated as important components of the patterns and regularities that researchers aim to discover. Interview and verbal accounts analysis should complement the analysis of actions based on observations. These verbal accounts provide another set of evidence to infer about underlying principles, but never give direct and unimpeded access to them. All verbal utterances and statements should be interpreted and should never be taken at face value.

In looking for patterns in actions and events, it is natural for researchers to inquire about the causal relations among them. In fact, for a realist ethnographic research, such inquiry is an important part of investigation. In understanding why people do what they do in different sociocultural settings, it is not only important to investigate the meanings behind these actions but also to hypothesize the factors that bring these meanings to action. This search for causality is a troubling question for sciences in general and for social sciences and ethnography in particular. Should ethnographers search for causality? Broad ideas on this matter were presented in Chapters 3 and 4 which can be summarized in the following way. Now that more and more social scientists are moving to realist or realist/interpretivist paradigms, searching for causal mechanisms and developing theories that account for such mechanisms is becoming a major trend. Scientists are starting to realize that in order to solve social problems and to do successful interventions, they have to know how the processes that constitute the problems are organized, what the causal mechanisms that drive the problematic phenomena are, and where these mechanisms malfunction need to be fixed. Both randomized experiments and case-based ethnographic and comparative studies should be used to discover the causal relations in sociocultural worlds (Maxwell, 2004a, 2004b).

Developing and Testing Hypotheses

This is the most important point in any analytical work: through the power of abductive or retroductive thinking, to instigate a breakthrough to a new understanding of the meanings, causes, and mechanisms that underlie the phenomena of interest. These are the conjectures and hypotheses that, when empirically verified, constitute the core of scientific theories. When these hypotheses are stated, a researcher should look for evidence that supports or falsifies them. He or she may look within the existing data or start purposefully collecting new data. Proposing a hypothesis about, for example, cultural models of communal life, is not the end of research, but the beginning of a new cycle of studies to verify this hypothesis and to validate empirically that such models exist and run the lives of a community. The arsenal of methods is wide. Researchers may continue collecting more observations and interviews and purposefully comparing them across cases; they may incorporate new methods of data generation: structured surveys, field experiments, document analysis, and psychological tests such as projective tests or psychosemantic methods. Among the last group the most popular are: The Semantic Differential (Osgood, Suci, & Tannenbaum, 1957; Triandis & Osgood, 1958), the Q-sort Technique (Brown, 1996; Shemmings & Ellingsen, 2012) and the Repertory Grid test (Fransella, Bell, & Bannister, 2004; Fromm, 2004). These techniques could be used to verify the hypotheses about collective and individual systems of meaning in standardized and quantitative forms. Remember the researcher-as-a-detective metaphor: everything goes if it can shed light on a solution of the problem.

Conclusion

By its nature ethnographic fieldwork for culture and psychology research is a process of entering, learning about, and navigating within the intentional and intersubjective worlds of others in order to extract, describe, and understand the cultural models that guide these worlds and to investigate the role these models play in the functioning, experience, and behavior of people. Ethnography constitutes not only another technique of data generation, but a different approach to thinking and researching people in sociocultural communities. There are two main targets of ethnographic work: communal cultural models and the structure and dynamics of the experience and behavior of the people guided by these models. The researcher's major tools are different forms of observation and interview accompanied by interpretation and the abductive/retroductive ways of inference. Person-centered ethnography/interviewing is especially relevant for culture and psychology research. It allows a researcher to treat members of communities both as informants and as participants, thus providing a rich empirical basis for theorizing about the relationships between the human mind and the sociocultural environment. "True ethnography" (Shweder, 1996) is a full-fledged scientific method that works within the interpretivist and realist paradigms by utilizing the abductive and retroductive modes of inference.

Questions

1. How do you understand ethnography as a way of thinking about culture and psychology research? Justify your answer.
2. What is moral/cultural community as an object of culture and psychology research? How does it differ from a simple congregation of people of a particular ethnic background?
3. Compare and contrast Shweder's presentation of the cultural models of moral communities with the theory of cultural models presented in Chapter 2.
4. Articulate and justify the twofold objective of ethnography for culture and psychology research. Compare these objectives with the theory of cultural models.

5. What are the challenges of and means for inquiring into the public aspects of cultural models in a community? Can this be done as a legitimate scientific enterprise? Justify your answers.
6. Is it possible to get to the internalized/private aspects of cultural models that are located in the individuals' minds? Is this a valid and justified procedure?
7. Why is ethnography considered an interpretive science? What are the main intellectual tools that an ethnographer should use? Justify your answers.
8. Can the results of ethnography be generalized? Explain your answer.
9. How do you understand person-centered ethnography and interviewing? How does this technique relate to the theory of cultural models?
10. Explain the logic behind the two types of person-centered interviews conducted by Quinn and Strauss.

Exercise

In the previous chapter you were asked to create an instrument to measure a particular construct cross-culturally. Continue this exercise by taking the same construct and inquiring about the cultural model of this idea or intentional thing by using ethnography. For this exercise, where you are not actually entering a cultural community, focus on conducting person-centered interviewing, treating your participants as informants and as respondents. Focus on inferring the taken-for-granted and hidden aspects of the cultural model. Use your own community as the object of investigation and surprise other people with your discovery!

Glossary

Ethnography: The term *ethnography* comes from the Greek words *ethnos*—people, nation, tribe, and *graphia*—description, writing. It means a study of people, their ways of life, customs, and traditions.

Gatekeepers are members of a cultural community who serve as liaisons, guides, and interpreters for a researcher entering and navigating through a community.

Moral/cultural community is a collectivity of people who live according to self-developed rules of engagement and conventions in the form of negotiated and co-constructed cultural models for different domains of life. Members of these communities internalize and share these models and, because of this, maintain the social order and harmony.

Person-centered ethnography and interviewing is a special kind of ethnography in which a person is interviewed as an informant and as respondent. The researcher asks interviewees about the public aspects of a cultural model of interest and about their personal experiences of enacting this model. This technique is well-suited for culture and psychology research because it allows researchers to address both the public and private aspects of a cultural model and their interactions.

Solicited verbal accounts are interviews that are conducted on purpose; they are specially organized and semiformal in their form.

Theoretical or analytic generalization of ethnographic results is concerned with extending hypothesized sociocultural and sociopsychological mechanisms, cultural models and their interactions with people's minds discovered in one setting to other settings where the same phenomena take place.

Theoretical sampling is a purposeful selection of settings, informants, participants, and events that allows an ethnographer to test the hypothesized theory about person-culture interactions.

Unsolicited verbal accounts are conversations and verbal statements that a researcher heard or participated in during observations. These are spontaneous, natural, situational, and contextual verbal accompaniments of actions and interactions.

Recommended Reading

DeWalt, K. M., DeWalt, B. R., & Wayland, C. B. (1998). Participant observation. In H. R. Bernard (Ed.), *Handbook of methods in cultural anthropology* (pp. 259–299). Walnut Creek, CA: AltaMira Press.

Emerson, R. M., Fretz, R. I., & Shaw, L. L. (2011). *Writing ethnographic fieldnotes*. Chicago, IL: University of Chicago Press.

Fetterman, D. (2010). *Ethnography: Step by step*. Thousand Oaks, CA: Sage.

Gobo, G. (2008). *Doing ethnography*. Los Angeles, CA: Sage.

Hammersley, M., & Atkinson, P. (2007). *Ethnography: Principles in practice* (3rd ed.). London, UK: Routledge.

Johnson, A., & Sackett, R. (1998). Direct systematic observation of behavior. In H. R. Bernard (Ed.), *Handbook of methods in cultural anthropology* (pp. 301–331). Walnut Creek, CA: AltaMira Press.

Konopinski, N. (Ed.). (2014). *Doing anthropological research: A practical guide*. New York, NY: Routledge.

Quinn, N. (Ed.). (2005c). *Finding culture in talk: A collection of methods*. New York, NY: Palgrave Macmillan

Schensul, S. L., Schensul, J. J., & LeCompte, M. D. (1999). *Essential ethnographic methods: Observations, interviews, and questionnaires*. Walnut Creek, CA: AltaMira Press.

Spradley, J. P. (1979). *The ethnographic interview*. New York, NY: Holt, Rinehart and Winston.

Spradley, J. P. (1980). *Participant observation*. New York, NY: Holt, Rinehart and Winston.

Stewart, A. (1998). *The ethnographer's method*. Thousand Oaks, CA: Sage.

References

Brown, S. R. (1996). Q methodology and qualitative research. *Qualitative Health Research, 6*(4), 561–567.

Bujra, J. (2006). Lost in translation? The use of interpreters in fieldwork. In V. Desai & R. B. Potter (Eds.), *Doing development research* (pp. 172–179). London, UK: Sage.

Cranq, M., & Cool, I. (2007). *Doing ethnographies*. Los Angeles, CA: Sage.

DeWalt, K. M., DeWalt, B. R., & Wayland, C. B. (1998). Participant observation. In H. R. Bernard (Ed.), *Handbook of methods in cultural anthropology* (pp. 259–299). Walnut Creek, CA: AltaMira Press.

Fransella, F., Bell, R., & Bannister, D. (2004). *A manual for Repertory Grid Technique* (2nd ed.). Chichester, UK: John Willey.

Fromm, M. (2004). *Introduction to the repertory grid interview*. New York, NY: Waxmann Munster.

Geertz, C. (1973). Religion as a cultural system. In C. Geertz (Ed.), *Interpretation of cultures*. (pp. 87–125). New York, NY: Basic Books.

Gobo, G. (2008). *Doing ethnography*. Los Angeles, CA: Sage.

Hammersley, M., & Atkinson, P. (2007). *Ethnography: Principles in practice* (3rd ed.). London, UK: Routledge.

Hollan, D. W. (2001). Developments in person-centered ehtnography. In C. C. Moore & H. F. Mathews (Eds.), *The psychology of cultural experience* (pp. 48–67). Cambridge, UK: Cambridge University Press.

Hollan, D. W. (2005). Setting a new standard: The person-centered interviewing and observation of Robert I. Levy. *Ethos, 33*(4), 459–466.

Johnson, A., & Sackett, R. (1998). Direct systematic observation of behavior. In H. R. Bernard (Ed.), *Handbook of methods in cultural anthropology* (pp. 301–331). Walnut Creek, CA: AltaMira Press.

Levy, R. I., & Hollan, D. W. (1998). Person-centered interviewing and observation. In H. R. Bernard (Ed.), *Handbook of methods in cultural anthropology* (pp. 333–364). Walnut Creek, CA: AltaMira Press.

Liamputtong, P. (Ed.). (2008). *Doing cross-cultural research: Ethical and methodological perspectives*. Dordrecht: The Netherlands: Springer.

Mason, J. (2002). *Qualitative researching*. Thousand Oaks, CA: Sage.

Maxwell, J. A. (2004a). Causal explanation, qualitative research, and scientific inquiry in education. *Educational Researcher, 33*(2), 3–11.

Maxwell, J. A. (2004b). Using qualitative methods for causal explanation. *Field methods, 16*(3), 243–264.

Osgood, C. E., Suci, G. J., & Tannenbaum, P. H. (1957). *The measurement of meaning*. Urbana, IL: University of Illinois Press.

Quinn, N. (2005a). How to reconstruct schemas people share, from what they say. In N. Quinn (Ed.), *Finding culture in talk: A collection of methods* (pp. 35–81). New York, NY: Palgrave Macmillan.

Quinn, N. (2005b). Introduction. In N. Quinn (Ed.), *Finding culture in talk: A collection of methods* (pp. 1–34). New York, NY: Palgrave Macmillan.

Quinn, N. (Ed.). (2005c). *Finding culture in talk: A collection of methods*. New York, NY: Palgrave Macmillan.

Schensul, S. L., Schensul, J. J., & LeCompte, M. D. (1999). *Essential ethnographic methods: Observations, interviews, and questionnaires*. Walnut Creek, CA: AltaMira Press.

Shemmings, D., & Ellingsen, I. T. (2012). Using Q methodology in qualitative interviews. In J. F. Gubrium, J. A. Holstein, A. B. Marvasti & K. D. McKinney (Eds.), *The Sage handbook of interview research: The complexity of the craft* (2nd ed., pp. 415–426). Thousand Oaks, CA: Sage.

Shweder, R. A. (1991). Cultural psychology: What is it? In R. A. Shweder (Ed.), *Thinking through cultures: Expeditions in cultural psychology*. (pp. 73–11). Cambridge, MA: Harvard University Press.

Shweder, R. A. (1996). True ethnography: The lore, the law, and the lure. In R. Jessor, A. Colby & R. Shweder (Eds.), *Ethnography and human development: Context and meaning in social inquiry*. (pp. 15–52). Chicago, IL: University of Chicago Press.

Shweder, R. A. (1997). The surprise of ethnography. *Ethos, 25*(2), 152–163.

Spradley, J. P. (1980). *Participant observation*. New York, NY: Holt, Rinehart and Winston.

Strauss, C. (2005). Analyzing discourse for cultural complexity. In N. Quinn (Ed.), *Finding culture in talk: A collection of methods* (pp. 203–242). New York, NY: Palgrave Macmillan.

Triandis, H. C., & Osgood, C. E. (1958). A comparative factorial analysis of semantic structures in monolingual Greek and American college students. *The Journal of Abnormal and Social Psychology, 57*(2), 187–196.

11
ETHICAL CONCERNS

This chapter will:

- Discuss the issues and controversies around informed consent
- Examine different positions of researchers and the related ethical consequences
- Review the danger of researchers' ethnocentrism
- Deliberate about building rapport and trust with informants and participants
- Consider various controversies with sharing knowledge and the problem of the beneficence of research
- Outline possible ethical positions for culture and psychology research.

Introduction

Ethics is about what is morally right and what is morally wrong. Each community creates its own ethical code for its members' behavior. Cultural researchers deal with, at least, two cultural or moral (by Shweder) communities: their own and the one that they investigate. And here is the difficulty: what is moral in one community may be immoral or ethically improper in the other one, and vice versa. So a researcher can be an ethical person by his or her community's standards, but behave unethically in the community of his or her research. Such improper behavior may offend and/or harm, at least emotionally, members of native communities, thus violating their trust, hospitality, and, ultimately, the very basic values of respect and dignity of all human beings. Such unintentional immorality may also jeopardize the research process or even make it impossible. Professional cultural psychologists cannot allow this to happen. That is why the topic of ethics in cross-cultural research is important to discuss. The issue of ethical behavior is equally relevant for quantitatively oriented cross-cultural psychologists who apply standardized tests and questionnaires, and also for cultural psychologists who conduct ethnographic investigations and live in native communities for some time. Both forms of investigation require entering the community of interest, establishing a rapport and trust with the people there, negotiating the conditions of research, conducting research, communicating results, thanking the members of the community, and exiting it. All these steps should be done ethically, respectfully and without any inconvenience for members of the host community or distortion of research. But this is easier said than done.

Major Ethical Concerns

Informed Consent

One of the first steps of ethical research is getting informed consent from the participants and informants. The requirement to get voluntary consent from and to protect participants of biomedical experiments gained prevalence after WWII, when Nazi doctors performed "scientific" experiments on humans in the Gestapo death camps. After the Nuremberg Trials, the Nuremberg code of ethical research on humans was proposed, and it lies at the core of research ethics regulation in every nation. By establishing such regulations, researchers wanted to make sure such experiments never happen in the future and ensure that all scholars take every step possible to protect participants of scientific investigations from any form of harm, either physical or psychological. Informed consent allows researchers to partner with their participants by explaining to them the purpose and details of their studies and to invite people to voluntarily participate in them. Such a decision on the part of the participants has to be verified by signing an informed consent form. So, what are the challenges with this requirement?

First, the idea of "scientific research" may be alien to members of non-Western cultural communities and efforts have to be made to explain to them what the newcomers want to do in their community. Researchers must be sure to inform and educate people about a study and its consequences and benefits for the members of their community. Community leaders and gatekeepers have to be informed first and must support the investigation. Their backing is crucial for its success. In the previous chapter, I discussed how much information should be revealed to the gatekeepers and other members of the community about a research program. Complete disclosure about the research may bias the behaviors and responses of the participants and informants, may scare them away, or may be an obstacle if the study requires changes in the future. Researchers should tell the truth but leave space for maneuvering if changes must be made, and they may reveal more details when greater trust and rapport have been established. If the study has been properly explained and people see its meaning and the benefits for themselves and/or for their community, and if they are eager to help, then it is time to get participants to sign the informed consent form.

Almost all modern scientific research involving humans *must* include a signed consent form. Researchers simply cannot risk not having it as this may jeopardize their study, its publication, and even their careers in the long run. Dawson and Kass (2005) identified three major tactics that researchers follow in obtaining informed consent: *regulatory*, *individual-oriented*, and *relational*. According to the *regulatory* tactics, researchers are focused primarily on obtaining a signed consent form in order to meet the requirements of the institutional review board (IRB). First, they translate the consent form into a native language and do its back translation to ensure that all the terms and conditions are clearly articulated. Sometimes they may try to avoid the legal and formal language of the original text and present it in more colloquial and understandable native terms. The matter of participants' reading and understanding the consent form can be an issue here. In some cultures, many people have limited reading abilities, but even if they can read, they may not understand the content of the form. Thus, special efforts have to be made to ensure that participants understand it. The best way is to tell participants about the research and the need for consent and then conduct a test of understanding (Dawson & Kass, 2005). This procedure ensures that participants comprehend what is conveyed to them and what rights they have in this research. Once it is clear that participants understand basic terms such as "scientific study," "fully agree to participate," "confidentiality," "right to withdraw," and some others, and the procedure of the study has been discussed in an open conversational manner, then it is time to sign the consent form. In some communities, signing any official/formal form is an intimidating act because such forms are typically related to a government, which these people may not trust. For example, refugees from Vietnam refused to sign a consent form because they were afraid that their government might learn about their whereabouts and might harm them (Birman, 2006). It is also possible that the act of formal signing does not have any meaning for participants. Sometimes signing a consent form may not be appropriate because of local traditions or other particular circumstances; in this case oral consent has to be secured. Liamputtong (2008a) reported about video recording participants providing oral consent (p. 13). The possibility of oral consent should be discussed with and secured by the institution review board (IRB).

Many collectivistic and paternalistic communities do not recognize individual consent but require a collective one. This means that a leader of the community, such as a chief of a village or the head of a family, should consent that the members of the community, or the family, be allowed to participate in the study (Dawson & Kass, 2005; Fisher et al., 2002; Liamputtong, 2008a). The Western idea of informed consent pertains only to an individual and his or her right to decide about participation. But in many communities, members will agree to participate only if the leaders give consent, so the collective consent is more appropriate in this case. One form of collective consent is recognized in Western scientific communities. For minors (children under the legal age), informed consent should be sought from parents or legal guardians. This is understandable, as children may not have a full account of their responsibilities and consequences regarding research, and the more mature and legally responsible individuals should make the decision for them. Nevertheless, an assent from a child him- or herself should too be solicited. This practice also has cultural variations. For example, Fisher et al., 2002, reported that "in some African American families, grandparents, aunts and uncles, or older siblings who do not have legal guardianship serve as the primary decision makers in the everyday activities of children or adolescents" and that in Asian countries "rendering consent [is] a family right rather than individual privilege" (p. 1030).

Some cross-cultural researchers believe that striving to obtain signed informed consent at any cost is often driven to protect researchers and their institutions and not the participants (Dawson & Kass, 2005). Marzano (2012) provided the following revealing view on the ethnocentric nature of an unquestionable requirement for signed informed consent:

> Problems arise for social scientists conducting research in foreign countries if it is decided in their home countries (usually by ethical committees) that indigenous norms should be ignored and that researchers should comply with their home country overkill ethical guidelines. This, in essence absolutizes informed consent and obliges researchers to obtain, for instance, written consent from people who may be illiterate . . . or who normally view a nod of the head as sufficient indication of agreement to participate. In these cases, a request for written consent . . . may even cause offence and introduce an element of suspicion into the research-participant relationship. (p. 445)

There are occasions when researchers fail to follow proper procedures in gaining consent, which results in them alienating participants and losing credibility. Ganesan (2006) described various mistakes made by researchers who were investigating post-tsunami victims in Sri Lanka. Many researchers did not acquire ethical clearance from the institutions in their own countries; instruments were often poorly translated and not validated on the local population; informed consent was rarely solicited or obtained from participants, and researchers did not articulate to the locals how the results would benefit them (p. 245).

The author also mentioned many procedural flaws. Standardized questionnaires were delivered to people who had never seen them before. Respondents signed consent under the assumption that "the questionnaires would lead to some financial or other help from the persons who were carrying out the interviewing" (p. 246). Researchers did not properly explain the purpose of their research and the participants' right to refuse taking part in it. When participants discovered this, they refused to answer the repeated surveys unless some benefits were promised (p. 246).

In the *individual decision-making* tactic outlined by Dawson and Kass (2005), researchers focus on securing an individual participant's voluntary consent. Researchers who embrace this approach believe that "ultimately, understanding of the research happens at the individual level" (p. 1217). The issue of voluntary participation and autonomous decision making is of concern here. Some researchers argue that the communal pressure, the difficulty of turning down research because of promised benefits, respect for researchers and their institutions, unequal distribution of power, false hopes of getting something good from researchers, and some other reasons may actually prevent participants from fully entertaining their free will in consenting. Concerns about anonymity and confidentiality are at issue here as well.

Anonymity means that a researcher removes any information that may identify participants, including replacing names with pseudonyms and avoiding using the real names of the communities or places where the research was done. *Confidentiality* means securing the information about the private and intimate aspects of participants' lives that researchers become exposed to from further distribution. Uncontrolled distribution of such information may harm the participants. These research requirements seem natural to Western researchers, but they may cause cross-cultural misunderstanding. Mohatt and Thomas (2006) reported that for Alaskan native communities, "not identifying yourself, your family, your homeland, and so forth is not acceptable" (p. 104). When the researchers told participants that they would destroy the data after 5 years of completing the research, "elders in the communities protested, stating that they could not imagine why they would tell their story if it would not be shared with others and would be destroyed" (p. 104). The solution was that the IRB agreed to give participants different degrees of confidentiality options. They could choose anonymity or they could choose to be "identified as participants and/or have their story published with their names included" (p. 104). These researchers concluded that "the issue of cross-cultural variation with respect to confidentiality must be carefully considered and negotiated between researchers, communities, and institutional review boards" (p. 104).

The *relational tactic* of dealing with the informed consent process is more than just securing the signing of a consent form. It is about building long-term relations with members of a community and future participants, acquiring their trust, and through this trust building ethical research relationships. This tactic is also known as "ethics of care" and "relational ethics" (Marzano, 2012, p. 451). Many researchers feel this tactic represents the real spirit of ethical cross-cultural research (Fluehr-Lobban, 1998; Wallace, 2006). According to Fluehr-Lobban (1998),

> Using the spirit of informed consent means that the researcher actually discusses the methods and likely research outcomes with the participant, thus the studier and the studied, develop an open relationship. Ideally, informed consent opens up a two-way channel of communication that, once opened, allows for continuous flow of information and ideas. (p. 185)

The main theme behind this spirit is acquiring the trust of participants: trust that they will not be harmed, exploited, or presented in a ridiculous or disgraceful manner; trust that the information they provide will be used to benefit them, their communities, and other people.

> For a researcher, adopting a relational approach means showing a concern for the well-being of the people studied that extends well beyond simple respect for their decision making autonomy or the transparency of the research objectives and methods. That is to say, it extends well beyond informed consent. (Marzano, 2012, p. 451)

This trust should be mutual, meaning that a researcher should also trust that informants/participants will be sincere in their answers and will provide the best available information regarding the questions asked, that they will not trick, deceive, or intentionally keep researchers ignorant about important aspects of the problem at hand. Researchers endorsing relational ethics also highlight a free exchange of information between the researcher and the participating communities and individuals. They also demonstrate high respect for values, and historical memories of participants and their attitudes toward research (Wallace, 2006). Researchers who endorse this tactic may experience tension if they need to get a consent form signed before such a trustful relationship has been developed. For them, entering a community, obtaining trust, securing informed consent, and conducting ethical research are all different sides of a single process of efficient, responsible, and professional research conduct (Dawson & Kass, 2005). Important components of the relational tactic are getting to know the community of interest, learning its beliefs and understanding its perspectives. It is also important for members of a community to understand the motives and intentions of the researchers and not to think, for example, that all Americans are CIA agents but that they can be trustworthy, "decent [and] honorable" individuals (Fluehr-Lobban, 1998, p. 187). The relational tactic also requires that researchers should be aware of the styles of communication prevalent in the community: status hierarchy, power distribution, schedule and appointment management, and many others, so that the communication of researchers with the community is congruent with these styles.

The issue of suspicion of and distrust toward foreigners and outsiders is important. Barata et al. (2006) studied the attitudes of Portuguese and Caribbean immigrants in Canada toward participating in health research and providing informed consent. Researchers discovered that many immigrants are suspicious of the real intentions of researchers and are afraid of being tricked. They look for different signs of trustworthiness, like hearing about the study from a trusted source like a radio announcement or a notification through a doctor's office, and they feel the researcher gains credibility by having a professional appearance. Investigators indicated that for the Caribbean participants, even the word "research" induced feelings of fear and anxiety. They also discovered that this mistrust may have been related to the researcher being of a different ethnicity and that the mediation of a trusted community leader was important for their participation. Another important theme was that participants wanted to receive more information about the research: what the study involved, what the risks and benefits were, and other related issues. In some communities, mistrust of research and the unwillingness to participate may be related to the fact that they do not see any benefits for themselves or their communities stemming from such participation. This means that researchers may have previously exploited such communities for their own academic benefits, or they may have simply failed to communicate the results of their previous studies adequately to members of the community. Both of these situations reflect unethical conduct, and the results of it are evident. Mistrust may come from the communities that were colonized and/or oppressed by the groups or countries researchers are from; in this case building rapport can be a challenging and long process (Liamputtong, 2008a), and in some cases it may even prove to be impossible.

Positions of Researchers: Insiders Versus Outsiders

In Chapters 1, 7, and 8, I introduced the etic and emic positions with regard to objects of investigation: in the etic stance scholars approach cultures, communities, or individuals from "outside" of these systems, and in the emic position they study them from "inside." These positions of researchers have not only methodological but also practical and ethical implications for cultural studies (Spradley, 1980). As was mentioned in Chapter 8, a researcher may be literally an *outsider* when he or she does not have intentions of and does not try to enter the world of others. This occurs when a researcher has tests and questionnaires that need to be answered in a standard fashion, or when he or she simply does not have the time and resources to enter the community of interest fully. Mainstream cross-cultural psychologists who are conducting quantitative comparative studies typically accept this position. Cultural researchers may also try to understand and accommodate a native point of view and look at different events and practices from the native perspective and this stance was labeled the *outsider-to-insider* position. Finally, a researcher may be in an *insider* position when doing research in his or her own cultural community. All three positions have their advantages and disadvantages, and researchers have to be aware of their particular positions and behave accordingly.

The outsider position is the most formal, least intimate, and requires minimal rapport with participants for generating data. An investigation from this position can be done through an interpreter, and a researcher does not even need to know the language of his or her participants. The power disparity between researchers and participants is the highest and the possibility of forming a deep rapport is the lowest. Studies conducted from this position are often labelled "helicopter" or "parachuting" research, meaning that researchers "jump from the sky" into a community of interest, do their business and "fly" away with little care for what is left behind. But even in this detached position, serious researchers have to be concerned with having knowledge about cultural models of communication, knowledge about folk psychology, and many other aspects of local life without which even the most standardized testing procedures may be ethnocentrically biased (see Chapter 9). To reduce potential ethical problems, cross-cultural psychologists (Tapp, Kelman, Triandis, Wrightsman, & Coelho, 1974) recommend including cultural insiders in the project and using them as translators, interpreters, mediators, gatekeepers, or even informants regarding various aspects of the project. These cultural insiders may be local researchers or educated members of the community who understand the structure, requirements, and value of scientific investigation, but are also sensitive of and concerned about their own community and its representation in the study. Birman (2006) provided a convincing account of various nuances of using cultural insiders in conducting research with immigrants when the primary researchers are outsiders.

The *outside-to-insider position* is typical for ethnographic and cultural psychological studies. Researchers who are outsiders to the community of interest—such as white scholars studying aboriginal communities, researchers investigating communities of immigrants and refugees, adult researchers studying children in kindergarten, education researchers investigating classroom cultures, or researchers ethnographically exploring gangs—enter these communities in order to understand "from within" the practices that exist there, the cultural models that guide these practices, and the norms and sanctions that stand behind them. It is not possible to do such investigations from the outsider stance. This is the most ethically loaded position because a bearer of one cultural ethical standard is trying to navigate his or her actions in a community driven by different ethical standards and is trying to collaborate with its members on their terms. This is where ethnocentrism and cultural incompetence may damage the research process. Although researchers in this position may work with interpreters, it is much more beneficial for them to know the language of their community of interest. Assistance from an interested insider/gatekeeper may be helpful here also.

In the *insider position*, researchers share the language and cultural background with their informants and participants. Many researchers believe that this is the best situation for establishing trust and rapport with members of a community, although there are still debates if this position is also beneficial for understanding culture and its models. The insider position allows the researcher to get access to communities that may be unavailable to outsiders. Birman (2006) provided examples of studying immigrants and refugees where insider-researchers had advantages in gaining access to and establishing rapport with their participants. She also mentioned that insiders have access to social networks in ethnic communities that may substantially enrich the investigation. If researchers and informants/participants are of the same ethnical and cultural background, there is no distrust aimed at outsiders. Beoku-Betts (1994) quoted the words of one black participant regarding working with a black researcher: "Black scholars have a sense of soul for our people because they have lived through it." (p. 7). Sharing ethnicity, experience, and language definitely reduces the social distance between researchers and their participants and this, in turn, benefits the research. However, researchers who are insiders by ethnicity and race may still be outsiders by class or other identifiers (religion, accent, personal history, etc.), and may still be treated with suspicion and distrust. Therefore, building rapport and trust is important here as well (see also (Dunbar, Rodriguez, & Parker, 2002; Ryen, 2002)).

But with strong concern about establishing trust and rapport in order to conduct ethical studies, researchers should not forget that their primary goal is to accomplish their research objectives and generate new knowledge. Some feel that an insider position is also beneficial for the scientific side of research: outsiders may be excluded from some important events or ideas or participants may simply decide not to share some information because they feel the outsider researcher may not understand and appreciate it. Beoku-Betts (1994) also stated that:

> Compared to a researcher with outsider status, a researcher with insider status is viewed as bringing a special sensitivity and engagement in the research process because of the shared experience and understanding of rules of conduct and nuances of behavior associated with that shared reality. (p. 416)

On the other hand, some researchers believe that too close familiarity with a culture and a deep involvement with it may prevent a researcher from having productive reflections on the cultural models that govern this community, and thus it may jeopardize the scientific purpose of research (Irvine, Roberts, & Bradbury-Jones, 2008).

Researchers' Ethnocentrism

When entering communities and getting access to participants, the main ethical concern is researchers' *ethnocentrism* and, related to it, cultural insensitivity and cultural incompetence. *Ethnocentrism* is the implicit and to a great extent natural attitude of people that their in-group (tribe, cast, community, ethnic group, or nation) is unique and at the center of the world. Because of this, these members have a feeling of superiority over other people and feel that everything that is conducted or happening in their group is morally right, good, just, and correct, whereas everything that other communities do differently is weird, immoral, bad, and should be scorned (LeVine & Campbell, 1972; A.D. Smith, 1986). Ethnocentrism is an implicit, taken-for-granted belief that, as social psychologists have suggested, works nearly automatically for members of different groups. Ethnocentrism lies at the roots of racism, nationalisms, and other forms of—isms, like sexism, ageism, and similar attitudes. This attitude nurtures stereotyping, prejudice, and discrimination. In Chapter 9, we discussed the ethnocentric bias of cross-cultural researchers. The same bias may prevent scholars from appreciating other communities' cultures and traditions and force them to act unethically there, without being fully aware of this.

Christopher, Wendt, Marecek, and Goodman (2014) provided examples of culturally insensitive forms of help that Western (mostly from the US) therapists and health workers imposed on victims of the 2004 tsunami in Sri Lanka. Following this disaster, Western mental health professionals expected "that posttraumatic stress disorder, depression, and suicide would reach epidemic proportions." But this actually did not happen and "in fact [there] was not an increase in suicidal behavior, or in admission to psychiatric services . . . in the tsunami-affected areas" (p. 646). It was reported that "some foreign psychologists organized group-based programs and therapeutic exercises in ways that violated the strictures of segregation by caste, religion, and sex that underpin local social organizations and stratification" (p. 646). Some psychologists offered one-on-one counselling—completely unaware of the stigma that exists in this area of having any mental health problems. This counselling singled out individuals and made them "the targets of gossip and teasing" (p. 647).

Other psychotherapists, who were ignorant of existing cultural models in Hindu and Buddhist cultures prohibiting intense public displays of emotions, "compelled people to take part in group sessions devoted to emotional catharsis ('Cry! Cry! It will make you feel better")" (p. 646). Despite the ethical demand "not to harm" these victims further, Christopher et al. indicated that "Local anxieties were heightened by culturally inappropriate demands to disclose private information about oneself or one's family in community 'awareness sessions'" (p. 646). They also reported that indiscriminate utilization of critical incident stress debriefing "exacerbated stress responses rather than relieved them" (p. 647). A local psychiatrist who faced such help from the Western colleagues "described the foreign helpers" "medical model orientation" and "lack of consideration of local culture and structures" as "disappointing and sometime shocking" (p. 646). These ethnocentric mental health professionals were not aware, for example, that psychologizing suffering (relating stress and the resulting suffering with mostly psychological consequences: cognitive and emotional disturbances) is not the cultural model for reacting to tragedies in Sri Lanka; that is why forms of psychotherapy used in Western cultures as a method of relieving the suffering were not needed there, and could not have been successful there. The local model for dealing with stress is that "'lamentation, complaint, and grieving' only increase sorrow, but [by] becoming composed, one can attain peace in mind" (p. 646).

The first step for researchers to account for their ethnocentrism is to be aware of it and be reflective about their own ethnocentric attitudes. Researchers must be aware of their community's cultural models, stereotypes, and attitudes that are accompanied by strong positive connotations and are taken for granted the by the majority of their communities' members—including the researchers themselves. Only by being self-aware of cultural biases may cross-cultural psychologists become sensitive to the cultures of others. Christopher et al. (2014) provided the sobering conclusion that American psychologists work abroad under unspoken assumptions that the psychological functioning of people in the rest of the world is described by the psychology that is currently researched, trained, and practiced in the United States (p. 647), thus demonstrating an ethnocentric bias.

A second way of accounting for ethnocentrism is to be knowledgeable of and sensitive to the cultures of others (Liamputtong, 2008a, 2008b). The starting point is to learn about the sociocultural communities of interest: their main values, prevailing cultural models, styles of communication, time management, appearance requirements, and many other aspects and things that constitute the uniqueness and peculiarity of that community. To make this understanding more substantial, it is important to learn about the history of the community and its socioeconomic and political systems. It is strongly recommended that researchers read previous ethnographic research on this or culturally similar communities, and learn what cultural models exist about gender, power distribution, and status hierarchy. This knowledge allows researchers to build their relationships in the community properly, and not offend its people, leaders, and elders. It is strongly recommended that an advisory committee for a project be developed and members of the local community and/or experts on the local culture are included on it. Guidance from such a committee will protect researchers from making mistakes and will help in the research progress.

Building Rapport

One of the main obstacles in building trust and rapport with informants and participants is differences in communication styles. A researcher may unwittingly violate the accepted standards of interacting with people, of greeting them, asking questions, complimenting, asking for favors, and many other communicative tasks, and this may be perceived by locals as improper, unethical, or even offensive. Intercultural communication specialists highlight the importance of *high-* versus *low-context communication styles*, discovered by anthropologist Edward Hall (1976). In communities where the high-context style dominates (mostly Asian, Middle Eastern, African, and aboriginal), the main content of the message is transmitted by the context and by reliance on internalized aspects of communication patterns. "A high-context . . . communication or message is one in which most of the information is either in the physical context or internalized in the person, while very little is in the coded, explicit, transmitted part of the message" (Hall, 1976, p. 91). The high-context communication style is mostly receiver-centered (where the responsibility on decoding and understanding the message lies on the receiver and not on the sender), has a differential linguistic code (meaning that the style of communication depends on the status, age, and familiarity of the communicators); it is not direct and wraps up even negative and harsh messages into smoothly worded style. This style allows both partners to save face and avoid embarrassment (Yum, 1999). Twins and intimate partners very often use high-context communication. When, for example, an Asian businessman provides several excuses why a project cannot be done instead of directly rejecting the offer, he is using high-context and indirect style of communication.

In contrast, the low-context communication style is common in Western Europe and North America (mostly the United States and Canada). This style relies on the verbal content of the message. "A low-context . . . communication is just the opposite [of the high-context one]; i.e., the mass of the information is vested in the explicit code" (Hall, 1976, p. 91) and much less information is in the context. A dialogue between two lawyers in a courtroom is an instance of low-context communication. This style is sender-centered (meaning that it is the responsibility of a sender to convey a message clearly and unambiguously, to be to the point and specific), has less emphasis on a differentiated linguistic code and more on an egalitarian type of interactions (students in cultures with a less differentiated linguistic code for status hierarchy may approach their professors by using their first names, which is absolutely unacceptable for cultures with a high-differentiated code); this style is direct, where a sender of a message expresses his or her ideas, intentions, complaints, or discontent directly and explicitly (Yum, 1999). Germans, Swiss, Scandinavians, and Russians are considered the most prominent examples of direct and low-context communicators. People from communities with the low-context communication style may have difficulties communicating with members of groups with the high-context style. Even more, such low-context and direct communicators may be perceived as rude, pushy, demanding and, ultimately, not people with whom you can have a good conversation. Low-context communicators may perceive people with the high-context style as slow in getting to the point, obscure, and, finally, not trustworthy.

Another important cross-cultural difference that may strongly influence a researcher's ability to establish rapport was also outlined by Hall (1983). This difference is about the way people perceive and manage time. When doing business with or research upon members of non-Western cultures, Westerners may become frustrated that these people are often late for appointments, they do not follow a schedule, and are difficult to plan future events with. Hall labeled the different time management systems of these groups *monochronic* (or M-time) and *polychronic* (or P-time). *Monochronic* literally means that time is perceived as one-dimensional; people in this system do one thing at a time. The term *polychronic* indicates that time is multidimensional and that people do many things at once.

> P-time stresses involvement of people and completion of transactions rather than adherence to preset schedules. Appointments are not taken as seriously and, as consequence, are frequently broken. P-time is treated as less tangible than M-time. For polychronic people time is seldom experienced as "wasted," and is apt to be considered a point rather than a ribbon or a road, but that point is often sacred. (p. 46)

> M-time is also tangible; we speak of it as being saved, spent, wasted, lost, made up, crawling, killed, and running out. These metaphors must be taken seriously. M-time scheduling is used as a classification system that orders life. The rules apply to everything except birth and

death. . . . Monochronic time is arbitrary and imposed, that is, learned. Because it is so thoroughly learned and so thoroughly integrated into our culture, it is treated as though it were the only natural and logical way of organizing life. Yet, it is not inherent in man's biological rhythms or his creative drives, nor it is existential in nature. (pp. 48–49)

Tension may arise when a monochronic researcher schedules an interview with a polychronic informant and discovers that at the time of the interview the informant's house is full of relatives and friends; thus a meaningful interview cannot be conducted. The researcher may become frustrated, feeling that the scheduled interview should have been a priority over all other matters. To the researcher, the appointment is sacred. For a polychronic informant, the appointment means next to nothing, especially if relatives arrive with interesting gossip that needs to be immediately discussed. Maintaining family relations and being up to date on all the community's affairs is much more important than talking to a researcher. If this happens, a cross-cultural conflict (subtle, and nearly invisible) may take place. A researcher must patiently wait until the visit ends, or, if the host will allow it, turn this visitation into a participant observation and even interview the relatives if conditions permit.

Researchers are frequently advised to show respect to locals. But what does respect mean to local people? This also must be discovered. In general, respect in cross-cultural research includes the researcher having personal self-control, self-awareness, and humbleness, combined with an understanding and deference toward local people, their values, sacred figures, and rituals. Liamputtong (2008a) advised researchers to "show respect for indigenous people like the Maori by showing their willingness 'to listen, to be humble, to be cautious, to avoid flaunting knowledge, and to avoid trampling over the *mana* of people'" (p. 6). Other cultural models of respect also exist and should be considered. Researchers can help to demonstrate respect and establish trust by sharing meals with locals, participating in their familial and communal activities, and helping them with important issues (p. 6).

Sharing Results

Another topic that fuels numerous discussions in social research communities is the sharing a study's results and distributing the knowledge obtained during the research. Ganesan (2006), a researcher who analyzed the flaws in organizing research in the tsunami-affected areas, noted that researchers and organizations were reluctant to communicate their results with other humanitarian organizations that were trying to help. Organizations felt they owned the information, even though this information also belonged to the population. This led to multiple assessments being done and delays in the planning and delivery of assistance (p. 246).

Failure to inform participants adequately of cultural and cross-cultural research about the results of the research in their communities and, even more, the inability to demonstrate how these results, even if they are shared, can benefit these participants personally as well as their communities constitute a serious ethical dilemma for all social science researchers. This is the problem of *beneficence* of research. If research results are not properly provided to the communities or if members of the communities do not see any benefits from participating in the research, then informants and participants may feel that they were exploited and used by researchers, leaving a feeling of injustice and domination. Feeding back the results of investigation and conducting beneficent research addresses the concern about the exploitation of participants by researchers who collect their data and disappear without bothering themselves about the people left on the site. One of the issues here is that the participants gave researchers what they needed—information—and received nothing in return. Other times, they receive back very little useful information or tangible compensations, which is usually money. It is not a secret that some participants take part in research exclusively for material reasons when they simply sell the information needed. Offering participants no benefits may prevent researchers from accessing the required information and/or using these participants/informants and their sites again. To avoid participants' exploitation, researchers are advised to at least "give something back, in the way of service or payment; that participants should be empowered by becoming part of the research process; or that research should be directed towards studying the powerful and not the powerless" (Hammersley & Atkinson, 2007, p. 218). All these recipes are not without problems. The issue of bargaining with participants is a tricky one, as it makes a commercial enterprise out of research; this may jeopardize the quality and validity of information provided. Involving participants in the research process may again threaten the validity of a study when some of its issues have to be hidden from the participants. And powerless people are the ones that need the most help and support from a society; in order to make this help efficient, most research should be directed toward them.

People and communities should at least know what kind of information was obtained so they can use this information to their benefit. Again this requirement is not without questions: to whom, how fully and in what form should this information be presented? And who owns the data researchers collect? Do people and their communities have any rights regarding the information they provided? A traditional approach to research requires researchers to protect the ideas and some of the procedural aspects of research from participants in order to get more valid results. Therefore, researchers are obliged to feed back some—but not all—information. In this case participants have little or no rights over the data, but have rights to be informed about the results. Another solution proposed by postcolonial researchers is to conduct *participatory research* where researchers work with members of a community to define the goals of and methodologies of a research, to discuss the results, and share their benefits (Simonsen & Robertson, 2013). The suggestion for participatory research emanated from Western white researchers who invited local researchers and people to contribute to an investigation. Another trend is when indigenous researchers develop and utilize *indigenous* or *decolonizing methodologies* that are conducted by these researchers for their communities (Chilisa, 2012; L. T. Smith, 2012) (some of these issues were discussed in Chapter 1). It is natural to expect that indigenous people have cultural models and practices for generating and distributing knowledge about the world, their communities, other people and themselves. They have generated such knowledge for centuries and have successfully used it for their own needs. Proponents of indigenous methodologies invite indigenous scholars to use these ways of generating knowledge and contributing to the indigenous knowledge production as an antithesis to Western-based academic and applied research, especially when this research is directed toward aboriginal communities and toward solving their problems. The indigenous approach is also considered to be ethically and culturally appropriate, eliminating most of the problems related to Western-based research in aboriginal cultural communities. The major issue here is what new knowledge do these participatory and indigenous methodologies generate and how do researchers reconcile this knowledge with Western methodologies. Only limited types of research may benefit from such methodologies, as blurring the boundaries between a researcher and his or her participants could be beneficial from political or activist perspectives, but has serious limitations for producing social scientific knowledge (Frideres, 1992). The methodology of participatory and indigenous research is beyond the scope of this book, so I send interested readers to relevant sources (Denzin, Lincoln, & Smith, 2008; Kovach, 2010; Simonsen & Robertson, 2013).

But there is another side to the problem of knowledge distribution. Distributing inaccurate or biased research results may damage the reputation, identity, or status of the communities and/or individuals who participated in the project. Ethical manuals and guidelines are full of examples where published research results damaged the reputation or well-being of the informants and communities being studied, especially when people and places became recognizable. Sometimes researchers may even be distributing valid and sound results, but they may be seen by some participants and their communities as harmful and disturbing because such results may present them in an unfavorable light. And what if researchers discover controversial practices and values that have been hidden from the public eye? Should they make them public? Institutions and communities that use these practices would become upset by such publicity, but society at large would benefit from eliminating these practices and keeping such institutions in order. This real or perceived damage by published results may be so substantial that informants/participants may search for retribution from researchers creating unpleasant and even dangerous situations for them (see some examples in (Hammersley & Atkinson, 2007). It is difficult to distribute knowledge in a way that always benefits participants. Then the question is: should potentially harmful results be published at all? Hammersley & Atkinson (2007) advised, based on Becker's opinion, that "one should refrain from publishing anything that will cause embarrassment or distress to the people studied if it is not central to the research or if its importance does not outweigh such consequences" (p. 221).

An additional issue with feeding (or not feeding) the results of research back to communities is the tension between applied (immediately usable) and theoretical (usable in the long-term) purposes of social research. There is an opinion that "the most important question that researchers need to ask is about the relevance of their research to the cultural groups and the likely outcomes" (Liamputtong, 2008a, p. 11). This means that almost any research on culturally different communities should have a nearly immediate impact or application to these communities and the studies that do not provide such effects should be considered unethical. But not all studies are applied and not all address local problems. Some researchers may argue that their research has a broader theoretical relevance and does not need to have a direct applied effect for the studied communities. Or they may argue that the research may address social issues that go beyond the community being studied. For example, refugee research is typically aimed toward developing policy recommendations for NGOs, the UN, and national governments rather than alleviating the problems and sufferings of the particular refugee groups that are the objects of the investigations (Jacobsen & Landau, 2003). And this is a legitimate argument. But participants usually do not have the big picture in their minds when they participate in research; they expect mitigation of their problems and concerns. Those who strongly suffer, like refugees, want their suffering alleviated. Hammersley and Atkinson (2007) cited Becker, who stated that there is an "irreconcilable conflict between the interests of science and the interest of those studied" and commented that this somewhat extreme statement points to "the fallacy of assuming that the researcher and the people studied usually see the research in the same way" (p. 219).

To address this tension, it is important to remind readers that the ultimate purpose of any sociocultural research is to gain new knowledge about societies, cultures, and people's functioning there and that building rapport and being ethical are only the means to this end and not the goals themselves. If researchers conduct a poorly designed study under the guise that this is the maximum that they can afford because of the ethical issues and/or local constraints and limitations, they are violating the primary ethical concern of any researcher: to be professional and rigorous to the highest available scientific and methodological standards. If this primary concern is not met, the study is a waste of time and resources: conducting such a study is fundamentally unethical and unprofessional. Researchers have to

> weigh the importance and contribution of their research against the chances and scale of any harm that is likely to be caused . . . against the values of honesty and fairness, against any infringement of privacy involved, and against any likely consequences for themselves and other researchers. (p. 225)

Because of the inevitable uncertainty and relativity of many of these issues, ethical conflicts will always be present in any cross-cultural research and violations will intentionally or unintentionally happen. Hammersley and Atkinson (2007) stated that

> the most effective strategies for pursuing research should be adopted unless there is clear evidence that these are ethically unacceptable. In other words, indeterminacy and uncertainty should for the most part be resolved by ethnographers [and other cross-cultural researchers] in favour of the interests of research, given that this is their primary task. (p. 225)

If a researcher does not take primary care about his or her research, its quality, validity, and relevance, then who will do this, even if all precautions regarding ethical and moral concerns and problems have been taken care of?

Outlining Possible Standpoints

This chapter indicated that nearly all aspects of the ethical requirements—informed consent, a free and open disclosure of information about research, anonymity, and confidentiality, not harming participants, etc.—may be violated intentionally or unintentionally because of the cultural and situational relativity of all these ethical requirements. So what should researchers do and how can they avoid being unethical and harmful with regard to both the nature of the research and the people being studied? Ethical considerations expressed by social researchers may be categorized into several standpoints that are useful for cultural researchers to reflect upon (Gobo, 2008; Hammersley & Atkinson, 2007; H. M. Smith, 1975). The first stance is *ethical absolutism* or *ethicism*, which treats the Western requirements for ethical research as absolute and the only possible ethical and moral ways of conducting research. This position identifies practices such as using deception or conducting undercover research as absolutely unethical under any circumstances. Then there is *ethical situationism* (also, *situated research ethics* (Gobo, 2008; Heggen & Guillemin, 2012)) that requires researchers to do their best in avoiding harm to participants by balancing the costs and benefits of their particular research. This balancing act is culture- and context-relative and cannot be done a priori based on a particular moral position. Research techniques are ethically neutral and their appropriateness should be evaluated regarding the particular contexts and circumstances of research. Basic concerns for the well-being and dignity of participants as well as for the integrity of research remain. *Ethical relativism* is a position where the ethics of a research is predetermined by the values and norms of the community wherein the study is conducted. "This position often leads to arguments to the effect that participants must be fully consulted or closely involved in the research, and that nothing must be done by researchers that transgresses their moral values" (Hammersley & Atkinson, 2007, p. 220). Its roots are found in the ideas of participatory ethnography and indigenous methodologies. Hammersley and Atkinson labeled the fourth position *Machiavellianism*: when researchers are completely committed to conducting research at any cost and they see ethical constraints as impediments that should be removed or very strongly restricted. Some researchers connect this position with ethical utilitarianism, where the ends justify the means (Gobo, 2008).

There is a trend of researchers advocating that the ethical situationist position is the most realistic, balanced, and practically executable. Hammersley & Atkinson (2007) argued that

> there are dangers in treating particular procedures as if they were intrinsically ethical and desirable, whether this involves ensuring fully informed consent, giving people control over

data relating to them, feeding back information about the research findings, or publishing information on the basis of the "public's right to know." What is appropriate and inappropriate depends upon the context to a larger extent, and sometimes actions that are motivated by genuine ethical ideals can cause severe problems, not just for researchers but for people they are studying as well. (p. 221)

Such a position may be associated with the above-discussed relational ethics that is based on thorough considerations about the people being studied and takes into account their points of view without jeopardizing the ultimate purposes of research. Hammersley and Atkinson continued:

Underlying the treatment of any procedures as absolute ethical requirements are assumptions about how social settings *ought to be* that may neglect *how they actually are*. Moreover, views about how they ought to be may well differ for those with different cultural backgrounds or political commitments. At the same time, it seems to us that there are values which most people, across most societies, would subscribe to in one form or another, and that these should guide researchers' judgments about what is and is not acceptable behavior. And the values and feelings of those being studied must also be considered. However, it is important to recognize that it may not always be possible or desirable to avoid acting in ways that run contrary to these values. (p. 222)

The ethical situationist position places strong emphasis on researchers' autonomous, rational, and reflective judgments about the ethics of their research and trusts that they are capable of exercising this autonomy responsibly and efficiently. Heggen & Guillemin (2012) talked about *ethical mindfulness* as a fundamental requirement for "situated research ethics" (p. 467). Such mindfulness asks researchers to attend to ethical issues at all stages of the research process, especially while interacting with participants.

Conclusion

Conducting ethical research is always of concern for sociocultural scholars. This concern is inherent in the very nature of any sociocultural project because researchers navigate across different moral communities. And there is no one-size-fits-all recipe for ethical conduct. The position supported in this chapter is that ethical conduct depends on a researcher's ethical mindfulness, sincere concern for the well-being of his or her informants and respondents, and the ability to balance academic responsibility and integrity with the contextual and situational conditions of a study. Therefore, relational and situated research ethics are considered to be most relevant for culture and psychology researchers. There are still many challenges and obstacles within this position. This chapter addressed some of them: how to get informed consent and not to offend local people, to be aware of the position from which a researcher approaches his or her study and what ethical responsibilities lie within each of them, how to avoid researchers' ethnocentrism, how to build trust and rapport with members of communities by learning their communication styles and time management systems, and how to share the results of research and make them beneficial for all participating parties. The list of these challenges and concerns is of course much longer, and the chapter invites readers to start exercising their ethical mindfulness by learning about other ethical issues that they may encounter and to engage in thinking about dealing with them in the most optimal fashion.

Questions

1. Why is informed consent important and required by all national research associations?
2. List the challenges of the regulatory tactic for getting informed consent.
3. The relational strategy of obtaining informed consent (and related to it relational ethics) is considered to be the most appropriate approach for culture and psychology research. Justify this position.
4. Why is the demand for anonymity and confidentiality controversial for cultural research? Find other examples when requirements for ethical research face cultural challenges.
5. Across several chapters, different positions of researchers are discussed: outsider; outsider-to-insider, and insider. Summarize these positions and outline the ethical demands for each of them.
6. Discuss in class the issue of ethnocentrism in sociocultural research. Bring your own examples and concerns. Outline the way to minimize the ethnocentric bias of researchers.
7. Communication style and time management systems may cause difficulties in building rapport with participants and may help to account for the ethnocentric bias.. Are there other aspects of communication, interactions, conducting research, etc. that should be considered by ethically mindful researchers?
8. Should researchers share their results of with communities? If you have done any of cultural or communal research, reflect on how this could be done. Discuss these issues in class.
9. Do you see any problems and controversies with participatory and indigenous research? You may decide to read more on these topics. Invite researchers who practice this type of research to your class and discuss the issues with them.
10. Outline the relational and situated research ethics: are they practical to use? When using them, how is it possible to meet the formal requirements of the institutional review boards?

Glossary

Anonymity: protecting a person's privacy by not identifying him or her by name.

Collective consent is given by a person in authority to his or her subordinates, allowing them to participate in research: in different cultures, parents give consent to (or for) their children, a husband to his wife and children; a head of a community to its members.

Confidentiality: keeping private information private.

Ethnocentrism is the implicit and to a great extent natural attitude of people that their in-group (tribe, caste, community, ethnic group, or nation) is unique and at the center of the world. Because of this, these members have a feeling of superiority over other people and feel that everything that is conducted or happening in their group is morally right, good, just, and correct, whereas everything that other communities do differently is weird, immoral, bad, and should be scorned.

Individual consent is given by an individual to a researcher.

Informed consent: permission granted to a researcher from participants based on information about risks, benefits, and procedures of a research.

Position of a researcher: *outsider:* when a researcher does not enter the intentional worlds of others; *outsider-to-insider:* when a researcher from outside of a cultural community enters it with the intention to understand from inside its intentional world; *insider:* when a researcher studies his or her own community, or a community with the same language and cultural traditions.

Relational and situated research ethics: an approach to research when researchers do their best to avoid harming participants by balancing the costs and benefits of their particular research. They do this by considering the culture of participants and the context of research, and building long-term relations with members of a community and future participants, acquiring their trust, and through this trust building ethical research relationships.

Styles of communication (by E. Hall): *high-context communication* happens when the main content of the message is transmitted by the context and by a reliance on the internalized aspects of communication patterns; *low-context communication* mostly relies on the direct verbal content of a message.

Time perception and management systems (by E. Hall): *Monochronic time* is perceived as one-dimensional; people in this system do one thing at a time; *polychromic time* indicates that time is multidimensional and that people do many things at once.

Recommended Reading

Christopher, J. C., Wendt, D. C., Marecek, J., & Goodman, D. M. (2014). Critical cultural awareness: Contributions to a globalizing psychology. *American Psychologist, 69*(7), 645–655.

Fisher, C. B., Hoagwood, K., Boyce, C., Duster, T., Frank, D. A., Grisso, T. . . . Zayas, L. H. (2002). Research ethics for mental health science involving ethnic minority children and youths. *American Psychologist, 57*(12), 1024–1040.

Hammersley, M., & Atkinson, P. (2007). *Ethnography: Principles in practice* (3rd ed.). London, UK: Routledge.

Liamputtong, P. (Ed.). (2008b). *Doing cross-cultural research: Ethical and methodological perspectives*. Dordrecht: The Netherlands: Springer.

Trimble, J. E. & Fisher, C. B. (Eds.), *The handbook of ethical research with ethnocultural populations & communities*. Thousand Oaks, CA: Sage.

References

Barata, P. C., Gucciardi, E., Ahmad, F., & Stewart, D. E. (2006). Cross-cultural perspectives on research participation and informed consent. *Social Science & Medicine, 62*(2), 479–490.

Beoku-Betts, J. (1994). When black is not enough: Doing field research among Gullah women. *NWSA Journal, 6*(3), 413–433.

Birman, D. (2006). Ethical issues in research with immigrants and refugees. In J. E. Trimble & C. B. Fisher (Eds.), *The handbook of ethical research with ethnocultural populations & communities* (pp. 155–177). Thousand Oaks, CA: Sage.

Chilisa, B. (2012). *Indigenous research methodologies*. Thousand Oaks, CA: Sage.

Christopher, J. C., Wendt, D. C., Marecek, J., & Goodman, D. M. (2014). Critical cultural awareness: Contributions to a globalizing psychology. *American Psychologist, 69*(7), 645–655.

Dawson, L., & Kass, N. E. (2005). Views of US researchers about informed consent in international collaborative research. *Social Science & Medicine, 61*(6), 1211–1222.

Denzin, N. K., Lincoln, Y. S., & Smith, L. T. (Eds.). (2008). *Handbook of critical and indigenous methodologies*. Los Angeles, CA: Sage.

Dunbar, C., Rodriguez, D., & Parker, L. (2002). Race, subjectivity, and the interview process. In J. F. Gubrium & J. A. Holstein (Eds.), *Handbook of interviwew research: Context & method* (pp. 279–298). Thousand Oaks, CA: Sage.

Fisher, C. B., Hoagwood, K., Boyce, C., Duster, T., Frank, D. A., Grisso, T. . . . Zayas, L. H. (2002). Research ethics for mental health science involving ethnic minority children and youths. *American Psychologist, 57*(12), 1024–1040.

Fluehr-Lobban, C. (1998). Ethics. In H. R. Bernard (Ed.), *Handbook of methods in cultural anthropology* (pp. 173–202). Walnut Creek, CA: AltaMira Press.

Frideres, J. S. (1992). Participatory research: An illusionary perspective. In J. S. Frideres (Ed.), *A world of communities: Participatory research perspectives* (pp. 1–13). North York, ON: Captus University Publications.

Ganesan, M. (2006). Psychosocial response to disasters—some concerns. *International Review of Psychiatry, 18*(3), 241-247.

Gobo, G. (2008). *Doing ethnography*. Los Angeles, CA: Sage.

Hall, E. T. (1976). *Beyond culture*. Garden City, NY: Anchor Books.
Hall, E. T. (1983). *The dance of life*. New York, NY: Anchor Books.
Hammersley, M., & Atkinson, P. (2007). *Ethnography: Principles in practice* (3rd ed.). London, UK: Routledge.
Heggen, K., & Guillemin, M. (2012). Protecting participants' confidentiality using a situated research ethics approach. In J. F. Gubrium, J. A. Holstein, A. B. Marvasti & k. D. McKinney (Eds.), *The Sage handbook of interview research: The complexity of the craft* (pp. 465–476). Thousand Oaks, CA: Sage.
Irvine, F., Roberts, G., & Bradbury-Jones, C. (2008). The researcher as insider versus the researcher as outsider: Enhancing rigor through language and cultural sensitivity. In P. Liamputtong (Ed.), *Doing cross-cultural research: Ethical and methodological perspectives* (pp. 35–48). Dordrecht, The Netherlands: Springer.
Jacobsen, K., & Landau, L. B. (2003). The dual imperative in refugee research: Some methodological and ethical considerations in social science research on forced migration. *Disasters, 27*(3), 185–206.
Kovach, M. E. (2010). *Indigenous methodologies: Characteristics, conversations, and contexts*. Toronto, ON: University of Toronto Press.
LeVine, R. A., & Campbell, D. T. (1972). *Ethnocentrism: Theories of conflict, ethnic attitudes, and group behavior*. New York, NY: John Wiley & Sons.
Liamputtong, P. (2008a). Doing research in cross-cultural context: Methodological and ethical issues. In P. Liamputtong (Ed.), *Doing cross-cultural research: Ethical and methodological perspectives* (pp. 3–20). Dordrecht, The Netherlands: Springer.
Liamputtong, P. (Ed.). (2008b). *Doing cross-cultural research: Ethical and methodological perspectives*. Dordrecht: The Netherlands: Springer.
Marzano, M. (2012). Informed consent. In J. F. Gubrium, J. A. Holstein, A. B. Marvasti & k. D. McKinney (Eds.), *The Sage handbook of interview research: The complexity of the craft* (pp. 443–456). Thousand Oaks, CA: Sage.
Mohatt, G. V., & Thomas, L. R. (2006). "I wonder, why would you do it that way?" Ethical dilemmas in doing participatory research with Alaska native communities. In J. E. Trimble & C. B. Fisher (Eds.), *The handbook of ethical research with ethnocultural populations & communities* (pp. 93–115). Thousand Oaks, CA: Sage.
Ryen, A. (2002). Cross-cultural interviewing. In J. F. Gubrium & J. A. Holstein (Eds.), *Handbook of interviwew research: Context & method* (pp. 335–354). Thousand Oaks, CA: Sage.
Simonsen, J., & Robertson, T. (Eds.). (2013). *Routledge international handbook of participatory design* New York, NY: Routledge.
Smith, A. D. (1986). *The ethnic origins of nations*. Oxford, UK: Blackwell.
Smith, H. M. (1975). *Strategies of social research: The methodological imagination*. Englewood Cliffs, NJ: Prentice-Hall.
Smith, L. T. (2012). *Decolonizing methodologies: Research and indigenous peoples* (2nd ed.). London, UK: Zed Books.
Spradley, J. P. (1980). *Participant observation*. New York, NY: Holt, Rinehart and Winston.
Tapp, J. L., Kelman, H. C., Triandis, H. C., Wrightsman, L. S., & Coelho, G. V. (1974). Continuing concern in cross-cultural ethics: A report. *International Journal of Psychology, 9*(3), 231–249.
Wallace, S. A. (2006). Addressing health disparities through relational ethics: An approach to increasing African American participation in biomedical and health research In J. E. Trimble & C. B. Fisher (Eds.), *The handbook of ethical research with ethnocultural populations & communities* (pp. 67–75). Thousand Oaks, CA: Sage.
Yum, J. O. (1999). The impact of Confucianism on interpersonal relationships and communication in East Asia. In L. A. Samovar & R. E. Porter (Eds.), *Intercultural communication: A reader* (9th ed., pp. 63–73). Belmont, CA: Wadsworth.

CONCLUSION

Final Words of Encouragement

This book argues that to address the events, conflicts, and problems that are related to cultural communities and people' interactions with them, culture and psychology researchers have to fully understand why people do, think, and feel as they do in particular cultural environments (and people always act, feel, and think in particular sociocultural circumstances). In order to gain this understanding, it is important to, first, investigate the collective intersubjective ideas of communities about various domains of people's lives (public aspects of cultural models), then study the learned and internalized facets of these models in people's minds (internalized aspects of cultural models), and, then examine how these aspects interact with each other and determine people's experiences and behaviors. This complex sociocultural-psychological mechanism of people's functioning in sociocultural environments constitutes the primary target of research on culture and psychology.

The major message of this textbook is that a problem-oriented, realist, and case-based research is the most productive way to conduct such studies and to advance knowledge in this area. Such studies should be guided by the realist paradigm accompanied by interpretivist thinking. This symbiosis provides the most comprehensive way to understand both the communal cultural models and their representations in people's minds. Within this broad framework, researchers may choose to use the *Homo Interpretans* theoretical perspective. This perspective could be best implemented through different fields of cultural/indigenous psychology and psychological and cognitive anthropology. It is recommended to use the idiographic strategy accompanied by the intensive design suggested by realist scholars. Thick description and the hermeneutic circle of interpretation should also be considered by experienced culture and psychology researchers. The goal of most projects should be to retroduct the hidden causal forces and mechanisms that drive and regulate people's functioning in different sociocultural environments. The primary candidates for this search are the various cultural models that exist in the communities and that regulate the behaviors of their members. These cultural models are taken-for-granted and thus not given directly to their bearers or to researchers. Scientists can discover them only through ampliative inferences. Special attention should be paid to the agency of members of communities in their interactions with existing cultural models. It is suggested here that a primary methodological tool should be person-centered ethnography and interviewing when members of a community are studied both as informants and as participants in order to infer their public and internalized aspects of the cultural models. Creativity, insightfulness, deep knowledge of the subject matter, and a diversity of methods and techniques will help investigators make these ampliative breakthroughs to the domain of unobservables.

A very important feature of the suggested logistics of research is that the retroducted ideas about the cultural models and mechanisms of sociocultural regulation are still hypotheses and conjectures—not final products of research. After proposing these hypotheses, researchers should start the elaborate work of verifying, testing, and validating these. At this stage standardized methods, including field experiments, can be implemented. The ultimate goal is to test if the proposed hypotheses reflect the actual sociocultural and psychological mechanisms that regulate the behavior of people in a community. A theory may be derived only after such testing.

Scientific generalizations are taking place at several levels here and are executed exclusively in a theoretical, and not enumerative, form. First, researchers generalize from individuals, as separate cases, to the mechanisms of the sociocultural regulation of all members of that particular community. These mechanisms have universal components and individual variations in their execution. Both universal and specific aspects should be considered when building the hypothetical theoretical model of these sociocultural mechanisms. If a researcher wants to generalize more broadly, say, about how culture interacts with human agency in regulating people's behaviors and experiences, he or she should work with a variety of communities that differ regarding their arrangements of cultural models and the freedom their members have to deviate from them. Researchers have to do a purposeful selection of different communities, hypothesize the mechanisms of regulation there, test and verify them and compare them with the mechanisms extracted in the first community. These between-case analyses and generalizations across different cultural communities allow scholars to move toward discovering more general mechanisms of a culture's individual interactions, thus contributing to theories of the sociocultural and psychological regulations of human experiences and actions.

Remember that real scientists are not research workers; they are discoverers and inventors. They penetrate into the unobservables, into the areas and domains where nobody except for true explorers with inquisitive and curious minds can inquire into. Only such discoveries can bring real delight to any scientific research. Follow this path and you will have the opportunity to advance knowledge and bring happiness and satisfaction to yourself and to people around the world.

INDEX

abduction 78–81; and interpretivism 82–6; *see also* modes of inference, abductive
acculturation 68, 78, 107, 133–5, 159, 192; definition of 150; operationalization of 70, 150, 237, 241
adaptation of assessment instruments 227
adoption of assessment instruments 227
agency: human 13, 18, 21, 48–9, 50, 83, 107, 300
aggregation bias 219 *see also* ecological fallacy
Allport, G. 171–2, 181, 218
analytic generalization *see* generalization, theoretical
analytic notes/memos 275
anonymity 285, 294, 296
anthropology 4, 8, 25, 172, 178, 207, 211; cognitive 14–15, 25; comparative 186, 211–12; cultural 4–6, 10, 26, 43, 120–1, 186; at a distance 12, 25, 121; of experience 13; interpretive 85–6; linguistic 8; phenomenological 13, 26; psychoanalytic 12; psychological 11–13, 19, 50; and realism 97, 98; social 4–5, 8, 10, 26–7, 43, 203; sociocultural 5, 27; and sociology 5
"anticipation of nature" (by Bacon) 96
Apel, K-O 83
argument by analogy 103
atomism 35
autonomy: psychological 13, 48, 49, 50, 74, 83, 215, 219; support of 246

Bacon, F. 60–1, 62, 96, 102, 159, 208
Bacon, R. 59
basic research 119–20
Bastian, A. 4, 5, 26
Benedict, R. 11–12, 90–1, 97, 120–1, 184, 185, 202
Berger, P. and Luckmann, T. 7, 35, 40, 43, 46, 83
Berkley, G. 64
Berry, J. 15–6, 68, 147, 183, 187, 191, 213, 217
Bhaskar, R. 69, 81–2, 95–6, 97, 105, 107, 108, 117, 129, 163, 174

bias 228, 230, 250, 251; cognition 228, 230, 232; communication 228, 230, 233; construct 228, 230–1, 234; definition of 228; ethnocentric or cultural 228, 230, 231, 234, 287–9; item 228, 230, 233; procedural or measurement 228, 230, 232–3; response 244; sampling 188–9, 250
Big Five personality theory 36, 144, 214, 216; *see also* trait theories of personality
Blumer, H. 97, 125, 141, 142, 147, 151
Boas, F. 5, 9, 11, 211
Bourdieu, P. 47, 59, 75, 97, 100–1, 155–7, 159, 162, 163
Bridgman, P. W. 149 *see also* operationalism
British empiricists 35–6, 64
Bruner, J. 19

case(s) 172, 175, 177, 184; definition of 184; extreme/deviant and pathological 103, 106–7, 192; sampling 192–3; typical 192
case-based approach/method/design 43, 50, 115, 145, 171, 177, 178, 183–5, 187, 194, 202, 208, 262; definition of 184; and realist research 106, 163–4, 186, 299; studies 40, 50, 176, 184, 191; *see also* research design and comparative case-based design/studies
categorical fallacy *see* fallacies
causality/causes 17, 35–7, 40, 49, 94, 105, 145, 173, 191, 201, 211, 265, 277
causal mechanisms *see* mechanisms
cognitive interviewing 242–3
coherence (by Whewell) 97, 164–6
Cole, M. 19, 50
comparative approach/method 10–11, 13, 43, 50, 136, 207–11, 221; in anthropology/ ethnography 10–11, 15, 43, 50, 132, 178, 186, 211–12, 277; before-and-after case study design 211; comparative case-based design 208–9, 221, 299; comparative *case* studies 99, 103, 192, 208, 277; of concomitant variations

(by Mill) 208; concurrent/synchronic design 208, 212; controlled comparison 209; cross-cultural psychological studies 16–18, 179–80, 186–8, 213–15, 228–52, 287; of difference (by Mill) 208–9; ecological-level studies 216–17, 221; historical/diachronic design 208, 212; individual-level studies 216, 222; methods of agreement (by Mill) 208–09; multicultural studies 188, 207, 212–13, 222; of residue (by Mill) 208; qualitative comparative method (by Ragin) 176, 209–11; within-case and cross/between-case analysis (by Miles, Huberman & Saldana) 209, 273, 300; variable-based design 213, 221, 228–52

concept(s) 121–123, 134, 141–3, 167; *see also* term(s); ambiguity and vagueness 147–9; definition of 143, 167; empirical/descriptive 142, 145, 167, 229; functional ambiguity of 148; in interpretivism 152–4, 234; nominalism versus realism 144–5; in positivism 151–2, 180, 235; in realism 146, 154–5; theoretical/explanatory 142, 145–6, 158, 167, 229, 237 (*see also* hypothetical constructs); and variables 145; *see also* definition

conceptual framework 122, 126–7, 141–3

conceptualization 100, 115, 125, 142, 276; epistemological tradition of 144, 167; in ethnographic study; "experience-near & experience-distant" (by Geertz) 152–5, 163, 167, 276; informant driven 276; observer driven 276; ontological tradition of 144, 167; the paradox of 158, 167

confidentiality 283, 285, 294, 296

confirmatory factor analysis (CFA) 236, 246, 250, 252

confirmatory studies 125, 139

confounding bias 219; *see also* ecological fallacy

consilience (by Whewell) 97, 164, 165

context of discovery 63, 64, 74, 79, 103

context of justification 63, 73, 74, 79

"correlation does not mean causation" 36, 183

counterfactual thinking 103, 104–5

country-level ecological studies 17, 187, 216–18, 221; *see also* unpackaging studies

covering laws model of science 65

Cronbach's alpha 244

cross-cultural research (in anthropology) *see* comparative approach

cultural determinism 41–2, 49, 52

cultural models 21, 22–4, 26, 43–9, 83, 153, 201, 205, 211–12, 222, 230, 233–4, 258–61, 265, 268–9, 287–8, 299–300; cultural models for and cultural models of 258, 273; definition of 44, 45, 52, 258, 259, 273; external/public (communal/public) aspects of 12, 44, 83, 259–61, 269–70, 299; foundational schemes (by Shore) 48; instituted models (by Shore) 48; internal/mental/internalized aspects of 12, 44, 91, 260–1, 269–70, 273, 299

cultural relativism 9, 26

culture xiii–xiv, xv, 5–6, 10, 13, 16–17, 20–1, 34, 38–9, 41–2, 43, 119–20; adaptationist theories 6–7, 38–9; as cognitive systems/systems of knowledge 7–8, 41; definitions of 6–9, 16–17, 148–9, 259; dimensional theories 17, 34, 217–18; ideational theories 7–8; as structural systems 8 (*see also* structuralist approach); as symbolic systems 8–9, 41 (*see also* interpretivism); functionalist approach 5, 11, 38–40, 52 (*see also* structural functionalism); theories of 6–9, 15, 20–1, 26; theory of cultural models 14, 20–1, 44; *see also* cultural determinism; cultural models, cultural relativism, essentialization of culture, moral/socio/cultural communities; reification of culture

culture and personality studies 5, 11–12, 25, 203, 204

D'Andrade, R. 9, 14, 20, 33, 41, 43, 46, 47, 83, 97, 144, 269

Darwin, C. 80–1, 91, 165

Dasen, P. R. 15

deduction 58, 65, 74, 80, 170; *see also* modes of inference

definition: nominal 148, 167; operational 145, 148, 149–50, 167 (*see also* operationalization, operationalism); theoretical/conceptual/real 148–9, 150, 167

Descartes, R. 33, 64

descriptive-exploratory studies 124–5

descriptive-inductive studies 125, 126–7, 128

development of assessment instruments 227–8

Dilthey, W. 83

ecological or decomposition fallacy *see* fallacies

effect size 73

elementarism/atomism 35, 37

emergent properties 71, 74, 218

empirical 64–5, 74; generalization (*see* generalizations); accidental regularities 68, 70–1, 102, 182; necessary regularities 68–9, 70, 102, 180, 182; regularities 36, 37, 62, 66–8, 69, 81, 95, 102, 105, 128, 129, 135–6, 158, 160, 174, 177, 181, 194, 195, 219, 276 (*see also* scientific law)

empiricism 33, 64, 66–8, 74–5, 81, 150–1, 160; logical 64, 68

enculturation 42, 44, 47, 49, 52, 82, 91

entering the field 261–4, 267

entering the intentional worlds of others 152, 259, 261, 296

enumerative generalization *see* generalization

epistemology 32, 56, 66, 74, 75, 94, 107, 232; epistemological fallacy (by Bhaskar) (*see* fallacies)

equivalence 19, 228, 245–8, 252; construct or concept 215, 227–37, 245, 249, 250, 251, 252; content 227–8, 237–8, 252; functional 235, 237, 247, 252; linguistic or semantic 227–8, 238–45, 252; structural 236–7, 252; *see also* measurement invariance

essence of things 57, 59, 62, 65, 75, 81, 82, 95, 134, 167, 171, 177, 208, 276

essentialist fallacy *see* fallacies

essentialization: of culture 35; of mental disorders 232

ethical mindfulness 295
ethical standpoints: ethical absolutism/ethicism 294; ethical relativism 294–5; ethical situationism (situated research ethics) 294–5
ethnocentrism 19, 23, 207, 287, 288–9, 295–6
ethnographic census-taking 265, 275
ethnographic journal 274–5
ethnographic mapping 9, 265, 275
ethnography/ethnographic method(s) 5, 9–10, 14, 21, 43, 50, 89, 90, 157, 162, 177, 202, 204, 206, 234, 241, 258–61; analysis of 276–8; covert 263, 267; definition of 257, 279 ethnographic fieldwork/fieldwork 121, 202, 257; person-centered 14, 92, 94, 268–74, 279 *see also* interviewing person-centered
etic and emic: approaches 9, 19, 21, 26, 176; -based criteria 10; stances (by Pike) 178–9; position of researchers 22, 43, 194
evaluative discourse (by Shweder) 260
Evans-Pritchard, E. E. (Sir) 5, 10, 211
evolutionary biology/biologists 38, 40, 81
evolutionary perspective/thinking 18, 38, 80
evolutionary psychology/psychologists 6, 17, 42
experience 13; anthropology of 13 (*see also* phenomenological anthropology); cultural 13–14, 202; and self 13
experiment 105, 204, 208–9, 213–15; in interpretivism 162; in positivism 37, 94, 105; in realism 98–9, 105–6, 164; social 98, 103, 106; thought 103
explanation 87, 128–30, 132–3, 159, 175; causal 37, 70, 94, 99, 130, 165, 177; mechanistic/mechanismic 100–1; in positivism 64, 67, 71, 129, 164, 195, 235; in realism 62, 93, 96, 102, 129–30
exploratory factor analysis (EFA) 236, 245
exploratory studies 125, 135; *see also* descriptive-exploratory studies
"explanatory understanding" (by Weber) 87, 92, 130
externalization 48

fallacies: "the average man fallacy" (by Mulaik) 181–2; categorical 231, 251–2; "cultural attribution fallacy" (by Matsumoto and Yoo) 188; epistemological (by Bhaskar) 108; ecological or decomposition 182, 208, 218–20, 221; essentialist (by Kleinman) 232; individual or compositions 208, 218, 222; inductivist (by Mulaik) 236
fallibilism 93, 94, 96, 101, 107, 146
fieldnotes 274–5
focus groups 126, 238, 239, 241, 242, 243
"foreknowledge" (by Gadamer) 87–8, 93, 163
Frazer, J. G. (Sir) 4
Freud, S. 11–12, 46, 81
"fusion of horizons" (by Gadamer) 88

Gadamer, H-G. 83, 85, 87–8
Galton's problem 10, 26

gatekeepers 263–4, 279, 283, 287
Geertz, C. 8–9, 42, 86, 90, 152–5, 207, 273
generalization: empirical 61–2, 64, 65, 66, 128, 262; enumerative 65, 73, 74, 75, 158, 177, 182, 187, 190–1, 262; "generalization with mechanisms" (by Bechtel) 186; theoretical 75, 158, 175, 177, 186, 262
Giddens, A. 97
Greenfield, P. 19, 230–4

Habermas, J. 83
habitus (by Bourdieu) 47, 101, 155–7, 159; research xv, 1, 59, 75
Heidegger, M. 83
Herder, J. G. von 4
hermeneutic circle, the 85–6, 88, 89, 92, 93, 94, 103, 110, 154, 176, 276, 299
hermeneutics 33, 83, 85–6; depth 8, 85–6, 89, 110, 130; double 88, 102, 152; single 152; surface 85, 89, 110, 130
Herskovits, M. 6
high- versus low-context communication styles (by Hall) 289–90, 297
Hirsch, E. D. 83, 93
Hofstede, G. 17, 187, 217, 219
Hofstede's cultural dimensions theory 17, 34, 36, 70, 128, 145, 150
holistic organismic thinking 39, 52, 184
Human Relations Area Files 11
Hume, D. 35, 60, 63, 64, 94, 105, 144–5
Husserl, E. 83, 174–5, 178
hypothetical construct 142, 145–6, 149, 150, 167, 226, 228, 229, 230, 233, 235, 236, 237, 272

indigenous/decolonizing methodologies *see* methodology
idiographic sciences 171–3, 175, 178, 194; approach 40, 115, 171, 175, 187, 299; interpretive idiographic approach 176
induction 58, 59–60, 65, 75, 165, 170; ampliative 58, 60, 61, 62, 65, 75, 79, 80, 96, 99, 107, 185, 191; analytic 97, 176, 208; eliminative 208; enumerative/naïve 58, 60, 61–2, 65–6, 67, 75, 84, 96, 165, 173, 181, 185, 190; explanatory 60; problem of 63; substantive 60; *see also* modes of inference, inductive
inductivist fallacy *see* fallacies
"inference to the best explanation" 80, 109; *see also* abduction
informants 88, 152, 182, 269–71, 287; key 189; specialized 189
informed consent 283–6, 296; collective 284; tactics to obtain, individual-oriented 283, 285; tactics to obtain, regulatory 283–4; tactics to obtain, relational 283, 285–6
insight 63, 64–5, 69, 74, 75, 81, 103–4, 121, 160, 207, 220, 261, 267, 274
instantiation 48–9
intelligence 150–1, 229–31, 233; intelligence scales 227, 237

intentional: states 20, 21, 26, 46, 258, 260–1, 265; things 13, 20, 26, 45, 46, 49, 97, 258, 260–1; worlds/realities 18, 20, 21, 26, 46, 81, 82, 83, 97, 111, 265; worlds of others 92, 152, 259, 261
intentionality 20, 46, 147, 148
internalization 46–8, 52, 63, 66, 75, 81, 99, 146, 154, 156
interpretation 8, 14, 20, 21, 64, 70, 75, 82, 83–5, 87, 88, 94, 97, 102, 102, 109–11, 130, 153, 177, 185, 206, 207, 261; act/process of 84, 85, 87–8, 163, 176, 275–6; "interpretation of nature" (by Bacon) 61, 96, 102; "surface" and "depth" 86, 259, 270; types of 89–92; validity of 92–4; *see also* "thin" and "thick" descriptions and hermeneutics
interpretive sciences 86, 92, 94, 176; anthropology 8, 85; "interpretive understanding" *see* verstehen; sociology 85; psychology 85
interpretivism 50, 78, 83, 85–6, 95, 110, 128, 161–3, 176; critique of 92–4; epistemology of 94; methodology of 94, 259; ontology of 94; two forms of 162; *see also* metatheoretical paradigms
intersubjective/intersubjectivity 8, 12, 20, 26, 35, 41, 45, 46, 49, 84, 89, 91, 97, 110, 158, 265, 299; nature of intentional things 18, 45, 52, 69, 83, 92, 258, 260; understanding 20, 26, 260–1, 265; *see also* meaning(s)
interview/interviewing 50, 89, 94, 98, 105, 126, 134, 137, 157, 177, 202, 205, 234, 238, 239, 241, 259, 264–5, 268; person-centered 261, 268–9, 279, 299; as informants 269–73; as respondents 273–4; solicited and unsolicited verbal accounts 269–70, 279, 280
intrapsychic 8, 46, 52
intuition 59, 63, 65, 80, 87, 103, 157, 164, 261, 272, 276

Kant, I. 4, 92, 144, 158
Kohlberg, L. 50, 213

law(s) 15, 16, 35, 57, 74, 134, 165, 171, 172, 174, 175–6, 182, 193, 194–5, 211, 213, 235, 252; empirical 64, 65, 67, 68, 128–9, 135, 157, 160, 173–4, 181, 186; scientific 36, 64, 65, 105, 128; theoretical 142, 156, 157, 158–9, 163, 167, 173, 174
Leibnitz, G. W. von 64
levels of analysis 199, 208, 216, 220, 222
Levi-Strauss, C. 4, 8
Lock, J. 64
Lonner, W. 15, 187, 191

Malinowski, B. 5, 10
Markus, H. 19
Maslow, A. 50
Mauss, M. 4, 162–3, 165
May, R. 50
meaning(s) 8, 10, 19, 20–1, 26, 47, 59, 81, 82, 83–90, 94, 98, 102–3, 109–10, 127, 130, 145, 151, 152, 155, 159, 162, 176, 202, 207, 229–30, 234, 238, 275; cultural/public and socio-cultural 8–9, 14, 41, 43, 82, 83, 89, 91, 92–3, 110, 205–6, 234, 270; in-depth/deep 86, 88–9, 91, 92, 93, 94, 102, 103, 110–11, 155, 176, 177, 191, 194, 213, 268, 276; "experiential meaning" (by Taylor) 91; idiosyncratic 43–4, 82, 83, 89, 91–2, 110, 273; "intersubjective constitutive meanings" (by Taylor) 89, 90, 91–2, 111; linguistic 82; meaning construction (by Shore) 48; nominal definition of 82; normative systems of 83, 89–90; realism 84, 95; systems of 8, 14, 41–2, 48, 69, 82, 83, 86, 89–92, 93, 95, 96, 110, 152, 156, 176, 202, 234, 259–60, 270, 277–8
measurement 18, 37, 40, 69–70, 94, 126, 164, 179, 194, 229–30, 234, 246, 251, 276
measurement equivalence/invariance 215, 228, 244, 245–250, 252; configural 236, 247; dimensional 236; error variance 248; factor covariance 248; factor variance 248; full and partial 248–9; metric 236, 248; multi-group mean and covariance structure analyses (MACS analyses) 246; scalar 248
mechanisms 6, 10, 13, 21, 62–3, 80–81, 95, 97, 98–9, 102, 107, 108, 119–20, 123, 128, 135, 138, 139, 145, 159, 164, 167, 174, 182–3, 185, 220, 277; causal 33, 57, 65–6, 69, 71, 78, 81, 95–6, 99–100, 102, 103, 105–6, 110, 128–30, 132, 135, 146, 155, 175–7, 186, 194, 203, 208–11, 215; cognitive 17, 18, 97; definition of 100–1; of sociocultural and psychological worlds 19, 26, 34, 40, 41–2, 44, 46–7, 52, 78, 95, 191–2, 218, 262, 269, 279, 299–300; unobservable 97, 102, 103, 105, 110, 134–5, 154, 162–4, 175–7, 185; *see also* explanation, mechanismic
mental models 44, 48; personal 44–5; conventional 44–5, 48; internalized aspects of cultural models 44
mental representations 20, 44, 46, 47, 92, 97, 143, 158, 258, 261; symbolic 120, 142
Merleau-Ponty, M. 83
metaphor(s) xv, 1, 6, 8, 33, 35, 37, 40, 43, 103, 205–6, 271–3, 275, 277, 278, 290; metaphorical thinking 103
metatheoretical or philosophical assumptions 32–3; interpretivist paradigm xv, 23, 43, 68, 78, 79, 81, 82, 85–6, 89, 92, 94, 98, 99, 110, 138, 152–5, 176, 191, 192, 202, 211, 260, 278; paradigms 58–9, 64, 160, 170, 191; positivist paradigm xv, 17, 23, 36, 37, 58, 64, 66–73, 75, 79, 94, 97, 105, 129, 130, 151, 164, 173, 180, 187, 191; realist paradigm xiv, 33, 68, 78, 79, 82, 95–6, 97, 99, 100, 105, 107, 110, 128, 151–2, 154–5, 160, 161, 163, 165, 166, 176, 185, 187, 191, 194, 202, 211, 260, 278, 299; thinking 56, 58–9, 299
method(s) xiv, xv, 9, 11, 22, 32, 36–7, 40, 43, 50, 59, 87, 89, 92, 96, 126, 135, 136, 171, 176, 177, 202, 204–5, 276, 278; statistical 10, 66, 71–3, 79, 211, 228, 245; *see also* case-based method; comparative method; ethnography; observation; interview

methodolatry 24, 59, 69, 137, 139; method-driven/oriented studies 137, 138, 139
methodology xv, 15, 18, 32, 36–7, 40, 43, 56, 66, 67, 69, 83, 98, 108, 126, 136, 171, 179, 184, 186, 191–2, 202, 213; indigenous/decolonizing 24, 292, 294
Mill, J. S. 35, 60, 64, 208–9
modes of inference 56, 58, 170; abductive 63, 78, 79, 99, 162, 164, 260; ampliative-deductive 58, 65–6, 74, 80, 107; deductive 58; deductive-nomological 58, 65–6, 74, 75, 235; hypothetico-deductive 68, 74; inductive 58, 65–6, 75; retroductive 63, 78, 79, 99, 162, 164, 260
monochronic versus polychronic time management (by Hall) 290–1, 297
monocultural studies 201–7, 209, 222, 262
de Montesquieu, C-L. 4
moral/socio/cultural communities xiii, 6, 8, 9, 10, 12, 13, 16, 19–23, 26, 43, 45–7, 82, 84, 89, 92, 97, 152, 156, 171, 176, 187, 202, 208, 229, 230, 241, 273, 258, 289
multicultural comparative studies *see* comparative approach
multidimensional scaling (MDS) 237
Murdock, G. 5, 11

natural philosophy 64
naturalistic observation *see* observation
Nisbett, R. 19, 204
nomological network 235, 252
nomothetic sciences 171–2, 174, 183, 194–5; approach 36, 171–3, 175, 176–8; in psychology 173; interpretive nomothetic approach 176; thinking 40, 172, 173, 175

observation 84, 135; naturalistic 9, 50, 89, 94, 98, 136, 150, 177, 184, 206, 234, 260, 264–6, 274–8; observational statements 89; participant 9, 10, 21, 50, 89, 94, 98, 177, 184, 234, 259, 264–5, 266–8, 274–8; units of 179, 184, 185, 194, 195
"onion peeling" metaphor of culture 6, 213, 232
ontology/ontological 32, 56, 58, 65–6, 85, 86, 94, 95, 107, 108, 110, 130, 144, 146, 167, 170, 174
operationalism 151

paradigm(s) *see* observation
participatory research 292
Pearson, K. 35–6
Peirce, C. 79–81, 99, 109, 117
phenomenological: analysis 13, 50, 124, 192, 234; cognitive psychology 50; neuroscience 50; psychology 50; paradigm 83; sociologists 20, 35; *see also* anthropology
phenomenon(a) xv, 6, 7, 18, 34, 35, 65–6, 67, 70, 79, 84, 85, 96–7, 100–1, 105, 108, 111, 119, 124–5, 128, 130, 132, 135, 138–9, 149, 150, 162, 164, 165, 166–7, 172, 176, 184, 208–9; definition of 75
Piaget, J. 50, 109

Pike, K. 9, 26, 178, 194; *see also* etic and emic approaches
pilot testing 239, 244, 245
Poortinga, Y. H. 15, 213, 233
position of researchers 37, 296; 'insider' 9, 10, 22–4, 43, 130, 202, 204, 205, 220, 267, 286, 286–8, 296; 'outsider' 9, 19, 23–4, 37, 82, 130, 178, 194, 204, 267, 286–8, 296; 'outsider-to-insider' 22, 202, 204, 207, 220, 287, 296
positivism 1, 16, 18, 36, 62, 68, 69–70, 75, 78, 79, 81, 94, 95, 128, 129, 151, 152, 159, 185, 195; logical 64, 68, 75; *see also* metatheoretical paradigms
prediction 37, 129, 235; categorical 129; in positivism 64, 67–8, 164, 129, 160–1, 177, 195; in realism 96, 129–30; symmetry of prediction and explanation 129–30; by Whewell 97, 164
problem-driven/oriented research xiv, 1, 107, 117, 137–8, 139, 161, 299
"psychic unity of mankind" (by Bastian) 4, 11, 21, 26, 229
psychological effects (by Cummins) 174
psychology, cross-cultural: critique of 18–19; definition of 15–16, 25–6; methodology 18, 21, 36–7, 40, 66–7, 128, 171, 176–8, 179–80, 180–3, 186–92, 213–20, 226–50, 282, 287, 289 (*see also* variable-based); understanding of culture 6, 16–17, 34–5, 38–9; understanding of psychological functioning 17–18, 35–6, 39–40
psychology, cultural: critique of 21; definition 19–20, 26; methodology 21, 50, 183–6, 192–3, 201–7, 212–13, 234, 257–78; understanding of culture 20–1, 43–9; understanding of psychological functioning 20–1, 49–50
psychology, existential-phenomenological 50
psychology: humanistic 50; humanistic cultural 50
psychology, indigenous 19, 21–2, 50, 201–2, 205, 230, 233–4; definition 23–4; methodology 24, 234, 257–78, 292, 294; sociocultural 5, 50; theoretical 161

qualitative: data 103; method(s) 74, 126, 176, 184, 209, 220, 221, 257; research 10, 18, 84, 93, 135, 137, 173, 187, 211, 218
quantitative: approach 5, 18, 191, 194, 226–50; data 103; method(s) 11, 74, 191, 204, 211, 252, 276, 278; research 84, 173, 287; sciences 183

Radcliffe-Brown, A. R. 5, 10, 211
rapport building 261, 263, 271, 282, 283, 286, 287, 289–91, 293, 295; "overrapport" (by Hammersley and Atkinson) 266
rational 64–5, 74, 75, 172; thinking 60, 66–7, 71, 75, 80, 81, 94, 110, 143, 158
rationalism 63–5, 75, 81
real 20, 26, 41, 46, 47, 70, 72, 81, 84, 92, 94, 95, 96, 97, 101, 105, 107, 108, 110, 144–5, 146, 147, 163, 166, 174, 183, 276; definition of 95
realism 8, 86, 96–7, 110, 129, 154–5, 160, 163–6; critical 96; critique of 107–8; depth 95; meaning

95; methodology of 98–9, 103–7; ontology of 107; philosophical (ontological) 95; shallow or naïve 66, 75, 95; scientific 96; *see also* metatheoretical paradigms
realist case-based research *see* case-based approach
reality 72; cultural/sociosymbolic/sociocultural 19, 34–5, 40, 41, 57, 72, 97, 104, 110, 258, 273; deep/indepth 66, 107, 145, 178; definition of 95, 110; denial of 107–8, 146, 162; empirical/observable 110, 150, 154, 163; linguistic 146; nature of 108; 'natural' 20, 46; multi-layered 94, 110, 191; physical 40, 57, 110; psychological 57, 72, 110, 144; 'valid/real' 41, 47, 82, 146 (*see also* taken-for-granted)
reductionism 35
reflection(s) xiv, 1, 3, 35, 41, 42, 59, 83, 91–2, 107, 119, 134, 135, 153, 170, 205, 219, 259, 265, 266, 274, 276, 288
reification of culture 34–5, 42–3
research design 36, 50, 117, 129, 131, 136, 157, 171, 178, 187, 213–14; extensive and intensive 103, 107, 175, 176, 204, 299; *see also* case-based and variable-based;
research habitus *see* habitus
research hypotheses 36, 62, 63, 65, 69, 74, 75, 80, 81, 94, 97, 98–9, 102, 105, 110, 120, 123, 125, 135–6, 154–5, 163, 175, 177, 186, 192, 209, 211, 215, 220, 246, 259, 268, 272, 275, 278, 300; definition of 135–6; theoretical versus statistical 135–6; *see also* research questions
research problem 33, 102, 117, 131–3, 136, 137–8, 139, 162, 170–1, 186, 195, 204, 227, 261, 275; applied 120–1, 139; formulation of 117–18, 121–4, 125–6, 261–3; functions 117–19; theoretical 119–20, 139; "thesis-antithesis-synthesis" strategy of formulation 123–4, 137–8; *see also* problem-oriented research
research questions 118, 131–2, 136, 137–8, 139, 141–2, 170, 261–2, 265, 274, 275; examples of 131–2, 206, 212, 214, 215, 216, 246; formulating 131–5; and hypotheses 135–6; main and subsidiary 133; wording 133–4; versus data generating questions 134–5
research purpose(s) 124, 137–8, 170, 201; descriptive 124–7; explanatory 124, 128–30; to understand 130–1
research strategies 170–2; extensive and intensive 176–7, 194
researchers' identities and roles 88, 264
response style 250; social desirability 250; acquiescence 250
retroduction 73, 81–2, 93, 96, 99–101, 103–4, 107, 108, 109, 117, 158, 163, 185, 192, 209; definition of 99, 110; *see also* modes of inference
Ricœur, P. 83, 85–6, 88, 94
Rogers, C. 50
Ryle, G. 86, 90

sampling 186, 195; cluster 190, 195; convenience 188, 190, 191; critical/extreme cases 192; maximum variation 192; participants 189–90; probability 73, 182, 187, 189–91, 195; purposive 188, 192–3, 195; random 188; representative 190; of settings 261–2, 265; theoretical 262, 279; theoretical of cultures 187–9; of time 265–6; *see also* case(s)
Sartre, J-P. 83
Schneider, D. 8
"scientists as spiders, ants, and bees" (by Bacon) 159–60
Segall, M. H. 15, 16, 17, 18, 34, 213
self 13, 19, 22, 24, 153, 203, 213, 234, 274; awareness 62, 289, 291; concept/construal 16, 62, 63, 229; determination 13, 49, 50, 83, 124, 215; development 50; identification 17; image 274; presentation 176, 267; production 40; realization 70; reflection(ive) 41, 51, 91, 202, 266; respect/esteem 126, 187, 244; sense of 49, 50, 154
Sextus Empiricus 59, 63
Shore, B. 42, 43–4, 45, 47, 48, 49, 83
Shweder, R. 19, 20–1, 46, 97, 147, 212, 258–61, 273, 277, 278, 282
significance testing 73
social constructionism xiv; epistemological 107, 108; strong version of 107, 146, 162; weak form of 146
"social stock of knowledge" (by Berger & Luckmann) 7, 44, 47, 83
socialization 42, 44, 47, 49, 52, 62, 63, 66, 81, 91, 120, 136, 158, 204; *see also* enculturation
sociocultural: attributes/characteristics 10, 250; communities/contexts 9, 13, 15, 26, 71, 82, 94, 107, 159, 180, 185, 289; conventions 46; existence 4; influences 13, 42, 106, 107, 246; institutions xiii, 44; phenomenon(a) 18, 37 70, 71–2, 83, 86 172–3, 178; research 10, 155, 185, 268, 293; sciences 33, 40, 71, 102, 145, 155; worlds/environments/realities/systems xiii, xiv, 1, 3, 4, 8, 10, 11, 12, 19, 20–1, 26, 35, 41, 42, 43, 44, 48, 57, 59, 70, 72, 81, 82, 83, 92, 94, 95, 97, 101, 110, 120, 125, 129, 136, 143, 147, 152, 156, 176, 202, 208, 216, 218, 257, 258, 261, 273, 277, 278, 299; variables 36; *see also* meaning(s) and mechanisms
socio/cultural-historical approach 50
Spinoza, B. 64
standard social science model 42, 52
structural equation modeling (SEM) 70, 250
structural functionalism 5
structuralist approach 4, 8
subjectivity *see* experience
symbolic environment *see* sociosymbolic; systems 7–8
symmetry of prediction and explanation (in positivism) *see* prediction and explanation
systemic: factor 218; methods 94; nature 10, 43, 71, 179; relations 40, 49, 94, 163, 185; thinking 39, 179, 216; wholes 9, 39, 52; *see also* emergent properties and systems
systems 5, 7, 9, 10, 14, 22–3, 32, 34, 39, 40, 41, 42, 44, 46, 52, 71, 88, 94, 97, 100–1, 152, 156, 157, 160–1, 174, 175, 176–7, 178–9, 184, 185, 194, 216, 276; open and closed (in realism) 105, 129, 177, 182; *see also* culture and meaning

taken-for-granted 1, 24, 27, 41, 45, 47, 59, 75, 92, 102, 123, 134, 156, 288, 299
term(s) 143; auxiliary 161; theoretical 143; scientific 143; substantive and notational 143, 167; and concept 143; *see also* concept
theoretical xv, xvi, 6, 17, 18, 20, 24, 25, 33, 56, 69, 70, 74, 75, 89, 101, 108, 115, 130–1, 132, 149, 151, 158, 160, 161, 162, 163, 164, 172, 175, 180–1, 186, 188, 191, 192, 219, 229, 236, 246, 249, 250, 252, 272, 276, 293, 300; theoretical perspectives: *Homo Bios* 7, 15, 16, 37–40; *Homo Interpretans* 15, 21, 23, 43–50, 299; *Homo Mechanicus* 16, 18, 33–7; *Homo Socius* 15, 21, 23, 40–3; sciences (by Husserl) 174–5; thinking xv, 1, 24, 32, 59, 63, 148, 160, 163–4, 214, 228; *see also* concept(s); definition, generalization; law, psychology, research hypotheses, research problem, sampling, terms
theory 22, 42, 107, 119, 123, 157–9, 167, 175, 186; of evolution 80–1, 165; in interpretivism 161–3; in positivism 63, 66, 70, 160–1, 180, 192–3, 208, 209, 213, 219, 235, 236, 237, 252, 263, 300; in realism 79, 81, 84, 96, 100, 105, 163–6 (*see also* prediction, consilience, coherence by Whewell); theory-laden 87, 163 (*see also* culture; Big Five theory, trait theories)
"thin" and/or "thick" descriptions (by Ryle) 67, 86, 89–90, 91–2, 94, 109, 110–11, 130, 176, 177, 184, 206, 207, 259, 270, 299
Tomasello, M. 50, 98–9, 119–20, 123, 136, 143–4, 158, 164
trait theories of personality 36, 149
translation 199, 227, 238, 239–45; centred or asymmetrical 239; decentered or symmetrical 239; TRAPD procedure 239; forward-and-back 239–40; committee-based 240
Triandis, H. C. 15, 17, 67, 187, 220, 278
Turner, V. 8, 13
Tylor, E. B. 4, 6, 7, 10

understanding or *verstehen* 20, 21, 70, 82, 85, 87–8, 89, 92, 93, 94, 102, 103, 107, 110, 111, 125, 128, 130, 132, 138, 152, 153, 161, 162, 178, 202, 205, 211, 212, 242–3, 260, 261, 270, 271, 275, 278, 289, 299; "direct observational" (by Weber) 89, 130; "explanatory" (by Weber) 87, 92, 130; interpretive 111, 162; intersubjective 26, 260; *see also* explanation
"universal psychological toolkit" (by Matsumoto & Juang) 38–9, 40
unpackaging cross-national studies 217–18
unsolicited and solicited verbal accounts *see* interview/interviewing

validity 16, 21, 63, 74, 92–3, 97, 98, 107, 129, 158, 164–6, 190, 230, 231, 244, 245, 247, 251, 252, 259, 261, 268, 271, 272, 292, 294; construct 229–30, 232, 235–6; content 237–8
Valsiner, J. 5, 19, 21, 50, 175, 181–4
Variables 15, 16, 17, 35, 36–7, 94, 126, 142–3, 145, 150, 151, 161, 167, 190, 237, 246–8, 250; critique of 181–3; design 105, 145, 170, 171, 177, 178, 180–181, 183, 185, 187, 188, 193, 194, 195; intervening 237; thinking 17; variable-based approach/method xvi, 18–19, 25–6, 34, 36–7, 67–8, 69–73, 79, 94, 106, 107, 115, 262; *see also* comparative approach/method, concept, country-level ecological studies, unpackaging cross-national studies
Vico, G. 4, 83
volkergeist (spirit of people) 4

Whewell, W. 96–7, 164–6
Whiting, B. B. and Whiting, J. W. M. 131, 134, 136, 185
Windelband, W. 171, 172, 174

Znaniecki, F. 57, 60, 71, 72, 97–176, 208